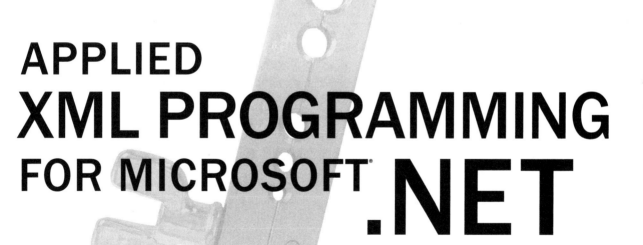

APPLIED
XML PROGRAMMING
FOR MICROSOFT .NET

Dino Esposito

Microsoft .net

Wintellect

PUBLISHED BY
Microsoft Press
A Division of Microsoft Corporation
One Microsoft Way
Redmond, Washington 98052-6399

Library of Congress Cataloging-in-Publication Data [pending.]
Esposito, Dino, 1965-
        Applied XML Programming for Microsoft .NET / Dino Esposito
            p. cm.
        Includes index.
        ISBN 0-7356-1801-1
        1. XML (Document markup language)   2. Microsoft .NET.   I. Title.

    QA76.76.H94 E85 2002
    005.7'2--dc21   2002029546

Printed and bound in the United States of America.

2 3 4 5 6 7 8 9   QWT   7 6 5 4

Distributed in Canada by H.B. Fenn and Company Ltd.

A CIP catalogue record for this book is available from the British Library.

Microsoft Press books are available through booksellers and distributors worldwide. For further information about international editions, contact your local Microsoft Corporation office or contact Microsoft Press International directly at fax (425) 936-7329. Visit our Web site at www.microsoft.com/mspress. Send comments to: *mspinput@microsoft.com*.

Acquisitions Editor: Anne Hamilton
Project Editor: Lynn Finnel
Technical Editor: Marc Young

Body Part No. X08-81851

To Silvia, Francesco, and Michela

Table of Contents

Part III   XML and Data Access

8   XML and Databases   347

Part IV   Applications Interoperability

Acknowledgments

I can say it now: Several times I was about to start an XML book project, but then for one reason or another the project never took off. So I'd like to start by saying thanks to the people who believed in a fairly confused book idea and worked to make it happen. These people are Anne Hamilton and Jeannine Gailey. (By the way, all the best, Jeannine!)

Lynn Finnel brought the usual fundamental contribution as project editor. As Lynn originally described her role in the first e-mail we exchanged, being an editor is a delicate art, as you have to reconcile the needs of many people while meeting your own deadlines. Thanks again, Lynn.

And a warm thanks goes to Jennifer Harris, who edited the book, and technical reviewers Marc Young, Jim Fuchs, Julie Xiao, and Jean Ross.

Other people were involved with this book, mostly as personal reviewers. Francesco Balena tested some of the code and provided a lot of insight. In particular, Giuseppe Dimauro and Giuseppe Guerrasio helped to figure out the intricacies of the *XmlSerializer* class, and Ralph Westphal did the same with custom readers. Kenn Scribner has been the ideal extension to the MSDN documentation about Web services. Rainer Heller of Siemens offered a really interesting perspective on Web services interoperability. It was nice to discuss Web services in the more general context of a conversation based on the World Football Championships—an indirect demonstration that Web services are still interoperable today!

Thanks to all the Wintellect guys, and Jason Clark and Jeffrey Richter, in particular, for their friendly and effective support.

And now my family. I've noticed that many authors, when writing acknowledgments, promise their families that they will never repeat the experience. Although rewarding for themselves, they explain, writing a book is too hard on the rest of the family to be repeated. I'll be honest and sincere here. So, Silvia, and Francesco and Michela, set your mind at rest. I will do all I can to write even more books. But I love you all beyond imagination.

—'til the next book

Dino

Introduction

It was about five years ago, a few days after I finished my first book, when the publisher came to me with a rather enticing proposal: "Why don't you start thinking about a new book?" Now I realize that all publishers make this sort of proposition, but at the time the proposal was definitely alluring, and a clear signal—I thought—of appreciation. "Because you seem to do so well with new technologies," they said, "we'd like you to have a look at this new stuff called XML." It was the first time I had heard about XML, which was not yet a W3C recommendation.

A lot of things have happened in the meantime, and XML did go a long way. You can be sure that, as I write this, a thousand or more IT managers are giving presentations that include XML in one way or another. Not many years ago, at a software conference, I heard a product manager emphasize the key role played by XML in the suite of products he was presenting. After the first dozen sentences to the effect that "this feature wouldn't have been possible without XML," one of the attendees asked a candid question: "Is there a function in which you didn't use XML?" The presenter's genuine enthusiasm led everyone there (including myself) to believe that programming would no longer be possible without a strong knowledge of XML. We were more than a little reassured by the speaker's answer: "Oh no, we didn't use XML in the compiler."

Regardless of the hype that often accompanies it, XML truly is a key element in software. Today, XML is more than just a software technology. XML is a fundamental aspect of all forms of programming, as essential as water and air to every human being. Just as human beings realistically need some infrastructure to take advantage of water and air, programming forms of life must be supported by software tools to be effective and express their potential in terms of interoperability, flexibility, and information. For XML, the most important of these tools is the parser.

An XML parser reads in XML text and outputs a mcmory representation of the contents. The input for an XML parser is always plain and platform-independent text, although potentially encoded in a variety of character sets, whereas the output of an XML parser is strictly tied to the underlying hardware and software platform. Depending on the operating system and the programming environment of choice, an XML parser can generate a Component Object Model (COM) object as well as a Java or a JScript class. No matter the kind of output, however, the end result is XML data in a programmable form.

The growing level of integration and orchestration that partner applications need makes the exchanged XML code more and more sophisticated and often requires the use of specialized dialects like Simple Object Access Protocol (SOAP) and XPath. As a result, XML programming requires ad hoc tools for reading and writing in these dialects; all the better if the tools are tightly integrated into some sort of programming framework.

Effective XML programming requires that you be able to generate XML in a more powerful way than merely concatenating strings. The XML API must be extensible enough to accommodate pluggable technologies and custom functionalities. And it must be serializable and integrate well with other elements of data storage and exchange, including databases, complex data types (arrays, tables, and lists), and—why not?—visual user interface elements. In simple terms, XML must no longer be a distinct API bolted onto the core framework, but instead be a fully integrated member of the family. This is just what XML is in the Microsoft .NET Framework. And this book is about XML programming with the .NET Framework.

What Is This Book About?

This book explores the array of XML tools provided by the .NET Framework. XML is everywhere in the .NET Framework, from remoting to Web services, and from data access to configuration. In the first part of this book, you'll find in-depth coverage of the key classes that implement XML in the .NET platform. Readers and writers, validation, and schemas are discussed with samples and reference information. Next the book moves on to XPath and XSL Transformations (XSLT) and the .NET version of the XML Document Object Model (XML DOM).

The final part of this book focuses on data access and interoperability and touches on SQL Server 2000 and its XML extensions and .NET Remoting and its cross-platform counterpart—XML Web services. You'll also find a couple of chapters about XML configuration files and XML data islands and browser/deployed managed controls.

What Does This Book Cover?

This book attempts to answer the following common questions:

- Can I read custom data as XML?

- What are the guidelines for writing custom XML readers?

- Is it possible to set up validating XML writers?

- How can I extend the XML DOM?

- Why should I use the XPath navigator object whenever possible?

- Can I embed my own managed classes in an XSLT script?

- How can I serialize a *DataSet* object efficiently?

- What is the DiffGram format?

- Are the SQL Server 2000 XML Extensions (SQLXML) worth using?

- Why does the XML serializer use a dynamic assembly?

- When should I use Web services instead of .NET Remoting?

- How can I embed managed controls in Web pages?

- How can managed controls access client-side XML data islands?

- How do I insert my own XML data in a configuration file?

All of the sample files discussed in this book (and even more) are available through the Web at the following address: *http://www.microsoft.com/mspress/books/6235.asp*. To open the Companion Content page, click on the Companion Content link in the More Information box on the right side of the page.

Although all the code shown in this book is in C#, the sample files are available both in C# and in Microsoft Visual Basic .NET. Here are some of the more interesting examples:

- An XML reader that reads CSV files and exposes their contents as XML

- An extended version of the XML DOM that detects changes to the disk file and automatically refreshes its data

- A Web service that offers dynamically created images

- An XML reader class with writing capabilities

- A class that serializes *DataTable* objects in a true binary format

- A tool to track the behavior of the XML serializer class

- A *ListView* control that retrieves its data from the host HTML page

These and other samples will get you on your way to XML in the .NET Framework.

What Do I Need to Use This Book?

Most of the examples in this book are Windows Forms or console applications. The key requirements for running these applications are the .NET Framework and Microsoft Visual Studio .NET. You also need to have SQL Server 2000 installed to make most of the samples work, and a few examples make use of Microsoft Access 2000 databases. The SQLXML 3.0 extensions are required for the samples in Chapter 8. The code has been tested with the .NET Framework SP1.

The SQL Server examples in this book assume that the sa account uses a blank password, although the use of such a blank password is strongly discouraged in any professional development environment. If your SQL Server sa account doesn't use a blank password, you'll need to add the sa password to the connection strings in the source code. For example, if your sa password is "Hello", the following connection string provides access to the Northwind database:

```
string nwind = "SERVER=localhost;UID=sa;pswd=Hello;DATABASE=northwind;";
```

Some of the applications in this book require SOAP Toolkit 2.0 and SQLXML 3.0. These products are available at the following locations:

- **SOAP Toolkit 2.0**   *http://msdn.microsoft.com/downloads/default .asp?URL=/downloads/sample.asp?url=/MSDN-FILES/027/001/580/ msdncompositedoc.xml*

- **SQLXML 3.0**   *http://msdn.microsoft.com/downloads/default.asp? URL=/downloads/sample.asp?url=/MSDN-FILES/027/001/824/msdn-compositedoc.xml*

Contacting the Author

Please feel free to send any questions about this book directly to the author. Dino Esposito can be reached via e-mail at one of the following addresses:

- dinoe@wintellect.com
- desposito@vb2themax.com

In addition, you can contact the author at the Wintellect (*http://www.wintellect.com*) and VB2-The-Max (*http://www.vb2themax.com*) Web sites.

Support

Every effort has been made to ensure the accuracy of this book and the contents of the sample files. Microsoft Press provides corrections for books through the Web at the following address:

http://www.microsoft.com/mspress/support/

To connect directly to the Microsoft Press Knowledge Base and enter a query regarding a question or issue that you might have, go to:

http://www.microsoft.com/mspress/support/search.asp

If you have comments, questions, or ideas regarding this book or the sample files, please send them to Microsoft Press using either of the following methods:

Postal mail:

Microsoft Press
Attn: *Microsoft .NET XML Programming* Editor
One Microsoft Way
Redmond, Wa 98052-6399

E-mail:

MSPINPUT@MICROSOFT.COM

Please note that product support is not offered through the above mail addresses. For support information, please visit the Microsoft Product Support Web site at

http://support.microsoft.com

Part I

XML Core Classes in the .NET Framework

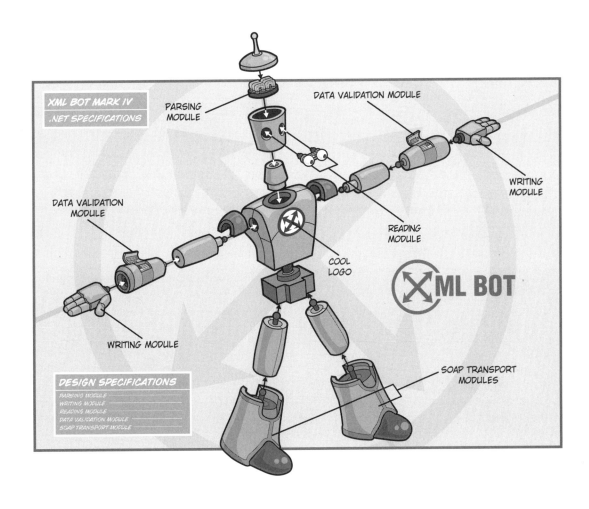

1

The .NET XML Parsing Model

XML is certainly a hot topic in the software community these days. As you read this, probably a thousand or more IT managers are giving presentations that include XML in one way or another. In fact, it's becoming almost redundant to emphasize the effect that the use of XML can have on applications.

Today, XML is a natural element of all forms of programming life, just as water, sun, and minerals are fundamental resources for every human being. To take full advantage of XML, applications need some infrastructure built into the operating system or into the underlying software platform. Normally, an XML infrastructure takes the form of tools that provide for parsing, document validation, schema design, and transformations.

The Microsoft .NET Framework provides a comprehensive set of classes that let you work with XML documents and related technologies at various levels and in strict accordance with the most recent World Wide Web Consortium (W3C) standards and recommendations. The XML support available in the .NET Framework covers XML 1.0, XML namespaces, Document Object Model (DOM) Level 2 Core, XML Schema Definition (XSD) Language, Extensible Stylesheet Language Transformations (XSLT), and XPath expressions. In addition, XML core classes are tightly integrated with other key portions of the .NET Framework, including data access, serialization, and applications configuration.

In this chapter, we'll take an overall look at XML as it is used in the .NET Framework. In particular, we'll focus on the new and innovative parsing model based on the concept of reader components. This first chapter is aimed at providing you with the big picture of the .NET Framework XML API, the key elements of transition from the previous Component Object Model (COM)–based Win32 API, and a bird's-eye view of the interconnections between XML and various parts of the .NET Framework.

XML in the .NET Framework

The .NET Framework XML core classes can be categorized according to their functions: reading and writing documents, validating documents, navigating and selecting nodes, managing schema information, and performing document transformations. The assembly in which the whole XML .NET Framework is implemented is system.xml.dll.

The most commonly used namespaces are listed here:

- *System.Xml*

- *System.Xml.Schema*

- *System.Xml.XPath*

- *System.Xml.Xsl*

The .NET Framework also provides for XML object serialization. The classes involved with this functionality are grouped in the *System.Xml.Serialization* namespace. XML serialization writes objects to, and reads them from, XML documents. This kind of serialization is particularly useful over the Web in combination with the Simple Object Access Protocol (SOAP) and within the boundaries of .NET Framework XML Web services.

Related XML Standards

Table 1-1 lists the XML-related standards that have been implemented in the .NET Framework. The table also provides the official URL for each standard for further reference.

Table 1-1   W3C Standards Supported in the .NET Framework

Standard	Reference
XML 1.0	*http://www.w3.org/TR/1998/REC-xml-19980210*
XML namespaces	*http://www.w3.org/TR/REC-xml-names*
XML Schema	*http://www.w3.org/TR/xmlschema-2*
DOM Level 1 and Level 2 Core	*http://www.w3.org/TR/DOM-Level-2*
XPath	*http://www.w3.org/TR/xpath*
XSLT	*http://www.w3.org/TR/xslt*
SOAP 1.1	*http://www.w3.org/TR/SOAP*

As a data exchange technology, XML is fully and tightly integrated into the .NET Framework. Table 1-2 provides a quick schematic view of the main areas of the .NET Framework in which significant traces of XML are clearly visible. Each area includes numerous classes and provides a set of application-level functions.

Table 1-2   Areas of the .NET Framework in Which XML Is Key

Category	Description
ADO.NET	Data container objects (for example, the *DataSet* object) are always transferred and remoted via XML. The .NET Framework also provides for two-way synchronized binding between data exposed in tabular format and XML format.
Configuration	Application settings are stored in XML files, making use of predefined and user-defined section readers. (More on readers later.)
Remoting	Remote .NET Framework objects can be accessed by using SOAP packets to prepare and perform the call.
Web services	SOAP is a lightweight XML protocol that Web services use for the exchange of information in a decentralized, distributed environment. Typically, you use SOAP to invoke methods on a Web service in a platform-independent fashion.
XML parsing	The core classes providing for XML parsing and manipulation through both the stream-based API and the XML Document Object Model (XMLDOM).
XML serialization	Supplies the ability to save and restore living instances of objects to and from XML documents.

Although not strictly part of the .NET Framework, another group of classes deserves mention: the managed classes defined in the SQL Server 2000 XML Extensions (SQLXML). SQLXML 3.0 extends the XML capabilities of SQL Server 2000 by introducing Web services support. SQLXML 3.0 makes it possible for you to export stored procedures as SOAP-based Web services and also extends ADO.NET capabilities with server-side XPath queries and XML views. SQLXML 3.0 is available as a separate download, but it seamlessly integrates with the existing installation of the .NET Framework. We'll look at SQLXML 3.0 in more detail in Chapter 8.

In general, the entire set of XML classes provided with the .NET Framework offers a standards-compliant, interoperable, extensible solution to today's software development challenges. This support is not a tacked-on API but a true part of the .NET Framework.

> **Note**   Almost all of today's XML parsers support the latest W3C specification for the DOM Level 2 Core. The current specification does not define a standard interface to persist and restore contents, however, although the most popular XML parsers, such as Microsoft's XML Core Services (MSXML)—formerly known as the Microsoft XML Parser—and some others based on Java, already have their own ways to persist objects to streams and to restore objects from them. These mechanisms have yet to be considered as custom and platform-specific extensions. An official API for serializing documents to and from XML format will not be available until DOM Level 3 Core achieves the status of a W3C recommendation. As of summer 2002, DOM Level 3 Core is qualified as a work in progress. The publicly available draft defines the specification for a pair of *Load* and *Save* methods designed to enable loading XML documents into a DOM representation and saving a DOM representation as an XML document. For more information, refer to *http://www.w3.org/TR/2002/WD-DOM-Level-3-Core-20020409*.
>
> A known parser that already provides an experimental implementation of DOM Level 3 Core is IBM's XML Parser for Java (Xml4J). See *http://www.alphaworks.ibm.com/tech/xml4j* for more information.

Core Classes for Parsing

Regardless of the underlying platform, the available XML parsers fall into one of two main categories: tree-based parsers and event-based parsers. Each parser category is designed according to a different philosophical approach and, subsequently, has its own pros and cons. The two categories are commonly identified with their two most popular implementations: XMLDOM and Simple API for XML (SAX). The XMLDOM parser is a generic tree-based API that renders an XML document as an in-memory structure. The SAX parser provides an event-based API for processing each significant element in a stream of XML data.

Conceptually speaking, a SAX parser is diametrically opposed to an XMLDOM parser, and the gap between the two models is indeed fairly large. XMLDOM seems to be clearly defined in its set of functionalities, and there is not much more one can reasonably expect from the evolution of this model. Regardless of whether you like the XMLDOM model or find it suitable for your needs, you can't really expect to radically improve or change its way of working. In a certain sense, the down sides of the XMLDOM model (memory footprint and bandwidth required to process large documents) are structural and stem directly from design choices.

SAX parsers work by letting client applications pass living instances of platform-specific objects to handle parser events. The parser controls the whole process and pushes data to the application, which is in turn free to accept or simply ignore the data. The SAX model is extremely lean and features a limited complexity in space.

The .NET Framework provides full support for the XMLDOM parsing model but not for the SAX model. The set of .NET Framework XML core classes supports two parser models: XMLDOM and a new model called an XML reader. The lack of support for SAX parsers does not mean that you have to renounce the functionality that a SAX parser can bring, however. All the functions of a SAX parser can be easily and even more effectively implemented using an XML reader. Unlike a SAX parser, a .NET Framework XML reader works under the total control of the client application, enabling the application to pull out only the data it really needs and skip over the remainder of the XML stream.

Readers are based on .NET Framework streams and work in much the same way as a database cursor. Interestingly, the classes that implement this cursor-like parsing model also provide the substrate for the .NET Framework implementation of the XMLDOM parser. Two abstract classes—*XmlReader* and

XmlWriter—are at the very foundation of all .NET Framework XML classes, including XMLDOM classes, ADO.NET-related classes, and configuration classes. So in the .NET Framework you have two possible approaches when it comes to processing XML data. You can use either any classes directly built onto *XmlReader* and *XmlWriter* or classes that expose information through the well-known XMLDOM.

The set of XML core classes also includes tailor-made class hierarchies to support other related XML technologies such as XSLT, XPath expressions, and the Schema Object Model (SOM).

We'll look at XML core classes and related standards in the following chapters. In particular, Chapter 2, Chapter 3, Chapter 4, and Chapter 5 describe the core classes and parsing models. Chapter 6 and Chapter 7 examine the related standards, such as XPath and XSL.

XML and ADO.NET

The interaction between ADO.NET classes and XML documents takes one of two forms:

■ Serialization of ADO.NET objects (in particular, the *DataSet* object) to XML documents and corresponding deserialization. Data can be saved to XML in a variety of formats, with or without schema information, as a full snapshot of the in-memory data including pending changes and errors, or with just the current instance of the data.

■ A dual-access model that lets you access and update the same piece of data either through a hierarchical programming interface or using the ADO.NET relational API. Basically, you can transform a *DataSet* object into an XMLDOM object and view the XMLDOM's subtrees as tables merged with the *DataSet* object's tables.

The ADO.NET *DataSet* class represents the only .NET Framework object that can be natively saved to XML. The XML representation of a *DataSet* object can have two different layouts: the ADO.NET normal form and the DiffGram format. In particular, the DiffGram format describes the history of the data and all recent changes. Each changed row in each table is represented by two nodes: the first node contains the snapshot of the row as it was originally read, and the second node contains the current values. The DiffGram represents a snapshot of the *DataSet* state and contents at a given moment. To write DiffGrams, ADO.NET uses an *XmlWriter* object.

The integration of and interaction between XML and ADO.NET classes is discussed in Chapter 8.

Application Configuration

Before Microsoft Windows 95, applications stored configuration settings to a text file with a .ini extension. INI files store information using name/value pairs grouped under sections. Ultimately, an INI file is a collection of sections, with each section consisting of any number of name/value pairs.

Windows 95 revamped the role of the *system registry*—a centralized data repository originally introduced with Windows NT. The registry is a collection of binary files that the operating system manages in exclusive mode. Client applications can read and write the contents of the registry only by using a tailor-made API. The registry works as a kind of hierarchical database consisting of root nodes (also known as *hives*), nodes, and entries. Each entry is a name/value pair.

All system, component, and application settings are supposed to be stored in the registry. The registry continues to increase in size, contributing to the creation of a configuration subsystem with a single (and critical) point of failure. More recently, applications have been encouraged to store custom settings and preferences in a local file stored in the application's root folder. For .NET Framework applications, this configuration file is an XML file written according to a specific schema.

In addition, the .NET Framework provides a specialized set of classes to read and write settings. The key class is named *AppSettingsReader* and works as a kind of parser for a small fragment of XML code—mostly a node or two with a few attributes.

ASP.NET applications store configuration settings in a file named web.config that is located in the root of the application's virtual folder. Windows Forms applications, on the other hand, store their preferences in a file with the same name as the executable plus a .config extension—for example, myprogram.exe.config. The CONFIG file must be available in the same folder as the main executable. The schema of the CONFIG file is the same regardless of the application model.

The contents of a CONFIG file is logically articulated into sections. The .NET Framework provides a number of predefined sections to accommodate Web and Windows Forms settings, remoting parameters, and ASP.NET run-time characteristics such as the authentication scheme and registered HTTP handlers and modules.

User-defined applications can extend the XML schema of the CONFIG file by defining custom sections with custom elements. By default, however, the *AppSettingsReader* class supports only settings expressed in a few formats, such as name/value pairs and a single tag with as many attributes as needed. This schema fits the bill in most cases, but when you have complex structured information, it soon becomes insufficient. Information is read from a section using special objects called *section handlers*. If no predefined section structure fits your needs, you can provide a tailor-made configuration section handler to read your own XML data, as shown here:

```
<configuration>
  <configSections>
    <section name="MySection"
      type="MySectionHandlerClass, assembly" />
  </configSections>
  <MySection>
    ⋮
  </MySection>
</configuration>
```

A configuration section handler is simply a .NET Framework class that parses a particular XML fragment extracted from the CONFIG file. We'll look at custom section handlers in more detail in Chapter 15.

Interoperability

XML is key to making .NET Framework applications interoperate with each other and with external applications running on other software and hardware platforms. *XML interoperability* is a sort of blanket term that covers three .NET-specific technologies: XML Web services, remoting, and XML object serialization.

By rolling functionality into an XML Web service, you can expose the functionality to any application on the Web that, irrespective of platform, speaks HTTP and understands XML. Based on open standards (HTTP and XML, but also SOAP), XML Web services are an emerging technology for system interoperation and are supported by the major players in the IT industry. The .NET Framework provides a special infrastructure to build both remote services and proxy-based clients.

Actually, in the .NET Framework, an XML Web service is treated as a special case of an ASP.NET application—one that is saved with a different file extension (.asmx) and accessible through the SOAP protocol as well as through HTTP GET and POST commands. Incoming calls for both .aspx files (ASP.NET pages) and .asmx files are processed by the same Internet Information Services

(IIS) extension module, which then dispatches the request to distinct down-stream factory components.

In an XML Web service, XML plays its role entirely behind the scenes. It is first used as the glue for the SOAP payloads that the communicating sides exchange. In addition, XML is used to express the results of a remote, cross-platform call. But what if you write a .NET XML Web service with one method returning, say, an ADO.NET *DataSet* object? How can a Java application handle the results? The answer is that the *DataSet* object is serialized to XML and then sent back to the client.

The .NET Framework provides two types of object serialization: serialization through formatters and XML serialization. The two live side by side but have different characteristics. XML serialization is the process that converts the public interface of an object to a particular XML schema. The goal is simplifying the process of data exchange between components rather than truly serializing objects that will then be deserialized to living and effective instances.

Remoting is the .NET Framework counterpart of the Distributed Component Object Model (DCOM) and uses XML to configure both the client and the remote components. In addition, XML is used through SOAP to serialize outbound parameters and inbound return values. Remoting is the official .NET Framework API for communicating applications, but it works only between .NET peers.

XML serialization, remoting, and XML Web services are covered in Part IV—specifically in Chapter 11, Chapter 12, and Chapter 13.

From MSXML to .NET Framework Classes

Prior to the advent of the .NET Framework, managing XML in the Microsoft world meant using the COM-based MSXML, now available in version 4.0, SP1. It goes without saying that Microsoft is still strongly committed to supporting XML the COM way, although this does not necessarily mean that we are going to have an MSXML 5.0 anytime soon. However, MSXML 4.0 represents an excellent parser for the Windows platform and has been updated to support W3C final recommendations for the XML Schema.

COM and .NET Framework XML Core Services

The first difference between MSXML and .NET Framework XML core classes that catches the eye is the fact that while MSXML supports XMLDOM and SAX parsers, the .NET Framework supplies an XMLDOM parser and XML readers and writers. (More on readers shortly.) This is just the most remarkable example of a common pattern, however. Quite a few key features of MSXML are *apparently* not supported in the .NET Framework XML core classes, but this hardly results in a loss of programming power.

In general, the biggest (and perhaps the only significant) difference between MSXML and .NET Framework XML classes is that the former represents a set of classes fully integrated into an all-encompassing, self-contained framework. Several functionalities that MSXML has to provide on its own come for free in the .NET Framework from other compartments. If you happen to use a certain MSXML function and you don't find a direct counterpart in the .NET Framework, check out the MSDN documentation before you panic. In the paragraphs that follow, we'll look at a few examples of .NET Framework functionality that provide the equivalent of some MSXML functionality.

MSXML supports asynchronous loading and validation while parsing. The .NET Framework XMLDOM parser, centered around the *XmlDocument* class, does not directly provide the same features, but proper use of the resources of the .NET Framework will let you obtain the same final behavior anyway.

MSXML also provides for a multithreaded HTTP client (the *XmlHttp* object) capable of issuing both synchronous and asynchronous calls to a remote URL. A similar feature is certainly available in the .NET Framework, but it has nothing to do with XML classes. If you just want your application to act as an HTTP client, use some of the classes in the *System.Net* namespace (for example, *HttpWebRequest* and *HttpWebResponse*).

In general, if you loved MSXML, you'll love .NET Framework XML classes too. The overall programming interface, especially for XMLDOM processing, is similar, although the underlying implementation is radically different, and several methods and properties have been renamed.

> **Note**   In MSXML 4.0, Microsoft introduced the same level of support for some relatively newer XML standards that are found in .NET Framework XML core classes—in particular, XSD, the XML Schema object model, and XPath. If you look at MSXML 3.0, however, the differences between managed and unmanaged XML processing are clearer.

Using MSXML in the .NET Framework

As with other COM objects, you can import the MSXML type library within the boundaries of a .NET application. The layer of system code providing for COM importation in the .NET Framework is the COM Interop Services (CIS). CIS provides access to existing COM components in a codeless and seamless way, without requiring modification of the original component.

The CIS consists of two distinct parts: one part makes COM components usable from within .NET applications, and the other part does the opposite—namely, making .NET classes callable from within a COM component. To incorporate a COM object into a managed application, you must first create a .NET wrapper class that exposes all the public methods and properties found in the component's type library. Microsoft Visual Studio .NET, for example, creates such a class on the fly, immediately after adding the proper library reference to the current project.

During the process, the involved types are converted from COM types and adapted to fit into the .NET Framework type system. After the importation is complete, the original COM object is ready for use in the .NET Framework, and more importantly, it has preserved the original interface while adding some .NET Framework–specific members such as *ToString* and *GetType*. In the end, for a Microsoft Visual Basic 6.0 programmer who happens to use Visual Basic .NET, the code to be written is nearly identical.

> **Note**   To generate a .NET wrapper class for a COM object, you can also use the tlbimp.exe utility from the command line. This utility gives you full control over the entire process, and by using command-line switches, you can intervene in many useful areas, including the (strong) name of the assembly and the wrapping namespace.

Although importing MSXML functionality into a .NET application is straightforward, you must have a good reason for doing so. Jumping continuously in and out of the .NET common language runtime (CLR) can result in a performance hit—not to mention the fact that you end up using a programming model that, although perfectly functional, is not the best suited for the surrounding environment.

The .NET Framework XML API

The essence of XML in the .NET Framework is found in two abstract classes—*XmlReader* and *XmlWriter*. These classes are at the core of all other .NET Framework XML classes, including the XMLDOM classes, and are used extensively by various subsystems to parse or generate XML text. For example, ADO.NET data adapters retrieve the data to store in a *DataSet* object using a database reader, and the *DataSet* object serializes its contents to the DiffGram format using an *XmlTextWriter* object, which derives from *XmlWriter*.

XML readers and writers constitute the primitive I/O functions for XML documents and are used to build more sophisticated functionalities. So overall, you have two possible approaches when it comes to processing XML data. You can use any of the specialized classes built on top of *XmlReader* and *XmlWriter* as well as document classes that expose the contents through the well-known and classic XMLDOM.

The direct use of readers represents a stream-based, but fast and stateless, approach to XML parsing. The use of XMLDOM classes (for example, *XmlDocument*) represents the traditional XMLDOM parsing model. Readers are representative of a pull model, as opposed to the SAX parser's typical push model. You can certainly build a push model atop a pull model–based API. Unfortunately, the reverse is never true, and that's why there is no SAX support in the .NET Framework. (In Chapter 2, you'll learn the basics of implementing a SAX parser using .NET Framework XML readers.)

The XML API for the .NET Framework comprises the following set of functionalities:

- XML readers
- XML writers
- XML document classes

All of these functionalities must overcome the rather subtle problem of type mapping. The .NET Framework XML type system has several things in common with the XSD Schema type system, and ad hoc conversion classes in the .NET Framework provide for applicable transformations.

Before we go any further into this overview of the key groups of classes, let's look at readers and writers in general. Readers and writers represent two rather generic software components that find several concrete (and powerful) implementations throughout the .NET Framework. The reader component provides a relatively common programming interface to read information out of a file or a stream. The writer component offers a common set of methods to write information down to a file or a stream in a format-independent way. Not surprisingly, readers operate in read-only mode, whereas writers accomplish their tasks operating in write-only mode.

.NET Framework Readers and Writers

In the .NET Framework, the classes available from the *System.IO* namespace provide for both synchronous and asynchronous read/write operations on two distinct categories of data: streams and files. A file is an ordered and named collection of bytes and is persistently stored to a disk. A stream represents a block of bytes that is read from, and written to, a data store. The data store can be based on a variety of storage media, including memory, disk files, and remote URLs. A stream is a kind of superset of a file, or in other words, a file that can be saved to a variety of storage media including memory. To work with streams, the .NET Framework defines several flavors of reader and writer classes. Figure 1-1 shows how each class relates to the others.

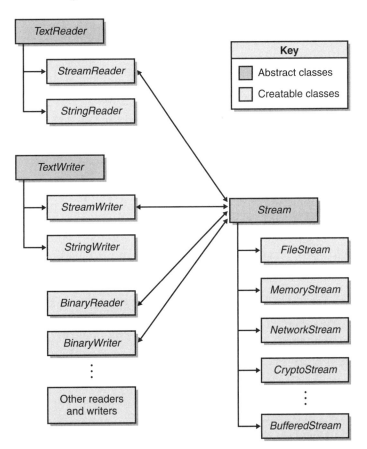

Figure 1-1   Streams can be read and written using made-to-measure reader and writer classes.

The base classes are *TextReader*, *TextWriter*, *BinaryReader*, *BinaryWriter*, and *Stream*. With the exception of the binary classes, all of these classes are marked as abstract (*MustInherit*, if you speak Visual Basic) and cannot be directly instantiated in code. You can use abstract classes to reference living instances of derived classes, however.

In the .NET Framework, base reader and writer classes find a number of concrete implementations, including *StreamReader* and *StringReader* and their writing counterparts. By design, reader and writer classes work on top of .NET streams and provide programmers with a customized user interface able to handle a particular type of underlying data or file format. Although each specific reader or writer class is tailor-made for the content of a given type of stream, they share a common set of methods and properties that defines the official .NET interface for reading and writing data.

The Cursor-Like Approach

A reader works in much the same way as a client-side database cursor. The underlying stream is seen as a logical sequence of units of information whose size and layout depend on the particular reader. Like a cursor, the reader moves through the data in a read-only, forward-only way. Normally, a reader is not expected to cache any information, but this is only common practice, rather than a strict requirement for all standard .NET readers.

ADO.NET data reader classes (for example, *SqlDataReader*) are simply .NET readers that move from one record to the next and expose the contents of the current record through a tailor-made interface. The unit of information read at every step is the database row. Similarly, a reader working on a disk file stream would consider as its own atomic unit of information the single byte, whereas a text reader would perhaps specialize in extracting one row of text at a time.

XML readers are simply another, very peculiar, type of .NET reader. The class parses the contents of an XML file, moving from one node to the next. In this case, the finer grain of the information processed is represented by the XML node—be it an element, an attribute, a comment, or a processing instruction.

XML Readers

An XML reader makes externally available a programming interface through which callers can connect and pull out all the data they need. This is in no way different from what happens when you connect to a database and fetch data. The database server returns a reference to an internal object—the cursor—

which manages all the query results and makes them available on demand. This statement applies regardless of the fact that the database world might provide several flavors of cursors—client, scrollable, server-side, and so on.

With XML readers, client applications are returned a reference to an instance of the reader class, which abstracts the underlying data stream. Methods on the reader class allow you to scroll forward through the contents, moving from node to node rather than from byte to byte or from record to record. When viewed from the perspective of readers, an XML document ceases to be a tagged text file and becomes a serialized collection of nodes. Such a cursor model is specific to the .NET platform, and to date, you will not find a similar programming API available for other platforms, including Microsoft Win32.

Readers vs. XMLDOM

XML readers don't require you to keep more data in memory than you actually need. When you open the XML document, a simple logical pointer that corresponds to a node is returned. You can easily skip over nodes to locate the one you need. In doing so, you don't tax in any way the application's memory with extra data other than that required to bufferize the currently selected node.

In contrast, the XMLDOM—a full read/write parser model—has the drawback that it might require a significant memory footprint and a long time to set up large documents in memory. Once in memory, however, the document can be easily and quickly read, edited, and serialized. To search a single node, or to change an individual property, you have to load the whole document in memory. As you can guess, this is not necessarily an optimal approach and might not be the appropriate way to go for most applications.

Taking the cursor-like approach to its limit, you can also observe an interesting convergence between readers and the XMLDOM. In fact, by visiting all element and attribute nodes in the stream and storing in a memory tree the related data, you build a dynamic and customized XMLDOM. Incidentally, this is just what happens in the .NET Framework when XMLDOM classes are instantiated using readers to load data and are serialized to disk using writers.

Readers vs. SAX

A SAX parser directly controls the evolution of the parsing process and pushes data to the client application. A cursor parser (that is, an XML reader), on the other hand, plays a more passive role and leaves client applications to control the process.

Giving applications, not the parser, control over the parsing process promotes the pull model (as opposed to the SAX parser's push model), in which the parser is invoked to obtain a reference to the underlying XML document. The parser also exposes methods for the client to navigate through the obtained document.

In addition to providing a simplified programming interface, the pull model is on average more efficient than the push model. For example, the pull model allows client applications to implement selective node processing and just skip over unneeded nodes. With SAX and the push model, all data has to pass through the application, which is the only entity that can reliably determine what is of interest and what can be discarded.

> **Note**   The push model, at least as implemented in SAX, can also be quite boring to code. SAX works by passing node contents to application-defined handlers. A handler is a living instance of an object that implements one or more interfaces according to the specification. So an application that needs to parse XML documents using SAX assigns instances of these objects to ad hoc properties on the SAX parser. Once started, the parser calls back the handlers through the predefined interfaces whenever it parses some content that relates to a given handler.

XML Writers

The .NET XML API separates parsing from editing and writing and offers a set of methods that provides effective results for performance as well as usability. When writing, you create new XML documents working at a considerably high level of abstraction and explicitly indicate the XML elements to create—nodes, attributes, comments, or processing instructions. The writer works on a stream, dumping content incrementally, one node after the next, without the random access capabilities of the XMLDOM but also without its memory footprint.

To grasp the importance of XML writers, consider that, in general, the only alternative you have for writing XML contents to any storage media consists of preparing the entire output as a string and then writing it off. In this case, the markup nature of XML is more hindrance than real help, because you must yourself take care of the intricacies of quotation marks, attributes, indentation, and end tags.

In the .NET Framework, XML writers come to the rescue and let you write XML documents programmatically in much the same way you write them through text editors. For example, you can specify whether you want a namespace prefix, the padding character and the size of the indentation, the quotation mark and the newline character, and even how you want white spaces to be treated. To create nodes, you simply use ad hoc methods to write comments, attributes, and element nodes. The overall method of working is simple and extremely effective.

The .NET Framework provides several types of writers that use heterogeneous output devices—strings, HTTP response, and HTML documents. You could also use an XML text writer to dump contents to a stream object or a new text file. In the latter two cases, you could also specify character encoding. If the encoding argument is *null*, the Unicode 8-bits-per-character schema (UTF-8) will be used.

XML writers, and in particular the *XmlTextWriter* class, are used throughout the .NET Framework for creating any sort of XML output. We'll look at XML writers in detail in Chapter 4.

The XML Document Object API in .NET

As mentioned, along with XML readers and writers, the .NET Framework also provides classes that load and edit XML documents according to the W3C DOM Level 1 and Level 2 Core. The key XMLDOM class in the .NET Framework is *XmlDocument*—not much different from the *DOMDocument* class, which you might recognize from working with MSXML.

The XMLDOM supplies an in-memory tree-based representation of XML documents and supports both navigation and editing of the document. In addition, the XMLDOM classes can handle both XPath queries and XSLT.

Tightly coupled with the *XmlDocument* class is the *XmlDataDocument* class. It extends *XmlDocument* and focuses on XML storage and retrieval of structured tabular data. In particular, *XmlDataDocument* can import data from an ADO.NET *DataSet* object and export regular XML contents to the *DataSet* relational format. Regular XML content is a set of nodes with exactly one level of subnodes, with each node having the same number of children. The ultimate goal of this requirement is enabling the XML contents to fit into a relational table.

The XMLDOM representation of an XML document is fully editable. Attributes and text can be randomly accessed, and nodes can be added and removed. You perform updates on a loaded XMLDOM document by first creating a node object (the *XmlNode* class) and then binding it to the existing tree. All in all, the underlying writing pattern is close to that of XML writers—you write nodes to the stream in one case, and you add nodes to the tree in the other. Of course, if you are using the XMLDOM, bear in mind that all changes occur in memory and must be flushed to the storage medium prior to return. (The XMLDOM API is described in detail in Chapter 5.)

XPath Expressions and XSLT

In the .NET Framework, XSLT and XPath expressions are fully supported but are implemented in classes distinct from those that parse and write XML text. This is a key feature of the overall .NET XML API. Any functionality is provided through a small hierarchy of objects, although each subtree connects and interoperates well with others. Figure 1-2 demonstrates the interconnection between constituent APIs.

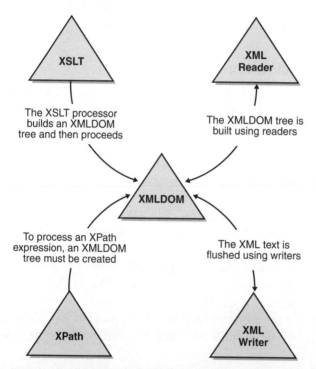

Figure 1-2   The XMLDOM API is built on top of readers and writers, but both XSLT and XPath expressions need to have a complete and XMLDOM-based vision of the entire XML document to process it.

XML readers and writers are the primitive elements of the .NET XML API. Whenever XML text must be parsed or written, all classes, directly or indirectly, refer to them. A more complex primitive element is the XMLDOM tree. Transformations and advanced queries must rely on the document in its entirety being held in memory and accessible through a well-known interface—the XMLDOM.

The XSLT Processor

The key class for XSLT is *XslTransform*. The class works as an XSLT processor and complies with version 1.0 of the XSLT recommendation. The class has two key methods, *Load* and *Transform*, whose behavior is for the most part self-explanatory.

Once you acquire an instance of the *XslTransform* class, you first load the source of an XSL document that contains the transformation rules. By calling the *Transform* method, you actually perform the conversion from native XML to the output format. Prior to applying the transformation, the underlying XML document is loaded as a kind of XMLDOM tree. (The details of XSLT are covered in Chapter 7.)

The XPath Query Engine

XPath is a language that allows you to navigate within XML documents. Think of XPath as a general-purpose query language for addressing, sorting, and filtering both the elements and the text of an XML document.

The XPath notation is basically declarative. Any XPath expression is a path within the XML document that identifies the information with the given characteristics. The path defines a pattern, and the resulting selection includes all the nodes that match it. The selection is expressed through a notation that emphasizes the hierarchical relationship between the nodes. It works in much the same way files and folders work. For example, the XPath expression *"book/publisher"* means find the *"publisher"* element within the *"book"* element. The XPath navigation model works in the context of a hierarchy of nodes in the XML document's tree. XPath makes use of a variation of the *XmlDocument* class, named *XPathDocument*.

Running an XPath query is not actually different from executing a Transact-SQL (T-SQL) query on SQL Server. Instead of getting back a collection of rows, a valid XPath expression returns a collection of nodes. To scroll the returned nodes, you just use an XPath-customized version of a reader. We'll look at XPath in more detail in Chapter 6.

Conclusion

In this chapter, we examined the building blocks of XML and explored the rationale behind XML readers and writers—a new and innovative way to perform basic operations on XML data sources. In the .NET Framework, XML readers introduce a database-like cursor model to navigate through data. The cursor model falls somewhere between the well-known XMLDOM and SAX models. Not as expensive as XMLDOM and more programmer-friendly than SAX, the .NET Framework cursor model presents XML as just another data format you can work on using a familiar approach.

As a developer, you are certainly familiar with I/O operations accomplished on a file or a database. Why should XML data sources be totally different? The *node* becomes just another atomic element, along with the *database row* or the *byte*. Ad hoc methods make it possible for you to move through nodes in a straightforward, effective way.

Readers and writers are not the only tools you can use to create XML-driven .NET applications. Another group of classes work according to the specification of the W3C DOM. XSLT and XPath expressions are a pair of XML-related technologies that are popular with developers and effective for arranging applications. In the .NET Framework, you find made-to-measure classes that make XML-to-XML transformation and query evaluation fast and easy.

All the XML technologies introduced in this chapter will be covered in depth in the chapters that follow, beginning with XML readers in Chapter 2.

Further Reading

The W3C organization is currently working on a draft of the DOM Level 3 Core to include support for an abstract modeling schema and I/O serialization. Check out the most recent draft at *http://www.w3.org/TR/2002/WD-DOM-Level-3-ASLS-20020409*. The approved standard—DOM Level 2 Core—is available at *http://www.w3.org/TR/DOM-Level-2*.

Relevant information about XML standards is available from the W3C Web site, at *http://www.w3.org*. If you want to learn more about the SAX specification, look at the new Web site for the SAX project, at *http://www.saxproject.org*.

A lot of useful developer-oriented documentation about XML is available on the Web sites of the companies that support XML. In addition to the

Microsoft Web site (*http://msdn.microsoft.com/xml*), check out the Intel Developer Services Web site *(http://cedar.intel.com)*. In particular, you'll find an essential guide to XML in the .NET Framework: *http://cedar.intel.com/media/pdf/dotnet/net_jumpstart.pdf.*

Finally, if you just want a good, all-encompassing book about XML programming, I heartily recommend the Microsoft Press Core Reference book *XML Programming (http://www.microsoft.com/mspress/books/4798.asp)*, by R. Allen Wyke, Sultan Rehman, and Brad Leupen (Microsoft Press, 2002). For a more general look into XML as a unifying technology, *Essential XML: Beyond Markup* (Addison Wesley, 2000), by Don Box, Aaron Skonnard, and John Lam, is still one of the best books available.

2

XML Readers

In the Microsoft .NET Framework, two distinct sets of classes provide for XML-driven reading and writing operations. These classes are known globally as *XML readers* and *writers*. The base class for readers is *XmlReader*, whereas *XmlWriter* provides the base programming interface for writers. In this chapter, we'll focus on a particular type of XML readers—the XML text readers. In Chapter 3, we'll zero in on validating readers and then move on to XML writers in Chapter 4.

The Programming Interface of Readers

XmlReader is an abstract class available from the *System.Xml* namespace. It defines the set of functionalities that an XML reader exposes to let developers access an XML stream in a noncached, forward-only, read-only way.

An XML reader works on a read-only stream by jumping from one node to the next in a forward-only direction. The XML reader maintains an internal pointer to the current node and its attributes and text but has no notion of previous and next nodes. You can't modify text or attributes, and you can move only forward from the current node. If you are visiting attribute nodes, however, you can move back to the parent node or access an attribute by index. The visit takes place in node-first order, but other visiting algorithms can be arranged in custom reader classes. See the note on page 72 for more information about visiting algorithms.

The specification for the *XmlReader* class recommends that any derived class should check at least whether the XML source is well-formed and throw exceptions if an error is encountered. XML exceptions are handled through the tailor-made *XmlException* class. The *XMLReader* class specification does not say anything about XML validation. Throughout this chapter, you'll see that the .NET Framework provides several reader classes with and without validation capabilities. Valid sources for an XML reader are disk files as well as any flavor of .NET streams and text readers (for example, string readers).

An OOP Refresher

Throughout this book, I'll often use terms such as *interface* and *class*, sometimes qualified by helper adjectives such as *abstract* or *base*. Although a full explanation of these terms and their related object-oriented programming (OOP) concepts is beyond the scope of this book, a quick terminology refresher will help you get to the heart of the XML class hierarchy in the .NET Framework.

In the .NET Framework, an *interface* is a container for a named collection of method, property, and event definitions referred to as a *contract*. An interface can be used as a reference type, but it is not a creatable type. Other types can implement one or more interfaces. In doing so, they adhere to the interface's contract and agree to provide actual implementation for all the methods, properties, and events in the contract.

A *class* is a container that can include data and function members (methods, properties, events, operators, and constructors). Classes support inheritance from other classes as well as from interfaces. Any class from which another class inherits is called a *base class*.

An *abstract class* simply declares its members without providing any implementation. Like interfaces, abstract classes are not creatable but can be used as reference types. An abstract class differs from an interface in that it has a slightly richer set of internal members (constructors, constants, and operators). Members of an abstract class can be scoped as private, public, or protected, whereas members of an interface are mostly public. In addition, child classes can implement multiple interfaces but can inherit from only one class.

The *XmlReader* Class

The *XmlReader* class defines methods that enable you to pull data from an XML source and to skip unwanted nodes. Bear in mind that each and every element in an XML stream is considered a node, meaning that *node* is a rather generic concept that applies to subtree roots as well as to attributes, processing instructions, entities, comments, and plain text.

The *XmlReader* class includes methods for reading XML content from an entire text file, returning the depth of the current XML node's subtree, and determining whether the contents of a given element is empty. You can also fairly easily read and navigate attributes and skip over elements and their contents. Valuable information such as the name and the contents of the current node is also returned via ad hoc properties.

Base Properties of XML Readers

Table 2-1 lists the public properties exposed by the *XmlReader* class. Notice that the values these properties contain depend on the actual reader class you are using in your code. The description of each property refers to the property's intended goal, but this description might not entirely reflect the actual role of the property in a derived reader class.

Table 2-1   Public Properties of the *XmlReader* Class

Property	Description
AttributeCount	Gets the number of attributes on the current node.
BaseURI	Gets the base URI of the current node.
CanResolveEntity	Gets a value indicating whether the reader can resolve entities.
Depth	Gets the depth of the current node in the XML document.
EOF	Indicates whether the reader has reached the end of the stream.
HasAttributes	Indicates whether the current node has any attributes.
HasValue	Indicates whether the current node can have a value.
IsDefault	Indicates whether the current node is an attribute that originated from the default value defined in the document type definition (DTD) or schema.
IsEmptyElement	Indicates whether the current node is an empty element with no attributes or value.
Item	Indexer property that returns the value of the specified attribute.

(continued)

Table 2-1   Public Properties of the *XmlReader* Class *(continued)*

Property	Description
LocalName	Gets the name of the current node with any prefix removed.
Name	Gets the fully qualified name of the current node.
NamespaceURI	Gets the namespace URI of the current node. Applies to *Element* and *Attribute* nodes only.
NameTable	Gets the name table object associated with the reader. (More on name table objects later.)
NodeType	Gets the type of the current node.
Prefix	Gets the namespace prefix associated with the current node.
QuoteChar	Gets the quotation mark character used to enclose the value of an attribute.
ReadState	Gets the state of the reader from the *ReadState* enumeration.
Value	Gets the text value of the current node.
XmlLang	Gets the *xml:lang* scope within which the current node resides.
XmlSpace	Gets the current *xml:space* scope from the *XmlSpace* enumeration (*Default*, *None*, or *Preserve*).

Note   When you read any sort of documentation about XML, you are usually bombarded by a storm of similar-looking acronyms: URI, URL, and URN. Let's review these terms. A Uniform Resource Identifier (URI) is a string that unequivocally identifies a resource over the network. There are two types of URI: Uniform Resource Locator (URL) and Uniform Resource Name (URN). A URL is specified by the protocol prefix, the host name or IP address, the port (optional), and the path. A URN is simply a unique descriptive string—for example, the human-readable form of a CLSID (the 128-bit identifier of a COM object) is a URN.

A bit misleading is the fact that URNs are often created using URL-like strings. This regularly happens with XML namespaces, for example. The reason for this practice is that a URL has a high likelihood of being unique, especially if you use a path within your company's Web site.

An XML reader can pass through several different states. All the possible states are defined by the *ReadState* enumeration and are listed in Table 2-2. The *ReadState* property contains a *ReadState* enumeration value and is expected to return the current state of the reader, but actual implementations of a reader class must ensure that the property always holds the correct value.

Table 2-2   Reader States

State	Description
Closed	The reader is closed.
EndOfFile	The end of the file has been reached successfully, but the reader is not yet closed.
Error	A critical error occurred, and the read operation can't continue.
Initial	The reader is in its initial position, waiting for the *Read* method to be called for the first time.
Interactive	The reader is open and functional.

The *BaseURI* property actually returns the URL of the node. Normally, the URL of a node—more generally, the URI—is bound to the resource name, be it a local file, a networked document, or a Web document. In these cases, the *BaseURI* property simply returns the URL-styled name of the resource. The following are examples of values that would be returned under these circumstances:

```
file://c:/myfolder/mydoc.xml
http://www.cpandl.com/myfolder/mydoc.xml
```

An XML document can result from the aggregation of various chunks of data—entities, schemas, and DTDs—coming from different network locations. In these cases, the *BaseURI* property tells you where these nodes come from. If the XML document is being processed through a stream (for example, an in-memory string), no URI is available and the *BaseURI* property returns the empty string.

Base Methods of XML Readers

Table 2-3 lists the public methods exposed by the *XmlReader* class. This table does not include the methods defined in the *Object* class and overridden in *XmlReader*—for example, *ToString*, *GetType*, and *Equals*.

Table 2-3   Public Methods of the *XmlReader* Class

Method	Description
Close	Closes the reader and sets the internal state to *Closed*.
GetAttribute	Gets the value of the specified attribute. An attribute can be accessed by index, local name, or qualified name.
IsStartElement	Indicates whether the current content node is a start tag.
LookupNamespace	Returns the namespace URI to which the given prefix maps.
MoveToAttribute	Moves the pointer to the specified attribute. An attribute can be accessed by index, local name, or qualified name.
MoveToContent	Moves the pointer ahead to the next content node or to the end of the file. This method returns immediately if the current node is already a content node, such as non-white-space text, CDATA, *Element*, *EndElement*, *EntityReference*, or *EndEntity*.
MoveToElement	Moves the pointer back to the element node that contains the current attribute node. Relevant only when the current node is an attribute.
MoveToFirstAttribute	Moves to the first attribute of the current *Element* node.
MoveToNextAttribute	Moves to the next attribute of the current *Element* node.
Read	Reads the next node and advances the pointer.
ReadAttributeValue	Parses the attribute value into one or more *Text*, *EndEntity*, or *EntityReference* nodes. (More on this in the section "Parsing Mixed-Content Attributes," on page 41.)
ReadElementString	Reads and returns the text from a text-only element.
ReadEndElement	Checks that the current content node is an end tag and advances the reader to the next node. Throws an exception if the node is not an end tag.
ReadInnerXml	Reads and returns all the content below the current node, including markup information.
ReadOuterXml	Reads and returns all the content in and below the current node, including markup information.
ReadStartElement	Checks that the current node is an element and advances the reader to the next node. Throws an exception if the node is not a start tag.
ReadString	Reads the contents of an element or a text node as a string. This method concatenates all the text up until the next markup. For attribute nodes, calling this method is equivalent to reading the attribute value.
ResolveEntity	Expands and resolves the current *EntityReference* node.
Skip	Skips the children of the current node.

In addition to the methods listed in Table 2-3, the *XmlReader* class also features a couple of static (shared, if you speak only Microsoft Visual Basic) methods named *IsName* and *IsNameToken*. Both take a string and return a Boolean value. The return value indicates whether the given string complies with the respective definitions of a *Name* and a *Nmtoken* (name token) according to the W3C XML 1.0 Recommendation.

In XML 1.0, a *Name* is a string that begins with a letter, an underscore (_), or a colon (:) and continues with letters, digits, hyphens, underscores, and colons. A *Nmtoken*, on the other hand, is any non-zero-length mixture of name characters—that is, letters, digits, hyphens, underscores, and colons.

> **Note**   A static member (as opposed to an instance member) of a class is a kind of global member that belongs to the type itself rather than to a specific instance of the class. Whereas an instance of a class contains a separate copy of all instance members, there is only one copy of each static member. Static members can't be referenced through an instance. Instead, you must reference them through the type name:
>
> ```
> Console.WriteLine(XmlReader.IsName("DinoEsposito"));
> ```
>
> Members that in C# are called static and declared with the *static* keyword, in Visual Basic .NET are called shared and are declared with the *Shared* keyword. Aside from this, their usage is identical.

Recognized Node Types

Each node in an XML source is of a certain type. The *NodeType* property is a read-only property that returns the type of the current node. The returned value belongs to the *XmlNodeType* enumeration, which comprises the node types listed in the Table 2-4.

Table 2-4   Types of Nodes in the *XmlNodeType* Enumeration

Node Type	Description
Attribute	Represents an attribute of an *Element* node. Attribute nodes can have two child node types, *Text* and *EntityReference*, which represent the value of the attribute. Note that an attribute is not the child of any other node type—in particular, it is not considered the child of an *Element* node.
CDATA	Represents a *CDATA* section. A *CDATA* section is a block of escaped text used as is and is not recognized as markup text. A *CDATA* node can't have any child nodes.
Comment	Represents a comment in the XML text. A *Comment* node can't have any child nodes.
Document	Represents a document object that is the root of the document tree. *Document* provides access to the whole XML document and can have the following child node types: only one *Element* node (the actual root of the XML tree), *ProcessingInstruction*, *Comment*, and *DocumentType*.
DocumentFragment	Represents a document fragment—namely, a node or an entire subtree—that is linked to a document without actually being part of it or contained in the same file.
DocumentType	Represents a document type. A document type node is characterized by the <*!DOCTYPE*> tag. A *DocumentType* node can have child nodes of type *Notation* and *Entity*.
Element	Represents the most common type of node found in XML documents. *Element* can have several types of child nodes, including other element nodes, text, comments, processing instructions, *CDATA*, and entity references.
EndElement	Represents the end tag of an element node.
EndEntity	Represents the end of an entity node.
Entity	Represents an entity declaration. In XML, entities are much the same as macros—that is, names that point to expanded text.
EntityReference	Represents a reference to an entity used in the body of XML documents.
None	The node type returned by the *XmlReader* class if the *Read* method has not yet been called.
Notation	Represents a notation in the document type declaration.
ProcessingInstruction	Represents a processing instruction at the beginning of the XML document.

Table 2-4   Types of Nodes in the *XmlNodeType* Enumeration

Node Type	Description
SignificantWhitespace	Represents a significant white space character between markup text in a mixed-content model or white space within the scope of *xml:space="preserve"*.
Text	Represents the text content of an element.
Whitespace	Represents an insignificant space between markup text.
XmlDeclaration	Represents the XML declaration node. *XmlDeclaration* must be the first node in the document and can't have children. The node can have attributes that provide version and encoding information.

Table 2-4 includes all the possible types of nodes found within the body of an XML document—at least when the document is parsed through a .NET XML reader. Notice that the XML element that is normally perceived as being *the* node—that is, marked up text—is said to be an *element node*. Attributes, comments, and even processing instructions are just other types of nodes. In light of this, when you move from one node to the next, you are not necessarily moving between nodes of the same type.

A lot of XML documents begin with several tags that do not represent any data content. The reader's *MoveToContent* method lets you skip all the heading information and position the pointer directly in the first content node. In doing so, the method skips over the following node types: *ProcessingInstruction*, *DocumentType*, *Comment*, *Whitespace*, and *SignificantWhitespace*.

Specialized Reader Classes

The *XmlReader* class defines only the clauses and appendices in the contract that .NET XML applications sign with the actual parser class. Because *XmlReader* is an abstract class, you'll use it in your code only as a reference type when type casting is needed. In lieu of *XmlReader*, you can use any of its derived classes already defined in the .NET Framework. In addition, you can use any other custom reader class that third-party vendors, or you yourself, might have written. All of these reader classes share the programming interface with *XmlReader*, however, and provide an actual, albeit custom, implementation for each of the methods and properties listed in Table 2-1, on page 27, and Table 2-3, on page 30.

Implementations of the *XmlReader* class extend the base class and vary in their design to support different scenarios. The .NET Framework supplies the following reader classes:

- **XmlTextReader**   Extremely fast; the reader ensures that the XML source is well-formed but neither validates it against a schema or a DTD nor resolves any embedded entity.

- **XmlValidatingReader**   An XML reader that can validate the source using a DTD, an XML-Data Reduced (XDR) schema, and an XML Schema Definition (XSD). In addition, the reader is capable of expanding entities and also supports default attributes as defined in the DTD or schema.

- **XmlNodeReader**   The reader specializes in parsing XML data from an XML Document Object Model (XML DOM) subtree and does not support validation.

In the next section, we'll examine the *XmlTextReader* class—probably the most frequently used .NET reader class. Validating readers will be covered in Chapter 3; node readers are discussed in Chapter 5. By the end of this chapter, you'll also have had in-depth exposure to the intricacies (and the flexibility) connected with the development of a custom reader class.

Parsing with the *XmlTextReader* Class

The *XmlTextReader* class is designed to provide fast access to streams of XML data in a forward-only and read-only manner. The reader verifies that the submitted XML is well-formed. It also performs a quick check for correctness on the referenced DTD, if one exists. In no case, though, does this reader validate against a schema or DTD. If you need more functionality (for example, validation), you must resort to other reader classes such as *XmlNodeReader* or *XmlValidatingReader*.

An instance of the *XmlTextReader* class can be created in a number of ways and from a variety of sources, including disk files, URLs, streams, and text readers. To process an XML file, you start by instantiating the constructor, as shown here:

```
XmlTextReader reader = new XmlTextReader(file);
```

Note that all the public constructors available require you to indicate the source of the data, be it a stream, a file, or whatever else. The default constructor of the

XmlTextReader class is marked as *protected* and, as such, is not intended to be used directly from user's code.

After the reader is up and running, you have to explicitly open it using the *Read* method. This behavior is not unique to XML readers, it is common to all .NET reader components. Readers move from their initial state to the first element using only the *Read* method. To move from any node to the next, you can continue using *Read* as well as a number of other more specialized methods, including *Skip*, *MoveToContent*, and *ReadInnerXml*.

To process the entire content of an XML source, you typically set up a loop based on the return value of the *Read* method. The *Read* method returns *true* if there's more content to be read, and *false* otherwise.

Accessing Nodes

The following example shows how to use an *XmlTextReader* object to parse the contents of an XML file and build the node layout. Let's begin by considering the following XML data:

```
<platforms type="software">
   <platform vendor="Microsoft">.NET</platform>
   <platform vendor="" OpenSource="yes">Linux</platform>
   <platform vendor="Microsoft">Win32</platform>
   <platform vendor="Sun">Java</platform>
</platforms>
```

The corresponding node layout that we want to extrapolate consists of a block of XML data that comprises all the element nodes of the source file, as shown here:

```
<platforms>
   <platform>
   </platform>
   <platform>
   </platform>
   <platform>
   </platform>
   <platform>
   </platform>
</platforms>
```

To produce these results, I created the *GetXmlFileNodeLayout* function. This function scans the entire contents of the XML file and processes each node found along the way. Only two types of nodes are relevant for this example: the start and end tags of *Element* nodes. The *NodeType* enumeration identifies these two types of nodes through the keywords *Element* and *EndElement*.

```
private string GetXmlFileNodeLayout(string file)
{
    // Open the stream
    XmlTextReader reader = new XmlTextReader(file);

    // Loop through the nodes
    StringWriter writer = new StringWriter();
    string tabPrefix = "";

    while (reader.Read())
    {
        // Write the start tag
        if (reader.NodeType == XmlNodeType.Element)
        {
            tabPrefix = new string('\t', reader.Depth);
            writer.WriteLine("{0}<{1}>", tabPrefix, reader.Name);
        }
        else
        {
            // Write the end tag
            if (reader.NodeType == XmlNodeType.EndElement)
            {
                tabPrefix = new string('\t', reader.Depth);
                writer.WriteLine("{0}</{1}>", tabPrefix, reader.Name);
            }
        }
    }

    // Write to the output window
    string buf = writer.ToString();
    writer.Close();

    // Close the stream
    reader.Close();

    return buf;
}
```

The Boolean value that controls the main loop stops the loop when the reader's internal pointer reaches the end of the stream. *GetXmlFileNodeLayout* is designed to analyze all nodes but process only those of type *Element* or *EndElement*. The name of the node, formatted to look like a tag name, is output to a memory string as a line of text.

After finding an *Element* or *EndElement* node, the function uses the reader's *Depth* property to get the nesting level of the current node and arranges a prefix string made of as many tab characters as the depth level. The prefix string is inserted into the output buffer before the node name to produce properly indented text.

You might have noticed that the *GetXmlFileNodeLayout* function accumulates the text that represents the node layout into a *StringWriter* object. The *StringWriter* object is a typical .NET writer class and offers a more friendly programming interface than the classic *String* class. *StringWriter* lets you express the content in lines and automatically provides for newline characters. In addition, its writing methods support placeholders and a variable-length parameters list. *GetXmlFileNodeLayout* then uses the *StringWriter* object's *ToString* method to return the accumulated text as a plain string.

> **Note**   The full source code for a Windows Forms application that uses the *GetXmlFileNodeLayout* function is available in this book's sample files. The application name is NodeLayout.

Reading and Converting Text

To read the content of the reader's current node, you normally use the *Value* property. This property, however, always returns a string that you might need to convert to a more specific type such as a date or a double. To convert a string to a .NET Framework type, you should use any of the *XmlConvert* class methods.

How is the *XmlConvert* class different from the *System.Convert* class—the .NET Framework primary tool for converting from one type to another? The two classes perform nearly identical tasks, but the *XmlConvert* class works according to the XSD data type specification and ignores the current locale. Let's look at an example that illustrates the difference between the two converting classes. Suppose that you have an XML fragment such as the following:

```
<employee>
    <hired>2-8-2001</hired>
    <salary>150,000</salary>
</employee>
```

The current locale dictates that the hire date is February 8, 2001, and the yearly salary is $150,000. If you convert the strings to specific .NET types using the *System.Convert* class, all will work as expected. If you convert using *Xml-Convert*, you'll get errors:

```
// Assume the reader points to <hired>
DateTime dt = XmlConvert.ToDateTime(reader.Value);

// Move the reader to <salary>
reader.Read();
double d = XmlConvert.ToDouble(reader.Value);
```

In particular, the *XmlConvert* class will not recognize the first string as a correct date. As for the salary, you'll get a message stating that the input string is not in the correct format.

If you had created the XML code programmatically using an XML writer (more on XML writers in Chapter 4) and .NET strong types, the XML fragment you're working with would be slightly different, as shown here:

```
<employee>
    <hired>2001-02-08</hired>
    <salary>150000</salary>
</employee>
```

To be understood in XML, a date must be in YYYY-MM-DD format and a double value should not include any locale-dependent element such as the digit group symbol. If the double value includes a fractional part, use a decimal point to separate it from the integer part. Likewise, *XmlConvert* recognizes Booleans only if they are expressed as true/false or 1/0 pairs.

Note   Another aspect that makes the difference between the *System.Convert* and *XmlConvert* classes even sharper is the fact that *XmlConvert* does not support custom format providers. The *XmlConvert* class works as a translator to and from .NET types and XSD types. When the conversion takes place, the result is rigorously locale independent.

Round-Tripping Non-XML Strings

Not all characters available on a given platform are necessarily valid XML characters. Only the characters included in the range of allowed characters defined in the XML specification (*www.w3.org/TR/2000/REC-xml-20001006.html*) can be safely used for element and attribute names.

The *XmlConvert* class provides key functions for tunneling non-XML names through XML over a round-trip to some servers. When names contain characters that are invalid in XML names, the methods *EncodeName* and *DecodeName* can adjust them to fit into an XML name schema. For example, several applications, including Microsoft SQL Server and Microsoft Office, allow and support Unicode characters in their documents. However, some of these characters are not valid in XML names. The typical circumstance that demonstrates the importance of *XmlConvert* occurs when you manipulate, say, a database column name containing blanks. Although SQL Server allows a column name such as *Invoice Details*, that would not be a valid name for an XML stream. The word space must be replaced with its hexadecimal encoding. A valid XML representation for the column name *Invoice Details* is the following string:

```
Invoice_0x0020_Details
```

You can obtain that string by using *EncodeName*, as shown here:

```
string xmlColName = XmlConvert.EncodeName("Invoice Details");
```

The reverse operation is accomplished by using *DecodeName*. This method translates an XML name back to its original form by unescaping any escaped sequence, as shown in the following code. Note that only fully escaped forms are detected. For example, only *_0x0020_* is rendered as a blank space.

```
string colName = XmlConvert.DecodeName("Invoice_0x0020_Details");
```

The only valid form of hexadecimal sequences is *_0xHHHH_*, where *HHHH* stands for a four-digit hexadecimal value. Similar forms are left unaltered, although they could easily be considered logically equivalent—for example, *_0x20_* is not processed.

Character Encoding

XML documents can contain an attribute to specify the encoding. Character encoding provides a mapping between numeric indexes and corresponding characters that users read from a document. The following declaration shows how to set the required encoding for an XML document:

```
<?xml version="1.0" encoding="ISO-8859-5"?>
```

The *Encoding* property of the XML reader returns the character encoding found in the document. The default encoding attribute is UTF-8 (UCS Transformation Format, 8 bits).

In the .NET Framework, the *System.Text.Encoding* class gathers all supported encodings. Most of these encodings can be used with XML documents, with just a few exceptions. Encodings such as UTF-7 are invalid for XML documents because they require different byte values than UTF-8. UTF-8 encodes Unicode characters using 8 bits per character. UTF-7, on the other hand, encodes Unicode characters using 7 bits per character.

Accessing Attributes

Of all the node types supplied in the .NET Framework, only *Element*, *Document-Type*, and *XmlDeclaration* support attributes. To check whether a given node contains attributes, use the *HasAttributes* Boolean property. The *AttributeCount* property returns the number of attributes available for the current node.

Once the internal reader's pointer is positioned on a certain node, you can directly read the value of a particular attribute using either the *GetAttribute* method or the indexer property *Item*. In both cases, overloads of the method and the property allow you to access attributes in various ways: by absolute position, by name, and by name and namespace. The returned value for an attribute is always a string; the task of converting it to a more specific data type is left to the programmer.

GetAttribute and *Item* provide a way to access attributes directly but require that you know the name or the ordinal position of the attribute being accessed. A third way to read attribute values is by moving the pointer to the attribute node itself and then using the *Value* property. You enumerate the attribute nodes using the *MoveToFirstAttribute* and *MoveToNextAttribute* methods. You can also change the pointer by moving directly to a given node using the *MoveTo-Attribute* method.

This next example demonstrates how to programmatically access any sequence of attributes for a node and concatenate their names and values in a single string. Consider the following XML fragment:

```
<employee id="1" lastname="Users" firstname="Joe" />
```

We want to create a method that, when run on this XML block of data, generates the following string:

```
id="1" lastname="Users" firstname="Joe"
```

The method we create to do this is the user-defined function *GetAttributeList*. *GetAttributeList* takes a reference to the reader and extracts attribute values for the currently selected node.

```
// Assume we call this method after having read the node
string GetAttributeList(XmlReader reader)
{
    String buf = "";
    if (reader.HasAttributes)
        while(reader.MoveToNextAttribute())
            buf += reader.Name + "=\"" + reader.Value + "\" ";

    reader.MoveToElement();
    return buf;
}
```

When the pointer is not already positioned on an attribute node, calling *MoveToNextAttribute* is equivalent to calling *MoveToFirstAttribute*, which moves the pointer to the first attribute node.

An XML reader can move only forward, which means that no previously visited node can be revisited once you have moved on to another node. This rule has a very specific exception. When the pointer is positioned on an attribute node, you can move back to the parent node using the *MoveTo-Element* method. This exception exists because, after all, an attribute is a particular type of node that is used to qualify the contents of the parent. From this point of view, an attribute is seen as a sort of subnode, and moving between the attributes of a given node does not logically change the index of the current element node. Using *MoveToAttribute* and *MoveToFirstAttribute*, you can jump from one attribute node to the next in both directions.

Parsing Mixed-Content Attributes

Normally, the content of an attribute consists of a simple string of text. If you need to use it as an instance of a more specific type (for example, a date or a Boolean value), you can convert the string using either the methods of the static classes *XmlConvert* (recommended) or even *System.Convert*.

In some situations, however, the content of an attribute is mixed and includes plain text along with entities. Although unable to resolve entity references, the *XmlTextReader* class can separate text from entities when both are embedded in an attribute's value. For this to happen, you must parse the attribute's content using the *ReadAttributeValue* method instead of simply reading the content via the *Value* property.

The following code demonstrates how to rewrite the *GetAttributeList* function so that it can preprocess mixed attributes and separate text from entities. The added code is shown in boldface.

```
// Assume we call this method after having read the node
string GetAttAttributeList(XmlReader reader)
{
    String buf = "";
    if (reader.HasAttributes)
        while(reader.MoveToNextAttribute())
        {
            buf += reader.Name + "=\"";
            while(reader.ReadAttributeValue())
            {
                if (reader.NodeType == XmlNodeType.EntityReference)
                    buf += "[" + reader.Name + "]";
                else
                    buf += reader.Value;
            }
            buf += "\" ";
        }

    reader.MoveToElement();
    return buf;
}
```

The *ReadAttributeValue* method parses the attribute value and isolates each constituent token, be it plain text or an entity. The function calls *ReadAttributeValue* repeatedly until the end of the attribute string is reached. Because by design the *XmlTextReader* parser does not resolve entities, there is not much you can do with the embedded entity other than recognizing and maybe skipping it. The preceding code, for instance, wraps the name of the entity in square brackets. When processing an element node such as this:

```
<book ISBN="61801-1" author="&author;, Italy">
```

the *GetAttAttributeList* function produces the following string:

```
ISBN="61801-1" author="[author], Italy"
```

Attribute Normalization

The W3C XML 1.0 Recommendation defines attribute normalization as the preliminary process that an attribute value should be subjected to prior to being returned to the application. The normalization process can be summarized in a few basic rules:

- Any referenced character (for example, * *) is expanded.

- Any white space character (blanks, carriage returns, linefeeds, and tabs) is replaced with a blank (ASCII *0x20*) character.

- Any leading or trailing sequence of blanks is discarded.

- Any other sequence of blanks is replaced with a single blank character (ASCII *0x20*).

All other characters (for example, the literals forming the value) are simply appended to the resulting normalized value. Any entity reference found in the attribute value is recursively normalized. Of course, the normalization process applies only to the attributes defined outside of any *CDATA* section.

The *XmlTextReader* parser lets you toggle the normalization process on and off through the *Normalization* Boolean property. By default, the *Normalization* property is set to *false*, meaning that attribute values are not normalized. If the normalization process is disabled, an attribute can contain any character, including characters in the *&#00;* to *&#20;* range, which are normally considered invalid and not permitted. When normalization is on, using any of those character entities results in an *XmlException* being thrown.

Consider the following attribute value, in which the entity character *
* denotes a linefeed character:

```
<book author="Dino Esposito" AuthorDisplayName="Dino&#10;Esposito">
```

Let's try to read the *AuthorDisplayName* attribute using the *XmlTextReader* parser when the normalization is off. The following code shows how:

```
reader.Normalization = false;
reader.Read();
Console.WriteLine(reader["AuthorDisplayName"]);
```

In the resulting string, the linefeed is preserved, and the output in the console window looks like this:

```
Dino
Esposito
```

Conversely, if you read the attribute when *Normalization* is set to *true*, the linefeed is replaced with a blank, and the output looks like this:

```
Dino Esposito
```

Handling XML Exceptions

The XML reader throws an exception whenever it encounters a parsing error in the XML source. The reader makes use of the *XmlException* class to return detailed information about the last parsing error. Ad hoc information includes the line number, the character position, and a text description. *LinePosition* and *Line-Number*, shown here, are the members that differentiate the *XmlException* class from the basic .NET *Exception* class:

```
public class XmlException : SystemException
{
    int LinePosition;
    int LineNumber;
}
```

Although you can still catch XML parsing and validation exceptions through the basic *Exception* class, catching them through *XmlException* gives you more information and the certainty that the error relates only to the code handling XML data.

> **Note**   If you have multiple XML documents in a single stream to parse in sequence, you can still use the same instance of the reader. However, prior to attacking a new stream, you must reset the internal state of the reader. The *XmlTextReader* class specifically defines a method, named *ResetState*, that simply resets the state of the reader to *Read-State.Initial*.
>
> *ResetState* resets all the properties to their default values, with a few exceptions. *Normalization*, *XmlResolver*, and *WhitespaceHandling* are not affected by the state reset.

Handling White Spaces

In XML, white spaces are a special type of node. White spaces found in the body of an XML document can be classified in two groups: *significant* and *insignificant*. A white space is said to be significant when it appears in the text of an element node or when it appears to be within the scope of a white space declaration, as shown here:

```
<MyTag xml:space="preserve">
<!-- Any space here is significant and must be preserved -->
    :
</MyTag>
```

Significant white spaces can't be removed from the document without affecting to some extent the validity and the contents of the document. An insignificant white space, on the other hand, is any white space that you do not need to preserve after reading the source document. *White space* is a blanket term that encompasses more than one character and does not refer only to blanks (ASCII *0x20*). White spaces are also carriage returns (ASCII *0x0D*), linefeeds (ASCII *0x0A*), and tabs (ASCII *0x09*).

The *XmlTextReader* class lets you control how white spaces are handled by using the property *WhitespaceHandling*. This property accepts and returns a value taken from the *WhitespaceHandling* enumeration, which lists three feasible options. The default option is *All* and indicates that both significant and insignificant spaces will be returned as distinct nodes—*SignificantWhitespace* and *Whitespace*, respectively. The *None* option indicates that no white space at all will be returned as a node. The third option, *Significant*, discards all insignificant white spaces and returns only nodes of type *SignificantWhitespace*. Interestingly, the *WhitespaceHandling* property is one of the few reader properties that can be changed at any time and will take effect immediately on the next read operation.

Resolving Entities

In XML, an *entity* is a named placeholder for some content or markup text. Entities can be declared both in-line and within a DTD or a schema. The declaration syntax is shown here:

```
<!ENTITY name "content">
```

The following statement declares an entity named *author* that is associated with the contents *"Dino Esposito"*:

```
<!ENTITY author "Dino Esposito">
```

When it is declared in-line, the entity must be part of an all-encompassing *<!DOCTYPE>* node, as in the following example:

```
<!DOCTYPE book [<!ENTITY author "Dino Esposito">]>
```

Once declared, entities are then used within the body of the XML document in place of their bound content. An entity can appear only within the scope of *Element*, *Attribute*, or *EntityReference* nodes. When used in an XML source, an entity is called an *entity reference*, and the parser connects to it through an *EntityReference* node. The following example shows how to use an entity in XML code:

```
<book ISBN="61801-1">
    <publisher>Microsoft Press</publisher>
    <author>&author;</author>
</book>
```

An entity reference consists of the entity name bracketed by an ampersand (&) and a semicolon (;). Not all parsers automatically expand entities upon document loading. When the *XmlTextReader* class encounters an entity reference, it returns an empty instance of the *XmlEntityReference* class in which the *Value* property is set to the empty string. By design, the *XmlTextReader* parser can't resolve entities, although it boasts a *ResolveEntity* method. Calling this method always throws an exception. You must use *XmlValidatingReader* to have entities properly expanded. (We'll cover validating readers and validation schemas in Chapter 3.)

Resolving External References

In the .NET Framework, external XML resources identified by a URI are resolved through classes derived from the abstract class *XmlResolver*. Typical external resources are entities and DTDs; however, the *XmlResolver* class can also successfully process include and import elements for both XSD schemas and XSL style sheets.

The .NET Framework provides only one concrete resolver class built atop *XmlResolver*: *XmlUrlResolver*. Programmers can design and implement custom resolvers, however, either by inheriting from the *XmlUrlResolver* class or completely from scratch by overriding the methods and properties of *XmlResolver*. Let's take a look at the key aspects, and the main tasks, of a resolver.

The activity of an XML resolver revolves around two methods: *GetEntity* and *ResolveUri*. The former takes the specified URI and returns the *Stream* object that represents the desired contents. How the method actually manages to resolve the URI is implementation-specific. *GetEntity*, however, assumes to have at its disposal an absolute URI. What if the URI read from the XML document is relative? Prior to calling *GetEntity*, you must be sure to call *ResolveUri*, passing both the relative URI and any base URI. *ResolveUri* is responsible for combining these URIs into an absolute URI.

Another problem a resolver must be ready to face arises when the resource referenced by the URI is protected and available only to authenticated users. In this case, the resolver must be passed valid credentials to carry out the task. Credentials are represented by an instance of the *NetworkCredential* class.

The *NetworkCredential* class can be used to support a variety of authentication schemes that make use of passwords. Among others, the list of authentication schemes includes basic and digest authentication and Kerberos. The class does not support other types of authentication such as those based on a public key. You provide the credentials to the resolver through the *XmlResolver.Credentials* property, as shown here:

```
XmlUrlResolver resolver = new XmlUrlResolver();
NetworkCredential cred = new NetworkCredential(user, pswd);
resolver.Credentials = cred;
reader.XmlResolver = resolver;
```

You can also use the *CredentialCache* class to bind the resolver in a single shot to a collection of URI/credential pairs, as shown in the following code. The collection will then be scanned, searching for a matching URI each time the resolver is called to action.

```
CredentialCache credCache = new CredentialCache();
credCache.Add(new Uri(url1), "Basic", cred);
credCache.Add(new Uri(url2), "Digest", cred);
resolver.Credentials = credCache;
```

If credentials are needed but not provided, the resolver makes an attempt using default credentials, available from the *CredentialCache.DefaultCredentials* property. If the default credentials still don't provide access, the resolve attempt will fail. Default credentials represents the system credentials for the application security context—that is, the credentials of the logged-in user or the user being impersonated.

Reading Large Streams

The *XmlTextReader* class provides a few methods—*ReadChars*, *ReadBinHex*, and *ReadBase64*—tailored to read chunks of data out of a large stream of embedded text. These methods share almost the same prototype and overall logic, but differ in how they preprocess and return the fetched data:

```
public int ReadChars (char[] array, int offset, int len);
public int ReadBinHex(byte[] array, int offset, int len);
public int ReadBase64(byte[] array, int offset, int len);
```

All three methods can be used only to read the text associated with an *Element* node. If you use any of them with nodes of other types, the method will fail. The read methods let you fetch the specified number of bytes (*len* argument) from the current reader starting at the given offset (*offset* argument).

The fetched bytes are then placed in the array argument. The return value indicates the number of bytes effectively read. This number equals *len* if the call was successful. The return value could be less than *len* if the stream is close to its end, however. Anomalous situations are identified through exceptions.

So what's the difference between these three methods? As their names imply, they differ in their decoding capabilities. The *ReadBinHex* method decodes BinHex content, whereas *ReadBase64* returns Base64 decoded binary bytes. The *ReadChars* method, on the other hand, reads the text as it is.

There are a few minor issues regarding the use of these methods. They do not perform any XML-specific tasks such as validating, resolving entities, or normalizing attribute values. While you're in the process of reading node content using a stream-based method, you can't read any attributes.

ReadChars, *ReadBinHex*, and *ReadBase64* always return everything found between the start tag and the end tag of the element node they are working on. If the embedded text includes any markup (for example, a mixed-content node), that is returned as well, just as if you were reading a binary or a text file from a disk.

Note   The full source code for an application demonstrating incremental access to XML files is available in this book's sample files. The application name is IncrementalRead.

Note   Earlier in this chapter, you learned how to use a single instance of an *XmlTextReader* reader to process multiple XML streams. In that case, the key was using the *ResetState* method to reinitialize the reader's internal state. If needed, however, you can also do the reverse—that is, use different readers (for example, a text reader and a validating reader) to process distinct pieces of a single XML stream. The method that makes this possible is *GetRemainder*, which returns the remainder of the buffered XML stream. *GetRemainder* scans and returns the portion of the buffer that has not yet been processed. The buffer is returned as a generic *TextReader* object.

The *NameTable* Object

One of the secrets behind the XML readers' great performance is the *NameTable* class—a helper class that works as a quickly accessible table of string objects. Several .NET classes, including, but not limited to, *XmlDocument* and *XmlText-Reader*, make use internally of a *NameTable* object. User applications too can use a *NameTable* object to store potentially duplicated strings more efficiently. When stored in a name table, a string is said to be an *atomized string*.

The net effect of atomized strings is that XML readers can manage elements and attributes as references rather than values and can therefore function more effectively, especially in terms of memory occupation and speed of comparison. Comparing two object references is much faster than comparing all the characters that form a string.

The *NameTable* class, which inherits from the abstract class *XmlNameTable*, has a relatively simple programming interface and provides methods to add new items and to read them back. You add a new item to a name table using the *Add* method.

```
NameTable table = new NameTable();
string name = table.Add("Author");
```

You get the atomized string with the specified value from the table using the *Get* method.

```
string name = table.Get("Author");
```

XML reader classes make internal use of name tables. The reader's name table can be accessed through the *NameTable* property. The reader's name table contains an *atom* (a reference to the string object) for each distinct element or attribute name, completed with namespace information for uniqueness. If the XML document being processed contains, say, 1000 nodes named *<Customer>*, only one atomized entry will be created in the name table. Don't mistake the *NameTable* object for a worker table in which the reader stores all the document's nodes. Instead, the *NameTable* object is just a worker collection of unique names stored in a way that allows for more effective storage, retrieval, and comparison.

The *NameTable* object is internally implemented using an array of structures that mimics a hash table. Like a hash table, the array manages strings using hash codes. So when a new string is added to the table, a new hash code is generated and compared to the others existing in the array. If a string with that hash code already exists in the table, a reference to the existing atom is returned; otherwise, a new entry is created and the relative reference (atom) returned. In case of overflow, the size of the array is doubled.

The *NameTable* object uses a homemade hash table rather than the official .NET *HashTable* object because the *HashTable* object is not as simple and compact as required in this context.

When creating a new instance of the *XmlTextReader* class, you can also indicate the specific *NameTable* object to use.

Designing a SAX Parser with .NET Tools

As mentioned in Chapter 1, significant differences exist between .NET XML readers—a kind of cursor-like parser—and Simple API for XML (SAX) parsers. All of these differences can be traced, directly or indirectly, to the differences existing between the push model, which is typical of SAX, and the pull model on which readers are based.

A SAX parser takes full control over the parsing process, extrapolates any predefined piece of XML code, duplicates it into local buffers, and finally pushes that data down to the calling application. The interaction between the parser and the application takes place through application-defined classes that, in turn, implement SAX-defined interfaces.

With SAX, the client application receives any data the parser is designed to push and can discard it if that result is of no interest. The data is always sent, however. The application has to build fairly sophisticated code to isolate the pieces of information it really needs (that is, the nodes of interest) and, more importantly, to add them to a custom data structure that represents the state.

XML readers tout the pull model, in which the parser is just one tool managed and governed by the caller application. This model allows for more selective processing—the application just skips over unneeded data—and even for an optimized interaction. In fact, the application puts data of interest directly in its final buffers rather than having the parser create and pass on temporary buffers.

The main advantage of SAX over XMLDOM—that is, the ability to visit XML data in a fast, forward-only, read-only way—is still the key feature of .NET XML readers. For this reason, you will not find any support for SAX in the .NET Framework, and frankly, the .NET XML infrastructure clearly works as a superset of SAX. However, if you still feel some nostalgia for the SAX model, consider that the pull model is flexible enough to let you build a push model on top of it. Let's see how.

Applications interact with a SAX parser by writing and registering their own handlers, as shown here:

```
Set saxParser.contentHandler = myCntHandler
' *** Set other handlers
```

```
saxParser.parseURL(file)
```

In Visual Basic .NET, you create a new .NET class named *SaxParser*:

```
Public Class SaxParser
    Public ContentHandler As SaxContentHandler

    Public Sub Parse(ByVal file As String)
        Dim reader As XmlTextReader = New XmlTextReader(file)
        While (reader.Read())
            ContentHandler.Process(reader.Name, reader.Value, reader.NodeType)
        End While

        reader.Close()
    End Sub
End Class
```

The *SaxParser* class has a property named *ContentHandler* that refers to a user-defined object in charge of processing the found nodes. The *Parse* method parses the content of the XML document using a reader, and whenever a new node is found, the method calls the content handler. The content handler class has a fixed interface represented by the following abstract class:

```
Public MustInherit Class SaxContentHandler
    Public MustOverride Sub Process( _
            ByVal name As String, _
            ByVal value As String, _
            ByVal type As XmlNodeType)
End Class
```

After the two classes have been compiled into an assembly, a client SAX application can simply reference and instantiate the parser and the content handler class. The world's simplest content handler class is shown here:

```
Public Class MyContentHandler
    Inherits SaxContentHandler
    Public Overrides Sub Process( _
            ByVal name As String, _
            ByVal value As String, _
            ByVal type As XmlNodeType)
        If type = XmlNodeType.Element Then
            MsgBox(name)
        End If
    End Sub
End Class
```

The SAX application initializes the parser as follows:

```
Dim saxParser As New SaxParser()
Dim myHandler As New MyContentHandler()
saxParser.ContentHandler = myHandler
saxParser.Parse(file)
```

Of course, the parser discussed here is fairly minimal, but the design guidelines are concrete and effective. As an aside, consider the fact that in the client application, the content handler class and the form are different classes, which makes updating the user interface from the content handler class a bit complicated.

> **Note**   The full source code discussed here is provided in this book's sample files. The application is named SaxParser.

Parsing XML Fragments

The *XmlTextReader* class provides the basic set of functionalities to process any XML data coming from a disk file, a stream, or a URL. This kind of reader works sequentially, reading one node after the next, and does not deliberately provide any ad hoc search function to parse only a particular subtree.

In the .NET Framework, to process only fragments of XML data, excerpted from a variety of sources, you can take one of two routes. You can initialize the text reader with the XML string that represents the fragment, or you can use another, more specific, reader class—the *XmlNodeReader* class.

The *XmlNodeReader* class works on the subtree rooted in the *XmlNode* object passed to the class constructor. A living instance of an *XmlNode* object is not something you can obtain through a text reader, however. Only the .NET XML DOM parser can create and return an *XmlNode* object. We'll examine the details of the *XmlNodeReader* class in Chapter 5, along with the .NET XML DOM parser.

If you have ever used Microsoft XML Core Services (MSXML)—the Microsoft COM XML parser—you have certainly noticed that it allows you to initialize the parser from a well-formed XML string. However, the long list of constructors that the *XmlTextReader* class boasts gives no clear indication that that same MSXML feature is also supplied by the .NET Framework. In this section, you'll learn how to parse XML data stored in a memory string. First I'll show you how to work with plain strings with no context information, and then

I'll show you how to process XML fragments using specific context information for the parser, such as namespaces and document type declarations.

Parsing Well-Formed XML Strings

The trick to initializing a text reader from a string is all in packing the string into a *StringReader* object. One of the *XmlTextReader* constructors looks like this:

```
public XmlTextReader(TextReader);
```

TextReader is an abstract class that represents a .NET reader object capable of reading a sequence of characters no matter where they are physically stored. The *StringReader* class inherits from *TextReader* and simply makes itself capable of reading the bytes of an in-memory string. Because *StringReader* derives from *TextReader*, you can safely use it to initialize *XmlTextReader*.

```
string xmlText = "…";
StringReader strReader = new StringReader(xmlText);
XmlTextReader reader = new XmlTextReader(strReader);
```

The net effect of this code snippet is that the XML code stored in the *xmlText* variable is parsed as it is read from a disk file or an open stream or downloaded from a URL.

> **Important**   Any class based on *TextReader* is inherently not thread-safe. Among other things, this means that the string object you are using to contain parsable XML data might be concurrently accessed from other threads. Of course, this happens only under special conditions, but it is definitely a plausible scenario. If you have a multi-threaded application and the string itself happens to be globally visible throughout the application, one thread could break the well-formedness of the string while another thread is parsing it. To avoid this situation, create a thread-safe wrapper for the *StringReader* class using the *TextReader* class's static member *Synchronized*, as shown here:
>
> ```
> String xmlText = "…";
> StringReader sr = new StringReader(xmlText);
> XmlTextReader reader = new XmlTextReader(sr);
> TextReader strReader = TextReader.Synchronized(sr);
> ```
>
> For performance reasons, you should use the thread-safe wrapper class only when strictly necessary. Even better, wherever possible, you should design your code to avoid the need for thread-safe classes.

Fragments and Parser Context

The context for an XML parser consists of all the information that can be used to customize the way in which the parser works. Context information includes the encoding character set, the DTD information needed to set all the default attributes and to expand entities, the namespaces, the language, and the white space handling.

If you specify the XML fragment using a *StringReader* object, as shown in the previous section, all elements of the parser context are set with default values. The parser context is fully defined by the *XmlParserContext* class. When instantiating an *XmlTextReader* class to operate on a string, you use the following constructor and specify a parser context:

```
public XmlTextReader(
    string xmlFragment,
    XmlNodeType fragType,
    XmlParserContext context
);
```

The *xmlFragment* parameter contains the XML string to parse. The *fragType* argument, on the other hand, represents the type of fragment. It specifies the type of the node at the root of the fragment. Only *Element*, *Attribute*, and *Document* nodes are permitted.

The *XmlParserContext* constructor has a few overloads. The one with the shortest list of arguments, shown here, is probably the overload you will use most often:

```
public XmlParserContext(
    XmlNameTable nt,
    XmlNamespaceManager nsMgr,
    string xmlLang,
    XmlSpace xmlSpace
);
```

Creating a new parser context is as easy as running the following statements:

```
NameTable table = new NameTable();
table.Add("Author");
XmlNamespaceManager mgr = new XmlNamespaceManager(table);
mgr.AddNamespace("company", "urn:ThisIsMyBook");
XmlParserContext context;
context = new XmlParserContext(table, mgr, "en-US", XmlSpace.None);
```

The first parameter to this *XmlParserContext* constructor is a *NameTable* object. The name table is used to look up prefixes and namespaces as atomized strings. For performance reasons, you also need to pass a *NameTable* object—

which inherits from the abstract *XmlNameTable* class—when creating a new instance of a namespace manager class.

> **Note**   If the namespace manager and the parser context happen to use different *NameTable* objects, the *XmlParserContext* might not be able to recognize the namespaces brought in by the manager, resulting in an XML exception.

The second parameter to the *XmlParserContext* constructor is an *XmlNamespaceManager* object. The *XmlNamespaceManager* class is a type of collection class designed to contain and manage namespace information. It provides methods to add, remove, and search for namespaces. Namespaces are stored with their prefix and URN, which are passed to it through the *AddNamespace* method. If the prefix is an empty string, the namespace is considered to be the default.

The *XmlParserContext* class makes use of a namespace manager to collect all the namespaces that the fragment might use. A fragment is simply a small piece of XML code and, as such, is not expected to contain all namespace definitions that its nodes and attributes might use.

When a namespace manager is created, the class constructor automatically adds a couple of frequently used prefixes. These prefixes are listed in Table 2-5.

Table 2-5   Standard Namespace Prefixes Added to *XmlNamespaceManager*

Prefix	Corresponding Namespace
xmlns	*http://www.w3.org/2000/xmlns*
xml	*http://www.w3.org/1998/namespace*

A third namespace prefix that is allowed is the empty string, which of course has no corresponding namespace URN. Thanks to this contrivance, you don't need to create a namespace manager instance to parse XML fragments unless nodes and attributes really contain custom namespaces. Added namespaces are not verified as conforming to the W3C Namespaces specification and are discarded if they do not conform.

As mentioned in the section "The *NameTable* Object," on page 49, the namespace names are atomized and placed in the related *NameTable* object as soon as they are added to the collection. When you call the XML reader's *LookupNamespace* method to search for the namespace that matches the specified prefix, the prefix string is atomized and added to the name table for additional, faster use.

Any namespace declaration has a clear and well-defined scope. The namespace declaration can appear anywhere in the document, not just at the very beginning of it. The place in the source where the declaration appears determines the scope. A namespace controls all the XML elements rooted in the node in which it appears. In the following example, the namespace is applied to the node *<author>* and all of its descendants:

```
<some_parent_node>
    ⋮
<author xmlns:dinoe="http://www.dinoe.com">
<firstname>Dino</firstname>
<lastname>Esposito</lastname>
<royalty>99</royalty>
</author>
    ⋮
</some_parent_node>
```

The namespace defined for the *<author>* element does not apply to elements outside that element. The namespace is effective from its point of declaration until the end of the element. After that, any other node not qualified with a namespace prefix is assumed to belong to whichever default namespace has been declared in the document.

You can specify other settings for the parser context using the properties of the *XmlParserContext* class, including *Encoding*, *BaseURI*, and *DocType-Name*. In particular, *BaseURI* is especially useful because it indicates the location from which the fragment was loaded.

Writing a Custom XML Reader

We have one more topic to consider on the subject of XML readers, which opens up a whole new world of opportunities: creating customized XML readers. An XML reader class is merely a programming interface for reading data that *appears* to be XML. The *XmlTextReader* class represents the simplest and the fastest of all possible XML readers but—and this is what really matters—it is just one reader. Its inherent simplicity and effectiveness stems from two key points. First, the class operates as a read-only, forward-only, nonvalidating parser. Second, the class is assumed to work on native XML data. It has no need, and no subsequent overhead, to map input data internally to XML data structures.

Virtually any data can be read, traversed, and queried as XML as long as a tailor-made piece of code takes care of mapping that data to an XML Schema. This mapping code can then be buried in a method that simply returns one of the standard reader objects or creates a custom XML reader class.

> **Note**   What's the advantage of exposing data through XML? XML provides a kind of universal model for defining a set of information (*infoset*), the type and layout of constituent items (XML Schema), and the query commands (XPath). In the .NET Framework, XML readers provide an effective way to deal with hierarchical, XML-shaped data. Because XML is just a metalanguage used to describe information, and not a data repository itself, the key difference between standard XML readers and custom XML readers is in the location and the modality of intervention of the code that exposes data as XML. Such code is not part of the basic .NET XML reader classes but constitutes the core of custom XML readers.

Mapping Data Structures to XML Nodes

For a long time, INI files have been a fundamental part of Microsoft Windows applications. Although with the advent of Microsoft Win32 they were officially declared obsolete, a lot of applications have not yet stopped using them. Understanding the reasons for this persistence is not of much importance here, but when they were designing the .NET Framework, the Microsoft architects decided not to insert any managed classes to handle INI files. Although overall I agree with their decision, keep in mind that if you need to access INI files from within a .NET Framework application, you'll find at your disposal only workarounds, not a direct solution.

You could, for instance, read and write the content of an INI file using file and I/O classes, or you might resort to making calls to the underlying Win32 unmanaged platform. Recently, however, I came across a rather illuminating MSDN article in which an even better approach is discussed. (See the section "Further Reading," on page 74, for details and the URL.) The idea is this: Why not wrap the contents of INI files into an XML reader? INI files are not well-formed XML files, but a custom reader could easily map the contents of an INI file's sections and entries to XML nodes and attributes.

In the next few sections of this chapter, you'll learn how to build a custom XML reader working on top of comma-delimited CSV files.

Mapping CSV Files to XML

A CSV file consists of one or more lines of text. Each line contains strings of text separated by commas. Each line of a CSV file can be naturally associated with a database row in which each token maps to a column. Likewise, a line in a CSV file can also be correlated to an XML node with as many attributes as the comma-separated tokens. The following code shows a typical CSV file:

```
Davolio,Nancy,Sales Representative
Fuller,Andrew,Sales Manager
Leverling,Janet,Sales Representative
```

A good XML representation of this structure is shown here:

```
<csv>
    <row col1="Davolio" col2="Nancy" col3="Sales Representative" />
    <row col1="Fuller" col2="Andrew" col3="Sales Manager" />
    <row col1="Leverling" col2="Janet" col3="Sales Representative" />
</csv>
```

Each row in the CSV file becomes a node in the XML representation, while each token is represented by a node attribute. In this case, the XML schema is ever-changing because the number of attributes varies with the number of commas in the CSV file. The number of total columns can be stored as an extra property. You can opt for an automatically generated sequence of attribute names such as *col1*, *col2*, and so on, or if the CSV file provides a header with column names, you can use those names. Of course, there is no way to know in advance, and in general, whether the first row has to be read as the first data row or just the header. A possible workaround is adding an extra property that tells the reader how to handle the first row.

Using the XML schema described so far, you can use the following pseudocode to read about a given item of information in the second row:

```
XmlCsvReader reader = new XmlCsvReader("employees.csv");
reader.Read();
reader.Read();
Console.WriteLine(reader[1].Value);
Console.WriteLine(reader["col2"].Value);
```

Another reasonable XML schema for a CSV file is shown here:

```
<csv>
    <row>
```

```
      <column name="col1">Davolio</column>
      <column name="col2">Nancy</column>
      <column name="col3">Sales Representative</column>
   </row>
   <row>
      <column name="col1">Fuller</column>
      <column name="col2">Andrew</column>
      <column name="col3">Sales Manager</column>
   </row>
   <row>
      <column name="col1">Leverling</column>
      <column name="col2">Janet</column>
      <column name="col3">Sales Representative</column>
   </row>
</csv>
```

Although more expressive, I find this format—an element normal form—to be a bit verbose, and more importantly, it would require more calls to *Read* or *Skip* methods to get to what you really need to know from CSV data—values.

Implementing a CSV-to-XML Reader

In this section, I'll take you through building a custom CSV-to-XML reader. A custom XML reader is built starting from the abstract *XmlReader* class, as shown in the following code. You override all abstract methods and properties and, if needed, add your own overloads and custom members.

```
public class XmlCsvReader : XmlReader
{
    ⋮
}
```

The *XmlCsvReader* class we're going to build is the reader class that processes CSV files as XML documents. Given the structure of a CSV file, not all methods and properties defined by the abstract XML reader interface make sense. For example, a CSV file does not contain namespaces or entities. Likewise, it does not need a name table property. Aside from these few exceptions, a large part of the *XmlReader* class basic interface is preserved.

The key method for our custom reader is still *Read*, and *Value* is the principal property. We'll use a *StreamReader* object to access the file and move from line to line as the user calls *Read*. From an XML point of view, the structure of a CSV file is rather simple. It consists of just one level of nodes—the *Depth* property is always 0—and, subsequently, there is no possibility for nested nodes. As you can imagine, this fact greatly simplifies the development and the internal logic of the reader.

Important   If you look at the full source code for the *XmlCsvReader* class, you'll notice that not all properties (see Table 2-1, on page 27) and methods (see Table 2-3, on page 30) defined for the *XmlReader* class are actually implemented or overridden. The reason is that although *XmlReader* is declared as an abstract class, not all methods and properties in the class are marked as abstract. Abstract methods and properties must be overridden in a derived class. Virtual methods and properties, on the other hand, can be overridden only if needed.

Notice that *abstract* and *virtual* are C# and C++ specific keywords. In Visual Basic .NET, to define an abstract class and a virtual method, you use the *MustInherit* and *MustOverride* keywords, respectively.

The Custom Reader's Constructors

The *XmlCsvReader* class comes with a couple of constructors: one takes the name of the file to open, and one, in addition to the file name, takes a Boolean value indicating whether the contents of the first line in the CSV file contains titles of the columns, as shown here:

```
LastName,FirstName,Title
Davolio,Nancy,Sales Representative
Fuller,Andrew,Sales Manager
Leverling,Janet,Sales Representative
```

Both constructors reference an internal helper routine, *InitializeClass*, that takes care of any initialization steps.

```
public XmlCsvReader(string filename)
{
    InitializeClass(filename, false);
}


public XmlCsvReader(string filename, bool hasColumnHeaders)
{
    InitializeClass(filename, hasColumnHeaders);
}


private void InitializeClass(string filename, bool hasColumnHeaders)
{
    m_hasColumnHeaders = hasColumnHeaders;
    m_fileName = filename;
    m_fileStream = new StreamReader(filename);
    m_readState = ReadState.Initial;
```

```
        m_tokenValues = new NameValueCollection();
        m_currentAttributeIndex = -1;
        m_currentLine = "";
}
```

In particular, the initialization routine creates a working instance of the *StreamReader* class and sets the internal state of the reader to the *ReadState.Initial* value. The CSV reader class needs a number of internal and protected members, as follows:

```
StreamReader m_fileStream;             // Stream reader
String m_fileName;                     // Name of the CSV file
ReadState m_readState;                 // Internal read state
NameValueCollection m_tokenValues;     // Current element node
String[] m_headerValues;               // Current headers for CSV tokens
bool m_hasColumnHeaders;               // Indicates whether the
                                       // CSV file has titles
int m_currentAttributeIndex;           // Current attribute index
string m_currentLine;                  // Text of the current CSV line
```

The currently selected row is represented through a *NameValueCollection* structure, and the current attribute is identified by its ordinal and zero-based index. In addition, if the CSV file has a preliminary header row, the column names are stored in an array of strings.

The *Read* Method

The CSV reader implementation of the *Read* method lets you move through the various rows of data that form the CSV file. First the method checks whether the CSV file has headers. The structure of the CSV file does not change regardless of whether headers are present. It's the programmer who declares, using a constructor's argument, whether the reader must consider the first row as the header row or just a data row. If the header row is present, it must be read only the first time a read operation is performed on the CSV file, and only if the read state of the reader is set to *Initial*.

```
public override bool Read()
{
    // First read extracts headers if any
    if (m_readState == ReadState.Initial)
    {
        if(m_hasColumnHeaders)
        {
            string headerLine = m_fileStream.ReadLine();
            m_headerValues = headerLine.Split(',');
```

(continued)

```
        }
    }

    // Read the new line and set the read state to interactive
    m_currentLine = m_fileStream.ReadLine();
    if (m_currentLine != null)
        m_readState = ReadState.Interactive;
    else
    {
        m_readState = ReadState.EndOfFile;
        return false;
    }

    // Populate the internal structure representing the current element
    m_tokenValues.Clear();
    String[] tokens = m_currentLine.Split(',');
    for (int i=0; i<tokens.Length; i++)
    {
        string key = "";
        if (m_hasColumnHeaders)
            key = m_headerValues[i].ToString();
        else
            key = CsvColumnPrefix + i.ToString();

        m_tokenValues.Add(key, tokens[i]);
    }

    // Exit
    return true;
}
```

The header values are stored in an array of strings (*m_headerValues*), which is automatically created by the *Split* method of the .NET *String* object. The *Split* method takes a character and splits into tokens all the parts of the string separated by that character. For a line of text read out of a CSV file, the separator must be a comma.

The reader reads one row at a time and ensures that the internal reader state is set to *Interactive* to indicate that the reader is ready to process requests and to *EndOfFile* when the end of the stream is reached. The text read is split into components, and each component is copied as the value of a name/value pair. In the following example, the row is split into *Davolio*, *Nancy*, and *Sales Representative*:

```
LastName,FirstName,Title
Davolio,Nancy,Sales Representative
```

If the reader has been set to support header names, each value is stored with the corresponding header. The resulting name/value pairs are shown here:

```
LastName/Davolio
FirstName/Nancy
Title/Sales Representative
```

If no header row is present, the name of each value takes a default form: *col1*, *col2*, *col3*, and so on. You can customize the prefix of the header by setting the *CsvColumnPrefix* property. As you might have guessed, *CsvColumn-Prefix* is a custom property defined for the *XmlCsvReader* class. The name/value pairs are stored in a *NameValueCollection* object, which is emptied each time the *Read* method is called.

The *Name* and *Value* Properties

The *Name* property represents the name of the current node—be it an element or an attribute node. Both the *Name* and the *Value* properties share a common design, as shown in the following code. Their content is determined by the node type.

```
public override string Name
{
    get
    {
        if(m_readState != ReadState.Interactive)
            return null;

        string buf = "";
        switch(NodeType)
        {
            case XmlNodeType.Attribute:
                buf = m_tokenValues.Keys[m_currentAttributeIndex].ToString();
                break;
            case XmlNodeType.Element:
                buf = CsvRowName;
                break;
        }

        return buf;
    }
}
```

If the reader is not in interactive mode, all properties return *null*, including *Name*. If the current node type is an attribute, *Name* is the header name for the CSV token that corresponds to the attribute index. For example, if the reader is currently positioned on the second attribute, and the CSV has headers as shown previously, the name of the attribute is *FirstName*. Otherwise, if the node is an element, the name is a string that you can control through the extra *CsvRowName* property. By default, the property equals the word *row*.

The *Value* property is implemented according to a nearly identical logic. The only difference is in the returned text, which is the value of the currently selected attribute if the node is *XmlNodeType.Attribute* or the raw text of the currently selected CSV line if the node is an element.

```
public override string Value
{
    get
    {
        if(m_readState != ReadState.Interactive)
            return "";

        string buf = "";
        switch(NodeType)
        {
            case XmlNodeType.Attribute:
                buf = this[m_currentAttributeIndex].ToString();
                break;
            case XmlNodeType.Element:
                buf = m_currentLine;
                break;
        }
        return buf;
    }
}
```

Who sets the node type? Actually, the node type is never explicitly set, but is instead retrieved from other data whenever needed. In particular, for this example, the index of the current attribute determines the type of the node. If the index is equal to −1 , the node is an element simply because no attribute is currently selected. Otherwise, the node can only be an attribute.

```
public override XmlNodeType NodeType
{
    get
    {
        if (m_currentAttributeIndex == -1)
            return XmlNodeType.Element;
        else
            return XmlNodeType.Attribute;
    }
}
```

The programming interface of an XML reader is quite general and abstract, so the actual implementation you provide (for example, for CSV files) is arbitrary to some extent, and several details can be changed at will. The *NodeType* property for a CSV file is an example of how customized the internal implementation can be. In fact, you return *Element* or *Attribute* based on logical conditions rather than the actual structure of the XML element read off disk.

Reading Attributes

Every piece of data in the CSV file is treated like an attribute. You access attributes using indexes or names. The methods in the *XmlReader* base interface that allow you to retrieve attribute values using a string name and a namespace URI are not implemented, simply because there is no notion of a namespace in a CSV file.

The following two function overrides demonstrate how to return the value of the currently selected attribute node by position as well as by name. The values of the current CSV row are stored as individual entries in the internal *m_tokenValues* collection.

```
public override string this[int i]
{
    get
    {
        return m_tokenValues[i].ToString();
    }
}
public override string this[string name]
{
    get
    {
        return m_tokenValues[name].ToString();
    }
}
```

The preceding code simply allows you to access an attribute using one of the following syntaxes:

```
Console.WriteLine(reader[i]);
Console.WriteLine(reader["col1"]);
```

You can also obtain the value of an attribute using one of the overloads of the *GetAttribute* method. The internal implementation for the CSV XML reader *GetAttribute* method is nearly identical to the *this* overrides.

Moving Through Attributes

When you call the *Read* method on the CSV XML reader, you move to the first available row of data. If the first row is managed as the header row, the first available row of data becomes the second row. The internal state of the reader is set to *Interactive*—meaning that it is ready to take commands—only after the first successful and content-effective reading.

Any single piece of information in the CSV file is treated as an attribute. In this way, the *Read* method can move you only from one row to the next. As with real XML data, when you want to access attributes, you must first select them. To move among attributes, you will not use the *Read* method; instead, you'll use a set of methods including *MoveToFirstAttribute*, *MoveToNextAttribute*, and *MoveToElement*.

The CSV XML reader implements attribute selection in a straightforward and effective way. Basically, the current attribute is tracked using a simple index that is set to −1 when no attribute is selected and to a zero-based value when an attribute has been selected. This index, stored in *m_currentAttributeIndex*, points to a particular entry in the collection of token values that represents each CSV row.

The CSV XML reader positions itself at the first attribute of the current row simply by setting the internal index to 0, as shown in the following code. It then moves to the next attribute by increasing the index by 1. In this case, though, you should also make sure that you're not specifying an index value that's out of range.

```
public override bool MoveToFirstAttribute()
{
    m_currentAttributeIndex = 0;
    return true;
}

public override bool MoveToNextAttribute()
{
    if (m_readState != ReadState.Interactive)
        return false;

    if (m_currentAttributeIndex < m_tokenValues.Count-1)
        m_currentAttributeIndex ++;
    else
        return false;
    return true;
}
```

You can also move to a particular attribute by index, and you can reset the attribute index to −1 to reposition the internal pointer on the parent element node.

```
public override void MoveToAttribute(int i)
{
    if (m_readState != ReadState.Interactive)
        return;

    m_currentAttributeIndex = i;
}

public override bool MoveToElement()
{
    if (m_readState != ReadState.Interactive)
        return false;

    m_currentAttributeIndex = -1;
    return true;
}
```

A bit trickier code is required if you just want to move to a particular attribute by name. The function providing this feature is an overload of the *MoveToAttribute* method.

```
public override bool MoveToAttribute(string name)
{
    if (m_readState != ReadState.Interactive)
        return false;

    for(int i=0; i<AttributeCount; i++)
    {
        if (m_tokenValues.Keys[i].ToString() == name)
        {
            m_currentAttributeIndex = i;
            return true;
        }
    }
    return false;
}
```

The name of the attribute—determined by a header row or set by default—is stored as the key of the *m_tokenValues* named collection. Unfortunately, the *NameValueCollection* class does not provide for search capabilities, so the only way to determine the ordinal position of a given key is by enumerating all the keys, tracking the index position, until you find the key that matches the specified name.

As you've probably noticed, almost all the methods and properties in the CSV reader begin with a piece of code that simply returns if the reader's state is not *Interactive*. This is a specification requirement that basically dictates that an XML reader can accept commands only after it has been correctly initialized.

Exposing Data as XML

In a true XML reader, methods like *ReadInnerXml* and *ReadOuterXml* serve the purpose of returning the XML source code embedded in, or sitting around, the currently selected node. For a CSV reader, of course, there is no XML source code to return. You might want to return an XML description of the current CSV node, however.

Assuming that this is how you want the CSV reader to work, the *ReadInnerXml* method for a CSV XML reader can only return either *null* or the empty string, as shown in the following code. By design, in fact, each element has an empty body.

```
public override string ReadInnerXml()
{
    if (m_readState != ReadState.Interactive)
        return null;

    return String.Empty;
}
```

In contrast, the outer XML text for a CSV node can be designed like a node with a sequence of attributes, as follows:

```
<row attr1="…" attr2="…" />
```

The source code to obtain this output is shown here:

```
public override string ReadOuterXml()
{
    if (m_readState != ReadState.Interactive)
        return null;

    StringBuilder sb = new StringBuilder("");
    sb.Append("<");
    sb.Append(CsvRowName);
    sb.Append(" ");
```

```
foreach(object o in m_tokenValues)
{
    sb.Append(o);
    sb.Append("=");
    sb.Append(QuoteChar);
    sb.Append(m_tokenValues[o.ToString()].ToString());
    sb.Append(QuoteChar);
    sb.Append(" ");
}

sb.Append("/>");
return sb.ToString();
}
```

The CSV XML Reader in Action

In this section, you'll see the CSV XML reader in action and learn how to instantiate and use it in the context of a realistic application. In particular, I'll show you how to load the contents of a CSV file into a *DataTable* object to appear in a Windows Forms *DataGrid* control. Figure 2-1 shows the application in action.

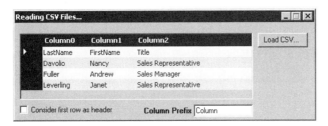

Figure 2-1   The CSV XML reader shows all the rows of a CSV file.

You start by instantiating the reader object, passing the name of the CSV file to be processed and a Boolean flag. The Boolean value indicates whether the values in the first row of the CSV source file must be read as the column names or as data. If you pass *false*, the row is considered a plain data row and each column name is formed by a prefix and a progressive number. You control the prefix through the *CsvColumnPrefix* property.

```
// Instantiate the reader on a CSV file
XmlCsvReader reader;
reader = new XmlCsvReader("employees.csv", hasHeader.Checked);
```

(continued)

```
reader.CsvColumnPrefix = colPrefix.Text;
reader.Read();

// Define the target table
DataTable dt = new DataTable();
for(int i=0; i<reader.AttributeCount; i++)
{
    reader.MoveToAttribute(i);
    DataColumn col = new DataColumn(reader.Name, typeof(string));
    dt.Columns.Add(col);
}
reader.MoveToElement();
```

Before you load data rows into the table and populate the data grid, you must define the layout of the target *DataTable* object. To do that, you must scroll the attributes of one row—typically the first row. You move to each of the attributes in the first row and create a *DataColumn* object with the same name as the attribute and specified as a string type. You then add the *DataColumn* object to the *DataTable* object and continue until you've added all the attributes. The *MoveToElement* call restores the focus to the CSV row element.

```
// Loop through the rows and populate a DataTable
do
{
    DataRow row = dt.NewRow();
    for(int i=0; i<reader.AttributeCount; i++)
    {
        row[i] = reader[i].ToString();
    }
    dt.Rows.Add(row);
}
while (reader.Read());
reader.Close();

// Bind the table to the grid
dataGrid1.DataSource = dt;
```

Next you walk through the various data rows of the CSV file and create a new *DataRow* object for each. The row will then be filled in with the values of the attributes. Because the reader is already positioned in the first row when the loop begins, you must use a *do…while* loop instead of the perhaps more natural *while* loop. At the end of the loop, you simply close the reader and bind the freshly created *DataTable* object to the *DataGrid* control for display.

Figure 2-2 shows the output generated by the sample application when it uses the values in the first row of the CSV file as column names.

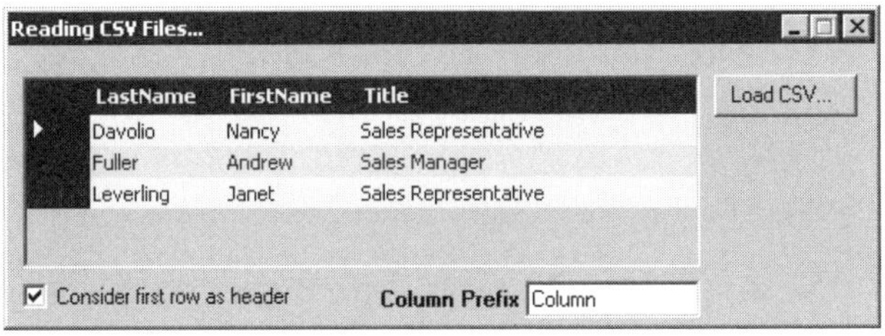

Figure 2-2   The CSV XML reader now reads the column names from the first row in the source file.

> **Caution**   I tried to keep this version of the CSV reader as simple as possible, which is always a good guideline. In this case, however, I went beyond my original intention and came up with a too simple reader! Don't be fooled by the fact that the sample code discussed here works just fine. As I built it, the CSV reader does not expose the CSV document as a well-formed XML document, but rather as a well-formed XML fragment. There is no root node, and no clear distinction is made between start and end element tags. In addition, the *Read-AttributeValue* method is not supported. As a result, if you use *ReadXml* to load the CSV into a *DataSet* object, only the first row would be loaded. If you run the CsvReader sample included in this book's sample files, you'll see an additional button on the form labeled Use ReadXML, which you can use to see this problem in action. In Chapter 9, after a thorough examination of the internals of *ReadXml*, we'll build an enhanced version of the CSV reader.

The *DataGrid* control shown in Figure 2-2 is read-only, but this does not mean that you can't modify rows in the underlying *DataTable* object and then save changes back to the CSV file. One way to accomplish this result would be by using a customized XML writer class—a kind of *XmlCsvWriter*. You'll learn how to create such a class in Chapter 4, while we're looking at XML writers.

> **Note**   The full source code for both the CSV XML reader and the sample application making use of it is available in this book's sample files. The folder of interest is named CsvReader.

> **Important**   The *XmlTextReader* class implements a visiting algorithm for the XML tree based on the so-called *node-first* approach. This means that for each XML subtree found, the root is visited first, and then recursively all of its children are visited, from the first to the last. Node-first is certainly not the most unique visiting algorithm you can implement, but it turns out to be the most sensible one for XML trees.
>
> Another well-known visiting algorithm is the *in-depth-first* approach, which goes straight to the leaves of the tree and then pops back to outer parent nodes. The node-first approach is more effective for XML trees because it visits nodes in the order they are written to disk. Choosing to implement a different visiting algorithm would make the code significantly more complex and less effective from the standpoint of memory footprint. In short, you should have a good reason to plan and code any algorithm other than node-first.
>
> In general, visiting algorithms other than node-first algorithms exist mostly for tree data structures, including well-balanced and binary trees. XML files are designed like a tree data structure but remain a very special type of tree.

Readers and XML Readers

To cap off our examination of XML readers and custom readers, let's spend a few moments looking at the difference between an XML reader and a generic reader for a non-XML data structure.

A *reader* is a basic and key concept in the .NET Framework. Several different types of reader classes do exist in the .NET Framework: binary readers, text readers, XML readers, and database readers, just to name a few. Of course, you can add your own data-specific readers to the list. But that's the point. How would you write your new reader? The simplest answer would be, you write the reader by inheriting from one of the existing reader classes.

A more precise answer should help you identify the best reader class to start from. The key criterion when you're choosing a base class is the kind of programming interface you expect from the new reader. Another minor, but not negligible, concern is whether the class allows for inheritance. Some reader classes are sealed and do not permit inheritance. (The data reader classes, such as *SqlDataReader*, belong to this category.)

Actually, you could build your own reader class from base classes such as *BinaryReader*, *TextReader*, and *XmlReader*. Typically, you choose the *Binary-Reader* class if you need to manipulate primitive types in binary rather than text format. You choose the *TextReader* class whenever character input is critical. To successfully build on top of *TextReader*, the most complicated thing you might need to do is read a line of text between two successive instances of a carriage return. You choose the *XmlReader* class as the base class if the content of the data you expose can be rendered, or at least traversed, as XML. Because XML is a very specific flavor of text, the *XmlReader* class happens to be more powerful and richer than any other reader class. Not all data, however, maps to some reasonable extent to XML. If this is the case, simply plan a brand-new reader on top of *BinaryReader* or *TextReader* as applicable.

If you just want to implement a specialized XML reader (for example, a SAX reader or an XML reader supporting a different visiting algorithm), you might also consider starting from *XmlTextReader*, *XmlNodeReader*, or *Xml-ValidatingReader*. An XML specialized reader is basically a reader designed to handle data that is natively stored as well-formed XML.

Conclusion

So far, we've covered the basics of XML readers. By now, you should know how to parse an XML document irrespective of its physical location and storage medium. You know how to move between nodes, how to skip unneeded nodes, and how to read contents and attributes. In short, you have gotten the gist of XML readers.

The reader is a general concept that crosses the whole spectrum of .NET Framework functionalities and applies to XML as well as databases, files, and network protocols. You can also create custom XML readers to process non-XML data structures such as CSV files.

We've only scratched the surface of this topic—there's a lot more to be done. For example, we haven't yet looked at validation, which is the topic of Chapter 3.

Further Reading

An article that summarizes in a few pages the essence of XML readers and writers was written for the January 2001 issue of *MSDN Magazine*. Although based on a beta version of .NET, it is still of significant value and can be found at *http://msdn.microsoft.com/msdnmag/issues/01/01/xml/xml.asp*. Fresh, up-to-date, and handy information about XML in the .NET world (and other topics) can be found monthly in the "Extreme XML" column on MSDN Online.

If you need to know more about ADO.NET and its integration with XML, you can check out my book *Building Web Solutions with ASP.NET and ADO.NET* (Microsoft Press, 2002) or David Sceppa's book *Microsoft ADO.NET (Core Reference)* (Microsoft Press, 2002).

XML extensions for SQL Server 2000 are described in detail in Chapter 2.

Finally, for a very informative article about the development of XML custom readers, see "Implementing XmlReader Classes for Non-XML Data Structures and Formats," available on MSDN at *http://msdn.microsoft.com/library/en-us/dndotnet/html/Custxmlread.asp*.

3

XML Data Validation

The base XML reader examined in Chapter 2—the *XmlTextReader* class—does not enable you to validate the contents of an XML source against a schema. The correctness of XML documents can be measured using two distinct and complementary metrics: the *well-formedness* of the document and the *validity*. Well-formedness of the document refers to the overall syntax of the document. Validation applies at a deeper level and involves the semantics of the document, which must be compliant with a user-defined layout.

The *XmlTextReader* class ensures only that the document being processed is syntactically correct. By design, the *XmlTextReader* class deliberately avoids making a more advanced analysis of the nodes in the document and checking their internal dependencies. A more specialized class is available in the Microsoft .NET Framework for accomplishing this more complex task—the *XmlValidatingReader* class. This chapter will focus on techniques and classes available in the .NET Framework to perform validation on XML data.

Although validation is a key aspect in projects that involve critical document exchange across heterogeneous platforms, it does come at a price. Validating a document means taking a while to analyze the constituent nodes; the number, type, and values of their attributes; and the node-to-node dependencies. When applications handle a fully validated document, they can be certain not only about the overall syntax but even about the contents. In a normal XML document, a node simply represents itself—a rather generic repository of hierarchical information. In a validated XML document, on the other hand, the same node to the application's eye represents a strongly typed and strongly defined piece of information. Basically, in a validated document, a node *<invoice_number>* ceases to be a node and becomes what it was intended to be—the number of the invoice.

Clearly, a nonvalidating reader (and, more generally, a nonvalidating XML parser) will run faster than a validating reader, and that's why XML parsers usually provide XML validation as an option that can be programmatically toggled on and off. In .NET applications, you use *XmlTextReader* if you simply need well-formedness; you resort to *XmlValidatingReader* if you need to validate the schema of the document.

The *XmlValidatingReader* Class

The *XmlValidatingReader* class is an implementation of the *XmlReader* class that provides support for several types of XML validation: document type definitions (DTDs), XML-Data Reduced (XDR) schemas, and XML Schemas. The XML Schema language is also referred to as XML Schema Definition (XSD). DTD and XSD are official recommendations issued by the W3C, whereas XDR is simply the Microsoft implementation of an early working draft of XML Schemas that will be superseded by XSD as time goes by.

You can use the *XmlValidatingReader* class to validate entire XML documents as well as *XML fragments*. An XML fragment is a string of XML code that does not have a root node. For example, the following XML string turns out to be a valid XML fragment but not a valid XML document. XML documents must have a root node.

```
<firstname>Dino</firstname>
<lastname>Esposito</lastname>
```

The *XmlValidatingReader* class works on top of an XML reader—typically an instance of the *XmlTextReader* class. The text reader is used to walk through the nodes of the document, and then the validating reader gets into the game, validating each piece of XML based on the requested validation type.

Supported Validation Types

What are the key differences between the validation mechanisms (DTD, XDR, and XSD) supported by the *XmlValidatingReader* class? Let's briefly review the main characteristics of each mechanism.

- **DTD** A DTD is a text file whose syntax stems directly from the Standard Generalized Markup Language (SGML)—the ancestor of XML as we know it today. A DTD follows a custom, non-XML syntax to define the set of valid tags, the attributes each tag can support, and the dependencies between tags. A DTD allows you to specify the children for each tag, their cardinality, their attributes, and a few other properties for both tags and attributes. *Cardinality* specifies the number of occurrences of each child element.

- **XDR** XDR is a schema language based on a proposal submitted by Microsoft to the W3C back in 1998. (For more information, see *http://www.w3.org/TR/1998/NOTE-XML-data-0105*.) XDRs are flexible and overcome some of the limitations of DTDs. Unlike DTDs, XDRs describe the structure of the document using the same syntax as the XML document. Additionally, in a DTD, all the data content is character data. XDR language schemas allow you to specify the data type of an element or an attribute.

- **XSD** XSD defines the elements and attributes that form an XML document. Each element is strongly typed. Based on a W3C recommendation, XSD describes the structure of XML documents using another XML document. XSDs include an all-encompassing type system composed of primitive and derived types. The XSD type system is also at the foundation of the Simple Object Access Protocol (SOAP) and XML Web services.

DTD was considered the cross-platform standard until a couple of years ago. Then the W3C officialized a newer standard—XSD—which is, technically speaking, far superior to DTD. Today, XSD is supported by almost all parsers on all platforms. Although the support for DTD will not be deprecated anytime soon, you'll be better positioned if you start migrating to XSD or building new XML-driven applications based on XSD instead of DTD or XDR.

As mentioned, XDR is an early hybrid specification that never reached the status of a W3C recommendation. It then evolved into XSD. The *XmlValidatingReader* class supports XDR mostly for backward compatibility, as XDR is fully supported by the Component Object Model (COM)–based Microsoft XML Core Services (MSXML).

> **Note**   The .NET Framework provides a handy utility, named xsd.exe, that among other things can automatically convert an XDR schema to XSD. If you pass an XDR schema file (typically, a .xdr extension), xsd.exe converts the XDR schema to an XSD schema, as shown here:
>
> ```
> xsd.exe myoldschema.xdr
> ```
>
>   The output file has the same name as the XDR schema, but with the .xsd extension.

The *XmlValidatingReader* Programming Interface

The *XmlValidatingReader* class inherits from the base class *XmlReader* but implements internally only a small set of all the functionalities that an XML reader exposes. The class always works on top of an existing XML reader, and many methods and properties are simply mirrored.

The dependency of validating readers on an existing text reader is particularly evident if you look at the class constructors. An XML validating reader, in fact, can't be directly initialized from a file or a URL. The list of available constructors comprises the following overloads:

```
public XmlValidatingReader(XmlReader);
public XmlValidatingReader(Stream, XmlNodeType, XmlParserContext);
public XmlValidatingReader(string, XmlNodeType, XmlParserContext);
```

A validating reader can parse only an XML document for which a reader is provided as well as any XML fragments accessible through a string or an open stream. In the section "Under the Hood of the Validation Process," on page 89, we'll look more closely at the internal architecture of an XML validating reader. In the meantime, let's analyze more closely the programming interface of such a class, starting with properties.

XmlValidatingReader Properties

Table 3-1 lists the key public properties exposed by the *XmlValidatingReader* class. This table does not include those properties defined in the *XmlReader* base class for which the *XmlValidatingReader* class simply mirrors the behavior of the underlying reader. Refer to Chapter 2 for more information about the base properties of *XmlReader*.

Table 3-1   Key Properties of the *XmlValidatingReader* Class

Property	Description
CanResolveEntity	Always returns *true* because the XML validating reader can always resolve entities.
EntityHandling	Indicates how entities are handled. Allowable values for this property come from the *EntityHandling* enumeration. The default value is *ExpandEntities*, which means that all entities are expanded. If set to *ExpandCharEntities*, only character entities are expanded (for example, *'*). General entities are returned as *EntityReference* node types.
Namespaces	Indicates whether namespace support is requested.
NameTable	Gets the name table object associated with the underlying reader.
Reader	Gets the *XmlReader* object used to construct this instance of the *XmlValidatingReader* class. The return value can be cast to a more specific reader type, such as *XmlTextReader*. Any change entered directly to the underlying reader object can lead to unpredictable results. Use the *XmlValidatingReader* interface to manipulate the properties of the underlying reader.
Schemas	Gets an *XmlSchemaCollection* object that holds a collection of preloaded XDRs and XSDs. Schema preloading is a trick used to speed up the validation process. Schemas, in fact, are cached, and there is no need to load them every time.
SchemaType	Gets the schema object that represents the current node in the underlying reader. This property is relevant only for XSD validation. The object describes whether the type of the node is one of the built-in XSD types or a user-defined simple or complex type.
ValidationType	Indicates the type of validation to perform. Feasible values come from the *ValidationType* enumeration: *Auto*, *None*, *DTD*, *XDR*, and *Schema*.
XmlResolver	Sets the *XmlResolver* object used for resolving external DTD and schema location references. The *XmlResolver* is also used to handle any import or include elements found in XSD schemas.

The validating reader uses the underlying reader to move around the document and implements most of its *XmlReader*-derived properties by simply mirroring the corresponding properties of the worker reader.

XmlValidatingReader Methods

Table 3-2 lists the methods exposed by the *XmlValidatingReader* class that are either new or whose behavior significantly differs from the corresponding methods of the *XmlReader* class.

Table 3-2   Public Methods of the *XmlValidatingReader* Class

Method	Description
Read	The underlying reader moves to the next node. At the same time, the validating reader gets the node information and validates it using the schema information and the previously cached information.
ReadTypedValue	Gets the value for the underlying node as a common language runtime (CLR) type. The mapping can take place only for XSDs. Whenever a direct mapping is not possible, the node value is returned as a string.
Skip	Skips the children of the current node in the underlying reader. You can't skip over badly formed XML text, however. In the *XmlValidatingReader* class, the *Skip* method also validates the skipped content.

As you can see, the programming interface of the *XmlValidatingReader* class does not explicitly provide a single method that can validate the entire contents of a document. The validating reader works incrementally, node by node, as the underlying reader does. Each validation error found along the way results in a particular event notification being returned to the caller application. The application is then responsible for defining an ad hoc event handler and behaving as needed.

The *ValidationEventHandler* Event

The *XmlValidatingReader* class contains a public event named *Validation-EventHandler*, which is defined as follows:

```
public event ValidationEventHandler ValidationEventHandler;
```

This event is used to pass information about any DTD, XDR, or XSD schema validation errors that have been detected. The handler for the event (also named *ValidationEventHandler*) has the following signature:

```
public delegate void ValidationEventHandler(
   object sender,
   ValidationEventArgs e
);
```

The *ValidationEventArgs* class is described by the following pseudocode:

```
public class ValidationEventArgs : EventArgs
{
    public XmlSchemaException Exception;
    public string Message;
    public XmlSeverityType Severity;
}
```

The *Message* field returns a description of the error. The *Exception* field, on the other hand, returns an ad hoc exception object (*XmlSchemaException*) with details about what happened. The schema exception class contains information about the line that originated the error, the source file, and, if available, the schema object that generated the error. The schema object (the *SourceSchema-Object* property) is available for XSD validation only.

The *Severity* field represents the severity of the validation event. The *XmlSeverityType* defines two levels of severity—*Error* and *Warning*. *Error* indicates that a serious validation error occurred when processing the document against a DTD, an XDR, or an XSD schema. If the current instance of the *XmlValidatingReader* class has no validation event handler set, an exception is thrown. Typically, a warning is raised when there is no DTD, XDR, or XSD schema to validate a particular element or attribute against. Unlike errors, warnings do not throw an exception if no validation event handler has been set.

The *XmlValidatingReader* in Action

Let's see how to validate an XML document. As mentioned, the *XmlValidating-Reader* class is still a reader class, so it proceeds with an incremental validation as nodes are actually read. The caller is notified of any schema exception found for a node by raising the *ValidationEventHandler* event. This section describes in detail how to validate an XML document, including initializing an XML reader, handling validation errors, and setting and detecting the validation types.

Initialization of the Reader

To validate the contents of an XML file, you must first create an XML text reader to work on the file and then use this reader to initialize an instance of a validating reader. A validating reader can be initialized using a living instance of an *XmlReader* class—typically, an *XmlTextReader* object—or using an XML fragment taken from a stream or a memory string, as shown here:

```
XmlTextReader _coreReader = new XmlTextReader(fileName);
XmlValidatingReader reader = new XmlValidatingReader(_coreReader);
```

You move around the input document using the *Read* method as usual. Actually, you use the validating reader as you would any other XML .NET reader. At each step, however, the structure of the currently visited node is validated against the specified schema and an exception is raised if an error is found.

To validate an entire XML document, you simply loop through its contents, as shown here:

```
private bool ValidateDocument(string fileName)
{
    // Initialize the validating reader
    XmlTextReader _coreReader = new XmlTextReader(fileName);
    XmlValidatingReader reader = new XmlValidatingReader(_coreReader);

    // Prepare for validation
    reader.ValidationType = ValidationType.Auto;
    reader.ValidationEventHandler += new
        ValidationEventHandler(MyHandler);

    // Parse and validate all the nodes in the document
    while(reader.Read()) {}

    // Close the reader
    reader.Close();
    return true;
}
```

The *ValidationType* property is set to the default value—*Validation-Type.Auto*. In this case, the reader determines what type of validation (DTD, XDR, or XSD) is required by looking at the contents of the file. The caller application is notified of any error through a *ValidationEventHandler* event. In the preceding code, the *MyHandler* procedure runs whenever a validation error is detected, as shown here:

```
private void MyHandler(object sender, ValidationEventArgs e)
{
// Logs the error that occurred
PrintOut(e.Exception.GetType().Name, e.Message);
}
```

Figure 3-1 shows the output of the sample program ValidateDocument. The list box tracks down all the errors that have been detected. The complete code listing for the sample application showing how to set up a validating parser is available in this book's sample files.

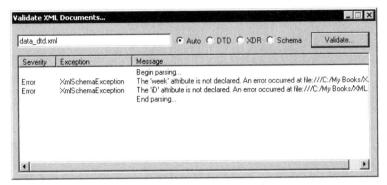

Figure 3-1   The sample application dumps the most significant events of its life cycle: when parsing begins, when parsing ends, and all the validation errors that have been detected in between.

When you've finished with the validation process, you close the reader using the *Close* method. This operation also resets the reader's internal state to *Closed*. Closing the validating reader automatically closes the underlying text reader. However, no exception is raised if you also attempt to programmatically close the internal reader. The *Close* method simply returns when it is called on a reader that is already closed.

Handling Validation Errors

If you need to know the details of validation errors, you must necessarily define an event handler and pass it along to the validating reader. Whenever an error is found, the reader fires the event and then continues to parse. As a result, the event fires for all the errors detected, thus giving the caller application a chance to handle the errors separately.

In some situations, you might want to know simply whether a given XML document complies with a given schema. In this case, you don't need to know anything about the error other than the fact that it occurred. The following code provides a class with a static method named *ValidateXmlDocument*. This method takes the name of an XML file, figures out the most appropriate validation schema, and returns a Boolean value.

```
using System;
using System.Xml;
using System.Xml.Schema;

public class XmlValidator
{
```

(continued)

```
private static bool m_isValid = false;

// Handle any validation errors detected
private static void ErrorHandler(object sender,
                                     ValidationEventArgs e)
{
    // Go on in case of warnings
        if (e.Severity == XmlSeverityType.Error)
            m_isValid = false;
}

// Validate the specified XML document (using Auto mode)
public static bool ValidateXmlDocument(string fileName)
{
    XmlTextReader _coreReader = new XmlTextReader(fileName);
    XmlValidatingReader reader = new XmlValidatingReader(_coreReader);
    reader.ValidationType = ValidationType.Auto;
    reader.ValidationEventHandler +=
        new ValidationEventHandler(XmlValidator.ErrorHandler);

    // Parse the document
    try
    {
        m_isValid = true;
        while(reader.Read() && m_isValid) {}
    }
    catch
    {
        m_isValid = false;
    }

    reader.Close();
    return m_isValid;
}
}
```

The *ValidateXmlDocument* method loops through the nodes of the document until the internal member *m_isValid* is *false* or the end of the stream is reached. The *m_isValid* member is set to *true* at the beginning of the loop and changes to *false* the first time an error is found. At this point, the document is certainly invalid, so there is no reason to continue looping.

Because the *ValidateXmlDocument* method is declared *static* (or *Shared* in Microsoft Visual Basic .NET), you don't need a particular instance of the base class to issue the call, as shown here:

```
if(!XmlValidator.ValidateXmlDocument("data.xml"))
    MessageBox.Show("Not a valid document!");
```

> **Note**   The reader's internal mechanisms responsible for checking a document's well-formedness and schema compliance are distinct. So if a validating reader happens to work on a badly formed XML document, no event is fired, but an *XmlException* exception is raised.

Setting the Validation Type

The *ValidationType* property indicates what type of validation must be performed on the current document. To be effective, the property must be set before the first call to *Read*. Setting the property after the first call to *Read* would originate an *InvalidOperationException* exception. If no value is explicitly assigned to the property, it defaults to the *ValidationType.Auto* value.

The *ValidationType* enumeration defines all the feasible values for the property, as listed in Table 3-3.

Table 3-3   Types of Validation

Type	Description
None	Creates a nonvalidating reader and ignores any validation errors
Auto	Determines the most appropriate type of validation by looking at the contents of the document
DTD	Validates according to the specified DTD
Schema	Validates according to the specified XSD schemas, including in-line schemas
XDR	Validates according to XDR schemas, including in-line schemas

When the validation type is set to *Auto*, the reader first attempts to locate a DTD declaration in the document. The DTD validation always takes precedence over other validation types. If a DTD is found, the document is validated accordingly. Otherwise, the reader looks for an XSD, either referenced or in-line. If no XSD is found, the reader makes a final attempt to find a referenced or an in-line XDR schema. If a schema is still not found, a nonvalidating reader is created. If more than one validation schema is specified in the document, only the first occurrence, in accordance with the order just discussed, is taken into account.

Detecting the Actual Validation Type

When the *ValidationType* property is set to *Auto*, you know at the end of the process whether the semantics of your XML document are valid. But valid against which schema? The *Auto* mode forces the parser to make various attempts until a validation schema type is found in the source code—whether it be DTD, XSD, or XDR. Is there a way to know what type of validation the parser is actually performing when working in *Auto* mode?

The validating reader class provides no help on this point, but with a bit of creativity you can easily identify the information you need. This information is not directly exposed, but it is right under your nose and can be inferred from the node type and the schema type without too much effort.

If the parser detects a node of type *DocumentType*, it can only be validating against a DTD. By definition, the *DOCTYPE* node must appear outside the information set (infoset). If no *DOCTYPE* node is found, check whether the *SchemaType* property evaluates to an *XmlSchemaType* object. This can happen only if an XML Schema Object Model (SOM) has been created, and hence only if XSD validation is taking place. The *XmlSchemaType* object has even more in store. By checking the contents of the *SourceUri* property, you can also determine whether the schema is in-line or a reference. If the schema is in-line, the *SourceUri* property matches the URI of the XML document being processed. Finally, if the validation type is neither DTD nor XSD, it can only be XDR! The following source code illustrates a function that determines the actual validation type:

```
string GetActualValidationType(XmlValidatingReader reader,
                               string filename)
{
    string realValidationType = "";
    if(reader.ValidationType == ValidationType.Auto)
    {
        if(reader.NodeType == XmlNodeType.DocumentType)
            realValidationType = "Auto.DTD";
        else
        {
            if(reader.SchemaType is XmlSchemaType)
            {
                XmlSchemaType xst = (XmlSchemaType) reader.SchemaType;
                string xsd = Path.GetFileName(xst.SourceUri);
                string doc = Path.GetFileName(filename);
                if (xsd == doc)
```

```
                    realValidationType = "Auto.Schema.Inline";
              else
                    realValidationType = "Auto.Schema.Ref (" + xsd + ")";
         }
      }
   }
   return realValidationType;
}
```

This code alone is not sufficient to produce the desired effect. It must be used in combination with the main parsing loop, as shown in the following code. The function should be called from within the loop as you read nodes, and at the end loop, you should check for the results. If neither DTD nor XSD has been detected, the document can be validated only through XDR.

```
string valtype = "";
while(reader.Read())
{
   if (valtype == "")
       valtype = GetActualValidationType(reader, filename);
}

// No DTD, no XSD, so it must be XDR...
if (valtype == "" && reader.ValidationType==ValidationType.Auto)
   valtype = "Auto.XDR";
```

Figure 3-2 shows how the ValidateDocument application implements this feature.

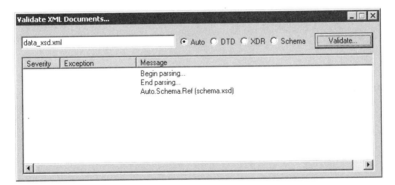

Figure 3-2   The ValidateDocument application determines the type of validation occurring under the umbrella of the *Auto* validation type.

Although it's easy to use, the *Auto* option is the most expensive of all in terms of performance because it must first figure out what type of validation to apply. Whenever possible, you should indicate explicitly the type of validation required.

> **Note**   When the *ValidationType* property is set to *None*, the DTD-specific *DOCTYPE* node, if present, is not used for validation purposes. However, default attributes in the DTD are correctly reported. General entities are not automatically expanded but can be resolved using the *ResolveEntity* method.

Events vs. Exceptions

The typical way to detect validation errors is by means of a validation event handler. If a validation event handler is specified, no validation exception is ever raised. In practice, once the reader has found an error, it looks for an event handler. If a handler is found, the handler raises the event; otherwise, it throws an *XmlSchemaException* exception.

For the reader class, handling an exception is much more expensive than firing an event, so use the *ValidationEventHandler* event whenever possible and do not abuse exceptions. Using exceptions automatically stops the validation process after the first error. As shown in the section "Detecting the Actual Validation Type," on page 86, you can obtain the same behavior from the event by using a slightly smarter Boolean guard for the loop. Instead of using the following statement:

```
while(reader.Read());
```

you resort to this:

```
while(reader.Read() && !m_errorFound)
```

where the *m_errorFound* private member is updated in the body of the event handler according to what you want to do.

A Word on XML DOM

So far, we've looked exclusively at how the validation process works for XML readers. But what about the *XmlDocument* class for XML Document Object Model (XML DOM) parsing? How can you validate against a schema while building an XML DOM? We'll examine XML DOM classes in detail in Chapter 5, but for now a quick preview, limited to validation, is in order.

The *XmlDocument* class—the key .NET Framework class for XML DOM parsing—uses the *Load* method to parse the entire contents of a document into memory. The *Load* method does not validate the XML source code against a DTD or a schema, however—*Load* can only check whether the XML is well-formed.

If you want to validate the in-memory tree while building it, use the following overload for the *XmlDocument* class's *Load* method:

```
public override void Load(XmlReader);
```

You can create an XML DOM from a variety of sources, including a stream, a text reader, and a file name. If you load the document through an XML validating reader, you hit your target and obtain a fully validated in-memory DOM, as shown here:

```
XmlTextReader _coreReader = new XmlTextReader(fileName);
XmlValidatingReader reader = new XmlValidatingReader(_coreReader);
XmlDocument doc = new XmlDocument();
doc.Load(reader);
```

As you'll see in Chapter 5, in the .NET Framework, an XML DOM is built using an internal reader. The programming interface of the *XmlDocument* class, however, in some cases allows you to specify the reader to use. If this reader happens to be a validating reader, you are automatically provided with a fully validated in-memory DOM.

Under the Hood of the Validation Process

Before going any further with the details of DTD, XDR, and XSD validation, let's review what happens under the hood of the validation process and how the *XmlValidatingReader* class really operates.

As mentioned, a validating reader works on top of a less-specialized reader, typically an XML text reader. You initialize the validating reader simply by passing a reference to this object. Upon initialization, the validating reader copies a few settings from the underlying reader. In particular, the properties *BaseURI*, *Normalization*, and *WhiteSpaceHandling* get the same values as the underlying reader. During the initialization step, an internal validator object is created to manage the schema information on a per-node basis.

> **Important** Although one of the *XmlValidatingReader* constructors takes an instance of the *XmlReader* class as its parameter, actually that reader can only be an instance of the *XmlTextReader* class, or a class that derives from it. You can't use just any class that happens to inherit from *XmlReader* (for example, a custom XML reader). Internally, the *XmlValidatingReader* class assumes that the underlying reader is an *XmlTextReader* object and specifically casts the input reader to *XmlTextReader*. If you use *XmlNodeReader* or a custom reader class, you will not get an error at compile time, but an exception will be thrown at run time.

Incremental Parsing

The validation takes place as the user moves the pointer forward using the *Read* method. After the node has been parsed and read, it is passed on to the internal validator object for further processing. The validator object operates based on the node type and the validation type requested. The validator object makes sure that the node has all the attributes and children it is expected to have.

The validator object internally invokes two flavors of objects: the DTD parser and the schema builder. The DTD parser processes the contents of the current node and its subtree against the DTD. The schema builder builds a SOM for the current node based on the XDR or XSD schema source code. The schema builder class is actually the base class for more specialized XDR and XSD schema builders. What matters, though, is that XDR and XSD schemas are treated in much the same way and with no difference in performance.

If a node has children, another temporary reader is used to read its XML subtree in such a way the schema information for the node can be fully investigated. The overall diagram is shown in Figure 3-3.

In general, an XML reader might or might not resolve entities, but an XML validating reader always does so. The *EntityHandling* property defines how entities are handled. The *EntityHandling* property can take one of two values defined in the *EntityHandling* enumeration, as described in Table 3-4.

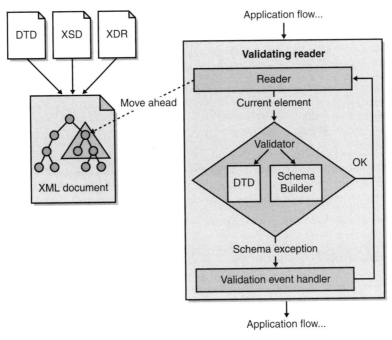

Figure 3-3   The validating reader coordinates the efforts of the internal reader, the validator, and the event handler.

Table 3-4   Ways to Handle Entities

Action	Description
ExpandCharEntities	Expands character entities and returns general entities as *EntityReference* nodes. You must then call the *ResolveEntity* method to expand a general entity.
ExpandEntities	Default setting; expands all entities and replaces them with their underlying text.

A *character entity* is an XML entity that evaluates to a character and is expressed through the character's decimal or hexadecimal representation. For example, *A* expands to *A*. Character entities are mostly used to guarantee the well-formedness of the overall document when this is potentially broken by that character.

A *general entity* is a normal XML entity that can expand to a string of any size, including a single character. A general entity is always expressed through text, even when it refers to a single character.

By default, the reader makes no distinction between the types of entities and expands them all when needed. By setting the *EntityHandling* property to *ExpandCharEntities*, however, you can optimize entity handling by expanding the general entities only when required. In this case, a call to *Read* expands only character entities. To expand general entities, you must resort to the *ResolveEntity* method or to *GetAttribute*, if the entity is part of an attribute.

The *EntityHandling* property can be changed on the fly; the new value takes effect when the next call to *Read* is made.

A Cache for Schemas

In the validating reader class, the *Schemas* property represents a collection—that is, an instance of the *XmlSchemaCollection* class—in which you can store one or more schemas that you plan to use later for validation. Using the schema collection improves overall performance because the various schemas are held in memory and don't need to be loaded each and every time validation occurs. You can add as many XSD and XDR schemas as you want, but bear in mind that the collection must be completed before the first *Read* call is made.

To add a new schema to the cache, you use the *Add* method of the *XmlSchemaCollection* object. The method has a few overloads, as follows:

```
public void Add(XmlSchemaCollection);
public XmlSchema Add(XmlSchema);
public XmlSchema Add(string, string);
public XmlSchema Add(string, XmlReader);
```

The first overload populates the current collection with all the schemas defined in the given collection. The remaining three overloads build from different data and return an instance of the *XmlSchema* class—the .NET Framework class that contains the definition of an XSD schema.

Populating the Schema Collection

The schema collection actually consists of instances of the *XmlSchema* class—a kind of compiled version of the schema. The various overloads of the *Add* method allow you to create an *XmlSchema* object from a variety of input arguments. For example, consider the following method:

```
public XmlSchema Add(
    string ns,
    string url
);
```

This method creates and adds a new schema object to the collection.

The compiled schema object is created using the namespace URI associated with the schema and the URL of the source. For example, let's assume that you have a clients.xsd file that begins as follows:

```
<xsd:schema xmlns:xsd="http://www.w3.org/2001/XMLSchema"
    xmlns="urn:my-company"
    elementFormDefault="qualified"

    targetNamespace="urn:my-company">
```

The corresponding *Add* statement to insert the schema into the collection looks like this:

```
XmlTextReader _coreReader = new XmlTextReader(file);
XmlValidatingReader reader = new XmlValidatingReader(_coreReader);
reader.Schemas.Add("urn:my-company", "clients.xsd");
```

While validating, the *XmlValidatingReader* class identifies the schema to use for a given XML source document by matching the document's namespace URI with the namespace URIs available in the collection. If the input document is an XDR schema, the source item to match in the schema collection is the contents of the *xmlns* attribute. If the input document is an XSD schema, the *targetNamespace* attribute in the XSD source code is used.

When you add a new schema to the collection and the namespace URI argument (the first argument) is *null* or empty, the *Add* method automatically brings in the value of the *xmlns* attribute if the source file is an XDR schema and the value of the *targetNamespace* attribute if you are adding an XSD schema, as shown here:

```
XmlTextReader _coreReader = new XmlTextReader(file);
XmlValidatingReader reader = new XmlValidatingReader(_coreReader);

reader.Schemas.Add(null, "Clients.xsd");
reader.ValidationType = ValidationType.Schema;
reader.ValidationEventHandler += new ValidationEventHandler(MyHandler);
```

If the namespace URI you use already exists in the schema collection, the schema being added replaces the original one.

If necessary, you could also load the schema from an XML reader object by using the overload shown here:

```
public XmlSchema Add(
    string ns,
    XmlReader reader
);
```

> **Note**   You can check whether a schema is already in the schema collection by using the *Contains* method. The *Contains* method can take either an *XmlSchema* object or a string representing the namespace URI associated with the schema. The former approach works only for XSD schemas. The latter covers both XSD and XDR schemas.

Different Treatments for XSD and XDR

Although you can store both XSD and XDR schemas in the schema collection, there are some differences in the way in which the *XmlSchemaCollection* object handles them internally. For example, the *Add* method returns an *XmlSchema* object if you add an XSD schema but returns *null* if the added schema is an XDR. In general, any method or property that manipulates the input or output of an *XmlSchema* object supports XSD schemas only.

Another difference concerns the behavior of the *Item* property in the *XmlSchemaCollection* class. The *Item* property takes a string representing the schema's namespace URI and returns the corresponding *XmlSchema* object. This happens only for XSDs, however. If you call the *Item* property on a namespace URI that corresponds to an XDR schema, *null* is returned.

The reason behind the different treatments for XDR and XSD schemas is that XDR schemas have no object model available in the .NET Framework, so when you need to handle them through objects, the system gracefully ignores the requests.

XDR schemas are there only to preserve backward compatibility; you will not find them supported outside the Microsoft Win32 platform. It is important to pay attention to the methods and the properties you use to manage XDR in your code. The overall programming interface makes the effort to unify the methods and the properties to work on both XDRs and XSDs. But in some circumstances, those same methods and properties might lead to unpleasant surprises.

In a nutshell, you can cache an XDR schema for further and repeated use by the *XmlValidatingReader* class, but that's all that you can do. You can't check for the existence of XDR schemas, nor can a reference to an XDR schema be returned. But you can do this, and more, for XSDs.

> **Important**   The *XmlSchemaCollection* object is important to improving the overall performance of the validation process. If you are validating more than one document against the same schema (XDR or XSD), preload the schema in the reader's internal cache, represented by the *Schemas* property. While doing so, bear in mind that any insertion in the schema collection must be done prior to starting the validation process. You can add to the schema collection only when the reader's state is set to *Initial*.

Validating XML Fragments

As mentioned, the *XmlValidatingReader* class has the ability to parse and validate entire documents as well as XML fragments. To parse an XML fragment, you must resort to one of the other two constructors that the *XmlValidating-Reader* class kindly provides, as shown here:

```
public XmlValidatingReader(Stream, XmlNodeType, XmlParserContext);
public XmlValidatingReader(string, XmlNodeType, XmlParserContext);
```

These constructors allow you to read XML fragments from a stream or a memory string and process them within the boundaries of a given parser context.

To bypass the root level rule for well-formed XML documents, you explicitly indicate what type of node the fragment happens to be. The node types for XML fragments are listed in Table 3-5.

Table 3-5   XML Fragment Node Types

Type	Fragment Contents
Attribute	The value of an attribute, including entities.
Document	An entire XML document in which all the rules of well-formedness apply, including the root level rules.
Element	Any valid element contents, including a combination of elements, comments, processing instructions, CDATA, and text. Root level rules are not enforced.

If you use any other element from the *XmlNodeType* enumeration, an exception is thrown. Entity references that are found in the element or the attribute body are expanded according to the value of the *EntityHandling* property.

When parsing a small XML fragment, you might need to take in extra information that can be used to resolve entities and add default attributes. For this purpose, you use the *XmlParserContext* class. (See Chapter 2 for more information about the *XmlParserContext* class.) The *XmlParserContext* argument of the *XmlTextReader* constructor is required if the requested validation mode is *DTD* or *Auto*. In this case, in fact, the parser context is expected to contain the reference to the DTD file against which the validation must be done. An exception is thrown if the *ValidationType* property is set to *DTD* and the *XmlParserContext* argument does not contain any DTD properties.

For all other validation types, the *XmlParserContext* argument can be specified without any DTD properties. Any schemas (XSDs or XDRs) used to validate the XML fragment must be referenced directly inside the XML fragment. When the validation is against schemas, the *XmlParserContext* argument is used primarily to provide information about namespace resolution.

Important   As mentioned, the *XmlValidatingReader* always works on top of an XML text reader and uses it to move around the nodes to validate. When you validate an XML fragment, however, you are not required to indicate a reader. So does the validating reader support a dual internal architecture to handle both cases? The fact that you don't have to pass an XML text reader to validate an XML fragment does not mean that a text reader can't be playing around in your code. Internally, both fragment-based constructors create a temporary text reader as their first task. The following pseudocode shows what happens:

```
XmlTextReader coreReader = new XmlTextReader(xml, type, context);
this = new XmlValidatingReader(coreReader);
```

At this point, the internal mechanisms of an XML validating reader and its programming interface should be clear. In the remainder of this chapter, we'll examine in more detail the three key types of validation—DTD, XDR, and XSD.

Using DTDs

The DTD validation guarantees that the source document complies with the validity constraints defined in a separate file—the DTD. A DTD file uses a formal grammar to describe both the structure and the syntax of XML documents. XML authors use DTDs to narrow the set of tags and attributes allowed in their documents. Validating against a DTD ensures that processed documents conform to the specified structure. From a language perspective, a DTD defines a newer and stricter XML-based syntax and a new tagged language tailor-made for a related group of documents.

Historically speaking, the DTD was the first tool capable of defining the structure of a document. The DTD standard was developed a few decades ago to work side by side with SGML—a recognized ISO standard for defining markup languages. SGML is considered the ancestor of today's XML, which actually sprang to life in the late 1990s as a way to simplify the too-rigid architecture of SGML.

DTDs use a proprietary syntax to define the syntax of markup constructs as well as additional definitions such as numeric and character entities. You can correctly think of DTDs as an early form of an XML schema. Although doomed to obsolescence, DTD is today supported by virtually all XML parsers.

An XML document is associated with a DTD file by using the *DOCTYPE* special tag. The validating parser (for example, the *XmlValidatingReader* class) recognizes this element and extracts from it the schema information. The *DOCTYPE* declaration can either point to an inline DTD or be a reference to an external DTD file.

Developing a DTD Grammar

Let's look more closely at a DTD file. To build a DTD, you normally start writing the file according to its syntax. In this case, however, we'll start from an XML file named data_dtd.xml that will actually be validated through the DTD, as shown here:

```
<?xml version="1.0" ?>
<!DOCTYPE class SYSTEM "class.dtd">
```

(continued)

```
<!-- Sample XML document (data_dtd.xml) using a DTD -->

<class title="Applied XML Programming for .NET"
    company="DinoEsposito's Own Company"
    author="Dino Esposito">
    <days total="5" expandable="true">
        <day id="1">XML Core Classes</day>
        <day id="2">Related Technologies</day>
        <day id="3">XML and ADO.NET</day>
        <day id="4" optional="true">XML and Applications</day>
        <day id="5" optional="true">XML Interoperability</day>
    </days>
</class>
```

As you can see, the file describes a class through its modules and topics covered. The general information about the class (title, author, training company) are written using attributes. Each module spans a full day, and its description is implemented using plain text.

Any XML document that must be validated against a given DTD file includes a *DOCTYPE* tag through which it simply links to the DTD of choice, as shown here:

```
<!DOCTYPE class SYSTEM "class.dtd">
```

The word following *DOCTYPE* identifies the metalanguage described by the DTD. This information is extremely important for the validation process. If that word—the document type name—does not match the root element of the DTD, a validation error is raised. The text following the *SYSTEM* attribute is the URL from which the DTD will actually be downloaded.

The following listing demonstrates a DTD that is tailor-made for the preceding XML document:

```
<!ELEMENT class (days)>
<!ATTLIST class title CDATA #REQUIRED
    author CDATA #IMPLIED
    company CDATA #IMPLIED>

<!ENTITY % Boolean "true | false">

<!ELEMENT days (day*)>
<!ATTLIST days total CDATA #REQUIRED
    expandable (%Boolean;) #REQUIRED>

<!ELEMENT day (#PCDATA)>
```

```
<!ATTLIST day id CDATA #REQUIRED
    optional (%Boolean;) #IMPLIED>
```

The *ELEMENT* tag identifies a node element, whereas *ATTLIST* is the tag that groups all attributes of a given node. Attributes are normally expressed through CDATA sections that contain unparsed data. In some cases, however, they can be allowed to take only the values defined by the specified entity. This is the case for the *expandable* attribute, whose only permitted values are *true* and *false*.

In the section "Further Reading," on page 133, you'll find references for learning more about the DTD syntax. What first catches the eye about DTDs is that they are written in a proprietary language that only mimics the typical markup of XML.

Validating Against a DTD

The following code snippet creates an *XmlValidatingReader* object that works on the sample XML file data_dtd.xml discussed in the section "Developing a DTD Grammar," on page 97. The document is bound to a DTD file and is validated using the DTD validation type.

```
XmlTextReader _coreReader = new XmlTextReader("data_dtd.xml");
XmlValidatingReader reader = new XmlValidatingReader(_coreReader);
reader.ValidationType = ValidationType.DTD;
reader.ValidationEventHandler += new ValidationEventHandler(MyHandler);
while(reader.Read());
```

Remember that when the validation type is set to *Auto*, the DTD option is the first to be considered.

When the validation mode is set to *DTD*, the validating parser returns a warning if the file has no link to any DTDs. Otherwise, if a DTD is correctly linked and accessible, the validation is performed, and in the process, entities are expanded. If the linked DTD file is not available, an exception is raised. What you'll get is not a schema exception but a simpler *FileNotFoundException* exception.

If you mistakenly use a DTD to validate an XML file with schema information, a schema exception is thrown, but with a low severity level. In practice, you get a warning informing you that no DTD has been found in the XML file. Figure 3-4 shows how the sample application handles this situation.

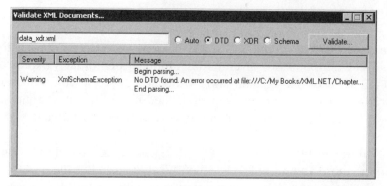

Figure 3-4   When you try to use a DTD to validate an XML document with schema information, the validating parser returns a warning.

In general, if you decide that schema warnings are not serious enough to break the ongoing validation process, you can skip them with the following code:

```
private void MyHandler(object sender, ValidationEventArgs e)
{
    if (e.Severity == XmlSeverityType.Error)
    {
        // Handle the schema exception
    }
}
```

Usage and Trade-Offs for DTDs

Unquestionably, the DTD validation format is an old one, albeit largely supported by virtually all available parsers. But if you are designing the validation layer for an XML-driven data exchange infrastructure today, there is no reason for you to discard XSDs. XSDs are more powerful than DTDs, and more important, they recently achieved W3C recommendation status, so they are a standard too.

So when should you use DTDs instead of XSDs, and under what circumstances will DTDs give you a better trade-off? Compatibility and legacy code are the only possible answers to these questions. Especially if your application handles complex DTDs, porting them to an XSD can be costly and is in no way an easy task. There is no official and totally reliable tool to automatically convert DTDs to schemas. On the W3C Web site (*www.w3.org*), you'll find a conversion tool available for download, but I wouldn't trust it to do the job unsupervised and then take the output as a trustworthy result.

Converting DTDs to schemas is no simple matter—in fact, it can be as complex as translating spoken languages. Translating from English to Italian, for example, requires a reengineering of the entire text, not just an adaptation of individual words and sentences. So design is deeply involved. When converting DTDs to schemas, you should also consider rearchitecting tags into types and perhaps rearchitecting the way you expose data in light of the new features.

Certainly XSDs provide you with more functions than DTDs can. For one thing, schemas are all written in XML and don't require you to learn a new language. If you look at our basic DTD example in this context, you might not be scared by its unusual format. As you move from textbook examples and enter the tough real world, the complexity of an inflexible language like DTD becomes more apparent.

XSDs provide you with a finer level of control over the cardinality of the tags and the attribute types. In addition, XSDs can be used to set up a system of schema inheritance in which more complex types are built atop existing ones.

All in all, if you currently have a huge, complex DTD, probably the best thing you can do is continue working with it while you carefully plan a migration to XSDs. DTDs and XSDs are both renowned standards, but especially if you are exchanging data between heterogeneous platforms, you're more likely to find a DTD-compliant parser than an XSD-compliant one. This situation will change over time, but not anytime soon. Check the supported functions for the XML parsers available on the target platform carefully before you drop DTDs.

Using XDR Schemas

As mentioned, XML-Data Reduced (XDR) schema validation is the result of a Microsoft implementation of an early draft of what today is XSDs. XDR was implemented for the first time in the version of MSXML that shipped with Microsoft Internet Explorer 5.0, back in the spring of 1999.

In the XDR schema specification, you'll find almost all of the ideas that characterize XSDs today. The main reason for XDR support in the .NET Framework is backward compatibility with existing MSXML-based applications. To enable these applications to upgrade properly to the .NET Framework, XDR support has been retained intact. You will not find XDR support anywhere else outside the Microsoft Windows platform, however.

If you have used Microsoft ActiveX Data Objects (ADO), and in particular the library's ability to persist the contents of a *Recordset* object to XML, you are probably a veteran of XDR. In fact, the XML schema used to persist ADO 2.x *Recordset* objects to XML is simply XDR.

Overview of XDR Schemas

The example XML document data_dtd.xml used to demonstrate DTDs contains information about the modules in which a given class is articulated. The following listing shows the XDR schema that provides a full description of the class:

```
<?xml version="1.0"?>

<Schema name="MyClass"
        xmlns="urn:schemas-microsoft-com:xml-data"
        xmlns:dt="urn:schemas-microsoft-com:datatypes">

<!-- Attribute Types -->
<AttributeType name="title" dt:type="string" />
<AttributeType name="company" dt:type="string" />
<AttributeType name="author" dt:type="string" />
<AttributeType name="total" dt:type="int" />
<AttributeType name="expandable" dt:type="enumeration"
               dt:values="true false" />
<AttributeType name="optional" dt:type="enumeration"
               dt:values="true false" />
<AttributeType name="id" dt:type="int" />

<!-- Element Types -->

<!-- CLASS -->
<ElementType name="class" content="eltOnly" model="closed" order="seq">
   <element type="days" minOccurs="1" maxOccurs="1" />
   <attribute type="title" required="yes" />
   <attribute type="author" required="no" />
   <attribute type="company" required="no" />
</ElementType>

<!-- DAYS -->
<ElementType name="days" content="eltOnly">
   <element type="day" minOccurs="1" maxOccurs="*" />
   <attribute type="total" required="yes" />
   <attribute type="expandable" required="no" />
</ElementType>
```

```
<!-- DAY -->
<ElementType name="day" content="textOnly">
   <attribute type="id" required="yes" />
   <attribute type="optional" required="no" />
</ElementType>
</Schema>
```

Compared to the DTD schema, this XDR schema is certainly more verbose, but it also provides more detailed information. The idea behind an XDR schema is that you define attribute and element types and then use those entities to construct the hierarchy that makes the target document. For example, let's analyze more closely the block that refers to the *<class>* root node, shown here:

```
<ElementType name="class" content="eltOnly" model="closed" order="seq">
   <element type="days" minOccurs="1" maxOccurs="1" />
   <attribute type="title" required="yes" />
   <attribute type="author" required="no" />
   <attribute type="company" required="no" />
</ElementType>
```

The *<class>* element is declared as an element type, with the subtree formed by all the nodes located one level down from it—in this case, only *<days>* and a few attributes.

Both attributes and child nodes have a *type* property that refers to other *ElementType* or *AttributeType* schema nodes. From this structure, it's easy to see how validating parsers work to verify the correctness of a node against a schema—be it XDR or XSD. They simply validate the node attributes and the child nodes one level down. By applying this simple algorithm recursively, they traverse and validate the entire tree.

From our sample XDR file, you can also appreciate the schema enhancements over the DTD model. In particular, you can set the type for each attribute and strictly control the cardinality of each node by using the *minOccurs* and *maxOccurs* properties. With DTDs, on the other hand, you can barely define a fixed range of occurrences for a given node.

Looking ahead to XSD, you'll notice that the key improvement concerns typing. XSD defines a type system that extends the XDR type system and that, more importantly, has a direct counterpart in the .NET Framework type system. (I'll have more to say about this in the section ".NET Type Mapping," on page 109.)

Validating Against an XDR

An XML document can include its XDR schema as in-line code or simply link it as an external resource. The *XmlValidatingReader* class determines that a given document requires XDR validation if an *x-schema* namespace declaration is found. The following sample document, named data_xdr.xml, points to an XDR schema stored in an external resource—the schema.xml file:

```
<?xml version="1.0" ?>
<!-- Sample XML document (data_xdr.xml) using XDR -->

<class xmlns="x-schema:Schema.xml"
       title="Applied XML Programming for .NET"
       company="Wintellect"
       author="DinoE">
   <days total="5" expandable="true">
     <day id="1">XML Core Classes</day>
     <day id="2">Related Technologies</day>
     <day id="3">XML and ADO.NET</day>
     <day id="4" optional="true">XML and Applications</day>
     <day id="5" optional="true">XML Interoperability</day>
   </days>
</class>
```

The following code snippet demonstrates how to set up an instance of the *XmlValidatingReader* class to make it validate a file using XDR:

```
XmlTextReader _coreReader = new XmlTextReader("data_xdr.xml");
XmlValidatingReader reader = new XmlValidatingReader(_coreReader);
reader.ValidationType = ValidationType.XDR;
reader.ValidationEventHandler += new ValidationEventHandler(MyHandler);
while(reader.Read());
```

This is in no way different from what you've seen for DTD and what you will see for XSD in the section "Validating Against an XSD Document," on page 130. When you require XDR validation and no XDR schema information exists in the XML document, the parser always returns a warning similar to the one shown in Figure 3-5.

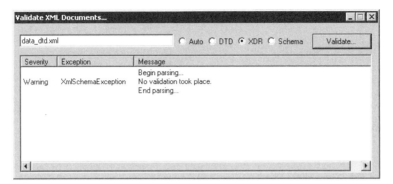

Figure 3-5   The parser has attempted to use XDR validation on a DTD-driven XML document.

The XML format for an ADO recordset provides the perfect, real-world example of an XML document that contains in-line XDR schema information, as shown here:

```
<!-- Northwind.xml, XML representation of an ADO recordset -->
<xml xmlns:s='uuid:BDC6E3F0-6DA3-11d1-A2A3-00AA00C14882'
     xmlns:dt='uuid:C2F41010-65B3-11d1-A29F-00AA00C14882'
     xmlns:rs='urn:schemas-microsoft-com:rowset'
     xmlns:z='#RowsetSchema'>
<s:Schema id='RowsetSchema'>
  <s:ElementType name='row' content='eltOnly'>
    <s:AttributeType name='employeeid' rs:number='1' />
    <s:AttributeType name='firstname' rs:number='2' />
    <s:AttributeType name='lastname' rs:number='3' />
    <s:extends type='rs:rowbase'/>
  </s:ElementType>
</s:Schema>
<rs:data>
  <z:row employeeid='1' firstname='Nancy' lastname='Davolio' />
  <z:row employeeid='2' firstname='Andrew' lastname='Fuller' />
  <z:row employeeid='3' firstname='Janet' lastname='Leverling' />
</rs:data>
</xml>
```

This simple recordset contains just three columns taken from the Employees table in the Microsoft SQL Server 2000 Northwind database. The XDR schema is placed in-line under the *<s:Schema>* tag. The structure of the document is expressed using a single element node (named *row*) and one attribute node per each column in the result set. Figure 3-6 demonstrates that this file (north-wind.xml) is perfectly validated by the .NET XDR parser.

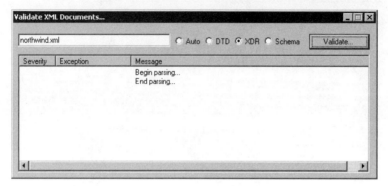

Figure 3-6 When the sample application operates in XDR validation mode, it can easily process XML files created by ADO.

Using the XML Schema API

As mentioned, XSD is a W3C recommendation that provides the tools you need to define the structure, contents, and semantics of an XML document. Compared to DTDs and XDRs, XSD has two key advantages. First, it is the official W3C recommendation for defining the structure of XML data. Second, it is the newest schema technology, and as such, has been built specifically to fix bugs and flaws in the other schemas (mostly problems with DTDs). And remember, more than an alternative schema technology, XDR is Microsoft's implementation of an early working draft of the XML Schema specification.

Although no developer can seriously think of denying the significance of XML, many perceive XML as a sort of extraneous entity that lies outside the main body of the code and that must be integrated through distinct objects. XML parsers process strings made of text and markup and come up with binary representations of that content. When you try to integrate this with the rest of the caller program, you must effectively transform text content into more specific data types.

The same issue arises in the other direction. To export your binary objects to XML, you perform a kind of text serialization that looks more like a normalization of involved types with subsequent loss of type information. You shouldn't be surprised by this information loss, because XML doesn't have a type system.

DTD is a format designed to describe the structure and the contents of a document rather than to endow XML with an effective type system. XDR, on the other hand, introduces the concept of typed attributes. XSD thinks a little bigger. Not only does it reinforce the importance of typed attributes, but it also distinguishes between simple and complex types, simplifies type inheritance, and exposes a full-blown and official XML type system.

The .NET Framework has been designed around XML standards, including XSD. Although the .NET Framework type system is a separate entity from the XML type system, a conversion API does exist that greatly simplifies software interaction through integration technologies such as SOAP and Web services.

What Is a Schema, Anyway?

A *schema* is an XML file (with typical extension .xsd) that describes the syntax and semantics of XML documents using a standard XML syntax. An XML schema specifies the content constraints and the vocabulary that compliant documents must accommodate. For example, compliant documents must fulfill any dependencies between nodes, assign attributes the correct type, and give child nodes the exact cardinality.

The XML Schema specification is articulated into two distinct parts. Part I contains the definition of a grammar for complex types—that is, composite XML elements. Part II describes a set of primitive types—the XML type system—plus a grammar for creating new primitive types, said to be simple types. New types are defined in terms of existing types.

An XML schema also supports rather advanced and object-oriented concepts such as type inheritance. In the .NET Framework, the SOM provides a suite of classes held in the *System.Xml.Schema* namespace to read a schema from an XSD file. These classes also enable you to programmatically create a schema that can be either compiled in memory or written to a disk file.

Simple and Complex Types

XML simple types consist of plain text and don't contain any other elements. Examples of simple types are *string*, *date*, and various flavors of numbers (*long*, *double*, and *integer*). XML complex types can include child elements and attributes. In practice, a complex type is always rendered as an XML subtree. A complex type can be associated only with an XML element node, whereas a simple type applies to both elements and attributes.

The diagram in Figure 3-7 illustrates the structure of the XSD type system.

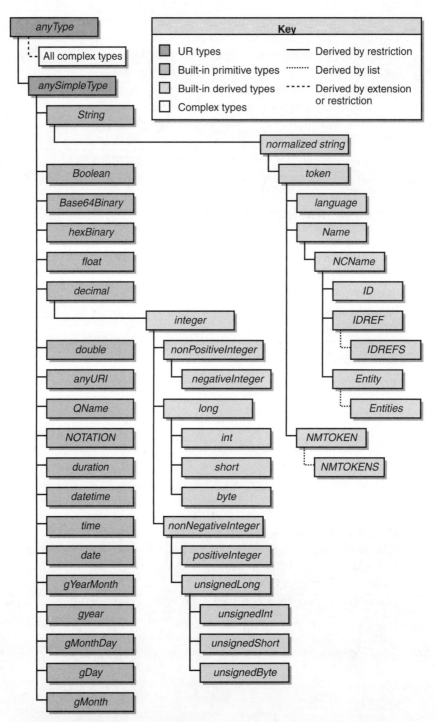

Figure 3-7 The XSD type hierarchy.

As you can see, both simple and complex types descend from the generic type *anyType*. Simple types also have their own base class, named *anySimpleType*. You can build new simple types from existing types and combine simple and existing complex types to create new ad hoc types by restricting, summing up, or listing features and values of the base types.

.NET Type Mapping

All the data types that can be used in XSD documents have a .NET Framework counterpart. After an XSD has been compiled into a .NET Framework representation object model, you can access it using the SOM classes. I'll have more to say on this in the section "Modifying a Schema Programmatically," on page 123.

The infoset that results from the schema compilation is also defined in the XSD recommendation and is said to be the post-schema-validation infoset (PSVI). The SOM renders the PSVI fields using read-only properties.

The pre-schema-validation infoset—that is, the infoset describing the source contents of the XSD—is built while the schema is being edited either from reading from a file or by using the SOM programmatically. The properties that express the pre-schema-validation infoset are all read/write.

In the SOM representation of the PSVI, the constituent elements of the schema are represented with instances of the *XmlSchemaDatatype* class. This class features two properties: *ValueType* and *TokenizedType*. The former returns the name of the XSD type, and the latter provides the name of the corresponding .NET Framework type. The return type is taken from the conversions listed in Table 3-6.

The schema compiler is a piece of code that translates between XSD types and the type system of a particular platform. In the .NET Framework, the schema compiler compiles XSD into an *XmlSchema* object that exposes the schema information through methods and properties.

Effective serialization between XSD and binary classes on a given platform is a feature with tremendous potential. It could supersede today's XML parsing by automatically creating an instance of a class instead of creating a generic and unwieldy XML DOM or simply passing raw data to the application. In the .NET Framework, XML serialization is accomplished using the *XmlSerializer* class and exploiting the services of the XML Schema definition tool (xsd.exe). I'll cover XML serialization extensively in Chapter 11.

Table 3-6   Mapping Between XSD and .NET Types

XSD Type	.NET Type	Description
anyURI	*System.Uri*	A URI reference
base64Binary	*System.Byte[]*	Base64-encoded binary data
Boolean	*System.Boolean*	Boolean values
Byte	*System.SByte*	A byte—that is, an 8-bit signed integer
Date	*System.DateTime*	Date based on the Gregorian calendar
dateTime	*System.DateTime*	An instant in time
decimal	*System.Decimal*	Decimal number with arbitrary precision
Double	*System.Double*	Double-precision floating number
duration	*System.TimeSpan*	An interval of time
ENTITIES	*System.String[]*	List of XML 1.0 entities
ENTITY	*System.String*	An XML 1.0 entity
Float	*System.Single*	Single-precision floating number
gDay	*System.DateTime*	Represents a day
gMonth	*System.DateTime*	Represents a month
gMonthDay	*System.DateTime*	Represents a period one day long
gYear	*System.DateTime*	Represents a year
gYearMonth	*System.DateTime*	Represents a period one month long
hexBinary	*System.Byte[]*	Hex-encoded binary data
ID	*System.String*	An XML 1.0 *ID* element
IDREF	*System.String*	An XML 1.0 *IDREF* element
IDREFS	*System.String[]*	List of XML 1.0 *IDREF* elements
int	*System.Int32*	32-bit signed integer
integer	*System.Decimal*	Arbitrary long integer
language	*System.String*	Language identifier (see RFC 1766 at *http://rfc.net/rfc1766.html*)
long	*System.Int64*	64-bit signed integer
Name	*System.String*	An XML name
NCName	*System.String*	Local name of XML elements (non-colonized)

Table 3-6   Mapping Between XSD and .NET Types

XSD Type	.NET Type	Description
negativeInteger	System.Decimal	Arbitrary long negative integer
NMTOKEN	System.String	An XML 1.0 NMTOKEN element
NMTOKENS	System.String[]	List of XML 1.0 NMTOKEN elements
nonNegativeInteger	System.Decimal	Arbitrary long integer = 0
nonPositiveInteger	System.Decimal	Arbitrary long integer = 0
normalizedString	System.String	String with normalized white spaces
NOTATION	System.String	An XML 1.0 NOTATION element
positiveInteger	System.Decimal	Arbitrary long positive integer
QName	System.Xml.XmlQualifiedName	An XML qualified name
short	System.Int16	16-bit signed integer
string	System.String	A string type
time	System.DateTime	An instant in time
timePeriod	System.DateTime	A period of time
token	System.String	Normalized string with leading and trailing white spaces removed
unsignedByte	System.Byte	8-bit unsigned integer
unsignedInt	System.UInt32	32-bit unsigned integer
unsignedLong	System.UInt64	64-bit unsigned integer
unsignedShort	System.UInt16	16-bit unsigned integer

> **Note**   The XML Schema definition tool (xsd.exe) is an executable available with the .NET Framework SDK. You'll find it in the BIN subdirectory of the .NET Framework installation path. Normally, this path is C:\Program Files\Microsoft Visual Studio .NET\FrameworkSDK.
>
> Among other things, xsd.exe can generate a C# or Visual Basic class from an XSD file and infer an XSD from a source XML file. This tool is also responsible for all the XSD-related magic performed by Visual Studio .NET.

Defining an XSD Schema

You have three options when creating an XSD schema. You can write it manually by combining the various tags defined by the XML Schema specification. A more effective option is represented by Visual Studio .NET, which provides a visual editor for XSD files with full IntelliSense support. The third option is based on the XML Schema definition tool (xsd.exe) mentioned in the previous section, which can infer the underlying schema from any well-formed XML document.

Of these options, the first is certainly the hardest to code and the one that you will probably use less frequently. It also happens to be the most useful tool for gaining an essential knowledge of the schema's structure and internals. Don't expect to find here an exhaustive explanation of the XSD syntax. For a comprehensive programmer's reference guide, use one of the resources listed in the section "Further Reading," on page 133.

Setting Up a Sample Schema

Let's start by creating a simple schema to describe an address. Like many real-world objects, an address too is rendered using a complex type—a kind of XML data structure. The following code shows the schema for an address. It's a fairly simple schema consisting of a sequence of five elements: *street*, *number*, *city*, *state*, and *zip*, plus an attribute named *country*. All constituent elements are string types.

```
<?xml version="1.0"?>
<xs:schema xmlns:xs="http://www.w3.org/2001/XMLSchema">
   <xs:element name="address" type="AddressType" />
   <xs:complexType name="AddressType">
      <xs:sequence>
         <xs:element name="street" type="xs:string" />
         <xs:element name="number" type="xs:string" />
         <xs:element name="city" type="xs:string" />
         <xs:element name="state" type="xs:string" />
         <xs:element name="zip" type="xs:string" />
      </xs:sequence>
      <xs:attribute name="country" type="xs:string" />
   </xs:complexType>
</xs:schema>
```

An XSD file begins with a *schema* node prefixed by the standard XML schema namespace: *http://www.w3.org/2001/XMLSchema*. In the schema's root node, you might want to set the *targetNamespace* attribute to specify the namespace of all components in the schema being defined and any schemas imported using the *include* element. Below the root node, you can find any of the top-level elements listed in Table 3-7.

Table 3-7   Top-Level Elements for XML Schema Files

Element	Description
Annotation	Contains a brief annotation about the structure.
Attribute	Indicates a global attribute declaration.
AttributeGroup	Groups attribute declarations for further use within the body of complex type definitions.
complexType	Defines an XML complex type.
element	Indicates a global element declaration.
group	Groups element declarations for further use within the body of complex type definitions.
import	Adds to the schema some definitions belonging to a different namespace. You reference the location of the external schema using the *schemaLocation* attribute.
include	Adds to the schema some definitions belonging to the same namespace as the current schema. The *schemaLocation* attribute lets you reference the external schema.
notation	Contains the definition of a notation to describe the format of non-XML data within an XML document.
redefine	Allows you to redefine in the current schema any components imported or included from an external schema.
simpleType	Defines an XML simple type.

In the preceding source code, the XSD file has one top-level *element* component of type *address*. It is followed by the declaration of the corresponding complex type—the *AddressType* sequence. The *sequence* element specifies the sequence of permitted nodes and related types. A complex type can be arranged using exactly one of the elements listed in Table 3-8. The element chosen specifies the content and the structure of the resultant type.

Table 3-8   Elements That Specify the Contents for Complex Types

Element	Description
simpleContent	Contains text or a *simpleType*; the type has no child elements.
complexContent	Contains only elements or is empty (has no element contents).
group	Contains the elements defined in the referenced group.
sequence	Contains the elements defined in the specified sequence.
choice	Lists the types of contents permitted for the type.
all	A group that allows elements to appear once and in any order.

Linking Documents and Schemas

You might want to know how an XML document can link to the schema. An XML schema can be associated with document files in two ways: as in-line code or through external references. The second option decouples the document instance and the schema. The first option, on the other hand, simplifies deployment and data transportation because all information resides in a single place.

The XSD is inserted prior to the document's root node, whether as in-line code or as an external reference. The following XML document links to the previously defined XSD through the *noNamespaceSchemaLocation* attribute:

```
<?xml version="1.0"?>
<address xmlns:xsi="http://www.w3.org/2001/XMLSchema-instance"
         xsi:noNamespaceSchemaLocation="address.xsd"
         country="Italy">
   <street>One Microsoft Way</street>
   <number>1</number>
   <city>Redmond</city>
   <state>WA</state>
   <zip>98052</zip>
</address>
```

The schema can be tied to a namespace by using the *schemaLocation* attribute, as shown here:

```
<?xml version="1.0"?>
<d:address xmlns:d="dino-e"
   xsi:schemaLocation="dino-e address1.xsd"
   xmlns:xsi="http://www.w3.org/2001/XMLSchema-instance"
   country="Italy">
   <street>One Microsoft Way</street>
   <number>1</number>
   <city>Redmond</city>
```

```
   <state>WA</state>
   <zip>98052</zip>
</d:address>
```

In this case, the XSD (address1.xsd) must be slightly modified by adding a *targetNamespace* attribute and setting an *xmlns* attribute to the target namespace URI, as follows:

```
<xs:schema targetNamespace="dino-e" xmlns="dino-e"
           xmlns:xs="http://www.w3.org/2001/XMLSchema">
```

Needless to say, the target namespace must match the designated namespace URI in the source document.

Complex Type Inheritance

With complex types, you simply define XML data structures that are in no logical way different from classes of object-oriented languages such as C# or Java. One key feature of those languages is the ability to derive new data types from existing classes. The same kind of inheritance can be achieved with XML schemas. To demonstrate, we'll build a new address type that, as in many European countries, takes into account also the province.

The address.xsd schema considered up to now contains more than just the definition of a complex type—it also contains a global element that will be included in any compliant document as an instance of the type. Let's first create a base class for the schema and name it xaddress.xsd, as shown in the following code. The new file differs from the earlier version in only one aspect: it now lacks the global element declaration.

```
<?xml version="1.0"?>
<xs:schema xmlns:xs="http://www.w3.org/2001/XMLSchema">

   <!-- Base definition for the Address type -->
   <xs:complexType name="AddressType">
     <xs:sequence>
        <xs:element name="street" type="xs:string" />
        <xs:element name="number" type="xs:string" />
        <xs:element name="city" type="xs:string" />
        <xs:element name="state" type="xs:string" />
        <xs:element name="zip" type="xs:string" />
     </xs:sequence>
     <xs:attribute name="country" type="xs:string" />
   </xs:complexType>
</xs:schema>
```

The next step is to define a new schema for a type named *EuAddressType*. You use the *include* tag to import the existing address construct from the base type declaration, as shown in the following code:

```
<xs:include schemaLocation="xaddress.xsd" />
```

At this point, you can declare the global element that, of course, will be of the new *EuAddressType* type, as follows:

```
<xs:element name="address" type="EuAddressType" />
```

Using the original xaddress.xsd schema (with a global element of type *AddressType*) raises a conflict because the *address* tag would be repeated. The final step is to define the extensions (or the restrictions) that characterize the new type. You use the *extension* tag or the *restriction* tag as needed. The following code adds a *<province>* string element to the definition:

```
<?xml version="1.0"?>
<xs:schema xmlns:xs="http://www.w3.org/2001/XMLSchema"
           targetNamespace="dino-e"
           xmlns="dino-e">

    <!-- Include the definition of the Address type -->
    <!-- xAddress.xsd does not include the global element -->
    <xs:include schemaLocation="xaddress.xsd" />

    <!-- Define the global element -->
    <xs:element name="address" type="EuAddressType" />

    <!-- Declare the new type inheriting from the base type -->
    <xs:complexType name="EuAddressType">
      <xs:complexContent>
        <xs:extension base="AddressType">
        <xs:sequence>
        <xs:element name="province" type="xs:string" />
        </xs:sequence>
        </xs:extension>
      </xs:complexContent>
    </xs:complexType>
</xs:schema>
```

The following XML file is now perfectly valid:

```
<?xml version="1.0"?>
<d:address xmlns:d="dino-e"
```

```
        xsi:schemaLocation="dino-e eu_address.xsd"
        xmlns:xsi="http://www.w3.org/2001/XMLSchema-instance"
        country="Italy">
<street>Via dei Tigli</street>
<number>123</number>
<city>Lamiacitta</city>
<state></state>
<zip>12345</zip>
<province>Rm</province>
</d:address>
```

The validation program ValidateDocument described in the section "The *XmlValidatingReader* in Action," on page 81, successfully checks the schema conformance of the preceding document, as shown in Figure 3-8. In the section "Validating Against an XSD Document," on page 130, we'll examine in more detail what happens when an instance of the *XmlValidatingReader* class is called to process an XML schema.

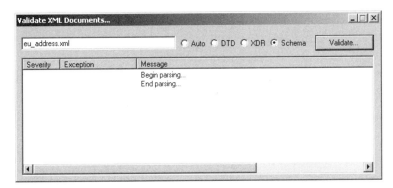

Figure 3-8   The *EuAddressType* schema is successfully checked.

Creating an XML Schema with Visual Studio .NET

Visual Studio .NET provides a visual editor, the XML Editor for XSD files. Instead of handling yourself the intricacies of schema markup, you can simply edit XML files using the drag and drop features and shortcut menus provided by the editor.

Figure 3-9 shows the XSD file from the previous section as it appears in the Visual Studio editor. The figure shows the components of the XSD file: a global element of type *AddressType* and the corresponding definition of the global element's complex type.

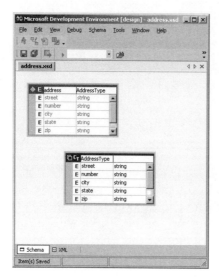

Figure 3-9   Sample XSD file edited with Visual Studio .NET.

As mentioned, Visual Studio .NET can also dynamically infer the schema from the currently displayed XML file. The task is actually accomplished by xsd.exe and can be easily repeated and controlled programmatically. The command line to use this tool is fairly straightforward, as shown here:

```
xsd.exe file.xml
```

Let's ask Visual Studio .NET to infer the schema for the sample address.xml file—the file we designed to be compliant with the address.xsd schema. One would expect to obtain a file nearly identical to address.xsd. However, surprisingly enough, the resultant schema seems to be different, as shown in the following code. The schema inferred is lexically different from address.xsd but completely equivalent in terms of semantics.

```
<?xml version="1.0"?>
<xs:schema id="NewDataSet"
        targetNamespace="http://tempuri.org/address1.xsd"
        xmlns:mstns="http://tempuri.org/address1.xsd"
        xmlns="http://tempuri.org/address1.xsd"
        xmlns:xs="http://www.w3.org/2001/XMLSchema"
        xmlns:msdata="urn:schemas-microsoft-com:xml-msdata"
        attributeFormDefault="qualified"
        elementFormDefault="qualified">
    <xs:element name="address">
        <xs:complexType>
            <xs:sequence>
                <xs:element name="street" type="xs:string"
```

```
                          minOccurs="0" msdata:Ordinal="0" />
          <xs:element name="number" type="xs:string"
                          minOccurs="0" msdata:Ordinal="1" />
          <xs:element name="city" type="xs:string"
                          minOccurs="0" msdata:Ordinal="2" />
          <xs:element name="state" type="xs:string"
                          minOccurs="0" msdata:Ordinal="3" />
          <xs:element name="zip" type="xs:string"
                          minOccurs="0" msdata:Ordinal="4" />
        </xs:sequence>
        <xs:attribute name="country" form="unqualified"
                          type="xs:string" />
      </xs:complexType>
  </xs:element>
  <xs:element name="NewDataSet" msdata:IsDataSet="true"
          msdata:EnforceConstraints="False">
    <xs:complexType>
      <xs:choice maxOccurs="unbounded">
        <xs:element ref="address" />
      </xs:choice>
    </xs:complexType>
  </xs:element>
</xs:schema>
```

If the difference isn't obvious from looking at the source code, take a quick look at the file in the XML Editor, as shown in Figure 3-10.

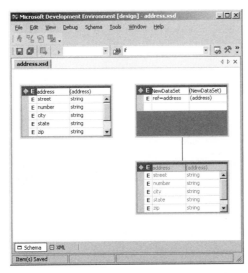

Figure 3-10   The graphical representation of the schema that Visual Studio inferred from the sample document.

The global *address* element is now described as simple content, as shown in the following code, and there is no reference to a named complex type like *AddressType*. In addition, the instance of the global element in the page is inserted using the *ref* keyword instead of the keyword pair *name/type*.

```
<xs:element ref="address" />
```

In the address.xsd schema, the *address* element was defined using the *name/ type* pair, like this:

```
<xs:element name="address" type="AddressType" />
```

The *ref* attribute lets you declare an element that uses an existing element definition. You use the *name/type* pair when the element is of a previously defined, or included, complex type. The *ref* and *name* attributes are mutually exclusive.

> **Note**   To understand the reason for such apparently odd behavior, consider the input data that you pass to Visual Studio .NET (and, under the hood, xsd.exe). Visual Studio .NET simply infers the schema, which means that it tries to figure out the schema based on the only observable source—the document text. In the source text, however, there is no mention of any complex type declarations. That's why the layout is correctly guessed but rendered using a simple content element.

The .NET Schema Object Model

Visual Studio .NET is not the only commercial tool capable of creating XML schemas in a visual fashion. XML Spy, for example, is another popular tool. The more powerful a tool is, however, the more details are hidden from the users.

For an effective programmatic manipulation of an XML schema, you need an object model. An object model enables you to build and edit schema information in memory. It also gives you access to each element that forms the schema and that exposes read/write properties in homage to the pre-schema-validation and post-schema-validation infoset specifications.

The .NET Framework provides a hierarchy of classes under the *System.Xml. Schema* namespace to edit existing schemas or create new ones from the ground up. The root class of the hierarchy is *XmlSchema*. Once your application holds an instance of the class, it can load an existing XSD file and populate the internal properties and collections with the contained information. By using the *XmlSchema* programming interface, you can then add or edit elements, attributes, and other schema components. Finally, the class exposes a *Write* method that allows you to persist to a valid stream object the current contents of the schema.

Reading a Schema from a File

You can create an instance of the *XmlSchema* class in two ways. You can use the default constructor, which returns a new, empty instance of the class, or you can use the static *Read* method.

The *Read* method operates on schema information available through a stream, a text reader, or an XML reader. The schema returned is not yet compiled. The *Read* method accepts a second argument—a validation event handler such as the ones discussed in the section "The *XmlValidatingReader* Programming Interface," on page 78. You can set this argument to *null*, but in this case you won't be able to catch and handle validation errors. The following code shows how to read and compile a schema using the .NET SOM:

```
XmlSchema schema;
XmlTextReader reader = new XmlTextReader(filename);
schema = XmlSchema.Read(reader, null);
schema.Compile(null);
//
// Do something here
//
⋮
reader.Close();
```

Once the schema has been compiled, you can access the constituent elements of the schema as defined by the PSVI. To access the actual types in the schema, you use the *SchemaTypes* collection. One of the differences between the information available before and after compilation is that an included complex type will not be detected until the schema is compiled. For example, in eu_address.xsd, we extended the *AddressType* type after importing it through the *<xs:include>* tag. To programmatically detect the presence of the *AddressType* complex type, however, you must first compile the schema, which would expand the *include* element that imports the type definition.

The following code snippet demonstrates how to get the list of complex types defined in the specified schema after compilation:

```
void ListComplexTypes(string filename)
{
    XmlSchema schema;

    // Open the XML reader
    XmlTextReader reader = new XmlTextReader(filename);
    try {
        schema = XmlSchema.Read(reader, null);
        schema.Compile(null);
    }
    catch {
        reader.Close();
        Console.WriteLine("Invalid schema specified.");
        return;
    }

    Console.WriteLine("{0} element(s) found.",
        schema.SchemaTypes.Count.ToString());

    // Loop through the collection of types
    foreach(XmlSchemaObject o in schema.SchemaTypes.Values)
    {
        if (o is XmlSchemaComplexType )
        {
            XmlSchemaComplexType t = (XmlSchemaComplexType) o;
            Console.WriteLine("{0} -- {1}", t.Name, o.ToString());
        }
        else
            Console.WriteLine("No complex types found");
    }
    reader.Close();
}
```

Figure 3-11 shows the tool in action on the eu_address.xsd schema.

Figure 3-11   Getting the list of complex types defined in the given XSD file.

Modifying a Schema Programmatically

After the schema has been read into memory, you can manipulate the structure of the schema, with the obvious limitation that indirect tags such as *include*, *import*, and *redefine* will be detected only as individual objects. These three tags, for example, will be detected as *XmlSchemaInclude*, *XmlSchemaImport*, and *XmlSchemaRedefine*, respectively, but the effect they have on the overall schema and contained types is not yet perceived.

Immediately after reading a schema, however, you can edit its child items by adding new elements and removing existing ones. When you have finished, you compile the schema and, if all went fine, save it to disk. Compiling the schema prior to persisting changes is not strictly necessary to get a valid schema, but it helps to verify whether any errors were introduced during editing.

The following applet reads a schema from disk, verifies that it contains a particular complex type, and then extends the structure of the type by adding a new element. The type processed is *AddressType*, which is edited with the addition of a new *<provinceInitials>* node. The node is expected to contain the first two uppercase initials of the province.

```
void EditComplexTypes(string filename)
{
    // Open and read the XML reader into a schema object
    XmlSchema schema;
    XmlTextReader reader = new XmlTextReader(filename);
    schema = XmlSchema.Read(reader, null);
    reader.Close();

    // Verify that the AddressType complex type is there
    XmlSchemaComplexType ct = GetComplexType(schema, "AddressType");
    if (ct == null)
    {
        Console.WriteLine("No type [AddressType] found.");
        return;
    }

    // Create the new <provinceInitials> element
    XmlSchemaElement provElem = new XmlSchemaElement();
    provElem.Name = "provinceInitials";

    // Define the in-line type of the element
```

(continued)

```
XmlSchemaSimpleType provinceType = new XmlSchemaSimpleType();
XmlSchemaSimpleTypeRestriction provinceRestriction;
provinceRestriction = new XmlSchemaSimpleTypeRestriction();
provinceRestriction.BaseTypeName = new XmlQualifiedName("string",
    "http://www.w3.org/2001/XMLSchema");
provinceType.Content = provinceRestriction;

// Set the (in-line) type of the element
provElem.SchemaType = provinceType;

// Define the pattern for the content
XmlSchemaPatternFacet provPattern = new XmlSchemaPatternFacet();
provPattern.Value = "[A-Z]{2}";
provinceRestriction.Facets.Add(provPattern);

// Get the sequence for the AddressType
XmlSchemaSequence seq = (XmlSchemaSequence) ct.Particle;
seq.Items.Add(provElem);

// Compile the schema
schema.Compile(null);

// Save the schema
XmlTextWriter writer = new XmlTextWriter("out.xsd", null);
writer.Formatting = Formatting.Indented;
schema.Write(writer);
writer.Close();
}
```

This code reads the schema using an XML reader and checks for a complex type named *AddressType*. If the type is not found, the application exits immediately. The search for a complex type is performed by scanning the contents of the schema's *Items* collection of *XmlSchemaObject* objects. *XmlSchemaObject* is the base class for all schema components. Figure 3-12 shows a non-exhaustive diagram of the schema object relationships. (See the section "Further Reading," on page 133, for additional references.)

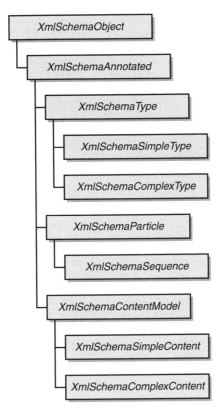

Figure 3-12   The *XmlSchemaObject* class and some of its descendants.

The *Items* collection picks up all the top-level elements found below the root *<xs:schema>* node. All elements that can be safely cast to *XmlSchema-ComplexType* have their *Name* property checked against the requested type, as shown here:

```
XmlSchemaComplexType GetComplexType(XmlSchema schema, string typeName)
{
    XmlSchemaComplexType ct;
    foreach(XmlSchemaObject o in schema.Items)
    {
        if (o is XmlSchemaComplexType)
        {
```

(continued)

```
            ct = (XmlSchemaComplexType) o;
            if (ct.Name == typeName)
               return ct;
         }
      }

      return null;
   }
```

Once a reference to the complex type has been found, the code proceeds by creating the new *<provinceInitials>* schema element. The relative type is declared in-line in the body of the element. It is a simple type defined as a restriction of the primitive XSD *string* type. When you define an XSD simple type by restriction you apply some facets to it. A *facet* is a property that narrows the set of values allowed for that element. For example, *length*, *minInclusive*, and *maxInclusive* are all facets that respectively determine the length of the type and the range of accepted values. Each facet defined in the XML Schema 1.0 specification has a corresponding class in the .NET SOM.

The *<provinceInitials>* element must fulfill a number of requirements. It has to be an uppercase string with a fixed length (2 characters). The *pattern* facet available in the XML Schema specification supports regular expressions to control the contents of an element at the finest level. The following code sets the uppercase and fixed-length constraints. (For more information about regular expressions, refer to the section "Further Reading," on page 133.)

```
XmlSchemaPatternFacet provPattern = new XmlSchemaPatternFacet();
provPattern.Value = "[A-Z]{2}";
provinceRestriction.Facets.Add(provPattern);
```

After the new element has been defined and given a type, you add it to the sequence of elements that form the type you want to extend. In this case, the *<provinceInitials>* element must become the next element in the *<xs:sequence>* compositor of the *AddressType* type. The programming interface of a complex type lets you access the sequence component through the *Particle* property, as shown here:

```
XmlSchemaSequence seq = (XmlSchemaSequence) ct.Particle;
seq.Items.Add(provElem);
```

At this point, the editing phase approaches an end. The new schema is now complete; all that remains is to save it to a disk file. The code discussed up to now, when applied to the address.xsd file, produces the following schema:

```
<?xml version="1.0"?>
<xs:schema xmlns:xs="http://www.w3.org/2001/XMLSchema">
    <xs:element name="address" type="AddressType" />
    <xs:complexType name="AddressType">
        <xs:sequence>
            <xs:element name="street" type="xs:string" />
            <xs:element name="number" type="xs:string" />
            <xs:element name="city" type="xs:string" />
            <xs:element name="state" type="xs:string" />
            <xs:element name="zip" type="xs:string" />
            <xs:element name="provinceInitials">
                <xs:simpleType>
                    <xs:restriction base="xs:string">
                        <xs:pattern value="[A-Z]{2}" />
                    </xs:restriction>
                </xs:simpleType>
            </xs:element>
        </xs:sequence>
        <xs:attribute name="country" type="xs:string" />
    </xs:complexType>
</xs:schema>
```

Application-Embedded Schemas

Schema information is fundamental for letting client applications know about the structure of the XML data they get from servers. Especially in distributed applications, however, schema information is just an extra burden that takes up a portion of the bandwidth.

In some situations, you can treat the schema like the debug information in Windows executables: indispensable during the development of the application; useless and unneeded once the application is released. This pattern does not apply to all applications but, where possible, constitutes an interesting form of optimization. After the two communicating modules agree on an XML format and this format is hard-coded in software, how can the format of the XML data being exchanged be different?

When the generation of XML documents is not completely controlled by the involved applications, schema validation ceases to be an optional feature. Thanks to the SOM, however, there's still room for optimizing the use of the bandwidth by not sending the schema information along with the document. The first option that comes to mind is that the client application stores the schema locally and loads it when needed to validate incoming documents. For

.NET Framework applications, the *XmlSchema.Read* static method is just what you need to load existing schema files.

An alternative option entails creating and compiling a schema object dynamically and then using it to validate documents. The code discussed in the previous section provides a concrete example of how .NET Framework applications can use the SOM to create schemas on the fly.

> **Note** Several applications in Windows incorporate an internal schema parser. Apparently, those applications don't require you to specify a schema. If you pass them an XML document that does not comply with the internal schema, however, an error is raised. An application that works in this way is the Windows Script Host (WSH) environment (wscript.exe)—the Windows shell-level script environment. Along with plain VBScript and JScript files, WSH supports an XML-based format characterized by a .wsf extension. Those files do not require schema information, but if you violate the documented layout rules, the file is not processed.

Deterministic and Nondeterministic Schemas

A schema validating parser works by matching the structure of the underlying XML document with the referenced XML schema document. By compiling the schema, the parser gets enough information to determine whether a given node in the source XML document conforms to the layout depicted by the XSD.

As the parser moves from one node to the next, two different situations can occur. Either the parser can unambiguously match the current node structure with a valid XSD sequence or it can't. If exactly one match is found, the process can continue. If no match is found, the source document does not follow the XML schema. Parsing stops, and an exception is raised. A schema in which the match between one XML node and one XSD sequence is unique (if any) is said to be *deterministic*. Our sample address schema is deterministic, and the SOM parser processes it successfully.

Other flavors of XML schemas are called *nondeterministic* because the number of matches found can exceed one. In this case, the parser must look ahead to try to determine the correct sequence and identify the correct piece of PSVI information. Nondeterministic does not mean invalid, but not all parsers can successfully handle such schemas. The .NET Framework schema parser, for example, does not support nondeterministic schemas. All files written according to the following (valid) schema are inevitably rejected:

```
<?xml version="1.0" encoding="utf-8" ?>
<xs:schema xmlns="" xmlns:xs="http://www.w3.org/2001/XMLSchema">
    <xs:element name="address">
        <xs:complexType>
            <xs:choice>
                <xs:sequence>
                    <xs:element name="street" type="xs:string" />
                    <xs:element name="number" type="xs:string" />
                    <xs:element name="city" type="xs:string" />
                    <xs:element name="state" type="xs:string" />
                    <xs:element name="zip" type="xs:string" />
                </xs:sequence>
                <xs:sequence>
                    <xs:element name="street" type="xs:string" />
                    <xs:element name="number" type="xs:string" />
                    <xs:element name="city" type="xs:string" />
                    <xs:element name="state" type="xs:string" />
                    <xs:element name="zip" type="xs:string" />
                    <xs:element name="country" type="xs:string" />
                </xs:sequence>
            </xs:choice>
        </xs:complexType>
    </xs:element>
</xs:schema>
```

The *<xs:choice>* element makes the schema inherently more prone to become nondeterministic. The *<xs:choice>* elements permits exactly one of the subsequent schema elements. However, when child elements are sequences, the schema automatically becomes nondeterministic.

In the preceding XSD, as soon as the parser moves to the *street* node, it detects an ambiguity. What is the correct *XmlSchemaSequence* class to take into account? The correct class can be determined only by looking a certain number of nodes ahead. In this very unfortunate case, the parser would need to look at least five nodes ahead. Some parsers support the forward-checking feature up to a fixed number of nodes; some do not. The .NET SOM parser requires the schema to be deterministic. Figure 3-13 shows what happens when the sample application ValidateDocument grapples with a nondeterministic schema.

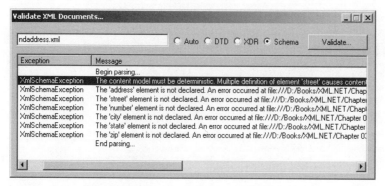

Figure 3-13   .NET SOM parser complaints about the nondeterministic nature of the schema.

Validating Against an XSD Document

After this long digression into the XML Schema API in the .NET Framework, let's conclude this chapter by looking at what happens when the *XmlValidating-Reader* class is called to operate on an XML file that includes, or references, an XML schema.

The following code shows how to set up the XML validator class to work on XSD files:

```
XmlTextReader _coreReader = new XmlTextReader(fileName);
XmlValidatingReader reader = new XmlValidatingReader(_coreReader);
reader.ValidationType = ValidationType.Schema;
reader.ValidationEventHandler += new ValidationEventHandler(MyHandler);
while(reader.Read());
```

When the *ValidationType* property is set to *Schema*, the parser tries to proceed anyway, regardless of the fact that the source file has no link to a schema file.

An interesting phenomenon occurs when the XML schema is embedded in the XML document that is being validated. In this case, the schema appears as a constituent part of the source document. In particular, it is a direct child of the document root element.

The schema is an XML subtree that is logically placed at the same level as the document to validate. A well-formed XML document can't have two roots, however. Thus an all-encompassing root node with two children, the schema and the document, must be created, as shown here:

```
<wrapper>
    <xs:schema xmlns:xs="http://www.w3.org/2001/XMLSchema"
            targetNamespace="sample">
      <xs:element name="book" type="xs:string" />
    </xs:schema>
```

```
    <smp:book xmlns:smp="sample">
        Applied XML Programming for Microsoft(r) .NET
    </smp:book>
</wrapper>
```

The root element can't be successfully validated because there is no schema information about it. When the *ValidationType* property is set to *Schema*, the *XmlValidatingReader* class returns a warning for the root element if an in-line schema is detected, as shown in Figure 3-14. Be aware of this when you set up your validation code. A too-strong filter for errors could signal as incorrect a perfectly legal XML document if the XSD code is embedded.

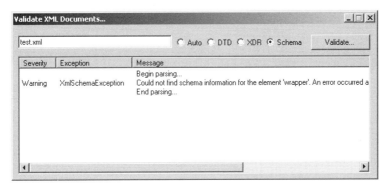

Figure 3-14   The validating parser returns a warning when the *ValidationType* property is set to *Schema* and an in-line schema is used.

> **Note**   The warning you get from *XmlValidatingReader* is only the tip of the iceberg. Although XML Schema as a format is definitely a widely accepted specification, the same can't be said for in-line schemas. An illustrious victim of this situation is the XML code you obtain from the *WriteXml* method of the *DataSet* object when the *XmlWriteMode.WriteSchema* option is set. The file you get has the XML schema in-line, but if you try to validate it using *XmlValidatingReader*, it does not work!
>
> In general, the guideline is to avoid in-line XML schemas whenever possible. This improves the bandwidth management (the schema is transferred one time at most) and shields you from bad surprises. As for the *DataSet* object, if you remove the schema to a separate file and reference it from within the *DataSet* object's serialized output, everything works just fine. Alternatively, with the *XmlValidatingReader* object, you can preload the schema in the schema cache and then proceed with the parsing of the source. We'll delve deeper into *DataSet* serialization issues in Chapter 9.

Conclusion

XML validation is the parser's ability to verify that a given XML source document is comformant to a specified layout. The intrinsic importance of validation, and related technologies, can't be denied, but a few considerations must be kept in mind.

For one thing, XML documents and schema information must be distinct elements. This improves performance when the document is transferred over the wire and keeps the memory footprint as lean as possible. In addition, validating a document to make sure it has the requested layout is not always necessary if the correctness of the data two applications exchange can be ensured by design. If the documents sent and received are generated programmatically and there is no (reasonable) way to hack them, validation can be an unneeded burden. In this case, you can rate the schema information as similar to debug information in Win32 executables: useful to speed up the development cycle, but useless in a production environment.

The real big thing behind XML validation is XSD—a W3C specification to define the structure, contents, and semantics of XML documents. XSD is another key element that enriches the collection of official and de facto current standards for interoperable software. It joins the group formed by HTTP for network transportation, XML for data description, SOAP for method invocation, XSL for data transformation, and XPath for queries.

With XSD, we have a standard but extremely rigorous way to describe the layout of the document that leaves nothing to the user's imagination. XSD is the constituent grammar for the XML type system, and thanks to the broad acceptance gained by XML, it is a candidate to become a universal and cross-platform type system.

This chapter uses the features and programming interface of a special reader class—the *XmlValidatingReader* class—to demonstrate how XML validation is accomplished in the .NET Framework. In doing so, we have inevitably touched on the technologies that are involved with the schema definition—from the still-flourishing DTD, to the newest and standard XSD, and passing through the intermediate, and mostly Microsoft proprietary, XDR.

For the most part, this chapter covers issues revolving around XML validating parsers. It also opens a window into the world of XML-related technologies.

Further Reading

XML sprang to life in the late 1990s as a metalanguage scientifically designed to definitively push aside SGML. If you want to learn more about this ancestor of XML, still in use in some legacy e-commerce applications, have a look at the tutorial available at *http://www.w3.org/TR/WD-html40-970708/intro/sgml-tut.html.*

In this chapter and in this book, you won't find detailed references to the syntax and structure of XML technologies. If you need to know all about DTD attributes and XSD components, you'll need to look elsewhere. One resource that I've found extremely valuable is *Essential XML Quick Reference*, written by Aaron Skonnard and Martin Gudgin (Addison Wesley, 2001). This book is an annotated review of all the markup code around XML, including XSD, XSL, XPath, and SOAP—not coincidentally, the same XML standards fully supported by the .NET Framework. Another resource I would recommend is *XML Pocket Consultant*, written by William R. Stanek (Microsoft Press, 2002). For online resources, check out in particular *http://www.xml.com.*

An excellent article that describes the big picture behind XSD, Web services, and SOAP can be found on the MSDN Magazine Web site, at *http://msdn.microsoft.com/msdnmag/issues/01/11/WebServ/WebServ0111.asp.* A detailed tutorial on XSD can be found at *http://www.w3.org/TR/xmlschema-0.* I especially recommend this tutorial if you need a complete step-by-step guide to the intricacies and wonders of the XSD as defined by the W3C.

As for regular expressions, I don't know of any book or online resource that specifically untangles this topic. On the other hand, regular expressions are covered in almost every book aimed at the .NET Framework. In particular, take a look at Chapter 12 of Francesco Balena's *Programming Visual Basic .NET Core Reference* (Microsoft Press, 2002).

4

XML Writers

Creating XML documents in a programmatic way has never been a particularly complicated issue. You simply concatenate a few strings into a buffer and then flush the buffer to a storage medium when you have finished. The process is quick, easy, and straightforward—could you ask for more? Well, actually, you should!

XML documents are text-based files, but they also contain a lot of markup text, and as you know, dealing with markup text can at times be boring or even annoying. More than just being a bother, you might find that supplying the necessary quotation marks and angle brackets can make your code more error-prone. Creating XML documents programmatically by simply putting one string of text after another is effective as long as you can absolutely guarantee that subtle errors will never sneak into the code mainstream, which is not much different from certifying that all of your manually created code is 100 percent bug-free.

The Microsoft .NET Framework provides a more productive, and even elegant, approach to writing XML code. Based on ad hoc tools, this approach simply applies the same pattern that has been the key to XML's rapid adoption—focus on the data and ignore the rest. Enter XML writers.

The XML Writer Programming Interface

An *XML writer* represents a component that provides a fast, forward-only way of outputting XML data to streams or files. More important, an XML writer guarantees—by design—that all the XML data it produces conforms to the W3C XML 1.0 and Namespace recommendations.

Suppose you have to render in XML the contents of a string array. The following code normally fits the bill:

```
void CreateXmlFile(String[] theArray, string filename)
{
    StringBuilder sb = new StringBuilder("");

    // Loop through the array and build the file
    sb.Append("<array>");
    foreach(string s in theArray)
    {
        sb.Append("<element value=\"");
        sb.Append(s);
        sb.Append("\"/>");
    }
    sb.Append("</array>");

    // Create the file
    StreamWriter sw = new StreamWriter(filename);
    sw.Write(sb.ToString());
    sw.Close();
}
```

The output is shown in Figure 4-1. Apparently, everything is working just fine.

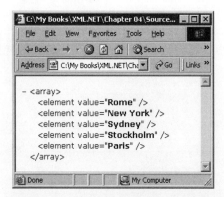

Figure 4-1   The sample XML file is successfully recognized and managed by Microsoft Internet Explorer.

One small drawback is that the XML code you get is not exactly in the format you expect—the format shown in Internet Explorer. The source code for the XML file in Figure 4-1 has no newline characters or indentation and appears to be an endless and hardly readable string of markup text. But this is no big deal. You can simply enhance the code a little bit by adding newline and tab characters.

In general, there is nothing really bad or wrong with this approach as long as the document file you need to create is simple, has minimal structure, and has only a few levels of nesting. When you have more advanced and stricter requirements such as processing instructions, namespaces, indentation, formatting, and entities, the complexity of your code can grow exponentially and, with it, the likelihood of introducing errors and bugs.

Let's rewrite our sample file using .NET XML writers, as shown in the following code. A .NET XML writer features ad hoc write methods for each possible XML node type and makes the creation of XML output more logical and much less dependent on the intricacies, and even the quirkiness, of the markup languages.

```
void CreateXmlFileUsingWriters(String[] theArray,
    string filename)
{
    // Open the XML writer (default encoding charset)
    XmlTextWriter xmlw = new XmlTextWriter(filename, null);
    xmlw.Formatting = Formatting.Indented;

    xmlw.WriteStartDocument();
    xmlw.WriteStartElement("array");
    foreach(string s in theArray)
    {
        xmlw.WriteStartElement("element");
        xmlw.WriteAttributeString("value", s);
        xmlw.WriteEndElement();
    }
    xmlw.WriteEndDocument();

    // Close the writer
    xmlw.Close();
}
```

Viewed in Internet Explorer, the final output for this file is the same as we saw in Figure 4-1. However, now newline and tab characters have been inserted as appropriate, and the source code truly looks like this:

```
<?xml version="1.0"?>
<array>
  <element value="Rome" />
  <element value="New York" />
  <element value="Sydney" />
  <element value="Stockholm" />
  <element value="Paris" />
</array>
```

An XML writer is a specialized class that knows only how to write XML data to a variety of storage media. It features ad hoc methods to write any special item that characterizes XML documents—from character entities to processing instructions, from comments to attributes, and from element nodes to plain text. In addition, and more important, an XML writer guarantees well-formed XML 1.0–compliant output. And you don't have to worry about a single angle bracket or the last element node that you left open.

> **Important** Because more often than not an XML writer class simply creates local or remote disk files, don't be too surprised if your code causes the .NET Code Access Security (CAS) system to throw a security exception. Partially trusted applications, and in particular Microsoft ASP.NET applications with default settings, have no access to the file system. Be aware that when you use XML writers, unless you take particular measures, sooner or later a security exception will be thrown.

The *XmlWriter* Base Class

XML writers are based on the *XmlWriter* abstract class that defines the .NET Framework interface for writing XML. The *XmlWriter* class is not directly creatable from user applications, but it can be used as a reference type for objects that are instances of classes derived from *XmlWriter*. Actually, the .NET Framework provides just one class that gives a concrete implementation of the *XmlWriter* interface—the *XmlTextWriter* class.

What the *XmlWriter* Class Can't Do

Although powerful and considerably feature-rich, an XML writer is not perfect; it still leaves some margin for errors. To be more precise, the *XmlWriter* class certainly generates 100-percent well-formed code, but only if you pass on correct information. In particular, an XML writer does not check for invalid characters in element and attribute names. It also does not guarantee that any Unicode characters you use fit into the current encoding schema. As a consequence, any characters outside the encoding schema are not escaped into character entities and might lead to incorrect output.

An XML writer also does not verify duplicate attributes; it simply dumps the text out when you call the appropriate method. Nor does an XML writer validate any identifiers (for example, the *SYSTEM* identifier) you specify when you create a *DOCTYPE* node.

In addition, the *XmlWriter* class does not validate against any schema or document type definition (DTD). Creating a validating writer is not difficult, however; I'll give you some tips on how to build one in the section "XML Validating Writers," on page 168. By the way, an *XmlValidatingWriter* class is just one of the extensions to the *System.Xml* namespace slated for the next version of the .NET Framework.

Properties of the *XmlWriter* Class

Table 4-1 lists the properties that belong to the *XmlWriter* class.

Table 4-1   Properties of the *XmlWriter* Class

Property	Description
WriteState	Read-only property that gets the state of the writer. The state can be any value taken from the *WriteState* enumeration and describes the element being written.
XmlLang	Read-only property that returns the current *xml:lang* scope. You set the language of the document by writing an *xml:lang* attribute to the output stream.
XmlSpace	Read-only property that indicates the current *xml:space* scope through a value taken from the *XmlSpace* enumeration (*Default*, *None*, or *Preserve*).

All of these properties are read-only and abstract—that is, they must be overridden in any derived class. The behavior described in Table 4-1 simply indicates what the properties have been designed for and does not necessarily reflect the actual behavior of these properties in a custom implementation.

In general, the *XmlWriter* class properties serve to track the state in which another component might have left the writer. Note that these properties belong to the current instance of the writer object. If you are using the same writer to generate more documents on the same stream, these properties are not automatically reset when you start a new document.

XML Writer States

Table 4-2 summarizes the allowable states for an XML writer. Values come from the *WriteState* enumeration type. Any XML writer is expected to properly and promptly update its *WriteState* property as various internal operations take place.

Table 4-2   States of an XML Writer

State	Description
Attribute	The writer enters this state when an attribute is being written.
Closed	The *Close* method has been called, and the writer is no longer available for writing operations.
Content	The writer enters this state when the contents of a node is being written.
Element	The writer enters this state when an element start tag is being written.
Prolog	The writer is writing the prolog (the section that declares the element names, attributes, and construction rules of valid markup for a data type) of a well-formed XML 1.0 document.
Start	The writer is in an initial state, waiting for a write call to be issued.

When you create a writer, its state is set to *Start*, meaning that you are still configuring the object and the actual writing phase has not yet begun. The next state is *Prolog*, which is reached as soon as you call *WriteStartDocument*—the first write method you call. After that, the state transition depends primarily on the type of document you are writing and its contents.

The writer remains in *Prolog* state while you add nonelement nodes, including comments, processing instructions, and document types. When the first element node is encountered—the document root node—the state changes to *Element*. The state switches to *Attribute* when you call the *WriteStartAttribute* method but not when you write attributes using the more direct *WriteAttribute-String* method. (In the latter case, the state remains set to *Element*.) Writing an end tag switches the state to *Content*, and when you have finished writing and call *WriteEndDocument*, the state returns to *Start* until you start another document or close the writer.

Methods of the *XmlWriter* Class

Table 4-3 lists some of the methods that belong to the *XmlWriter* class. Only methods that are not directly involved with the writing of XML elements are included here.

Table 4-3   Nonwriting Methods of the *XmlWriter* Class

Method	Description
Close	Closes both the writer and the underlying stream. The writer can't be used to write additional text. Any attempt would cause an invalid operation exception to be thrown.
Flush	Flushes whatever is in the buffer to the underlying streams and also flushes the underlying stream. After this method is called, the writer remains active and ready to write more to the same stream.
LookupPrefix	Takes a namespace URI and returns the corresponding prefix. In doing so, the method looks for the closest matching prefix defined in the current namespace scope.

An XML writer accumulates text in an internal buffer. Normally, the buffer is flushed, and the XML text actually written, only when the writer is closed. By calling the *Flush* method, however, you can empty the buffer and write the current contents down to the stream. Some working memory is freed, the writer is not closed, and the operation can continue.

For example, let's assume that you use a file as the output stream. At some point, while generating the XML content, you call *Flush*. As a result, the file (existing or already created by the time *Flush* is called) is partially populated. However, it can't be accessed by other processes because the file is locked by your process. The XML file will be unlocked and made available to other processes only when the writer is closed—an action that, in turn, closes the stream and releases any underlying resources.

Table 4-4 summarizes the key methods of the *XmlWriter* class for writing specific XML elements such as attributes, entities, and nodes.

Table 4-4   Writing Methods of the *XmlWriter* Class

Method	Description
WriteAttributeString	Writes an attribute with the specified value. The method adds start and end quotation marks.
WriteCData	Writes a *CDATA* block containing the specified text. The method adds start (*<![CDATA[*) and end (*]]>*) blocks for the element.
WriteCharEntity	Writes the specified Unicode character in hexadecimal character entity reference format. For example, the & (ampersand) character is written as *&*.
WriteComment	Writes a comment. The method adds start (*<!--*) and end (*-->*) blocks for the element.
WriteDocType	Writes the *DOCTYPE* declaration with the specified name and optional attributes.
WriteElementString	Writes an element node with the specified contents. It can produce the following output with a single call: *<city>Rome</city>*, where *city* is the name of the element and *Rome* is the contents to write.
WriteEndAttribute	Closes a previous call made to *WriteStartAttribute*.
WriteEndDocument	Closes any open elements or attributes and returns the writer to its initial state (*Start*).
WriteEndElement	Closes the innermost open element using the short end tag (*/>*) where appropriate. The namespace scope moves one level up.
WriteEntityRef	Writes an entity reference with the specified name. Takes care of the leading *&* and the trailing semicolon (*;*).
WriteFullEndElement	Closes one element by using a full end tag (for example, *</element>*). This method is similar to *WriteEndElement*, but it always closes the innermost element using a full end tag. Just as with *WriteEndElement*, the namespace scope is moved one level up.
WriteName	Writes the specified name, ensuring that it is a valid name according to the W3C XML 1.0 recommendation.
WriteNmToken	Writes the specified name, ensuring that it is a valid *NmToken* according to the W3C XML 1.0 recommendation.
WriteProcessingInstruction	Writes a processing instruction using the required syntax *<?name value?>*.
WriteQualifiedName	Writes the namespace-qualified name after looking up the prefix that is in scope for the specified namespace.

Table 4-4   Writing Methods of the *XmlWriter* Class

Method	Description
WriteStartAttribute	Writes the start of an attribute. Switches the writer's state to *Attribute*.
WriteStartDocument	Writes the XML 1.0 standard prolog declaration.
WriteStartElement	Writes the specified start tag for the specified element node.
WriteString	Writes the specified text contents. Can be used with open attributes or element nodes.
WriteWhitespace	Writes the specified white space.

Some of these methods are abstract; some are not. In particular, the *Xml-Writer* class provides an implementation for one-shot methods that group a few more basic calls. For example, *WriteAttributeString* is implemented in *Xml-Writer* like this:

```
public void WriteAttributeString(string localName, string value)
{
    WriteStartAttribute(null, localName, null);
    WriteString(value);
    WriteEndAttribute();
}
```

Other, more specialized, writing methods available in the *XmlWriter* interface are listed in Table 4-5.

Table 4-5   Miscellaneous Writing Methods

Method	Description
WriteAttributes	Writes all the attributes found at the current position in the specified *XmlReader* object. This method is actually implemented in *XmlWriter*. (This method will be discussed in more detail in the section "A Read/Write XML Streaming Parser," on page 179.)
WriteBase64	Encodes the specified binary bytes as base64 and writes out the resulting text. (Base64 encoding is designed to represent arbitrary byte sequences in a text form comprised of the 65 US-ASCII characters [A-Za-z0-9+/=], where each character encodes 6 bits of the binary data.) You decrypt this text using the *XmlReader* class's *ReadBase64* method. (These methods will be discussed in more detail in the section "Writing Encoded Data," on page 162.)

(continued)

Table 4-5   Miscellaneous Writing Methods   *(continued)*

Method	Description
WriteBinHex	Encodes the specified binary bytes as BinHex and writes out the resulting text. (BinHex is an encoding scheme that converts binary data to ASCII characters.) You decrypt this text using the *XmlReader* class's *ReadBinHex* method. (These methods will be discussed in more detail in the section "Writing Encoded Data," on page 162.)
WriteChars	Writes a block of bytes as text to the XML stream. This method is useful when you have to write a lot of text and want to do it one chunk at a time.
WriteNode	Copies everything from the specified reader to the writer, moving the *XmlReader* object to the end of the current element. This method is actually implemented in *XmlWriter*. (This method will be discussed in more detail in the section "A Read/Write XML Streaming Parser," on page 179.)
WriteRaw	Writes unencoded text either from a string or from a buffer of bytes as is. Can contain markup text that would be parsed as appropriate.
WriteSurrogate-CharEntity	Generates and writes the surrogate character entity for the surrogate character pair.

A *surrogate* (or *surrogate pair*) is a pair of 16-bit Unicode encoding values that together represent a single character. Surrogate pairs are in effect 32-bit atomic characters, although they are represented by a pair of characters (low and high char). Surrogates are critical when you use the *WriteChars* method to split a large amount of text. If that text, arbitrarily split, contains surrogates, some special handling must be done to ensure that surrogate pairs are not split across different chunks.

If a split happens, a generic exception (*Exception* class) is thrown. By catching this exception, you force the application to continue writing until the erroneously split surrogate pair is safely copied into the output buffer.

The *XmlTextWriter* Class

As mentioned, *XmlWriter* is an abstract class, although a few of its methods have a concrete implementation. In the .NET Framework, there is just one class built on top of the base *XmlWriter* class—the *XmlTextWriter* class.

XmlTextWriter provides a standard implementation for all the methods and the properties described up to now, plus a few more. It maintains an internal stack to keep track of XML elements that have been opened but not yet closed. Each element node can be directly associated with a namespace, thus becoming the root of a namespace scope. If a namespace is not specified, the element is associated with the last declared namespace.

The *XmlTextWriter* class has three constructors. You can have the writer work on a file or on an open stream. In both cases, you must also specify the required encoding schema, as shown in the following code. If this argument is *null*, the Universal Character Set Transformation Format, 8-bit form (UTF-8) character encoding set is assumed.

```
public XmlTextWriter(Stream w, Encoding encoding);
public XmlTextWriter(string filename, Encoding encoding);
```

The third constructor allows you build an XML text writer starting from a *TextWriter* object.

Encoding Schemas

In the .NET Framework, four different character encoding schemas are defined. Each schema corresponds to a class that inherits from the *Encoding* class. The classes are listed in Table 4-6.

Table 4-6   Available Character Encoding Schemas

Property	Class	Description
Encoding.ASCII	*ASCIIEncoding*	Encodes Unicode characters as single 7-bit ASCII characters.
Encoding.Unicode	*UnicodeEncoding*	Encodes each Unicode character as two consecutive bytes.
Encoding.UTF7	*UTF7Encoding*	Encodes Unicode characters using the UTF-7 character encoding set. (UTF-7 stands for Universal Character Set Transformation Format, 7-bit form.)
Encoding.UTF8	*UTF8Encoding*	Encodes Unicode characters using the UTF-8 character encoding set.

The default character encoding schema is UTF-8, which supports all Unicode character values and surrogates. UTF-8 uses a variable number of bytes per character and is optimized for the lower 127 ASCII characters.

If you want to use the default encoding, omit the second argument in the constructor. Otherwise, use the static properties of the *Encoding* class to indicate which type of encoding you want. You don't need to create a new instance of an encoding class to create a writer that encodes data in a certain way. For example, to create an ASCII stream, you use the following code:

```
XmlTextWriter xmlw = new XmlTextWriter(file, Encoding.ASCII);
```

If you want to get just the default setting, use *Encoding.Default* instead. Keep in mind that character encoding classes are located in the *System.Text* namespace.

Properties of the XML Text Writer

Table 4-7 lists the properties that are specific to the *XmlTextWriter* class—that is, the properties that the class does not inherit from *XmlWriter*.

Table 4-7   Properties of the *XmlTextWriter* Class

Property	Description
BaseStream	Returns the underlying stream object. If you created the writer from a file, this result is a *FileStream* object.
Formatting	Indicates how the output is formatted. Allowed values are found in the *Formatting* enumeration type: *None* or *Indented*.
Indentation	Gets or sets the number of times to write the *IndentChar* white space character for each level of nesting in the XML data. This property is ignored when *Formatting* is set to *None*.
IndentChar	Gets or sets the white space character to be used for indenting when *Formatting* is set to *Indented*.
Namespaces	Gets or sets support for namespaces. When this property is set to *false*, *xmlns* declarations are not written. Set to *true* by default.
QuoteChar	Gets or sets the character to be used to surround attribute values. Can be a single (') or a double (") quotation mark; the default is a double quotation mark.

In theory, the indentation character can be any character; the property does not exercise any control over what you choose. To create XML 1.0–compliant code, however, the value of the *IndentChar* property must be a white space character such as a tab, a blank, or a carriage return. By default, each level of indentation is rendered with two blanks.

> **Note**   When the XML text writer works on a file, it opens the file in exclusive write mode. If the file does not exist, it will be created. If the file exists already, it will be truncated to zero length.

The *XmlTextWriter* class has no data methods in addition to those described in Table 4-3, Table 4-4, and Table 4-5 as part of the *XmlWriter* class interface.

Writing Well-Formed XML Text

The *XmlTextWriter* class takes a number of precautions to ensure that the final XML code is perfectly compliant with the XML 1.0 standard of well-formedness. In particular, the class verifies that any special character found in the passed text is automatically escaped and that no elements are written in the wrong order (such as attributes outside nodes, or *CDATA* sections within attributes). Finally, the *Close* method performs a full check of well-formedness immediately prior to return. If the verification is successful, the method ends gracefully; otherwise, an exception is thrown.

Other controls that the *XmlTextWriter* class performs on the generated XML output ensure that each document starts with the standard XML prolog, shown in the following code, and that any *DOCTYPE* node always precedes the document root node:

```
<?xml version="1.0" ?>
```

This said, there is no absolute guarantee that users won't write badly formed code. If the bad format can be detected, the writer throws an exception. Otherwise, the file is considered correctly written, but client applications might complain about it, as in Figure 4-2.

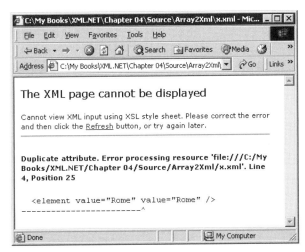

Figure 4-2   An XML file created with the *XmlTextWriter* class has a duplicated attribute that the class did not discover.

The following code demonstrates how to write two identical attributes for a specified node:

```
xmlw.WriteStartElement("element");
xmlw.WriteAttributeString("value", s);
xmlw.WriteAttributeString("value", s);
xmlw.WriteEndElement();
```

In the check made just before dumping data out, the writer neither verifies the names and semantics of the attributes nor validates the schema of the resultant document, thus authorizing this code to generate bad XML.

Building an XML Document

Up to now, we've looked at several code snippets showing the XML text writer in action, but without going into details. Let's make up for this now. The necessary steps to create an XML document can be summarized as follows:

- **Initialize the document**   The output stream is already open, and at this stage you simply write the XML prolog, including the XML 1.0 default declaration and any other heading information that the recommendation mandates to precede actual data nodes. (Typically, this information consists of processing instructions, schema references, and the DTD.)

- **Write data**   At this stage, you create XML nodes such as element nodes, attributes, *CDATA* and parsable text, entities, white space, and whatever else you might need that the writer supports. The writer maintains an internal node stack and uses it to detect and block erroneous calls such as attributes being created outside the start tag. The writer is smart enough to complete the markup for nodes automatically. This means, for example, that the writer automatically inserts all missing end tags when the writer is closed and completes the markup for the start tag when writing of text or child nodes begins.

- **Close the document**   At this stage, you close the writer to flush both the contents of the writer and the underlying stream object. At this time only (or prior, if you call the *Flush* method), the XML text accumulated in an internal buffer is written out and undergoes a summary check for XML well-formedness.

Writing the XML Prolog

Once you have a living and functional instance of the *XmlTextWriter* class, the first XML element you add to it is the official XML 1.0 signature. You obtain this signature in a very natural and transparent way simply by calling the *WriteStart-Document* method. This method starts a new document and marks the XML declaration with the *version* attribute set to "*1.0*", as shown in the following code:

```
// produces: <?xml version="1.0"?>
writer.WriteStartDocument();
```

By using one of the *WriteStartDocument* overloads, you can also set the *standalone* attribute to "*yes*", as shown here:

```
// produces: <?xml version="1.0" standalone="yes"?>
writer.WriteStartDocument(true);
```

> **Note**   A *stand-alone XML document* is declared to be totally independent of external resources such as DTDs or entities.

You close the document writing phase by calling the *WriteEndDocument* method, as shown in the following code. At this stage, all pending nodes are automatically closed, the internal stack is entirely cleared, and the writer is switched back to its initial state.

```
writer.WriteStartDocument();
// ...
// Build the document here
// ...
writer.WriteEndDocument();
```

> **Important**   The *WriteStartDocument/WriteEndDocument* pair is not required to produce an XML file. If you omit such calls, the writer will still work just fine. However, instead of a well-formed XML 1.0 document, you can get a well-formed XML fragment with no root rules applied.

When you need to insert a comment, use the *WriteComment* method. The syntax is straightforward, as shown here:

```
writer.WriteComment("Do something here");
```

No exception is raised if the comment text is null or empty. The following code is generated by an empty comment:

```
<!---->
```

Another XML element you often find at the beginning of an XML document is the *processing instruction*. The method that writes such instructions is *WriteProcessingInstruction*. It takes two arguments: the name of the instruction and a value. The following code demonstrates a typical processing instruction:

```
<?xml-stylesheet type="text/xsl" href="transform.xsl"?>
```

The processing instruction dictates that the contents of the current document must be transformed using the source of the specified style sheet document. A processing instruction consists of a name (*xml-stylesheet* in this example) plus a value. The value can be a combination of one or more name/value pairs, however. When you create a processing instruction with the .NET XML API, you group all the name/value pairs in a single string, using blanks to separate consecutive pairs, as shown here:

```
String text = "type=\"text/xsl\" href=\"transform.xsl\"";
writer.WriteProcessingInstruction("xml-stylesheet", text);
```

The preceding code creates the following XML line:

```
<?xml-stylesheet type="text/xsl" href="transform.xsl"?>
```

> **Important**   The *XML declaration* is a kind of processing instruction. However, you can't create a typical XML 1.0 signature using the *WriteProcessingInstruction* method because *WriteProcessingInstruction* can be called only after the XML document has been initialized—that is, after *WriteStartDocument* has been called. At this point, any attempt to write the *xml* processing instruction would raise an argument exception.

Writing *DOCTYPE* and Entities

In an XML document, the document type subtree is a unique graph that contains references to external markup resources such as a DTD or a list of entities. As mentioned in the previous section, XML documents without such external references are said to be stand-alone and can declare their status in the XML signature through the *standalone* attribute.

To identify an external markup resource, two types of identifiers can be used: *public* and *system*. In the .NET Framework, both identifiers are found in the body of the *WriteDocType* method, as shown here:

```
public override void WriteDocType(
    string name, string pubid, string sysid, string subset);
```

The *name* argument is mandatory and represents the name of *DOCTYPE* root node. The *subset* argument, on the other hand, represents the text being written in the *!DOCTYPE* XML node. The *pubid* and *sysid* arguments represent the identifier of the *DOCTYPE* resource being defined. The key identifier is *sysid*, rendered in XML through the *SYSTEM* attribute. It normally evaluates to a URL that points to the remote location where the resource is stored. For example, the following code associates the *MyDoc* resource with the *file.dtd* URL:

```
<!DOCTYPE MyDoc SYSTEM "http://server/file.dtd" >
```

By using the *pubid* argument (*PUBLIC* attribute in XML code), you can reinforce the identification of the resource by also using a location-independent public name for it, as shown here:

```
<!DOCTYPE MyDoc PUBLIC "MyDtd" "http://server/file.dtd" >
```

You can use *SYSTEM* without *PUBLIC*, or both, or neither. You can't use *PUBLIC* alone.

You use the *WriteDocType* method to insert a reference to an in-line or external DTD file to be used for validation purposes. Alternatively, you can use the *WriteDocType* method to insert entity definitions. In this case, specify *null* values for both *sysid* and *pubid* arguments. The following XML code creates an entity named *dinoe* that evaluates to *"Dino Esposito"*:

```
writer.WriteDocType(
    "MyDef",
    null,
    null,
    "<!ENTITY dinoe 'Dino Esposito'>");
```

The resulting XML text looks like this:

```
<!DOCTYPE MyDef[<!ENTITY dinoe 'Dino Esposito'>]>
```

An entity declaration defines a macro to access pieces of XML text using a symbolic name. When a previously defined entity is then used in code, another method does the job of expanding the content—*WriteEntityRef*. (More on this expansion in the next section.)

Writing Element Nodes and Attributes

The .NET XML API provides two methods for writing nodes. You use the *WriteElementString* method if you need to write a simple node around some text. You use the *WriteStartElement/WriteEndElement* pair if you need to specify attributes or if you need to control what's written as the body of the node.

The following instruction creates a node named *MyNode* and wraps it around the specified text. If needed, the method also provides an overload in which you can add namespace information.

```
writer.WriteElementString("MyNode", "Sample text");
```

The output looks like this:

```
<MyNode>Sample text</MyNode>
```

By writing the start tag and the end tag of an element node as distinct pieces, you can add attributes, reference entities, and create *CDATA* sections. Here's how:

```
// Open the document
writer.WriteStartDocument();

// Write DOCTYPE and entities
writer.WriteDocType("MyDef", null, null,
    "<!ENTITY I 'Italy'><!ENTITY I-Capital 'Rome'>");

// Open the root <Cities>
writer.WriteStartElement("Cities");

// Open the child <City>
writer.WriteStartElement("City");

// Write the Zip attribute
writer.WriteAttributeString("Zip", "12345");

// Write the State attribute (reference an entity)
writer.WriteStartAttribute("State", "");
writer.WriteEntityRef("I");
writer.WriteEndAttribute();

// Write the body of the node (reference an entity)
writer.WriteEntityRef("I-Capital");

// Close the current innermost element (City)
writer.WriteEndElement();

// Close the current innermost element (Cities)
```

```
writer.WriteEndDocument();

// Close the document
writer.WriteEndDocument();
```

All the instructions in the preceding code work together to populate a single element node named *City*. The *City* node contains an attribute named *Zip*, which is created in one shot using the *WriteAttributeString* method. As with element nodes, attribute nodes too can be written in two ways, using either a one-shot method or a pair of start/end methods.

The instructions in boldface demonstrate the alternative approach. The *State* attribute is opened and closed with separate statements. Meanwhile, a *WriteEntityRef* call determines the entity's contents by expanding a previously defined entity. The final output is shown here:

```
<Cities>
    <City Zip="12345" Country="&I;">&I-Capital;</City>
</Cities>
```

Internet Explorer correctly displays the document and expands all of its entities, as shown in Figure 4-3.

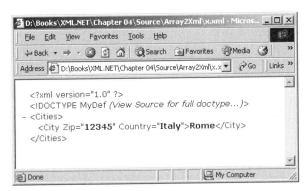

Figure 4-3   A dynamically created XML document with entities and *DOCTYPE* definitions.

If you need to concatenate entities with plain text or if you just want to write the contents of an attribute, use the *WriteString* method. For example, the following code adds "*, Europe*" to the attribute *Country*:

```
writer.WriteStartAttribute("Country", "");
writer.WriteEntityRef("I");
writer.WriteString(", Europe");
writer.WriteEndAttribute();
```

Figure 4-4 shows the results of the concatenation.

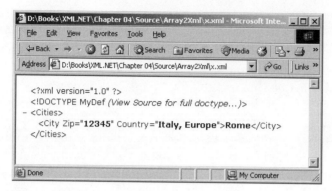

Figure 4-4   The *Country* attribute is created by concatenating an entity reference and plain text.

As you might have noticed, the end tags for both attributes and nodes do not take any arguments. The writer maintains an internal stack of opened attributes and nodes and automatically pops the innermost element when you close a node. Likewise, when a new node or attribute is opened, the writer simply pushes a new element onto the stack. If the newly added element is a node, in the resulting XML code, the node is nested one additional level.

At the end of the document—that is, when *WriteEndDocument* is called—all pending nodes are automatically popped off the stack and closed according to the last in, first out (LIFO) method. Let's consider what can happen if you disregard this simple rule and omit a call to *WriteEndElement* in a loop. The following code translates an array of strings into XML:

```
writer.WriteStartDocument();
writer.WriteStartElement("array");
foreach(string s in theArray)
{
    writer.WriteStartElement("element");
    writer.WriteAttributeString("value", s);
    writer.WriteEndElement();
}
writer.WriteEndDocument();
```

The root node is *array* and contains a series of child nodes named *element*, each with an attribute *value*, as shown here:

```
<?xml version="1.0"?>
<array>
  <element value="Rome" />
  <element value="New York" />
  <element value="Sydney" />
  <element value="Stockholm" />
  <element value="Paris" />
</array>
```

The *element* node is created entirely in the loop. If you don't explicitly close it by calling *WriteEndElement*, the final output would look like this:

```
<?xml version="1.0"?>
<array>
  <element value="Rome">
    <element value="New York">
      <element value="Sydney">
        <element value="Stockholm">
          <element value="Paris" />
        </element>
      </element>
    </element>
  </element>
</array>
```

Writing Raw XML Data

As we've seen, the XML writer saves the developer from a lot of the details concerning the markup text in an XML document. So what happens if you try to run the following command?

```
writer.WriteString("<");
```

This command executes normally, but any occurrence of markup-sensitive characters is replaced by escaped characters—mostly entities. Thus, the less than sign (<) is written using the *<* entity. This behavior might be acceptable at times, and sometimes not. If you just need to write out a particular sequence of markup characters as is, use *WriteRaw* method, as follows

```
writer.WriteRaw("<");
```

Unlike other writing methods, *WriteRaw* does not parse the string being passed. The method counts two overloads and allows you to write markup text manually either from a string or from a buffer of characters. If you use *WriteRaw* and make yourself responsible for the manual handling of the markup text, the writer can no longer guarantee the well-formedness of the final XML output.

In addition to *WriteRaw*, the *WriteCData* method writes out text in a somewhat protected way. *WriteCData* writes the text wrapped by a CDATA block, thus marking the text as unparsable by XML parsers. Typically, you use a *CDATA* section for XML code that might contain sensitive symbols such as less than (<), greater than (>), or ampersand (&), as shown here

```
writer.WriteCData("More >");
```

The text passed on to *WriteCData* is rendered like this:

```
<![CDATA[More >]]>
```

If you try to write the same text using *WriteString*, the effect is different, as the following XML text demonstrates:

```
More &gt;
```

> **Tip**   The *XmlConvert* class represents a handy tool that can be used to achieve a couple of goals. First, it provides methods for converting XML Schema Definition (XSD) data types to the .NET Framework type system. For example, the method *ToDateTime* converts an XSD *Date* type to *System.DateTime*. In addition, the *XmlConvert* class also lets you encode and decode XML names so that they comply with the W3C standards. The encoding process escapes any invalid characters into entities consisting of the character's numeric representation in the current encoding set.

Formatting Text

The *XmlTextWriter* class allows you to specify a few properties to configure the way in which newline characters, quotation marks, and indentation are defined. Normally, XML documents use tab characters or blanks to indent child nodes, although an XML document rendered as an endless string is by all means a perfectly valid XML document.

As mentioned, the properties involved with XML formatting are *Formatting*, *IndentChar*, *Indentation*, and *QuoteChar*. The first three are somewhat correlated, whereas the latter simply indicates the character to be used to enclose attributes—by default, the double quotation mark.

Formatting lets you control the formatting style by toggling it on and off altogether. When *Formatting* is set to *Formatting.Indented* (the other possible value is *Formatting.None*), the XML writer attributes a special role to *IndentChar* and *Indentation* that would otherwise be ignored. *Indentation* specifies the number of characters to indent for each level in the document's hierarchy. Conversely, *IndentChar* represents the character that will be used to indent the text of the new node. By default, formatting is on and the indentation is two blanks.

Note that all the XML writer's formatting is managed by the writer only before the document is actually opened—that is, prior to the *WriteStartDocument* call. The following code snippet demonstrates how to write a new XML document, indenting with a tab character any level of the hierarchy:

```
XmlTextWriter writer = new XmlTextWriter(filename, null);
writer.Formatting = Formatting.Indented;
writer.Indentation = 1;
writer.IndentChar = "\t";
```

As a final note, keep in mind that XML formatting normally indents element contents only and does not format mixed contents.

Supporting Namespaces

In the *XmlTextWriter* class, all the methods available for writing element nodes and attributes have overloads to work with namespaces. You simply add a new argument to the call and specify the namespace prefix of choice. A namespace is identified by a URN and is used to qualify both attribute and node names so that they belong to a particular domain of names.

Namespace Declaration

You insert a namespace declaration in the current node using the *xmlns* attribute. You can also optionally specify a namespace prefix. The prefix is a symbolic name that uniquely identifies the namespace. To declare a namespace, add a special attribute to the node that roots the target scope of the namespace, as shown here:

```
<node xmlns:prefix="namespace-urn">
```

You can write this XML text as raw text or use one of the methods of the writer object. Typically, you use one of the overloads of the *WriteAttribute-String* method, as shown here:

```
public void WriteAttributeString(
    string prefix,
    string attr,
    string ns,
    string value);
```

You can use this method to declare a namespace, but it remains primarily a method to add attributes. To obtain a namespace declaration like the one in our earlier examples, a few exceptions to the signature apply. In particular, for an *xmlns* attribute being written, you instruct the method to add an attribute whose name matches the prefix and whose prefix equals *xmlns*.

The third argument is expected to be the URN of the namespace for the attribute. In this case, however, the namespace prefix named *xmlns* points to the default XML namespace, so the *ns* argument must be set to *null*. Note that any attempt to set *ns* to a non-null value would result in an exception because the specified URN would not match the URN of the *xmlns* namespace prefix. The fourth and final argument, *value*, contains the URN of the namespace you are declaring. The following code shows how to declare a sample namespace rooted in the node *<MyNode>*:

```
writer.WriteStartElement("MyNode");
writer.WriteAttributeString("xmlns", "x", null,
    "dinoe:isbn-0735618011");
```

This code produces the following output:

```
<MyNode xmlns:x="dinoe:isbn-0735618011">
```

Qualified Nodes

A namespace is unequivocally identified by a URN. Thus, whenever you need to indicate a namespace for an XML node, you should specify the URN. The following code shows how to use *WriteElementString* to write a qualified node based on the namespace declared in the previous section:

```
writer.WriteElementString("value", "dinoe:isbn-0735618011",
    "...");
```

The output looks like the following XML code:

```
<x:value>...</x:value>
```

As you can see, the method uses the specified URN to look up the closest prefix and then uses that prefix to generate the output text.

The *LookupPrefix* method is a public method that takes a URN and returns the closest prefix that matches it. By *closest*, I mean the topmost prefix available on the namespace stack. In other words, you can have the same namespace being referenced through different prefixes in different document's subtrees. *LookupPrefix* simply scans the namespaces declared within the current document and returns when the most recent one has been found. The method traverses the XML tree starting from the current node and moving up from parent to parent until the root is reached.

The following code shows an alternative way to write the preceding XML data using *LookupPrefix*:

```
string prefix = writer.LookupPrefix("dinoe:isbn-0735618011");
writer.WriteStartElement(prefix, "value", null);
writer.WriteString("...");
writer.WriteEndElement();
```

The *WriteStartElement* method takes the prefix and the node name. It can also accept a third argument, the URN of the namespace. If this argument is *null* or matches the closest URN for the prefix, the looked-up, existing namespace is used. The final XML code looks like this:

```
<x:value>...</x:value>
```

If the third argument of *WriteStartElement* represents an unknown URN, the namespace is declared and prefixed in place. In this case, its scope ranges over the XML subtree rooted in the node being created. Consider the following statements:

```
// Get the topmost prefix for the URN.
string prefix = writer.LookupPrefix("dinoe:isbn-0735618011");

// Write a <prefix:value> node. Identify the namespace
// using the most recent prefix/URN binding.
writer.WriteStartElement(prefix, "value", null);
writer.WriteString("...");
writer.WriteEndElement();

// Write a <prefix:value> node. Since the URN associated with
// the prefix does not match the specified URN, a new prefix/URN
// binding is generated rooting in the new <prefix:value> node.
writer.WriteStartElement(prefix, "value",
    "despos:isbn-0735618011");
writer.WriteString("...");
writer.WriteEndElement();
```

The two nodes created look like the XML source code shown here:

```
<x:value>...</x:value>
<x:value xmlns:x="despos:isbn-0735618011">...</x:value>
```

The two *<x:value>* nodes are scoped in different namespaces although they have the same name and even the same namespace prefix.

Qualified Attributes

To write qualified attributes, you use some of the overloads of the *Write-AttributeString* and *WriteStartAttribute* methods. According to the W3C XML 1.0 and Namespaces specifications, element nodes can have an associated namespace without a prefix, as shown here:

```
<value xmlns="despos:isbn-0735618011">...</value>
```

This namespace can be obtained with the following code:

```
writer.WriteStartElement("value", "despos:isbn-0735618011");
writer.WriteString("...");
writer.WriteEndElement();
```

Attributes, on the other hand, can't do without a prefix once they are bound to a namespace. If you don't indicate the prefix explicitly, one is generated automatically. Try the following code:

```
writer.WriteStartElement("element");
writer.WriteStartAttribute("value", "despos:isbn-0735618011");
writer.WriteString(s);
writer.WriteEndAttribute();
writer.WriteEndElement();
```

The *value* attribute is associated with a namespace URN, but no prefix is set or retrieved through *LookupPrefix*. The resultant XML text is shown here:

```
<element d2p1:value="..." xmlns:d2p1="despos:isbn-0735618011" />
```

An automatic prefix is generated to scope the attribute. There are two elements in the .NET Framework–generated prefix: the depth level, *d{n}*, and the prefix index, *p{n}*. The depth level is a one-based value that counts the depth of the node in the XML tree. The prefix index counts the number of namespaces defined in the body of the node. For example, consider the following code:

```
writer.WriteStartElement("parent");
writer.WriteStartElement("element");

// First <element value=".."> attribute
writer.WriteStartAttribute("value", "despos:isbn-0735618011");
writer.WriteString("...");
```

```
writer.WriteEndAttribute();

// Second <element value=".."> attribute
writer.WriteAttributeString("value", "urn:my-namespace", "...");
writer.WriteEndElement();
writer.WriteEndElement();
```

The corresponding output that the *XmlTextWriter* class generates is shown in the following code. Notice the presence of an extra parent node.

```
<parent>
  <element d3p1:value="..." d3p2:value="..."
    xmlns:d3p2="urn:my-namespace"
    xmlns:d3p1="despos:isbn-0735618011" />
</parent>
```

As you can see, the depth increased by 1 due to the extra parent node. In addition, the prefix index ranges from 1 to 2 to include all the namespaces in the node.

Getting the Qualified Name

The methods described up to now only allow you to create element and attribute nodes with fully qualified names. *WriteQualifiedName* is a method you can use to write out both element and attribute namespace-qualified names.

The *WriteQualifiedName* method takes two arguments, one for the node name and one for the namespace URN. Next it looks for the prefix associated with that URN and outputs the combined name in the form *prefix:name*. If you are writing element content, you get an exception if the namespace declaration does not exist. If the namespace argument maps to the current default namespace, the method generates no prefix. For attributes, if the specified namespace is not found, it is automatically registered and a related prefix is created as described in the previous section.

The *WriteQualifiedName* method, however, simply returns the name of the node and can't be used to create the node itself. From this point of view, it is only complementary to methods like *WriteStartElement* and *WriteStart-Attribute*. You need this method only when you have to write out the name of a node. When the writer is configured to support namespaces (which is the default), the *WriteQualifiedName* method also ensures that the output name conforms to the W3C Namespaces recommendation as defined in the XML 1.0 specification. You can turn namespace support on and off in a writer by setting the *Namespaces* property with a Boolean value as appropriate.

> **Tip**   As the W3C XML Namespaces specification recommends, the prefix should be considered only as a placeholder for a namespace URN. Although you could use prefixes and real names interchangeably within the range of a document, bear in mind that an intensive use of prefixes can soon become misleading when the document must be accessed by different applications and when you use the same prefix repeatedly in the same document. Whenever possible, applications should use the namespace name rather than a prefix. The use of a prefix is more acceptable when only unique prefixes are used and possibly only one namespace is defined in the document.

Writing Encoded Data

As mentioned in the section "Methods of the *XmlWriter* Class," on page 141, the XML text writer object has two methods that write out XML data in a softly encrypted way using base64 and BinHex algorithms. The methods involved—*WriteBase64* and *WriteBinHex*—have a rather straightforward interface. They simply take an array of bytes and write it out starting at a specified offset and for the specified number of bytes. (As you saw in Chapter 2, XML reader classes have matching *ReadBase64* and *ReadBinHex* methods to comfortably read back encoded information.)

> **Note**   In the .NET Framework, base64 encoding can also be performed through static methods exposed by the *Convert* class. In particular, the *ToBase64String* method takes an array of bytes and returns a base64-encoded string. Likewise, the *FromBase64String* method decodes a previously encoded string and returns it as an array of bytes. For some reason, the .NET Framework does not provide similar support for BinHex. BinHex, therefore, is supported only through XML readers and writers.

In the section "The XML Writer Programming Interface," on page 136, you learned how to serialize an array of strings to XML using the following array:

```
string[] theArray = {"Rome", "New York", "Sydney",
    "Stockholm", "Paris"};
```

Let's look at how to write this array to a base64-encoded form. The structure of the code we analyzed earlier does not need to be altered much. Only a couple of issues need to be addressed. The first concerns how strings are actually turned into an array of bytes. The second concerns the signature of the encoding methods. You can use *WriteBinHex* to write both element and attribute content in BinHex format, instead of using *WriteBase64*, as shown here:

```
XmlTextWriter xmlw = new XmlTextWriter(filename, null);
writer.Formatting = Formatting.Indented;

writer.WriteStartDocument();
writer.WriteComment("Array to Base64 XML");

writer.WriteStartElement("array");
writer.WriteAttributeString("xmlns", "x", null,
    "dinoe:isbn-0735618011");
foreach(string s in theArray)
{
    writer.WriteStartElement("x", "element", null);
    writer.WriteBase64(Encoding.Unicode.GetBytes(s),
        0, s.Length*2);
    writer.WriteEndElement();
}
writer.WriteEndDocument();
writer.Close();
```

Encoding-derived classes provide the *GetBytes* method, which simply translates strings into an array of bytes. You use *Encoding.Unicode* because that is the native format of .NET Framework strings in memory. When translating a Unicode string to an array of bytes, keep in mind that each Unicode character takes up two bytes. This code is slightly more efficient than using the following instruction, in which the conversion is performed internally:

```
writer.WriteBase64(Encoding.Default.GetBytes(s), 0, s.Length);
```

In the case of very large arrays, you can consider using direct pointers and the *unsafe* copy method. The *unsafe* method has the clear advantage of reducing memory allocations, so the resulting code is slightly faster. (See the section "Further Reading," on page 199, for references to more information.)

Figure 4-5 shows the final output of this code.

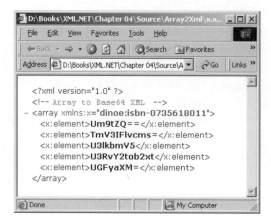

Figure 4-5   The contents of an array serialized to base64-encoded XML text.

Encoding using BinHex is nearly identical, as Figure 4-6 demonstrates.

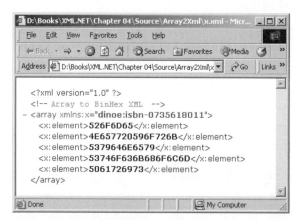

Figure 4-6   The contents of an array serialized to BinHex-encoded XML text.

As for the code, simply change the boldfaced line to the following and you're pretty much done:

```
writer.WriteBinHex(Encoding.Unicode.GetBytes(s), 0, s.Length*2);
```

Decoding Base64 and BinHex Data

Reading encoded data is a bit trickier, but not because the *ReadBase64* and *ReadBinHex* methods feature a more complex interface. The difficulty lies in the fact that you have to allocate a buffer to hold the data and make some decision about its size. If the buffer is too large, you can easily waste memory; if the buffer is too small, you must set up a potentially lengthy loop to read all the data. In addition, if you can't process data as you read it, you need another buffer or stream in which you can accumulate incoming data.

Aside from this, however, decoding is as easy as encoding. The following code shows how to read the base64 XML document created in the previous section. The XML reader opens the file and loops over the contained nodes. The *ReadBase64* method copies the specified number of bytes, starting at the specified offset, into a buffer that is assumed to be large enough. *ReadBase64* returns a value denoting the actual number of bytes read.

Encoding-derived classes also provide a method—*GetString*—to transform an array of bytes into a string, as shown here:

```
XmlTextReader reader = new XmlTextReader(filename);
while(reader.Read())
{
    if (reader.LocalName == "element")
    {
        byte[] bytes = new byte[1000];
        int n = reader.ReadBase64(bytes, 0, 1000);

        string buf = Encoding.Unicode.GetString(bytes);

        // Output the decoded data
        Console.WriteLine(buf.Substring(0,n));
    }
}
reader.Close();
```

If in this code you replace the call to *ReadBase64* with a call to *ReadBinHex*, you obtain a BinHex decoder as well.

Embedding Images in XML Documents

The technique described in the previous section can be used with any sort of binary data that can be expressed with an array of bytes, including images. Let's look at how to embed a JPEG image in an XML document.

The structure of the sample XML document is extremely simple. It will consist of a single *<jpeg>* node holding the BinHex data plus an attribute containing the original name, as shown here:

```
writer.WriteStartDocument();
writer.WriteComment("Contains a BinHex JPEG image");
writer.WriteStartElement("jpeg");
writer.WriteAttributeString("FileName", filename);

// Get the size of the file
FileInfo fi = new FileInfo(jpegFileName);
int size = (int) fi.Length;

// Read the JPEG file
byte[] img = new byte[size];
FileStream fs = new FileStream(jpegFileName, FileMode.Open);
BinaryReader f = new BinaryReader(fs);
img = f.ReadBytes(size);
f.Close();

// Write the JPEG data
writer.WriteBinHex(img, 0, size);

// Close the document
writer.WriteEndElement();
writer.WriteEndDocument();
```

This code uses the *FileInfo* class to determine the size of the JPEG file. *FileInfo* is a helper class in the *System.IO* namespace used to retrieve information about individual files. The contents of the JPEG file is extracted using the *ReadBytes* method of the .NET binary reader. The contents are then encoded as BinHex and written to the XML document. Figure 4-7 shows the source code of the XML just created.

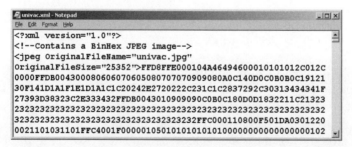

Figure 4-7   An XML file containing a BinHex-encoded JPEG file.

The BinHex stream is now part of the XML document and, as such, can be reread using an XML reader and decoded into an array of bytes. The sample application shown in the following code does just that and, in addition, translates the bytes into a *Bitmap* object to display within a Windows Forms *Picture-Box* control:

```
XmlTextReader reader = new XmlTextReader(filename);
reader.Read();
reader.MoveToContent();

if (reader.LocalName == "jpeg")
{
    FileInfo fi = new FileInfo(filename);
    int size = (int) fi.Length;
    byte[] img = new byte[size];
    reader.ReadBinHex(img, 0, size);

    // Bytes to Image object
    MemoryStream ms = new MemoryStream();
    ms.Write(img, 0, img.Length);
    Bitmap bmp = new Bitmap(ms);
    ms.Close();

    // Fill the PictureBox control
    JpegImage.Image = bmp;
}
reader.Close();
```

The reader opens the XML file and jumps to the root node using *MoveTo-Content*. Next it gets the size of the XML file to oversize the buffer destined to contain the decoded JPEG file. Bear in mind that a BinHex stream is always significantly larger then a binary JPEG file, but this is the price you must pay to string encoding algorithms. The *ReadBinHex* method decodes the JPEG stream and stores it in a *MemoryStream* object. This step is necessary if you want to transform the array of bytes into a .NET Framework graphics object—say, the *Bitmap* object—that can be then bound to a *PictureBox* control, as shown in Figure 4-8.

Figure 4-8   A *PictureBox* control displays a JPEG file just extracted from an XML file and properly decoded.

If you want to extract the image bits and create a brand-new JPEG file, use the following code. The name of the JPEG file is read out of the *OriginalFile-Name* attribute in the XML encoded document.

```
string originalFileName = reader["OriginalFileName"];
FileStream fs = new FileStream(originalFileName,
    FileMode.Create);
BinaryWriter writer = new BinaryWriter(fs);
writer.Write(img);
writer.Close();
```

XML Validating Writers

As mentioned, XML text writers do not validate against schema or DTD files. In fact, writing the XML document and validating its contents are two distinct operations that can't occur at the same time. However, if you need to make sure that the document just written is valid against, say, a schema, you can proceed in the following way: write the document and, when finished, validate it using a validating reader. Sounds straightforward? Well, it isn't.

The difficulty lies in the fact that, to validate, you must reread the text just written. If you are using a file, you can simply open the file using an XML reader and then instantiate a validating reader. The task is trickier if you happen to use an output stream—in many cases, you can't read the contents of an output (and mostly write-only) stream. In this case, a possible workaround is caching the entire XML document into a string. When you've finished, you simply pass the XML fragment to the validating reader. If all went fine, you write out the string to the expected output stream. To accumulate the XML output into a string, you use a *StringWriter* object to build the XML writer. The *StringWriter* class inherits from *TextWriter* and, as such, can be used to initialize an XML text writer using the following constructor:

```
public XmlTextWriter(TextWriter w);
```

Because this constructor is not stream-based, you can't indicate an encoding schema. Once you have run the statements listed in the following code, the remainder of the code does not need to be changed or altered. The big difference, though, is that now the text is accumulated in an in-memory buffer managed by *StringWriter*. Incidentally, this buffer is implemented using a *StringBuilder* object.

```
StringWriter sw = new StringWriter();
XmlTextWriter writer = new XmlTextWriter(sw);
//
```

```
// Write as usual
//
writer.Close();
```

Only after the XML writer has been closed does the string contain all the XML text generated by the application. You can copy that text into a local string variable using the *ToString* method and post-process it as appropriate, as shown here:

```
string xml = sw.ToString();
sw.Close();
```

In particular, you might want to pass down this string to an instance of the *XmlValidatingReader* class to apply schema validation. You can initialize the *XmlValidatingReader* class by passing the string as a whole and a node type of *Document*. Alternatively, you can use an *XmlTextReader* object working on the XML string through a *StringReader* object, as shown here:

```
StringReader sr = new StringReader(xml);
XmlTextReader xr = new XmlTextReader(sr);
XmlValidatingReader reader = new XmlValidatingReader(xr);
```

Yet another option is to use the special all-inclusive validator object built in Chapter 3—the global *XmlValidator* object—as shown here:

```
StringReader sr = new StringReader(xml);
XmlTextReader xr = new XmlTextReader(sr);
bool b = XmlValidator.ValidateXmlDocument(xr);
```

The *XmlValidator* object takes an *XmlReader*-derived class (or a file name) and handles internally all the details of the validation process, returning a Boolean value that indicates the success of the operation. Figure 4-9 shows the output of the sample application.

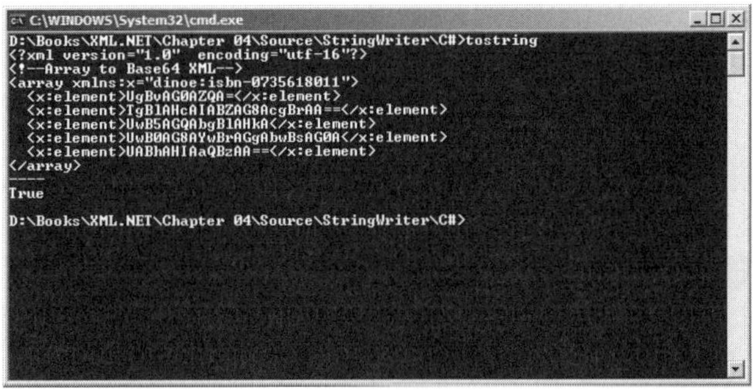

Figure 4-9   The sample XML validating writer in action. It dumps out the XML text and the Boolean value resulting from the schema validation.

> **Note**   The entire source code for a sample XML validating writer application can be found in this book's sample files. It is a console application named ValidatingWriter.

Writing a Custom XML Writer

As we've seen, an XML writer is a .NET Framework class that specializes in writing out XML text. Because there is just one flavor of XML, the need for customized versions of *XmlTextWriter* is extremely low. However, a lot of documents and objects out there might take significant advantage of an ad hoc, specialized, and seamless XML serialization class.

In the .NET Framework, all the XML files being used—from ADO.NET DiffGram objects to Web .config files—are written using XML writers. (ADO.NET *DataSet* objects are always remoted and serialized in a special XML format called the *DiffGram*; see Chapter 10.) In addition, the XML serializer saves and restores .NET Framework objects to and from XML documents. (I'll cover XML serialization in Chapter 11) So the .NET Framework provides you with some tools to save existing objects into an XML layout.

The XML serializer is designed to map living instances of objects to an XML schema. Sometimes, though, you just need to produce a particular XML output, and the use of XML schemas is not a strict requirement. In situations like this, what you can do is create an XML writer class and add to it as many specialized methods and properties as required by the structure you want to obtain.

Earlier in this chapter, we looked at a couple of simple XML writers that were used to create XML representations of string arrays and even JPEG images. In those cases, however, the expected output was so simple that there was no need to set up a class with more than one method. The next step is to analyze a more complex case—arranging a .NET XML writer class to produce the XML version of an ADO recordset starting from ADO.NET objects.

Implementing an ADO Recordset XML Writer

In Microsoft ADO.NET, the *OleDbDataAdapter* class allows you to import the contents of an ADO *Recordset* object into one or more *DataTable* objects. This kind of binding is unidirectional, however. You can import recordsets into

ADO.NET objects, but you can't create an ADO *Recordset* object starting from, say, a *DataSet* or a *DataTable* object.

The two-way binding between ADO.NET and ADO is important because it can save you from planning hasty porting of Windows Distributed interNet Applications (DNA) applications to the .NET platform. If you have a Windows DNA application with middle-tier objects that use ADO to fetch data, chances are good that you can import ADO recordsets into ASP.NET pages. In this way, as the first step of the porting, you simply refresh the user interface but leave unaltered the middle tier—the most critical part of a distributed system.

With this approach, you soon run into a subtle problem. How can you send down updated recordsets to the middle-tier objects? A possible workaround to create a recordset from scratch is by importing the ADO library in .NET Framework applications and then using the native methods to instantiate and populate the *Recordset* object. In this section, we'll look at an alternative approach: creating an ADO-specific XML file that COM-based middle-tier objects can read and internally transform into a living instance of the object.

Although the ADO.NET *DataSet* object can be easily serialized to XML, the schema used is not compatible with ADO. The XML schema used by ADO is based on XML Data-Reduced (XDR) schemas (see Chapter 3) and a few specific namespaces. In addition, it makes use of the XDR type system, which has no direct correspondence with the .NET Framework type system. But one thing at a time. Let's start with the new *XmlRecordsetWriter* class.

The *XmlRecordsetWriter* Programming Interface

The *XmlRecordsetWriter* class embeds an instance of the *XmlTextWriter* class but does not inherit from it. All the hard work of creating the XML output is accomplished through the internal writer, but the class programming interface is completely customized and largely simplified.

By design, the set of constructors of the *XmlRecordsetWriter* class is nearly identical to the constructors of the *XmlTextWriter* class, as shown here:

```
protected XmlTextWriter Writer;
public XmlRecordsetWriter(string filename)
{
    Writer = new XmlTextWriter(filename, null);
    SetupWriter();
}
public XmlRecordsetWriter(Stream s)
{
```

(continued)

```
    Writer = new XmlTextWriter(s, null);
    SetupWriter();
}
public XmlRecordsetWriter(TextWriter tw)
{
    Writer = new XmlTextWriter(tw);
    SetupWriter();
}
```

The only difference is that the *XmlRecordsetWriter* constructors do not support an encoding character set. The parameter for encoding is always set to *null*.

Table 4-8 lists the methods exposed by the *XmlRecordsetWriter* class.

Table 4-8 Public Methods of the *XmlRecordsetWriter* Class

Method	Description
WriteContent	Loops on the specified ADO.NET source object and writes a row of data. This method features overloads to read from *DataSet*, *DataTable*, and *DataView* objects.
WriteEndDocument	Ensures that all the pending nodes are closed and releases the underlying writer and stream.
WriteRecordset	One-shot method that groups together all the steps necessary to create an XML recordset file. This method features overloads to read from *DataSet*, *DataTable*, and *DataView* objects.
WriteSchema	Writes the schema information according to the XDR syntax and reads column metadata from ADO.NET objects. This method features overloads to read from *DataSet*, *DataTable*, and *DataView* objects.
WriteStartDocument	Writes the document's prolog, including the root node with all the needed namespace declarations.

For writing schemas and content, the *XmlRecordsetWriter* class needs to read information out of some ADO.NET objects. For this reason, methods like *WriteSchema*, *WriteContent*, and *WriteRecordset* have the following four overloads:

```
public void WriteXXX(DataSet ds)
{
    WriteXXX(ds.Tables[0]);
}
public void WriteXXX(DataSet ds, string tableName)
{
```

```
    WriteXXX(ds.Tables[tableName]);
}
public void WriteXXX(DataView dv)
{
    WriteXXX(dv.Table);
}
public void WriteXXX(DataTable dt)
{
    // Actual implementation here
}
```

The node layout of an ADO *Recordset* object is shown in Figure 4-10.

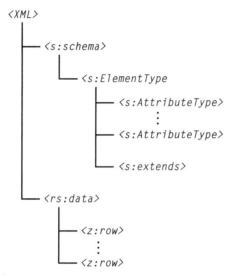

Figure 4-10   Layout of the XML schema for ADO *Recordset* objects.

Creating an XML *Recordset* object involves four steps: writing the prolog, writing the schema, writing the contents, and, finally, closing all pending nodes. The *XmlRecordsetWriter* class allows you to create the XML code by controlling each step yourself or by calling one of the *WriteRecordset* overloads, shown here:

```
public void WriteRecordset(DataTable dt)
{
    WriteStartDocument();
    WriteSchema(dt);
    WriteContent(dt);
    WriteEndDocument();
}
```

Creating the Recordset-Based Document

The *WriteStartDocument* method writes the root node, named *xml*, and all of the namespaces the document needs to reference, as follows:

```
public void WriteStartDocument()
{
    Writer.WriteStartDocument();
    Writer.WriteComment("Created by XmlRecordsetWriter");

    Writer.WriteStartElement("xml");
    Writer.WriteAttributeString("xmlns", "s", null,
        "uuid:BDC6E3F0-6DA3-11d1-A2A3-00AA00C14882");
    Writer.WriteAttributeString("xmlns", "dt", null,
        "uuid:C2F41010-65B3-11d1-A29F-00AA00C14882");
    Writer.WriteAttributeString("xmlns", "rs", null,
        "urn:schemas-microsoft-com:rowset");
    Writer.WriteAttributeString("xmlns", "z", null,
        "#RowsetSchema");
}
```

The next step is creating the schema. The following listing demonstrates a sample, but valid, XML schema for an ADO *Recordset* object with two fields, *firstname* and *lastname*:

```
<s:Schema id="RowsetSchema">
  <s:ElementType name="row" content="eltOnly">
    <s:AttributeType name="firstname" rs:number="2" />
    <s:AttributeType name="lastname" rs:number="3" />
    <s:extends type="rs:rowbase" />
  </s:ElementType>
</s:Schema>
```

As you can see, this syntax is based on the Microsoft XDR schema, an early subset of today's XML schema, shown here:

```
public void WriteSchema(DataTable dt)
{
    // Open the schema tag (XDR)
    Writer.WriteStartElement("s", "Schema", null);
    Writer.WriteAttributeString("id", "RowsetSchema");
    Writer.WriteStartElement("s", "ElementType", null);
    Writer.WriteAttributeString("name", "row");
    Writer.WriteAttributeString("content", "eltOnly");
```

```
    // Write the column info based on the table passed
    int index=0;
    foreach(DataColumn dc in dt.Columns)
    {
        index ++;
        Writer.WriteStartElement("s", "AttributeType", null);
        Writer.WriteAttributeString("name", dc.ColumnName);
        Writer.WriteAttributeString("rs", "number", null,
            index.ToString());
        Writer.WriteEndElement();
    }
    Writer.WriteStartElement("s", "extends", null);
    Writer.WriteAttributeString("type", "rs:rowbase");

    // Close the schema tag(s)
    Writer.WriteEndElement();
    Writer.WriteEndElement();
    Writer.WriteEndElement();
}
```

The information exposed by the schema depends on the source table used. The *XmlRecordsetWriter* class can do its job starting from data contained in any of the following objects: *DataSet*, *DataTable*, and *DataView*. However, because the *DataTable* object is the ADO.NET object that more closely matches the ADO *Recordset* object, the overloaded methods that receive a *DataSet* or a *DataView* object simply pass the related *DataTable* object to the overloaded method that receives a *DataTable* object. As mentioned, the XML recordset is built using a particular table in the specified *DataSet* object or using the table for the specified *DataView* object.

Processing Record Contents

The serialized contents of an ADO *Recordset* object consist of a bunch of *<z:row>* nodes grouped below a parent *<rs:data>* node. The *WriteContent* method simply loops through the rows in the table and creates the *<z:row>* nodes, as shown in the following code. Next it loops over all the columns and adds an attribute for each data column found.

```
public void WriteContent(DataTable dt)
{
    // Write data
```

(continued)

```
Writer.WriteStartElement("rs", "data", null);
foreach(DataRow row in dt.Rows)
{
    Writer.WriteStartElement("z", "row", null);
    foreach(DataColumn dc in dt.Columns)
        Writer.WriteAttributeString(dc.ColumnName,
            row[dc.ColumnName].ToString());
    Writer.WriteEndElement();
}
Writer.WriteEndElement();
}
```

ADO *Recordset* objects do not support embedding more result sets in a single XML file. For this reason, you must either develop a new XML format or use separate files, one for each result set.

Testing the *XmlRecordsetWriter* Class

For .NET Framework applications, using the *XmlRecordsetWriter* class is no big deal. You simply instantiate the class and call its methods, as shown here:

```
void ButtonLoad_Click(object sender, System.EventArgs e)
{
    // Create and display the XML document
    CreateDocument("adors.xml");
    UpdateUI("adors.xml");
}

void CreateDocument(string filename)
{
    DataSet ds = LoadDataFromDatabase();
    XmlRecordsetWriter writer = new XmlRecordsetWriter(filename);
    writer.WriteRecordset(ds);
}
```

Figure 4-11 shows the output of a sample application that creates the XML file and then displays it in a text box on the form.

The source *DataSet* object is fetched from the SQL Server Northwind database by executing the following query:

```
SELECT employeeid, firstname, lastname FROM employees
```

```
Testing the XML Recordset Writer...                                    _ □ ×

  Load Data...

<?xml version="1.0"?>
<!--Created by XmlRecordsetWriter-->
<xml xmlns:s="uuid:BDC6E3F0-6DA3-11d1-A2A3-00AA00C14882"
xmlns:dt="uuid:C2F41010-65B3-11d1-A29F-00AA00C14882"
xmlns:rs="urn:schemas-microsoft-com:rowset" xmlns:z="#RowsetSchema">
    <s:Schema id="RowsetSchema">
        <s:ElementType name="row" content="eltonly">
            <s:AttributeType name="employeeid" rs:number="1" />
            <s:AttributeType name="firstname" rs:number="2" />
            <s:AttributeType name="lastname" rs:number="3" />
            <s:extends type="rs:rowbase" />
        </s:ElementType>
    </s:Schema>
    <rs:data>
        <z:row employeeid="1" firstname="Nancy" lastname="Davolio" />
        <z:row employeeid="2" firstname="Andrew" lastname="Fuller" />
        <z:row employeeid="3" firstname="Janet" lastname="Leverling" />
        <z:row employeeid="4" firstname="Margaret" lastname="Peacock" />
        <z:row employeeid="5" firstname="Steve" lastname="Buchanan" />
        <z:row employeeid="6" firstname="Michael" lastname="Suyama" />
        <z:row employeeid="7" firstname="Robert" lastname="King" />
        <z:row employeeid="8" firstname="Laura" lastname="Callahan" />
        <z:row employeeid="9" firstname="Anne" lastname="Dodsworth" />
    </rs:data>
</xml>
```

Figure 4-11   An ADO XML *Recordset* object that has just been created
and its contents displayed in a text box on the form.

The XML file that is created in this way is successfully recognized by ADO-
driven applications, as shown in Figure 4-12.

Figure 4-12   COM-based applications based on ADO interoperate perfectly with the document that the XML writer has created by exporting
ADO.NET data.

The following VBScript script proves just that:

```
Const adClipString = 2
Const adCmdFile = 256
Set rs = CreateObject("ADODB.Recordset")
rs.Open filename, Nothing, -1, -1, adCmdFile
MsgBox rs.GetString(adClipString),, filename
```

> **Important** In the XML document that represents the data originally stored in an ADO.NET DataTable object, no type information exists. In spite of this, the XML document built so far is technically legal and correct, and all ADO-based applications can successfully manage it. All the various pieces of information in the document are rendered in the same way—that is, using Unicode strings, by means of the ADO *adLongVarWChar* data type.
>
> Making those fields type-aware means adding some type information to the *<AttributeType>* node in the XML schema. You do this using a pair of attributes in the *dt* namespace—one of the namespaces defined in the root node—as shown here:
>
> ```
> <s:AttributeType name='lastname' rs:number='2'>
>     <s:datatype dt:type='string' dt:maxLength='20' />
> </s:AttributeType>
> ```
>
> The *<s:datatype>* element describes the type of corresponding character data used in the parent attribute value. The main attribute of *<s:datatype>* is the *dt:type* attribute. For variable-length data types, XDR also allows you to specify a maximum length via the *dt:max-Length* attribute.
>
> The .NET Framework type system and the ADO *Recordset* object recognize different types. And ADO types are, in turn, different from predefined XDR data types. There's no easy way to obtain the XDR data type that corresponds to a .NET Framework *Type* object. Whenever type information is critical for the health of your application, you should figure out how to map a *DataTable* object's column .NET Framework type to an XDR type. In fact, you should exhaustively consider each .NET Framework type and map each to an element in another set of data types.

Comparing Writers and XML Writers

In the .NET Framework, a writer class is merely a document-producer object. It exposes ad hoc methods to let developers create the desired output using high-level tools. A method named *WriteSchema* that internally handles primitives to add nodes and attributes is much more understandable than, say, a *String-Builder* object that you use to build markup text. An XML writer is just a specialized writer that handles XML text.

You can certainly design your own writer classes to quickly and easily enable developers to create certain compound documents. In doing so, though, you don't need to inherit from *XmlWriter*, *XmlTextWriter*, or *BinaryWriter*. Although you can, and often must, use those objects internally, the user-level interface should comprehend methods and properties that reflect the nature and the structure of the final document.

As a general guideline, try to provide constructors that work over streams and text writers and to provide as many overloads as you can. For example, the *XmlRecordsetWriter* class can output its contents to streams and *TextWriter*-derived objects, including *StringWriter* objects. The modular architecture of the .NET Framework makes achieving these goals relatively inexpensive and, therefore, there is no good reason for not exploiting it to the fullest.

A Read/Write XML Streaming Parser

XML readers and writers work in separate compartments and in an extremely specialized way. Readers just read, and writers just write. There is no way to force things to go differently, and in fact, the underlying streams are read-only or write-only as required. Suppose that your application manages lengthy XML documents that contain rather volatile data. Readers provide a powerful and effective way to read that contents. Writers, on the other hand, offer a fantastic tool to create that document from scratch. But if you want to read *and* write the document at the same time, you must necessarily resort to a full-fledged XML Document Object Model (XML DOM). What can you do to read and write an XML document without loading it entirely into memory?

In Chapter 5, I'll tackle the XML DOM model of a parser, which is the classic tool for performing read/write operations on an XML tree. The strength of the XML DOM parsers, but also their greatest drawback, lies in the fact that an XML DOM parser loads the whole XML document in memory, creates an ad hoc image of the tree, and lets you perform any sort of modification and search on the mapped nodes. Keeping the nitty-gritty details of XML DOM warm for Chapter 5, in this section, we'll look at how to set up a mixed type of streaming parser that works as a kind of lightweight XML DOM parser.

The idea is that this parser will allow you read the contents of a document one node at a time as with an XML (validating) reader but that, if needed, it can also perform some simple updates. By *simple updates*, I mean simply changing the value of an existing attribute, changing the contents of a node, or adding new attributes or nodes. For more complex operations, realistically nothing compares to XML DOM parsers.

Designing a Writer on Top of a Reader

In the .NET Framework, the XML DOM classes make intensive use of streaming readers and writers to build the in-memory tree and to flush it out to disk. Thus, readers and writers are definitely the only XML primitives available in the .NET Framework. Consequently, to build up a sort of lightweight XML DOM parser, we can only rely, once more, on readers and writers.

The inspiration for designing such a read/write streaming parser is database server cursors. With database server cursors, you visit records one after the next and, if needed, can apply changes on the fly. Database changes are immediately effective, and actually the canvas on which your code operates is simply the database table. The same model can be arranged to work with XML documents.

You will use a normal XML (validating) reader to visit the nodes in sequence. While reading, however, you are given the opportunity to change attribute values and node contents. Unlike the XML DOM, changes will have immediate effect. How can you obtain these results? The idea is to use an XML writer on top of the reader.

You use the reader to read each node in the source document and an underlying writer to create a hidden copy of it. In the copy, you can add some new nodes and ignore or edit some others. When you have finished, you simply replace the old document with the new one. You can decide to write the copy in memory or flush it in a temporary medium. The latter approach makes better use of the system's memory and saves you from possible troubles with the application's security level and zones. (For example, partially trusted Windows Forms applications and default running ASP.NET applications can't create or edit disk files.)

Built-In Support for Read/Write Operations

When I first began thinking about this lightweight XML DOM component, one of key points I identified was an efficient way to copy (in bulk) blocks of nodes from the read-only stream to the write stream. Luckily enough, two somewhat underappreciated *XmlTextWriter* methods just happen to cover this tricky but boring aspect of two-way streaming: *WriteAttributes* and *WriteNode*.

The *WriteAttributes* method reads all the attributes available on the currently selected node in the specified reader. It then copies them as a single string to the current output stream. Likewise, the *WriteNode* method does the same for any other type of node. Note that *WriteNode* does nothing if the node type is *XmlNodeType.Attribute*.

The following code shows how to use these methods to create a copy of the original XML file, modified to skip some nodes. The XML tree is visited in the usual node-first approach using an XML reader. Each node is then processed and written out to the associated XML writer according to the index. This code scans a document and writes out every other node.

```
XmlTextReader reader = new XmlTextReader(inputFile);
XmlTextWriter writer = new XmlTextWriter(outputFile);

// Configure reader and writer
writer.Formatting = Formatting.Indented;
reader.MoveToContent();

// Write the root
writer.WriteStartElement(reader.LocalName);

// Read and output every other node
int i=0;
while(reader.Read())
{
    if (i % 2)
        writer.WriteNode(reader, false);
    i++;
}

// Close the root
writer.WriteEndElement();

// Close reader and writer
writer.Close();
reader.Close();
```

You can aggregate the reader and the writer in a single new class and build a brand-new programming interface to allow for easy read/write streaming access to attributes or nodes.

Designing the *XmlTextReadWriter* Class

The *XmlTextReadWriter* class does not inherit from *XmlReader* or *XmlWriter* but, instead, coordinates the activity of running instances of both classes—one operating on a read-only stream, and one working on a write-only stream. The methods of the *XmlTextReadWriter* class read from the reader and write to the writer, applying any requested changes in the middle.

The *XmlTextReadWriter* class features three constructors, shown in the following code. These constructors let you indicate an input file and an optional output stream, which can be a stream as well as a disk file. If the names of input and output files coincide, or if you omit the output file, the *Xml-TextReadWriter* class uses a temporary file to collect the output and then automatically overwrites the input file. The net effect of this procedure is that you simply modify your XML document without holding it all in memory, as XML DOM does.

```
public XmlTextReadWriter(string inputFile)
public XmlTextReadWriter(string inputFile, string outputFile)
public XmlTextReadWriter(string inputFile, Stream outputStream)
```

The internal reader and writer are exposed through read-only properties named *Reader* and *Writer*, as shown here:

```
public XmlTextReader Reader
{
    get {return m_reader;}
}
public XmlTextWriter Writer
{
    get {return m_writer;}
}
```

For simplicity, I assume that all the XML documents the class processes have no significant prolog (for example, processing instructions, comments, declarations, and *DOCTYPE* definitions). On the other hand, the primary goal of this class is to provide for quick modification of simple XML files—mostly filled with any kind of settings. For more complete read/write manipulation of documents, you should resort to XML DOM trees.

Configuring the *XmlTextReadWriter* Class

Immediately after class initialization, the reader and the writer are configured to work properly. This process entails setting the policy for white spaces and setting the formatting options, as shown here:

```
m_reader = new XmlTextReader(m_InputFile);
m_writer = new XmlTextWriter(m_OutputStream, null);
m_reader.WhitespaceHandling = WhitespaceHandling.None;
m_writer.Formatting = Formatting.Indented;

// Skip all noncontent nodes
m_reader.Read();
m_reader.MoveToContent();
```

I recommend that you configure the reader to ignore any white space so that it never returns any white space as a distinct node. This setting is correlated to the autoformatting feature you might need on the writer. If the reader returns white spaces as nodes and the writer indents any node being created, the use of the writer's *WriteNode* method can cause double formatting.

As you can see in the preceding code, the *XmlTextReadWriter* class also moves the internal reader pointer directly to the first contents node, skipping any prolog node found in the source.

The *XmlTextReadWriter* Programming Interface

I designed the *XmlTextReadWriter* class with a minimal programming interface because, in most cases, what you really need is to combine the features of the reader and the writer to create a new and application-specific behavior such as updating a particular attribute on a certain node, deleting nodes according to criteria, or adding new trees of nodes. The class provides the methods listed in Table 4-9.

Table 4-9   Methods of the *XmlTextReadWriter* Class

Method	Description
AddAttributeChange	Caches all the information needed to perform a change on a node attribute. All the changes cached through this method are processed during a successive call to *Write-Attributes*.
Read	Simple wrapper around the internal reader's *Read* method.
WriteAttributes	Specialized version of the writer's *WriteAttributes* method. Writes out all the attributes for the specified node, taking into account all the changes cached through the *Add-AttributeChange* method.
WriteEndDocument	Terminates the current document in the writer and closes both the reader and the writer.
WriteStartDocument	Prepares the internal writer to output the document and adds default comment text and the standard XML prolog.

A read/write XML document is processed between two calls to *WriteStart-Document* and *WriteEndDocument*, shown in the following code. The former method initializes the underlying writer and writes a standard comment. The latter method completes the document by closing any pending tags and then closes both the reader and the writer.

```
public void WriteStartDocument()
{
    m_writer.WriteStartDocument();
    string text = String.Format("Modified: {0}",
        DateTime.Now.ToString());
    m_writer.WriteComment(text);
}
public void WriteEndDocument()
{
    m_writer.WriteEndDocument();
    m_reader.Close();
    m_writer.Close();

    // If using a temp file name, overwrite the input
    if (m_ReplaceFile)
    {
        File.Copy(m_tempOutputFile, m_InputFile, true);
        File.Delete(m_tempOutputFile);
    }
}
```

If you are not using a distinct file for output, *WriteEndDocument* also over-writes the original document with the temporary file in which the output has been accumulated in the meantime.

You can use any of the methods of the native interfaces of the *XmlText-Writer* and *XmlTextReader* classes. For simplicity, however, I endowed the *XmlTextReadWriter* class with a *Read* method and a *NodeType* property. Both are little more than wrappers for the corresponding method and property on the reader. Here's how you initialize and start using the *XmlTextReadWriter* class:

```
XmlTextReadWriter rw = new XmlTextReadWriter(inputFile);
rw.WriteStartDocument();
// Process the file
rw.WriteEndDocument();
```

What happens between these two calls depends primarily on the nature and the goals of the application. You could, for example, change the value of one or more attributes, delete nodes, or replace the namespace. To accomplish whatever goal the application pursues, you can issue direct calls on the interface of the internal reader and writer as well as use the few methods specific to the *XmlTextReadWriter* class.

Bear in mind that reading and writing are completely distinct and independent processes that work according to slightly different models and strategies. When the reader is positioned on a node, no direct method can be called on the writer to make sure that just the value or the name of that node is modified. The following pseudocode, for example, does not correspond to reality:

```
if (reader.Value >100)
    writer.Value = 2*reader.Value;
```

To double the value of each node, you simply write a new document that mirrors the structure of the original, applying the necessary changes. To change the value of a node, you must first collect all the information about that node (including attributes) and then proceed with writing. One of the reasons for such an asymmetry in the reader's and writer's working model is that XML documents are hierarchical by nature and not flat like an INI or a CSV file. In the section "A Full-Access CSV Editor," on page 192, I'll discuss a full read/write editor for CSV files for which the preceding pseudocode is much more realistic.

Testing the *XmlTextReadWriter* Class

Let's review three examples of how the *XmlTextReadWriter* class can be used to modify XML documents without using the full-blown XML DOM. Looking at the source code, you'll realize that a read/write streaming parser is mostly achieved by a smart and combined use of readers and writers.

By making assumptions about the structure of the XML source file, you can simplify that code while building the arsenal of the *XmlTextReadWriter* class with ad hoc properties such as *Value* or *Name* and new methods such as *SetAttribute* (which would be paired with the reader's *GetAttribute* method).

Changing the Namespace

For our first example, consider the problem of changing the namespace of all the nodes in a specified XML file. The *XmlTextReadWriter* parser will provide for this eventuality with a simple loop, as shown here:

```
void ChangeNamespace(string prefix, string ns)
{
    XmlTextReadWriter rw;
    rw = new XmlTextReadWriter(inputFile);
    rw.WriteStartDocument();
```

(continued)

```
// Modify the root tag manually
rw.Writer.WriteStartElement(rw.Reader.LocalName);
rw.Writer.WriteAttributeString("xmlns", prefix, null, ns);

// Loop through the document
while(rw.Read())
{
    switch(rw.NodeType)
    {
    case XmlNodeType.Element:
        rw.Writer.WriteStartElement(prefix,
            rw.Reader.LocalName, null);
        rw.Writer.WriteAttributes(rw.Reader, false);
        if (rw.Reader.IsEmptyElement)
            rw.Writer.WriteEndElement();
        break;
    }
}

// Close the root tag
rw.Writer.WriteEndElement();

// Close the document and any internal resources
rw.WriteEndDocument();
}
```

The code starts by manually writing the root node of the source file. Next it adds an *xmlns* attribute with the specified prefix and the URN. The main loop scans all the contents of the XML file below the root node. For each element node, it writes a fully qualified new node whose name is the just-read local name with a prefix and namespace URN supplied by the caller, as shown here:

```
rw.Writer.WriteStartElement(prefix, rw.Reader.LocalName, null);
```

Because attributes are unchanged, they are simply copied using the writer's *WriteAttributes* method, as shown here:

```
rw.Writer.WriteAttributes(rw.Reader, false);
```

The node is closed within the loop only if it has no further contents to process. Figure 4-13 shows the sample application. In the upper text box, you see the original file. The bottom text box contains the modified document with the specified namespace information.

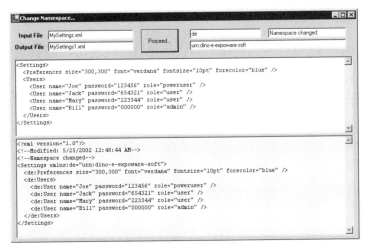

Figure 4-13   All the nodes in the XML document shown in the bottom text box now belong to the specified namespace.

Updating Attribute Values

The ultimate goal of our second example is changing the values of one or more attributes on a specified node. The *XmlTextReadWriter* class lets you do that in a single visit to the XML tree. You specify the node and the attribute name as well as the old and the new value for the attribute.

In general, the old value is necessary just to ensure that you update the correct attribute on the correct node. In fact, if an XML document contains other nodes with the same name, you have no automatic way to determine which is the appropriate node to update. Checking the old value of the attribute is just one possible workaround. If you can make some assumptions about the structure of the XML document, this constraint can be easily released.

As mentioned, the update takes place by essentially rewriting the source document, one node at a time. In doing so, you can use updated values for both node contents and attributes. The attributes of a node are written in one shot, so multiple changes must be cached somewhere. There are two possibilities. One approach passes through the addition of enrichment of a set of properties and methods that more closely mimics the reader. You could expose a read/write *Value* property. Next, when the property is written, you internally cache the new value and make use of it when the attributes of the parent node are serialized.

Another approach—the one you see implemented in the following code—is based on an explicit and application-driven cache. Each update is registered using an internal *DataTable* object made up of four fields: node name, attribute name, old value, and new value.

```
rw.AddAttributeChange(nodeName, attribName, oldVal, newVal);
```

The same *DataTable* object will contain attribute updates for each node in the document. To persist the changes relative to a specified node, you use the *XmlTextReadWriter* class's *WriteAttributes* method, shown here:

```
public void WriteAttributes(string nodeName)
{
    if (m_reader.HasAttributes)
    {
        // Consider only the attribute changes for the given node
        DataView view = new DataView(m_tableOfChanges);
        view.RowFilter = "Node='" + nodeName + "'";

        while(m_reader.MoveToNextAttribute())
        {
            // Begin writing the attribute
            m_writer.WriteStartAttribute(m_reader.Prefix,
                m_reader.LocalName, m_reader.NamespaceURI);

            // Search for a corresponding entry
            // in the table of changes
            DataRow[] rows =
                m_tableOfChanges.Select("Attribute='" +
                m_reader.LocalName + "' AND OldValue='" +
                m_reader.Value + "'");
            if (rows.Length >0)
            {
                DataRow row = rows[0];
                m_writer.WriteString(row["NewValue"].ToString());
            }
            else
                m_writer.WriteString(m_reader.Value);
        }
    }

    // Move back the internal pointer
    m_reader.MoveToElement();

    // Clear the table of changes
    m_tableOfChanges.Rows.Clear();
```

```
        m_tableOfChanges.AcceptChanges();
}
```

The following code, called by a client application, creates a copy of the source document and updates node attributes:

```
void UpdateValues(string nodeName, string attribName,
    string oldVal, string newVal)
{
    XmlTextReadWriter rw;
    rw = new XmlTextReadWriter(inputFile, outputFile);
    rw.WriteStartDocument();

    // Modify the root tag manually
    rw.Writer.WriteStartElement(rw.Reader.LocalName);

    // Prepare attribute changes
    rw.AddAttributeChange(nodeName, attribName, oldVal, newVal);

    // Loop through the document
    while(rw.Read())
    {
        switch(rw.NodeType)
        {
        case XmlNodeType.Element:
            rw.Writer.WriteStartElement(rw.Reader.LocalName);
            if (nodeName == rw.Reader.LocalName)
                rw.WriteAttributes(nodeName);
            else
                rw.Writer.WriteAttributes(rw.Reader, false);

            if (rw.Reader.IsEmptyElement)
                rw.Writer.WriteEndElement();
            break;
        }
    }

    // Close the root tag
    rw.Writer.WriteEndElement();

    // Close the document and any internal resources
    rw.WriteEndDocument();
}
```

Figure 4-14 shows the output of the sample application from which the preceding code is excerpted.

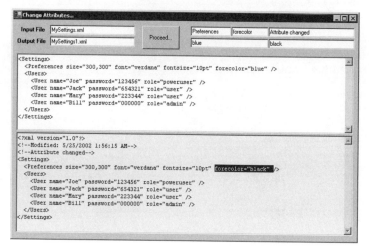

Figure 4-14   The code can be used to change the value of the *forecolor* attribute from blue to black.

Adding and Deleting Nodes

A source XML document can also be easily read and modified by adding or deleting nodes. Let's look at a couple of examples.

To add a new node, you simply read until the parent is found and then write an extra set of nodes to the XML writer. Because there might be other nodes with the same name as the parent, use a Boolean guard to ensure that the insertion takes place only once. The following code demonstrates how to proceed:

```
void AddUser(string name, string pswd, string role)
{
    XmlTextReadWriter rw;
    rw = new XmlTextReadWriter(inputFile, outputFile);
    rw.WriteStartDocument();

    // Modify the root tag manually
    rw.Writer.WriteStartElement(rw.Reader.LocalName);

    // Loop through the document
    bool mustAddNode = true;    // Only once
    while(rw.Read())
    {
        switch(rw.NodeType)
        {
        case XmlNodeType.Element:
            rw.Writer.WriteStartElement(rw.Reader.LocalName);
            if ("Users" == rw.Reader.LocalName && mustAddNode)
```

```
        {
            mustAddNode = false;
            rw.Writer.WriteStartElement("User");
            rw.Writer.WriteAttributeString("name", name);
            rw.Writer.WriteAttributeString("password", pswd);
            rw.Writer.WriteAttributeString("role", role);
            rw.Writer.WriteEndElement();
        }
        else
            rw.Writer.WriteAttributes(rw.Reader, false);
            if (rw.Reader.IsEmptyElement)
                rw.Writer.WriteEndElement();
        break;
    }
}

// Close the root tag
rw.Writer.WriteEndElement();

// Close the document and any internal resources
rw.WriteEndDocument();
}
```

To delete a node, you simply ignore it while reading the document. For example, the following code removes a *<User>* node in which the *name* attribute matches a specified string:

```
while(rw.Read())
{
    switch(rw.NodeType)
    {
    case XmlNodeType.Element:
        if ("User" == rw.Reader.LocalName)
        {
            // Skip if name matches
            string userName = rw.Reader.GetAttribute("name");
            if (userName == name)
                break;
        }

        // Write in the output file if no match has been found
        rw.Writer.WriteStartElement(rw.Reader.LocalName);
        rw.Writer.WriteAttributes(rw.Reader, false);
        if (rw.Reader.IsEmptyElement)
            rw.Writer.WriteEndElement();
        break;
    }
}
```

Figure 4-15 shows this code in action. The highlighted record has been deleted because of the matching value of the *name* attribute.

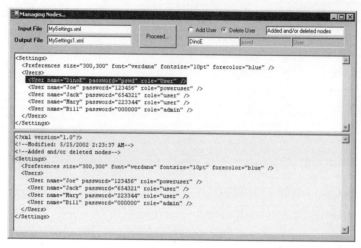

Figure 4-15   A sample application to test the class's ability to add and delete nodes.

> **Note**   The entire sample code illustrating the *XmlTextReadWriter* class and its way of working is available in this book's sample files. The all-encompassing Microsoft Visual Studio .NET solution is named XmlReadWriter.

A Full-Access CSV Editor

In Chapter 2, we looked at the *XmlCsvReader* class as an example of a custom XML reader. The *XmlCsvReader* class enables you to review the contents of a CSV file through nodes and attributes and the now-familiar semantics of XML readers. In this section, I'll go one step further and illustrate a full-access CSV reader capable of reading and writing—the *XmlCsvReadWriter* class.

The new class inherits from *XmlCsvReader* and modifies only a few methods and properties. The *XmlCsvReadWriter* class works by using a companion output stream in which each row read and modified is then persisted prior to reading a new row. The *XmlCsvReadWriter* class is declared as follows:

```
public class XmlCsvReadWriter : XmlCsvReader
{
public XmlCsvReadWriter(
```

```
string filename, bool hasColumnHeaders, bool enableOutput)
    { ... }
    ...
}
```

The class has a new constructor with a third argument—the Boolean value *enableOutput*, which specifies whether the class should use a hidden output stream. Basically, by setting *enableOutput* to *true*, you declare your intent to use the class as a reader/writer instead of a simple reader. When this happens, the constructor creates a temporary file and a stream writer to work on it. At the end of the reading, this output file contains the modified version of the CSV and is used to replace the original file. A new property, named *EnableOutput*, can be used to programmatically enable and disable the output stream.

Shadowing the Class Indexer

The *Item* indexer property—that is, the property that permits the popular *reader[index]* syntax—is declared as read-only in the abstract *XmlReader* base class. This means that any derived class can't replace that property with another one that is read/write. However, the *XmlCsvReader* class provides a total implementation of the abstract functionality defined in *XmlReader*. So when deriving from *XmlCsvReader*, you can simply shadow the base *Item* property and replace it with a brand-new one with both *get* and *set* accessors.

The following code is at the heart of the new CSV reader/writer class. It extends the *Item* property to make it work in a read/write fashion. The *get* accessor is identical to the base class. The *set* accessor copies the specified value in the *m_tokenValues* collection, in which the attributes of the current CSV row are stored. (See Chapter 2 for more details about the internal architecture of the CSV sample XML reader.)

```
new public string this[int i]
{
    get
    {
        return base[i].ToString();
    }
    set
    {
        // The Item[index] property is read-only, so
        // use the Item[string] overload
        string key = m_tokenValues.Keys[i].ToString();
        m_tokenValues[key] = value;
    }
}
```

Notice the use of the *new* keyword to shadow the same property defined on the base class. This trick alone paves the road for the read/write feature.

> **Note**   The *new* keyword is C#-specific. To achieve the same effect with Microsoft Visual Basic .NET, you must use the *Shadows* keyword. Also note that, when it comes to overloading a method in a derived class, you don't need to mark it in any way if the language of choice is C#. If you use Visual Basic .NET, the overload must be explicitly declared using the *Overloads* keyword.

In addition, bear in mind that a standard *NameValueCollection* object allows you to update a value only if you can pass the key string to the indexer, as shown here:

```
public string this[int] {get;}
public string this[string] {get; set;}
```

The new *Item* indexer property allows you to write code, as the following code snippet demonstrates:

```
for(int i=0; i<reader.AttributeCount; i++)
{
    if (reader[i] == "Sales Representative")
        reader[i] = "SalesMan";
    ...
}
```

The reader's *Read* method copies the contents of the current CSV row in the input stream, and from there the indexer will draw the values to return. When updated, the indexer overwrites values in the internal memory collection. When will changes actually be persisted to the CSV output stream?

Persisting Changes During the Next Read

The *Read* method moves the internal pointer of an XML reader one element ahead. An XML CSV reader moves that pointer to the next row. The contents of the newly selected row is buffered into a local and transient structure—the *m_tokenValues* collection—for further use and investigation.

However, when the *Read* method is called to move ahead, all the changes on the current element have been performed. This is a great time to persist those changes to the output stream if a stream is enabled. After that, you go on as usual with the *Read* base class's implementation, as shown here:

```
public override bool Read()
{
    if (!EnableOutput)
    return base.Read();

    // If we're not reading the first row, then save the
    // current status to the output stream. (If we're reading the
    // first row, then the token collection is empty and there's
    // nothing to persist.
    if (m_tokenValues.Count >0)
    {
        // If writing the first row, and used the first source
        // row for headers, now add that prior to writing the
        // first data row.
        if (HasColumnHeaders && !m_firstRowRead)
        {
            m_firstRowRead = true;
            string header = "";
            foreach(string tmp in m_tokenValues)
                header += tmp + ",";
            m_outputStream.WriteLine(header.TrimEnd(','));
        }

        // Prepare and write the current CSV row
        string row = "";
        foreach(string tmp in m_tokenValues)
            row += m_tokenValues[tmp] + ",";
        m_outputStream.WriteLine(row.TrimEnd(','));
    }

    // Move ahead as usual
    return base.Read();
}
```

If the first row in the source CSV file has been interpreted as the headers of the columns (*HasColumnHeaders* property set to *true*), this implementation of the *Read* method ensures that the very first row written to the output stream contains just those headers. After that, the current contents of the *m_tokenValues* collection is serialized to a comma-separated string and is written to the output stream. Once this has been done, the *Read* method finally moves to the next line.

Closing the Output Stream

When you close the reader, the output stream is also closed. In addition, because the output stream was writing to a temporary file, that file is also copied over by the source CSV replacing it, as shown here:

```
public override void Close()
{
    base.Close();

    if (EnableOutput)
    {
        m_outputStream.Close();
        File.Copy(m_tempFileName, m_fileName, true);
        File.Delete(m_tempFileName);
    }
}
```

The net effect of this code is that any changes entered in the source CSV document are cached to a temporary file, which then replaces the original. The user won't perceive anything of these workings, however.

The CSV Reader/Writer in Action

Let's take a sample CSV file, read it, and apply some changes to the contents so that they will automatically be persisted when the reader is closed. Here is the source CSV file:

```
LastName,FirstName,Title,Country
Davolio,Nancy,Sales Representative,USA
Fuller,Andrew,Sales Manager,USA
Leverling,Janet,Sales Representative,UK
Suyama,Michael,Sales Representative,UK
```

The idea is to replacing the expression *Sales Representative* with another one—say, *Sales Force*. The sample application, nearly identical to the one in Chapter 2, loads the CSV file, applies the changes, and then displays it through a desktop *DataGrid* control, as follows:

```
// Instantiate the reader on a CSV file
XmlCsvReadWriter reader;
reader = new XmlCsvReadWriter("employees.csv",
    hasHeader.Checked);
reader.EnableOutput = true;
reader.Read();

// Define the schema of the table to bind to the grid
```

```
DataTable dt = new DataTable();
for(int i=0; i<reader.AttributeCount; i++)
{
    reader.MoveToAttribute(i);
    DataColumn col = new DataColumn(reader.Name,
        typeof(string));
    dt.Columns.Add(col);
}
reader.MoveToElement();

// Loop through the CSV rows and populate the DataTable
do
{
    DataRow row = dt.NewRow();
    for(int i=0; i<reader.AttributeCount; i++)
    {
        if (reader[i] == "Sales Representative")
            reader[i] = "Sales Force";
        row[i] = reader[i].ToString();
    }
    dt.Rows.Add(row);
}
while (reader.Read());    // Persist changes and move ahead

// Flushes the changes to disk
reader.Close();

// Bind the table to the grid
dataGrid1.DataSource = dt;
```

If the contents of a specified CSV attribute matches the specified string, it is replaced. The change occurs initially on an internal collection and is then transferred to the output stream during the execution of the *Read* method. Finally, the reader is closed and the output stream flushed. Figure 4-16 shows the program in action.

Figure 4-16   The original CSV file has been read and updated on disk.

Conclusion

Readers and writers are at the foundation of every I/O operation in the .NET Framework. You find them at work when you operate on disk and on network files, when you serialize and deserialize, while you perform data access, even when you read and write configuration settings.

XML writers are ad hoc tools for creating XML documents using a higher-level metaphor and putting more abstraction between your code and the markup. By using XML writers, you go far beyond markup to reach a node-oriented dimension in which, instead of just accumulating bytes in a block of contiguous memory, you assemble nodes and entities to create the desired schema and infoset.

In this chapter, we looked primarily at the programming interface of .NET XML writers—specifically, the *XmlTextWriter* class. You learned how to create well-formed XML documents, how to add nodes and attributes, how to support namespaces, and how to encode text using BinHex and base64 encoding algorithms.

.NET XML writers only ensure the well-formedness of each individual XML element being generated. Writers can in no way guarantee the well-formedness of the entire document and can do even less to validate a document against a DTD or a schema. Although badly formed XML documents can only result from actual gross programming errors, the need for an extra step of validation is often felt in production environments, especially when the creation of the document depends on a number of variable factors and run-time conditions. For this reason, we've also examined the key points involved in the design and implementation of a validating XML writer.

This chapter also featured a few custom XML-driven writers. In this chapter, you learned how to write string arrays, JPEG images, and *DataTable* objects to specific XML schemas. It goes without saying that the techniques discussed here do not exhaust the options available in the .NET Framework for those tasks. For example, the XML serializer can sometimes be more effectively employed to obtain the same results. (XML serializers are covered in Chapter 11.)

These examples were provided with a double goal: to show one way to solve a problem, and to demonstrate custom XML writers. As a general guideline, bear in mind that the more specific an XML-based format is, the more a specialized writer class can help. The key advantage of a writer class is perhaps not so much raw performance savings but the resultant elegance, reusability, and efficiency of the design.

We've also looked at an intermediate level of XML parser that falls somewhere between streaming parsers such as readers and XML DOM. XML readers are great for parsing XML documents, but they work in a read-only way. XML DOM parsers, on the other hand, make updating documents a snap—but only after the documents have been fully loaded in memory. The *XmlTextReadWriter* class incorporates a reader and a writer and coordinates their independent activity through a simple new API. As a result, you can parse a document one node at a time while maintaining the ability to add, update, or delete nodes. The new class is not the cure-all for any XML pains, but it can be an interesting option in some situations.

In Chapter 5, we'll examine the XML DOM classes that you must use when full read/write access to XML documents is critical and when the ability to perform searches takes precedence over the memory footprint.

Further Reading

This chapter touches on a number of topics that you might want to know more about. Some are XML-related, but not so much .NET-related as to find an ideal place for discussion here. Some are not really XML-related but definitely belong to the .NET Framework and, as such, deserve at least a reference here.

One topic we spent a lot of time on in this chapter is XML namespaces and qualified names. The official site where the specification can be found is *http://www.w3.org/TR/REC-xml-names*. In Chapter 3, I covered XML validation and the various schema involved in the process. If you think you need an XML crash course from a higher, non-.NET-Framework-related perspective, I can recommend two books. One is *Essential XML,* by Don Box, John Lam, and Aaron Skonnard (Addison-Wesley, 2000). This reference is great if you need to get the gist of XML in a platform-independent and language-independent context. Otherwise, look at the *XML Programming Core Reference*, by R. Allen Wyke, Sultan Rehman, Brad Leupen, and Ash Rofail (Microsoft Press, 2002), for more development-related considerations and tips.

A great source for learning about underdocumented features and tricks of the .NET Framework is certainly Jeffrey Richter's most recent book, *Applied .NET Framework Programming* (Microsoft Press, 2002). This book is a gold mine for all that boring stuff that revolves around string manipulation, character encoding, and memory management.

One of the examples discussed in this chapter entails the creation of an XML ADO *Recordset* object from ADO.NET–specific objects such as *DataSet*, *DataTable*, and *DataView*. A more thorough discussion of the integration between ADO and ADO.NET can be found in Chapter 8 of my book *Building Web Solutions with ASP.NET and ADO.NET* (Microsoft Press, 2002). Although that book is markedly ASP.NET-specific, the theme of how to efficiently use ADO from .NET Framework applications is fairly platform-independent and can be applied to Windows Forms as well.

Finally, this chapter touches on .NET code security. If you need to get started with security and are looking for a long-range perspective with concrete code snippets sprinkled here and there, by all means check out Jason Clark's excellent article at *http://msdn.microsoft.com/msdnmag/issues/02/06/rich/rich.asp*.

Part II

XML Data Manipulation

5

The XML .NET Document Object Model

In addition to XML readers and writers, the Microsoft .NET Framework provides classes that parse XML documents according to the W3C Document Object Model (DOM) Level 1 Core and the DOM Level 2 Core. These classes, available in the *System.Xml* namespace, build a complete in-memory representation of the contents of an XML document and make it programmatically accessible during both read and write operations.

The structure of the XML Document Object Model (XML DOM) is a general specification that is implemented using platform-specific features and components. The MSXML library provides a COM-based XML DOM implementation for the Microsoft Win32 platform. The *System.Xml* assembly provides a .NET Framework–specific implementation of the XML DOM centered on the *XmlDocument* class.

Although it is stored as flat text in a linear text file, XML content is inherently hierarchical. Readers simply parse the text as it is read out of the input stream. They never cache read information and work in a stateless fashion. As a result of this arrangement, you can neither edit nodes nor move backward.

The limited navigation capabilities also prevent you from implementing node queries of any complexity. The XML DOM philosophy is quite different. XML DOM loads all the XML content in memory and exposes it through a suite of collections that, overall, offer a tree-based representation of the original content. In addition, the supplied data structure is fully searchable and editable.

Advanced searching and editing are the primary functions of the XML DOM, whereas readers (and Simple API for XML [SAX] parsers as well) are optimized for document inspection, simple searching, and any sort of read-only activity. In Chapter 2, we explored the characteristics of pull mode readers. Let's analyze now the .NET Framework programming interface for full-access XML document processing.

The XML DOM Programming Interface

The central element in the .NET XML DOM implementation is the *XmlDocument* class. The *XmlDocument* class represents an XML document and makes it programmable by exposing its nodes and attributes through ad hoc collections. Let's consider a simple XML document:

```
<MyDataSet>
    <NorthwindEmployees count="3">
        <Employee>
            <employeeid>1</employeeid>
            <firstname>Nancy</firstname>
            <lastname>Davolio</lastname>
        </Employee>
        <Employee>
            <employeeid>2</employeeid>
            <firstname>Andrew</firstname>
            <lastname>Fuller</lastname>
        <Employee>
            <employeeid>3</employeeid>
            <firstname>Janet</firstname>
            <lastname>Leverling</lastname>
        </Employee>
    </NorthwindEmployees>
</MyDataSet>
```

When processed by an instance of the *XmlDocument* class, this file creates a tree like the one shown in Figure 5-1.

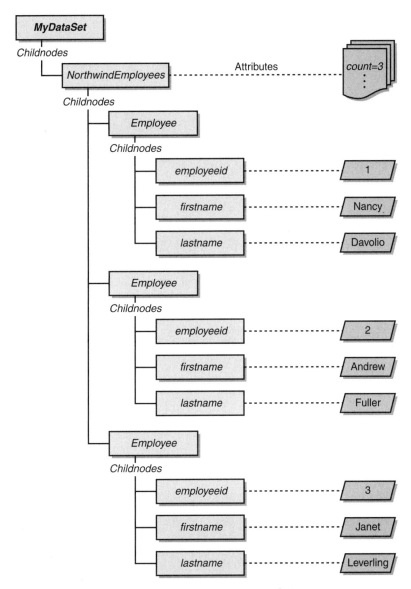

Figure 5-1   Graphical representation of an XML DOM tree.

The *XmlDocument* class represents the entry point in the binary structure and the central console that lets you move through nodes, reading and writing contents. Each element in the original XML document is mapped to a particular .NET Framework class with its own set of properties and methods. Each element can be reached from the parent and can access all of its children and siblings. Element-specific information such as contents and attributes are available via properties.

Any change you enter is applied immediately, but only in memory. The *XmlDocument* class does provide an I/O interface to load from, and save to, a variety of storage media, including disk files. Subsequently, all the changes to constituent elements of an XML DOM tree are normally persisted all at once.

> **Note**   The W3C DOM Level 1 Core and Level 2 Core do not yet mandate an official API for serializing documents to and from XML format. Such an API will come only with the DOM Level 3 specification, which at this time is only a working draft.

Before we look at the key tasks you might want to accomplish using the XML DOM programming interface, let's review the tools that this interface provides. In particular, we'll focus here on two major classes—the *XmlDocument* class and the *XmlNode* class. A third class, *XmlDataDocument*, that is tightly coupled with XML DOM in general, and *XmlDocument* in particular, will be covered in Chapter 8. *XmlDataDocument* represents the connecting link between the hierarchical world of XML and the relational world of ADO.NET *DataSet* objects.

The *XmlDocument* Class

When you need to load an XML document into memory for full-access processing, you start by creating a new instance of the *XmlDocument* class. The class features two public constructors, one of which is the default parameterless constructor, as shown here:

```
public XmlDocument();
public XmlDocument(XmlNameTable);
```

While initializing the *XmlDocument* class, you can also specify an existing *XmlNameTable* object to help the class work faster with attribute and node names and optimize memory management. Just as the *XmlReader* class does, *XmlDocument* builds its own name table incrementally while processing the document. However, passing a precompiled name table can only speed up the overall execution. The following code snippet demonstrates how to load an XML document into a living instance of the *XmlDocument* class:

```
XmlDocument doc = new XmlDocument();
doc.Load(fileName);
```

The *Load* method always work synchronously, so when it returns, the document has been completely (and successfully, we hope) mapped to memory and is ready for further processing through the properties and methods exposed by the class. As you'll see in a bit more detail later in this section, the *XmlDocument* class uses an XML reader internally to perform any read operation and to build the final tree structure for the source document.

> **Note**   In spite of what the beginning of this chapter might suggest, the *XmlDocument* class is just the logical root class of the XML DOM class hierarchy. The *XmlDocument* class actually inherits from the *XmlNode* class and is placed at the same level as classes like *XmlElement*, *XmlAttribute*, and *XmlEntity* that you manipulate as child elements when processing an XML document. In other words, *XmlDocument* is not designed as a wrapper class for XML node classes. Its design follows the XML key guideline, according to which everything in a document is a node, including the document itself.

Properties of the *XmlDocument* Class

Table 5-1 lists the properties supported by the *XmlDocument* class. The table includes only the properties that the class introduces or overrides. These properties are specific to the *XmlDocument* class or have a class-specific implementation. More properties are available through the base class *Xml-Node*, which we'll examine in more detail in the section "The *XmlNode* Base Class," on page 213.

> **Note**   In Table 5-1, you'll find the description of the property for a special type of XML node—the *XmlNodeType.Document* node. In some instances, this same property is shared with other nodes, in which case it behaves in a slightly different manner. So read this table with a grain of salt and replace the word *document* with the more generic word *node* when appropriate. For example, the *Owner-Document* property returns *null* if the node is *Document* but returns the owner *XmlDocument* object in all other cases. Similarly, both *Name* and *LocalName* always return *#document* for *XmlDocument*, but they actually represent the qualified and simple (namespace-less) name of the particular node.

Table 5-1   Properties of the *XmlDocument* Class

Property	Description
BaseURI	Gets the base URI of the document (for example, the file path).
DocumentElement	Gets the root of the document as an *XmlElement* object.
DocumentType	Gets the node with the *DOCTYPE* declaration (if any).
Implementation	Gets the *XmlImplementation* object for the document.
InnerXml	Gets or sets the markup representing the body of the document.
IsReadOnly	Indicates whether the document is read-only.
LocalName	Returns the string *#document*.
Name	Returns the string *#document*.
NameTable	Gets the *NameTable* object associated with this implementation of the *XmlDocument* class.
NodeType	Returns the value *XmlNodeType.Document*.
OwnerDocument	Returns *null*. The *XmlDocument* object is not owned.
PreserveWhitespace	Gets or sets a Boolean value indicating whether to preserve white space during the load and save process. Set to *false* by default.
XmlResolver	Write-only property that specifies the *XmlResolver* object to use for resolving external resources. Set to *null* by default.

By default, the *PreserveWhitespace* property is set to *false*, which indicates that only significant white spaces will be preserved while the document is loaded. A significant white space is any white space found between markup in a mixed-contents node or any white space found within the subtree affected by the following declaration:

```
xml:space="preserve"
```

All spaces are preserved throughout the document if *PreserveWhitespace* is set to *true* before the *Load* method is called. As for writing, if *Preserve-Whitespace* is set to *true* when the *Save* method is called, all spaces are preserved in the output. Otherwise, the serialized output is automatically indented. This behavior represents a proprietary extension over the standard DOM specification.

The *XmlDocument* Implementation

The *Implementation* property of the *XmlDocument* class defines the operating context for the document object. *Implementation* returns an instance of the *XmlImplementation* class, which provides methods for performing operations that are independent of any particular instance of the DOM.

In the base implementation of the *XmlImplementation* class, the list of operations that various instances of *XmlDocument* classes can share is relatively short. These operations include creating new documents, testing for supported features, and more important, sharing the same name table.

The *XmlImplementation* class is not sealed, so you could try to define a custom implementation object and use that to create new *XmlDocument* objects with some nonstandard settings (for example, *PreserveWhitespace* set to *true* by default). The following code snippet shows how to create two documents from the same implementation:

```
XmlImplementation imp = new XmlImplementation();
XmlDocument doc1 = imp.CreateDocument();
XmlDocument doc2 = imp.CreateDocument();
```

The following code shows how *XmlImplementation* could work with a custom implementation object:

```
MyImplementation imp = new MyImplementation();
XmlDocument doc = imp.CreateDocument();
```

In the section "Custom Node Classes," on page 234, when we examine XML DOM extensions, I'll have more to say about custom implementations.

> **Note** Two instances of *XmlDocument* can share the same imple-
> mentation when the implementation is custom. Actually, all instances
> of *XmlDocument* share the same standard *XmlImplementation* object.
> Sharing the same implementation does not mean that the two objects
> are each other's clone, however. The XML implementation is a kind of
> common runtime that services both objects.

Methods of the *XmlDocument* Class

Table 5-2 lists the methods supported by the *XmlDocument* class. The list
includes only the methods that *XmlDocument* introduces or overrides; more
methods are available through the base class *XmlNode*. (See the section "The
XmlNode Base Class," on page 213.)

Table 5-2   Methods of the *XmlDocument* Class

Method	Description
CloneNode	Creates a duplicate of the document.
CreateAttribute	Creates an attribute with the specified name.
CreateCDataSection	Creates a CDATA section with the specified data.
CreateComment	Creates a comment with the specified text.
CreateDocumentFragment	Creates an XML fragment. Note that a fragment node can't be inserted into a document; however, you can insert any of its children into a document.
CreateDocumentType	Creates a *DOCTYPE* element.
CreateElement	Creates a node element.
CreateEntityReference	Creates an entity reference with the specified name.
CreateNode	Creates a node of the specified type.
CreateProcessingInstruction	Creates a processing instruction.
CreateSignificantWhitespace	Creates a significant white space node.
CreateTextNode	Creates a text node. Note that text nodes are allowed only as children of elements, attributes, and entities.
CreateWhitespace	Creates a white space node.

Table 5-2   Methods of the *XmlDocument* Class

Method	Description
CreateXmlDeclaration	Creates the standard XML declaration.
GetElementById	Gets the element in the document with the given ID.
GetElementsByTagName	Returns the list of child nodes that match the specified tag name.
ImportNode	Imports a node from another document.
Load	Loads XML data from the specified source.
LoadXml	Loads XML data from the specified string.
ReadNode	Creates an *XmlNode* object based on the information read from the given XML reader.
Save	Saves the current document to the specified location.
WriteContentTo	Saves all the children of the current document to the specified *XmlWriter* object.
WriteTo	Saves the current document to the specified writer.

As you can see, the *XmlDocument* class has a lot of methods that create and return instances of node objects. In the .NET Framework, all the objects that represent a node type (*Comment, Element, Attribute,* and so on) do not have any publicly usable constructors. For this reason, you must resort to the corresponding method.

How can the *XmlDocument* class create and return instances of other node objects if no public constructor for them is available? The trick is that node classes mark their constructors with the *internal* modifier (*Friend* in Microsoft Visual Basic). The *internal* keyword restricts the default visibility of a type method or property to the boundaries of the assembly. The internal keyword works on top of other modifiers like *public* and *protected*. *XmlDocument* and other node classes are all defined in the *System.Xml* assembly, which ensures the effective working of factory methods. The following pseudocode shows the internal architecture of a factory method:

```
public virtual XmlXXX CreateXXX( params )
{
    return new XmlXXX ( params );
}
```

> **Note**   When the node class is *XmlDocument*, the methods *WriteTo* and *WriteContentTo* happen to produce the same output, although they definitely run different code. *WriteTo* is designed to persist the entire contents of the node, including the markup for the node, attributes, and children. *WriteContentTo*, on the other hand, walks its way through the collection of child nodes and persists the contents of each using *WriteTo*. Here's the pseudocode:
>
> ```
> void WriteContentTo(XmlWriter w) {
>     foreach(XmlNode n in this)
>             n.WriteTo(w);
> }
> ```
>
> A *Document* node is a kind of super root node, so the loop on all child nodes begins with the actual root node of the XML document. In this case, *WriteTo* simply writes out the entire contents of the document but the super root node has no markup. As a result, the two methods produce the same output for the *XmlDocument* class.

Events of the *XmlDocument* Class

Table 5-3 lists the events that the *XmlDocument* class fires under the following specific conditions: when the value of a node (any node) is being edited, and when a node is being inserted into or removed from the document.

Table 5-3   Events of the *XmlDocument* Class

Events	Description
NodeChanging, NodeChanged	The *Value* property of a node belonging to this document is about to be changed or has been changed already.
NodeInserting, NodeInserted	A node is about to be inserted into another node in this document or has been inserted already. The event fires whether you are inserting a new node, duplicating an existing node, or importing a node from another document.
NodeRemoving, NodeRemoved	A node belonging to this document is about to be removed from the document or has been removed from its parent already.

All these events require the same delegate for the event handler, as follows:

```
public delegate void XmlNodeChangedEventHandler(
    object sender,
    XmlNodeChangedEventArgs e
);
```

The *XmlNodeChangedEventArgs* structure contains the event data. The structure has four interesting fields:

- **Action**   Contains a value indicating what type of change is occurring on the node. Allowable values, listed in the *XmlNodeChanged-Action* enumeration type, are *Insert*, *Remove*, and *Change*.

- **NewParent**   Returns an *XmlNode* object representing the new parent of the node once the operation is complete. The property will be set to *null* if the node is being removed. If the node is an attribute, the property returns the node to which the attribute refers.

- **Node**   Returns an *XmlNode* object that denotes the node that is being added, removed, or changed. Can't be set to *null*.

- **OldParent**   Returns an *XmlNode* object representing the parent of the node before the operation began. Returns *null* if the node has no parent—for example, when you add a new node.

Some of the actions you can take on an XML DOM are compound actions consisting of several steps, each of which could raise its own event. For example, be prepared to handle several events when you set the *InnerXml* property. In this case, multiple nodes could be created and appended, resulting in as many *NodeInserting/NodeInserted* pairs. In some cases, the *XmlNode* class's *AppendChild* method might fire a pair of *NodeRemoving/NodeRemoved* events prior to actually proceeding with the insertion. By design, to ensure XML well-formedness, *AppendChild* checks whether the node you are adding already exists in the document. If it does, the existing node is first removed to avoid identical nodes in the same subtree.

The *XmlNode* Base Class

When you work with XML DOM parsers, you mainly use the *XmlDocument* class. The *XmlDocument* class, however, derives from a base class, *XmlNode*, which provides all the core functions to navigate and create nodes.

XmlNode is the abstract parent class of a handful of node-related classes that are available in the .NET Framework. Figure 5-2 shows the hierarchy of node classes.

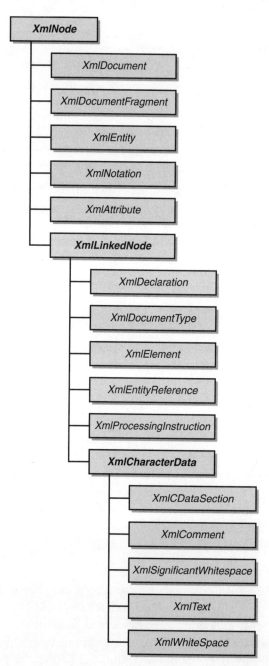

Figure 5-2 Graphical representation of the hierarchy of node classes and their relationships in the .NET Framework.

Both *XmlLinkedNode* and *XmlCharacterData* are abstract classes that provide basic functionality for more specialized types of nodes. Linked nodes are nodes that you might find as constituent elements of an XML document just linked to a preceding or a following node. Character data nodes, on the other hand, are nodes that contain and manipulate only text.

Properties of the *XmlNode* Class

Table 5-4 lists the properties of the *XmlNode* class that derived classes can override if necessary. For example, not all node types support attributes and not all have child nodes or siblings. For situations such as this, the overridden properties can simply return *null* or the empty string. By design, all node types must provide a concrete implementation for each property.

Table 5-4   Properties of the *XmlNode* Class

Property	Description
Attributes	Returns a collection containing the attributes of the current node. The collection is of type *XmlAttributeCollection*.
BaseURI	Gets the base URI of the current node.
ChildNodes	Returns an enumerable list object that allows you to access all the children of the current node. The object returned derives from the base class *XmlNodeList*, which is a linked list connecting all the nodes with the same parent and the same depth level (siblings). No information is cached (not even the objects count), and any changes to the nodes are detected in real time.
FirstChild	Returns the first child of the current node or *null*. The order of child nodes reflects the order in which they have been added. In turn, the insertion order reflects the visiting algorithm implemented by the reader. (See Chapter 2.)
HasChildNodes	Indicates whether the current node has children.
InnerText	Gets or sets the text of the current node and all its children. Setting this property replaces all the children with the contents of the given string. If the string contains markup, the text will be escaped first.
InnerXml	Gets or sets the markup representing the body of the current node. The contents of the node is replaced with the contents of the given string. Any markup text will be parsed and resulting nodes inserted.
IsReadOnly	Indicates whether the current node is read-only.
Item	Indexer property that gets the child element node with the specified (qualified) name.

(continued)

Table 5-4   Properties of the *XmlNode* Class *(continued)*

Property	Description
LastChild	Gets the last child of the current node. Again, which node is the last one depends ultimately on the visiting algorithm implemented by the reader. Normally, it is the last child node in the source document.
LocalName	Returns the name of the node, minus the namespace.
Name	Returns the fully qualified name of the node.
NamespaceURI	Gets the namespace URI of the current node.
NextSibling	Gets the node immediately following the current node. Siblings are nodes with the same parent and the same depth.
NodeType	Returns the type of the current node as a value taken from the *XmlNodeType* enumeration.
OuterXml	Gets the markup code representing the current node and all of its children. Unlike *InnerXml*, *OuterXml* also includes the node itself in the markup with all of its attributes. *InnerXml*, on the other hand, returns only the markup found below the node, including text.
OwnerDocument	Gets the *XmlDocument* object to which the current node belongs.
ParentNode	Gets the parent of the current node (if any).
Prefix	Gets or sets the namespace prefix of the current node.
PreviousSibling	Gets the node immediately preceding the current node.
Value	Gets or sets the value of the current node.

The collection of child nodes is implemented as a linked list. The *Child-Nodes* property returns an internal object of type *XmlChildNodes*. (The object is not documented, but you can easily verify this claim by simply checking the type of the object that *ChildNodes* returns.) You don't need to use this object directly, however. Suffice to say that it merely represents a concrete implementation of the *XmlNodeList* class, whose methods are, for the most part, marked as abstract. In particular, *XmlChildNodes* implements the *Item* and *Count* properties and the *GetEnumerator* method.

XmlChildNodes is not a true collection and does not cache any information. When you access the *Count* property, for example, it scrolls the entire list, counting the number of nodes on the fly. When you ask for a particular node through the *Item* property, the list is scanned from the beginning until a matching node is found. To move through the list, the *XmlChildNodes* class relies on the node's *NextSibling* method. But which class actually implements the *NextSibling* method? Both *NextSibling* and *PreviousSibling* are defined in the *XmlLinkedNode* base class.

XmlLinkedNode stores an internal pointer to the next node in the list. The object referenced is simply what *NextSibling* returns. Figure 5-3 how things work.

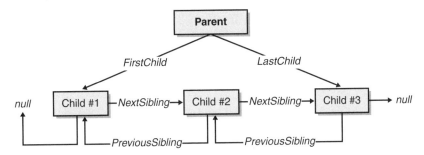

Figure 5-3   The *XmlLinkedNode* class's *NextSibling* method lets applications navigate through the children of each node.

Scrolling forward through the list of child nodes is fast and effective. The same can't be said for backward scrolling. The list of nodes is not double-linked, and each node doesn't also store a pointer to the previous one in the list. For this reason, *PreviousSibling* reaches the target node by walking through the list from the beginning to the node that precedes the current one.

> Tip   To summarize, when you are processing XML subtrees, try to minimize calls to *PreviousSibling*, *Item*, and *Count* because they always walk through the entire collection of subnodes to get their expected output. Whenever possible, design your code to take advantage of forward-only movements and perform them using *NextSibling*.

Methods of the *XmlNode* Class
Table 5-5 lists the methods exposed by the *XmlNode* class.

Table 5-5 Methods of the *XmlNode* Class

Method	Description
AppendChild	Adds the specified node to the list of children of the current node. The node is inserted at the bottom of the list.
Clone	Creates a duplicate of the current node. For element nodes, duplication includes child nodes and attributes.
CloneNode	Creates a duplicate of the current node. Takes a Boolean argument indicating whether cloning should proceed recursively. If this argument is *true*, calling the *CloneNode* method is equivalent to calling *Clone*. Entity and notation nodes can't be cloned.
GetEnumerator	Returns an internal and node-specific object that implements the *IEnumerator* interface. The returned object provides the support needed to arrange *for-each* iterations.
GetNamespaceOfPrefix	Returns the closest *xmlns* declaration for the given prefix.
GetPrefixOfNamespace	Returns the closest *xmlns* declaration for the given namespace URI.
InsertAfter	Inserts the specified node immediately after the specified node. If the node already exists, it is first removed. If the reference node is *null*, the insertion occurs at the beginning of the list.
InsertBefore	Inserts the specified node immediately before the specified reference node. If the node already exists, it is first removed. If the reference node is *null*, the insertion occurs at the bottom of the list.
Normalize	Ensures that there are no adjacent *XmlText* nodes by merging all adjacent text nodes into a single one according to a series of precedence rules.
PrependChild	Adds the specified node to the beginning of the list of children of the current node.
RemoveAll	Removes all the children of the current node, including attributes.
RemoveChild	Removes the specified child node.
ReplaceChild	Replaces the specified child node with a new one.
SelectNodes	Returns a list (*XmlNodeList*) of all the nodes that match a given XPath expression.
SelectSingleNode	Returns only the first node that matches the given XPath expression.
Supports	Verifies whether the current *XmlImplementation* object supports a specific feature.

Table 5-5   **Methods of the *XmlNode* Class**

Method	Description
WriteContentTo	Saves all the children of the current node to the specified *XmlWriter* object. Equivalent to *InnerXml*.
WriteTo	Saves the entire current node to the specified writer. Equivalent to *OuterXml*.

To locate one or more nodes in an XML DOM object, you can use either the *ChildNodes* collection or the *SelectNodes* method. With the former technique, you are given access to the unfiltered collection of child nodes. Note that in this context, *child nodes* means all and only the sibling nodes located one level below the current node.

The *SelectNodes* (and the ancillary *SelectSingleNode*) method exploits the XPath query language to let you extract nodes based on logical conditions. In addition, XPath queries can go deeper than one level and even work on all descendants of a node. The .NET Framework XPath implementation is covered in Chapter 6. See the section "Further Reading," on page 244, for resources providing detailed coverage of the XPath query language.

Working with XML Documents

To be fully accessible, an XML document must be entirely loaded in memory and its nodes and attributes mapped to relative objects derived from the *Xml-Node* class. The process that builds the XML DOM triggers when you call the *Load* method. You can use a variety of sources to indicate the XML document to work on, including disk files and URLs and also streams and text readers.

Loading XML Documents

The *Load* method always transforms the data source into an *XmlTextReader* object and passes it down to an internal loader object, as shown here:

```
public virtual void Load(Stream);
public virtual void Load(string);
public virtual void Load(TextReader);
public virtual void Load(XmlReader);
```

The loader is responsible for reading all the nodes in the document and does that through a nonvalidating reader. After a node has been read, it is analyzed and the corresponding *XmlNode* object created and added to the document tree. The entire process is illustrated in Figure 5-4.

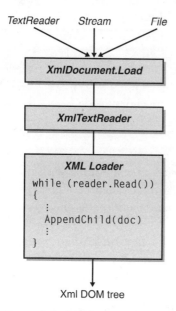

Figure 5-4 The loading process of an *XmlDocument* object.

Note that before a new *XmlDocument* object is loaded, the current instance of the *XmlDocument* object is cleared. This means that if you reuse the same instance of the *XmlDocument* class to load a second document, the existing contents are entirely removed before proceeding.

> **Important** Although an XML reader is always used to build an XML DOM, some differences can be noticed when the reader is built internally—that is, you call *Load* on a file or a stream—or explicitly passed by the programmer. In the latter case, if the reader is already positioned on a nonroot node, only the siblings of that node are read and added to the DOM. If the current reader's node can't be used as the root of a document (for example, attributes or processing instructions), the reader reads on until it finds a node that can be used as the root. Pay attention to the state of the reader before you pass it on to the XML DOM loader.

Let's see how to use the XML DOM to build a relatively simple example—
the same code that we saw in action in Chapter 2 with readers. The following
code parses the contents of an XML document and outputs its element node
layout, discarding everything else, including text, attributes, and other nonelement nodes:

```
using System;
using System.Xml;

class XmlDomLayoutApp
{
    public static void Main(String[] args)
    {
        try {
            String fileName = args[0];
            XmlDocument doc = new XmlDocument();
            doc.Load(fileName);
            XmlElement root = doc.DocumentElement;
            LoopThroughChildren(root);
        }
        catch (Exception e) {
            Console.WriteLine("Error:\t{0}\n", e.Message);
        }

        return;
    }

    private static void LoopThroughChildren(XmlNode root)
    {
        Console.WriteLine("<{0}>", root.Name);
        foreach(XmlNode n in root.ChildNodes)
        {
            if (n.NodeType == XmlNodeType.Element)
                LoopThroughChildren(n);
        }
        Console.WriteLine("</{0}>", root.Name);
    }
}
```

After creating the XML DOM, the program begins a recursive visit that
touches on all internal nodes of all types. The *ChildNodes* list returns only the first-
level children of a given node. Of course, this is not enough to traverse the tree
from the root to the leaves, so the *LoopThroughChildren* method is recursively

called on each element node found. Let's call the program to work on the following XML file:

```
<platforms type="software">
  <platform vendor="Microsoft">.NET</platform>
  <platform vendor="" OpenSource="yes">Linux</platform>
  <platform vendor="Microsoft">Win32</platform>
  <platform vendor="Sun">Java</platform>
</platforms>
```

The result we get using the XML DOM is shown here and is identical to what we got from readers in Chapter 2:

```
<platforms>
<platform></platform>
<platform></platform>
<platform></platform>
<platform></platform>
</platforms>
```

Well-Formedness and Validation

The XML document loader checks only input data for well-formedness. If parsing errors are found, an *XmlException* exception is thrown and the resulting *XmlDocument* object remains empty. To load a document and validate it against a DTD or a schema file, you must use the *Load* method's overload, which accepts an *XmlReader* object. You pass the *Load* method a properly initialized instance of the *XmlValidatingReader* class, as shown in the following code, and proceed as usual:

```
XmlTextReader _coreReader;
XmlValidatingReader reader;
_coreReader = new XmlTextReader(xmlFile);
reader = new XmlValidatingReader(_coreReader);
doc.Load(reader);
```

Any schema information found in the file is taken into account and the contents are validated. Parser errors, if any, are passed on to the validation handler you might have defined. (See Chapter 3 for more details on the working of .NET Framework validating readers.) If your validating reader does not have an event handler, the first exception stops the loading. Otherwise, the operation continues unless the handler itself throws an exception.

Loading from a String

The XML DOM programming interface also provides you with a method to build a DOM from a well-formed XML string. The method is *LoadXml* and is shown here:

```
public virtual void LoadXml(string xml);
```

This method neither supports validation nor preserves white spaces. Any context-specific information you might need (DTD, entities, namespaces) must necessarily be embedded in the string to be taken into account.

Loading Documents Asynchronously

The .NET Framework implementation of the XML DOM does not provide for asynchronous loading. The *Load* method, in fact, always work synchronously and does not pass the control back to the caller until completed. As you might guess, this can become a serious problem when you have huge files to process and a rich user interface.

In similar situations—that is, when you are writing a Windows Forms rich client—using threads can be the most effective solution. You transfer to a worker thread the burden of loading the XML document and update the user interface when the thread returns, as shown here:

```
void StartDocumentLoading()
{
    // Create the worker thread
    Thread t = new Thread(new ThreadStart(this.LoadXmlDocument));

    statusBar.Text = "Loading document...";
    t.Start();
}

void LoadXmlDocument()
{
    XmlDocument doc = new XmlDocument();
    doc.Load(InputFile.Text);

    // Update the user interface
    statusBar.Text = "Document loaded.";
    Output.Text = doc.OuterXml;
    Output.ReadOnly = false;

    return;
}
```

While the secondary thread works, the user can freely use the application's user interface and the huge size of the XML file is no longer a serious issue—at least as it pertains to loading.

Extracting XML DOM Subtrees

You normally build the XML DOM by loading the entire XML document into memory. However, the *XmlDocument* class also provides the means to extract only a portion of the document and return it as an XML DOM subtree. The key method to achieve this result is *ReadNode*, shown here:

```
public virtual XmlNode ReadNode(XmlReader reader);
```

The *ReadNode* method begins to read from the current position of the given reader and doesn't stop until the end tag of the current node is reached. The reader is then left immediately after the end tag. For the method to work, the reader must be positioned on an element or an attribute node.

ReadNode returns an *XmlNode* object that contains the subtree representing everything that has been read, including attributes. *ReadNode* is different from *ChildNodes* in that it recursively processes children at any level and does not stop at the first level of siblings.

Visiting an XML DOM Subtree

So far, we've examined ways to get XML DOM objects out of an XML reader. Is it possible to call an XML reader to work on an XML DOM document and have the reader visit the whole subtree, one node after the next?

Chapter 2 introduced the XmlNodeReader class, with the promise to return to it later. Let's do that now. The XmlNodeReader class is an XML reader that enables you to read nodes out of a given XML DOM subtree.

Just as *XmlTextReader* visits all the nodes of the specified XML file, *XmlNodeReader* visits all the nodes that form an XML DOM subtree. Note that the node reader is really capable of traversing all the nodes in the subtree no matter the level of depth. Let's review a situation in which you might want to take advantage of *XmlNodeReader*.

The *XmlNodeReader* Class

Suppose you have selected a node about which you need more information. To scan all the nodes that form the subtree using XML DOM, your only option is to use a recursive algorithm like the one discussed with the *LoopThroughChildren* method in the section "Loading XML Documents," on page 219. The *XmlNodeReader* class gives you an effective, and ready-to-use, alternative, shown here:

```
// Select the root of the subtree to process
XmlNode n = root.SelectSingleNode("Employee[@id=2]");
if (n != null)
{
```

```
    // Instantiate a node reader object
    XmlNodeReader nodeReader = new XmlNodeReader(n);

    // Visit the subtree
     while (nodeReader.Read())
    {
        // Do something with the node...
        Console.WriteLine(nodeReader.Value);
    }
}
```

The *while* loop visits all the nodes belonging to the specified XML DOM subtree. The node reader class is initialized using the *XmlNode* object that is the root of the XML DOM subtree.

Updating Text and Markup

Once an XML document is loaded in memory, you can enter all the needed changes by simply accessing the property of interest and modifying the underlying value. For example, to change the value of an attribute, you proceed as follows:

```
// Retrieve a particular node and update an attribute
XmlNode n = root.SelectSingleNode("days");
n.Attributes["module"] = 1;
```

To insert many nodes at the same time and in the same parent, you can exploit a little trick based on the concept of a document fragment. In essence, you concatenate all the necessary markup into a string and then create a document fragment, as shown here:

```
XmlDocumentFragment df = doc.CreateDocumentFragment();
df.InnerXml = "<extra>Value</extra><extra>Another Value</extra>";
parentNode.AppendChild(df);
```

Set the *InnerXml* property of the document fragment node with the string, and then add the newly created node to the parent. The nodes defined in the body of the fragment will be inserted one after the next.

In general, when you set the *InnerXml* property on an *XmlNode*-based class, any detected markup text will be parsed, and the new contents will replace the existing contents. For this reason, if you want simply to add new children to a node, pass through the *XmlDocumentFragment* class, as described in the previous paragraph, and avoid using *InnerXml* directly on the target node.

Detecting Changes

Callers are notified of any changes that affect nodes through events. You can set event handlers at any time and even prior to loading the document, as shown here:

```
XmlDocument doc = new XmlDocument();
doc.NodeInserted += new XmlNodeChangedEventHandler(Changed);
doc.Load(fileName);
```

If you use the preceding code, you will get events for each insertion during the building of the XML DOM. The following code illustrates a minimal event handler:

```
void Changed(object sender, XmlNodeChangedEventArgs e)
{
    Console.WriteLine(e.Action.ToString());
}
```

Note that by design XML DOM events give you a chance to intervene before and after a node is added, removed, or updated.

Limitations of the XML DOM Eventing Model

Although you receive notifications before and after an action takes place, you can't alter the predefined flow of operations. In other words, you can perform any action while handling the event, but you can't cancel the ongoing operation. This also means that you can't just skip some nodes based on run-time conditions. In fact, the event handler function is *void*, and all the arguments passed with the event data structure are read-only. Programmers have no way to pass information back to the reader and skip the current node. There is only one way in which the event handler can affect the behavior of the reader. If the event handler throws an exception, the reader will stop working. In this case, however, the XML DOM will not be built.

Selecting Nodes by Query

As mentioned, the XML DOM provides a few ways to traverse the document forest to locate a particular node. The *ChildNodes* property returns a linked list formed by the child nodes placed at the same level. You move back and forth in this list using the *NextSibling* and *PreviousSibling* methods.

You can also enumerate the contents of the *ChildNodes* list using a *foreach*-style enumerator. This enumerator is built into the *XmlDocument* class and returned on demand by the *GetEnumerator* method, as shown here:

```
foreach(XmlNode n in node.ChildNodes)
{
    // Do something
}
```

Direct Access to Elements

The *GetElementById* method returns the first child node below the current node that has an ID attribute with the specified value. Note that ID is a particular XML type and not simply an attribute with that name. An attribute can be declared as an ID only in an XML Schema Definition (XSD) or a DTD schema. The following XML fragment defines an *employeeid* attribute of type ID. The attribute belongs to the *Employee* node.

```
<!ATTLIST Employee employeeid ID #REQUIRED>
```

A corresponding XML node might look like this:

```
<Employee employeeid="1" LastName="Davolio" FirstName="Nancy" />
```

As you can see, the source XML is apparently unaffected by the use of an ID attribute.

An ID attribute can be seen as an XML primary key, and the *GetElement-ById* method—part of the W3C DOM specification—represents the search method that applications use to locate nodes. The following code retrieves the node element in the document whose ID attribute (*employeeid*) matches the specified value:

```
employeeNode = node.GetElementById("1");
```

If you call *GetElementById* on a node whose children have no ID attributes or matching values, the method returns *null*. The search for a matching node stops when the first match is found.

Another query method at your disposal is *GetElementsByTagName*. As the name suggests, this method returns a list of nodes with the specified name. *GetElementsByTagName* looks similar to *ChildNodes* but differs in one aspect. Whereas *ChildNodes* returns all the child nodes found, including all elements and leaves, *GetElementsByTagName* returns only the element nodes with a particular name. The name specified can be expressed as a local as well as a namespace-qualified name.

XPath-Driven Access to Elements

The methods *SelectNodes* and *SelectSingleNode* provide more flexibility when it comes to selecting child nodes. Both methods support an XPath syntax (see

Chapter 6) to select nodes along the XML subtree rooted in the current node. There are two main differences between these methods and the other methods we've examined, such as *ReadNode* and *XmlNodeReader*.

The first difference is that an XPath query lets you base the search at a deeper level than the current node. In other words, the query expression can select the level of child nodes on which the search will be based. All other search methods can work only on the first level of child nodes.

The second difference is that an XPath expression lets you select nodes based on logical criteria. The code in this section is based on the following XML layout:

```
<MyDataSet>
    <NorthwindEmployees>
        <Employee id="1" />
        ...
    </NorthwindEmployees>
</MyDataSet>
```

By default, the *SelectNodes* and *SelectSingleNode* methods work on the children of the node that calls it, as follows:

```
root.SelectNodes("NorthwindEmployees");
root.SelectNodes("NorthwindEmployees/Employee");
root.SelectNodes("NorthwindEmployees/Employee[@id>4]");
```

An XPath expression, however, can traverse the tree and move the context for the query one or more levels ahead, or even back. The first query selects all the *NorthwindEmployees* nodes found below the root (the *MyDataSet* node). The second query starts from the root but goes two levels deeper to select all the nodes named *Employee* below the first *NorthwindEmployees* node. Finally, the third query adds a stricter condition and further narrows the result set by selecting only the *Employee* nodes whose *id* attribute is greater than 4. By using special syntax constructs, you can have XPath queries start from the root node or any other node ancestor, regardless of which node runs the query. (More on this topic in Chapter 6.)

Creating XML Documents

If your primary goal is analyzing the contents of an XML document, you will probably find the XML DOM parsing model much more effective than readers in spite of the larger memory footprint and set-up time it requires. A document loaded through XML DOM can be modified, extended, shrunk, and, more important, searched. The same can't be done with XML readers; XML readers follow a different design center. But what are the advantages of creating XML documents using XML DOM?

To create an XML document using the XML DOM API, you must first create the document in memory and then call the *Save* method or one of its overloads. This system gives you great flexibility because no changes you make are set in stone until you save the document. In general, however, using the XML DOM API to create a new XML document is often overkill unless the creation of the document is driven by a complex and sophisticated logic.

In terms of the internal implementation, it is worth noting that the XML DOM's *Save* method makes use of an XML text writer to create the document. So unless the content to be generated is complex and subject to a lot of conditions, using an XML text writer to create XML documents is faster.

The *XmlDocument* class provides a bunch of methods to create new nodes. These methods are named consistently with the writing methods of the *XmlTextWriter* class we encountered in Chapter 4. You'll find a *CreateXXX* method for each *WriteXXX* method provided by the writer. Actually, each *CreateXXX* method simply creates a new node in memory, and the corresponding *WriteXXX* method on the writer simply writes the node to the output stream.

Appending Nodes

Let's look at how to create a brand-new XML document persisting to XML the subdirectories found below a given path. The basic algorithm to implement can be summarized in the following steps:

1.   Create any necessary nodes.

2.   Link the nodes to create a tree.

3.   Append the tree to the in-memory XML document.

4.   Save the document.

The expected final output has the following layout:

```
<folders ...>
    <folder ...>text</folder>
    <folder ...>text</folder>
    ...
</folders>
```

The following code creates the XML prolog and appends to the *Xml-Document* instance the standard XML declaration and a comment node:

```
XmlDocument doc = new XmlDocument();
XmlNode n;

// Write and append the XML heading
n = doc.CreateXmlDeclaration("1.0", "", "");
doc.AppendChild(n);

// Write and append some comment
n = doc.CreateComment(" Content of the \"" + path + "\" folder ");
doc.AppendChild(n);
```

The *CreateXmlDeclaration* method takes three arguments: the XML version, the required encoding, and a Boolean value denoting whether the document can be considered stand-alone or has dependencies on other documents. All arguments are strings, including the *encoding* argument, as shown here:

```
<?xml version="1.0" standalone="yes" encoding="utf-7"?>
```

If specified, the encoding is written in the XML declaration and used by *Save* to create the actual output stream. If the encoding is *null* or empty, no *encoding* attribute is set, and the default Unicode Universal Character Set Transformation Format, 8-bit form (UTF-8) encoding is used.

CreateXmlDeclaration returns an *XmlDeclaration* node that you add as a child to the *XmlDocument* class. *CreateComment*, on the other hand, creates an *XmlComment* node that represents an XML comment, as shown here:

```
<!-- Content of the c:\ folder -->
```

Element nodes are created using the *CreateElement* method. The node is first configured with all of its expected child nodes and then added to the document, as shown here:

```
XmlNode root = doc.CreateElement("folders");
```

For the purposes of this example, we need a way to access all the subdirectories of a given folder. In the .NET Framework, this kind of functionality is provided by the *DirectoryInfo* class in the *System.IO* namespace:

```
DirectoryInfo dir = new DirectoryInfo(path);
```

To scan the subdirectories of the given path, you arrange a loop on top of the array of *DirectoryInfo* objects returned by the *GetDirectories* method, as follows:

```
foreach (DirectoryInfo d in dir.GetDirectories())
{
    n = doc.CreateElement("folder");

    //
    // Create attributes for the <folder> node
    //

    // Set the text for the node
    n.InnerText = "Content of " + d.Name;

    // Append the node to the rest of the document
    root.AppendChild(n);
}
```

In the loop, you create any needed *<folder>* node, configure the node with attributes and text, and then append the node to the parent *<folders>* node.

When creating an element node using the *CreateElement* method, you can specify a namespace URI as well as a namespace prefix. With the following code, you add an *xmlns* attribute to the node declaration:

```
XmlNode root = doc.CreateElement("folders", "urn:dino-e");
```

The final result is shown here:

```
<folders xmlns="urn:dino-e">
```

If you use a namespace, you might reasonably want to use a prefix too. To specify a namespace prefix, resort to another overload for the *CreateElement* method in which you pass in the order, the prefix, the local name of the element, and the namespace URI, as shown here:

```
XmlNode root = doc.CreateElement("d", "folders", "urn:dino-e");
```

The node XML code changes to this:

```
<folders xmlns:d="urn:dino-e">
```

At this point, to also qualify the successive *<folder>* nodes with this namespace, call *CreateElement* with the prefix and the URI, as shown here:

```
n = doc.CreateElement("d", "folder", "urn:dino-e");
```

> **Note**   Bear in mind that although all the *CreateXXX* methods avail-able in the *XmlDocument* class can create an XML node, that node is not automatically added to the XML DOM. You must do that explicitly using one of the several methods defined to extend the current DOM.

Appending Attributes

An attribute is simply a special type of node that you create using the *Create-Attribute* method. The method returns an *XmlAttribute* object. The following code shows how to create a new attribute named *path* and how to associate it with a parent node:

```
XmlAttribute a;
a = doc.CreateAttribute("path");
a.Value = path;
node.Attributes.SetNamedItem(a);
```

Like *CreateElement*, *CreateAttribute* too allows you to qualify the name of the attribute using a namespace URI and optionally a prefix. The overloads for both methods have the same signature.

You set the value of an attribute using the *Value* property. At this point, however, the attribute node is not yet bound to an element node. To associate the attribute with a node, you must add the attribute to the node's *Attributes* collection. The *SetNamedItem* method does this for you. The following code shows the finalized version of the loop that creates the XML file for our example:

```
foreach (DirectoryInfo d in dir.GetDirectories())
{
    n = doc.CreateElement("folder");
    a = doc.CreateAttribute("name");
    a.Value = d.Name;
    n.Attributes.SetNamedItem(a);

    a = doc.CreateAttribute("created");
    a.Value = d.CreationTime.ToString();
    n.Attributes.SetNamedItem(a);
    root.AppendChild(n);
    n.InnerText = "Content of " + d.Name;
}
```

Figure 5-5 demonstrates the structure of the newly created XML file.

```
<?xml version="1.0" ?>
<!-- Content of the "c:\" folder  -->
<d:folders path="c:\" count="21" xmlns:d="urn:dino-e">
  <d:folder name="Config.Msi" created="7/8/2001 4:51:58 PM">Content of Config.Msi</d:folder>
  <d:folder name="Documents and Settings" created="3/19/2001 6:02:54 PM">Content of Documents and Settings</d:folder>
  <d:folder name="Ftt" created="5/24/2001 4:44:24 PM">Content of Ftt</d:folder>
  <d:folder name="Inetpub" created="3/19/2001 5:45:42 PM">Content of Inetpub</d:folder>
  <d:folder name="My Apps" created="3/20/2001 3:57:05 PM">Content of My Apps</d:folder>
  <d:folder name="My Articles" created="3/27/2001 10:45:31 PM">Content of My Articles</d:folder>
  <d:folder name="My Books" created="3/27/2001 8:11:46 PM">Content of My Books</d:folder>
  <d:folder name="My Clients" created="3/27/2001 10:46:31 PM">Content of My Clients</d:folder>
  <d:folder name="My Conferences" created="3/29/2001 10:46:15 AM">Content of My Conferences</d:folder>
  <d:folder name="My Downloads" created="6/6/2001 10:15:41 AM">Content of My Downloads</d:folder>
  <d:folder name="My Email" created="4/12/2001 9:09:17 AM">Content of My Email</d:folder>
  <d:folder name="My Icons" created="5/30/2001 7:50:00 PM">Content of My Icons</d:folder>
  <d:folder name="My Info Seminars" created="3/27/2001 8:12:28 PM">Content of My Info Seminars</d:folder>
  <d:folder name="My Labs" created="4/13/2001 5:57:57 PM">Content of My Labs</d:folder>
  <d:folder name="My Seminars" created="7/12/2001 6:36:34 PM">Content of My Seminars</d:folder>
  <d:folder name="My Technical Papers" created="3/20/2001 4:28:26 PM">Content of My Technical Papers</d:folder>
  <d:folder name="PPC650" created="3/21/2001 9:00:01 AM">Content of PPC650</d:folder>
  <d:folder name="Program Files" created="3/19/2001 6:03:51 PM">Content of Program Files</d:folder>
  <d:folder name="WINNT" created="3/19/2001 5:58:11 PM">Content of WINNT</d:folder>
</d:folders>
```

Figure 5-5   An XML file representing a directory listing created using the XML DOM API.

Persisting Changes

The final step in saving the XML document we have created is to attach the *<folders>* node to the rest of the document and save the document, as shown here:

```
doc.AppendChild(root);
doc.Save(fileName);
```

To persist all the changes to a storage medium, you call the *Save* method, which contains four overloads, shown here:

```
public virtual void Save(Stream);
public virtual void Save(string);
public virtual void Save(TextWriter);
public virtual void Save(XmlWriter);
```

The XML document can be saved to a disk file as well as to an output stream, including network and compressed streams. You can also integrate the class that manages the document with other .NET Framework applications by using writers, and you can combine more XML documents using, in particular, XML writers.

Whatever overload you choose, it is always an XML writer that does the job of persisting XML nodes to a storage medium. The *XmlDocument* class makes use of a specialized version of the *XmlTextWriter* class that simply works around one of the limitations of XML writers.

XML writers do not allow you to write element and attribute nodes for which you have a prefix but an empty namespace. If the namespace URI is set to *null*, the writer successfully looks up the closest definition for that prefix and figures out the namespace, if one exists. If the namespace is simply an empty string, however, an *ArgumentException* exception is thrown. The XML DOM internal writer overrides the *WriteStartElement* and *WriteStartAttribute* methods. If the namespace URI is empty when the prefix is not, the new overrides reset the prefix to the empty string and no exception is raised.

Extending the XML DOM

Although the .NET Framework provides a suite of rich classes to navigate, query, and modify the contents of an XML document, there might be situations in which you need more functionality. For example, you might want a node class with more informative properties or a document class with extra functions. To obtain that class, you simply derive a new class from *XmlNode*, *XmlDocument*, or whatever XML DOM class you want to override. Let's see how.

Custom Node Classes

As a general rule of thumb, you should avoid deriving node classes from the base class *XmlNode*. If necessary, derive node classes from a specialized and concrete node class like *XmlElement* or *XmlAttribute*. This will ensure that no key behavior of the node is lost in your implementation. But what kind of extensions can you reasonably build for a node?

I haven't encountered any huge flaws in the design of the XML DOM node classes, so if you need extensions, it's probably because you want to give nodes new methods or properties that simplify a particular operation you carry out quite often.

The Microsoft Developer Network (MSDN) documentation already provides an example of XML DOM extensions that adds line information to each node and then counts the number of element nodes a given document contains. (See the section "Further Reading," on page 244, for more information about this example.) As mentioned, the *ChildNodes* property of the *XmlDocument* class does not cache the number of elements in the list. As a result, whenever you need to know the number of children and call the *Count* property, the entire list of nodes is walked from top to bottom. In addition, you have no way to distinguish between element nodes and leaf nodes.

In the MSDN documentation, you'll find a class that attempts to solve this problem by extending the *XmlDocument* class with a custom *GetCount* method, shown here:

```
class LineInfoDocument : XmlDocument
{
    ...
    public int GetCount()
    {
        return elementCount;
    }
    ...
}
```

In the remainder of this section, however, we'll look at a more substantial improvement to the *XmlDocument* class. In particular, you'll learn how to build a kind of "sensitive" XML DOM that can detect any changes to the underlying disk file and automatically reload the new contents.

Building a Hot-Plugging XML DOM

Being able to detect changes to files and folders as they occur is a feature that many developers would welcome. Win32 provides a set of functions to get notifications of incoming changes to the size, the contents, or the attributes of a given file or folder. Unfortunately, the feature is limited to notifying registered applications that a certain event occurred in the watched file or folder but provides no further information about what happened to which file or folder and why.

To clarify, this feature was introduced with Microsoft Windows 95 and was tailor-made for Windows Explorer. Have you ever noticed that when you have a Windows Explorer view open and you modify a file shown in that view, the Windows Explorer view automatically refreshes to show updated data? The trick behind this apparently magical behavior is that, just before a new folder view is opened, Windows Explorer registers a file notification object for the contents of that folder. When it gets a notification that something occurred to that folder's contents, Windows Explorer simply refreshes the view to show the new contents, whatever that is.

Later, Microsoft introduced only for the Windows NT platform an even more sophisticated mechanism that not only notifies applications of the event but also provides information about the type of change that occurred and the file or files affected. This extended feature relies on Win32 API functions supported only on Windows NT platforms, starting with Windows NT 4.0.

The .NET Framework wraps all this functionality into the *FileSystem-Watcher* class, available from the *System.IO* namespace. This class takes advantage of the Windows NT–based API and for this reason is not available with Microsoft Windows 98, Microsoft Windows Me, and older platforms.

> **Note** Because *FileSystemWatcher* is a wrapper for the Windows NT API, it works only on computers running Windows NT, Windows 2000, or Windows XP. But you could write a wrapper class using a less powerful Win32 API and have it work on all Win32 platforms.

An instance of the *FileSystemWatcher* class is at the foundation of the extended version of the *XmlDocument* class that we'll build in the next section. The new class, named *XmlHotDocument*, is capable of detecting any changes that have occurred in the underlying file and automatically notifies the host application of these changes.

The *XmlHotDocument* Class Programming Interface

The *XmlHotDocument* class inherits from *XmlDocument* and provides a new event and a couple of new properties, as shown in the following code. In addition, it overrides one of the overloads of the *Load* method—the method overload that works on files. In general, however, nothing would really prevent you from extending the feature to also cover streams or text readers as long as those streams and readers are based on disk files.

```
public class XmlHotDocument : XmlDocument
{
    public XmlHotDocument() : base()
    {
        m_watcher = new FileSystemWatcher();
        HasChanges = false;
        EnableFileChanges = false;
    }
    ...
}
```

As you can see, the preceding code includes the class declaration and the constructor's code. Upon initialization, the class creates an instance of the file system watcher and sets the new public properties—*HasChanges* and *Enable-FileChanges*—to *false*. Table 5-6 summarizes what's really new with the programming interface of the *XmlHotDocument* class.

Table 5-6   Programming Interface of the *XmlHotDocument* Class

Property or Event	Description
EnableFileChanges	Boolean property that you use to toggle on and off the watching system. If set to *true*, the application receives notifications for each change made to the file loaded in the DOM. Set to *false* by default.
HasChanges	Boolean property that the class sets to *true* whenever there are changes in the underlying XML file that the application has not yet processed. Set to *false* by default; is reset when you call the *Load* method again.
UnderlyingDocumentChanged	Represents an event that the class fires whenever a change is detected in the watched file.

In addition, the *XmlHotDocument* class has one private member—the reference to the *FileSystemWatcher* object used to monitor file system changes.

The Watching Mechanism

An instance of the *FileSystemWatcher* class is created in the class constructor but is not set to work until the caller application sets the *EnableFileChanges* property to *true*, as shown here:

```
public bool EnableFileChanges
{
    get { return m_watcher.EnableRaisingEvents; }
    set {
        if (value == true)
        {
            // Get the local path of the current file
            Uri u = new Uri(BaseURI);
            string filename = u.LocalPath;

            // Set the path to watch for
            FileInfo fi = new FileInfo(filename);
            m_watcher.Path = fi.DirectoryName;
```

(continued)

```
        m_watcher.Filter = filename;

        // Set hooks for writing changes
        m_watcher.NotifyFilter = NotifyFilters.LastWrite;
        m_watcher.Changed +=
            new FileSystemEventHandler(this.OnChanged);

        // Start getting notifications
        m_watcher.EnableRaisingEvents = true;
    }
    else
        m_watcher.EnableRaisingEvents = false;
}
}
```

EnableFileChanges is a read/write property that is responsible for setting up the watching system when set to *true*. The watching system consists of *Path* and *Filter* properties that you use to narrow the set of files and folders that must be watched for changes.

The *Path* property sets the folder to watch, while the *Filter* property restricts the number of files monitored in that folder. If you set the *Filter* property to an empty string, the entire contents of the folder will be watched; otherwise, only the files matching the filter string will be taken into account. In this case, we just need to monitor a single file, so we'll set the *Filter* property to the name of the document used to populate the current XML DOM.

> **Note**   When setting the *Filter* property, avoid using fully qualified path names. Internally, the *FileSystemWatcher* class will be concatenating the *Path* and *Filter* properties to obtain the fully qualified path to filter out files and folders involved in any file-system-level event caught.

The *XmlDocument* class stores the name of the document being processed in its *BaseURI* property. Although the *BaseURI* property is a string, it stores the file name as a URI. As a result, a file name such as c:\data.xml is stored in the *BaseURI* property as file:///c:/data.xml. Note that in the .NET Framework, URIs are rendered through an ad hoc type—the *Uri* class. To obtain the local path from a URI, you must first create a new *Uri* object and query its *LocalPath* property, as shown here:

```
Uri u = new Uri(BaseURI);
string filename = u.LocalPath;
```

Why can't we just use the file name in the URI form? To avoid the rather boring task of parsing the path string to extract the directory information, I use the *FileInfo* class and its handy *DirectoryName* property. Unfortunately, however, the *FileInfo* class can't handle file names in the URI format. The following code will throw an exception if *filename* is a URI:

```
FileInfo fi = new FileInfo(filename);
m_watcher.Path = fi.DirectoryName;
m_watcher.Filter = fi.Name;
```

To finalize the watcher setup, you also need to define the change events that will be detected and register a proper event handler for each of them. You set the *NotifyFilter* property with any bitwise combination of flags defined in the *NotifyFilters* enumeration. In particular, you can choose values to detect changes in the size, attributes, name, contents, date, and security settings of each watched file. The following code simply configures the watcher to control whether the monitored file has something new written to it. The *LastWrite* flag actually causes an event to fire whenever the timestamp of the file changes, irrespective of the contents that you might have written to the file. In other words, the event also fires if you simply open and save the file without entering any changes.

```
m_watcher.NotifyFilter = NotifyFilters.LastWrite;
m_watcher.Changed += new FileSystemEventHandler(this.OnChanged);

// Start getting notifications
m_watcher.EnableRaisingEvents = true;
```

The changes you can register to be detected are originated by four events: *Changed*, *Created*, *Deleted*, and *Renamed*. In this example, we are interested only in the changes that modify an existing file, so let's handle only the *Changed* event, as shown here:

```
private void OnChanged(object source, FileSystemEventArgs e)
{
    HasChanges = true;
    if (UnderlyingDocumentChanged != null)
        UnderlyingDocumentChanged(this, EventArgs.Empty);
}
```

Any file system event passes to the handlers a *FileSystemEventArgs* object that contains information about the event—for example, the name of the files involved and a description of the event that just occurred. The *XmlHotDocument* class processes the *Changed* event by simply setting the *HasChanges* property to *true* and bubbling the event up to the caller application. In the process, the original event is renamed to a class-specific event named *Underlying-DocumentChanged*. In addition, no argument is passed because the client application using the XML DOM needs to know only that some changes have occurred to the underlying documents currently being processed.

After it is completely set up, the *FileSystemWatcher* class starts raising file system events only if you set its *EnableRaisingEvents* property to *true*. Changing the value of this property to *false* is the only way you have to stop the watcher from sending further events.

> **Note**   When monitoring a file or a folder through a *FileSystem-Watcher* class, don't be surprised if you receive too many events and some events that are not strictly solicited. The class is a watchful observer of what happens at the file system level and correctly reports any change you registered for. Many operations that look like individual operations are actually implemented in several steps, each of which can cause an independent event. In addition, you might have software running in the background (for example, antivirus software) that performs disk operations that will be detected as well.

Using the *XmlHotDocument* Class

To take advantage of the new class in a client application, start by declaring and instantiating a variable of that type, as follows:

```
XmlHotDocument m_hotDocument = new XmlHotDocument();
```

Next you register an event handler for the *UnderlyingDocumentChanged* event and call the *Load* method to build the XML DOM. When you think you are ready to start receiving file system notifications, set the *EnableFileChanges* property to *true*, as shown here:

```
m_hotDocument.UnderlyingDocumentChanged +=
    new EventHandler(FileChanged);
m_hotDocument.Load("data.xml");
m_hotDocument.EnableFileChanges = true;
```

Note that you can't set *EnableFileChanges* to *true* before the XML DOM is built—that is, before the *Load* method has been called.

Registering a handler for the custom *UnderlyingDocumentChanged* event is not mandatory, but doing so gives your application an immediate notification about what happened. The value of the *HasChanges* property automatically indicates any underlying changes that the current XML DOM does not yet reflect, however. When you build an XML DOM, the *HasChanges* property is reset to *false*. Figure 5-6 shows the sample application immediately after startup.

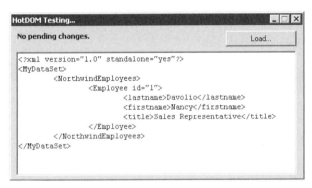

Figure 5-6   A sample application making use of the *XmlHotDocument* class. No pending changes have been detected yet on the displayed XML file.

When another user, or another application, modifies the XML file that is being processed by the current instance of the *XmlHotDocument* object, an *UnderlyingDocumentChanged* event reaches the application. The sample program shown in Figure 5-6 handles the event using the following code:

```
void FileChanged(object sender, EventArgs e)
{
    UpdateUI();
}
```

The internal *UpdateUI* method simply refreshes the user interface, checking the state of the *HasChanges* property, as shown here:

```
if (m_hotDocument.HasChanges)
    PendingChanges.Text = "*** Pending changes ***";
```

Figure 5-7 shows the application when it detects a change.

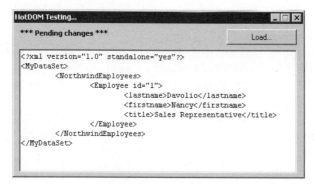

Figure 5-7 The sample application detects changes in the underlying XML file and updates the user interface.

At this point, the user can reload the XML DOM using the *Load* method again, as shown in the following code. As mentioned, calling the *Load* method resets the status of the *HasChanges* property, resulting in an up-to-date user interface.

```
public override void Load(string filename)
{
    // Load the DOM the usual way
    base.Load(filename);

    // Reset pending changes
HasChanges = false;
}
```

Figure 5-8 shows the application displaying the change.

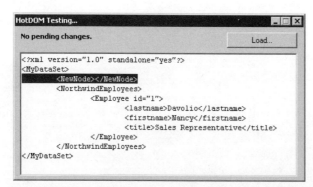

Figure 5-8 Changes dynamically occurring in the XML document are now correctly reflected by the XML DOM used by the application.

A hot-plugging XML DOM is more than a made-to-measure example. It is a piece of code that you might find useful in all those circumstances in which you make use of extremely volatile XML documents.

Conclusion

This chapter presented the .NET Framework classes that provide XML DOM capabilities. Using these classes—primarily *XmlDocument* and *XmlNode*—you can parse XML documents, building in-memory and fully accessible representations of data.

The overall programming interface of the *XmlDocument* class might look familiar to those of you who have spent some time working with the Microsoft COM-based MSXML library. The *XmlDocument* class provides methods to load XML documents from a variety of sources, including XML readers and streams. The loading of a document can happen only synchronously, but you can significantly lessen the impact of this design issue by using multiple threads.

To locate a node in the in-memory tree that represents the original XML document, you can proceed with a collection that returns only the first level of child nodes, or you can, more effectively, use an XPath query string to locate nodes by condition. If your goal is visiting all the nodes that are part of a given DOM subtree, you have two options, both of which have been described with code in this chapter. One possibility is writing your own recursive algorithm to visit all the child nodes below a given root. An alternative approach is based on the *XmlNodeReader* class—an XML reader class capable of reading nodes from an XML DOM source.

You also learned how to build XML documents from scratch using the XML DOM classes and the methods offered by the *XmlDocument* class. Creating new documents using XML DOM is not as efficient as using XML writers, but because the document is first built in memory, you have an unprecedented level of flexibility and can fine-tune your document before it is written to the output stream.

XML DOM is a powerful object model that provides you with a rich set of methods and properties to manipulate the schema and contents of XML documents. Under the hood of the XML DOM interface, however, you still find XML reader and writer objects working hard to provide input and output functionalities. Extending the DOM is as easy as deriving a new class from *XmlDocument*, as you saw when we created a "sensitive" XML DOM class that detects incoming changes in the underlying XML file and fires ad hoc events to the caller application. In Chapter 6, we'll take the plunge into XPath and the .NET Framework classes that make it happen.

Further Reading

This chapter repeatedly mentions the XML DOM as the starting point for defining the set of methods and properties for the *XmlDocument* class. The .NET Framework classes support the interface defined by the DOM Level 1 Core and DOM Level 2 Core specifications. If you are interested in the official papers, you can find them at *http://www.w3.org/TR/REC-DOM-Level-1* and *http://www.w3.org/TR/DOM-Level-2*.

Another topic that has been mentioned quite often is XPath. We'll be looking at XPath in Chapter 6, but you won't find a complete reference to the syntax elements of the XPath query language there. (In general, this book is not a comprehensive reference for any of the XML-related standards.) For a thorough treatment of this topic, refer to *Essential XML Quick Reference*, by Aaron Skonnard and Martin Gudgin (Addison-Wesley, 2001), which provides short comments and descriptions and not much background information, but does cover in detail every single element of the syntax. By combining the information in that book with the general information available in this one, you should end up with a good grasp of the technology.

In this chapter, I developed an XML DOM extension that enables XML applications to detect ongoing changes in the XML files they are processing through the DOM. Another example of XML DOM extensions is available for download at *http://www.gotdotnet.com/userfiles/XMLDom/extendDOM.zip*.

6

XML Query Language and Navigation

XML sprang to life as a metalanguage that can be used to describe any sort of data and documents using a truly hierarchical representation, or a representation that simply looks hierarchical. As XML gained broad acceptance from the software industry, the need for additional and related standards promptly arose. In Chapter 5, we looked at the XML Document Object Model (XML DOM), which represents the official object model for XML data containers.

Although it is rich and powerful, XML DOM alone does not address the needs of XML data retrieval. One of the key advantages of XML markup text over plain text is that it can be used to mark portions of the text with special tags and attributes. So how do you effectively retrieve parts of an XML document that have been marked in a certain way?

The need for an effective XML-based query language is as old as the need for a general-purpose data description language. In fact, a W3C-ratified standard for an XML query language followed shortly after the XML 1.0 recommendation. XPath is the query language defined to address parts of an XML document using a compact, relatively simple, but not XML-based syntax. More importantly, XPath is designed to define and provide a common syntax for accessing XML nodes through the XML DOM as well as from XML Stylesheet Language Transformation (XSLT) scripts. (We'll look at XSLT in Chapter 7.)

In the Microsoft .NET Framework, XPath is fully supported through the classes defined in the *System.Xml.XPath* namespace. The .NET Framework implementation of XPath is based on a language parser and an evaluation engine. The overall architecture is similar to database queries. As with SQL commands, you prepare XPath expressions and submit them to a run-time engine evaluation. The query is parsed and executed against a data source—an instance of the XML DOM. Next you get back some information representing the result set of the query.

What Is XPath, Anyway?

XPath is a general-purpose query language for addressing and filtering both the elements and the text of an XML document. As the name suggests, the XPath notation is basically declarative. A valid XPath expression looks like a path to a particular set of nodes or a value excerpted from the source document.

XPath works on top of a tree-based representation of the source document. The path expresses a node pattern using a notation that emphasizes the hierarchical relationship between the nodes. Although semantically speaking the closest similarity is with the SQL query language, from a syntax point of view, XPath expressions look a lot like a file system path composed of folder and file names. For example, consider the following simple XPath expression:

```
customer/address
```

This expression states: find all the *address* nodes that happen to be children of the *customer* element. But on which nodes is this expression evaluated? An XPath expression is always evaluated in the context of a node. The *context node* is designated by the application and represents the starting point of the query. Expressing the concept of the context node in terms of file system paths, we could say that the appropriate file system counterpart for the context node is the current directory.

The nodes affected by the expression form the *context node-set*. The final set of nodes that is actually returned to the application is a subset of the context node-set that includes only those nodes that match the specified criteria.

Context of XPath Queries

The context of an XPath query includes, but is not limited to, a context node and a context node-set. The XPath context also contains position and namespace information, variable bindings, and a standard library of functions. We'll look at the contents of the XPath context in detail in this section.

In the .NET Framework, the context node is the *XmlNode* object on which you call either the *SelectNodes* or the *SelectSingleNode* method. The context node-set is determined by the so-called *axis* of the query. The axis is a keyword that specifies the group of nodes that will then be filtered out by the XPath expression.

XPath Axes

Continuing with the file system parallel, the axis is similar to the drive information in a file system path. Like the drive identifier, axis information is not strictly necessary, and a default value can be assumed if the axis is omitted.

If an XPath query has no axis element, the context node-set contains the direct children of the context node. As with drives, when specified, an axis defines the entire set of nodes that the following path will evaluate. Table 6-1 lists the available axes.

Table 6-1   XPath Axes

Axis	Description	Context Node-Set
self	The context node.	7
child	Children of the context node.	8, 9
parent	Parent of the context node.	5
descendant	Nodes in the subtree rooted in the context node. The variant *descendant-or-self* adds the context node to the set.	8, 9, 10
ancestor	Parent of the context node and then parent's parent, up to the document root. The variant *ancestor-or-self* adds the context node to the set.	5, 1
Following	All the nodes that will be visited after the context node. The XPath specification dictates that the document be visited in depth-first order, going as deep as possible on a path.	> 7
following-sibling	Following sibling nodes of the context node.	11
Preceding	All the nodes already visited according to the standard algorithm.	< 7
preceding-sibling	Preceding sibling of the context node.	6

The context node-set numbers in Table 6-1 refer to the XML tree in Figure 6-1 and indicate the nodes that would form the corresponding node-set once a given axis is specified. The context node is labeled 7.

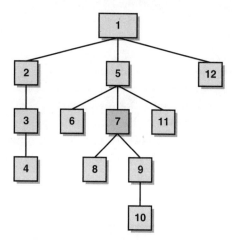

Figure 6-1 A sample XML tree in which the node numbers indicate the order in which nodes are visited by the XPath query processor.

The XPath specification requires that the nodes be visited in depth-first order, starting from the root and then proceeding with all the children from left to right until a leaf is found. This order corresponds to the order in which nodes are read from an XML disk file.

Position Information

An XPath context is characterized by a position and a size. The *position* attribute is a one-based value that indicates the ordinal position of the context node in the context node-set to which it belongs. The *size* attribute, on the other hand, returns the size of the context node-set—that is, the number of nodes being processed by the expression. The number does not necessarily match the size of the final node-set returned to the caller application.

XPath and Namespaces

The XPath processor uses node information to determine whether a match exists with the current expression. The most important information used by XPath expressions is the node's name, type, and attributes. XPath fully supports XML namespaces and splits the name of a node into two constituent parts: the namespace URI and the local name. The set of namespaces declared in scope for the context node is used to qualify node names in the expression.

Variable Bindings

An XPath expression can contain variable references that are resolved through a set of in-memory bindings established between variable names and actual values. Each variable holds a value whose type is normally one of the four base types—*node-set*, *string*, *Boolean*, and *number*. It is still possible, however, for a variable reference to contain a value of some other type.

XPath Functions

Any implementation of the XPath parser must provide a function library that is used to evaluate expressions. Functions in the core library have no namespace information, but extension functions can have a namespace. Extension functions are defined within vendor-specific XPath implementations but can also be provided by specialized and XPath-based programming APIs such as XSLT and XML Pointer Language (XPointer) APIs.

The functions in the XPath core library work on the base XPath types: *node-set*, *Boolean*, *string*, and *number*. Type conversion is automatically performed whenever possible. The only type conversion not permitted is from any other type to node-sets. Table 6-2 lists just the commonly used functions included in the library.

Table 6-2   Some Members of the XPath Core Library

Function	Description
last	A node-set function that returns the number of nodes in the current node-set
name	A node-set function that returns the fully qualified name of the specified node
text	A node-set function that returns the text of the specified node
position	A node-set function that returns the index of the context node in the current node-set
boolean	A Boolean function that converts a value to a Boolean
contains	A string function that indicates whether a string contains the specified substring
substring	A string function that returns the specified substring
starts-with	A string function that indicates whether the string begins with a given substring
ceiling	A number function that rounds a number up to the next integer
floor	A number function that rounds a number down to the next integer
round	A number function that rounds a number to the nearest integer

You will likely use the node-set functions most often. While being processed, an XPath expression is tokenized into subexpressions, and each subexpression is individually evaluated. The XPath processor is passed the subexpression and the context node-set. It returns a possibly narrowed node-set that will be iteratively used as the input argument for the next subexpression. During this process, the context node, position, and size can vary, whereas variable and function references as well as namespace declarations remain intact.

Location Paths

As mentioned, an XPath expression can return any of the following types: *Boolean*, *string*, *number*, or *node-set*. In most cases, however, it will return a set of nodes. The most frequently used type of XPath expression is the *location path*.

A location path looks a lot like a file system path and, like a file system path, can be either absolute or relative to the context node. When absolute, a location path begins with the forward slash (/). The following expression, for example, locates all the *<invoice>* nodes, irrespective of the node on which the expression is evaluated.

```
/archive/invoices/invoice
```

In contrast, this expression attempts to retrieve the nodes at the end of a particular path that starts from the current node:

```
archive/invoices/invoice
```

Unabbreviated Syntax for a Location Path

A fully qualified location path consists of three pieces: an optional *axis*, a *node test*, and an optional *predicate*. The axis information defines the initial context node-set for the expression, whereas the node test is a sequence of node names that identifies a path in the node-set. The predicate is a logical expression that defines the criteria to filter the current node-set.

If the location path lacks any of its optional components, it is said to be in *abbreviated* form. The general, *unabbreviated*, syntax for a location path expression is shown here:

```
axis::node-test[predicate]
```

The syntax dictates that the axis be separated from the rest of the expression by a double colon (::). This special separator once again recalls the parallel between axis information and drive information in a file system. The predicate is enclosed in square brackets. A location path can include multiple predicates that are written one after another like indexes in a multidimensional array.

The node test is a node-based expression that is evaluated for each node in the context node-set. If the expression returns *true*, the node remains in the node-set; otherwise, it is removed. Typically, the node test takes the form of a path. Read as an expression, it returns *true* if the specified path exists below the context node and *false* otherwise. The following code demonstrates a fully qualified XPath location:

```
descendant::invoice[@year = 2002]
```

The XPath processor first selects all the descendants of the context node. Next it selects from this set all the *<invoice>* nodes whose *year* attribute equals 2002.

> **Tip**   You can use the wildcard character (*) to indicate all the nodes in a given axis. For example, the expression *child::** denotes all the children of the current context node. Likewise, *descendant-or-self::** means all the descendants and the node itself.

Location Steps

A location path is composed of several child elements called *location steps*. Each location step is actually a location path and, as such, can be expressed in an abbreviated or fully qualified form, as appropriate. Location steps are separated by forward slashes, as shown in Figure 6-2.

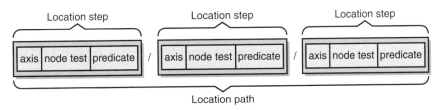

Figure 6-2   A location path consists of one or more location steps, each of which can be expressed in full or abbreviated form.

Consider the following three-step expression:

```
invoices/descendant::invoice[@year = 2002]/child::country[text() = 'USA']
```

The first step selects all the nodes named *<invoices>* below the context node. This node-set is then passed as the context node-set to the next location step. The second location step is expressed in an unabbreviated form and loops through all the descendants of each previously selected *<invoices>* node. When processed, each node plays the role of the context node and provides different position information. At the end of the second step, the node-set contains only the *<invoice>* nodes that have a parent *<invoices>* and a *year* attribute set to 2002.

The final step further narrows the node-set by excluding all the nodes that have no *<country>* child whose text equals *USA*.

> **Note**   The at sign (@) that you use to indicate a node attribute is actually an abbreviation for another particular axis type: the *attribute*. The full syntax for the year attribute is *attribute::year*. The XPath specification recommends a number of abbreviations that are commonly used in coding, including the following shortcuts: Use a period (.) to indicate the context node and two periods (..) to refer to the parent. When no axis is specified, *child::* is assumed. Finally, *[n]* means the *n*th node in the current context node-set; this array-like notation is equivalent to *[position() = n]*.

Links Between Documents

The XPath query language is used to select a set of nodes in a given XML document. You typically use XPath to search for nodes in an XML DOM implementation of a data source and to filter the nodes to which a given transformation template in an XSL script must be applied.

Recently, another possible use for the XPath syntax has boldly emerged. I'm talking about XPointer, which is designed to become the standard way to link portions of external documents to XML documents.

What Is XPointer?

XPointer is used to locate data within an XML document. When XML documents need to point to external resources, they can declare an entity reference or, more effectively, include the whole resource, using the XML Inclusion (XInclude) syntax. XInclude—a W3C recommendation candidate—links the host document to an external resource, or a portion of it. XPointer defines the syntax you use to specify the addressed portion of the document.

Normally, to indicate a particular position in an XML document, you attach a fragment identifier to the document's URL. A fragment identifier is marked by a number sign (#) and follows the document's URL. For example, the URL *http://www.w3.org/TR/xptr/#conformance* points to the portion of the document labeled with the *conformance* name.

With XPointer, you can use the XPath syntax to identify with greater flexibility a particular location in the external document.

How XPointer Uses XPath

An XPointer fragment identifier can be the name of a particular portion of the target document, but it could also be a more complex and expressive XPath query. For example, you could link a piece of information using the following syntax:

```
invoices.xml#xpointer(/descendant::invoice[@id=201])
```

This expression references the particular descendant node named *<invoice>* having an *id* attribute equal to *201*.

XPath in the XML DOM

In the .NET Framework, you can make use of XPath expressions in two ways: through the XML DOM or by means of a new and more flexible API based on the concept of the *XPath navigator.*

In the former case, you use XPath expressions to select nodes within the context of a living instance of the *XmlDocument* class. As we saw in Chapter 5, the *XmlDocument* class is the .NET Framework class that renders a given XML document as a hierarchical object model (XML DOM). This approach keeps the API close to the old MSXML programming style and has probably been supplied mostly for compatibility reasons.

The alternative approach consists of creating an instance of the *XPath-Document* class and obtaining from it an XPath navigator object. The navigator object is a generic XPath processor that works on top of any XML data store that exposes the *IXPathNavigable* interface. Rendered through the *XPathNavigator* class, the XPath navigator object parses and executes expressions using its *Select* method. XPath expressions can be passed as plain text or as preprocessed, compiled expressions. As you can see, although the classes involved are different, the overall programming style is not much different from those pushed by MSXML and the .NET Framework XML DOM classes.

This said, though, the XPath navigator object represents a quantum leap from the *SelectNodes* method of the *XmlDocument* class. For one thing, it works on top of highly specialized document classes that implement *IXPathNavigable* and are optimized to perform both XPath queries and XSL transformations. In contrast, the *XmlDocument* class is a generic data container class that incorporates an XPath processor but is not built around it.

Several classes in the .NET Framework implement the *IXPathNavigable* interface, thus making their contents automatically selectable by XPath expressions. We'll look at the navigation API in more detail in the section "The .NET XPath Navigation API," on page 263. For now, let's review the XPath support built into the *XmlDocument* class.

The XML DOM Node Retrieval API

When using XPath queries to query an XML DOM instance, you can use the *SelectNodes* method of the *XmlDocument* class. In particular, *SelectNodes* returns a collection that contains instances of all the *XmlNode* objects that match the specified expression. If you don't need the entire node-set, but instead plan to use the query to locate the root of a particular subtree, use the *SelectSingleNode* method. *SelectSingleNode* takes an XPath expression and returns a reference to the first match found.

The *SelectNodes* and *SelectSingleNode* methods perform identical functionality to the methods available from the Component Object Model (COM)–based MSXML library that script and Microsoft Win32 applications normally use. It is worth noting that these methods are not part of the official W3C XML DOM specification but represent, instead, Microsoft extensions to the standard XML DOM.

At the application level, XML DOM methods and the XPath navigator supply different programming interfaces, but internally they run absolutely equivalent code.

The *SelectNodes* Internal Implementation

The *SelectNodes* method internally employs a navigator object to retrieve the list of matching nodes. The return value of the navigator's *Select* method is then used to initialize an undocumented internal node list class named *System.Xml.XPath .XPathNodeList*. As you have probably guessed, this class inherits from *Xml-NodeList*, which is a documented class. To verify this statement, compile and run the following simple code:

```
XmlDocument doc = new XmlDocument();
doc.Load(fileName);
```

```
XmlNodeList nodes = doc.SelectNodes("child::*");
Console.WriteLine(nodes.ToString());
```

The true type of the variable nodes is *XPathNodeList*. If you try to reference that type in your code, you get a compile error due to the protection level of the class.

What's the difference between using *SelectNodes* and the XPath navigator object? The *SelectNodes* method uses a navigator that works on top of a generic XML document class—the *XmlDocument* class. The *SelectNodes* method's navigator object is, in fact, created by the *XmlDocument* class's *CreateNavigator* method. If you choose to publicly manage a navigator, you normally create it from a more specific and XPath-optimized document class—the *XPathDocument* class.

The XPath expression is passed to the navigator as plain text:

```
XmlNodeList SelectNodes(string xpathExpr, XmlNamespaceManager nsm)
```

Interestingly enough, however, if you use this overload of the *SelectNodes* method that handles namespace information, the XPath expression is first compiled and then passed to the processor.

As we'll see in the section "Compiling Expressions," on page 274, only compiled XPath expressions support namespace information. In particular, they get namespace information through an instance of the *XmlNamespaceManager* class.

The *SelectSingleNode* Internal Implementation

The *SelectSingleNode* method is really a special case of *SelectNodes*. Unfortunately, there is no performance advantage in using *SelectSingleNode* in lieu of *SelectNodes*. The following pseudocode illustrates the current implementation of the *SelectSingleNode* method:

```
public XmlNode SelectSingleNode(string xpathExpr)
{
    XmlNodeList nodes = SelectNodes(xpathExpr);
    return nodes[0];
}
```

The *SelectSingleNode* method internally calls *SelectNodes* and retrieves all the nodes that match a given XPath expression. Next it simply returns the first selected node to the caller. Using *SelectSingleNode* perhaps results in a more easily readable code, but doing so certainly does not improve the performance of the application when you need just one node.

In the next section, we'll build a sample Microsoft Windows Forms application to start practicing with XPath expressions, thus turning into concrete programming calls all that theory about the XPath query language.

The Sample XPath Evaluator

The sample XPath Evaluator application is a Windows Forms application that loads an XML document and then performs an XPath query on it. The application's user interface lets you type in both the context node and the query string. Next it creates an XML DOM for the document and calls *SelectNodes*.

The output of the expression is rendered as an XML string rooted in an arbitrary *<results>* node, as shown here:

```
<results>
    ... XML nodes that match ...
</results>
```

The sample application is shown in Figure 6-3. You can find the code listing for this application in this book's sample files.

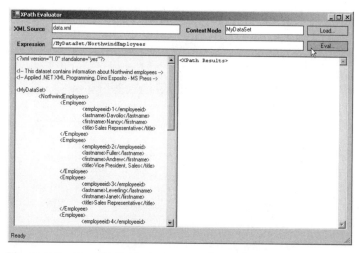

Figure 6-3   The XPath Evaluator sample application in action.

Initializing the Application

When the user clicks the Load button, a *StreamReader* object is used to load the specified XML document and refresh the left text box, which displays the contents of the XPath source document. I used the I/O API to read the document to preserve the newline characters. An alternative approach consists of loading the document into the *XmlDocument* class and then getting the source through the document element's *OuterXml* property. In this case, however, what you get is a string of contiguous characters that does not display well in a fixed-width text box.

Setting the Context Node

As mentioned, the context node is the starting point of the query. The context node is important if you specify a relative expression. In this case, the context node—that is, the *XmlNode* object from which you call *SelectNodes*—determines the full path. The context node is simply ignored if the expression contains an absolute location path, in which case, the path must start from the XML root node.

The sample application first initializes the XML DOM and then sets the context node by calling *SelectSingleNode* on the document object. For the sake of generality, this application's user interface accepts a reference to the context node using an XPath expression, as shown here:

```
XmlDocument doc = new XmlDocument();
doc.Load(xmlFile);
XmlNode cxtNode = doc.SelectSingleNode(ContextNode.Text);
```

In a real-world situation, you normally know what the context node is (typically, the XML document root) and can locate it more efficiently using the *ChildNodes* collection. For example, the following code shows how to set the context node to the document's root:

```
XmlNode cxtNode = doc.DocumentElement;
XmlNodeList nodes = cxtNode.SelectNodes(xpathExpr);
```

Performing the XPath Query

After you type the XPath expression, you click the Eval button to run the query. Note that the node names in an XPath expression are case-sensitive and must perfectly match the names in the original source document.

After the processor has processed the node list, the output string is built by calling the *BuildOutputString* method and then displayed in the form's results panel via the *ShowResults* method, as shown here:

```
string buf = "";
int nodeCount = 0;
XmlNodeList nodes = null;
try {
   nodes = cxtNode.SelectNodes(xpathExpr);
   nodeCount = nodes.Count;
} catch {}
if (nodes == null || nodeCount <= 0)
   buf = "<results>No nodes selected</results>";
else
   buf = BuildOutputString(nodes);
ShowResults(buf, nodeCount);
```

The results of the XPath query are rendered as an XML document. The root node is **, which contains the outer XML code of each node found.

Post-Processing the Node-Set

Post-processing the output of an XPath query is a relatively common task if you have to transfer the results to a different process or machine. In similar situations, you don't have formatting concerns and can quickly arrange a final XML document, as follows:

```
StringBuilder sb = new StringBuilder("<results>");
foreach(XmlNode n in nodes)
    sb.Append(n.OuterXml);
sb.Append("</results>");
return sb.ToString();
```

Our sample application intentionally follows a more sophisticated approach to display formatted output in the text box. In addition, this code turns out to be a useful exercise for understanding the logic of XML writers.

If you want to generate XML output in the .NET Framework, unless the text is short and straightforward, you have no good reason for not using XML writers. Using XML writers also provides automatic and free indentation. Don't think that choosing an XML writer ties you to using a specific output stream. As the following code demonstrates, the output of an XML writer can be easily redirected to a string:

```
string BuildOutputString(XmlNodeList nodes)
{
    // Create a string writer to hold the XML text. For efficiency,
    // the string writer is based on a StringBuilder object.
    StringBuilder sb = new StringBuilder("");
    StringWriter sw = new StringWriter(sb);

    // Instantiate the XML writer
    XmlTextWriter writer = new XmlTextWriter(sw);
    writer.Formatting = Formatting.Indented;

    // Write the first element (No WriteStartDocument call is needed)
    writer.WriteStartElement("results");

    // Loop through the children of each selected node and
    // recursively output attributes and text
    foreach(XmlNode n in nodes)
        LoopThroughChildren(writer, n);
```

```
// Complete pending nodes and then close the writer
writer.WriteEndElement();
writer.Close();

// Flush the contents accumulated in the string writer
return sw.ToString();
}
```

Let's see what happens when we process the following XML document:

```
<MyDataSet>
   <NorthwindEmployees>
     <Employee>
        <employeeid>1</employeeid>
        <lastname>Davolio</lastname>
        <firstname>Nancy</firstname>
        <title>Sales Representative</title>
     </Employee>
        ⋮
   </NorthwindEmployees>
</MyDataSet>
```

This document is the same XML representation of the Northwind's Employees database that we used in previous chapters. To see the application in action, let's set *MyDataSet* (the root) as the context node and try the following expression:

```
NorthwindEmployees/Employee[employeeid > 7]
```

The XPath query has two steps. The first step restricts the search to all the *<NorthwindEmployees>* nodes in the source document. In this case, there is only one node with that name. The second step moves the search one level down and then focuses on the *<Employee>* nodes that are children of the current *<NorthwindEmployees>* context node. The predicate *[employeeid > 7]* includes in the final result only the *<Employee>* nodes with a child *<employeeid>* element greater than 7. The following XML output is what XPath Evaluator returns:

```
<results>
  <Employee>
     <employeeid>8</employeeid>
     <lastname>Callahan</lastname>
     <firstname>Laura</firstname>
     <title>Inside Sales Coordinator</title>
  </Employee>
```

(continued)

```
<Employee>
    <employeeid>9</employeeid>
    <lastname>Dodsworth</lastname>
    <firstname>Anne</firstname>
    <title>Sales Representative</title>
</Employee>
</results>
```

Figure 6-4 shows the user interface of XPath Evaluator when it is set to work on our sample document and expression.

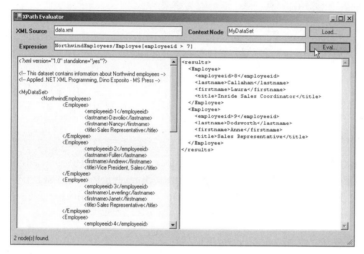

Figure 6-4   The node set returned by XPath Evaluator.

> **Note**   The preceding expression is an abbreviated form that could have been more precisely expressed as follows:
>
> ```
> NorthwindEmployees/Employee/self::*[child::employeeid > 7]
> ```
>
> You apply the predicate to the context node in person (*self*) and verify that the *employeeid* node on its children has a value greater than 7.

The contents of the final node-set is determined by the node that appears in the last step of the XPath expression. Predicates allow you to perform a sort of forward checking—that is, selecting nodes at a certain level but based on the values of child nodes. The expression *NorthwindEmployees/Employee[employeeid > 7]* is different from this one:

```
NorthwindEmployees/Employee/employeeid[node() > 7]
```

In this case, the node set consists of *<employeeid>* nodes, as shown here:

```
<results>
   <employeeid>8</employeeid>
   <employeeid>9</employeeid>
</results>
```

Concatenating Multiple Predicates

An XPath expression can contain any number of predicates. If no predicate is specified, *child::** is assumed, and all the children are returned. Otherwise, the conditions set with the various predicates are logically concatenated using a short-circuited *AND* operator.

Predicates are processed in the order in which they appear, and the next predicate always works on the node-set generated by the previous one, as shown here:

```
Employee[contains(title, 'Representative')][employeeid >7]
```

This example set first selects all the *<Employee>* nodes whose *<title>* child node contains the word *Representative*. Next the returned set is further filtered by discarding all the nodes with an *<employeeid>* not greater than 7.

Accessing the Selected Nodes

The *SelectNodes* method returns the XPath node set through an *XmlNodeList* data structure—that is, a list of references to *XmlNode* objects. If you need simply to pass on this information to another application module, you can serialize the list to XML using a plain *for-each* statement and the *XmlNode* class's *OuterXml* property.

Suppose, instead, that you want to access and process all the nodes in the result set. In this case, you set up a recursive procedure, like the following *LoopThroughChildren* routine, and start it up with a *for-each* statement that touches on the first-level nodes in the XPath node-set:

```
foreach(XmlNode n in nodes)
     LoopThroughChildren(writer, n);
```

The following procedure is designed to output the node contents to an XML writer, but you can easily modify the procedure to meet your own needs.

```
void LoopThroughChildren(XmlTextWriter writer, XmlNode rootNode)
{
    // Process the start tag
    if (rootNode.NodeType == XmlNodeType.Element)
    {
        writer.WriteStartElement(rootNode.Name);

        // Process any attributes
        foreach(XmlAttribute a in rootNode.Attributes)
            writer.WriteAttributeString(a.Name, a.Value);

        // Recursively process any child nodes
        foreach(XmlNode n in rootNode.ChildNodes)
            LoopThroughChildren(writer, n);

        // Process the end tag
        writer.WriteEndElement();
    }
    else
        // Process any content text
        if (rootNode.NodeType == XmlNodeType.Text)
            writer.WriteString(rootNode.Value);
}
```

This version of the *LoopThroughChildren* routine is an adaptation of the routine we analyzed in Chapter 5.

A Better Way to Select a Single Node

In the section "The *SelectSingleNode* Internal Implementation," on page 255, I pointed out that *SelectSingleNode* is not as efficient as its signature and description might suggest. This XML DOM method is expected to perform an XPath query and then return only the first node. You might think that the method works smartly, returning to the caller as soon as the first node has been found.

Unfortunately, that isn't what happens. *SelectSingleNode* internally calls *SelectNodes*, downloads all the nodes (potentially a large number), and then returns only the first node to the caller. The inefficiency of this implementation lies in the fact that a significant memory footprint might be required, albeit for a very short time.

So in situations in which you need to perform an XPath query to get only a subset of the final node-set (for example, exactly one node), you can use a smarter XPath expression. The basic idea is that you avoid generic wildcard expressions like the following:

```
doc.SelectSingleNode("NorthwindEmployees/Employee");
```

Instead, place a stronger filter on the XPath expression so that it returns just the subset you want. For example, to get only the first node, use the following query:

```
doc.SelectSingleNode("NorthwindEmployees/Employee[position() = 1");
```

The same pattern can be applied to get a matching node in a particular position. For example, if you need to get the *n*th matching node, use the following expression:

```
doc.SelectSingleNode("NorthwindEmployees/Employee[position() < n+1");
```

Using such XPath expressions with *SelectSingleNode* does not change the internal implementation of the method, but those expressions require downloading a smaller subset of nodes prior to returning the first matching node to the caller.

The same XPath expression, if used with *SelectNodes*, returns a subset of the first *n* matching nodes:

```
doc.SelectNodes("NorthwindEmployees/Employee[position() < n+1");
```

The .NET XPath Navigation API

The XML DOM support for XPath expressions has a double goal. First, it smooths the transition from MSXML COM code to the .NET Framework. Second, it gives you a built-in and easy-to-use mechanism to search for nodes in a memory-mapped XML document. As mentioned, the core .NET API for processing XPath expressions is built into a tailor-made class named *XPathNavigator*.

You access the navigator object either from the *XmlDocument* class or from the newest *XPathDocument* class. Figure 6-5 illustrates the relationship between the two ways of accessing XPath functions in the .NET Framework.

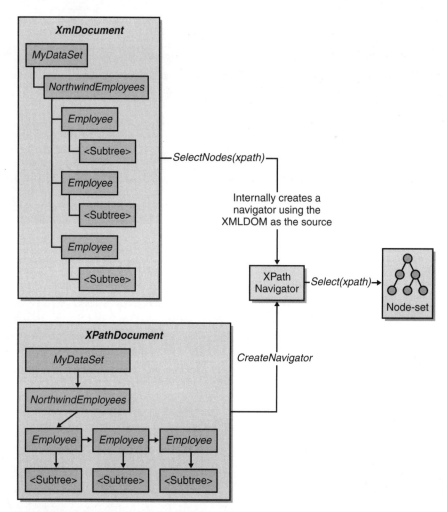

Figure 6-5 Applications can access XPath through either *XmlDocument* or *XPathDocument*. In both cases, the actual query is performed by a .NET XPath navigator object.

As you can see, the *XmlDocument* and *XPathDocument* classes have different internal layouts. *XmlDocument* implements XML DOM, whereas *XPathDocument* provides a more agile and compact structure, designed to speed XPath-driven navigation. (Later in this chapter, in the section "The *XPathDocument* Class," on page 281, I'll have more to say about this.)

No matter the application-level API, the sequence of steps necessary to execute XPath queries on an XML data source is always the same:

1. Get a reference to an XPath-enabled document class (for example, an instance of an *XPathDocument* or *XmlDocument* class).

2. Create a navigator object for the class instance.

3. Optionally, precompile the XPath expression.

4. Call the *Select* method on the navigator object to act on the specified XPath expression.

The *XPathNavigator* Class

The programming interface of the navigator object is defined in the *XPathNavigator* abstract class. The *XPathNavigator* class represents a generic interface designed to act as a reader for any data that exposes its contents as XML.

Functionally speaking, the *XPathNavigator* class is not much different from a pseudo-class that simply groups together all the XML DOM methods (*ChildNodes*, *SelectNodes*, and *SelectSingleNode*) to navigate the document contents. The big difference lies in the fact that *XPathNavigator* is a distinct component completely decoupled from the document class. As mentioned, *XPathNavigator* represents a generic interface to navigate and read data from any XML-based, or XML-looking, contents.

The *XPathNavigator* class enables you to move from one node to the next and perform XPath queries. In the .NET Framework, only three classes support XPath navigators: *XmlDocument*, *XPathDocument*, and *XmlDataDocument*.

An XPath navigator works on top of a special breed of XML document class that is generically referred to as an *XPath data store*. An XPath data store is simply any .NET Framework class that exposes its contents as XML and that can be queried using XPath expressions. An XPath data store can be based on a native XML stream or other data sources exposed as XML. For example, both the *XmlDocument* and *XPathDocument* classes are built from well-formed XML data. In contrast, the *XmlDataDocument* class exposes as XML the contents of an ADO.NET *DataSet* object. In all cases, however, the XPath query and navigation API works just fine.

As a stand-alone class providing a programming interface, the navigator is much more than a simple collection of XPath-related methods. The XPath navigator is not bound to a particular class document and can be associated with a number of data container classes.

A .NET Framework class becomes XPath-enabled simply by implementing the *IXPathNavigable* interface. This interface consists of a single method, *CreateNavigator*, that creates and returns an instance of a document-specific navigator object, as shown here:

```
public interface IXPathNavigable
{
    XPathNavigator CreateNavigator();
}
```

All document-specific navigators derive from the *XPathNavigator* abstract class.

XPath Navigators and XML Readers

The MSDN documentation defines an XPath navigator as a class that reads data from an XML-based data store using a cursor model. *XPathNavigator*, therefore, provides read-only, random access to the underlying XML-based data. The navigator has a notion of the current node and advances the internal pointer using a series of move methods. When the navigator is positioned on a given node, all of its properties reflect the value of that node. How is this different from the XML readers that we encountered in Chapter 2?

XPath navigators and XML readers are radically different objects, although both look like client-side cursors for reading XML data. Let's review the key differences:

- **Connection model**   Both readers and navigators work on top of a data source. Readers, however, work connected to the input stream, which is often a persistent storage medium like a disk file. Navigators always work on memory-mapped data sources like XML DOM or more optimized and specialized structures. Readers must be closed when you have finished with them; navigators are simply garbage-collected when they go out of scope. A parallel can be drawn with ADO.NET data readers and *DataSet* objects. An XML data reader object, like the *SqlDataReader* base class, is connected to the data source, whereas a *DataSet* object is a disconnected object.

- **Navigation interface**   Readers are simple read-only and forward-only cursors. Navigators too are read-only, but they let you move forward and backward. The navigator's set of move methods is significantly richer. In particular, the set includes methods for going to the root of the underlying document, for reaching the parent node, for reaching the next and the previous sibling, for reaching the node where the given namespace is defined, and even more. In addition, you can synchronize the navigator position with the current position on another navigator object.

■   **Programming interface**   Navigators provide rich XPath capabilities and supply methods that perform XPath queries and return groups of related nodes. You have a generic *Select* method but also ad hoc selection methods that specialize on the most common XPath axes, such as *descendant*, *ancestor*, and *child*. In addition, navigators can simply evaluate an XPath expression and return the value.

Conceptually, XPath navigators and XML readers occupy diametrically opposed positions in the .NET XML puzzle. Moreover, this difference clearly stems from their names. Navigators are thought to traverse XML-based or XML-looking data. XML readers are simply lower-level tools that you can use to read XML-based or XML-looking data and build in-memory data structures that navigators rely on.

> **Note**   As mentioned, XML readers and navigators work on XML-based or XML-looking data. *XML-based data* refers to data persisted, or just read, as well-formed XML. As we saw in Chapter 2, however, you can use specialized reader classes to publish non-XML data through a virtual XML tree. Likewise, a navigator can be built to work on top of a data store that creates a virtual XML tree from non-XML data. *XML-looking data* refers to just such virtual XML trees.

The *XPathNavigator* Programming Interface

Let's briefly review the properties and methods that form the programming interface of the *XPathNavigator* class. A valid instance of the class can be obtained by calling the *CreateNavigator* method on any .NET Framework class that implements the *IXPathNavigable* interface.

Properties of the *XPathNavigator* Class

Table 6-3 summarizes the properties of the *XPathNavigator* class. As you can see, most of these properties reflect the characteristics of the currently selected node.

Table 6-3   Properties of the *XPathNavigator* Class

Property	Description
BaseURI	Gets the base URI of the current node
HasAttributes	Indicates whether the current node has any attributes
HasChildren	Indicates whether the current node has any child nodes
IsEmptyElement	Indicates whether the current node is empty (for example, *<node />*)
LocalName	Gets the name of the current node without the namespace prefix
Name	Gets the fully qualified name of the current node
NamespaceURI	Gets the URI of the namespace associated with the current node
NameTable	Gets the name table associated with the navigator
NodeType	Gets the type of the current node
Prefix	Gets the namespace prefix associated with the current node
Value	Returns a string denoting the value of the current node
XmlLang	Gets the *xml:lang* scope for the current node

Like XML readers and XML DOM documents, an XPath navigator employs a name table to more efficiently store strings. The set of properties looks like the subset of properties that in the *XmlTextReader* class characterizes the current node.

Methods of the *XPathNavigator* Class

The tables in this section group the methods available in the *XPathNavigator* class into three main categories: move methods, selection methods, and miscellaneous methods. Table 6-4 lists the move methods.

Table 6-4   *XPathNavigator* Move Methods

Method	Description
MoveTo	Moves to the same position as the specified *XPathNavigator* object.
MoveToAttribute	Moves to the specified attribute of the current node.
MoveToFirst	Moves to the first sibling of the current node.

Table 6-4 *XPathNavigator* **Move Methods**

Method	Description
MoveToFirstAttribute	Moves to the first attribute of the current node.
MoveToFirstChild	Moves to the first child of the current node.
MoveToFirstNamespace	Moves to the first namespace in the current element node.
MoveToId	Moves to the node with an attribute of type ID whose value matches the given string.
MoveToNamespace	Moves to the namespace node with the specified prefix in the current element node. A namespace node is seen as an attribute node with the *xmlns* name. The real name of the namespace node is the prefix.
MoveToNext	Moves to the next sibling of the current node.
MoveToNextAttribute	Moves to the next attribute of the current node.
MoveToNextNamespace	Moves to the next namespace in the current element node.
MoveToParent	Moves to the parent of the current node.
MoveToPrevious	Moves to the previous sibling of the current node.
MoveToRoot	Moves to the root node of the document.

The *MoveTo* method attempts to synchronize the current instance of the *XPathNavigator* object with another instance. *MoveTo* returns *true* or *false* depending on the success or failure of the operation. Note that the synchronization always fails if the two navigators are actually implemented through different and incompatible classes. Two navigators have different implementations if the other navigator can't be cast to the current type.

Consider the following pseudocode:

```
public bool MoveTo(XPathNavigator other)
{
   InternalXPathNavigator nav = other as InternalXPathNavigator;
   if (nav == null)
     return false;
   ⋮
}
```

In C#, the *as* operator behaves like a cast except that, when the conversion fails, it returns *null* rather than raising an exception. In the preceding pseudocode, the *InternalXPathNavigator* class represents the actual (and internal) navigator class you got from the document's *CreateNavigator* method. Each XPath-enabled document class actually instantiates a custom navigator class and returns that class when you call its *CreateNavigator* method.

The *MoveTo* method also might fail when the two navigators share the same implementation but point to different document instances. What happens in this case, however, depends on the specific implementation. In particular, *MoveTo* fails when the document class is *XmlDocument* or *XmlDataDocument*, but not when the underlying data object is an instance of *XPathDocument*.

Namespace Node Navigation

As you might have noticed in Table 6-4, there are three types of move methods: for element, attribute, and namespace nodes. Calling the wrong method on a node causes the whole operation to fail, and there is no change in the position of the navigator. Only *MoveTo* and *MoveToRoot* can be called on any node, irrespective of the type. In addition, attributes and namespaces also have ad hoc methods to return their values: *GetAttribute* and *GetNamespace*.

When you call either *MoveToFirstNamespace* or *MoveToNextNamespace*, you can specify an argument of type *XPathNamespaceScope*. The *XPathNamespaceScope* enumeration has three values: *All*, *ExcludeXML*, and *Local*. *All* returns all namespaces defined in the scope of the current node, including *xmlns:xml*, which is always declared implicitly. *ExcludeXml* returns all namespaces defined in the scope of the current node, excluding *xmlns:xml*. *Local* returns all namespaces that are defined locally at the current node. Whatever value you specify, the order of the namespaces returned is not defined.A namespace node is a special type of attribute node. When selected, the navigator's *Name* property returns the namespace prefix. The *Value* property, on the other hand, returns the URI.

Table 6-5 lists the *XPathNavigator* class's methods for selecting nodes through XPath queries.

Table 6-5 *XPathNavigator'* **Selection Methods**

Method	Description
Select	Returns the node-set selected by the specified XPath expression. The context for the selection is the position of the navigator when the method is called. The XPath expression can be passed in as plain text or in a compiled form.
SelectAncestors	Selects all the ancestor element nodes of the current node. You can narrow the returned node-set by specifying a node name and a namespace URI to match.
SelectChildren	Selects all the child nodes of the current node. You can narrow the node-set by specifying a node name and a namespace URI to match. Attributes and namespace nodes are not included.
SelectDescendants	Selects all the descendant nodes of the current node. You can narrow the node-set by specifying a node name and a namespace URI to match. Attributes and namespace nodes are not included.

None of these methods produces any effect on the state of the *XPathNavigator* object. The following code snippet demonstrates how to select the descendants of a node. The code to get the ancestors is nearly identical.

```
// Create the underlying XPath-enabled document object
XPathDocument doc = new XPathDocument(fileName);

// Create the navigator for the specified object
XPathNavigator nav = doc.CreateNavigator();

// Select the descendants of the current node that match
// the specified criteria
nav.SelectDescendants(nodeName, nsUri, selfIncluded);
```

SelectDescendants, as well as *SelectAncestors*, has the following two overloads. The former takes a node type and returns only the nodes of that type, if any. The latter takes a node name and a namespace URI.

```
XPathNodeIterator SelectDescendants(XPathNodeType, bool);
XPathNodeIterator SelectDescendants(string, string, bool);
```

If you pass both the node name and the namespace URI as empty strings, all descendant nodes with no namespace information are selected. This method, and the homologous *SelectAncestors* and *SelectChildren* methods, is a specialized query performed along the corresponding XPath axis.

The Boolean argument you specify in the method signatures indicates whether the context node must be included in the final node-set. Setting the argument to *true* is equivalent to working along the *descendant-or-self* axis.

> **Important** As you might have noticed, all selection methods return a new type of object—the *XPathNodeIterator* class. This class will be covered in detail in the section "The *XPathNodeIterator* Class," on page 285. For now, suffice to say that an XPath iterator provides a generic way to visit a set of selected nodes. From this point of view, an iterator is not much different from an enumerator—just a bit more specialized.

Table 6-6 lists the remaining *XPathNavigator* methods.

Table 6-6 *XPathNavigator* **Miscellaneous Methods**

Method	Description
Clone	Clones the navigator and returns a new object with the same current node.
ComparePosition	Compares the position of the current navigator with the position of the specified *XPathNavigator* object.
Compile	Compiles an XPath expression.
Evaluate	Evaluates the given XPath expression and returns the result.
GetAttribute	Gets the value of the specified attribute, if such an attribute exists on the current node.
GetNamespace	Gets the URI of the specified namespace prefix, if such a namespace exists on the current node.
IsDescendant	Indicates whether the specified navigator is a descendant of the current navigator. A navigator is a descendant of another navigator if it is positioned in a descendant node.
IsSamePosition	Indicates whether the current navigator is at the same position as the specified navigator.
Matches	Determines whether the current node matches the specified XPath expression.

As you can see, several methods have to do with XPath expressions that are often rendered as instances of the *XPathExpression* class. But why do we need to express an XPath command using a new class?

XPath Expressions in the .NET Framework

An XPath expression is first of all a string that represents a location path, but an XPath expression is a bit more than a plain command string. It has a surrounding context that is just what the .NET Framework *XPathExpression* class encapsulates. The context of an expression includes the return type and the namespace information to handle the involved nodes.

The *XPathExpression* Class

Table 6-7 lists the methods and properties that characterize a .NET Framework XPath expression.

Table 6-7   Properties and Methods of the *XPathExpression* Class

Name	Description
Expression	Property that returns the XPath expression as a string.
ReturnType	Property that returns the computed result type of the expression.
AddSort	Method that sorts the nodes selected by the expression.
Clone	Method that clones the *XPathExpression* object.
SetContext	Method that sets the necessary information to use for resolving nodes namespaces. The information is passed, packed into an object of type *XmlNamespaceManager*.

Looking at the programming interface of the *XPathExpression* class, you'll notice the methods *Clone* and *AddSort*. As its name suggests, *Clone* makes a deep copy of the object, creating a brand-new and identical object. *AddSort*, on the other hand, associates the expression with a sorting algorithm that will be automatically run once the node-set for the expression has been retrieved.

The *XPathExpression* class is not publicly creatable. To get a new instance of this class, you must take a plain XPath string expression and compile it into an *XPathExpression* object.

Compiling Expressions

Both the XML DOM *SelectNodes* method and the navigator object's *Select* method let you execute an XPath query indicating the expression as plain text. In spite of this simplified programming interface, in the .NET Framework, an XPath expression can execute only in its compiled form. This means that both the aforementioned methods silently compile the provided text into an *XPathExpression* before proceeding.

> **Note**   In this context, the term *compile* does not mean that the XPath expression is transformed into an executable (and/or managed) piece of code. More simply, the action of compiling must be literally seen as the process that produces an object by collecting and putting together many pieces of information.

There are several advantages to compiling the expression yourself. For one thing, you can reuse the compiled object over and over. If you repeatedly call an XPath selection method to work on the same expression, each time the method will instantiate the same object. If you have a compiled expression, you save a few operations.

In addition, a compiled expression lets you know in advance about the expected return type. The return type is one of the values defined in the *XPathResultType* enumeration, shown in Table 6-8.

Table 6-8   XPath Return Types

Type	Description
Any	Represents any of the XPath node types
Boolean	Represents a Boolean value
Error	When returned, the expression does not evaluate to a correct XPath type
Navigator	Described as a value that returns a tree fragment; in the current version of the .NET Framework, implemented as a synonym of *String*
NodeSet	Represents a collection of nodes
Number	Represents a numeric, floating-point value
String	Represents a string value

The *Boolean, NodeSet, Number,* and *String* types come directly from the W3C specification; the others represent extensions. However, *Any* and *Error* do not introduce any new functionality but simply make more consistent the enumeration type.

If you use a compiled expression, you can add namespace information to process the nodes and define a sorting algorithm for the resultant node-set. All this extra information remains associated with the *XPathExpression* object and can be reused at will.

To compile an expression, you use the *Compile* method of the *XPathNavigator* class. The method takes a string and returns an *XPathExpression* object, as shown here:

```
XPathDocument doc = new XPathDocument(fileName);
XPathNavigator nav = doc.CreateNavigator();
XPathExpression expr = nav.Compile(xpathExpr);

// Output the expected return type
Console.WriteLine(expr.ReturnType.ToString());

// Execute the expression
nav.Select(expr);
```

A compiled XPath expression can be consumed by a few navigator methods, including *Select, Evaluate,* and *Matches*.

> **Important**   Unlike the navigator's *Select* method, the XML DOM *SelectNodes* method can't accept a compiled XPath expression. Internally, the *SelectNodes* method creates an instance of the navigator object that actually compiles the XPath string into an *XPathExpression* object. In this case, however, there is no object reuse.

Setting Namespace Information

The information you can pass through the *SetContext* method helps the XPath processor to resolve any namespace references in the expression. If no prefix appears in the expression, it is assumed that the namespace URI for all nodes is the empty namespace. Otherwise, you must let the processor know about defined prefix and namespace URI mappings.

You create an *XmlNamespaceManager* object, pack it with all the needed information, and then use the *SetContext* method to register it with the XPath expression object, as shown here:

```
// Create the navigator
XPathDocument doc = new XPathDocument(fileName);
XPathNavigator xnm = doc.CreateNavigator();

// Create and populate the XML namespace manager
XmlNamespaceManager xnm = new XmlNamespaceManager(nav.NameTable);
xnm.AddNamespace("dd", "urn:dino-e");
xnm.AddNamespace("es", "http://www.contoso.com");

// Set the expression's context
XPathExpression expr = nav.Compile(xpathExpr);
expr.SetContext(xnm);
```

The .NET XPath processor is designed to look for the namespace manager on the XPath expression object prior to proceeding.

Evaluating Expressions

As mentioned, when evaluated, an XPath expression can return any of four basic types: *node-set*, *Boolean*, *number*, or *string*. If the return type is a *node-set*, you can run the expression through both the *Select* method and the *Evaluate* method.

The *Select* method returns an object of type *XPathNodeIterator* that you can use to walk your way through the members of the node-set. Unlike *Select*, the *Evaluate* method returns a generic *object* type, which it is your responsibility to cast to the correct strong type, as in the following example:

```
XPathNodeIterator iterator = (XPathNodeIterator) nav.Evaluate(expr);
```

Expressions that do not return a node-set can be used only with the *Evaluate* method. In this case, however, you must also cast the returned object to a strong type, as shown here:

```
string buf = (string) nav.Evaluate(expr);
```

The *Evaluate* method has no effect on the state of the navigator. An interesting overload for the method is shown here:

```
public object Evaluate(
   XPathExpression expr,
   XPathNodeIterator context
);
```

Normally, the expression is evaluated using the current node in the navigator as the context node. Using this overload, however, you can control the context node for the expression. If the *context* argument is *null*, the method works as usual. Otherwise, if *context* points to a valid iterator object, the current node in the iterator is used to determine the context node for the XPath expression.

Sorting the Node-Set

An interesting extension to the XPath programming model built into the *XPathExpression* class and the XPath processor is the ability to sort the node-set before it is passed back to the caller. To add a sorting algorithm, call the *AddSort* method of the *XPathExpression* object. *AddSort* allows for two overloads, as follows:

```
public void AddSort(
   object expr,
   IComparer comparer
);
public void AddSort(
   object expr,
   XmlSortOrder order,
   XmlCaseOrder caseOrder,
   string lang,
   XmlDataType dataType
);
```

The *expr* argument denotes the sort key. It can be a string representing a node name or another *XPathExpression* object that evaluates to a node name. In the first overload, the *comparer* argument refers to an instance of a class that implements the *IComparer* interface. The interface supplies a *Compare* method that is actually used for comparing a pair of values. Use this overload if you need to specify a custom algorithm to sort nodes.

Using the *Comparer* Object

To sort arrays of objects, the .NET Framework provides a few predefined comparer classes, including *Comparer* and *CaseInsensitiveComparer*. The former class compares objects (including strings) with respect to the case. The latter class does the same, but irrespective of the case. To use both classes in your code, be sure to import the *System.Collections* namespace.

The *Comparer* class has no public constructor but provides a singleton instance through the *Default* static property, as shown here:

```
expr.AddSort("lastname", Comparer.Default);
```

If you need to create your own comparer class, do as follows:

```
class MyOwnStringComparer : IComparer
{
    public int Compare(object x, object y)
    {
        string strX = (string) x;
        string strY = (string) y;

        // 0 if equals, >0 if x>y, <0 if x<y
        return String.Compare(strX, strY);
    }
}
```

This class can also be defined within the body of your application and does not necessarily require a separate assembly.

The second overload of the *AddSort* method always performs a numeric or text comparison according to the value of the *dataType* argument. In addition, you can specify a sorting order (ascending or descending) and even the sort order for uppercase and lowercase letters. In practice, you can decide whether lowercase letters must come before or after uppercase letters. The constant *XmlCaseOrder.None* simply ignores the case. Finally, the *lang* argument indicates the language to use for comparison—for example, "*us-en*" for U.S. English.

The following code snippet selects all the *<Employee>* nodes from our original sample XML file. This time, we make use of a compiled expression with sorting capabilities.

```
XPathDocument doc = new XPathDocument(fileName);
XPathNavigator nav = doc.CreateNavigator();
XPathExpression expr;
expr = nav.Compile("/MyDataSet/NorthwindEmployees/Employee");
expr.AddSort("lastname",
            XmlSortOrder.Ascending, XmlCaseOrder.None,
            "", XmlDataType.Text);
XPathNodeIterator iterator = nav.Select(expr);
```

The iterator now returns nodes sorted in ascending order on the values stored in the *lastname* child nodes.

Is there a way to sort by multiple fields? As mentioned, the *expr* argument of the *AddSort* method can also be an XPath expression, and by exploiting this feature, you can involve more nodes in the sort process. When sorting database tables, you normally indicate the sortable columns in a comma-separated string. In this case, you must provide a valid XPath expression. The expression will be evaluated to a string and the actual value used to sort nodes. To concatenate the contents of two or more nodes, you must resort to the XPath *concat* core function—the only XPath way to concatenate strings. The following code sorts by *title* and *lastname*. To demonstrate the flexibility of the solution, the node contents are separated with an unnecessary comma.

```
string sortKey = "concat(concat(title, ','), lastname)";
```

Figure 6-6 demonstrates that using the *AddSort* method does change the structure of the final node-set.

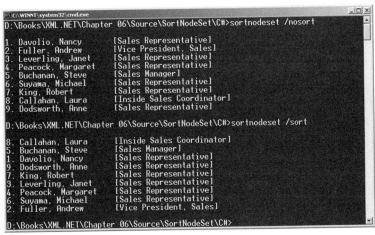

Figure 6-6   The sample application sorts nodes by *title* and *lastname*.

To generate the output shown in this figure, I made use of an XPath iterator to visit all the nodes and their own subtrees. We'll examine this code in detail in the section "Visiting the Selected Nodes," on page 286, but first we'll take a look at the internal layout of the XML document classes the navigator relies on.

XPath Data Stores

As mentioned, an XPath navigator works on top of an ad hoc document class. The .NET Framework provides three XPath-enabled classes: *XmlPathDocument*, *XmlDocument*, and *XmlDataDocument*. These classes have in common the *IXPathNavigable* interface.

In theory, each .NET Framework class can become XPath-enabled. In practice, however, only a subset of classes is a good candidate. In the first place, the class must act as the in-memory repository of some sort of content. Second, this content must be, or must be exposed as, XML. When these two prerequisites are met, classes can reasonably implement the *IXPathNavigable* interface and create their own navigators.

An XPath navigator is always class-specific and is built by inheriting from the abstract class *XPathNavigator*. Although in practice you always use navigators through the generic reference type of *XPathNavigator*, each class has its own navigator object. Table 6-9 lists these internal, undocumented classes; they are programmatically unaccessible, and often each is implemented in a different way. Despite this complexity, however, the classes' application-level programming interface is common and is based on their base class *XPathNavigator*.

Table 6-9   Document-Specific Navigator Classes

Document Class	Corresponding Internal Navigator Class
XPathDocument	*System.Xml.XPath.XPathDocumentNavigator*
XmlDocument	*System.Xml.DocumentXPathNavigator*
XmlDataDocument	*System.Xml.DataDocumentXPathNavigator*

The document-specific navigator exploits the internal layout of the document class to provide the navigation API. A document-specific navigator can also have new methods and properties that make sense to a particular implementation. In this case, however, the navigator's author must carefully document the new features; otherwise, it would be hard for a caller to exploit them through the generic *XPathNavigator* interface.

In the following sections, we'll review the characteristics of the various XPath-enabled document classes.

The *XPathDocument* Class

The *XPathDocument* class provides a highly optimized, read-only in-memory cache for XML documents. Specifically designed to serve as an XPath data container, the class does not provide any information or identity for nodes. *XPathDocument* simply creates an underlying web of node references to let the navigator operate quickly and effectively. *XPathDocument* does not respect any XML DOM specification and has only one method—*CreateNavigator*.

The internal architecture of the *XPathDocument* class looks like a linked list of node references. Nodes are managed through an internal class (*XPathNode*) that represents a small subset of the *XmlNode* class, which is the official XML DOM node class in the .NET Framework. You can access the XML nodes of the document only through the properties exposed by the navigator object. (See Table 6-3.)

The following code shows how to create a new, *XPathDocument*-driven navigator object:

```
XPathDocument doc = new XPathDocument(fileName);
XPathNavigator nav = doc.CreateNavigator();
```

The returned navigator is positioned at the root of the document. The *XPathDocument* class supports only XML-based data sources, and you can initialize it from disk files, streams, text, and XML readers.

> **Tip**   You can also initialize an XPath document using the output returned by the *ExecuteXmlReader* method of the *SqlCommand* ADO.NET class. The method builds and returns an XML reader using the result set of a SQL query, as shown here:
>
> ```
> SqlCommand cmd = new SqlCommand(query, conn);
> XmlTextReader reader = (XmlTextReader) cmd.ExecuteXmlReader();
> XPathDocument doc = new XPathDocument(reader);
> ```

The *XmlDocument* Class

XmlDocument is the class that represents the .NET Framework implementation of the W3C-compliant XML DOM. This aspect of *XmlDocument* was covered in detail in Chapter 5.

Unlike *XPathDocument*, the *XmlDocument* class provides read/write access to the nodes of the underlying XML document. In addition, each node can be individually accessed and sets of nodes can be selected through XPath queries run by the *SelectSingleNode* and *SelectNodes* methods, respectively.

The *XmlDocument* class also enables you to create a navigator object. In this case, however, the navigator will work on a much more rich and complex web of node references. The following code shows how to get the navigator for the *XmlDocument* class:

```
XmlDocument doc = new XmlDocument();
doc.Load(fileName);
XPathNavigator nav = doc.CreateNavigator();
```

In particular, *XmlDocument*'s navigator class extends the interface of the standard navigator by implementing the *IHasXmlNode* interface. This interface defines just one method, *GetNode*, as shown here:

```
public interface IHasXmlNode
{
    XmlNode GetNode();
}
```

Using this method, callers can access and query the currently selected node of the navigator. This feature is simply impossible to implement for navigators based on *XPathDocument* because it exploits the different internal layout of the *XmlDocument* class. By design, the *XPathDocument* class minimizes the memory footprint and does not provide node identity.

If the *GetNode* method is an extension to the *XPathNavigator* base class, how can callers take advantage of it? Here's a code snippet:

```
XmlDocument doc = new XmlDocument();
doc.Load(fileName);
XPathNavigator nav = doc.CreateNavigator();
XmlNode node = ((IHasXmlNode) nav).GetNode();
```

At this point, the caller program has gained full access to the node and can read and update it at will.

> **Note** When created, the *XmlDocument* navigator is not positioned on the root of the document. Instead, it is positioned on the node from which the *CreateNavigator* method was called.

The *XmlDataDocument* Class

The *XmlDataDocument* class is an extension of *XmlDocument* designed to allow the manipulation of a relational *DataSet* object through XML. The class also allows for rendering XML data as a relational *DataSet* object; but this aspect is less important here. (We will return to this topic in Chapter 8.)

The *XmlDataDocument* class provides a *CreateNavigator* method to let callers navigate the XML representation of an ADO.NET *DataSet* object. This is a neat example of the fact that the .NET Framework navigation API can be indifferently applied to XML-based data as well as XML-looking data. Like the *XmlDocument* navigator, the *XmlDataDocument* navigator also is not positioned on the root of the document but is positioned on the node from which the *CreateNavigator* method was called.

Custom Navigator Objects

The .NET Framework navigation API is extensible with navigator objects that work on top of particular XML documents or any other data exposed through a virtual XML node structure. To XPath-enable a given data source, you create a class that inherits from *XPathNavigator*. You can associate this new navigator class with a document class or make it a stand-alone creatable class. The MSDN documentation includes an example class named *FileSystemNavigator*. I extracted it from the documentation and compiled the C# and Microsoft Visual Basic code into an assembly. The assembly is available in this book's sample files.

The file system navigator supports a virtual node structure similar to the following:

```
<root Name="…" CreationTime="…">
   <folder Name="…" CreationTime="…" />
   <folder Name="…" CreationTime="…">
   <file Name="…" CreationTime="…" Length="…" />
   <file Name="…" CreationTime="…" Length="…" />
   ⋮
   </folder>
</root>
```

Notice that the sample file system navigator places all subfolders of the context folder at the same level, thus losing any hierarchical information. The following code snippet shows how the custom navigator can be created and used:

```
XPathNavigator nav = new FileSystemNavigator("c:\\folder");

// Exclude the folder itself but not all the subfolders.
// (If you run this on c:\ a VERY LONG list of nodes is returned...)
```

(continued)

```
XPathNodeIterator it = nav.Select("descendant::*[position() >1]");
while(it.MoveNext())
    Console.WriteLine(it.Current.Name);
```

In this case, the architecture of the sample code makes it significantly harder to execute a query that selects only the children of the context folder. The preceding listing returns all the folders and files below the c:\ folder despite the effective parent folder. The predicate *[position() >1]* skips over the context folder name.

> **Tip**   When you plan to build a navigator for a persistent data source (for example, a database, the file system, or the registry), you can do without a document class. A document class is key when there is no other API to provide the in-memory infrastructure for navigation. In the previous example, the *DirectoryInfo* and *FileInfo* classes provide the core API used by the *FileSystemNavigator* object. In this case, they actually play the role of the XPath document class.

XPath Iterators

When the XPath expression originates a node-set, the navigator object always returns it using a new breed of object—the *node iterator*. The node iterator is a relatively simple object that provides an agile, common interface to navigate an array of nodes. The base class for XPath iterators is *XPathNodeIterator*.

The node iterator does not cache any information about the identity of the nodes involved. It simply works as an indexer on top of the navigator object that operated the XPath query. All the functionalities you might find in the implementation of any *XPathNodeIterator* classes could have been easily packed into the navigator itself. Why then does the .NET Framework provide the navigation and the iteration API as distinct components?

First, decoupling data containers from navigators, and navigators from iterators, represents a good bargain from the software standpoint. The ultimate reason for keeping the navigation and the iteration API distinct, however, is that in this way the results of any XPath query can be easily accessed and processed from different programming environments—XML DOM, XPath, and, last but not least, XSLT.

The *XPathNodeIterator* Class

The *XPathNodeIterator* class has no public constructor and can be created only by the parent navigator object. The iterator provides forward-only access to the nodes selected by XPath query. Callers use the iterator's methods and properties to access all the nodes included in the node-set. Figure 6-7 illustrates the relationship between callers, navigators, and iterators. A caller passes an XPath expression. The navigator executes the command and gets a node-set. The caller then receives an iterator object to access the members of the node-set. *Current*, *Count*, and *MoveNext* are the key members of the iterator's programming interface.

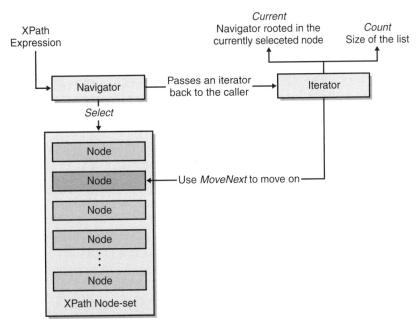

Figure 6-7   The relationship between callers, navigators, and iterators.

Properties of the Iterator Object

Table 6-10 summarizes the properties exposed by the *XPathNodeIterator* class.

Table 6-10   Properties of the *XPathNodeIterator* Class

Property	Description
Count	Returns the number of elements in the node-set. This value refers to the top-level nodes and does not consider child nodes.
Current	Returns a reference to a navigator object rooted in the iterator's current node.
CurrentPosition	Gets the index of the currently selected node.

The *Current* property is the key property for callers to drill down into the structure of the selected node. In the XPath Evaluator sample application we discussed earlier in this chapter, at a certain point we had to examine the subtree of each node included in the node-set. The code in Figure 6-4 uses a recursive routine (named *LoopThroughChildren*) to navigate the subtree of a given node.

The navigator/iterator pair makes that task quite straightforward to accomplish. The *Current* property already returns a reference to the *XPathNavigator* object rooted in the currently selected node. Pay attention to the fact that what you get is not a copy of the navigator but a simple reference. If you need to dig into the node structure, make a deep copy of the navigator first. For the purpose, you can use the navigator's *Clone* method.

Methods of the Iterator Object

Table 6-11 lists the public methods of an iterator object.

Table 6-11   Methods of the *XPathNodeIterator* Class

Method	Description
Clone	Makes a deep copy of the current *XPathNodeIterator* object
MoveNext	Moves to the next node in the navigator's selected node-set

When *MoveNext* is called, the iterator adjusts some internal pointers and refreshes its *Current* and *CurrentPosition* properties. When the iterator is first returned to the caller, there is no currently selected node. Only after the first call to *MoveNext* does the *Current* property point to a valid navigator object.

Visiting the Selected Nodes

Let's review the typical way in which an XPath iterator works. Suppose that you just executed an XPath command using an *XPathNavigator* object, as shown here:

```
XPathDocument doc = new XPathDocument(fileName);
XPathNavigator nav = doc.CreateNavigator();
XPathNodeIterator iterator = nav.Select(expr);
```

To visit all the selected nodes, you set up a loop controlled by the iterator's *MoveNext* method, as follows:

```
while (iterator.MoveNext())
{
    XPathNavigator nav2 = iterator.Current.Clone();
    ⋮
}
```

In real-world applications, you need to drill down into the subtree of each node referenced in the XPath node-set. You should not use the navigator returned by the *Current* property to move away from the node-set. Instead, you should clone the object and use the cloned navigator to perform any additional moves. The following code snippet generates the output shown in Figure 6-6:

```
while (iterator.MoveNext())
{
    XPathNavigator _copy = iterator.Current.Clone();
    string buf = "";

    // Select the <employeeid> node and read the current value
    _copy.MoveToFirstChild();
    buf += _copy.Value + ". ";

    // Select the <lastname> node and read the current value
    _copy.MoveToNext();
    buf += _copy.Value;

    // Select the <firstname> node and read the current value
    _copy.MoveToNext();
    buf += ", " + _copy.Value;

    // Select the <title> node and read the current value
    _copy.MoveToNext();
    buf += "   \t[" + _copy.Value + "]";

    // Write out the final result
    Console.WriteLine(buf);
}
```

Of course, the cloned and the original *XPathNavigator* objects are totally distinct and independent objects, and the clone is not affected by any subsequent changes made to the original navigator.

Conclusion

On the long road to standardization, XPath seems like the first significant step toward a universal query language to keep up with the universal protocol (HTTP), the universal data description language (XML), and the universal remote procedure call protocol (SOAP).

With XPath, you gain the ability to identify and process a group of related nodes from an XML-driven data source. This ability can be exploited by a number of different client environments. XML DOM classes, for example, can use XPath for in-memory data retrieval. XPath is also great for querying XML representations of relational data held both in disconnected structures (such as *XmlDataDocument*) and in more traditional APIs like XML Extensions for SQL Server 2000. (See Chapter 10.)

XSLT is another programming environment that successfully leverages XPath. XSLT is particularly powerful when it comes to applying code templates to XML subtrees. XPath supplies the underlying means to identify those nodes declaratively. *XPathNavigator* supports XSLT and can be used as an input mechanism to the *XslTransform* class. We'll look at XSLT in more detail in Chapter 7.

This chapter presented two high-level APIs to evaluate XPath expressions: the XML DOM–based API and the newest, .NET Framework–specific navigation API. As we've seen, under the hood, the two APIs make use of the same core code. What's new with XPath in the .NET Framework is the concept of the navigator object, especially in conjunction with the iterator object.

The navigator is a self-contained API used to navigate an XML-based, or XML-looking, data source. The iterator is a child object that comes in handy for accessing the results of XPath queries run by the navigator. All the underlying data structures are extremely optimized and compact. So if you're looking for efficiency, run your XPath queries using the navigation API.

Further Reading

The official XPath specification is available at *http://www.w3.org/TR/xpath*. This chapter also mentioned XPointer and XInclude as XPath-related technologies. You can find their current W3C status and most recent specifications at *http://www.w3.org/TR/xptr* and *http://www.w3.org/TR/xinclude*.

Like many other XML-related technologies, XPath is well covered in different forms in *Essential XML Quick Reference,* written by Aaron Skonnard and Martin Gudgin (Addison-Wesley, 2001) and mentioned in previous chapters. For even quicker and more compact references, check out the "The XML Files," a monthly column in *MSDN Magazine,* at *http://msdn.microsoft.com/msdnmag.* Finally, the following URL points you to a recent and useful article about XPath and namespaces: *http://msdn.microsoft.com/library/en-us/dnexxml/html/ xml05202002.asp.*

7

XML Data Transformation

XML was first introduced as a metalanguage for data description. Why is it a *metalanguage* and not just a language? In general, the prefix *meta* indicates an evolutionary transformation process. A metalanguage represents a well-defined interface that evolves and is transformed into derived languages. XML is simply the foundation interface for a number of specific markup languages, each of which is based on its own vocabulary and schema.

The schema syntactically differentiates XML languages from each other. XML is key for data exchange and interoperability, and the schema is essential for providing XML documents with a typed and well-defined structure. Unfortunately, in the imperfect world in which we live, schemas often express the same semantics through different syntaxes.

An XML transformation is simply the XML workaround for this relatively common situation. An XML transformation is a user-defined algorithm that attempts to express the semantics of a given document using another equivalent syntax. A transformation is much like a type cast in programming. You can always try to coerce the type, but in doing so you could face and accept compromises like syntax adaptations and, sometimes, loss of data and logic.

In XML, the transformation process is seen as the application of a style sheet to the source document. The style sheet is a declarative and user-defined document that is referred to as *extensible*. The term *Extensible Stylesheet Language* (XSL) indicates a metalanguage designed for expressing style sheets for XML documents. An XSL file contains the set of rules that will be used to transform a document into another, possibly equivalent, document.

XSL files were originally conceived as the XML counterpart of HTML's *cascading style sheets* (CSS). In this context, XSL files were simply extensible and user-definable tools to render an XML markup in HTML for display purposes. The growing complexity of style sheets, as well as the advent of XML schemas, changed the perspective of XSL and led to XSL Transformations (XSLT).

What Is XSLT, Anyway?

The goal of XSL has evolved over time. Today, XSL is a blanket term for a number of derived technologies that altogether better qualify and implement the original idea of styling XML documents. The various components that fall under the umbrella of XSL are the actual software entities that you use in your code:

- **XSLT**   Rule-based language for transforming XML documents into any other text-based format. XSLT provides for XML-to-XML transformation, which mostly means schema transformation. An XSLT program is a generic set of transformation rules whose output can be any text-based language, including HTML, Rich Text Format (RTF), and Wireless Markup Language (WML), to name just a few.

- **XPath**   Query language that XSLT programs use to select specific parts of an XML document. The result of XPath expressions is then parsed and elaborated by the XSLT processor. Normally, the XSLT processor works sequentially on the source document, but it resorts to XPath if it needs to access and refer to particular groups of nodes. XPath was covered in Chapter 6.

- **XSL Formatting Objects (XSL-FO)**   Advanced styling features expressed by an XML vocabulary that define the semantics of a set of formatting elements. Most of these formatting objects are borrowed from CSS, Level 2 (CSS2) properties, but others have been added. (See the section "Further Reading," on page 343, for more information.)

XSL and XSLT are not the same thing. XSL still refers to the page styling, of which XML transformations to arbitrary text are just one aspect, albeit the most important aspect. This chapter will accentuate the Microsoft .NET Framework implementation of XSLT. Before going any further with the .NET Framework core classes for data transformation, let's briefly recap the main concepts of XSLT and the programming tools it provides to developers.

XSLT Template Programming

XSLT is a process that combines two XML documents—the XML source file and the style sheet—to produce a third document. The resultant document can be an XML document, an HTML page, or any text-based file the style sheet has been instructed to generate.

The source document must meet only one requirement: it must be a well-formed XML document. The style sheet must be a valid XML document that contains the transformation logic expressed using the elements in the XSLT vocabulary. An XSLT style sheet can be seen as a sequence of *templates*. Each template takes one or more source elements as input and returns some output text based on literals as well as transformed input data. Figure 7-1 illustrates the transformation process.

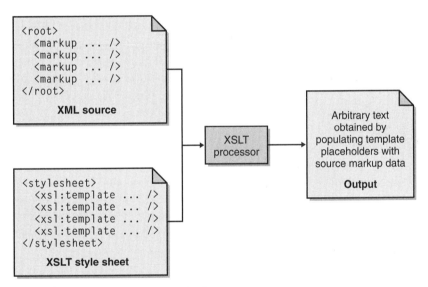

Figure 7-1   An overview of the XSLT process.

The core part of the transformation process is the application of templates to XML source elements. Other ancillary steps might include the expansion of elements to text, the execution of some script code, and the selection of a subset of nodes using XPath queries. The layout of a generic XSLT script is shown here:

```
<xsl:stylesheet xmlns:xsl="http://www.w3.org/1999/xsl/transform">
  <xsl:template match="/">
  ⋮
  </xsl:template>
```

(continued)

```
<xsl:template match="...">
   ⋮
</xsl:template>
   ⋮
</xsl:stylesheet>
```

The root node of an XSLT script is *<stylesheet>*. The *<stylesheet>* node belongs to the official W3C namespace for XSLT 1.0. (Note that the .NET Framework supports only XSLT 1.0, but the W3C committees are currently working on a draft of XSLT 1.1.) Below the *<stylesheet>* node are a variety of *<template>* nodes, each of which contains a *match* attribute. The *match* attribute contains a valid XPath expression that selects the source node (or nodes) that will be used to fill the template.

The template consists of some output literal text interspersed with XSLT placeholder tags. At compile time, the XSLT processor reads source data for any matching nodes and dynamically populates all the placeholders. The source markup text is poured into the template in various forms according to the particular XSLT instruction used. Text or attribute values can be copied or preprocessed using script code or extension objects. In addition, you can apply some basic flow constructs such as *if*, *when*, and *for-each* as well as process nodes in a particular order or filtered by an ad hoc XPath expression.

The final output of each template must form a syntactically valid fragment in the target language—be it XML, HTML, RTF, or some other language. You are not required to indicate the target language explicitly, although the XSLT vocabulary provides a tailor-made instruction to declare what the expected output will be. The main requirement for the XSLT style sheet is that its overall text be well-formed XML. In addition, it must make syntactically correct use of all the XSLT instructions it needs. The syntax of each embedded XSLT command, therefore, is validated against the official XSLT schema.

Although an XSLT style sheet is not necessarily composed of explicitly declared templates, in many real-world cases, it is. In other situations, you can have an XSLT style sheet that consists of plain XSLT instructions not grouped as individually callable templates.

A template to the XSLT language is much like a function to other high-level programming languages. You can group more instructions under a function or a method, but you can also embed in the source program instructions to run sequentially.

In the body of an XSLT style sheet, a template is always defined with inline code, but it can be configured, and subsequently invoked, in two ways: it can have implicit or explicit arguments. With implicit arguments, you use the *match* attribute to select the nodes for the template to process. In this case, you *apply* the template to the matching nodes.

With explicit arguments, you give the template a name and optionally some arguments and let other templates call it explicitly. Like a DLL function, the invoked template can try to determine its context by using XPath expressions, or it can work in isolation, using only the passed arguments. In this case, you *call* the template to operate on some arguments. We'll look at some examples of template calls in the section "From XML to HTML," on page 299. In the meantime, Figure 7-2 illustrates the process of applying templates to nodes.

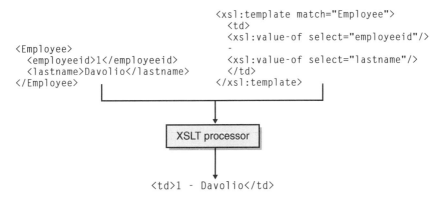

Figure 7-2   Applying an XSLT template to source markup text.

XSLT Instructions

The XSLT vocabulary consists of special tags that represent particular operations you can perform on the source markup text or passed arguments. Although the overall syntax is that of a rigorous XML dialect, you can easily recognize the main constructs of a high-level programming language.

The following subsections summarize the main XSLT instructions you are likely to run across in your XSLT experience. The XSLT instructions are divided into four categories: templates, data manipulation, control flow, and layout.

Template Instructions

An XSLT template is a mixed-content template consisting of verbatim text and expandable placeholders. A template can be applied to a selected group of nodes as well as invoked by other templates with or without arguments. Table 7-1 lists the main commands for working with templates. All of these XSLT elements are qualified with the *xsl* prefix, but bear in mind that *xsl* is just an arbitrary, although common, namespace prefix. Feel free to replace it with another prefix in your own code.

Table 7-1   XSLT Instructions for Templates

Instruction	Description
<xsl:template match="…" | *name="…">*	Defines the transformation rules for the nodes that match the XPath expression set in the *match* attribute. The template must be explicitly applied to its nodes using the *<xsl:apply-templates>* command. The instruction can also be used to declare a template that will then be called by name using the *<xsl:call-template>* command. In this case, use the *name* attribute instead of *match*.
<xsl:apply-template select="…">	Applies all the possible templates to the elements that match the XPath description. The *select* attribute selects the target elements. In general, a single element can be affected by multiple templates.
<xsl:call-template name="…">	Executes the specified template. The *name* attribute indicates the name of the previously declared template to execute.
<xsl:param name="…" select="…"> </xsl:param>	Defines a formal argument for a named template. The *name* attribute indicates the name of the argument. The parameter can have a default argument. You specify a default value using either an XPath expression (via the *select* attribute) or a template as the body of the element.
<xsl:with-param name="…" select="…"> </xsl:with-param>	Defines an actual parameter for a template call. The *name* attribute indicates the matching parameter. The actual value can be expressed using either an XPath expression (via the *select* attribute) or the body of the element.

When you set the *select* attribute, the template (or the parameter) will execute in the context of the selected nodes. Any further XPath expression to locate the text of a particular node or attribute must be based in that context.

Data Manipulation Instructions
The commands listed in Table 7-2 are helpful for extracting data out of source nodes and then preprocessing it using in-place code.

Table 7-2   XSLT Instructions for Data Manipulation

Instruction	Description
<xsl:value-of select="...">	Returns the value of the specified attribute or the text associated with the given node. You select nodes using XPath expressions. Of course, attributes must be prefixed with an at sign (@). This command works more or less as a macro that expands at run time.
<xsl:copy-of select="...">	Returns the entire node-set that corresponds to the results of the specified XPath expression.
<xsl:sort select="..." data-type="..." order="..." case-order="...">	Specifies sort criteria for the node-set being processed by *<xsl:for-each>* or *<xsl:apply-templates>* instructions. In this case, you use the *select* keyword to indicate the sort key and *data-type* for the type of sorting (text or number). The *order* attribute indicates the direction, and *case-order* designates which case comes first in the sort.
<xsl:eval>FuncName() </xsl:eval>	Evaluates a user-defined function and returns the output. The function can access the underlying XML Document Object Model (XML DOM) using the *this* keyword as the entry point to the document root node. The *<xsl:eval>* tag is a Microsoft extension to the XSL implementation.

Each XSLT implementation supports a different set of languages for writing user-defined functions. For example, Microsoft's XML Core Services (MSXML) supports only Microsoft Visual Basic, Scripting Edition (VBScript) and JScript. The .NET Framework transformation classes, on the other hand, include support for C# and Microsoft Visual Basic .NET. (More on this later.)

> **Note**   The syntax shown for the XSLT instructions is largely incomplete. I limited the descriptions to the most important and most frequently used attributes. More attributes are actually available; you can find them documented and explained in the MSDN documentation as well as in the resources listed in the section "Further Reading," on page 343.

Control Flow Instructions

The XSLT vocabulary includes some tags that represents control flow statements such as conditional and iterative statements. Table 7-3 summarizes the most important commands.

Table 7-3   XSLT Instructions for Control Flow

Instruction	Description
<xsl:for-each select="…"> </br> *</xsl:for-each>*	Applies the rules in the body to each element that matches the given XPath expression. The node-set can be sorted by putting an *<xsl:sort>* in the body.
<xsl:if test="…"> </br> *</xsl:if>*	Applies the internal template only if the specified XPath expression evaluates to *true*.
<xsl:choose> <xsl:when </br> *test="…">…* </br> *</xsl:when>* </br> *<xsl:otherwise>…* </br> *</xsl:otherwise><xsl:choose>*	Similar to the C# *switch* statement; represents a multiple-choice statement. Each test is expressed using an *<xsl:when>* statement, while the *<xsl:otherwise>* element represents the default choice. The statement evaluates all the *<xsl:when>* blocks until the test expression returns *true*. When that happens, the corresponding template is applied. If no test is successful, the *<xsl:otherwise>* template is invoked.

Although this list of commands lacks a *for* statement, you can still realize a loop that runs a specified number of times by using the XPath *position* function. Of course, *position* returns the index of the current context node and is not a general variable counter. On the other hand, XSLT instructions are designed to work on XPath node-sets, not to arrange general-purpose programs.

Layout Instructions

A typical task for an XSLT script is the creation of new elements and attributes. Sometimes attributes and node elements can be hard-coded in script; sometimes this is just impossible to do. The XSLT statements listed in Table 7-4 let you programmatically create layout elements.

Table 7-4   XSLT Instructions for Layout

Instruction	Description
<xsl:element name = "…" *namespace = "…">* *</xsl:element>*	Creates an element with the specified name. The *namespace* attribute indicates the URI of the created element, if any. The *<xsl:element>* element contains a template for the attributes and children of the created element.
<xsl:attribute name = "…" *namespace = "…">* *</xsl:attribute>*	Creates an attribute node and attaches it to an output element. The *name* attribute denotes the name of the attribute, and *namespace* indicates the namespace URI, if any. The contents of this element specify the value of the attribute. Note that *<xsl:attribute>* can also be used directly on output elements, not only in conjunction with *<xsl:element>*.
<xsl:processing-instruction *name="…">* *</xsl:processing-instruction>*	Generates a processing instruction in the output text. The *name* attribute represents the name of the processing instruction. The contents of the element provide the text of the processing instruction.
<xsl:comment>	Generates a comment node in the output text. The text generated by the body of *<xsl:comment>* appears between the typical comment wrappers <!-- and -->.

In addition to the instructions described in this section, the XSLT vocabulary contains a few more elements to define data-bound variables (*<xsl:variable>*), raw text (*<xsl:text>*), or numbers (*<xsl:number>*). In particular, a data-bound variable can be given a name and its value calculated either by evaluating an XPath expression or by applying the template in the body of the tag.

After our brief but intensive tour of the XSLT programming interface, let's see how to turn some of these instructions into concrete calls in a real XSLT script. We'll look at a couple of typical examples: converting XML documents to HTML pages, and transforming an XML document into an equivalent schema.

From XML to HTML

Let's return to our faithful XML document (data.xml) from previous chapters and turn it into a compelling HTML page. This sample XML document contains information about the employees in the Northwind database's Employees table.

The idea is to create a final HTML page that renders the information about employees through a table. The structure of the XSLT script is shown in the following code:

```
<xsl:stylesheet
    xmlns:xsl="http://www.w3.org/1999/XSL/Transform"
    version="1.0">

  <xsl:template match="/">
    <HTML>
      <BODY>
      <H1>Northwind's Employees</H1>
        <TABLE>
          <xsl:apply-templates
              select="MyDataSet/NorthwindEmployees/Employee" />
        </TABLE>
      </BODY>
    </HTML>
  </xsl:template>

  ⋮
  more templates here
  ⋮
</xsl:stylesheet>
```

As the *match* attribute indicates, the main *<xsl:template>* instruction applies to the root of the XML document. The XSLT script produces a simple HTML page with a fixed H1 heading and a table. The table is generated by applying all matching templates to the nodes that match the following XPath expression:

```
MyDataSet/NorthwindEmployees/Employee
```

The actual templates that make the final HTML page are defined later in the document. To start off, you define a template for each *<Employee>* node, as shown here:

```
<xsl:template match="Employee">
  <TR>
    <xsl:apply-templates select="employeeid" />
    <xsl:apply-templates select="lastname" />
    <xsl:apply-templates select="title" />
  </TR>
</xsl:template>
```

The template defines a wrapper table row and then calls into the child templates, one for each significant piece of information to be rendered. As you've probably guessed, each child template defines a table cell. For example, the following template selects the *<employeeid>* node below the current *Employee* and renders the text of the node in boldface:

```
<xsl:template match="employeeid">
  <TD bgcolor="yellow" style="border:1px solid black">
    <B><xsl:value-of select="." /></B>
  </TD>
</xsl:template>
```

As you can see, the node selection is always performed using XPath expressions. The "*.*" expression for the *<xsl:value-of>* node refers to the text of the current node. A similar pattern is used for other templates, as follows:

```
<xsl:template match="lastname">
  <TD style="border:1px solid black">
    <B><xsl:value-of select="."/></B>,
      <xsl:value-of select="../firstname"/>
  </TD>
</xsl:template>

<xsl:template match="title">
  <TD style="border:1px solid black">
    <I><xsl:value-of select="."/></I>
  </TD>
</xsl:template>
```

In the first template, the context node is *<lastname>*, but at a certain point, we need to access a sibling node—the *<firstname>* node. The XPath syntax includes the double-dot symbol (..), which is a shortcut for the parent of the current context node. (See Chapter 6.)

The final HTML output for the source XML document is shown Figure 7-3.

Northwind's Employees

1	**Davolio**, Nancy	*Sales Representative*
2	**Fuller**, Andrew	*Vice President, Sales*
3	**Leverling**, Janet	*Sales Representative*
4	**Peacock**, Margaret	*Sales Representative*
5	**Buchanan**, Steve	*Sales Manager*
6	**Suyama**, Michael	*Sales Representative*
7	**King**, Robert	*Sales Representative*
8	**Callahan**, Laura	*Inside Sales Coordinator*
9	**Dodsworth**, Anne	*Sales Representative*

Figure 7-3   The HTML page generated from a source XML file.

To display the HTML output as plain text, you must perform the transformation programmatically, using either the MSXML object model or the newest .NET Framework classes. Alternatively, you can view the output using a specialized browser with the direct browsing functionality. Microsoft Internet Explorer has provided this capability since version 5.0.

Linking the Style Sheet to the HTML Page

Internet Explorer applies a silent and automatic transformation to all XML documents you view through it. However, an XML document can override the default Internet Explorer style sheet by using a processing instruction that simply links an XSLT script.

The following code demonstrates how to add the style sheet from the previous section (emplist.xsl) to the source file (data.xml) so that double-clicking it generates the output shown in Figure 7-3. A style sheet can have either a .xsl or a .xml extension.

```
<!-- Directly browsable using a custom XSLT script -->
<?xml-stylesheet type="text/xsl" href="emplist.xsl"?>
```

You register a style sheet with an XML document using a processing instruction with a couple of attributes: *type* and *href*. The *type* attribute must be set to the string *text/xsl*. The *href* attribute instead references the URL of the XSLT script. If you insert more than one processing instruction for XSLT scripts, only the final instruction will be considered.

Calling Templates

The previous example used *<xsl:apply-templates>* exclusively to perform template-based transformations. When you know that only one template applies to a given block of XML source code, you might want to use a more direct instruction: *<xsl:call-template>*.

If you plan to use the *<xsl:call-template>* instruction, you must first give the target template a name. For example, the following code defines a template named *EmployeeIdTemplate*:

```
<xsl:template name="EmployeeIdTemplate">
  <TD bgcolor="yellow" style="border:1px solid black">
    <B><xsl:value-of select="employeeid"/></B>
  </TD>
</xsl:template>
```

How do you call into this template? Just use the following code:

```
<xsl:template match="Employee">
  <TR>
```

```
      <xsl:call-template name="EmployeeIdTemplate" />
      <xsl:apply-templates select="lastname" />
      <xsl:apply-templates select="title" />
   </TR>
</xsl:template>
```

There is one difference you should be aware of. With *<xsl:apply-templates>*, you use the *select* attribute to select a node-set for the template, as shown here:

```
   <xsl:apply-templates select="employeeid" />
```

As a result, the template works on the *<employeeid>* node and retrieves the value with the following expression:

```
<xsl:value-of select="." />
```

When you use the *<xsl:call-template>* instruction, on the other hand, you call the template by name, but it works on the currently selected context node. The ongoing context node is *<Employee>*, and you must explicitly indicate the child node in the body of *<xsl:value-of>*, as shown here:

```
<xsl:value-of select="employeeid" />
```

From Schema to Schema

Transforming an XML document into an XML document with another schema is in no way different from transforming XML into HTML. The real difference is that you use another target XML vocabulary.

The following XSLT script is designed to simplify the structure of our sample data.xml file. The original file is structured like this:

```
<MyDataSet>
  <NorthwindEmployees>
    <Employee>
      <employeeid>…</employeeid>
      <lastname>…</lastname>
      <firstname>…</firstname>
      <title>…</title>
    </Employee>
    ⋮
  </NorthwindEmployees>
</MyDataSet>
```

The expected target schema is simpler and contains only two levels of nodes, as shown in the following code. In addition, all employee information is now coded using attributes instead of child nodes, and last and first names are merged into a single value.

```
<Employees database="northwind">
  <Employee id="1" name="Davolio, Nancy"
      title="Sales Representative" />
  ⋮
  </Employee>
</Employees>
```

The following script performs the magic:

```
<xsl:stylesheet
    xmlns:xsl="http://www.w3.org/1999/XSL/Transform"
    version="1.0">
  <xsl:template match="MyDataSet/NorthwindEmployees">
    <Employees database="northwind">
      <xsl:for-each select="Employee">
        <xsl:element name="Employee">
          <xsl:attribute name="id">
            <xsl:value-of select="employeeid" />
          </xsl:attribute>
          <xsl:attribute name="name">
            <xsl:value-of select="lastname" />,
            <xsl:value-of select="firstname" />
          </xsl:attribute>
          <xsl:attribute name="title">
            <xsl:value-of select="title" />
          </xsl:attribute>
        </xsl:element>
      </xsl:for-each>
    </Employees>
  </xsl:template>
</xsl:stylesheet>
```

This script includes only one template rooted in the *<NorthwindEmployees>* node and creates a new element for each child *<Employee>* node. The node has a few attributes: *id*, *name*, and *title*. The *<xsl:value-of>* instruction is used to read node values into the newly created attributes. The final output is shown here:

```
<?xml version="1.0" encoding="utf-8"?>
<Employees database="northwind">
  <Employee id="1" name="Davolio, Nancy"
      title="Sales Representative"></Employee>
  <Employee id="2" name="Fuller, Andrew"
      title="Vice President, Sales"></Employee>
```

```
   <Employee id="3" name="Leverling, Janet"
      title="Sales Representative"></Employee>
   <Employee id="4" name="Peacock, Margaret"
      title="Sales Representative"></Employee>
   <Employee id="5" name="Buchanan, Steve"
      title="Sales Manager"></Employee>
   <Employee id="6" name="Suyama, Michael"
      title="Sales Representative"></Employee>
   <Employee id="7" name="King, Robert"
      title="Sales Representative"></Employee>
   <Employee id="8" name="Callahan, Laura"
      title="Inside Sales Coordinator"></Employee>
   <Employee id="9" name="Dodsworth, Anne"
      title="Sales Representative"></Employee>
</Employees>
```

As you can see, transforming XML into another arbitrary text-based language is simply a matter of becoming familiar with a relatively small vocabulary of ad hoc tags. The XSLT vocabulary is a bit peculiar because some of its tags look a lot like high-level programming language statements. But grasping the essence of XSLT is not all that difficult.

The .NET Framework XSLT Processor

In the .NET Framework, the core class for XSLT is *XslTransform*. Located in the *System.Xml.Xsl* namespace, the *XslTransform* class implements the XSLT processor. You make use of this class in two steps: first you load the style sheet in the processor, and then you apply transformations to as many source documents as you need.

The *XslTransform* class supports only the XSLT 1.0 specification. A style sheet declares itself compliant with this version of the specification by including the following namespace:

```
<xsl:stylesheet xmlns:xsl="http://www.w3.org/1999/XSL/Transform"
   version="1.0">
```

By the way, note that the *version* attribute is mandatory to ensure the correctness of the style sheet document.

The key methods in the *XslTransform* class are *Load* and *Transform*. They perform the two steps just mentioned. In particular, you use the *Load* method to read the style sheet from a variety of sources. The *Transform* method, on the other hand, applies the transformation rules set in the style sheet to a given XML source document.

A Quick XSLT Transformer

Earlier in the chapter, we used XSLT scripts to transform an XML source document into something else—say, an HTML page or another XML schema. The scripts were tested simply by adding a processing instruction to the XML source document. Such an instruction tells specialized browsers, like Internet Explorer 5 and later, to use the referenced XSLT script to transform the XML document before displaying it.

A .NET Framework application can programmatically control the entire transformation process using the *XslTransform* class. The following console application represents a quick command-line XSLT transformer. It takes three arguments (the XML source, the XSLT style sheet, and the output file), sets up the processor, and saves the results of the transformation to the output file.

```
using System;
using System.Xml;
using System.Xml.Xsl;

class QuickXslTransformer
{
    public QuickXslTransformer(string source, string stylesheet,
        string output)
    {
        XslTransform xslt = new XslTransform();
        xslt.Load(stylesheet);
        xslt.Transform(source, output);
    }

    public static void Main(string[] args)
    {
        try {
            QuickXslTransformer o;
            o = new QuickXslTransformer(args[0], args[1], args[2]);
        }
        catch (Exception e)
        {
            Console.WriteLine(
                "Unable to apply the XSLT transformation.");
            Console.WriteLine("Error:\t{0}", e.Message);
            Console.WriteLine("Exception: {0}", e.GetType().ToString());
        }

        return;
    }
}
```

The heart of the application is found in the following three lines of rather self-explanatory code:

```
XslTransform xslt = new XslTransform();
xslt.Load(stylesheet);
xslt.Transform(source, output);
```

The style sheet can be loaded from a variety of sources, including XPath documents, XML readers, local disk files, and URLs. The *Load* method compiles the style sheet and uses the stored information to initialize the XSLT processor. When *Load* returns, the processor is ready to perform any requested transformation.

The *Transform* method loads an XML document, runs the XSLT script, and writes the results to the specified stream. *Transform* is particularly handy, because it saves you from explicitly loading the source document and creating the output file. As we'll see more in detail in the section "Performing Transformations," on page 314, *Transform* uses an intermediate XPath document to transform the XML.

Note   Several other programming environments allow you to exercise total control over the XSLT process. In particular, in Microsoft Win32, the combined use of two distinct instances of the *Microsoft.XMLDOM* COM object lets you programmatically perform an XSLT transformation. The following JScript code illustrates how to proceed:

```
// Collects arguments from the WSH command line
source = WScript.Arguments(0);
stylesheet = WScript.Arguments(1);
output = WScript.Arguments(2);

// Instantiates the XMLDOM for the source
xml = new ActiveXObject("Microsoft.XMLDOM");
xml.load(source);

// Instantiates the XMLDOM for the style sheet
xsl = new ActiveXObject("Microsoft.XMLDOM");
xsl.load(stylesheet);

// Creates the output
fso = new ActiveXObject("Scripting.FileSystemObject");
f = fso.CreateTextFile(output);
f.Write(xml.transformNode(xsl.documentElement));
f.Close();
```

The *XslTransform* Class

Now that we've seen how the *XslTransform* class implements the .NET Framework processor to transform XML data into arbitrary text using XSL style sheets, let's look more closely at its programming interface.

As shown in the following code, *XslTransform* has only the default constructor. In addition, it is a *sealed class*, meaning that you can use it only as is and other classes can't inherit from it.

```
public sealed class XslTransform
{
    ⋮
}
```

The programming interface of the class is fairly simple and consists of just one public property and a couple of methods.

Properties of the *XslTransform* Class

The only property that the *XslTransform* class exposes is *XmlResolver*, which handles an instance of the *XmlResolver* class. Interestingly, the *XmlResolver* property is write-only—that is, you can set it, but you can't check the currently set resolver object.

As we've seen in previous chapters, the *XmlResolver* object is used to resolve external references found in the documents being processed. In this context, the *XmlResolver* property is used only during the transformation process. It is not used, for example, to resolve external resources during load operations.

If you don't create a custom resolver object, an instance of the *XmlUrlResolver* class is used.

Methods of the *XslTransform* Class

The *XslTransform* class supplies two methods specific to its activity—the *Load* and *Transform* methods mentioned earlier. The *Load* and *Transform* methods are described in more detail in Table 7-5.

Table 7-5   Methods of the XSLT Processor

Method	Description
Load	Loads the specified XSLT style sheet document from a number of possible sources, including remote URLs and XML readers. The method has several overloads, including overloads that let you specify a custom *XmlResolver* object to load any style sheets referenced through *xsl:import* and *xsl:include* statements.
Transform	Transforms the specified XML data using the loaded XSLT style sheet and writes the results to a given stream. Some of the method's overloads let you specify an argument list as input to the transformation.

The following code snippet shows how to use an *XmlResolver* object with credentials to access a remote XSLT style sheet:

```
XmlUrlResolver resolver = new XmlUrlResolver();
NetworkCredential cred = new NetworkCredential(uid, pswd, domain);
resolver.Credentials = cred;
XslTransform xslt = new XslTransform();
xslt.Load(stylesheet, resolver);
```

The *XslTransform* class is also unique from the threading and security standpoints. Let's see why.

Threading Considerations

XslTransform is guaranteed to operate in a thread-safe way only during transform operations. In other words, although an instance of the class can be shared by multiple threads, only the *Transform* method can be called safely from multiple threads. For the sake of your code, you must ensure that both of the following conditions are met:

- The *Load* method is not concurrently called from within different threads.

- No other method (for example, *Transform*) is called on the object during load operations.

In a nutshell, the *XslTransform* class is multithreaded only with respect to transformations. The reasons for this behavior stem from the internal architecture of the class, which is summarized in Figure 7-4.

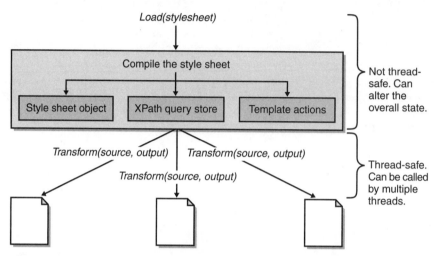

Figure 7-4   The *Load* method is not thread-safe, and its state can be overwritten and spoiled by concurrent calls. The *Transform* method, on the other hand, reads the shared state and can run concurrently from multiple threads.

When the *Load* method is called, the style sheet is compiled and its contents are used to set the internal state of the object. For performance reasons, this code is not grouped into a critical section, which would serialize the threads' access to the internal state. After loading the style sheet, the XSLT processor needs to modify its state to reflect the loaded document. The operation does not occur atomically within the virtual boundaries created by a *lock* statement. As a result, concurrently running threads could in theory access the same instance of the processor and break the data consistency. The load operation is thread-sensitive because it alters the global state of the object.

The transform operation, on the other hand, is inherently thread-safe because it performs read-only access to the processor's state. Nothing bad can happen if concurrent threads apply transformations using the same processor.

To avoid threading risks, be aware that loading a style sheet is an unprotected operation. Either lock the operation yourself, or avoid spawning concurrent threads that perform style sheet loading on the same processor.

Security Considerations

The *XslTransform* class has a *link demand* permission set attached. A link demand specifies which permissions direct callers must have to run the code, as shown in the following example. Callers' rights are checked during just-in-time compilation.

```
[PermissionSet(SecurityAction.LinkDemand, Name="FullTrust")]
public sealed class XslTransform
{
    ⋮
}
```

The permission set attribute for the *XslTransform* class is expressed by name and points to one of the built-in permission sets—*FullTrust*. What does this mean to you? Only callers (direct callers are involved with the check, not caller's callers) with fully trusted access to all the local resources can safely call into the XSLT processor.

Try running the XSLT Quick Security Tester sample application over a network. Because of the class security settings, a security exception is thrown. Figure 7-5 shows the security exception dialog box.

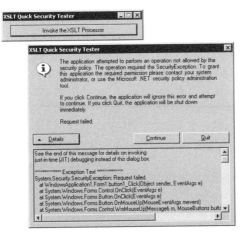

Figure 7-5 The XSLT processor class works only if called by locally trusted callers. An XSLT application can work well as long as you invoke it locally, but it will raise a security exception if you run it over a network share.

Under the Hood of the XSLT Processor

In the overall behavior of the .NET Framework XSLT processor, three phases can be clearly identified: loading the style sheet document, setting up the internal state, and performing the transformations. Although you see, and interact with, only a single class (*XslTransform*), a lot of internal classes are involved in the process.

The first two phases occur within the context of the *Load* method. Of course, you can't call the *Transform* method before a previous call to *Load* has successfully terminated. If you do, you will experience an *XsltException* exception on the *Transform* method.

Load always works synchronously, so when it returns, you can be sure that the loading step has been completed. You will not get from *Load* any return value that denotes the failure or the success of the operation. When something goes wrong with the *Load* method, however, some exceptions are thrown. In particular, you will get a *FileNotFoundException* exception if you are pointing to a missing style sheet, and you will get a more generic *XsltCompile-Exception* exception if the XSLT script contains errors. An *XsltCompileException* exception provides you with a line position and number indicating where the error occurred in the style sheet.

Loading the Style Sheet

The input style sheet can be loaded from four sources: a URL, an XML reader, an XPath document, or an XPath navigator. Whatever the source, the *Load* method first expresses it as an XPath navigator. As discussed in Chapter 6, an XPath navigator represents a generic interface able to navigate over any XML-based, or XML-looking, data store. The *XPathNavigator* class enables you to move from one node to the next and to retrieve node-sets using XPath queries.

The source style sheet is normalized to an XPath navigator mostly for performance reasons. The style sheet must be compiled and, given the compiler's architecture, a navigator is an extremely efficient object for performing the task. Compiling is a process that simply excerpts information from the original style sheet and stores it in handy data structures for further use. The entire set of these data structures is said to be the *state* of the XSLT processor. Figure 7-6 illustrates the flow of the *Load* method.

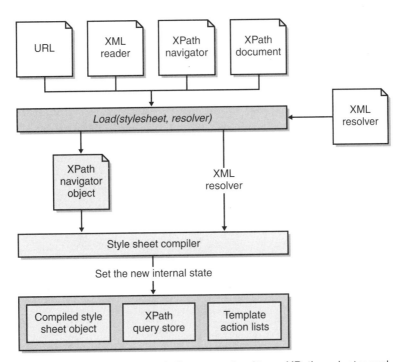

Figure 7-6   The style sheet is first normalized to an XPath navigator and then compiled.

Managing the Processor's State

The style sheet compiler populates three internal data structures with the data read from the source. The compiled style sheet object shown in Figure 7-6 represents an index of the style sheet contents. The other two data structures are tables containing compiled versions of the XPath queries to execute and the actions that the various templates require.

As mentioned, the state of the XSLT processor is not set atomically, which might pose problems if you are using the XSLT processor from within a multi-threaded application. Once set by the *Load* method, the processor's state is not modified until the same *Load* method is called again.

Performing Transformations

The transformation method, depicted in Figure 7-7, takes at least two explicit arguments—the source XML document and the output stream—plus a couple of implicit parameters. The compiled style sheet object is of course one of the implicit input arguments. The second implicit parameter is the *XmlResolver* property. As mentioned, the *XmlResolver* property is designed to help the processor resolve external resources.

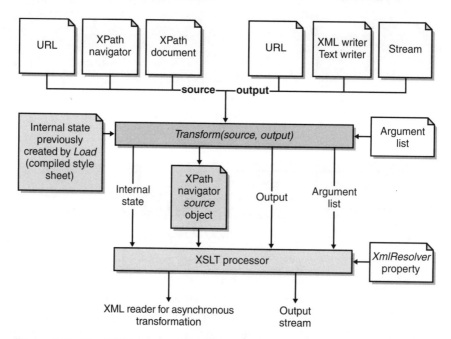

Figure 7-7   The XSLT processor generates the output text based on the source XML document and the internally stored information about the style sheet.

The *Transform* method can also take a third explicit argument—an object of class *XsltArgumentList*. The argument contains the namespace-qualified arguments used as input to the transformation process. (More on this in the section "Creating a .NET Framework Argument List," on page 324.)

The XML source document is normalized as an XPath navigator and passed down in this form to the XSLT processor. Interestingly, the internal processor class has two types of overloads. Some of the overloads work as *void* methods and simply write to the specified stream. Others work as functions and specifically return an XML reader object. As you'll see in a moment, this feature provides an interesting opportunity: implementing asynchronous XSLT transformations.

> **Note**   How easy is it to normalize XML readers, URLs, and documents to XPath navigators? Remember that you can always create an *XPathDocument* object from any XML file or reader. Once you have a reference to an *XPathDocument* object, or an instance of any other object that implements the *IXPathNavigable* interface, you simply call the *CreateNavigator* method and you're done. The *CreateNavigator* method, of course, is part of the *IXPathNavigable* interface.

Applying Transformations

The XSL style sheet and the XML source can be loaded from a variety of sources, including local disk files and remote URLs. You can't load style sheets and source documents from a stream, but because you can easily obtain an XML reader from a stream, a workaround is quickly found. Whatever the input format, the content is transformed into an XPath navigator object immediately after reading.

In light of this, passing style sheet and XML source data directly as XPath documents or navigators is advantageous from two standpoints: you save conversion time, and you work with objects whose internal storage mechanism is lighter and more compact.

Choosing optimized forms of storage like XPath documents binds you to a read-only manipulation of the data. If you need to edit the document before a transformation is performed, load it into an *XmlDocument* object and apply all the changes. When you have finished, pass the *XmlDocument* object to the *XslTransform* class. As you'll recall from Chapter 6, *XmlDocument* implements the *IXPathNavigable* interface and as such can be used with the *Transform* method.

The *Load* and *Transform* methods have several overloads each. In all this richness of call opportunities, not all possible combinations of input and output channels are always supported. For example, you can load the source document from a URL, but only if you output to another URL or disk file. Likewise, if you want to transform to a text writer, you can't load the source from a file. Table 7-6 and Table 7-7 provide a quick-access view of the available overloads.

Table 7-6 *Load* **Method Overloads**

Return Type	Style Sheet Source	XML Resolver
void	File or URL	No
void	XPath document	No
void	XPath navigator	No
void	XML reader	No
void	File or URL	Yes
void	XPath document	Yes
void	XPath navigator	Yes
void	XML reader	Yes

The interface of the *Load* method is fairly regular. It always returns *void*, and it supports four reading media, with or without an XML resolver object.

Table 7-7 *Transform* **Method Overloads**

Return Type	XML Source	Argument List	Output
void	File or URL		File or URL
void	XPath document	*XsltArgumentList*	Stream
void	XPath navigator	*XsltArgumentList*	Stream
void	XPath document	*XsltArgumentList*	Text writer
void	XPath navigator	*XsltArgumentList*	Text writer
void	XPath document	*XsltArgumentList*	XML writer
void	XPath navigator	*XsltArgumentList*	XML writer
XmlReader	XPath document	*XsltArgumentList*	
XmlReader	XPath navigator	*XsltArgumentList*	

The programming interface of the *Transform* method is much less regular. The overloads that return an XML reader work only on XPath documents or navigators. The overload that manages URLs or files is an exception, perhaps provided for the sake of simplicity. The remaining overloads are grouped by the type of the output media: stream, text, or XML writer. For each of them, you can have a source XML document read from an XPath document or an XPath navigator.

Design Considerations

The style sheet and the source XML document are two equally important arguments for the XSLT processor. The *XslTransform* programming interface requires that you indicate them in different steps, however. In doing so, the accent goes on a particular use—transforming multiple documents using the same style sheet.

Although optimized for a particular scenario, such a design doesn't tax those programmers who use the style sheet for a single transformation. In this case, the only, and very minimal, drawback is that you have to write three lines of code instead of one! Look at the following class. It provides a static method for performing XSLT transformations. It doesn't explicitly provide for style sheet reuse, but it does save you two lines of code!

```
public class QuickXslt
{
    public static bool Transform(
        string source, string stylesheet, string output)
    {
        try
        {
            XslTransform xslt = new XslTransform();
            xslt.Load(stylesheet);
            xslt.Transform(source, output);
            return true;
        }
        catch (Exception e)
        {
            return false;
        }
    }
}
```

The *Transform* method shown in the preceding code also catches any exceptions and flattens them into a Boolean value. Using this global method is as easy as writing the following code:

```
public static void Main(string[] args)
{
    bool b = QuickXslt.Transform(args[0], args[1], args[2]);
    Console.WriteLine(b.ToString());
}
```

By design, the static *Transform* method accepts only disk files or URLs.

> **Tip** By passing an XML reader to the *XslTransform* class's *Load* and *Transform* methods, you can load both the style sheet and the source document from an XML subtree. In this case, in fact, the *XslTransform* class will start reading from the reader's current node and continue through the entire subtree.

Another interesting consideration that applies to XSLT concerns the process as a whole. The style sheet is always loaded synchronously. The transformation, on the other hand, can occur asynchronously—at least to some extent. Let's see why.

Asynchronous Transformations

The *Transform* method has a couple of overloads that return an XML reader, as shown here:

```
public XmlReader Transform(XPathNavigator input,
    XsltArgumentList args);
public XmlReader Transform(IXPathNavigable input,
    XsltArgumentList args);
```

The signature, and the behavior, of these overloads is slightly different from the others. As you can see, the method does not accept any argument representing the output stream. The second argument can be an *XsltArgumentList* object, which serves other purposes that we'll get into in the section "Creating a .NET Framework Argument List," on page 324. The input document must be an XPath navigator or an XPath document referenced through the *IXPathNavigable* interface.

XSLT Output Records

The output of the transformation process is not written out to a stream but created in memory and returned to the user via an XML reader. The overall transformation process works by creating an intermediate data structure (referred to as the *navigator input*) in which the content of the style sheet is used as the underlying surface. Any XSLT tag found in the style sheet source is replaced with expanded text or any sequence of calls that results from embedded templates.

The final output looks like a compiled program in which direct statements are interspersed with calls to subroutines. In an XSLT program, these statements are called *output records*, while templates play the role of subroutines. Figure 7-8 shows how the XSLT processor generates its output.

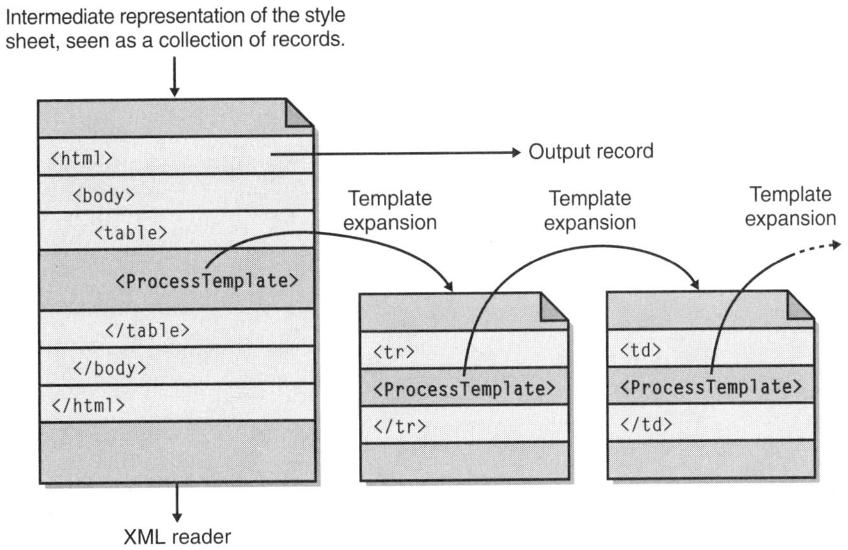

Intermediate representation of the style
sheet, seen as a collection of records.

Figure 7-8   An XML reader lets you access the output records one at a time.

When the *Transform* method gets an output stream to write to, the XSLT processor loops through all the records and accumulates the text into the specified buffer. If an XML reader has been requested, the processor creates an instance of an internal reader class and returns that to the caller. The exact name of the internal reader is *System.Xml.Xsl.ReaderOutput*. No transformation is performed until the caller explicitly asks to read the cached output records. Figure 7-9 shows how the XSLT processor returns its output.

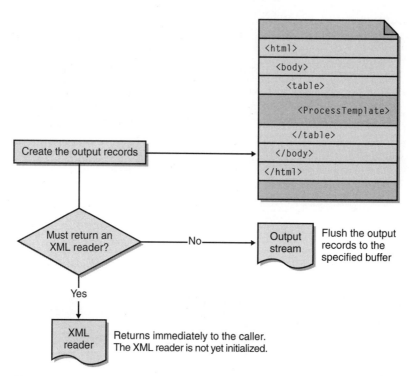

Figure 7-9   The XSLT processor instantiates a reader object and returns. No transformation is performed until you "read" the internal data using the methods and the properties of the returned reader.

The XSLT Record Reader

The *ReaderOutput* class builds a virtual XML tree on top of the compiled style sheet, thus making it navigable using the standard XML reader interface. When the *Transform* method returns, the reader is in its initial state (and therefore it is not yet initialized for reading).

Each time you pop an element from the reader, a new output record is properly expanded and returned. In this way, you have total control over the transformation process and can plan and realize a number of fancy features. For example, you could provide feedback to the user, discard nodes based on run-time conditions and user roles, or cause the process to occur asynchronously on a secondary thread.

The reader interface exposes the XSLT records as XML nodes—the same XML nodes you will find by visiting the output document. The following code snippet demonstrates how to set up a user-controlled transformation:

```
// The XML source must be an XPath document or an XPath navigator
XPathDocument doc = new XPathDocument(source);

// No arg-list to provide in this case
XmlReader reader = xslt.Transform(doc, null);

// Perform the transformation, record by record
while (reader.Read())
{
    // Do something
}
```

Figure 7-10 shows the user interface of a sample application. It includes a list box control that is iteratively populated with information excerpted from the reader's current node. Each row in the list box corresponds to an output record generated by the XSLT processor.

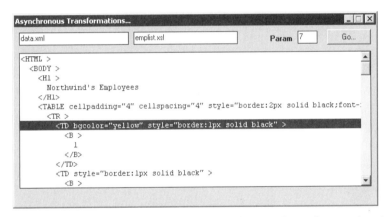

Figure 7-10   The HTML file generated by the transformation, rendered as a node tree, is received one row at a time.

In the reading loop, all nodes are analyzed and serialized to XML text, as shown in the following code. In this way, each row in the list box corresponds to the line of text that is sent to an output stream if you opt for a synchronous transformation.

```
void ReadOutputRecords(XmlReader reader)
{
    // Clear the list box
    OutputList.Items.Clear();

    // Read the records
    while(reader.Read())
    {
```

(continued)

```
            string buf = "";
            switch(reader.NodeType)
            {
                case XmlNodeType.Element:
                    buf = String.Format("{0}<{1} {2}>",
                        new String(' ', 2*reader.Depth),
                        reader.Name,
                        GetNodeAttributes(reader));
                    break;
                case XmlNodeType.EndElement:
                    buf = String.Format("{0}</{1}>",
                        new String(' ', 2*reader.Depth),
                        reader.Name);
                    break;
                case XmlNodeType.Text:
                    buf = String.Format("{0}{1}",
                        new String(' ', 2*reader.Depth),
                        reader.Value);
                    break;
            }
            OutputList.Items.Add(buf);
        }
    }
}
```

The final text is indented using a padding string whose size depends on the reader's *Depth* property. Node names and values are returned by the *Name* and *Value* properties. For element nodes, attributes are read using a piece of code that we examined in detail in Chapter 2:

```
string GetNodeAttributes(XmlReader reader)
{
    if (!reader.HasAttributes)
        return "";

    string buf = "";
    while(reader.MoveToNextAttribute())
        buf += String.Format("{0}=\"{1}\" ", reader.Name, reader.Value);

    reader.MoveToElement();
    return buf;
}
```

Output Formats

An XSLT style sheet can declare the output format of the serialized text using the *<xsl:output>* statement. This statement features several attributes, the most important of which is *method*. The *method* attribute can be set with any of the following keywords: *xml*, *html*, or *text*. By default, the output format is XML unless the root tag of the results document equals *<html>*. In this case, the output is in HTML.

Differences between XML and HTML are minimal. If the output format is HTML, the XML well-formedness is sacrificed in the name of a greater programmer-friendliness. This means that, for example, empty tags will not have an end tag. In addition to *method*, other attributes of interest are *indent*, *encoding*, and *omit-xml-declaration*, which respectively indent the text, set the preferred character encoding, and omit the typical XML prolog.

If you add an *<xsl:output>* statement to the previously considered style sheets, the source code of the results document will be significantly different, but not its overall meaning. If you choose to output plain text, on the other hand, the XSLT processor will discard any markup text in the style sheet and output only text.

As a final note, consider that *<xsl:output>* is a discretionary behavior that not all XSLT processors provide and not all in the same way. In particular, when the *Transform* method is writing to a text writer or an XML writer, the .NET Framework XSLT processor ignores the *encoding* attribute in favor of the corresponding property on the object.

Passing and Retrieving Arguments

As mentioned, XSLT scripts can take arguments. You can declare arguments globally for the entire script or locally to a particular template. Arguments can have a default value that will make them always available as a variable in the scope. Aside from the default value, in XSLT there are no other differences between arguments and variables.

The following code shows a style sheet snippet in which a parameter named *MaxNumOfRows* is declared and initialized with a default value of 6:

```
<xsl:template match="Employee">
 <xsl:param name="MaxNumOfRows" select="6" />
 <xsl:if test="$MaxNumOfRows > position()">
   <TR>
     <xsl:apply-templates select="employeeid" />
     <xsl:apply-templates select="lastname" />
     <xsl:apply-templates select="title" />
   </TR>
 </xsl:if>
</xsl:template>
```

The script retrieves the argument using its public name prefixed with a dollar sign ($). In particular, the conditional statement shown here applies to the template only if five employee nodes have not yet been processed:

```
<xsl:if test="$MaxNumOfRows > position()">
  <!-- Apply the template -->
</xsl:if>
```

Note that you can't use the less than sign (<) in an XSLT expression because it could confuse the processor. Instead, use the escaped version of the character: *<*. The greater than sign (>) can be safely used, however. If, like me, you don't like escaped strings, you can invert the terms of the comparison.

> **Note** Parameters can be associated only with templates or with the global script. You can't associate parameters with other XSLT instructions such as a *<xsl:for-each>*.

Calling Templates with Arguments

When you call a parameterized XSLT template, you give actual values to formal parameters using the *<xsl:with-param>* instruction. Here's an example that calls the sample *Employee* template, giving the *MaxNumOfRows* argument a value of 7:

```
<xsl:apply-templates select="MyDataSet/NorthwindEmployees/Employee">
  <xsl:with-param name="MaxNumOfRows" select="7" />
</xsl:apply-templates>
```

If the called template has no such parameter, nothing happens, and the argument will be ignored. The *<xsl:with-param>* instruction can be associated with both *<xsl:apply-templates>* and *<xsl:call-template>* instructions.

Creating a .NET Framework Argument List

The *Transform* method lets you pass arguments to the style sheet using an instance of the *XsltArgumentList* class. When you pass arguments to an XSLT script in this way, you can't specify what template call will actually use those arguments. You just pass arguments globally to the XSLT processor. The internal modules responsible for processing templates will then read and import those arguments as appropriate.

Creating an argument list is straightforward. You create an instance of the *XsltArgumentList* class and populate it with values, as shown here:

```
XsltArgumentList args = new XsltArgumentList();
args.AddParam("MaxNumOfRows", "", 7);
```

The *AddParam* method creates a new entry in the argument list. *AddParam* requires three parameters: the (qualified) name of the parameter, the namespace URI (if the name is qualified by a namespace prefix), and an object representing the actual value. Regardless of the .NET Framework type you use to pack the entry into the argument list, the parameter value must correspond to a valid XPath type: string, Boolean, number, node fragment, and node-set. The number type corresponds to a .NET Framework *double* type, whereas node fragments and node-sets are equivalent to XPath navigators and XPath node iterators. (See Chapter 6 for more information about these data types.)

The *XsltArgumentList* Class

Despite what its name suggests, *XsltArgumentList* is not a collection-based class. It does not derive from *ArrayList* or from a collection class, nor does it implement any of the typical list interfaces like *IList* or *ICollection*.

The *XsltArgumentList* class is built around a couple of child hash tables: one to hold XSLT parameters and one to gather the so-called *extension objects*. An extension object is simply a living instance of a .NET Framework object that you can pass as an argument to the style sheet. Of course, this feature is specific to the .NET XSLT processor. We'll look at extension objects in more detail in the section "XSLT Extension Objects," on page 336.

The programming interface of the *XsltArgumentList* class is described in Table 7-8. It provides only methods.

Table 7-8   Methods of the *XsltArgumentList* Class

Method	Description
AddExtensionObject	Adds a new managed object to the list. You can specify the namespace URI or use the default namespace by passing an empty string. If you pass *null*, an exception is thrown.
AddParam	Adds a parameter value to the list. Must indicate the name of the argument and optionally the associated namespace URI.
Clear	Removes all parameters and extension objects from the list.
GetExtensionObject	Returns the object associated with the given namespace.
GetParam	Gets the value of the parameter with the specified (qualified) name.
RemoveExtensionObject	Removes the specified object from the list.
RemoveParam	Removes the specified parameter from the list.

As with parameters, the style sheet identifies an extension object through its class name and an associated namespace prefix.

Practical Examples

Before we take the plunge into more advanced topics such as using managed objects with XSLT style sheets, let's recap and summarize what we've looked at so far in a couple of real-world examples. First we'll transform a Microsoft ADO.NET *DataSet* object into a Microsoft ActiveX Data Objects (ADO) *Recordset* object. Of course, this transformation will not involve the binary image of the objects, just their XML representation.

Second we'll look at a Microsoft ASP.NET example to introduce you to the use of a very handy control: the XML Web server control. The XML Web server control is capable of rendering an XML document in the body of a Web page with or without XSLT formatting.

Transforming *DataSet* Objects into *Recordset* Objects

Exporting the contents of ADO.NET *DataSet* objects to legacy ADO applications is a problem that we encountered and solved in Chapter 4. That solution was based on a special breed of XML writer. In this section, we'll reconsider that approach and use an XSLT style sheet to accomplish the same task.

Bear in mind that using a style sheet to convert a *DataSet* object to a *Recordset* object does not necessarily lead to faster code. If we merely consider the transformation process, I do recommend that you always use the writer. Your code is not taxed by the XSLT processor and, perhaps more importantly, you can use a more familiar programming style. The writer is written in C# or Visual Basic and, as such, provides you with total control over the generated output. An XSLT style sheet is something different, even though it is often referred to as a program.

A style sheet is a kind of mask that you put on top of a document to change its appearance; the document can then be saved in its new form. Using a style sheet also decouples the transformation process from the rest of the application. You can modify the logic of the transformation without touching or recompiling a single line of code.

Writing an XSLT style sheet to transform a *DataSet* object into a *Recordset* object is useful for other reasons as well. First, the style sheet code needed is not trivial and requires a good working knowledge of both XPath and XSLT. Look at it as a useful exercise to test your level of familiarity with the technologies. Second, you can apply the style sheet directly to the binary *DataSet* object, without first serializing the object to XML.

The ability to style a binary *DataSet* object is provided by the *XmlDataDocument* class. As mentioned in Chapter 6, *XmlDataDocument* is an XPath document class. It implements the *IXPathNavigable* interface and, as such, can be directly passed as an argument to the *Transform* method. (We'll examine the *XmlDataDocument* class in detail in Chapter 8.)

Getting the *DataSet* Object

The following code fetches some records from the Northwind database's Employees table and stores them into a *DataSet* object:

```
string conn = "DATABASE=northwind;SERVER=localhost;UID=sa;";
string comm = "SELECT firstname, lastname, title, notes FROM employees";
SqlDataAdapter adapter = new SqlDataAdapter(comm, conn);
DataSet data = new DataSet("Northwind");
adapter.Fill(data, "Employees");
```

The *DataSet* object is named *Northwind* and contains just one *DataTable* object, *Employees*. As we'll see in a moment, the names of the *DataSet* and *DataTable* objects play a key role in the XML representation of the objects. By default, a *DataSet* object is named *NewDataSet*, and a *DataTable* object is named *Table*. (We'll look at ADO.NET XML serialization in great detail in Chapter 9 and Chapter 10.)

The XML representation of a *DataSet* object looks like this:

```
<DataSetName>
  <TableName>
    <employeeid>...</employeeid>
    <lastname>...</lastname>
    ⋮
  </TableName>
  ⋮
</DataSetName>
```

> **Tip**   You can get the string representing the XML version of the *DataSet* object through the *DataSet* method *GetXml*. The text does not include schema information. You can get the schema script separately by calling the *GetXmlSchema* method. To persist the XML representation to a stream, use the *WriteXml* method instead.

Transforming the *DataSet* Object

Transforming a *DataSet* object into a *Recordset* object poses a couple of problems. The first is that you have to infer and write the *Recordset* object's schema. The second is that the XML layout of the *DataSet* object depends on a number of different parameters. In particular, the root of the XML version of the *DataSet* object depends on the object's *DataSetName* property. Likewise, each table record is grouped under a node whose name matches the *DataTable* object's *TableName* property.

You could easily work around the first issue by writing a more generic XSLT script. As for the second problem, because a *DataSet* object can contain multiple tables, you must necessarily know the name of the table you want to process and render as a *Recordset* object. The name of the table must be passed to the XSLT processor through the argument list.

The following code shows how to transform the *DataSet* object into an XPath document and load it into the processor. The result of the transformation is directly written out to an auto-indent XML writer. The argument passed to the style sheet is the name of the first table in the specified *DataSet* object.

```
// Set up the style sheet
XslTransform xslt = new XslTransform();
xslt.Load("ado.xsl");

// Create an XPath document from the DataSet
XmlDataDocument doc = new XmlDataDocument(data);

// Prepare the output writer
XmlTextWriter writer = new XmlTextWriter(outputFile, null);
writer.Formatting = Formatting.Indented;

// Set some arguments
XsltArgumentList args = new XsltArgumentList();
args.AddParam("TableName", "", data.Tables[0].TableName);

// Call the transfomer and close the writer upon completion
xslt.Transform(doc, args, writer);
writer.Close();
```

The *XmlDataDocument* class internally creates an XML DOM representation of the *DataSet* content. That content then becomes the input for the XSLT style sheet.

The ADO Style Sheet

Let's analyze the XSLT code necessary to transform a *DataSet* object into the XML version of an ADO *Recordset* object. The following listing shows the overall layout:

```
<xsl:stylesheet version="1.0"
    xmlns:xsl="http://www.w3.org/1999/XSL/Transform">
<xsl:output method="xml" />

<!-- Matches the DataSet's root, whatever the name -->
```

```
<xsl:template match="/child::*[position()=1]">

  <!-- PARAM:: Name of the table to consider -->
  <xsl:param name="TableName" select="string('Table')" />

  <!-- The XML-based ADO Recordset  -->
  ⋮
  <!-- End of the XML-based ADO Recordset  -->

</xsl:template>
</xsl:stylesheet>
```

The style sheet contains a single template that applies to the first node in the document—that is, the *DataSet* object's root. Because the match is found using a generic XPath expression that selects the first child, the template will work on the *DataSet* object's root, whatever its name might be.

The style sheet can accept one argument (*TableName*) that defaults to the string *Table*. Note that if you omit the XPath *string* function, *Table* denotes a node-set value rather than a string.

The XML version of an ADO *Recordset* object consists of two distinct blocks—schema and rows—grouped under an *<xml>* node. Here's the code for the *Recordset* schema:

```
<xml
    xmlns:s="uuid:BDC6E3F0-6DA3-11d1-A2A3-00AA00C14882"
    xmlns:dt="uuid:C2F41010-65B3-11d1-A29F-00AA00C14882"
    xmlns:rs="urn:schemas-microsoft-com:rowset"
    xmlns:z="#RowsetSchema">

  <!-- Create the schema -->
  <xsl:element name="s:schema"
      namespace="uuid:BDC6E3F0-6DA3-11d1-A2A3-00AA00C14882">
    <xsl:attribute name="id">RowsetSchema</xsl:attribute>

    <xsl:element name="s:ElementType"
        namespace="uuid:BDC6E3F0-6DA3-11d1-A2A3-00AA00C14882">
      <xsl:attribute name="name">row</xsl:attribute>
      <xsl:attribute name="content">eltOnly</xsl:attribute>

      <!-- Take the first table tree and walk its children
           to enumerate the fields in the schema -->
      <xsl:for-each
          select="child::*[local-name()=$TableName][position()=1]">
        <xsl:for-each select="child::*">
          <xsl:element name="s:AttributeType"
              namespace="uuid:BDC6E3F0-6DA3-11d1-A2A3-00AA00C14882">
            <xsl:attribute name="name">
```

(continued)

```
            <xsl:value-of select="local-name()" />
          </xsl:attribute>
        </xsl:element>
    </xsl:for-each>
  </xsl:for-each>
</xsl:element>

<xsl:element name="s:extends"
    namespace="uuid:BDC6E3F0-6DA3-11d1-A2A3-00AA00C14882">
  <xsl:attribute name="type">rs:rowbase</xsl:attribute>
</xsl:element>
</xsl:element>
```

After you create the *<xml>* node with all of its required namespace declarations, you create a *<s:schema>* node with an *id* attribute. The schema tree contains the definitions of all the element and attribute types that will be used later. Note that ADO expresses the *Recordset* object in XML using the XML-Data Reduced (XDR) schema instead of the newer XML Schema Definition (XSD) schema. (See Chapter 3.)

In particular, the *Recordset* schema defines a *<row>* element to render a table row. The node will contain as many attributes as there are columns in the source table. To define all the attributes in the *Recordset* schema, you must visit all the children of a *<TableName>* node in the *DataSet* object. The actual name of the *<TableName>* node will be specified by the *$TableName* style sheet argument.

The sample listing emphasizes a couple of *for-each* statements. The first statement selects the first node whose local, unqualified name matches the *$TableName* argument. The second loop enumerates the children of this node and creates an attribute schema definition for each.

The final step involves the creation of the data rows. Each source row corresponds to a *<z:row>* node whose attributes map to the source columns, as shown here:

```
<xsl:element name="rs:data"
    namespace="urn:schemas-microsoft-com:rowset">
  <xsl:for-each select="child::*[local-name()=$TableName]" >
    <xsl:element name="z:row" namespace="#RowsetSchema">
      <xsl:for-each select="child::*">
        <xsl:attribute name="{local-name()}">
          <xsl:value-of select="." />
```

```
            </xsl:attribute>
          </xsl:for-each>
      </xsl:element>
    </xsl:for-each>
</xsl:element>
```

This listing also includes a couple of nested *for-each* statements that run in the context of the *DataSet* object's root. The outer loop selects all the nodes whose name matches the *$TableName* parameter, whereas the innermost loop creates an attribute for each child node found. The *<z:row>* node is expected to have as many attributes as the child nodes of the corresponding source tree and be named after them. In other words, the name of the attribute must be determined dynamically.

In an XSLT script, you create an attribute using the *<xsl:attribute>* instruction. The instruction has a *name* attribute to let you assign a name to the attribute. The *name* attribute can only be set with a literal, however. What if you must use an XPath expression to decide the name? In that case, you use the following special XPath syntax:

```
<xsl:attribute name="{local-name()}">
```

By wrapping the expression in curly brackets, you tell the processor that the attribute must be assigned the result of the specified expression.

Figure 7-11 illustrates a sample application that runs a query against SQL Server and saves the output in ADO-compliant XML.

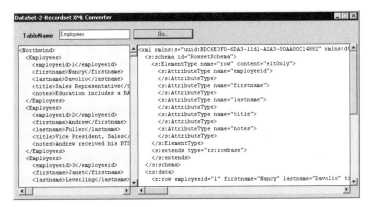

Figure 7-11   The *DataSet*-to-*Recordset* style sheet converter in action.

> **Caution**   The style sheet discussed in this example works well even if the *DataSet* object contains multiple tables. In fact, it has been designed to process only the nodes that match a given table name. The style sheet will produce incorrect XML output if a relationship exists between two tables and the corresponding *DataRelation* object has the *Nested* property set to *true*. In this case, the records of the child table are serialized below each parent row, thus resulting in a discrepancy between the declared schema and the actual contents of each row.
>
> A possible workaround is to use a second parameter, *n*, that specifies the number of columns in the table to be processed. While you define the schema, you stop the loop after the first *n* child rows, discarding all the rows set there because of the nested relationship.

The XML Web Server Control

The XML Web server control is used to output the contents of an XML document directly in an ASP.NET page. The control can display the source XML as is or as the results of an XSLT transformation.

The XML Web server control, denoted by the *<asp:xml>* tag, is a declarative counterpart to the *XslTransform* class. The XML Web server control has no more features than the *XslTransform* class. More precisely, the XML Web server control makes use of the *XslTransform* class internally.

You use the XML Web server control when you need to embed XML documents in a Web page. For example, the control is extremely handy when you need to create XML *data islands* for the client to consume. Data islands consist of XML data referenced or included in an HTML page. The XML data can be included in-line within the HTML, or it can be in an external file. By combining this control's ability with the ADO XML style sheet we created in the previous section, you can transform a *DataSet* object into an ADO *Recordset* object and send it to the browser to be processed by client script procedures.

Let's take a closer look at the programming interface of the XML Web server control.

Programming the XML Web Server Control

In addition to the typical and standard properties of all server controls, the XML Web server control provides the properties listed in Table 7-9. The document properties represent the source XML data, and the transform properties handle the instance of the *XslTransform* class to be used and the style sheet.

Table 7-9   Properties of the XML Web Server Control

Property	Description
Document	Sets the XML source document using an *XmlDocument* object
DocumentContent	Sets the XML source document using a string
DocumentSource	Sets the XML source document using a file
Transform	Sets the *XslTransform* class to use for transformations
TransformArgumentList	Gets or sets the argument list for transformations
TransformSource	Sets the style sheet to use for transformations

You can specify a source document using a file, a string, or an XML DOM object. A style sheet, on the other hand, can be specified using a file or a pre-configured *XslTransform* object. The output of the transformation, if any, is the Web page output stream.

The settings are mutually exclusive, and the last setting always wins. For example, if you set both *Document* and *DocumentSource*, no exception is thrown, but the first assignment is overridden. Although Table 7-9 emphasizes the writing of these properties, they are all read/write properties. For the *DocumentContent* property, however, only the set accessor has a significant implementation. If you attempt to read the property, an empty string is returned.

The *DocumentContent* property can be set programmatically by using a string variable or declaratively by placing text between the start and end tags of the control, as shown here:

```
<asp:xml runat="server" id="theXml">
  ... xml data ...
</asp.xml>
```

You can optionally specify an XSL style sheet document that formats the XML document before it is written to the output. The output of the style sheet must be HTML, XML, or plain text. It can't be, for example, ASP.NET source code or a combination of ASP.NET layout declarations. Let's look at a few practical examples.

Server-Side Transformations

The following listing demonstrates a simple but effective way to describe a portion of your Web page using XML code. The actual XML-to-HTML transformation is automatically and silently performed by the style sheet.

```
<!-- Show employee info -->
<asp:xml runat="server" TransformSource="EmpInfo.xsl">
  <MyDataSet>
    <NorthwindEmployees>
      <Employee>
        <employeeid>1</employeeid>
        <firstname>Nancy</firstname>
        <lastname>Davolio</lastname>
        <title>Sales Representative</title>
        <notes>...</notes>
      </Employee>
    </NorthwindEmployees>
  </MyDataSet>
</asp:xml>
```

The XML Web server control can have an ID and can be programmatically accessed. This opens up a new possibility. You can now check the browser's capabilities and decide dynamically which style sheet is most appropriate.

You can also describe the entire page with XML and use a style sheet to translate the page into HTML, as shown in the following code. This is not always, and not necessarily, the best solution to gain flexibility, but the XML Web server control definitely makes implementing that solution considerably easier.

```
<asp:xml runat="server"
    DocumentSource="Employees.xml"
    TransformSource="EmpInfo.xsl" />
```

If you need to pass in an argument, simply create and populate an instance of the *XsltArgumentList* class and pass it to the control using the *TransformArgumentList* property.

Creating Client-Side Data Islands

A data island is a block of data that is embedded in the body of an HTML page and is invisible to the user. Storing data in hidden fields is certainly the oldest and more widely supported way of implementing data islands. You can think of XML data islands as islands of XML data dispersed in the sea of HTML pages.

Modern browsers (Internet Explorer 5.0 and later) support an ad hoc client-side tag, *<xml>*, to store islands of data, hiding them from view, as shown here:

```
<xml id="data">
  ... XML data goes here ...
</xml>
```

Don't confuse the Internet Explorer 5.0 client-side HTML tag with the *<asp:xml>* server-side control. In Chapter 14, we'll return to data islands, and you'll learn how to define them from within server pages. For now, let's just say that an XML data island is XML text wrapped in an *<xml>* HTML tag. Not all browsers support this. The example described here requires Internet Explorer 5.0 or later.

Used in conjunction with the *<xml>* tag, the XML Web server control can be very helpful and effective. The following code flushes the contents of the specified XML file in a particular data island:

```
<xml id="data">
    <asp:xml runat="server" documentsource="employees.xml" />
</xml>
```

If needed, you can first apply a transformation. For example, you can embed an ADO XML *Recordset* object in a data island. In this case, set the *Transform-Source* property of the XML Web server control with the proper style sheet.

Internet Explorer 5.0 automatically exposes the contents of the *<xml>* tag through an XML DOM object. Hold on, though—that's not managed code! What you get is a scriptable MSXML COM object. The following ASP.NET page includes some VBScript code that retrieves the contents of the data island. (More on this in Chapter 14.)

```
<script runat="server">
<!-- Add a client-side onclick handler to the button -->
void Page_Load(object sender, EventArgs e)
{
    button.Attributes["onclick"] = "ReadXmlData()";
}
</script>

<html>
  <script language="VBScript">
  Sub ReadXmlData()
     ' data is the name of the <xml> tag and
     ' represents an MSXML XML DOM object
     window.alert(data.DocumentElement.nodeName)
  End Sub
  </script>
```

(continued)

```
<body>
  <h1>Client-side Data Islands</h1>

  <!-- Client-side XML data island -->
  <xml id="data">
    <asp:xml runat="server" documentsource="employees.xml" />
  </xml>
  <!-- End of the data island -->

  <form runat="server">
    <asp:button runat="server" id="button" text="Click..." />
  </form>

</body>
</html>
```

XSLT Extension Objects

Let's complete our examination of transformations by analyzing the XSLT
extension objects. As mentioned, the *XsltArgumentList* class can contain both
parameters and extension objects. Parameters are simply value types, whereas
extension objects are instances of .NET classes. When passed to the *Transform* method, both parameters and extension objects can be invoked from
style sheets.

The behavior of a style sheet can be extended in various ways. For example, you can use the *<xsl:eval>* instruction to run VBScript or JScript interpreted
code. Before the advent of the .NET Framework, this was the only option available. With the .NET Framework, given the other characteristics of the XSLT processor, the *<xsl:eval>* instruction is by far the less interesting alternative.

In addition, in the .NET Framework, the *<xsl:eval>* instruction has been
superseded by the *<msxsl:script>* element. This new instruction works in much
the same way as *<xsl:eval>*, but it supports managed languages, thus providing
access to the entire .NET Framework.

Processing Embedded Scripts

When the style sheet is loaded in the *XslTransform* class, all defined functions are
wrapped in a class and compiled to the .NET Framework intermediate language
(IL). They then become available to XPath expressions as native functions.

The .NET Framework XSLT processor accepts external scripts through the
<msxsl:script> element. The script must use only XPath-compliant types even
though, in most cases, type coercion is automatically provided by the processor.

The type conformance is fundamental for input parameters and return values. Each script can internally use any .NET Framework type, paying some attention to the required namespaces. The following namespaces are imported by default: *System*, *System.Text*, *System.Xml*, *System.Text.RegularExpressions*, *System.Xml.XPath*, *System.Xml.Xsl*, *System.Collections*, and *Microsoft.VisualBasic*. Classes in other system namespaces can be used too, but their names must be fully qualified. For example, to use a *DataSet* object, you must call it *System.Data.DataSet*.

> **Important**   An embedded script can't call into a user-defined namespace. The XSLT subsystem knows nothing about dependent assemblies and so can't reference them at compile time. To work around this issue, use extension objects.

The *<msxsl:script>* Instruction

The *<msxsl:script>* instruction has the following syntax:

```
<msxsl:script
  language = "language"
  implements-prefix = "prefix">
</msxsl:script>
```

Supported languages are C#, Visual Basic, and JScript. The *language* attribute is not mandatory and, if not specified, defaults to JScript. The *implements-prefix* attribute is mandatory, however. It declares a namespace and associates the user-defined code with it. The namespace must be defined somewhere in the style sheet. In addition, to make use of the *<msxsl:script>* instruction, the style sheet must include the following namespace:

```
xmlns:msxsl=urn:schemas-microsoft-com:xslt
```

Let's see how to define a simple script. To start off, we'll declare the extra namespaces in the the style sheet's root node, as shown here:

```
<xsl:stylesheet version="1.0"
    xmlns:xsl="http://www.w3.org/1999/XSL/Transform"
    xmlns:msxsl="urn:schemas-microsoft-com:xslt"
    xmlns:dino="urn:dino-scripts">
```

This declaration is necessary to be able to call the *<msxsl:script>* instruction. The namespace simply groups under a single roof some user-defined scripts. The prefix *dino* is now necessary to qualify any calls to any functions defined in a *<msxsl:script>* block. Script blocks can be defined as children of the *<stylesheet>* node, at the same level as templates.

The following script concatenates first and last names, separated by a comma:

```
<msxsl:script implements-prefix="dino" language="C#">
public string PrepareName(string last, string first)
{
    return last + ", " + first;
}
</msxsl:script>
```

In the body of the style sheet—typically in a template—you call the function, as follows:

```
<xsl:template match="lastname">
  <TD style="border:1px solid black">
    <xsl:value-of select="dino:PrepareName(., ../firstname)" />
  </TD>
</xsl:template>
```

If you enclose parameters in quotation marks, they will be treated as literals. To ensure that the function receives only node values, use the same expressions you would use with the *select* attribute of an *<xsl:value-of>* instruction. The preceding script runs from the context of a *<lastname>* node in the following schema:

```
<Employee>
  <lastname>...</lastname>
  <firstname>...<firstname>
</Employee>
```

The dot symbol (.) indicates the value of the current node, whereas *../firstname* stands for the sibling of the current context node, named *<firstname>*.

When a function is declared, it is contained in a script block. Style sheets, however, can contain multiple blocks. All blocks are namespace-scoped and independent from each other. You can call a function defined in another block only when both functions share the same namespace and language.

Why should we use the same language to call into a function defined in another block? Isn't the .NET Framework totally language-neutral? The explanation for this discrepancy is found under the hood of *<msxsl:script>*. The instruction works as a mere code runner. It groups all script blocks in one or more all-encompassing classes. Blocks with the same namespace flow in the same dynamically created class.

In light of this, calling into external blocks is only possible because both involved functions—the caller and the callee—are members of the same managed class. For the same reasons, you can't use different languages. What the .NET Framework provides is the ability to invoke a compiled class irrespective of its source language. In no way does the .NET Framework provide you with the ability to write and compile a single class using different languages.

The CDATA Section

When an *<msxsl:script>* element is declared, you should enclose all of its code in a CDATA section. The main purpose of the CDATA delimitors is to protect the source code from the XML parser. A style sheet document is in fact still an XML document and as such gets parsed, as shown here:

```
<msxsl:script implements-prefix="dino" language="C#">
<![CDATA[
  code goes here
]]>
</msxsl:script>
```

Wrapped in a CDATA section, the user-defined code can contain any unescaped character that would otherwise confuse the parser. The most common example is <. If you omit the CDATA section and need to use < in a Boolean expression, you must use it in the escaped form *<* or you'll get an error.

Node Fragments in Transformations

As mentioned, you must always use XPath types when you pass arguments to *<msxsl:script>* blocks or return values from within a user-defined function. Let's have a second look at the command we used to invoke our previously defined extension function:

```
<xsl:value-of select="dino:PrepareName(., ../firstname)" />
```

As you can see, the *PrepareName* function is actually passed a couple of *XPathNodeIterator* objects. Chapter 6 defined *XPathNodeIterator* objects as the .NET Framework implementation of XPath node-sets. What any function receives is always the .NET Framework type that represents the results of a particular XPath query. The XSLT processor attempts to coerce types whenever possible. In this example, the *PrepareName* function takes two *string* objects, and the processor coerces the results of the . and *../firstname* expressions to *string* types.

When you need to process an entire node-set, declare your function to use an *XPathNodeIterator* argument, as shown here:

```
double CalculateSubTotal(XPathNodeIterator nodeset)
{
    double total = 0;

    while (nodeset.MoveNext())
        total += System.Convert.ToDouble(nodeset.Value);

    return total;
}
```

You call this function passing an XPath expression that evaluates to a node-set and then use the iterator's methods to navigate the nodes.

Passing Managed Objects to the Style Sheet

Using the *<msxsl:script>* instruction lets you execute managed code, which is advantageous from at least two standpoints. First, you write extension code using high-level languages, thus accessing the true power of the .NET Framework. Second, you move some of the style sheet logic into functions, thus rendering it with more appropriate tools than XSLT instructions.

The *<msxsl:script>* instruction does not represent the optimal solution, however. The main problem is that you still have code defined in the body of the style sheet. In addition, this code is silently and automatically transformed into managed code through the intervention of a system tool— the *<msxsl:script>* instruction—whose activity is neither monitored nor controllable. For this reason, the XSLT processor allows you to define a second group of parameters—extension objects.

How Managed Extension Objects Work

The idea behind extension objects is simple. Instead of defining embedded scripts and leaving the *<msxsl:script>* instruction the task of grouping them into a dynamically created and compiled class, you just create and pass a managed class yourself!

Unlike embedded scripts, which are natively defined in the body of the style sheet, extension objects are external resources that must be plugged into the style sheet in some way. You can't use the *<xsl:param>* mechanism, however, because XSLT parameters must be XPath types. On the other hand, conceptually speaking, an extension object is just an external argument you pass to the style sheet. For this reason, the *XsltArgumentList* class defines a parallel array of methods specifically to handle extension objects. (See the section "Passing and Retrieving Arguments," on page 323.)

The XSLT processor maps the parameters in the argument list to the *<xsl:param>* instructions in the style sheet. The extension objects, on the other hand, are plugged in using the same internal mechanism that triggers when the *<msxsl:script>* code is gathered and then compiled. In abstract terms, using embedded scripts and using extension objects are somewhat equivalent. But using extension objects provides you with greater flexibility and improves the overall software design.

Script and Extension Object Trade-Offs

Using extension objects is preferable over using embedded scripts for at least three reasons. First, extension objects provide much better code encapsulation, not to mention the possibility of class reuse. Second, you end up with more compact, layered style sheets, with significant advantages also in terms of more seamless code maintenance.

Finally, using classes lets you exploit the true potential of the .NET Framework more easily. You no longer have to worry about CDATA sections. And you can cascade calls from one class to another, with each class compiled separately and written in any language. An additional pleasant side effect is that you can call methods in classes belonging to custom namespaces as well as system namespaces.

Extension Objects in Action

The following code demonstrates how to register extension objects for use with the XSLT processor:

```
// Create and configure the extension object
ExtensionObject o = new ExtensionObject();
// *** set properties on the object if needed

// Register the object with the XSLT processor
XsltArgumentList args = new XsltArgumentList();
args.AddExtensionObject("urn:dino-objects", o);

XslTransform xslt = new XslTransform();
xslt.Transform(doc, args, writer);
```

The *ExtensionObject* class in this code snippet is any .NET class that is visible to the caller program. When you add a living instance of the object to the argument list, you must specify the namespace URI that will be used throughout the style sheet to qualify the object.

The style sheet must include the corresponding namespace declaration with its own style sheet–wide prefix, as in the following example:

```
<xsl:stylesheet version="1.0"
    xmlns:xsl="http://www.w3.org/1999/XSL/Transform"
    xmlns:dino="urn:dino-objects">
```

Finally, you invoke the methods on the object's interface using XPath expressions, as with embedded scripts. For example, if the *ExtensionObject* class has a *DoSomething* method, the following would be perfectly valid code:

```
<xsl:template match="lastname">
  <TD style="border:1px solid black">
    <xsl:value-of select="dino:DoSomething(., ../firstname)" />
  </TD>
</xsl:template>
```

As with embedded scripts, methods of extension objects must publicly handle .NET Framework types that can be converted to XPath types.

Conclusion

XML data is a key element for any modern distributed and tiered system. But XML data alone is not really usable, and even when it is usable, it turns out to be not very profitable, because XML is a metalanguage that needs further instantiation and specialization.

You can think of XML as an abstract class for data description languages. Like abstract classes, you can use XML as a reference but not to perform complex tasks. So XML does matter but only if you pair it with other related technologies. In Chapter 6, we analyzed XPath as the emerging language for performing queries. I can't say whether XPath is the definitive query tool or just a temporary technology that will soon be replaced by something else—perhaps XQuery. XPath is a key technology to enable powerful and effective data transformation, which is just what this whole chapter has been all about.

In abstract terms, transforming XML data means making data usable by actual applications and by end-users. XSLT is simply a subset of the XML style sheet language, but it probably represents the core part. This chapter provided a quick refresher course in the XSLT vocabulary of instructions and then focused on the .NET Framework implementation of the XSLT processor.

In the .NET Framework, the XSLT processor is contained in a single class—the *XslTransform* class. This chapter explained the programming interface of the XSLT processor and unveiled some of its internal features. We also looked at security and threading aspects and a few concrete examples of style sheet definitions and use.

With this chapter, the second part of the book, dedicated to data manipulation via XML-related standards, has come to the end. In Part III, we'll look at a new programming aspect of XML—XML and databases. Chapter 8 in particular will discuss how to read and write data from and to databases in XML format.

Further Reading

For further study of the XSL initiative and XSLT in particular, the official specification is available at *http://www.w3.org/TR/xslt*. It refers to XSLT 1.0, which is the version currently supported by the .NET Framework. For a sneak preview of what's coming next, the working draft of XSLT 1.1 is downloadable from *http://www.w3.org/TR/xslt11*. In our examination of the XSL technology as a whole, XSL Formatting Objects (XSL-FO) were introduced. To learn more, have a look at the following online tutorial: *http://www.dpawson.co.uk/xsl/sect3/bk/index.html*. In general, useful links for online material about XSL and related technologies are listed at *http://www.w3.org/Style/XSL*.

Part III
XML and Data Access

8

XML and Databases

Most likely, the majority of today's computer experts and students would associate the idea of a database with a relational database. Since their introduction in the early 1970s, relational databases have gained an extraordinary success. Relational databases have grown so steadily and progressively that along the way they've lost the qualifying adjective *relational* and become the only commonly accepted way to design a database.

Today, relational databases like Microsoft SQL Server 2000, Oracle 9i, and IBM DB2 are the favorite tools for storing and working with data. Modern databases do a lot of things, but what a (relational) database still does best is store data. Relational databases won out over other data models such as the hierarchical and reticular models mostly because of their inherent simplicity and natural way of modeling data and arranging queries. Relational databases exploit the structured query language (SQL) to search for contained information.

Recent developments in the computer industry have raised the need for total software integration and communication. As a side effect, data modeled into a system must often be transformed into analogous, but not identical, models in order to be stored or linked on different systems. Enter XML and its innate ability to describe data.

More and more often today you need to extract data out of databases and model it into a particular data schema using XML. So why not just ask the database itself to return data as XML, possibly formatted in a supplied schema? XML support is built into (or will be built into) almost all database management systems (DBMS) currently available. In particular, Microsoft SQL Server 2000 comes with an embedded engine capable of returning data as XML. This feature is built as an extension to the traditional SELECT command, and data is rendered as XML before being sent back to the client. Oracle 9i provides a slightly different model that treats XML as a native data type. XML data can be stored in ad hoc relational tables as well as in binary large object (BLOB) fields that can be either binary or ASCII.

Whatever the vendor approach, XML and databases represent a key alliance for the present and the future of data-driven and interoperable applications. In this chapter, we'll review the essential aspects of XML in SQL Server 2000, and you'll learn how to take advantage of these features from within a Microsoft .NET Framework environment.

Reading XML Data from Databases

With SQL Server 2000, you have two basic ways to retrieve data as XML: you can use the XML extensions to the SELECT command, or you can execute a query on a particular text or BLOB field that is known to contain XML data. SQL Server does not mark these fields with a special attribute or data type to indicate that they contain XML data, however.

With the first technique, you typically use the FOR XML clause in a traditional query command. In response, the DBMS executes the query in two steps. First it executes the SELECT statement, and next it applies the FOR XML transformation to a rowset. The resulting XML is then sent to the client as a one-column rowset.

> **Note**   Although specific to the OLE DB specification, the term *rowset* is often used generically to indicate a set of rows that contain columns of data. Rowsets are key objects that enable all OLE DB data providers to expose query result set data in a tabular format.

The FOR XML extensions let you consider XML mostly as a data output format. With the alternative technique for retrieving data as XML, you can store raw XML data in a text or BLOB field and retrieve that data using an ordinary query—preferably a scalar, single-field query. In both cases, the Microsoft ADO.NET object model, along with the Microsoft .NET Framework XML core classes, provide a number of handy features to extract XML data quickly and effectively.

SQL Server 2000 XML Extensions

The XML support in SQL Server 2000 provides URL-driven access to the database resources, XML-driven data management, and the possibility of using XPath queries to select data from relational tables. SQL Server 2000 does not create ad hoc storage structures for XML data. It does provide an ad hoc infrastructure for reading, writing, and querying relational data through the XML logical filter.

The following list gives you a bird's-eye view of the key XML features available in SQL Server 2000 and its latest extension, SQLXML 3.0:

- **Access SQL Server through a URL.**   An ISAPI filter running on top of the Internet Information Services (IIS) allows you to directly query commands to SQL Server using HTTP. You simply point to a properly formatted URL, and what you get back is the result set data formatted as XML data.

- **Create XML schema-driven views of relational data.**   Similar to CREATE VIEW, this feature lets you represent a result set as an XML document written according to a given XML Schema Definition (XSD) or XML-Data Reduced (XDR) schema. You specify the mapping rules between the native fields and XML attributes and elements. The resultant XML document can be treated as a regular XML Document Object Model (XML DOM) object and queried using XPath expressions.

- **Return fetched data as XML.**   This feature is at the foundation of the entire XML support in SQL Server 2000. A database internal engine is capable of formatting raw column data into XML fragments and exposing those fragments as strings to callers. This capability is incorporated in the SELECT statement and can be controlled through a number of clauses and attributes.

- **Insert data represented as an XML document.**   Just as you can read relational data into hierarchical XML documents, you can write XML data into tables. The source document is preprocessed by a system stored procedure named *sp_xml_preparedocument*. The parsed document is then passed on to a special module—named OPENXML—that provides a rowset view of the XML data. At this point, to ordinary Transact-SQL (T-SQL) commands, XML native data looks like ordinary result sets.

(continued)

SQL Server 2000 XML Extensions   *(continued)*

SQLXML 3.0 is an extension to SQL Server 2000 designed to keep current with evolving W3C standards for XML and other requested functions. Available as a free download at *http://msdn.microsoft.com/downloads*, SQLXML 3.0 also provides a bunch of managed classes for exposing some of the functionalities to .NET Framework applications. SQLXML 3.0 includes the ability to expose stored procedures as Web services via the Simple Object Access Protocol (SOAP) and adds support for ADO.NET DiffGrams and client-side XML transformations.

XML Extensions to the SELECT Statement

In SQL Server 2000, you can query existing relational tables and return results as XML documents rather than as standard rowsets. The query is written and runs normally. If the SELECT statement contains a trailing FOR XML clause, the result set is then transformed into a string of XML text. Within the FOR XML clause, you can specify one of the XML modes described in Table 8-1.

Table 8-1   Modes of the FOR XML Extension

Mode	Description
AUTO	Returns query results as a sequence of *<table>* XML elements, where *table* is the name of the table. Fields are rendered as node attributes. If the additional ELEMENTS clause is specified, rows are rendered as child nodes instead of attributes.
EXPLICIT	The query defines the schema of the XML document being returned.
RAW	Returns query results as a sequence of generic *<row>* nodes with as many attributes as the selected fields.

The mode is valid only in the SELECT command for which it has been set. In no way does the mode affect any subsequent queries. XML-driven queries can be executed directly or from within stored procedures.

> **Tip**   The XML data contains an XDR schema if you append the XML-DATA attribute to the FOR XML mode of choice, as shown here:
>
> ```
> SELECT * FROM Employees FOR XML, XMLDATA
> ```
>
> Schema information is incorporated in a *<schema>* node prepended to the document.

The FOR XML AUTO Mode

The AUTO mode returns data packed as XML fragments—that is, without a root node. The alias of the table determines the name of each node. If the query joins two tables on the value of a column, the resulting XML schema provides nested elements.

Let's consider the following simple query:

```
SELECT CustomerID, ContactName FROM Customers FOR XML AUTO
```

The XML result set has the form shown here:

```
<Customers CustomerID="ALFKI" ContactName="Maria Anders" />
<Customers CustomerID="ANATR" ContactName="Ana Trujillo" />
...
```

Try now with a command that contains an INNER JOIN, as follows:

```
SELECT Customers.CustomerID, Customers.ContactName,
  Orders.OrderID
FROM Customers
INNER JOIN Orders ON Customers.CustomerID = Orders.CustomerID
FOR XML AUTO
```

Interestingly, in this case the XML output automatically groups child records below the parent:

```
<Customers CustomerID="ALFKI" ContactName="Maria Anders">
  <Orders OrderID="10643"/>
  <Orders OrderID="10692"/>
  <Orders OrderID="10783"/>
  ...
</Customers>
<Customers CustomerID="ALFKI" ContactName="Ana Trujillo">
  <Orders OrderID="11459"/>
  <Orders OrderID="10987"/>
  ...
</Customers>
...
```

If the ELEMENTS attribute is also specified, the data rows are rendered in XML through elements rather than as attributes. Let's consider the following query:

```
SELECT CustomerID, ContactName FROM Customers FOR XML AUTO,
  ELEMENTS
```

The XML output is similar to this:

```
<Customers>
  <CustomerID>ALFKI</CustomerID>
  <ContactName>Maria Anders</ContactName>
</Customers>
<Customers>
  <CustomerID>ANATR</CustomerID>
  <ContactName>Ana Trujillo</ContactName>
</Customers>
...
```

In the case of INNER JOINs, the output becomes the following:

```
<Customers>
  <CustomerID>ALFKI</CustomerID>
  <ContactName>Maria Anders</ContactName>
  <Orders>
    <OrderID>10643</OrderID>
  </Orders>
  <Orders>
    <OrderID>10692</OrderID>
  </Orders>
  ...
</Customers>
...
```

The FOR XML AUTO mode always resolves table dependencies in terms of nested rows. The overall XML stream is not completely well-formed. Instead of an XML document, the output is an XML fragment, making it easier for clients to concatenate more result sets into a single structure.

> **Note**   If you also add the BINARY BASE64 option to a FOR XML query, any binary data that is returned will automatically be encoded using a base64 algorithm.

The FOR XML RAW Mode

As its name suggests, the FOR XML RAW mode is the least rich mode in terms of features and options. When designed using this mode, the query returns an XML fragment that, at a first glance, might look a lot like the fragment produced by the FOR XML AUTO option. You obtain an XML fragment made of *<row>* nodes with as many attributes as the columns. For example, consider the following simple query:

```
SELECT CustomerID, ContactName FROM Customers FOR XML RAW
```

The output is shown here:

```
<row CustomerID="ALFKI" ContactName="Maria Anders" />
<row CustomerID="ANATR" ContactName="Ana Trujillo" />
...
```

You can't change the name of the node, nor can you render attributes as nested nodes. So far, so good—the RAW mode is only a bit less flexible than the AUTO mode. However, the situation changes when you use joined tables.

The schema of XML data remains intact even when you process multiple tables. The INNER JOIN statement from the previous section run in FOR XML RAW mode originates the following output:

```
<row CustomerID="ALFKI" ContactName="Maria Anders"
  OrderID="10643"/>
<row CustomerID="ALFKI" ContactName="Maria Anders"
  OrderID="10692"/>
<row CustomerID="ALFKI" ContactName="Maria Anders"
  OrderID="10783"/>
...
```

Even with the naked eye, you can see that the RAW mode produces a less optimized and more redundant output than the AUTO mode. The ELEMENTS clause is not supported in RAW mode, whereas XMLDATA and BINARY BASE64 are perfectly legitimate.

Limitations of FOR XML

The FOR XML clause is not valid in all cases in which a SELECT statement is acceptable. In general, FOR XML can be used only when the selection produces direct output going to the SQL Server client, whatever that output is. Let's review a couple of common scenarios in which you can't make use of the FOR XML clause. For a more complete overview, please refer to SQL Server's Books Online.

FOR XML Can't Be Used in Subselections

SQL Server 2000 allows you to use the output of an inner SELECT statement as a virtual table to which an outer SELECT statement can refer. The inner query can't return XML data if you plan to use its output to perform further operations. For example, the following query is not valid:

```
SELECT * FROM (SELECT * FROM Employees FOR XML AUTO) AS t
```

Likewise, the FOR XML clause is not valid in a SELECT statement that is used to create a view. For example, the following statement is not allowed:

```
CREATE VIEW MyOrders AS
    SELECT OrderId, OrderDate FROM Orders FOR XML AUTO
```

In contrast, you can select data from a view and return it as XML. In addition, FOR XML can't be used with cursors.

FOR XML Can't Be Used with Computed Columns

The current version of SQL Server does not permit GROUP BY and aggregate functions to be used with FOR XML AUTO. Aggregate functions and GROUP BY clauses can be safely used if the XML query is expressed in RAW mode, however. The following code returns the expected results:

```
SELECT min(unitprice) AS price, max(quantity) AS quantity
FROM [order details] FOR XML RAW
```

The only caveat is that you must explicity name the computed columns using the AS keyword. The output is shown here:

```
<row price="2.0000" quantity="130" />
```

Table 8-1 mentioned a third FOR XML mode—the EXPLICIT mode. The EXPLICIT mode goes beyond the rather basic goals of both AUTO and RAW. It is designed to enable users to build a personal schema to render relational data in XML. The EXPLICIT mode is one of the ways that programmers have to create custom XML views of stored data.

Client-Side XML Formatting

SQLXML 3.0 extends the base set of SQL Server 2000 XML extensions by including client-side formatting capabilities in addition to the default server-side XML formatting. From within a .NET Framework application, you use SQLXML 3.0 managed classes (more on this in the section "SQLXML Managed Classes," on page 386) to set up a command that returns XML data.

When the command executes, the managed classes—at least in this version of the SQLXML library—call into a middle-tier OLE DB provider

(SQLXMLOLEDB) object, which in turn calls into the OLE DB provider for SQL Server. The command that hits the database does not contain the FOR XML clause. When the rowset gets back to the SQLXMLOLEDB provider, it is transformed into XML according to the syntax of the FOR XML clause and returned to the client. Figure 8-1 compares server-side and client-side XML formatting.

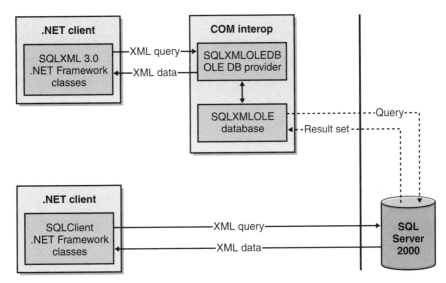

Figure 8-1   The client-side XML formatting feature of SQLXML 3.0 makes use of intermediate OLE DB providers to execute the query and transform the results.

As you'd expect, the two intermediate OLE DB providers cause more performance problems than they ever attempt to resolve. On the other hand, SQLXML 3.0 is not specifically designed for the .NET Framework, although it contains a few managed classes that we'll look at in the section "SQLXML Managed Classes," on page 386. In a nutshell, keep in mind that SQLXML 3.0 provides client-side XML formatting but that this feature is rather inefficient. For .NET Framework applications, a much better approach for client-side XML rendering is represented by the *XmlDataDocument* class. (See the section "The *XmlDataDocument* Class," on page 372.)

Creating XML Views

Just as a CREATE VIEW statement in SQL lets you create a virtual table by collecting columns from one or more tables, an XML view provides an alternative and highly customizable way to present relational data in XML.

Building an XML view consists of defining a custom XML schema and mapping to its elements the columns and the tables selected by the query. Once built, an XML view can be used like its close cousin, SQL view. In particular, an XML view can be queried using XPath expressions and transformed using XSL Transformation (XSLT) scripts. An XML view is simply a stream of XML data and can be used as allowed by .NET. In the .NET Framework, you can use XML views through readers, XML DOM, or even specialized classes, such as those in SQLXML 3.0.

There are two possible ways to create XML views: you can use the FOR XML EXPLICIT mode of the SELECT statement, or you can build an annotated XDR or XSD schema. To use an XSD schema, you must install SQLXML 3.0 first.

The FOR XML EXPLICIT Mode

The query defines the shape of the generated XML document. The ultimate goal of the query is making hierarchical data fit into a tabular rowset. An EXPLICIT mode query creates a virtual table in which all the information fetched from the tables is organized in such a way that it can then be easily rendered in XML. The definition of the schema is free, and of course, programmers must ensure that the final output is well-formed XML.

Any FOR XML EXPLICIT query requires two extra metacolumns, named *Tag* and *Parent*. The values in these columns are used to generate the XML hierarchy. The *Tag* column contains a unique numeric index for each XML root node that is expected to have children in the XML schema. The *Parent* column contains a tag value that links a given node to a particular, and previously defined, subtree.

To add columns, you must use a relatively complex syntax for column aliases. Each selected column must have an alias defined according to the following syntax:

```
SELECT column_name AS [ParentNode!ParentTag!TagName!Directive]
```

The *ParentNode* item represents the name of the node element that is expected to be the parent of the column data. The *ParentTag* is the tag number of the parent. The *TagName* item indicates the name of the XML element that contains the column data. Finally, the *Directive* element can take various values, the most common ones being no value or *element*. If no value is specified, the column data is rendered as an attribute named *TagName*; otherwise, it will be an *element* attribute.

It's interesting to note that an EXPLICIT mode query consists of one or more tables that result from SELECT statements potentially involving multiple tables and joined data. Let's see what's needed to obtain the following XML representation of the rows in the Northwind database's Employees table:

```
<Employee id="employeeid"
  name="titleOfCourtesy lastname, firstname">
  <PersonalData>
    <Birth>birthdate</Birth>
    <City>city</City>
  </PersonalData>
  <JobData>
    <Hired>hiredate</Hired>
    <Title>title</Title>
  </JobData>
  <Notes>notes</Notes>
</Employee>
```

The boldface lines in this code represent the roots of the three subtrees of XML data being created. Each subtree corresponds to a different tag, and each must be filled by resorting to a different SELECT statement.

To begin filling the subtrees, consider the following query:

```
SELECT 1 AS Tag,
       NULL AS Parent,
       employeeid AS [Employee!1!ID],
       lastname AS [Employee!1!Name]
```

This statement fills in the first tag—the fragment's root—which has no parent and contains two attributes, *ID* and *Name*. The *employeeid* and the *lastname* columns will fill respectively the *ID* and the *Name* attributes of an *<Employee>* node with no parent.

The first table always defines the structure of the XML view. Successive tables can only fill in holes—nothing new will be added. Consequently, to obtain the previous schema, you must write the first tag as follows:

```
SELECT 1 AS Tag,
  NULL AS Parent,
  employeeid AS [Employee!1!ID],
  titleofcourtesy + ' ' + lastname + ', ' + firstname
       AS [Employee!1!Name],
  NULL AS [PersonalData!2!BirthDate!element],
  NULL AS [PersonalData!2!City!element],
  NULL AS [JobData!3!HireDate!element],
  NULL AS [JobData!3!Title!element],
  lastname AS [Employee!1!Notes!element]
FROM Employees
```

The columns with *NULL* values will be selected by successive queries. In particular, you'll notice *PersonalData* and *JobData* trees with tag IDs of *2* and *3*, respectively. The former contains a pair of *BirthDate* and *City* elements. The latter holds elements named *Title* and *HireDate*.

To unify all the subtables, you must use the UNION ALL statement. The complete statement is shown here:

```
SELECT
  1 AS Tag,
  NULL AS Parent,
  employeeid AS [Employee!1!ID],
  titleofcourtesy + ' ' + lastname + ', ' + firstname
      AS [Employee!1!Name],
  NULL AS [PersonalData!2!BirthDate!element],
  NULL AS [PersonalData!2!City!element],
  NULL AS [JobData!3!HireDate!element],
  NULL AS [JobData!3!Title!element],
  lastname AS [Employee!1!Notes!element]
FROM Employees

UNION ALL
SELECT
  2, 1,
  employeeid,
  titleofcourtesy + ' ' + lastname + ', ' + firstname,
  birthdate,
  city,
  hiredate,
  title,
  notes
FROM Employees

UNION ALL
SELECT
  3, 1,
  employeeid,
  titleofcourtesy + ' ' + lastname + ', ' + firstname,
  birthdate,
  city,
  hiredate,
  title,
  notes
FROM Employees
ORDER BY [Employee!1!ID]
FOR XML EXPLICIT
```

The T-SQL UNION ALL operator combines the results of two or more SELECT statements into a single result set. All participating result sets must have the same number of columns, and corresponding columns must have compatible data types.

Using an Annotated Mapping Schema

A more lightweight alternative to FOR XML EXPLICIT views is the annotated schema. SQL Server 2000 lets you create XML views by defining an XDR schema with special annotations that work like placeholders for selected data. Basically, instead of defining the schema using a new syntax and combining multiple virtual tables, you use a standard XML data definition language and map elements to columns using ad hoc annotations.

The base version of SQL Server 2000 supports only XDR. If you want to use XSD, you must install SQLXML 3.0. (To review the differences between XDR and XSD, see Chapter 3)

The following listing shows a simple XSD annotated schema that defines an *<Employee>* node with a couple of child nodes—*<FirstName>* and *<LastName>*:

```
<xsd:schema
    xmlns:xsd="http://www.w3.org/2001/XMLSchema"
    xmlns:sql="urn:schemas-microsoft-com:mapping-schema">
    <xsd:element name="Employee" sql:relation="Employees" >
      <xsd:complexType>
        <xsd:sequence>
          <xsd:element name="FName"
             sql:field="FirstName" type="xsd:string" />
          <xsd:element name="LName"
             sql:field="LastName" type="xsd:string" />
        </xsd:sequence>
        <xsd:attribute name="EmployeeID" type="xsd:integer" />
      </xsd:complexType>
    </xsd:element>
</xsd:schema>
```

The annotations *sql:relation* and *sql:field* facilitate the mapping between the source table and the resulting XML data. In particular, *sql:relation* indicates that the given node is related to the specified table. The *sql:field* annotation indicates the column that should be used to populate the given element. If no *sql:field* annotation is provided, SQL Server expects to find a perfect match between the element or attribute name and a column. In the preceding schema, the *EmployeeID* attribute is linked directly by name.

> **Note**   Annotated schemas do not allow you to use expressions when selecting columns. The *sql:field* annotation can accept only the name of an existing column; it can't accept an expression that evaluates to a column name.

Are XML Views Effective?

The FOR XML EXPLICIT clause and annotated schemas are two somewhat equivalent ways to query relational tables and return data formatted according to a particular XML schema. XSD mapping is more powerful than XDR, but all in all, in terms of raw functionalities, explicit and schema mapping are two nearly identical options for building XML views.

Certainly the FOR XML EXPLICIT clause can lead to hard-to-maintain code, whereas annotated schemas are probably easier to read and maintain and, in addition, keep the schema distinct from the query and the data.

The real XML mapping schema issue is this: What's the added value that XML views bring to your code? Are you sure that the ability to execute XPath queries justifies the creation of an XML view? The XPath query engine is certainly inferior to the SQL Server's query engine, at least for complex queries like the ones you might need to perform on real-world data. In addition, for read/write solutions, writing data back to the native relational tables can be less than effective if done through XML. We'll return to this topic when we look at the OPENXML provider in the section "The OPENXML Rowset Provider," on page 376.

One scenario in which reading relational data as XML turns out to be really and clearly effective is when you need to turn fetched data into more manageable or easily interoperable structures. If you need to exchange an invoice document with commercial partners, using an XML representation of the data is certainly useful, because you process data in an intermediate, platform-independent and application-independent format, while preserving the ability to create views and perform queries locally. In addition, having the database return and accept XML data with a custom layout can only help considerably.

In this scenario, another reasonable step you might need to take is transforming the XML data into high-level data structures such as classes. For .NET Framework applications, *XML serialization* is key technology that you must absolutely be familiar with. We'll examine XML serialization in Chapter 11.

Let's look now at how ADO.NET and XML classes can be used to read and process relational data expressed in a hierarchical shape.

XML Data Readers

.NET Framework applications delegate all their low-level data access tasks to a special breed of connector objects called *managed data providers*. The object model around these connector components is known as ADO.NET. Basically, a data provider is the software component that enables any .NET Framework application to connect to a data source and execute commands to retrieve and modify data.

A .NET Framework data provider component interfaces client applications through the objects in the ADO.NET namespace and exposes any provider-specific behavior directly to consumers. A .NET Framework data provider component creates a minimal layer between the physical data source and the client code, thereby increasing performance without sacrificing functionality.

A .NET Framework data provider is fully integrated with the surrounding environment—the .NET Framework—so any results that a command generates are promptly and automatically packed into a familiar data structure—the ADO.NET and XML classes—for further use.

A key architectural goal for .NET Framework data providers is that they must be designed to work on a rigorous per-data source basis. They expose connection, transaction, command, and reader objects, all working according to the internal capabilities and structure of the DBMS. As a result, the programming interface of, say, the Microsoft Access data provider will not be completely identical to that of the SQL Server provider. An area in which this difference is palpable is in XML data queries.

OLE DB and .NET Framework Managed Data Providers

Prior to the advent of the .NET Framework, OLE DB was considered the emerging data access technology. It was well positioned to definitively replace in the heart, and the code, of developers another well-known standard for universal data access—open database connectivity (ODBC).

OLE DB is the data access technology that translates the Universal Data Access (UDA) vision into concrete programming calls. Introduced about five years ago, UDA describes a scenario in which all the data that can be expressed in a tabular format can be accessed and manipulated through a common API, no matter the actual binary format and the storage medium. According to the UDA vision, special modules—the OLE DB providers—would be called to expose the contents of a data source to the world. Another family of components—the OLE DB consumers—would consume such contents by interacting with the providers through a common API.

(continued)

OLE DB and .NET Framework Managed Data Providers   *(continued)*

In designing the intermediate API for OLE DB providers and consumers to communicate through, Microsoft decided to use the key software technology of the time: the Component Object Model (COM). In this design approach, the consumer had to instantiate a COM object, query for a number of interfaces, and handle the results. The provider had to implement the same number of interfaces (and even more) and access the wrapped data source at every method invocation. The methods defined in the OLE DB interfaces are quite general and are not tied to the features of a particular data source.

Compared to OLE DB providers, .NET Framework data providers implement a much smaller set of interfaces and always work within the boundaries of the .NET Framework common language runtime (CLR). A .NET Framework managed data provider and an OLE DB provider are different components mostly in the outermost interface, which clients use to communicate. Under the hood, they look much more similar than you may expect. In particular, both components use the same low-level API to talk to the physical data source. For example, both the .NET Framework data provider and the OLE DB provider access SQL Server 7.0 and later using Tabular Data Stream (TDS) packets. Both components hook up SQL Server at the wire level, thereby providing a nearly identical performance, each from their native environment—Microsoft Win32 for OLE DB and the .NET Framework for managed data providers.

Reading from XML Queries

The SQL Server .NET Framework data provider makes available a particular method in its command class, *SqlCommand*, that explicitly lets you obtain an XML reader whenever the command text returns XML data. In other words, you can choose to execute a SQL command with a trailing FOR XML clause and then pick up the results directly using an XML reader. Let's see how.

The following code sets up a command that returns XML information about all the employees in the Northwind database:

```
string nwind = "DATABASE=northwind;SERVER=localhost;UID=sa;";
string query = "SELECT * FROM Employees FOR XML AUTO, ELEMENTS";
SqlConnection conn = new SqlConnection(nwind);
SqlCommand cmd = new SqlCommand(query, conn);
```

In general, an ADO.NET command can be run using a variety of execute methods, including *ExecuteNonQuery*, *ExecuteReader*, and *ExecuteScalar*. These methods differ in the format in which the result set is packed. The SQL Server 2000 ad hoc command class—*SqlCommand*—supplies a fourth execute method, *ExecuteXmlReader*, which simply returns the result set as an XML reader.

You use the *ExecuteXmlReader* method as a special type of constructor for an *XmlTextReader* object, as shown here:

```
conn.Open();
XmlTextReader reader = (XmlTextReader) cmd.ExecuteXmlReader();
ProcessXmlData(reader);
reader.Close();
conn.Close();
```

The *ExecuteXmlReader* method executes the command and returns an instance of an *XmlTextReader* object to access the result set. Of course, *ExecuteXml-Reader* fails, throwing an *InvalidOperationException* exception, if the command does not return an XML result.

The *SqlCommand* class performs no preliminary check on the structure of the T-SQL command being executed to statically determine whether the command returns XML data. This means that any error that invalidates the operation is detected on the server. A client-side check could verify that the command text incorporates a correct FOR XML clause prior to sending the text to the database. However, such a test would also catch as erroneous a perfectly legitimate situation: selecting XML data from a text or a BLOB field. So while performing a preliminary check could still make sense for some user applications, it would be ineffective if done from within the command class.

> **Note**   Although the *ExecuteXmlReader* method returns a generic *XmlReader* object, the true type of the returned object is always *Xml-TextReader*. You can use this object at will—for example, to create a validating reader. Bear in mind, however, that the more you use the XML reader, the longer the connection stays open.

The application shown in Figure 8-2 uses the schema we analyzed in the section "The FOR XML EXPLICIT Mode," on page 356, while examining the FOR XML EXPLICIT clause. The application runs the same SELECT command we used in that section and then walks its way through the result set using an XML reader. The information read is used to fill up a treeview control.

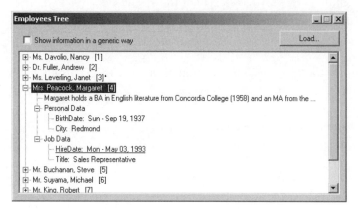

Figure 8-2 The application retrieves data from SQL Server using an explicit schema, reads the information through an XML reader, and populates a treeview control.

The following code illustrates how to extract information from the previously described schema and add nodes to the treeview. The *ProcessXmlData* routine has an extra Boolean argument used to specify whether you want the application's user interface to be generic. If the user interface is not generic, it makes assumptions about the structure of the XML data and attributes specific semantics to each element. If the user interface is generic, the sample application treats the data as a generic XML stream.

```
void ProcessXmlData(XmlTextReader reader, bool bUseGenericMode)
{
    // Clear the treeview
    dataTree.Nodes.Clear();
    dataTree.BeginUpdate();

    // Process elements
    while(reader.Read())
    {
        if(reader.NodeType == XmlNodeType.Element)
        {
            // Creates an hash table of nodes at various
            // depths so that each element can figure out
            // what its parent is
            int depth = reader.Depth;
            int parentDepth = depth -1;
            string text = "";
```

```
        if (m_ParentNodes.ContainsKey(parentDepth))
        {
            TreeNode n =
                (TreeNode) m_ParentNodes[parentDepth];
            text = PrepareOtherDataDisplayText(reader,
                bUseGenericMode);
            m_ParentNodes[depth] = n.Nodes.Add(text);
        }
        else
        {
            // Only first-level nodes
            text = PrepareEmployeeDisplayText(reader,
                bUseGenericMode);
            m_ParentNodes[depth] = dataTree.Nodes.Add(text);
        }
    }
}
dataTree.EndUpdate();
}
```

Figure 8-3 shows the user interface in generic mode.

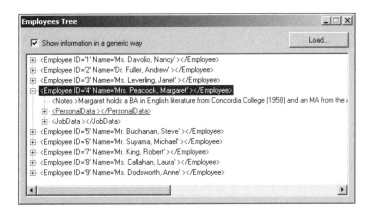

Figure 8-3   The user interface of the application now shows only XML elements.

A quick comment regarding the algorithm used to populate this treeview object: I make use of a small hash table to keep track of the latest node inserted at a given level—the *Depth* property of the XML text reader. Each element that is expected to have a parent—that is, a depth greater than 0—looks upward for a *TreeNode* object in the table and adds its description to the node. Next, the node itself registers as a parent node for its own level of depth.

Under the Hood of *ExecuteXmlReader*

Internally, the *ExecuteXmlReader* method first calls *ExecuteReader* and then creates a new instance of an *XmlTextReader* object. The XML reader is configured to work on an internal stream object whose class name is *SqlStream*. The *SqlStream* class represents the data stream that SQL Server uses to return rows to callers. The format of the SQL Server data stream is the TDS.

> **Note** The *SqlStream* class is defined internally to the *System.Data* assembly and is marked with the *internal* modifier. This keyword makes the class accessible only to the other classes defined in the same assembly. The Microsoft Visual Basic .NET counterpart to the *internal* keyword is *Friend*.

The following listing shows the pseudocode of *ExecuteXmlReader*. What happens under the lid of this method leads straight to the conclusion that the ability to execute a database command to XML can also be added to the *OleDbCommand* class as well as to the command classes in a number of other managed providers. We'll examine this concept in more detail in a moment.

```
public XmlReader ExecuteXmlReader()
{
    // Execute the command
    SqlDataReader datareader = ExecuteReader();

    // Obtain the TDS stream for the command
    SqlStream tdsdata = new SqlStream(datareader);

    // Create the XML text reader
    // (No context information specified)
    XmlReader xmlreader = new XmlTextReader(tdsdata,
        XmlNodeType.Element, null);

    // Close the temporary data reader but leaves the
    // stream open
    datareader.Close();

    return xmlreader;
}
```

As long as the XML reader is open and in use, the underlying database connection remains open.

At the end of the day, the trick that makes it possible to access the result set as XML is simply the availability of the data through a stand-alone XML reader object. SQL Server 2000 transforms the contents of its low-level TDS stream into XML and then builds an XML text reader from that. The whole process takes place on the server.

Reading from Text Fields

Most important with XML readers working on top of SQL commands is that the commands return XML data. With SQL Server 2000, this certainly happens if you use any of the *FOR XML* clauses. It also happens if the query returns one or more rows that, in combination, can be seen as a unique XML stream.

Text or *ntext* fields that contain XML data can be selected and then processed using an XML text reader. (The *ntext* data type is a variable-length Unicode data type that can hold a maximum of 1,073,741,823 characters. An *ntext* column stores a 16-byte pointer in the data row, and the data is stored separately.) Of course, the query must include a single column and possibly a single record. Let's consider the following query from a modified version of the Northwind database. I created the XmlNet database by duplicating the Northwind databases Employees table and then wrapping all the strings stored in the Notes column in a *<notes></notes>* pair. The Notes column is of type *ntext*.

```
SELECT notes FROM employees
```

Although the SELECT command listed here does not explicitly return XML data, you can run it through the *ExecuteXmlReader* method, as shown here:

```
string nwind = "DATABASE=xmlnet;SERVER=localhost;UID=sa;";
string query = "SELECT notes FROM employees";
SqlConnection conn = new SqlConnection(nwind);
SqlCommand cmd = new SqlCommand(query, conn);

conn.Open();
XmlTextReader reader = (XmlTextReader) cmd.ExecuteXmlReader();
ProcessNotes(reader);
reader.Close();
conn.Close();
```

The XML reader will loop through the nodes, moving from one record to the next, as shown here:

```
void ProcessNotes(XmlTextReader reader)
{
    try
    {
        while(reader.Read())
```

(continued)

```
            {
                if (reader.NodeType == XmlNodeType.Text)
                    MessageBox.Show(reader.Value);
            }
        }
        catch {}
        finally
        {
            MessageBox.Show("Closed...");
        }
    }
```

The connection remains open until the reader is closed. Next store the results in a string variable and use that string to create a new *XmlTextReader* object. (See Chapter 2.) This technique gives you an extra advantage: you can work with the reader while you are disconnected from the database.

An XML Reader for Data Readers

An XML reader can work on top of different data containers, including streams, files, and text readers. By writing a custom XML reader, you can also navigate non-XML data using the same XML reader metaphor. In this case, you create a virtual XML tree and make the underlying data look like XML. (In Chapter 2, you learned how to visit CSV files the XML way.)

The ability to expose result sets via XML is specific to SQL Server 2000 and potentially to any other native managed provider for DBMS systems with full support for XML queries. You can't, for example, use the *ExecuteXmlReader* method with an object of class *OleDbCommand*.

Recall from the section "Under the Hood of *ExecuteXmlReader*," on page 366, the internal structure of *ExecuteXmlReader*. The *ExecuteXmlReader* method simply creates an XML text reader based on the internal stream used to carry data back and forth. What about creating a custom XML reader by building a virtual XML tree around the provider-specific data reader? In this way, you could easily extend any .NET Framework data provider by using the *ExecuteXmlReader* method. This method is not as effective as using the internal stream, but it does work and can be applied to all data providers.

Building the XML Data Reader

Let's rework the CSV reader example from Chapter 2 and build an *XmlDataReader* class inheriting from *XmlReader*, as follows:

```
public class XmlDataReader : XmlReader
{
    ...
}
```

The base class is for the most part abstract, thus requiring you to override several methods and properties. When designing an XML reader, a key step is defining the XML virtual tree that underlying data will populate. In this case, we'll try for a relatively simple XML schema that closely resembles the schema of the FOR XML RAW mode, as shown here:

```
<row field1="..." field2="..." ... />
<row field1="..." field2="..." ... />
...
```

The *XmlDataReader* class features only one constructor, which takes any object that implements the *IDataReader* interface. The programming interface of a data reader object like *OleDbDataReader* and *SqlDataReader* consists of two distinct groups of functions: the *IDataReader* and *IDataRecord* interfaces. The former includes basic methods such as *Read*, *Close*, and *GetSchemaTable*. The latter contains specific reading methods including *GetName*, *GetValue*, and the *Item* indexer property.

By making the constructor accept a reference to the *IDataReader* interface, you enable the *XmlDataReader* class to support any data reader object. Internally, the class defines the following private properties:

```
protected IDataReader m_dataReader;
protected IDataRecord m_dataRecord;
protected ReadState m_readState;
protected int m_currentAttributeIndex;
```

The idea is to map the reading methods of the *XmlDataReader* class to the data reader object and use the *m_currentAttributeIndex* member to track down the currently selected attribute, as shown in the following code. Of course, each XML attribute corresponds to a column in the underlying result set.

```
public XmlDataReader(IDataReader dr)
{
    m_dataReader = dr;
    m_readState = ReadState.Initial;
    m_dataRecord = (IDataRecord) dr;
    m_currentAttributeIndex = -1;
}
```

Notice that the same object is passed as a reference to *IDataReader* but can also be cast to *IDataRecord*. This is possible as long as the real object implements both interfaces, but for data reader objects this is true by design.

The *XmlDataReader* Implementation

Let's review the implementation of a few properties and methods to grasp the essence of the reader, as shown in the following code. The entire source code is available for download in this book's sample files.

```
// Return the number of attributes (for example, the field count)
public override int AttributeCount
{
    get {return m_dataRecord.FieldCount;}
}

// Indexer property that works by index and name
public override string this[int i]
{
    get {return m_dataRecord.GetValue(i).ToString();}
}
public override string this[string name]
{
    get {return m_dataRecord[name].ToString();}
}

// Return the value of the current attribute
public override string Value
{
    get {
        if(m_readState != ReadState.Interactive)
            return "";

        string buf = "";
        if (NodeType == XmlNodeType.Attribute)
            buf = this[m_currentAttributeIndex].ToString();
        return buf;
    }
}
```

The *Read* method calls into the *Read* method of the data reader and updates its state accordingly, as shown in the following code. The *Close* method closes the data reader and resets the internal state.

```
public override bool Read()
{
    // Read the new row and set the state
    bool canReadMore = m_dataReader.Read();
    m_readState = (canReadMore
        ?ReadState.Interactive :ReadState.EndOfFile);

    return canReadMore;
}
```

```
public override void Close()
{
    m_dataReader.Close();
    m_readState = ReadState.Closed;
}
```

The XML data reader object can work atop any provider-specific data readers, thus providing a free XML transformation service that is functionally equivalent to *ExecuteXmlReader*. The so-called XML transformation takes place on the client, but the connection with the database remains open until you close the reader.

> **Note** A custom XML reader does not really transform rows into XML schemas. The *XmlDataReader* object simply causes a data record to look like an XML fragment. You can derive new classes from *XmlData-Reader* to support more complex XML schemas. For such simple XML layouts at least, this approach is even slightly more efficient than using FOR XML. Both solutions use an underlying data reader and expose an XML reader, but *XmlDataReader* requires no server-side rowset-to-XML transformation.

Using XML with OLE DB Data Providers

Let's see how to use the *XmlDataReader* class with an instance of the OLE DB data reader. As usual, you create an *OleDbCommand* object, execute the command, and get a living instance of the *OleDbDataReader* class. Next you pass the OLE DB data reader to the *XmlDataReader* constructor, as shown here:

```
string nwind, query;
nwind = "PROVIDER=sqloledb;SERVER=localhost;" +
    "DATABASE=northwind;UID=sa;";
query = "SELECT employeeid, firstname, lastname," +
    " title FROM employees";

OleDbConnection conn = new OleDbConnection(nwind);
OleDbCommand cmd = new OleDbCommand(query, conn);

// Create the XML data reader
conn.Open();
OleDbDataReader dr = cmd.ExecuteReader();
```

(continued)

```
XmlDataReader reader = new XmlDataReader(dr);
ProcessDataReader(reader);
reader.Close();
conn.Close();
```

The reader can be used on demand to walk through the contents of the result set, as shown here:

```
private void ProcessDataReader(XmlReader reader)
{
    ResultsListBox.Items.Clear();
    while(reader.Read())
        ResultsListBox.Items.Add(reader.ReadOuterXml());
    reader.Close();
}
```

This code generates the output shown in Figure 8-4.

Figure 8-4   *FOR XML RAW* output obtained using the *XmlDataReader* class and an OLE DB data provider.

A Disconnected XML Data Reader

By design, a data reader object works while connected, and so do any XML readers you might build on top of it. However, the .NET Framework provides a class that has the ability to expose a disconnected set of rows—a *DataSet* object—as XML. The *DataSet* object is designed as a disconnected object with no relationship to any living instance of a DBMS. The *XmlDataDocument* class takes a *DataSet* object and transforms it into an XML DOM object—that is, the *XmlDocument* class we analyzed in Chapter 5. In a nutshell, the *XmlDataDocument* class provides a client-side and an XML DOM representation of a disconnected set of rows. Let's see how.

The *XmlDataDocument* Class

The *XmlDataDocument* class inherits from *XmlDocument*, and although it is defined in the *system.data* assembly, it belongs to the *System.Xml* namespace.

A combined use of the *XmlDataDocument* class and the *DataSet* class provides access to the same data using two otherwise alternative approaches: *relational* and *hierarchical*. When a *DataSet* class and an *XmlDataDocument* class are synchronized, they work on the same set of data and detect each other's changes in real time.

The *XmlDataDocument* class has a *DataSet* property that is bound to the related *DataSet* object. The class does not duplicate the *DataSet* contents but simply holds a reference to the object. When the *DataSet* property is set, the *XmlDataDocument* registers a listener module for each *DataSet* event that indicates a change in the data. By hooking the events, the *XmlDataDocument* class can stay in sync with the *DataSet* contents.

Event hooking also works the other way around. In Chapter 5, we saw that whenever an application changes the contents of the XML DOM, a *NodeChanged* event fires. The *XmlDataDocument* class registers an event handler for *NodeChanged* and passes the changes down to the referenced *DataSet* object.

Synchronizing with a *DataSet* Object

You can synchronize a *DataSet* object with an *XmlDataDocument* object in various ways. For example, you can start by populating a *DataSet* object with schema and data and then pass it on to a new *XmlDataDocument* object, as shown here:

```
DataSet data = new DataSet();
// Populate the DataSet with schema and data
XmlDataDocument dataDoc = new XmlDataDocument(data);
```

In this case, the XML DOM object is created from the relational data. Alternatively, you can set up the *DataSet* object with schema only, associate it with the *XmlDataDocument* class, and then populate the XML DOM object with XML data, as shown in the following code. In this way, the *DataSet* object is filled with hierarchical data.

```
DataSet data = new DataSet();
// Populate the DataSet only with schema information
XmlDataDocument dataDoc = new XmlDataDocument(data);
dataDoc.Load(xmlfile);
```

Note that an exception is thrown if you attempt to load an *XmlDataDocument* object synchronized with a *DataSet* object that contains data.

You can take a third route. You can instantiate and load an *XmlDataDocument* object and then extract the corresponding *DataSet* object from it, as shown here:

```
XmlDataDocument dataDoc = new XmlDataDocument();
DataSet data = dataDoc.DataSet;
// Add schema information to the DataSet
dataDoc.Load(xmlfile);
```

In this case, no *DataSet* object is explicitly passed in by the user. The default constructor creates an empty *DataSet* object anyway that is then filled when the *XmlDataDocument* object is loaded. A client application can get a reference to the internal *DataSet* object by using the *DataSet* property.

An important issue to consider is that the *DataSet* object can't be filled if no schema information has been set. You can manually create tables and columns in the *DataSet* object or read the information from an XML stream using the *ReadXmlSchema* method. (More on this topic in Chapter 9.)

XML Data Fidelity

To fill a *DataSet* object with XML data, you can use one of two methods. The first method is to use the *DataSet* object's *ReadXml* method (see Chapter 9). The second method is to load the data as XML into an instance of the *XmlData-Document* class, and then use the *XmlDataDocument.DataSet* method to fill the *DataSet* object. The two approaches differ significantly in terms of data fidelity.

When *ReadXml* is used and the data is written back as XML, all extra XML information such as white spaces, processing instructions, and CDATA sections is irreversibly lost. This happens because the *DataSet* relational format simply does not know how to handle information that is meaningful only to the hierarchical model.

When the *DataSet* object is filled using an XML document loaded into *XmlDataDocument*, the *DataSet* object still contains a simplified and adapted representation of the hierarchical contents but the original XML document is preserved intact.

Nested Data Relations

If the *DataSet* object to be synchronized with an *XmlDataDocument* object contains one or more relations (instances of the *DataRelation* object), you should set the *Nested* property of the *DataRelation* object to *true*. In this way, the child rows of the relation will be nested within the parent column when written as XML data or synchronized with an *XmlDataDocument* object. By default, the *Nested* property of the *DataRelation* object is *false*.

Reading Data as XML

Representing a *DataSet* object with an instance of the *XmlDataDocument* class allows you to use XPath expressions to select data. In general, using XPath queries to select XML data makes sense especially if you have XML DOM data disconnected and stored in memory—that is, if you use *XmlDataDocument*. In doing so, you actually work on an XML DOM object and don't in any way tax the database. Pay attention when using this technique in Microsoft ASP.NET applications. In this case, the *client* lives on the Web server, and you end up occupying the Web server's memory with potential hits on the overall performance and scalability.

Using XPath to query XML representations of data relationally stored in SQL Server (for example, annotated schemas) seems to be a rather twisted and ineffective way to execute queries. The query engine of SQL Server, therefore, outperforms the XPath query engine—not to mention that to run slower queries, you still have to pay the price of transforming relational data in XML.

Reading database contents as XML makes sense only if you need to represent that information in an intermediate format for further transformations and processing. Currently, the best approach is still relying on *FOR XML* using the EXPLICIT operator if you need complex schemas. SQL Server 2000 supports XDR schemas, and to use XSD, you should resort to SQLXML 3.0. Unfortunately, SQLXML 3.0 relies on the OLE DB provider for data access and is not recommended for .NET Framework applications. If you find the FOR XML EXPLICIT syntax too quirky, look ahead to the discussion of .NET Framework XML serialization in Chapter 11.

Writing XML Data to Databases

So much for reading database contents as XML. Now let's review the options available for persisting data to relational DBMS systems using XML representations of data. SQL Server 2000 supports three basic ways for expressing database changes using XML: OPENXML, XML bulk loading, and Updategrams.

OPENXML is a SQL Server 2000 keyword that represents a rowset provider such as a table or a view. The net effect of OPENXML is not really different from that of another relatively popular T-SQL keyword—OPENROWSET. The OPEN-ROWSET keyword represents an alternative to accessing tables in a linked server and an ad hoc method of accessing data using any OLE DB providers. Both keywords can be referenced as if they were actual table names in the FROM clause of a query and in an INSERT or UPDATE command. The difference between the two keywords is that OPENXML renders the contents of an XML file as a rowset, whereas OPENROWSET does the same with the results of an OLE DB query.

XML bulk loading is a technique that lets you load semistructured XML data into SQL Server tables. Functionally similar to OPENXML, bulk loading is implemented through a COM object and provides higher performance when large amounts of XML data must be processed.

Finally, Updategrams are an XML description of the changes that must be applied to the database. Updategrams are a syntax that applies to an annotated XML view to denote insertions, deletions, and updates. The mapping schema of the XML view contains the necessary information to map XML elements and attributes to tables and columns in the database. From a .NET Framework perspective, Updategrams look a lot like DiffGrams. In SQL Server 2000, however, Updategrams are the native XML language to denote database changes.

The OPENXML Rowset Provider

OPENXML is a T-SQL function that takes care of inserting data represented as an XML document. OPENXML parses the contents of the XML document and exposes it as a rowset. As a result, the records in the rowset can be stored in database tables. OPENXML is not a write-only keyword that you can use only with INSERT or UPDATE. Because it is a generic rowset provider, you can use it with statements such as SELECT and SELECT INTO, and in general wherever a source table or view is accepted.

OPENXML takes up to three arguments, as shown here:

```
OPENXML (handle, rowpattern [, flags])
[WITH (SchemaDeclaration | TableName)]
```

The first argument (*handle*) is the handle of the internal representation of an XML document. The document handle is created by the *sp_xml_preparedocument* system stored procedure. The *rowpattern* argument is the XPath expression that selects the nodes in the source XML that must be processed as database rows.

The *flags* argument is optional and, if specified, indicates how attributes and elements in the selected nodes should be processed. By default, the flag is set to *1*, which indicates *attribute-centric mapping*. Attribute-centric mapping accepts input values only from the attributes of the selected nodes. The mapping between attributes and columns is determined by name. Alternatively, you can specify *element-centric mapping* (a value of 2). Element-centric mapping is similar to attribute-centric mapping except for the fact that it accepts input values from the text of child element nodes.

Caution   You could also opt for mixed mapping—a value of 3—by combining attribute-centric and element-centric mapping. In this case, attribute-centric mapping is applied first, and then for all still unmatched columns, an element-centric mapping is applied. You should use this feature only when absolutely necessary. Using a double flag can significantly slow performance.

The WITH clause is optional and can be used to define the schema of the target table. If a table with the desired schema already exists, you simply indicate the table name. This is what commonly happens when you use OPENXML to write data. When you use OPENXML with a SELECT statement, you can specify the schema of the columns being returned. (More details on the syntax of OPENXML can be found in SQL Server 2000 Books Online.)

OPENXML in Action

The first step in using OPENXML is calling the *sp_xml_preparedocument* stored procedure to parse the XML document. The stored procedure returns a tree representation of the nodes in the XML document, and this in-memory image becomes the input for OPENXML. The stored procedure returns the handle of the document as an output parameter. Here's an example of how to use OPENXML:

```
DECLARE @handle int
EXEC sp_xml_preparedocument @handle OUTPUT,
   N'<ROOT>
      <Employees LastName="Esposito" FirstName="Dino" />
      <Employees LastName="Esposito" FirstName="Michela" />
      </ROOT>'

INSERT Employees
SELECT * FROM OPENXML(@handle, N'/ROOT/Employees') WITH Employees
EXEC sp_xml_removedocument @handle
```

This code adds a couple of records to the Employees table in the Northwind database. Notice that the XPath expression selects all the *<Employees>* nodes in the source document.

The *sp_xml_removedocument* stored procedure removes the internal representation of the specified XML document that was previously built by *sp_xml_preparedocument*. If not explicitly invalidated, the handle of the document is valid for the duration of the connection to SQL Server.

Threshold and Performance

OPENXML uses the Microsoft XML Core Services (MSXML) COM parser to build a binary representation of the source document. Next it performs some XPath queries to select the proper node-set to be processed to build the physical rowset to interface with SQL Server.

In general, you should avoid using XPath beyond a certain threshold. If you realize that your code is relying on XPath for complex queries that run often, you are probably using the wrong tool to address your needs. A temporary relational table would probably serve you better.

A parsed document is stored in the internal cache of SQL Server 2000. The memory that the MSXML parser can use to generate binary images of the source XML can reach up to one-eighth of the total memory available to SQL Server. To avoid running out of memory, free up binary images as soon as document handles go out of scope by using *sp_xml_removedocument*. Be sure to use the stored procedure in a timely manner, however. If you free up memory that will be used later, SQL Server can only reparse the source document, which is probably worse than occupying more memory. To be on the safe side, keep the number of documents in memory under control, and don't forget to call *sp_xml_removedocument* too.

Keep in mind that OPENXML has been designed and optimized to handle documents up to 50 KB in size. Over that threshold, monitor constantly the response time, and decide whether you can still continue with OPENXML or you need something different, like XML bulk loading.

XML Bulk Loading

XML Bulk Load is a COM component available for SQL Server 2000 that reads data out of an XML file and according to an XDR or XSD schema copies the data into database tables and columns. Unlike OPENXML, XML bulk loading is optimized to work with large quantities of data.

The bulk loader reads the XML data as a stream. Step by step, it identifies the database tables and columns involved and prepares and executes SQL statements against SQL Server. When the bulk loader encounters an XML element, it uses the schema information to associate the element with a record in a table. The record is actually written when the end tag for that element is found. This algorithm ensures that in the case of parent-child relationships, all the children are processed before the parent row.

Transacted Loading

Unlike the T-SQL BULK INSERT statement, XML bulk loading is a sort of add-on. Because XML bulk loading is not natively part of SQL Server 2000, it never runs within an implicit transaction, as normally happens with T-SQL statements. As a result, you must manage transactions yourself. On the other hand, bulk loading is the kind of operation that sometimes does need to run in a transacted context.

It goes without saying that if you can afford to run bulk loading without transactions, doing so would be greatly beneficial to the overall performance of the application. Nontransacted loading makes a lot of sense when you have to fill up empty databases. In a transactionless scenario, you lose the ability to roll back changes, but because your databases were originally empty, if something goes wrong, you can clear the database and start over.

> **Note**   In nontransacted mode, XML bulk loading takes advantage of the methods of the OLE DB *IRowsetFastLoad* interface to do the job. Not all OLE DB providers supply the *IRowsetFastLoad* interface, but the SQLOLEDB provider does.

When XML bulk loading works in transacted mode, the component creates a temporary file for each table involved in the operation. The files will gather all the changes for the tables. When a commit occurs, the contents of the various files are flushed into the corresponding SQL Server table using the BULK INSERT statement.

XML Bulk Loading in Action

Let's see how XML bulk loading really works. As mentioned, XML bulk loading is implemented through a COM object whose *progID* attribute is *SQLXMLBulk-Load*. The following Visual Basic 6.0 code shows how to use the object:

```
conn = "PROVIDER=sqloledb;SERVER=localhost;" & _
    "database=Northwind;UID=sa"
Set bulk = CreateObject("SQLXMLBulkLoad.SQLXMLBulkload.3.0")
bulk.ConnectionString = conn
bulk.Execute "schema.xml", "data.xml"
```

To perform bulk loading, you set the connection string and then call the *Execute* method. The method takes two arguments: the schema and the XML source data. In-line schemas are ignored, as are schema files referenced in the source file. As a result, you must always supply schema information and data through distinct XML files. Finally, note that XML documents are checked for well-formedness, but their contents are never validated against any schema. Any contents outside the root node of the document—the *<ROOT>* node—are simply discarded.

The following listing shows a typical source for a bulk loading operation. It adds a couple of employees, each with a few related territories.

```
<ROOT>
  <Employees>
    <EmployeeID>991</EmployeeID>
    <FirstName>Dino</FirstName>
    <LastName>Esposito</LastName>
    <City>Roma</City>
    <Territory TerritoryID="1" />
    <Territory TerritoryID="2" />
  </Employees>
  <Employees>
    <EmployeeID>992</EmployeeID>
    <FirstName>Francesco</FirstName>
    <LastName>Esposito</LastName>
    <City>Roma</City>
    <Territory TerritoryID="5" />
  </Employees>
</ROOT>
```

The schema that would make it possible for the bulk loader to interpret and process this information is shown here:

```
<xsd:schema xmlns:xsd="http://www.w3.org/2001/XMLSchema"
  xmlns:sql="urn:schemas-microsoft-com:mapping-schema">
<xsd:annotation>
  <xsd:appinfo>
    <sql:relationship name="Employees2Territories"
         parent="Employees"
         parent-key="EmployeeID"
         child="EmployeeTerritories"
         child-key="EmployeeID" />
  </xsd:appinfo>
</xsd:annotation>
```

```
    <xsd:element name="Employees" sql:relation="Employees" >
  <xsd:complexType>
    <xsd:sequence>
      <xsd:element name="EmployeeID" type="xsd:int" />
      <xsd:element name="FirstName" type="xsd:string" />
      <xsd:element name="LastName" type="xsd:string" />
      <xsd:element name="City" type="xsd:string" />
      <xsd:element name="Territory"
          sql:relation="EmployeeTerritories"
          sql:relationship="Employees2Territories" >
        <xsd:complexType>
         <xsd:attribute name="TerritoryID" type="xsd:integer" />
        </xsd:complexType>
      </xsd:element>
    </xsd:sequence>
  </xsd:complexType>
  </xsd:element>
</xsd:schema>
```

This schema first defines a relationship between the Employees table and the
EmployeeTerritories table. The relationship is based on the common field
EmployeeID. Next the schema describes the elements and the attributes that
form the data source. The *sql:relation* annotation identifies the source table,
whereas *sql:relationship* points to the relationship.

Bulk Loading in .NET Framework Applications

As you've probably noticed, very little about XML bulk loading is specifically
related to the .NET Framework world. XML bulk loading and, more generally,
a lot of SQLXML 3.0 features are still based on COM. This means a couple of
things. First, the only way you can take advantage of such features is through
the .NET Framework COM interop layer. (COM interop allows COM clients to
access .NET objects and .NET code to access COM objects.) Be aware that,
although highly optimized, the performance of COM interop services isn't the
same as you get by calling managed code. If you have no alternative, you
should use COM interop services; otherwise, choose a more .NET Framework–
specific approach.

XML bulk loading can't be directly invoked from within managed code.
Managed code must yield to COM code to do the job. As of SQLXML 3.0 SP1,
the COM object that provides XML bulk loading is named *xblkld3.dll* and is normally located under the following path: *C:\Program Files\Common Files\Sys-
tem\Ole DB*. You can use either Microsoft Visual Studio .NET or the tlbimp.exe
command-line utility to generate a .NET Framework wrapper class.

The Updategram Template

An Updategram is an XML file that contains information about the changes that must be entered in one or more database tables. In addition to incoming changes, the Updategram can also contain optional mapping information to better associate elements in the XML source with columns in the database.

Below the <*ROOT*> tag, an Updategram can have one or more <*sync*> blocks. Each of these blocks can contain one or more pairs of <*before*> and <*after*> blocks. Using <*before*> and <*after*> blocks, you can specify the new expected state of the source. If a record exists only in the <*before*> block, a DELETE operation is performed. If the record appears only in the <*after*> block, an INSERT operation occurs. If the record appears in both blocks, an UPDATE statement is run. Records that do not appear in either block are left intact.

Structure of an Updategram

The schema of an Updategram is illustrated here:

```
<ROOT>
<sync>
  <before>
    <Customers customerid="999" ... />
  </before>
  <after>
    <Customers customerid="1999" ... />
  </after>
</sync>
<sync>
  ...
</sync>
</ROOT>
```

The contents of each <*sync*> block represent an atomic unit of processing for which the Updategram guarantees a transactional behavior—either all the changes take effect or none do. You can use different pairs of <*before*> and <*after*> blocks to group changes that must be executed in a certain order.

All the keywords in an Updategram are defined in the namespace *urn:schemas-microsoft-com:xml-updategram*. The namespace must be associated with each Updategram, although with arbitrary prefixes, as in the following example:

```
<ROOT xmlns:u="urn:schemas-microsoft-com:xml-updategram">
<u:sync>
  <u:before>
    <Customers customerid="999" ... />
  </u:before>
```

```
<u:after>
  <Customers customerid="1999" ... />
</u:after>
</u:sync>
```

By default, the Updategram maps any first-level element below the *<before>* and *<after>* blocks to a table of the same name in the current database. Any attribute in that node is implicitly mapped to columns in that table. For example, in the preceding sample script, the Updategram would work on the Customers table, removing the row with a *customerid* attribute of 999 and replacing it with a new row with a *customerid* attribute of 1999.

You can specify a mapping schema using the *mapping-schema* attribute, as shown in the following code. The attribute references an XML file (typically an XDR or XSD file) that describes the nature of the mapping in much the same way as described earlier for XML bulk loading. (See the section "XML Bulk Loading in Action," on page 379.)

```
<u:sync mapping-schema="schema.xml">
```

> **Note**   The schema for XML bulk loading does not recognize the *sql:identity* annotation to flag identity auto-increment columns, which means that XML bulk loading is unable to handle tables with this feature. On the other hand, Updategrams handle identity columns nicely. You simply annotate the column in the schema and set the *sql:identity* attribute to *Ignore* if you need to rely on the SQL Server–generated values or to *useValue* if a user-provided value should be used instead.
>
> *NULL* values also require special handling. In practice, you declare an alternative text-based representation for NULL values and use that throughout the Updategram. The *nullvalue* attribute indicates the alternative text, as shown here:
>
> ```
> <u:sync u:nullvalue="IsNULL"  >
>     <u:before>
>         <Employees EmployeeID="1" Title="IsNULL" />
>     </u:before>
>     ...
> ```

Submitting Commands Through Updategrams

Updategrams can be executed in various ways. You can send the Updategram text to SQL Server over HTTP. Alternatively, you can write the XML contents out to a file and then point the browser (or any other HTTP-enabled software) to that URL so that the contents are executed. Or you can use an Updategram with ADO.

The following Visual Basic 6.0 code shows how to proceed. Notice that you must copy the Updategram to a stream and receive the response over another stream object.

```
Dim cmd As New ADODB.Command
Dim conn As New ADODB.Connection
Dim strIn As New ADODB.Stream
Dim strOut As New ADODB.Stream

conn.Provider = "SQLOLEDB"
conn.Open "SERVER=localhost;DATABASE=northwind;UID=sa;"
conn.Properties("SQLXML Version") = "SQLXML.3.0"

Set cmd.ActiveConnection = conn
cmd.Dialect = "{5d531cb2-e6ed-11d2-b252-00c04f681b71}"

strIn.Open
strIn.WriteText SQLxml
strIn.Position = 0
Set cmd.CommandStream = strIn

strOut.Open
cmd.Properties("Output Stream").Value = strOut
cmd.Properties("Output Encoding").Value = "UTF-8"
cmd.Execute , , adExecuteStream
```

Notice also that you need to set the command dialect to a particular globally unique identifier (GUID)—DBGUID_MSSQLXML—and set a few properties on the command and the connection objects.

Concurrency Issues

Updategrams are batches that work by looping on source data and executing a sequence of commands. What happens if, due to the system concurrency, rows that you are going to modify have been changed since the time you last read them? Updategrams have been designed to provide three levels of protection against this kind of conflict, as follows:

■   **Blind updates**   You specify only the primary key of the record in the *<before>* block. In this case, the change is persisted without first checking whether the current status of the record is consistent with the expected one.

■   **Partial conflict detection**   The *<before>* block contains the primary key as well as any other field you plan to update. When the Updategram executes, the change is applied only if the specified fields haven't been changed in the meantime.

■   **Total conflict detection**   All the columns in the row are checked, and the change fails if any of them has been modified. You can obtain this form of protection either by listing all the fields in the *<before>* block or by using the table *timestamp* column, if one exists. A *timestamp* column will be updated whenever a user writes something to the row.

Updategrams and DiffGrams

If you're familiar with ADO.NET, you'll no doubt notice a close similarity, both conceptual and physical, between Updategrams and DiffGrams. Although ADO.NET DiffGrams are a newer format—and perhaps the format of the future—currently, SQL Server 2000 natively supports only Updategrams.

In the section "SQLXML Managed Classes," on page 386, we'll take a quick tour of the managed classes in SQLXML 3.0. You'll notice that some of these classes apparently enable you to send DiffGrams to SQL Server. Although this is possible, the actual implementation is not particularly effective. The source DiffGram is in fact internally transformed into an Updategram and then processed by SQL Server.

Apart from the patent similarity in their schemas, Updategrams and DiffGrams have slightly different goals. Updategrams have been designed to update SQL Server; DiffGrams are mostly a stateful way to persist the contents of a *DataSet* object. (ADO.NET DiffGrams are covered in Chapter 10.) Converting DiffGrams to Updategrams is certainly possible at the schema level, but Updategrams are unquestionably more powerful objects. Together with SQLXML 3.0 and the SQL Server XML extensions, Updategrams let you control concurrency, control the order of updates, perform transactional updates, and specify parameters.

On the other hand, there is not yet a .NET Framework class that works like an Updategram. (And SQLXML 3.0 is still a hybrid, half COM and half managed code.) Most of the batch update features you find in Updategrams can be implemented in ADO.NET using the *DataSet* object's *Update* method and the provider-specific data adapter object. Nothing comes for free, though, and you must write a lot of code to emulate Updategrams in the .NET Framework.

XML Batch Update

In ADO.NET, as well as in ADO, you can persist the changes made to a set of records stored in memory using a procedure called a *batch update*. This procedure consists of a loop that looks up for changed records in the *DataSet* object (or the *Recordset* object in ADO) and issues a command to the back-end database. From the programmer's perspective, a batch update is ideal for working in disconnected scenarios and in ADO.NET— although it is not yet perfect, it has been significantly improved and made applicable to real-world usage.

Thanks to the ADO.NET XML serialization mechanism (see Chapter 9), you can load a *DataSet* object from XML data, enter the needed changes, and then proceed with the batch update. The ADO.NET Diff-Gram is one of the possible XML representations for a *DataSet* object. Although, all in all, the Updategram is a more powerful and richer object for XML-driven updates, an ADO.NET batch update is still an option to consider when you're updating a database starting with XML data.

The ADO.NET batch update is a step-by-step procedure implemented through a sequence of individual statements, all running from the client environment. Once again, this is different from Updategrams, in which all data is downloaded to SQL Server and applied as a server-side batch.

The closest you can get to this model with ADO.NET is using a data-tier component that decouples any middle-tier objects from the database. The middle-tier object applies all the needed changes to the *DataSet* object and then passes the object on to another component, possibly located on the same machine as SQL Server. The *DataSet* object is remoted as XML and is rebuilt at the destination. Finally, the changes are applied in batch update mode but through a specialized and scalable data-tier component and with a more effective use of the bandwidth.

SQLXML Managed Classes

SQLXML 3.0 comes with a handful of managed classes designed to expose the functionality of SQLXML 3.0 inside the .NET Framework. SQLXML managed classes allow you bring XML data read from SQL Server into .NET Framework applications, process the data, and send any updates back to SQL Server as an ADO.NET DiffGram. The managed classes are exposed by the *microsoft.data.sqlxml* assembly.

SQLXML does not get along perfectly with the .NET Framework data provider for SQL Server. SQLXML needs to address special XML-driven functionalities of SQL Server 2000 that the .NET Framework data provider simply does not support. As a result, the SQL Server .NET Framework provider can handle traditional SQL queries, including FOR XML queries, but it can't execute XML templates (for example, Updategrams) or server-side XPath queries over XML views. For this reason, SQLXML managed classes rely on the SQLXMLOLEDB OLE DB provider for all of the tasks that involve a SQL Server connection.

Figure 8-5 illustrates the key role that the *SqlXmlCommand* class and its *ExecuteStream* method play in the overall SQLXML 3.0 architecture.

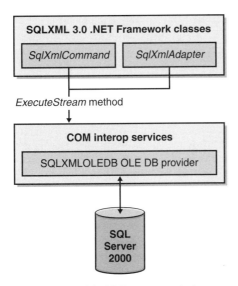

Figure 8-5   SQLXML managed classes go to SQL Server 2000 using the *ExecuteStream* method of the *SqlXmlCommand* class and the SQLXMLOLEDB OLE DB provider.

The set of SQLXML managed classes consists of two main classes—*SqlXmlCommand* and *SqlXmlAdapter*—plus a few ancillary classes like *SqlXmlParameter* and *SqlXmlException*. *SqlXmlCommand* is the fundamental class used to execute an XML-driven command against SQL Server. The *SqlXmlAdapter* class is actually a wrapper for the command that simply exposes the results through a *DataSet* object.

The *SqlXmlCommand* Class

The *SqlXmlCommand* class represents any XML command you can send to SQL Server 2000. As mentioned, you should use this class only to issue those XML-related commands that the .NET Framework data provider for SQL Server does not natively support. The class reliance on an OLE DB provider makes rather ineffective any kind of abuse from within a .NET Framework application.

Do not use *SqlXmlCommand* to execute a simple FOR XML query, but take it into account when you need to work with Updategrams, server-side XPath queries (assuming that an XPath query makes sense at all in the context of the application), or XML views.

SqlXmlCommand Properties

The properties available in the *SqlXmlCommand* class let you configure the query. Unlike most ADO.NET command classes, the *SqlXmlCommand* class provides a command stream property that applications can use to pass potentially lengthy input data such as Updategrams. Table 8-2 summarizes the properties of the *SqlXmlCommand* class.

Table 8-2   Properties of the *SqlXmlCommand* Class

Property	Description
BasePath	Gets or sets the base path used to resolve an XSL file (*XslPath* property), a mapping schema file (*SchemaPath* property), or any other external schema reference in an XML template.
ClientSideXml	Boolean property, indicates that the conversion of the rowset to XML should occur on the client instead of on the server.
CommandStream	Gets or sets the input stream for the command. Use this property to execute a command from a file (for example, a template or an Updategram). *CommandStream* and *CommandText* are mutually exclusive; if you set *CommandStream*, *CommandText* is automatically set to *null*.
CommandText	Gets or sets the text of the command to execute. *CommandText* and *CommandStream* are mutually exclusive; if you set *CommandText*, *CommandStream* is automatically set to *null*.
CommandType	Identifies the type of the command you want to execute. Feasible values are defined in the *SqlXmlCommandType* enumeration.
Namespaces	Enables the execution of XPath queries that use namespaces.
OutputEncoding	Specifies the encoding for the stream that is returned when the command executes. UTF-8 is the default encoding.
RootTag	Gets or sets the name of the root element for XML generated by command execution. Set to <*ROOT*> by default.

Table 8-2 **Properties of the *SqlXmlCommand* Class**

Property	Description
SchemaPath	Gets or sets the name of the mapping schema for XPath queries. The path can be absolute or relative. If relative, the *BasePath* property is used to resolve the path.
XslPath	Gets or sets the name of the XSL file to use for XML data transformations. The path can be absolute or relative.

Streams play a key role in the *SqlXmlCommand* class. Not only can you use a stream to specify the input of a command, but you can also pick up the results of the command from an output stream. You can also control the encoding of this output stream. For a better understanding of these properties, review the ADO example about Updategrams in the section "Submitting Commands Through Updategrams," on page 383.

Supported Command Types

The *SqlXmlCommand* class can execute a variety of commands. The allowable command types are defined in the *SqlXmlCommandType* enumeration and are shown in Table 8-3.

Table 8-3 **Command Types**

Type	Description
Diffgram	Executes an ADO.NET DiffGram.
Sql	Executes an ordinary SQL command that returns XML. The default setting.
Template	Executes an XML template (for example, creates an XPath-driven view). The command text is specified via the command input stream.
TemplateFile	Executes an XML template via the specified file. The name of the file is set through the *CommandText* property.
UpdateGram	Executes an updategram.
XPath	Executes an XPath command.

A template is an XML document that contains T-SQL commands wrapped in ad hoc XML attributes, as shown here:

```
<ROOT xmlns:sql="urn:schemas-microsoft-com:xml-sql">
  <sql:query>
    SELECT * FROM Employees FOR XML AUTO
  </sql:query>
</ROOT>
```

The template specifies a sequence of commands to produce a particular result set. Overall, a template is a dynamically defined stored procedure expressed using XML syntax and supporting XPath queries.

SqlXmlCommand Methods

On instantiation, the *SqlXmlCommand* class creates an instance of the SQLXMLOLEDB provider. Interestingly, it does not make use of an explicit wrapper assembly but instead gets a COM object type using the static method *GetTypeFromCLSID* from the *Type* class. Next it instantiates the COM object using the *Activator* class.

> **Note** The *Activator* class contains methods to create types of objects locally or remotely, or obtain references to existing remote objects. Functionally equivalent to the *new* operator, *Activator* enables you to create instances of objects whose type is passed as an argument. With *Activator*, you can sometimes experience difficulties addressing a particular parameter-rich constructor. The *Activator* object will be covered in detail in Chapter 12.

The methods provided by the *SqlXmlCommand* class are described in Table 8-4.

Table 8-4 Methods of the *SqlXmlCommand* Class

Method	Description
CreateParameter	Creates an *SqlXmlParameter* object that represents a parameter for the command
ClearParameters	Clears the parameters that were created for the command
ExecuteNonQuery	Executes the command but does not return anything
ExecuteStream	Executes the command and returns a new *Stream* object
ExecuteToStream	Executes the command and writes the query results to the specified existing stream
ExecuteXmlReader	Executes the command and returns an *XmlReader* object

ExecuteStream is the key method in the interface in the sense that all other execute methods fall back internally to it. In particular, *ExecuteNonQuery* merely wraps a call to *ExecuteStream*, whereas *ExecuteXmlReader* creates and returns an *XmlTextReader* object built using the stream obtained from *Execute-Stream*.

ExecuteToStream does not use *ExecuteStream* internally, but the two methods have a similar architecture and use the same internal worker method. Basically, *ExecuteStream* calls an internal executor and sets it to work on a memory stream. The memory stream (*MemoryStream* class) is then returned as a generic *Stream* object. *ExecuteToStream*, instead, reads from, and writes to, the user-provided stream object. Figure 8-6 shows these two methods in action.

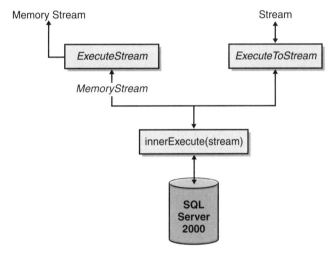

Figure 8-6   *ExecuteStream* and *ExecuteToStream* in action.

The following code shows how to use a *SqlXmlCommand* object. Notice that the connection string for *SqlXmlCommand* must necessarily use the SQLOLEDB provider because SQLXML 3.0 does not support the .NET Framework managed data provider.

```
string conn = "PROVIDER=sqloledb;SERVER=(local);" +
    "DATABASE=northwind;UID=sa";
SqlXmlCommand cmd = new SqlXmlCommand(conn);
cmd.CommandText = "SELECT * FROM Employees" +
    " FOR XML AUTO, BINARY BASE64";
Stream stm = cmd.ExecuteStream();

// Consumes the stream content
StreamReader sr = new StreamReader(stm)
Console.WriteLine(sr.ReadToEnd());
sr.Close();
```

The Employees table contains a BLOB field with a picture of each employee. If you want the binary field returned encoded as a string, use the BINARY BASE64 keyword in the FOR XML clause.

If the command that *SqlXmlCommand* executes does not return XML, an exception is raised because streaming is not supported over a result set with multiple columns. *SqlXmlCommand* works just fine on non-XML queries as long as they return a single column of data.

> **Tip** The *ExecuteToStream* method comes in handy for automatically sending the result set over a special stream like the output stream of an ASP.NET page or the console.

Executing Server-Side XPath Queries

A typical functionality of the SQLXML library is executing server-side XPath queries over SQL Server data. Personally, I would not recommend this practice—I believe that a well-designed SQL query outperforms any XPath engine. The XPath language does let you address hierarchically structured data more easily, however, but keep in mind that a server-side XPath query requires a preliminary step—the relational-to-XML data transformation, as shown here:

```
SqlXmlCommand cmd = new SqlXmlCommand(conn);
cmd.CommandText = "Emp[@EmployeeID >3]";
cmd.CommandType = SqlXmlCommandType.XPath;
cmd.SchemaPath = "MappingSchema.xml";
cmd.RootTag = "Northwind";
Stream stOut = cmd.ExecuteStream();
```

When the command type is XPath, you must necessarily set the *Schema-Path* property on the *SqlXmlCommand* object. The property points to an XSD or XDR file that defines the XML schema on which the XPath expression is called to operate. For example, consider the following schema:

```
<xsd:schema xmlns:xsd="http://www.w3.org/2001/XMLSchema"
    xmlns:sql="urn:schemas-microsoft-com:mapping-schema">
  <xsd:element name="Emp" sql:relation="Employees" >
   <xsd:complexType>
    <xsd:sequence>
      <xsd:element name="FName" sql:field="FirstName"
        type="xsd:string" />
      <xsd:element name="LName" sql:field="LastName"
```

```
            type="xsd:string" />
        </xsd:sequence>
        <xsd:attribute name="EmployeeID" type="xsd:integer" />
      </xsd:complexType>
    </xsd:element>
</xsd:schema>
```

This schema addresses a layout such as the following, in which *FName* and *LName* map to *FirstName* and *LastName* and the target table is Employees:

```
<Emp employeeid="...">
  <FName>...<FName>
  <LName>...<LName>
</Emp>
```

Given this underlying XML schema, using the following command text to select all the employees with an ID greater than 3 makes sense:

```
Emp[@EmployeeID >3]
```

The *SqlXmlParameter* Class

To pass parameters to a *SqlXmlCommand* object, you must use instances of the *SqlXmlParameter* class. Here's an example:

```
string conn = "PROVIDER=sqloledb;SERVER=(local);" +
    "DATABASE=northwind;UID=sa";
SqlXmlCommand cmd = new SqlXmlCommand(conn);

// Define the command text
StringBuilder sb = new StringBuilder("");
sb.Append("SELECT * FROM Employees ");
sb.Append("WHERE employeeid=? ");
sb.Append("FOR XML AUTO, BINARY BASE64");
cmd.CommandText = sb.ToString();

// Set the parameter
SqlXmlParameter p = cmd.CreateParameter();
p.Value = 2;

// Execute the command
Stream stm = cmd.ExecuteStream();
```

When you have several parameters set on a particular instance of a *SqlXmlCommand* object and you want to reuse that instance for another command, use the *ClearParameters* method to clear in a single shot the parameters collection.

The *SqlXmlAdapter* Class

The *SqlXmlAdapter* class is a shrink-wrapped adapter class. It does not implement the *IDataAdapter* interface, so technically speaking, it can't be presented as an adapter object. Nevertheless, the class provides adapter-like methods such as *Fill* and *Update*, as shown in the following code. These are also the only public methods for the class.

```
void Fill(DataSet ds);
void Update(DataSet ds);
```

The *SqlXmlAdapter* class also provides three constructors, shown in the following code, whose signatures reinforce the idea that this adapter is a mere wrapper class for *SqlXmlCommand*. In other words, the *SqlXmlAdapter* class is more a command that manages *DataSet* objects than a true data adapter object as it is described in the ADO.NET specification.

```
public SqlXmlAdapter(SqlXmlCommand cmd)
public SqlXmlAdapter(string commandText,
    SqlXmlCommandType cmdType,
    string connectionString)
public SqlXmlAdapter(Stream commandStream,
    SqlXmlCommandType cmdType,
    string connectionString)
```

These constructors use the information they receive to set up an internal instance of the *SqlXmlCommand* class. The *Fill* method makes full use of all the information passed through the constructor. For the *Update* method, on the other hand, only the connection string information is actually needed.

Filling an XML Adapter

The *Fill* method is rather simple. First it executes the embedded XML command using *ExecuteStream*. Next it uses the returned memory stream to fill the specified *DataSet* object through its *ReadXml* method.

The *ReadXml* method populates a *DataSet* object by reading XML data from a variety of sources, including streams and text readers, and inferring the schema. We'll examine the inference process in detail in Chapter 9. For now, suffice to say that *ReadXml* can detect any in-line or referenced XSD schema or determine the schema dynamically.

Once the *DataSet* object has been filled from the XML stream generated by the command execution, all the changes are accepted so that the *DataSet* object appears intact and with no pending changes.

Updating Using an XML Adapter

The *Update* method takes a *DataSet* object and applies its pending changes to the target database. The parameters specified on instantiation contain the details about the connection string. The embedded *SqlXmlCommand* object has command text and a command type that are simply ignored during *Update*. Let's see why.

When *Update* executes, the embedded command object is used to perform the task, but its command text and command type properties are silently and temporarily overwritten with *DataSet*-specific settings.

The *Update* method writes the contents of the *DataSet* object to a newly created memory stream. The *DataSet* object is serialized as a DiffGram. Next the contents of the stream—that is, the DiffGram representation of the *DataSet* object—are copied into the *CommandText* property of the underlying *SqlXml-Command* object. The *CommandType* property is set to *Template*, and *Execute-Stream* is called to update the database. If all goes well, the *DataSet* changes are committed using the *DataSet* object's *AcceptChanges* method.

Although COM is still involved, the *SqlXmlAdapter* object represents a way to architecturally improve the batch update mechanism in ADO.NET. By using *SqlXmlAdapter*, you actually obtain a *DataSet* object that is serialized as a DiffGram directly to SQL Server and processed entirely on the server. To optimize the bandwidth, you can pass a *DataSet* object that contains only changed rows. The *GetChanges* method provides for that.

> **Note**   Using *GetChanges* with ADO.NET batch updating is not a significant optimization—it simply reduces the total number of iterations, but the eliminated iterations are no-op by design. Instead, using *GetChanges* with *SqlXmlAdapter* can be a key optimization, as it truly minimizes the amount of data being transferred from the client to SQL Server.

Conclusion

In this chapter, we have explored the connections between databases (SQL Server 2000 in particular) and XML. Several DBMS systems provide XML support in various forms. The industry standard, however, requires that a DBMS provide for direct XML result sets and accept changes expressed as XML streams. SQL Server 2000 adheres to these requirements.

The difficulty lies in .NET and the different connecting model it introduces—.NET Framework data providers instead of OLE DB providers. For .NET Framework applications, fetching data as XML is much easier and more effective than persisting changes as XML. For COM applications, the same features are more balanced. The reason is that SQL Server 2000 came out much earlier than the .NET Framework, but the .NET Framework still came too soon to allow the managed provider to be designed with a broader perspective.

As a result, the SQL Server managed provider is unaware of XML extensions to support FOR XML queries and their limitations. Incidentally, this feature, combined with the power of .NET Framework XML readers, produces a really powerful toolkit. The truth, however, is that today the SQL Server managed provider is designed and optimized for traditional SQL commands—period.

SQLXML 3.0 is an add-on conceived to extend the SQL Server 2000 support for XML. SQLXML 3.0 is just that, however; in no way does it represent an integration to the .NET Framework managed provider model. For this reason, it is entirely based on COM OLE DB providers. The managed classes are wrappers around the SQLXMLOLEDB provider and, as such, require your code to silently jump out of the CLR during execution. This does not mean that you should not use SQLXML 3.0—just be aware of the managed classes' understandable, but still not optimal, design.

Hopes for the future? That's easy—my wish is that SQLXML 3.0 will be improved and integrated with the .NET Framework managed provider. As a side effect of this integration, ADO.NET should be enriched with a kind of Updategram object specifically designed for server-side batch updates.

In Chapter 9, we'll tackle *DataSet* serialization and the theme of XML serialization for key ADO.NET objects in general, including *DataTable* and *DataView* objects. We'll also take another look at DiffGrams. DiffGrams will be explored in depth in Chapter 10.

Further Reading

This chapter touched on a number of SQL Server 2000 issues and, in particular, a number of points related to T-SQL—the SQL dialect of SQL Server. The online documentation that comes with the product (SQL Server's Books Online) is certainly a good starting point to learn more. If you're interested in SQL Server 2000 from an architectural point of view, I recommend Kalen Delaney's *Inside SQL Server 2000* (Microsoft Press, 2000). Delaney's book covers the basics of the T-SQL language, but it is not an in-depth guide to T-SQL, and should be accompanied with another text more specifically targeted to the SQL Server dialect. One that I've found useful is Ken Henderson's *The Guru's Guide to Transact-SQL*, (Addison Wesley, 2000).

Programming Microsoft SQL Server 2000 with XML by Graeme Malcolm (Microsoft Press, 2001) is a good introductory text for exploring XML extensions in SQL Server 2000. Because the book is a bit outdated, it does not cover SQLXML 3.0 and managed extensions.

Another topic introduced in this chapter is ADO.NET and batch updating. My book *Building Web Solutions with ASP.NET and ADO.NET* (Microsoft Press, 2002) includes a practical chapter on batch updating from the ASP.NET perspective. A broader and in some respects more thoughtful and technology-oriented coverage can be found in Francesco Balena's *Programming Visual Basic .NET* (Microsoft Press, 2002). If you're interested in the entire spectrum of ADO.NET technologies, take a look at David Sceppa's *Microsoft ADO.NET* (Microsoft Press, 2002).

9

ADO.NET XML Data Serialization

XML is the key element responsible for the greatly improved interoperability of the Microsoft ADO.NET object model when compared to Microsoft ActiveX Data Objects (ADO). In ADO, XML was merely an I/O format (nondefault) used to persist the contents of a disconnected recordset. The participation of XML in the building and in the interworkings of ADO.NET is much deeper. The aspects of ADO.NET in which the interaction and integration with XML is stronger can be summarized in two categories: object serialization and remoting and a dual programming interface.

In ADO.NET, you have several options for saving objects to, and restoring objects from, XML documents. In effect, this capability belongs to one object only—the *DataSet* object—but it can be extended to other container objects with minimal coding. Saving objects like *DataTable* and *DataView* to XML is essentially a special case of the *DataSet* object serialization.

As we saw in Chapter 8, ADO.NET and XML classes provide for a unified, intermediate API that is made available to programmers through a dual, synchronized programming interface—the *XmlDataDocument* class. You can access and update data using either the hierarchical node-based approach of XML or the relational approach of column-based tabular data sets. At any time, you can switch from a *DataSet* representation of the data to an XML Document Object Model (XML DOM) representation, and vice versa. Data is synchronized, and any change you enter in either model is immediately reflected and visible in the other.

In this chapter, we'll explore the XML features built around the *DataSet* object and other ADO.NET objects for data serialization and deserialization.

You'll learn how to persist and restore data contents, how to deal with schema information, and even how schema information is automatically inferred from the XML source.

Serializing *DataSet* Objects

Like any other .NET Framework object, a *DataSet* object is stored in memory in a binary format. Unlike other objects, however, the *DataSet* object is always remoted and serialized in a special XML format, called a DiffGram. (We'll look at the DiffGram format and the relative API in more detail in Chapter 10.) When the *DataSet* object trespasses across the boundaries of the application domains (AppDomains), or the physical borders of the machine, it is automatically rendered as a DiffGram. At its destination, the *DataSet* object is silently rebuilt as a binary and immediately usable object.

In ADO.NET, serialization of an object is performed either through the public *ISerializable* interface or through public methods that expose the object's internal serialization mechanism. As .NET Framework objects, ADO.NET objects can plug into the standard .NET Framework serialization mechanism and output their contents to standard and user-defined formatters. The .NET Framework provides a couple of built-in formatters: the binary formatter and the Simple Object Access Protocol (SOAP) formatter. A .NET Framework object makes itself serializable by implementing the methods of the *ISerializable* interface—specifically, the *GetObjectData* method, plus a particular flavor of the constructor. According to this definition, both the *DataSet* and the *DataTable* objects are serializable.

In addition to the official serialization interface, the *DataSet* object supplies an alternative, and more direct, series of methods to serialize and deserialize itself, but in a class-defined XML format only. To serialize using the standard method, you create instances of the formatter object of choice (binary, SOAP, or whatever) and let the formatter access the source data through the methods of the *ISerializable* interface. The formatter obtains raw data that it then packs into the expected output stream.

In the alternative serialization model, the *DataSet* object itself starts and controls the serialization and deserialization process through a group of extra methods. The *DataTable* object does not offer public methods to support such an alternative and embedded serialization interface, nor does the *DataView* object.

In the end, both the official and the embedded serialization engines share the same set of methods. The overall architecture of *DataSet* and *DataTable* serialization is graphically rendered in Figure 9-1.

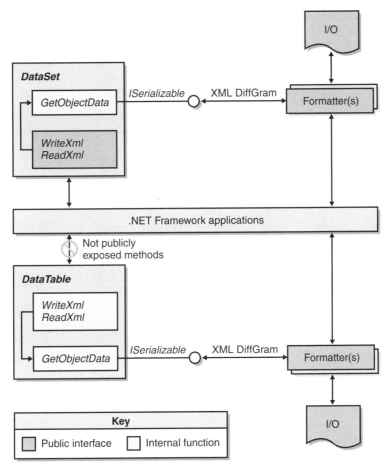

Figure 9-1   Both the *DataSet* object and the *DataTable* object implement the *ISerializable* interface for classic .NET Framework serialization. The *DataSet* object also publicly exposes the internal API used to support classic serialization.

All the methods that the *DataSet* object uses internally to support the .NET Framework serialization process are publicly exposed to applications through a group of methods, one pair of which clearly stands out—*ReadXml* and *WriteXml*. The *DataTable* object, on the other hand, does not publish the same methods, although this feature can be easily obtained with a little code. (I'll demonstrate this in the section "Serializing Filtered Views," on page 417.)

As you can see in the architecture depicted in Figure 9-1, both objects always pass XML data to .NET Framework formatters. This means that there is no .NET Framework–provided way to serialize ADO.NET objects in binary formats. We'll return to this topic in the section "Custom Binary Serialization," on page 424.

The *DataSet* Object's Embedded API for XML

Table 9-1 presents the *DataSet* object methods you can use to work with XML, both in reading and in writing. This list represents the *DataSet* object's internal XML API, which is at the foundation of the serialization and deserialization processes for the object.

Table 9-1   The *DataSet* Object's Embedded Serialization API

Method	Description
GetXml	Returns an XML representation of the data currently stored in the *DataSet* object. No schema information is included.
GetXmlSchema	Returns a string that represents the XML schema information for the data currently stored in the object.
ReadXml	Populates the *DataSet* object with the specified XML data read from a stream or a file. During the process, schema information is read or inferred from the data.
ReadXmlSchema	Loads the specified XML schema information into the current *DataSet* object.
WriteXml	Writes out the XML data, and optionally the schema, that represents the *DataSet* object to a storage medium—that is, a stream or a file.
WriteXmlSchema	Writes out a string that represents the XML schema information for the *DataSet* object. Can write to a stream or a file.

Note that *GetXml* returns a string that contains XML data. As such, it requires more overhead than simply using *WriteXml* to write XML to a file. You should not use *GetXml* and *GetXmlSchema* unless you really need to obtain the *DataSet* representation or schema as distinct strings for in-memory manipulation. The *GetXmlSchema* method returns the *DataSet* object's XML Schema Definition (XSD) schema; there is no way to obtain the *DataSet* object's XML-Data Reduced (XDR) schema.

As Table 9-1 shows, when you're working with *DataSet* and XML, you can manage data and schema information as distinct entities. You can take the XML schema out of the object and use it as a string. Alternatively, you could write the schema to a disk file or load it into an empty *DataSet* object. Alongside the methods listed in Table 9-1, the *DataSet* object also features two XML-related properties: *Namespace* and *Prefix*. *Namespace* specifies the XML namespace used to scope XML attributes and elements when you read them into a *DataSet* object. The prefix to alias the namespace is stored in the *Prefix* property. The namespace can't be set if the *DataSet* object already contains data.

Writing Data as XML

The contents of a *DataSet* object can be serialized as XML in two ways that I'll call *stateless* and *stateful*. Although these expressions are not common throughout the ADO.NET documentation, I believe that they capture the gist of the two XML schemas that can be used to persist a *DataSet* object's contents. A stateless representation takes a snapshot of the current instance of the data and renders it according to a particular XML schema (defined in Chapter 1 as the ADO.NET normal form). A stateful representation, on the other hand, contains the history of the data in the object and includes information about changes as well as pending errors. Keep in mind that *stateless* and *stateful* refer to the data in the *DataSet* object but not to the *DataSet* object as a whole.

In this chapter, we'll focus on the stateless representation of the *DataSet* object, with just a glimpse at the stateful representation—the DiffGram format. In Chapter 10, we'll delve into the DiffGram's structure and goals.

The XML representation of a *DataSet* object can be written to a file, a stream, an *XmlWriter* object, or a string using the *WriteXml* method. It can include, or not include, XSD schema information. The actual behavior of the *WriteXml* method can be controlled by passing the optional *XmlWriteMode* parameter. The values in the *XmlWriteMode* enumeration determine the output's layout. The overloads of the method are shown in the following listing:

```
public void WriteXml(Stream, XmlWriteMode);
public void WriteXml(string, XmlWriteMode);
public void WriteXml(TextWriter, XmlWriteMode);
public void WriteXml(XmlWriter, XmlWriteMode);
```

WriteXml provides four additional overloads with the same structure as this code but with no explicit *XmlWriteMode* argument.

The stateless representation of the *DataSet* object takes a snapshot of the current status of the object. In addition to data, the representation includes tables, relations, and constraints definitions. The rows in the tables are written only in their current versions, unless you use the DiffGram format—which would make this a stateful representation. The following schema shows the

ADO.NET normal form—that is, the XML stateless representation of a *DataSet* object:

```
<DataSetName>
  <xs:schema ... />
  <Table #1>
    <field #1>...</field #1>
    <field #2>...</field #2>
  </Table #1>
  <Table #2>
    <field #1>...</field #1>
    <field #2>...</field #2>
    <field #3>...</field #3>
  </Table #2>
    ⋮
</DataSetName>
```

The root tag is named after the *DataSet* object. If the *DataSet* object has no name, the string *NewDataSet* is used. The name of the *DataSet* object can be set at any time through the *DataSetName* property or via the constructor upon instantiation. Each table in the *DataSet* object is represented as a block of rows. Each row is a subtree rooted in a node with the name of the table. You can control the name of a *DataTable* object via the *TableName* property. By default, the first unnamed table added to a *DataSet* object is named *Table*. A trailing index is appended if a table with that name already exists. The following listing shows the XML data of a *DataSet* object named *NorthwindInfo*:

```
<NorthwindInfo>
  <Employees>
    <employeeid>1</employeeid>
    <lastname>Davolio</lastname>
    <firstname>Nancy</firstname>
  </Employees>
    ⋮
  <Territories>
    <employeeid>1</employeeid>
    <territoryid>06897</territoryid>
  </Territories>
    ⋮
</NorthwindInfo>
```

Basically, the XML representation of a *DataSet* object contains rows of data grouped under a root node. Each row is rendered with a subtree in which child nodes represent columns. The contents of each column are stored as the text of the node. The link between a row and the parent table is established through the name of the row node. In the preceding listing, the *<Employees>...</Employees>* subtree represents a row in a *DataTable* object named *Employees*.

Modes of Writing

Table 9-2 summarizes the writing options available for use with *WriteXml* through the *XmlWriteMode* enumeration.

Table 9-2   The *XmlWriteMode* Enumeration

Write Mode	Description
DiffGram	Writes the contents of the *DataSet* object as a DiffGram, including original and current values.
IgnoreSchema	Writes the contents of the *DataSet* object as XML data without a schema.
WriteSchema	Writes the contents of the *DataSet* object, including an in-line XSD schema. The schema can't be inserted as XDR, nor can it be added as a reference.

IgnoreSchema is the default option. The following code demonstrates the typical way to serialize a *DataSet* object to an XML file:

```
StreamWriter sw = new StreamWriter(fileName);
dataset.WriteXml(sw);     // Defaults to IgnoreSchema
sw.Close();
```

Tip   In terms of functionality, calling the *GetXml* method and then writing its contents to a data store is identical to calling *WriteXml* with *XmlWriteMode* set to *IgnoreSchema*. Using *GetXml* can be comfortable, but in terms of raw overhead, calling *WriteXml* on a *StringWriter* object is slightly more efficient, as shown here:

```
StringWriter sw = new StringWriter();
ds.WriteXml(sw, XmlWriteMode.IgnoreSchema);
// Access the string using sw.ToString()
```

The same considerations apply to *GetXmlSchema* and *WriteXmlSchema*.

Preserving Schema and Type Information

The stateless XML format is a flat format. Unless you explicitly add schema information, the XML output is weakly typed. There is no information about tables and columns, and the original content of each column is normalized to a string. If you need a higher level of type and schema fidelity, start by adding an in-line XSD schema.

In general, a few factors can influence the final structure of the XML document that *WriteXml* creates for you. In addition to the overall XML format—DiffGram or a plain hierarchical representation of the current contents—important factors include the presence of schema information, nested relations, and how table columns are mapped to XML elements.

> **Note**   To optimize the resulting XML code, the *WriteXml* method drops column fields with *null* values. Dropping the *null* column fields doesn't affect the usability of the *DataSet* object—you can successfully rebuild the object from XML, and data-bound controls can easily manage *null* values. This feature can become a problem, however, if you send the *DataSet* object's XML output to a non-.NET platform. Other parsers, unaware that *null* values are omitted for brevity, might fail to parse the document. If you want to represent *null* values in the XML output, replace the *null* values (*System.DBNull* type) with other neutral values (for example, blank spaces).

Writing Schema Information

When you serialize a *DataSet* object, schema information is important for two reasons. First, it adds structured information about the layout of the constituent tables and their relations and constraints. Second, extra table properties are persisted only within the schema. Note, however, that schema information describes the structure of the XML document being created and is not a transcript of the database metadata.

The schema contains information about the constituent columns of each *DataTable* object. (Column information includes name, type, any expression, and all the contents of the *ExtendedProperties* collection.)

The schema is always written as an in-line XSD. As mentioned, there is no way for you to write the schema as XDR, as a document type definition (DTD), or even as an added reference to an external file. The following listing shows the schema source for a *DataSet* object named *NorthwindInfo* that consists of two tables: Employees and Territories. The Employees table has three columns—*employeeid*, *lastname*, and *firstname*. The Territories table includes *employeeid* and *territoryid* columns. (These elements appear in boldface in this listing.)

```
<xs:schema id="NorthwindInfo" xmlns=""
    xmlns:xs="http://www.w3.org/2001/XMLSchema"
    xmlns:msdata="urn:schemas-microsoft-com:xml-msdata">
  <xs:element name="NorthwindInfo" msdata:IsDataSet="true">
    <xs:complexType>
      <xs:choice maxOccurs="unbounded">
        <xs:element name="Employees">
          <xs:complexType>
            <xs:sequence>
              <xs:element name="employeeid" type="xs:int" />
              <xs:element name="lastname" type="xs:string" />
              <xs:element name="firstname" type="xs:string" />
            </xs:sequence>
          </xs:complexType>
        </xs:element>
        <xs:element name="Territories">
          <xs:complexType>
            <xs:sequence>
              <xs:element name="employeeid" type="xs:int" />
              <xs:element name="territoryid" type="xs:string" />
            </xs:sequence>
          </xs:complexType>
        </xs:element>
      </xs:choice>
    </xs:complexType>
  </xs:element>
</xs:schema>
```

The *<xs:choice>* element describes the body of the root node *<North-windInfo>* as an unbounded sequence of *<Employees>* and *<Territories>* nodes. These first-level nodes indicate the tables in the *DataSet* object. The children of each table denote the schema of the *DataTable* object. (See Chapter 3 for more information about XML schemas.)

The schema can be slightly more complex if relations exist between two or more pairs of tables. The *msdata* namespace contains ad hoc attributes that are used to annotate the schema with ADO.NET–specific information, mostly about indexes, table relationships, and constraints.

In-Line Schemas and Validation

Chapter 3 hinted at why the XmlValidatingReader class is paradoxically unable to validate the XML code that WriteXml generates for a DataSet object with an in-line schema, as shown here:

```
<DataSetName>
  <schema>...</schema>
  <Table1>...</Table1>
  <Table2>...</Table2>
<DataSetName>
```

In the final XML layout, schema information is placed at the same level as the table nodes, but includes information about the common root (*DataSetName*, in the preceding code) as well as the tables (*Table1* and *Table2*). Because the validating parser is a forward-only reader, it can match the schema only for nodes placed after the schema block. The idea is that the parser first reads the schema and then checks the compliance of the remainder of the tree with the just-read information, as shown in Figure 9-2.

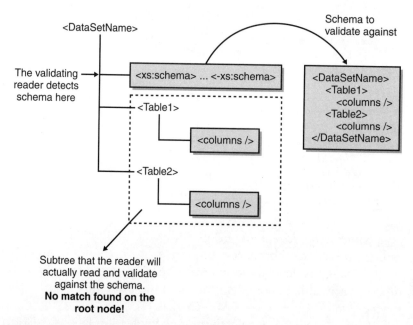

Figure 9-2   How the .NET Framework validating reader parses a serialized *DataSet* object with an in-line schema.

Due to the structure of the XML document being generated, what comes after the schema does not match the schema! Figure 9-3 shows that the validating parser we built in Chapter 3 around the *XmlValidatingReader* class does not recognize (I'd say, by design) a serialized *DataSet* object when an in-line schema is incorporated.

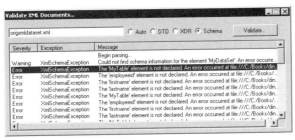

Figure 9-3   The validating parser built in Chapter 3 does not validate an XML *DataSet* object with an in-line schema.

Is there a way to serialize the *DataSet* object so that its XML representation remains parsable when an in-line schema is included? The workaround is fairly simple.

Serializing to Valid XML

As you can see in Figure 9-2, the rub lies in the fact that the in-line schema is written in the middle of the document it is called to describe. This fact, in addition to the forward-only nature of the parser, irreversibly alters the parser's perception of what the real document schema is. The solution is simple: move the schema out of the *DataSet* XML serialization output, and group both nodes under a new common root, as shown here:

```
<Wrapper>
  <xs:schema> ... </xs:schema>
  <DataSet>
  ⋮
  </DataSet>
</Wrapper>
```

Here's a code snippet that shows how to implement this solution:

```
XmlTextWriter writer = new XmlTextWriter(file);
writer.Formatting = Formatting.Indented;
writer.WriteStartElement("Wrapper");
ds.WriteXmlSchema(writer);
ds.WriteXml(writer);
writer.WriteEndElement();
writer.Close();
```

If you don't use an XML writer, the *WriteXmlSchema* method would write the XML declaration in the middle of the document, thus making the document wholly unparsable. You can also mark this workaround with your own credentials using a custom namespace, as shown here:

```
writer.WriteStartElement("de", "Wrapper", "dinoe-xml-07356-1801-1");
```

Figure 9-4 shows the new document displayed in Microsoft Internet Explorer.

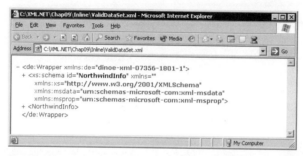

Figure 9-4   The *DataSet* object's XML output after modification.

Figure 9-5 shows that this new XML file (validdataset.xml) is successfully validated by the *XmlValidatingReader* class. The validating parser raises a warning about the new root node; this feature was covered in Chapter 3.

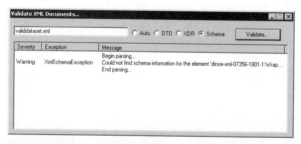

Figure 9-5   The validating parser raises a warning but accepts the updated XML file.

A reasonable concern you might have is about the *DataSet* object's ability to read back such a modified XML stream. No worries! The *ReadXml* method is still perfectly able to read and process the modified schema, as shown here:

```
DataSet ds = new DataSet();
ds.ReadXml("ValidDataset.xml", XmlReadMode.ReadSchema);
ds.WriteXml("standard.xml");
```

> **Note**   Although paradoxical, this behavior (whether it's by design or a bug) does not deserve much hype. At first glance, this behavior seems to limit true cross-platform interoperability, but after a more thoughtful look, you can't help but realize that very few XML parsers today support in-line XML schemas. In other words, what appears to be a clamorous and incapacitating bug is actually a rather innocuous behavior that today has a very limited impact on real applications. Real-world cross-platform data exchange, in fact, must be done using distinct files for schema and data.

Customizing the XML Representation

The schema of the *DataSet* object's XML representation is not set in stone and can be modified to some extent. In particular, each column in each *DataTable* object can specify how the internal serializer should render its content. By default, each column is rendered as an element, but this feature can be changed to any of the values in the *MappingType* enumeration. The *DataColumn* property that specifies the mapping type is *ColumnMapping*.

Customizing Column Mapping

Each row in a *DataTable* object originates an XML subtree whose structure depends on the value assigned to the *DataColumn* object's *ColumnMapping* property. Table 9-3 lists the allowable column mappings.

Table 9-3   The *MappingType* Enumeration

Mapping	Description
Attribute	The column is mapped to an XML attribute on the row node.
Element	The column is mapped to an XML node element. The default setting.
Hidden	The column is not included in the XML output unless the DiffGram format is used.
SimpleContent	The column is mapped to simple text. (Only for tables containing exactly one column.)

The column data depends on the row node. If *ColumnMapping* is set to *Element*, the column value is rendered as a child node, as shown here:

```
<Table>
  <Column>value</Column>
    ⋮
</Table>
```

If *ColumnMapping* is set to *Attribute*, the column data becomes an attribute on the row node, as shown here:

```
<Table Column="value">
    ⋮
</Table>
```

By setting *ColumnMapping* to *Hidden*, you can filter the column out of the XML representation. Unlike the two preceding settings, which are maintained in the DiffGram format, a column marked with *Hidden* is still serialized in the DiffGram format, but with a special attribute that indicates that it was originally marked hidden for serialization. The reason is that the DiffGram format is meant to provide a stateful and high-fidelity representation of the *DataSet* object.

Finally, the *SimpleContent* attribute renders the column content as the text of the row node, as shown here:

```
<Table>value</Table>
```

For this reason, this attribute is applicable only to tables that have a single column.

Persisting Extended Properties

Many ADO.NET classes, including *DataSet*, *DataTable*, and *DataColumn*, use the *ExtendedProperties* property to enable users to add custom information. Think of the *ExtendedProperties* property as a kind of generic cargo variable similar to the *Tag* property of many ActiveX controls. You populate it with name/value pairs and manage the contents using the typical and familiar programming interface of collections. For example, you can use the *DataTable* object's *ExtendedProperties* collection to store the SQL command that should be used to refresh the table itself.

The set of extended properties is lost at serialization time, unless you choose to add schema information. The *WriteXml* method adds extended properties to the schema using an ad hoc attribute prefixed with the *msprop* namespace prefix. Consider the following code:

```
ds.Tables["Employees"].ExtendedProperties.Add("Command",
    EmployeesCommand.Text);
ds.Tables["Territories"].ExtendedProperties.Add("Command",
    TerritoriesCommand.Text);
```

When the tables are serialized, the *Command* slot is rendered as follows:

```
<xs:element name="Employees" msprop:Command="...">
<xs:element name="Territories" msprop:Command="...">
```

ExtendedProperties holds a collection of *objects* and can accept values of any type, but you might run into trouble if you store values other than strings there. When the object is serialized, any extended property is serialized as a string. In particular, the string is what the object's *ToString* method returns. This can pose problems when the *DataSet* object is deserialized.

Not all types can be successfully and seamlessly rebuilt from a string. For example, consider the *Color* class. If you call *ToString* on a *Color* object (say, *Blue*), you get something like *Color [Blue]*. However, no constructor on the *Color* class can rebuild a valid object from such a string. For this reason, pay careful attention to the nonstring types you store in the *ExtendedProperties* collection.

Rendering Data Relations

A *DataSet* object can contain one or more relations gathered under the *Relations* collection property. A *DataRelation* object represents a parent/child relationship set between two *DataTable* objects. The connection takes place on the value of a matching column and is similar to a primary key/foreign key relationship. In ADO.NET, the relation is entirely implemented in memory and can have any cardinality: one-to-one, one-to-many, and even many-to-one.

More often than not, a relation entails table constraints. In ADO.NET, you have two types of constraints: *foreign-key constraints* and *unique constraints*. A foreign-key constraint denotes an action that occurs on the columns involved in the relation when a row is either deleted or updated. A unique constraint denotes a restriction on the parent column whereby duplicate values are not allowed. How are relations rendered in XML?

If no schema information is required, relations are simply ignored. When a schema is not explicitly required, the XML representation of the *DataSet* object is a plain snapshot of the currently stored data; any ancillary information is ignored. There are two ways to accurately represent a *DataRelation* relation within an XML schema: you can use the *<msdata:Relationship>* annotation or specify an *<xs:keyref>* element. The *WriteXml* procedure uses the latter solution.

The *msdata:Relationship* Annotation

The *msdata:Relationship* annotation is a Microsoft XSD extension that ADO.NET and XML programmers can use to explicitly specify a parent/child relationship between non-nested tables in a schema. This annotation is ideal for expressing the content of a *DataRelation* object. In turn, the content of an *msdata:Relationship* annotation is transformed into a *DataRelation* object when *ReadXml* processes the XML file.

Let's consider the following relation:

```
DataRelation rel = new DataRelation("Emp2Terr",
        ds.Tables["Employees"].Columns["employeeid"],
    ds.Tables["Territories"].Columns["employeeid"]);
ds.Relations.Add(rel);
```

The following listing shows how to serialize this relation to XML:

```
<xs:schema id="NorthwindInfo" ... >
  <xs:annotation>
    <xs:appinfo>
      <msdata:Relationship name="Emp2Terr"
          msdata:parent="Employees"
          msdata:child="Territories"
          msdata:parentkey="employeeid"
          msdata:childkey="employeeid" />
    </xs:appinfo>
  </xs:annotation>

  <xs:element name="NorthwindInfo" msdata:IsDataSet="true">
    ⋮
  </xs:element>
</xs:schema>
```

This syntax is simple and effective, but it has one little drawback—it is simply targeted to describe a relation. When you serialize a *DataSet* object to XML, you might want to obtain a hierarchical representation of the data, if a parent/child relationship is present. For example, which of the following XML documents do you find more expressive? The sequential layout shown here is the default:

```
<Employees employeeid="1" lastname="Davolio" firstname="Nancy" />
<Territories employeeid="1" territoryid="06897" />
<Territories employeeid="1" territoryid="19713" />
```

The following layout provides a hierarchical view of the data—all the territories' rows are nested below the logical parent row:

```
<Employees employeeid="1" lastname="Davolio" firstname="Nancy">
  <Territories employeeid="1" territoryid="06897" />
  <Territories employeeid="1" territoryid="19713" />
</Employees>
```

As an annotation, *msdata:Relationship* can't express this schema-specific information. Another piece of information is still needed. For this reason, the *WriteXml* method uses the *<xs:keyref>* element to describe the relationship along with nested type definitions to create a hierarchy of nodes.

The XSD *keyref* Element

In XSD, the *keyref* element allows you to establish links between elements within a document in much the same way a parent/child relationship does. The *WriteXml* method uses *keyref* to express a relation within a *DataSet* object, as shown here:

```
<xs:keyref name="Emp2Terr" refer="Constraint1">
  <xs:selector xpath=".//Territories" />
  <xs:field xpath="@employeeid" />
</xs:keyref>
```

The *name* attribute is set to the name of the *DataRelation* object. By design, the *refer* attribute points to the name of a *key* or *unique* element defined in the same schema. For a *DataRelation* object, *refer* points to an automatically generated *unique* element that represents the parent table, as shown in the following code. The child table of a *DataRelation* object, on the other hand, is represented by the contents of the *keyref* element.

```
<xs:unique name="Constraint1">
  <xs:selector xpath=".//Employees" />
  <xs:field xpath="employeeid" />
</xs:unique>
```

The *keyref* element's contents consist of two mandatory subelements—*selector* and *field*—both of which contain an XPath expression. The *selector* subelement specifies the node-set across which the values selected by the expression in *field* must be unique. Put more simply, *selector* denotes the parent or the child table, and *field* indicates the parent or the child column. The final XML representation of our sample *DataRelation* object is shown here:

```
<xs:unique name="Constraint1">
  <xs:selector xpath=".//Employees" />
  <xs:field xpath="employeeid" />
</xs:unique>
<xs:keyref name="Emp2Terr" refer="Constraint1">
  <xs:selector xpath=".//Territories" />
  <xs:field xpath="@employeeid" />
</xs:keyref>
```

This code is functionally equivalent to the *msdata:Relationship* annotation, but it is completely expressed using the XSD syntax.

Nested Data and Nested Types

The XSD syntax is also important for expressing relations in XML using nested subtrees. Neither *msdata:Relationship* nor *keyref* are adequate to express the relation when nested tables are required. Nested relations are expressed using nested types in the XML schema.

In the following code, the *Territories* type is defined within the *Employees* type, thus matching the hierarchical relationship between the corresponding tables:

```
<xs:element name="Employees">
  <xs:complexType>
    <xs:sequence>
        ⋮
      <xs:element name="Territories" minOccurs="0" maxOccurs="unbounded">
        <xs:complexType>
          <xs:sequence>
            <xs:element name="employeeid" type="xs:int" />
            <xs:element name="territoryid" type="xs:string" />
          </xs:sequence>
        </xs:complexType>
      </xs:element>
    </xs:sequence>
  </xs:complexType>
</xs:element>
```

By using *keyref* and nested types, you have a single syntax—the XML Schema language—to render in XML the contents of any ADO.NET *DataRelation* object. The *Nested* property of the *DataRelation* object specifies whether the relation must be rendered hierarchically—that is, with child rows nested under the parent—or sequentially—that is, with all rows treated as children of the root node.

> **Important** When reading an XML stream to build a *DataSet* object, the *ReadXml* method treats the *<msdata:Relationship>* annotation and the *<xs:keyref>* element as perfectly equivalent pieces of syntax. Both are resolved by creating and adding a *DataRelation* object with the specified characteristics. When *ReadXml* meets nested types, in the absence of explicit relationship information, it ensures that the resultant *DataSet* object has tables that reflect the hierarchy of types and creates a *DataRelation* object between them. This relation is given an auto-generated name and is set on a pair of automatically created columns.

Serializing Filtered Views

As mentioned, in ADO.NET both the *DataSet* object and the *DataTable* object implement the *ISerializable* interface, thus making themselves accessible to any .NET Framework serializers. Only the *DataSet* object, however, exposes additional methods (for example, *WriteXml*) to let you explicitly save the contents to XML. We'll explore the various aspects of ADO.NET object serialization in the section "Binary Data Serialization," on page 422.

In the meantime, let's see how to extend the *DataTable* and *DataView* objects with the equivalent of a *WriteXml* method.

Serializing *DataTable* Objects

The .NET Framework does not allow you to save a stand-alone *DataTable* object to XML. (A stand-alone *DataTable* object is an object not included in any parent *DataSet* object.) Unlike the *DataSet* object, the *DataTable* object does not provide you with a *WriteXml* method. Nevertheless, when you persist a *DataSet* object to XML, any contained *DataTable* object is regularly rendered to XML. How is this possible?

The *DataSet* class includes internal methods that can be used to persist an individual *DataTable* object to XML. Unfortunately, these methods are not publicly available. Saving the contents of a stand-alone *DataTable* object to XML is not particularly difficult, however, and requires only one small trick.

The idea is that you create a temporary, empty *DataSet* object, add the table to it, and then serialize the *DataSet* object to XML. Here's some sample code:

```
public static
void WriteDataTable(DataTable dt, string outputFile, XmlWriteMode mode)
{
    DataSet tmp = CreateTempDataSet(dt);
    tmp.WriteXml(outputFile, mode);
}
```

This code is excerpted from a sample class library that provides static methods to save *DataTable* and *DataView* objects to XML. Each method has several overloads and mimics as much as possible the *DataSet* object's *WriteXml* method. In the preceding sample code, the input *DataTable* object is incorporated in a temporary *DataSet* object that is then saved to a disk file. The following code creates the temporary *DataSet* object and adds the *DataTable* object to it:

```
private static DataSet CreateTempDataSet(DataTable dt)
{
    // Create a temporary DataSet
    DataSet ds = new DataSet("DataTable");
```

(continued)

```
    // Make sure the DataTable does not already belong to a DataSet
    if (dt.DataSet == null)
        ds.Tables.Add(dt);
    else
        ds.Tables.Add(dt.Copy());
    return ds;
}
```

Note that a *DataTable* object can't be linked to more than one *DataSet* object at a time. If a given *DataTable* object has a parent object, its *DataSet* property is not *null*. If the property is not *null*, the temporary *DataSet* object must be linked to an in-memory copy of the table.

The class library that contains the various *WriteDataTable* overloads is available in this book's sample files and is named AdoNetXmlSerializer. A client application uses the library as follows:

```
StringWriter writer = new StringWriter();
AdoNetXmlSerializer.WriteDataTable(m_data, writer);

// Show the serialization output
OutputText.Text = writer.ToString();
writer.Close();
```

Figure 9-6 shows the sample application in action.

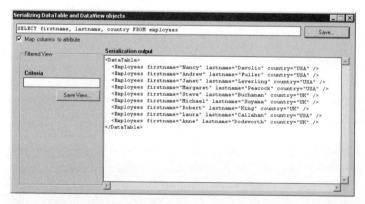

Figure 9-6 An application that passes some data to a *DataTable* object and then persists it to XML.

So much for *DataTable* objects. Let's see what you can do to serialize to XML the contents of an in-memory, possibly filtered, view.

Inside the *DataView* Object

The *DataView* class represents a customized view of a *DataTable* object. The relationship between *DataTable* and *DataView* objects is governed by the rules of a well-known design pattern: the document/view model. According to this model, the *DataTable* object acts as the document, and the *DataView* object acts as the view. At any moment, you can have multiple, different views of the same underlying data. More important, you can manage each view as an independent object with its own set of properties, methods, and events.

The view is implemented by maintaining a separate array with the indexes of the original rows that match the criteria set on the view. By default, the table view is unfiltered and contains all the records included in the table. By configuring the *RowFilter* and *RowStateFilter* properties, you can narrow the set of rows that fit into a particular view. Using the *Sort* property, you can apply a sort expression to the rows in the view. Figure 9-7 illustrates the internal architecture of the *DataView* object.

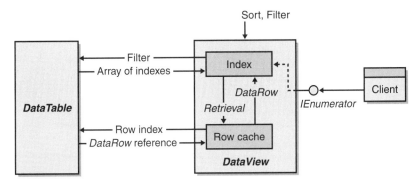

Figure 9-7 A *DataView* object maintains an index of the table rows that match the criteria.

When any of the filter properties is set, the *DataView* object gets from the underlying *DataTable* object an updated index of the rows that match the criteria. The index is a simple array of positions. No row objects are physically copied or referenced at this time.

Linking Tables and Views

The link between the *DataTable* object and the *DataView* object is typically established at creation time through the constructor, as shown here:

```
public DataView(DataTable table);
```

However, you could also create a new view and associate it with a table at a later time using the *DataView* object's *Table* property, as in the following example:

```
DataView dv = new DataView();
dv.Table = dataSet.Tables["Employees"];
```

You can also obtain a *DataView* object from any table. In fact, the *Default-View* property of a *DataTable* object simply returns a *DataView* object initialized to work on that table, as shown here:

```
DataView dv = dt.DefaultView;
```

Originally, the view is unfiltered, and the index array contains as many elements as there are rows in the table.

Getting Views of Rows

The contents of a *DataView* object can be scrolled through a variety of programming interfaces, including collections, lists, and enumerators. The *GetEnumerator* method in particular ensures that you can walk your way through the records in the view using the familiar *foreach* statement.

The following code shows how to access all the rows that fit into the view:

```
DataView myView = new DataView(table);
foreach(DataRowView rowview in myView)
{
    // Dereferences the DataRow object
    DataRow row = rowview.Row;
    ⋮
}
```

When client applications access a particular row in the view, the class expects to find it in an internal rows cache. If the rows cache is not empty, the specified row is returned to the caller via an intermediate *DataRowView* object. The *DataRowView* object is a wrapper for the *DataRow* object that contains the actual data. You access row data through the *Row* property. If the rows cache is empty, the *DataView* class fills it with an array of *DataRowView* objects, each of which references an original *DataRow* object. The rows cache can be empty either because it has not yet been used or because the sort expression or the filter string has been changed in the meantime.

Serializing *DataView* Objects

The *AdoNetXmlSerializer* class also provides overloaded methods to serialize a *DataView* object. You build a copy of the original *DataTable* object with all the rows (and only those rows) that match the view, as shown here:

```
public static
void WriteDataView(DataView dv, string outputFile, XmlWriteMode mode)
{
    DataTable dt = CreateTempTable(dv);
    WriteDataTable(dt, outputFile, mode);
}
```

You create a temporary *DataTable* object and then serialize it to XML using the previously defined methods. The structure of the internal *CreateTempTable* routine is fairly simple, as shown here:

```
private static DataTable CreateTempTable(DataView dv)
{
    // Create a temporary DataTable with the same structure
    // as the original
    DataTable dt = dv.Table.Clone();

    // Fill the DataTable with all the rows in the view
    foreach(DataRowView rowview in dv)
        dt.ImportRow(rowview.Row);

    return dt;
}
```

The *ImportRow* method creates a new row object in the context of the table. Like many other ADO.NET objects, the *DataRow* object can't be referenced by two container objects at the same time. Using *ImportRow* is logically equivalent to cloning the row and then adding the clone as a reference to the table. Figure 9-8 shows a *DataView* object saved to XML.

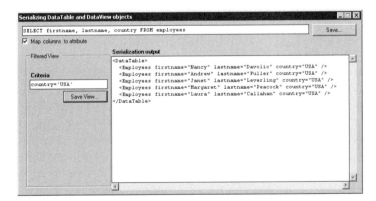

Figure 9-8   Saving a *DataView* object to XML.

Binary Data Serialization

There are basically two ways to serialize ADO.NET objects: using the object's own XML interface, and using .NET Framework data formatters. So far, we have reviewed the *DataSet* object's methods for serializing data to XML, and you've learned how to persist other objects like *DataTable* and *DataView* to XML. Let's look now at what's needed to serialize ADO.NET objects using the standard .NET Framework data formatters.

The big difference between methods like *WriteXml* and .NET Framework data formatters is that in the former case, the object itself controls its own serialization process. When .NET Framework data formatters are involved, any object can behave in one of two ways. The object can declare itself as serializable (using the *Serializable* attribute) and passively let the formatter extrapolate any significant information that needs to be serialized. This type of object serialization uses .NET Framework reflection to list all the properties that make up the state of an object.

The second behavior entails the object implementing the *ISerializable* interface, thus passing the formatters the data to be serialized. After this step, however, the object no longer controls the process. A class that neither is marked with the *Serializable* attribute nor implements the *ISerializable* interface can't be serialized. No ADO.NET class declares itself as serializable, and only *DataSet* and *DataTable* implement the *ISerializable* interface. For example, you can't serialize to any .NET Framework formatters a *DataColumn* or a *DataRow* object.

Ordinary .NET Framework Serialization

The .NET Framework comes with two predefined formatter objects defined in the *System.Runtime.Serialization.Formatters* namespace—the binary formatter and the SOAP formatter. The classes that provide these two serializers are *Binary-Formatter* and *SoapFormatter*. The former is more efficient, is faster, and produces more compact code. The latter is designed for interoperability and generates a SOAP-based description of the class that can be easily consumed on non-.NET platforms.

> **Note**   A *formatter object* is merely a class that implements the *IFor-matter* interface to support the serialization of a graph of objects. The *SoapFormatter* and *BinaryFormatter* classes also implement the *IRe-motingFormatter* interface to support remote procedure calls across AppDomains. No technical reasons prevent you from implementing custom formatters. In most cases, however, you only need to tweak the serialization process of a given class instead of creating an extension to the general serialization mechanism. Quite often, this objective can be reached simply by implementing the *ISerializable* interface.

The following code shows what's needed to serialize a *DataTable* object using a binary formatter:

```
BinaryFormatter bf = new BinaryFormatter();
StreamWriter swDat = new StreamWriter(outputFile);
bf.Serialize(swDat.BaseStream, dataTable);
swDat.Close();
```

The *Serialize* method causes the formatter to flush the contents of an object to a binary stream. The *Deserialize* method does the reverse—it reads from a previously created binary stream, rebuilds the object, and returns it to the caller, as shown here:

```
DataTable dt = new DataTable();
BinaryFormatter bf = new BinaryFormatter();
StreamReader sr = new StreamReader(sourceFile);
dt = (DataTable) bf.Deserialize(sr.BaseStream);
sr.Close();
```

When you run this code, something surprising happens. Have you ever tried to serialize a *DataTable* object, or a *DataSet* object, using the binary formatter? If so, you certainly got a binary file, but with a ton of XML in it. Unfortunately, XML data in serialized binary files only makes them huge, without the portability and readability advantages that XML normally offers. As a result, deserializing such files might take a while to complete—usually seconds.

There is an architectural reason for this odd behavior. The *DataTable* and *DataSet* classes implement the *ISerializable* interface, thus making themselves responsible for the data being serialized. The *ISerializable* interface consists of a single method—*GetObjectData*—whose output the formatter takes and flushes into the output stream.

Can you guess what happens next? By design, the *DataTable* and *DataSet* classes describe themselves to serializers using an XML DiffGram document. The binary formatter takes this rather long string and appends it to the stream. In this way, *DataSet* and *DataTable* objects are always remoted and transferred using XML—which is great. Unfortunately, if you are searching for a more compact representation of persisted tables, the ordinary .NET Framework run-time serialization for ADO.NET objects is not for you. Let's see how to work around it.

Custom Binary Serialization

To optimize the binary representation of a *DataTable* object (or a *DataSet* object), you have no other choice than mapping the class to an intermediate object whose serialization process is under your control. The entire operation is articulated into a few steps:

1. Create a custom class, and mark it as serializable (or, alternatively, implement the *ISerializable* interface).

2. Copy the key properties of the *DataTable* object to the members of the class. Which members you actually map is up to you. However, the list must certainly include the column names and types, plus the rows.

3. Serialize this new class to the binary formatter, and when deserialization occurs, use the restored information to build a new instance of the *DataTable* object.

Let's analyze these steps in more detail.

Creating a Serializable Ghost Class

Assuming that you need to persist only columns and rows of a *DataTable* object, a ghost class can be quickly created. In the following example, this ghost class is named *GhostDataTable*:

```
[Serializable]
public class GhostDataTable
{
    public GhostDataTable()
    {
        colNames = new ArrayList();
        colTypes = new ArrayList();
        dataRows = new ArrayList();
    }
```

```
    public ArrayList colNames;
    public ArrayList colTypes;
    public ArrayList dataRows;
}
```

This class consists of three, serializable *ArrayList* objects that contain column names, column types, and data rows.

The serialization process now involves the *GhostDataTable* class rather than the *DataTable* object, as shown here:

```
private void BinarySerialize(DataTable dt, string outputFile)
{
    BinaryFormatter bf = new BinaryFormatter();
    StreamWriter swBin = new StreamWriter(outputFile);

    // Instantiate and fill the worker class
    GhostDataTable ghost = new GhostDataTable();
    CreateTableGraph(dt, ghost);

    // Serialize the object
    bf.Serialize(swBin.BaseStream, ghost);
    swBin.Close();
}
```

The key event here is how the *DataTable* object is mapped to the *GhostData-Table* class. The mapping takes place in the folds of the *CreateTableGraph* routine.

Mapping Table Information

The *CreateTableGraph* routine populates the *colNames* array with column names and the *colTypes* array with the names of the data types, as shown in the following code. The *dataRows* array is filled with an array that represents all the values in the row.

```
void CreateTableGraph(DataTable dt, GhostDataTable ghost)
{
    // Insert column information (names and types)
    foreach(DataColumn col in dt.Columns)
    {
        ghost.colNames.Add(col.ColumnName);
        ghost.colTypes.Add(col.DataType.FullName);
    }

    // Insert rows information
    foreach(DataRow row in dt.Rows)
        ghost.dataRows.Add(row.ItemArray);
}
```

The *DataRow* object's *ItemArray* property is an array of objects. It turns out to be particularly handy, as it lets you handle the contents of the entire row as a single, monolithic piece of data. Internally, the *get* accessor of *ItemArray* is implemented as a simple loop that reads and stores one column after the next. The *set* accessor is even more valuable, because it automatically groups all the changes in a pair of *BeginEdit/EndEdit* calls and fires column-changed events as appropriate.

Sizing Up Serialized Data

The sample application shown in Figure 9-9 demonstrates that a *DataTable* object serialized using a ghost class can be up to 80 percent smaller than an identical object serialized the standard way.

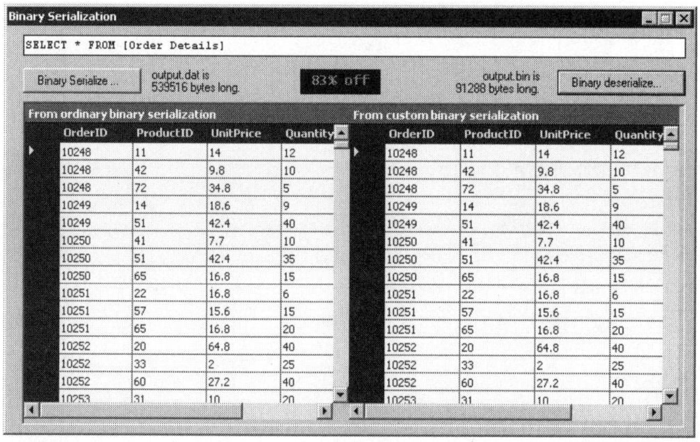

Figure 9-9   The difference between ordinary and custom binary serialization.

In particular, consider the *DataTable* object resulting from the following query:

```
SELECT * FROM [Order Details]
```

The table contains five columns and 2155 records. It would take up half a megabyte if serialized to the binary formatter as a *DataTable* object. By using an intermediate ghost class, the size of the output is 83 percent less. Looking at things the other way round, the results of the standard serialization process is about 490 percent larger than the results you obtain using the ghost class.

Of course, not all cases give you such an impressive result. In all the tests I ran on the Northwind database, however, I got an average 60 percent reduction. The more the table content consists of numbers, the more space you save. The more BLOB fields you have, the less space you save. Try running the following query, in which *photo* is the BLOB field that contains an employee's picture:

```
SELECT photo FROM employees
```

The ratio of savings here is only 25 percent and represents the bottom end of the Northwind test results. Interestingly, if you add only a couple of traditional fields to the query, the ratio increases to 28 percent. The application shown in Figure 9-9 (included in this book's sample files) is a useful tool for fine-tuning the structure of the table and the queries for better serialization results.

Deserializing Data

Once the binary data has been deserialized, you hold an instance of the ghost class that must be transformed back into a usable *DataTable* object. Here's how the sample application accomplishes this:

```
DataTable BinaryDeserialize(string sourceFile)
{
    BinaryFormatter bf = new BinaryFormatter();
    StreamReader sr = new StreamReader(sourceFile);
    GhostDataTable ghost =
        (GhostDataTable) bf.Deserialize(sr.BaseStream);
    sr.Close();

    // Rebuild the DataTable object
    DataTable dt = new DataTable();

    // Add columns
    for(int i=0; i<ghost.colNames.Count; i++)
    {
        DataColumn col = new DataColumn(ghost.colNames[i].ToString(),
            Type.GetType(ghost.colTypes[i].ToString()));
        dt.Columns.Add(col);
    }

    // Add rows
    for(int i=0; i<ghost.dataRows.Count; i++)
    {
        DataRow row = dt.NewRow();
        row.ItemArray = (object[]) ghost.dataRows[i];
        dt.Rows.Add(row);
    }

    dt.AcceptChanges();
    return dt;
}
```

The information stored in the ghost arrays is used to add columns and rows to a newly created *DataTable* object. Figure 9-9 demonstrates the perfect equivalence of the objects obtained by deserializing a *DataTable* and a ghost class.

Caution   The ghost class used in the preceding sample code serializes the minimal amount of information necessary to rebuild the *DataTable* object. You should add new properties to track other *DataColumn* or *DataRow* properties that are significant in your own application. Note that you can't simply serialize the *DataColumn* and *DataRow* objects as a whole because none of them is marked as serializable.

Loading *DataSet* Objects from XML

The contents of an ADO.NET *DataSet* object can be loaded from an XML stream or document—for example, from an XML stream previously created using the *WriteXml* method. To fill a *DataSet* object with XML data, you use the *ReadXml* method of the class.

The *ReadXml* method fills a *DataSet* object by reading from a variety of sources, including disk files, .NET Framework streams, or instances of *XmlReader* objects. In general, the *ReadXml* method can process any type of XML file, but of course the nontabular and rather irregularly shaped structure of XML files might create some problems and originate unexpected results when the files are rendered in terms of rows and columns.

In addition, the *ReadXml* method is extremely flexible and lets you load data according to a particular schema or even infer the schema from the data.

Building *DataSet* Objects

The *ReadXml* method has several overloads, all of which are similar. They take the XML source plus an optional *XmlReadMode* value as arguments, as shown here:

```
public XmlReadMode ReadXml(Stream, XmlReadMode);
public XmlReadMode ReadXml(string, XmlReadMode);
public XmlReadMode ReadXml(TextReader, XmlReadMode);
public XmlReadMode ReadXml(XmlReader, XmlReadMode);
```

The *ReadXml* method creates the relational schema for the *DataSet* object according to the read mode specified and regardless of whether a schema already exists in the *DataSet* object. The following code snippet is typical code you would use to load a *DataSet* object from XML:

```
StreamReader sr = new StreamReader(fileName);
DataSet ds = new DataSet();
ds.ReadXml(sr);
sr.Close();
```

The return value of the *ReadXml* method is an *XmlReadMode* value that indicates the modality used to read the data. This information is particularly important when no reading mode is specified or when the automatic default mode is set. In either case, you don't really know how the schema for the target *DataSet* object has been generated.

Modes of Reading

Table 9-4 summarizes the reading options available for use with the *ReadXml* method; allowable options are grouped in the *XmlReadMode* enumeration.

Table 9-4   *XmlReadMode* Enumeration Values

Read Mode	Description
Auto	Default option; indicates the most appropriate way of reading by looking at the source data.
DiffGram	Reads a DiffGram and adds the data to the current schema. If no schema exists, an exception is thrown. Information that doesn't match the existing schema is discarded.
Fragment	Reads and adds XML fragments until the end of the stream is reached.
IgnoreSchema	Ignores any in-line schema that might be available and relies on the *DataSet* object's existing schema. If no schema exists, no data is loaded. Information that doesn't match the existing schema is discarded.
InferSchema	Ignores any in-line schema and infers the schema from the XML data. If the *DataSet* object already contains a schema, the current schema is extended. An exception is thrown in the case of conflicting table namespaces and column data types.
ReadSchema	Reads any in-line schema and loads both data and schema. An existing schema is extended with new columns and tables, but an exception is thrown if a given table already exists in the *DataSet* object.

The default read mode is *XmlReadMode.Auto*. When this mode is set, or when no read mode has been explicitly set, the *ReadXml* method examines the XML source and chooses the most appropriate option.

The first possibility checked is whether the XML data is a DiffGram. If it is, the *XmlReadMode.DiffGram* mode is used. If the XML data is not a DiffGram but references an XDR or an XSD schema, the *InferSchema* mode is used. *Read-Schema* is used only if the document contains an in-line schema. In both the *InferSchema* and *ReadSchema* cases, the *ReadXml* method checks first for an XDR (referenced or in-line) schema and then for an XSD schema. If the *DataSet* object already has a schema, the read mode is set to *IgnoreSchema*. Finally, if no schema information can be found, the *InferSchema* mode is used.

Reading XML Data

Although *ReadXml* supports various types of sources—streams, files, and text readers—the underlying routine used in all cases reads data using an XML reader. The following pseudocode illustrates the internal architecture of the *ReadXml* overloads:

```
public XmlReadMode ReadXml(Stream stream)
{
    return ReadXml(new XmlTextReader(stream));
}
public XmlReadMode ReadXml(TextReader reader)
{
    return ReadXml(new XmlTextReader(reader));
}
public XmlReadMode ReadXml(string fileName)
{
    return ReadXml(new XmlTextReader(fileName));
}
```

The XML source is read one node after the next until the end is reached. The information read is transformed into a *DataRow* object that is added to a *DataTable* object. Of course, the layout of both the *DataTable* object and the *DataRow* object is determined based on the schema read or inferred.

Merging *DataSet* Objects

When loading the contents of XML sources into a *DataSet* object, the *ReadXml* method does not merge new and existing rows whose primary key information matches. To merge an existing *DataSet* object with a *DataSet* object just loaded from an XML source, you must proceed in a particular way.

First you create a new *DataSet* object and fill it with the XML data. Next you merge the two objects by calling the *Merge* method on either object, as shown in the following code. The *Merge* method is used to merge two *DataSet* objects that have largely similar schemas.

```
target.Merge(source);
```

The target *DataSet* object is the object on which the merge occurs. The source *DataSet* object provides the information to merge but is not affected by the operation. Determining which *DataSet* object must be the target and which will be the source is up to you and depends on the data your application needs to obtain. During the merging, the rows that get overwritten are those with matching primary keys.

An alternative way to merge existing *DataSet* objects with contents read from XML is through the DiffGram format. Loading a DiffGram using *ReadXml* will automatically merge rows that have matching primary keys. When using the *XmlReadMode.DiffGram* format, the target *DataSet* object must have the same schema as the DiffGram; otherwise, the merge operation fails and an exception is thrown.

Reading Schema Information

The *XmlReadMode.IgnoreSchema* option causes the *ReadXml* method to ignore any referenced or in-line schema. The data is loaded into the existing *DataSet* schema, and any data that does not fit is discarded. If no schema exists in the *DataSet* object, no data will be loaded. Of course, an empty *DataSet* object has no schema information, as shown in the following listing. If the XML source is in the DiffGram format, the *IgnoreSchema* option has the same effect as *XmlReadMode.DiffGram*.

```
// No schema in the DataSet, no data will be loaded
DataSet ds = new DataSet();
StreamReader sr = new StreamReader(fileName);
ds.ReadXml(sr, XmlReadMode.IgnoreSchema);
```

Reading In-Line Schemas

The *XmlReadMode.ReadSchema* option works only with in-line schemas and does not recognize external references to schema files. The *ReadSchema* mode causes the *ReadXml* method to add new tables to the *DataSet* object, but if any tables defined in the in-line schema already exist in the *DataSet* object, an exception is thrown. You can't use the *ReadSchema* option to change the schema of an existing table.

If the *DataSet* object does not contain a schema (that is, the *DataSet* object is empty) and there is no in-line schema, no data is read or loaded. *ReadXml* can read only in-line schemas defined using the XDR or XSD schema. DTD documents are not supported.

Reading External Schemas

An XML source that imports XDR or XSD schema information from an external resource can't be handled through *ReadSchema*. External references are resolved through the *InferSchema* option by inferring the schema from the external file.

The *InferSchema* option is generally quite slow because it has to determine the structure by reading the source. With externally referenced schemas, however, the procedure is considerably faster. The *ReadXml* method simply reads the schema information from the given URL in the same way as the *ReadXmlSchema* method does—no true inferential process is started.

By design, external schema resolution is implemented in the *InferSchema* reading mode rather than in *ReadSchema*. When called to operate in automatic mode on a file that references an external schema, the *ReadXml* method returns *InferSchema*. In turn, *ReadSchema* does not work if called to work on external schemas.

The *ReadSchema* and *InferSchema* options are complementary. The former reads only in-line schema and ignores external references. The latter does the reverse, ignoring any in-line schema that might be present in the source.

Reading Fragments

When the *XmlReadMode.Fragment* option is set, the *DataSet* object is loaded from an XML fragment. An XML fragment is a valid piece of XML that identifies elements, attributes, and documents. The XML fragment for an element is the markup text that fully qualifies the XML element (node, CDATA, processing instruction, or comment). The fragment for an attribute is the *Value* attribute; the fragment for a document is the entire content set.

When the XML data is a fragment, the root level rules for well-formed XML documents are not applied. Fragments that match the existing schema are appended to the appropriate tables, and fragments that do not match the schema are discarded. *ReadXml* reads from the current position to the end of the stream. The *XmlReadMode.Fragment* option should not be used to populate an empty, and subsequently schemaless, *DataSet* object.

Inferring Schema Information

When the *ReadXml* method works with the *XmlReadMode.InferSchema* option set, the data is loaded only after the schema has been completely read from an external source or after the schema has been inferred. Existing schemas are extended by adding new tables or by adding new columns to existing tables, as appropriate.

In addition to the *ReadXml* method, you can use the *DataSet* object's *InferXmlSchema* method to load the schema from a specified XML file into the *DataSet* object. You can control, to some extent, the XML elements processed during the schema inference operation. The signature of the *InferXmlSchema* method allows you to specify an array of namespaces whose elements will be excluded from inference, as shown here:

```
void InferXmlSchema(String fileName, String[] rgNamespace);
```

The *InferXmlSchema* method creates an XML DOM representation of the XML source data and then walks its way through the nodes, creating tables and columns as appropriate.

A Sample Application

To demonstrate the various effects of *ReadXml* and other reading modes, I've created a sample application and a few sample XML documents. Using the application is straightforward. You select an XML file, and the code attempts to load it into a *DataSet* object using the *XmlReadMode* option you specify. The results are shown in a *DataGrid* control. As shown in Figure 9-10, the bottom text box displays the schema of the *DataSet* object as read or inferred by the reading method.

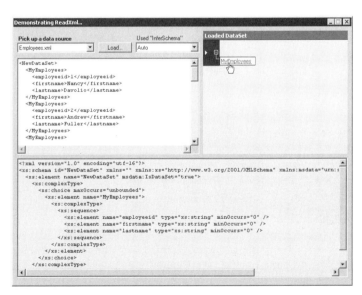

Figure 9-10   *ReadXml* correctly recognizes an XML document in ADO.NET normal form.

In Figure 9-10, the selected XML document is expressed in the ADO.NET normal form—that is, the default schema generated by *WriteXml*—and the *ReadXml* method handles it correctly.

Not all XML sources smoothly fill out a *DataSet* object, however. Let's consider what happens with the following XML document:

```xml
<?xml version="1.0" ?>
<class title="Programming XML.NET" company="Wintellect" author="DinoE">
  <days total="4" expandable="true">
    <day id="1">XML Core Classes</day>
    <day id="2">XML-related Technologies</day>
    <day id="3">XML and ADO.NET</day>
    <day id="4">Remoting and Web services</day>
    <day id="5" optional="true">Miscellaneous and Samples</day>
  </days>
</class>
```

This document is not in ADO.NET normal form even though it contains information that can easily fit in a table of data. As you can see in Figure 9-11, the .NET Framework inference algorithm identifies three distinct tables in this document: *class*, *days*, and *day*. Although acceptable, this is not probably what one would expect.

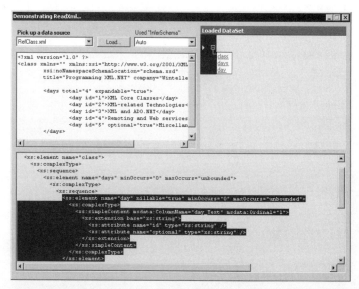

Figure 9-11   The schema that *ReadXml* infers from the specified and nonstandard XML file.

I would read this information as a single table—*day*—contained in a *DataSet* object. My interpretation is a logical rather than an algorithmic reading of the data, however. The final schema consists of three connected tables, shown in Figure 9-12, of which the first two tables simply contain a foreign key field that normalizes the entire data structure.

Figure 9-12   How Microsoft Visual Studio .NET renders the XML schema inferred by *ReadXml*.

Choosing the Correct Reading Mode

If you save the contents of a *DataSet* object to XML and then read it back via *ReadXml*, pay attention to the reading mode you choose. Each reading mode has its own set of features and to the extent that it is possible, you should exploit those features.

Although it is fairly easy to use, the *XmlReadMode.Auto* mode is certainly not the most effective way to read XML data into a *DataSet* object. Avoid using this mode as much as possible, and instead use a more direct, and data-specific, option.

Binding XML to Data-Bound Controls

XML data sources are not in the official list of allowable data sources for the .NET Framework data-bound client and server controls. Many .NET Framework classes can be used as data sources—not just those dealing with database contents. In general, any object that exposes the *ICollection* interface is a potential source for data binding. As a result, you can bind a Microsoft Windows Forms data-bound control or a Web Forms data-bound control to any of the following data structures:

- In-memory .NET Framework collection classes, including arrays, dictionaries, sorted and linked lists, hash tables, stacks, and queues

- User-defined data structures, as long as the structure exposes *ICollection* or one of its child interfaces, such as *IList*

- Database-oriented classes such as *DataTable* and *DataSet*

- Views of data represented by the *DataView* class

You can't directly bind XML documents, however, unless you load XML data in one of the aforementioned classes. Typically, you load XML data into a *DataTable* or a *DataSet* object. This operation can be accomplished in a couple of ways. You can load the XML document into a *DataSet* object using the *ReadXml* method. Alternatively, you can load the XML document into an instance of the *XmlDataDocument* class and access the internally created *DataSet* object.

Loading from Custom Readers

In Chapter 2, we built a custom XML reader for loading CSV files into a *DataTable* object. As mentioned, however, that reader is not fully functional and does not work through *ReadXml*. Let's see how to rewrite the class to make it render the CSV content as a well-formed XML document.

Our target XML schema for the CSV document would be the following:

```
<csv>
  <row col1="..." col2="..." col3="..." />
  <row col1="..." col2="..." col3="..." />
  ⋮
</csv>
```

Of course, this is not the only schema you can choose. I have chosen it because it is both compact and readable. If you decide to use another schema, the code for the reader should be changed accordingly. The target XML schema is a crucial aspect, as it specifies how the *Read* method should be implemented. Figure 9-13 illustrates the behavior of the *Read* method.

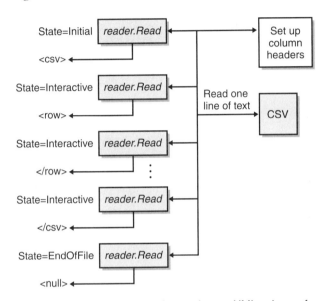

Figure 9-13   The process of returning an XML schema for a CSV file.

The reader tracks the current node and sets internal variables to influence the next node to be returned. For example, when returning an *Element* node, the reader annotates that there's an open node to close. Given this extremely simple schema, a Boolean member is enough to implement this behavior. In fact, no embedded nodes are allowed in a CSV file. In more complex scenarios, you might want to use a stack object.

The *Read* Method

When a new node is returned, the reader updates the node's depth and state. In addition, the reader stores fresh information in node-specific properties such as *Name*, *NodeType*, and *Value*, as shown here:

```
public override bool Read()
{
    if (m_readState == ReadState.Initial)
    {
        if (m_hasColumnHeaders)
```

(continued)

```
        {
            string m_headerLine = m_fileStream.ReadLine();
            m_headerValues = m_headerLine.Split(',');
        }

        SetupRootNode();
        m_readState = ReadState.Interactive;
        return true;
    }

    if (m_readState != ReadState.Interactive)
        return false;

    // Return an end tag if there's one opened
    if (m_mustCloseRow)
    {
        SetupEndElement();
        return true;
    }

    // Return an end tag if the document must be closed
    if (m_mustCloseDocument)
    {
        m_readState = ReadState.EndOfFile;
        return false;
    }

    // Open a new tag
    m_currentLine = m_fileStream.ReadLine();
    if (m_currentLine != null)
        m_readState = ReadState.Interactive;
    else
    {
        SetupEndRootNode();
        return true;
    }

    // Populate the internal structure representing the current element
    m_tokenValues.Clear();
    string[] tokens = m_currentLine.Split(',');
    for (int i=0; i<tokens.Length; i++)
    {
        string key = "";
        if (m_hasColumnHeaders)
            key = m_headerValues[i].ToString();
        else
            key = CsvColumnPrefix + i.ToString();
```

```
            m_tokenValues.Add(key, tokens[i]);
    }

    SetupElement();
    return true;
}
```

For example, when the start tag of a new element is returned, the following code runs:

```
private void SetupElement()
{
    m_isRoot = false;
    m_mustCloseRow = true;
    m_mustCloseDocument = false;

    m_name = CsvRowName;
    m_nodeType = XmlNodeType.Element;
    m_depth = 1;
    m_value = null;

    // Reset the attribute index
    m_currentAttributeIndex = -1;
}
```

When traversing a document using an XML reader, the *ReadXml* method visits attributes in a loop and reads attribute values using *ReadAttributeValue*.

Setting Attributes

Attributes are not read through calls made to the *Read* method. A reader provides ad hoc methods to access attributes either randomly or sequentially. When one of these methods is called—say, *MoveToNextAttribute*—the reader calls an internal method that refreshes the state so that *Name* and *NodeType* can now point to the correct content, as shown here:

```
private void SetupAttribute()
{
    m_nodeType = XmlNodeType.Attribute;
    m_name = m_tokenValues.Keys[m_currentAttributeIndex];
    m_value = m_tokenValues[m_currentAttributeIndex].ToString();
    if (m_parentNode == "")
        m_parentNode = m_name;
}
```

A node is associated with a line of text read from the CSV file. Each token of information becomes an attribute, and attributes are stored in a collection of name/value pairs. (This part of the architecture was described in detail in Chapter 2.) The *m_parentNode* property tracks the name of the element acting as the parent of the current attribute. Basically, it represents the node to move to when *MoveToElement* is called. Again, in this rather simple scenario, a string is sufficient to identify the parent node of an attribute. For more complex XML layouts, you might need to use a custom class.

Reading Attributes Using *ReadXml*

The *ReadXml* method accesses all the attributes of an element using a loop like this:

```
while (reader.MoveToNextAttribute())
{
    // Use ReadAttributeValue to read attribute values
    :
}
```

To load XML data into a *DataSet* object, the *ReadXml* method uses an XML loader class that basically reads the source and builds an *XmlDocument* object. This document is then parsed, and *DataRow* and *DataTable* objects are created and added to the target *DataSet* object. While building the temporary *XmlDocument* object, the loader scrolls attributes using *MoveToNextAttribute* and reads values using *ReadAttributeValue*.

ReadAttributeValue does not really return the value of the current attribute. This method, in fact, simply returns a Boolean value indicating whether there's more to read about the attribute. By using *ReadAttributeValue*, however, you can read through the text and entity reference nodes that make up the attribute value. Let's say that this is a more general way to read the content of an attribute; certainly, it is the method that *ReadXml* uses indirectly. To let *ReadXml* read the value of an attribute, you must provide a significant implementation for *ReadAttributeValue*. In particular, if the current node is an attribute, your implementation should set the new node type to *XmlNodeType.Text*, increase the depth by 1, and return *true*.

```
public override bool ReadAttributeValue()
{
    if (m_nodeType == XmlNodeType.Attribute)
    {
        m_nodeType = XmlNodeType.Text;
        m_depth ++;
        return true;
    }

    return false;
}
```

ReadAttributeValue parses the attribute value into one or more *Text*, *EntityReference*, or *EndEntity* nodes. This means that the XML loader won't be able to read the value unless you explicitly set the node type to *Text*. (We don't support references in our sample CSV reader.) At this point, the loader will ask the reader for the value of a node of type *Text*. Our implementation of the *Value* property does not distinguish between node types, but assumes that *Read* and other move methods (for example, *MoveToNextAttribute*) have already stored the correct value in *Value*. This is just what happens. In fact, the attribute value is read and stored in *Value* right after positioning on the attribute, before *ReadAttributeValue* is called. In other cases, you might want to check the node type in the *Value* property's *get* accessor prior to returning a value.

In general, understanding the role of *ReadAttributeValue* and integrating this method with the rest of the code is key to writing effective custom readers. Nevertheless, as you saw in Chapter 2, if you don't care about *ReadXml* support, you can write XML readers even simpler than this. But the specialness of an XML reader is precisely that you can use it with any method that accepts an XML reader! So dropping the support for the *DataSet* object's *ReadXml* method would be a significant loss.

> **Note**   How *ReadXml* works with custom readers is in no way different from the way it works with system-provided XML readers. However, understanding how *ReadXml* works with XML readers can help you to build effective and functional custom XML readers.

Conclusion

In ADO.NET, XML is much more than a simple output format for serializing data. You can use XML to streamline the entire contents of a *DataSet* object, but you can also choose the actual XML schema and control the structure of the resulting XML document.

There are several ways to persist a *DataSet* object's contents. You can create a snapshot of the currently stored data using a standard layout referred to here as the ADO.NET normal form. This data format can include schema information or not. Saving to the ADO.NET normal form does not preserve the state of the *DataSet* object and discards any information about the previous state of each row. If you want stateful persistence, resort to the DiffGram XML format. DiffGrams are the subject of Chapter 10.

In this chapter, we also examined how ADO.NET objects integrate with the standard .NET Framework run-time serialization mechanism. *DataSet* and *DataTable* objects always expose themselves to data formatters as XML Diff-Grams, thus resulting in larger output files. We looked at a technique for reducing the size of the serialized data as much as 500 percent.

In ADO.NET, the deserialization process is tightly coupled with the inference engine, which basically attempts to algorithmically extract the layout of the XML stream. When loading XML into a *DataSet* object, the inference engine is involved more frequently than not. Because it is not a lightweight piece of code, you should always opt for a clear and effective reading mode and use the inference engine only when absolutely necessary.

As mentioned, in the next chapter we'll tackle a very special XML serialization format—the DiffGram. Among other things, the DiffGram format is the format used to deliver *DataSet* objects to other platforms through Web services. It is also ideal for setting up intermittent applications—that is, applications that can work both connected to and disconnected from the system.

Further Reading

Object serialization and ADO.NET are the key topics of this chapter. You'll find a lot of books out there covering ADO.NET from various perspectives. I recommend *Microsoft ADO.NET, Core Reference*, by David Sceppa (Microsoft Press, 2002).

It's more difficult to locate a book that provides thorough coverage of object serialization. Chapter 11 in *Programming Microsoft Visual Basic .NET, Core Reference,* by Francesco Balena (Microsoft Press, 2002), is an excellent and self-contained reference. If you want a shorter but complete overview, have a look at the following online article: *http://msdn.microsoft.com/library/en-us/dnadvnet/html/vbnet09252001.asp.*

10

Stateful Data Serialization

The *DataSet* object is designed with data disconnection in mind and with the assumption that optimistic concurrency is the default. In a multiple-user environment, optimistic concurrency occurs when applications do not lock a row while reading it. In contrast, a pessimistic form of concurrency involves locking rows at the data source to prevent users from modifying data in a way that affects other users. The *DataSet* object abstracts from the physical data source and qualifies itself as a superarray component capable of containing in-memory data.

As a container of disconnected data, the *DataSet* object accepts any sort of update to the rows it contains, so you can add new rows to any child tables, and you can update or delete existing rows. All these changes are persisted in memory and are not passed on to a persistent storage medium until an explicit update operation is conducted. Such an update requires a new connection and applies an array of changes in a single shot. For this reason, a *DataSet* update operation is often referred to as a *batch update*. When the batch update is completed, the *DataSet* in-memory changes are automatically committed to ensure consistency between the in-memory cache and the underlying storage medium.

As a result, each row of data stored in a *DataSet* object can have a history of changes that applications might be interested in knowing about and exploiting. All this information is irreversibly lost when you serialize a *DataSet* object to the Microsoft ADO.NET normal form using the standard option of the *WriteXml* method. (We examined this type of serialization in Chapter 9.)

An alternative XML schema for serializing the contents of a *DataSet* object is the DiffGram format. The DiffGram format of the *WriteXml* method can provide a stateful representation of the *DataSet* contents, as opposed to the stateless nature of the normal form. Because of its ability to preserve the state of the constituent rows, the DiffGram format is also used to remote a *DataSet* object through both the Microsoft .NET Framework remoting architecture and Web services. But let's start by taking a closer look at the structure of a DiffGram script.

Overview of the DiffGram Format

A DiffGram is an XML serialization format that includes both the original values and the current values of each row in each table. In particular, a DiffGram contains the current instance of rows with the up-to-date values, plus a section where all the original values for changed rows are grouped.

Each row is given a unique identifier that is used to track changes between the two sections of the DiffGram. This relationship looks a lot like a foreign key relationship. The following listing outlines the structure of a DiffGram:.

```
<diffgr:diffgram
  xmlns:msdata="urn:schemas-microsoft-com:xml-msdata"
  xmlns:diffgr="urn:schemas-microsoft-com:xml-diffgram-v1">
  <DataSet>
  ...
  </DataSet>

  <diffgr:before>
  ...
  </diffgr:before>

  <diffgr:errors>
  ...
  </diffgr:errors>
</diffgr:diffgram>
```

The *<diffgr:diffgram>* root node can have up to three children. The first is the *DataSet* object with its current contents, including newly added rows and modified rows but not deleted rows. The actual name of this subtree depends on the *DataSetName* property of the source *DataSet* object. If the *DataSet* object has no name, the subtree's root is *NewDataSet*.

The subtree rooted in the *<diffgr:before>* node contains enough information to restore the original state of all modified rows. For example, it still contains any row that has been deleted as well as the original contents of any modified row. All columns affected by any change are tracked in the *<diffgr:before>* subtree.

The last subtree is *<diffgr:errors>*, which contains information about any errors that have occurred in a particular row. The *DataRow* class provides a few methods and properties that programmers can use to set an error on any column in the row. Errors can be set at any time, not necessarily when the data is entered. For example, in distributed applications, it's typical for one user to create some data that another user has to validate. In this situation, the reviewer can set an error message on each column of a row to signal that something is wrong with that column. Amazingly, the Microsoft Windows Forms *DataGrid* control then detects any pending errors on displayed rows and marks them with a red exclamation point, providing the user with visual feedback that a particular column contains an error.

The following listing shows a sample DiffGram in which row 1 has been modified, row 2 has been deleted, row 3 has an error, and a new row has been added:

```
<diffgr:diffgram
  xmlns:msdata="urn:schemas-microsoft-com:xml-msdata"
  xmlns:diffgr="urn:schemas-microsoft-com:xml-diffgram-v1">

  <NorthwindInfo>
    <Employees diffgr:id="Employees1" msdata:rowOrder="0"
      diffgr:hasChanges="modified"
      employeeid="1" lastname="Davolio" firstname="Michela" />
    <Employees diffgr:id="Employees4" msdata:rowOrder="3"
      diffgr:hasErrors="true"
      employeeid="4" lastname="Peacock" firstname="Margaret" />
    <Employees diffgr:id="Employees10" msdata:rowOrder="9"
      diffgr:hasChanges="inserted"
      employeeid="10" lastname="Esposito" firstname="Dino" />
  </NorthwindInfo>

  <diffgr:before>
    <Employees diffgr:id="Employees1" msdata:rowOrder="0"
      employeeid="1" lastname="Davolio" firstname="Nancy" />
    <Employees diffgr:id="Employees2" msdata:rowOrder="1"
      employeeid="2" lastname="Fuller" firstname="Andrew" />
  </diffgr:before>

  <diffgr:errors>
    <Employees diffgr:id="Employees3"
      diffgr:Error="Check out the first name!!!" />
  </diffgr:errors>

</diffgr:diffgram>
```

Some of the attributes and nodes that form a DiffGram come from a couple of Microsoft proprietary namespaces. The default prefixes are *msdata* and *diffgr*. In particular, the *msdata* namespace contains a number of attributes that are annotations for the data in the stream. We'll look at these attributes and the entire structure of the DiffGram in the section "DiffGram Format Annotations," on page 448.

The Current Data Instance

The first section of the DiffGram represents the current instance of the data. Although it's not strictly mandatory from a syntax standpoint, of the three constituent subtrees, the data instance is the only subtree that you will always find in a DiffGram. A DiffGram without data is just the representation of an empty *DataSet* object. The *<diffgr:before>* and *<diffgr:errors>* subtrees are not present if the source *DataSet* object has no pending changes and errors.

A DiffGram is stateful and is like a superset of the ADO.NET XML normal form. The data instance is nearly identical to the normal form, which is a simple, stateless snapshot of data. The major difference between the DiffGram's data instance and the normal form is that the DiffGram format does not include schema information. To make the overall DiffGram format truly stateful, you must combine the data with two other subtrees—the original data and the pending errors. By combining the contents of the three subtrees, a client can rebuild a faithful representation of the original *DataSet* contents.

> **Note**   Like the normal form, not even the DiffGram can be considered a serialization format for the *DataSet* as an object. The DiffGram is a serialization format for the contents of a *DataSet* object. To be a valid serialization of the *DataSet* object itself, the DiffGram would need to contain schema information. Incidentally, the implementation of the *ISerializable* interface that both the *DataSet* object and the *DataTable* object provide manages to return a special version of the DiffGram format that differs from this because it incorporates schema information. You'll learn how to build DiffGram documents that contain a schema in the section "The DiffGram Viewer Application," on page 457.

Data Generator Objects

As mentioned, the data subtree in a DiffGram is similar to the ADO.NET normal form for XML we looked at in Chapter 9. In both cases, the XML code being generated by the *WriteXml* method represents a snapshot of the data currently stored in the *DataSet* object's tables. The data written out faithfully tracks any pending updates and deletions that have occurred in the meantime. As Figure 10-1 shows, the similarity between the first block of a DiffGram and the XML normal form is not just cosmetic, nor it is due to a mere chance.

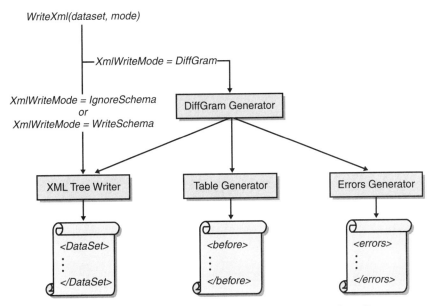

Figure 10-1 Components that work under the hood of the *DataSet* object's *WriteXml* method.

The same internal component, the XML tree writer, is used to generate both the ADO.NET XML normal form and the data instance block in a Diff-Gram. A pleasant side effect of this architecture is that all the mapping features for *DataColumn* objects we examined in Chapter 9 (see the discussion of the *MappingType* enumeration in the section "Customizing the XML Representation," on page 411) are still valid in the context of a DiffGram. You can decide whether a given column is better rendered using an attribute or an element, or whether the column should be hidden altogether.

The *Hidden* Flag

The *MappingType.Hidden* flag reveals a slight difference in the XML code that *WriteXml* generates for DiffGrams. A column mapped as hidden text is still part of DiffGram's data instance, but qualified with a particular attribute, as shown here:

```
<diffgr:diffgram
  xmlns:msdata="urn:schemas-microsoft-com:xml-msdata"
  xmlns:diffgr="urn:schemas-microsoft-com:xml-diffgram-v1">
  <NorthwindInfo>
    <Employees diffgr:id="Employees1" msdata:rowOrder="0"
      msdata:hiddenemployeeid="1">
      <lastname>Davolio</lastname>
```

(continued)

```
        <firstname>Nancy</firstname>
      </Employees>
      ...
  </NorthwindInfo>
</diffgr:diffgram>
```

For example, assume that you marked the *employeeid* column as hidden, as shown here:

```
DataColumn col = ds.Tables["Employees"].Columns["employeeid"];
col.ColumnMapping = MappingType.Hidden;
```

The *employeeid* column is not rendered as an *<employeeid>* element or an *employeeid* attribute, but a custom attribute is always used. The name of this attribute is *hiddenXXX*, where *XXX* represents the name of the column—in this case, *hiddenemployeeid*. The new attribute belongs to the *msdata* namespace.

> **Note**   In the context of the DiffGram, the *msdata:hiddenXXX* attribute is a full replacement for the hidden column—in other words, the information is not hidden at all, but the name of the column is a bit camouflaged.

DiffGram Format Annotations

Another remarkable difference between the ADO.NET XML normal form and the DiffGram's data instance is that the latter includes extra attributes such as *id*, *hasChanges*, *hasErrors*, and *rowOrder*. The extra attributes come from a couple of custom namespaces that are referenced at the beginning of the DiffGram. These special attributes are used to flag nodes, thus relating elements across the various sections—data instance, changes, and errors.

Table 10-1 lists all the DiffGram special attributes, also commonly referred to as *annotations*.

Table 10-1   DiffGram Annotations

Attribute	Description
diffgr:error	Contains the text that describes the error for the row or a column on the row.
diffgr:hasChanges	Indicates that the row has been modified or inserted.
diffgr:hasErrors	Indicates that the row contains an error.
diffgr:id	Returns the unique ID used to couple rows across sections.

Table 10-1 **DiffGram Annotations**

Attribute	Description
diffgr:parentId	Returns the unique ID for the parent row.
msdata:hiddenXXX	Replacement attribute for columns marked as hidden. *XXX* denotes the actual name of the column.
msdata:rowOrder	Tracks the ordinal position of the row in the *DataSet* object.

There's no special reason for annotations to come from different namespaces—it's just a more rational categorization. Attributes in the *diffgr* namespace relate elements from different blocks. Attributes in the *msdata* namespace represent working information that is useful to know when you're processing the DiffGram.

Cross-Section Links

Each row rendered in a DiffGram is given a unique ID. The ID is automatically generated and consists of the table name followed by a one-based index—for example, Employees1, Employees2, and so on. The *diffgr:id* attribute is used as a key to retrieve the original data and the errors of a row from the *<diffgr:before>* and *<diffgr:errors>* sections.

The following DiffGram contains a modified row:

```
<diffgr:diffgram
  xmlns:msdata="urn:schemas-microsoft-com:xml-msdata"
  xmlns:diffgr="urn:schemas-microsoft-com:xml-diffgram-v1">
  <NorthwindInfo>
    <Employees diffgr:id="Employees1" msdata:rowOrder="0"
      diffgr:hasChanges="modified"
      employeeid="1" lastname="Davolio" firstname="Michela" />
    ...
  </NorthwindInfo>
  <diffgr:before>
    <Employees diffgr:id="Employees1" msdata:rowOrder="0"
      employeeid="1" lastname="Davolio" firstname="Nancy" />
  </diffgr:before>
</diffgr:diffgram>
```

The same row can be referenced in any, or even all, of the DiffGram blocks. If the row is currently part of the *DataSet* object, you will find it in the data instance block. If the row has been updated or deleted, it will have a corresponding entry in the *<diffgr:before>* section. If error messages have been associated with any of the row's columns, another record will be found in the *<diffgr:errors>* section. The *diffgr:id* attribute is used to pair related elements.

The *msdata:rowOrder* attribute is a simple zero-based index that tracks the ordinal position of the row in the source *DataSet* object. This information is not updated when a row is deleted. An *msdata:rowOrder* value of 1 indicates that the row was the second in the table when the DiffGram was created.

Catching Changes in the Data

The *diffgr:hasChanges* attribute indicates the type of change that has occurred in the row. This attribute can take any of the values listed in Table 10-2.

Table 10-2   Values for the *diffgr:hasChanges* Attribute

Value	Description
descent	Indicates that the row received has one or more children from a parent/child relationship that have been modified.
inserted	Indicates that the row has been added.
modified	Indicates that the row has been modified. The original values are stored in the corresponding row in the *<diffgr:before>* section.

An added row has no corresponding element in the *<diffgr:before>* section. A deleted row has no corresponding element in the data instance block, but there will be an entry in the *<diffgr:before>* block. Looking at the data instance, you can quickly and easily identify the modified and added rows—each has a *diffgr:hasChanges* attribute set to a self-explanatory value. But what about deleted rows?

By design, any hole in the sequence of *msdata:rowOrder* values denotes a deleted row. The *msdata:rowOrder* values must necessarily be consecutive. Let's look more closely at how a DiffGram is actually loaded in memory and transformed into a *DataSet* object.

Reading Back DiffGrams

When reading a DiffGram, the *DataSet* object's *ReadXml* method first loads the data instance and creates all the necessary tables and rows. Each row is put in the added or modified state, as appropriate. All the *diffgr:id* values are temporarily copied into an internal hash table defined as a property of the *DataSet* object. Each entry in the hash table references a *DataRow* object in the table being created.

Next *ReadXml* processes the *<diffgr:before>* section and reads the old values for the available rows. If a match can be found between a row in the *<diffgr:before>* section and a row already loaded in the table, the just-read values are stored as the original values of the table row. *ReadXml* looks for a match between the *diffgr:id* attribute in the *<diffgr:before>* section and the contents of the hash table. Figure 10-2 shows how the *DataSet* object is built.

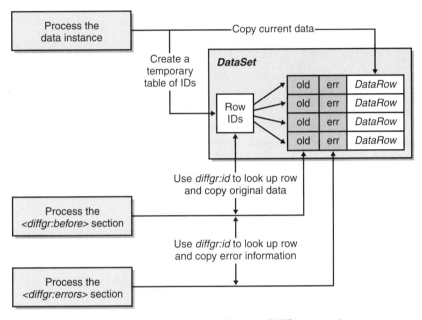

Figure 10-2   The *DataSet* is built by reading the DiffGram sections one after the next and using the row IDs to pair elements in the various blocks.

If no match is found, *ReadXml* deduces that the row in the *<diffgr:before>* section was deleted from the table when it was at the position that the *msdata:rowOrder* attribute indicates. The method inserts a new row in the table at the same position and populates it with the values read from the *<diffgr:before>* section. Next the row is marked for deletion using the *Delete* method of the *DataRow* object.

The final step consists of reading the values from the *<diffgr:errors>* section and updating accordingly the *RowError* property of the corresponding *DataRow* object in the table.

The Row Commit Model

The *DataSet*, *DataTable*, and *DataRow* objects maintain a local cache of changes. When a row is modified, deleted, or added, its state changes to one of the values of the *DataRowState* enumeration. (See the .NET Framework documentation for details.) Similarly, when a row is added, modified, or deleted from a table, the internal state of the table is altered, resulting in pending changes for the affected rows.

Pending changes can be either accepted or rejected at the *DataSet*, *DataTable*, or *DataRow* level. Accepting a pending change means that the row (changes always involve a row) updates are committed to the table. Rejecting a pending change rolls back the state of the table, and the table appears as though the change never occurred.

A DiffGram can track pending changes—that is, in-memory changes that have not yet been committed. Table 10-3 lists the allowable states for a *DataRow* object.

Table 10-3   States of a *DataRow* Object

State	Description
Added	The row has been added to the table, but *AcceptChanges* has not yet been called.
Deleted	The row is marked for deletion from the parent table.
Detached	Either the row has been created but not yet added to the table, or the row has been removed from the rows collection.
Modified	Some columns within the row have been changed.
Unchanged	No changes have been made since the last call to *AcceptChanges*. This is also the state of all rows when the table is first created.

The *AcceptChanges* method has the power to commit all the changes and accept the current values as the new original values of the table, clearing pending changes. *RejectChanges* rolls back all the pending changes. We'll encounter the row commit model again in the section "A Save-And-Resume Application," on page 464, when we look at save-and-resume applications.

The Original Data Section

The DiffGram has a layered structure in which current values, original values for the modified rows, and pending errors are stored in distinct sections. The state of the *DataSet* object is rebuilt by combining the contents of these sections. The original values are stored in the *<diffgr:before>* section as a change with respect to the current data instance.

The *DataRow* object maintains several versions of itself that are internally stored in an array of rows. The versions are grouped in the *DataRowVersion* enumeration, shown in Table 10-4.

Table 10-4   Values for the *DataRowVersion* Enumeration

Value	Description
Current	Contains the current values of the row
Default	The default row version, according to the current state of the row
Original	Contains the original values for the row—that is, the values stored when *AcceptChanges* was last called
Proposed	Contains proposed values for the row

Only the *Current* and *Original* versions are permanently stored in the *DataRow* object. The *Proposed* versions have a shorter life and are available only during the row edit phase. A row is in edit mode only during the time that elapses between two successive calls to the *BeginEdit* and *EndEdit* methods. When reading values from a *DataRow* object, you can also specify which of the available versions you want, as shown here:

```
if(row[0] == row[0, DataRowVersion.Original])
{...}
```

The *<diffgr:before>* section contains information that the *ReadXml* method will use to restore the *Original* version of each row referenced in the data instance. Newly added rows have no previous state and, subsequently, are not listed in the *<diffgr:before>* section.

Deleted rows are present only in the *<diffgr:before>* section, as they have no current data to show. Deleted rows are detected by matching the *diffgr:id* attribute of original rows in the DiffGram with the IDs of the rows in the current data instance. Rows in the *<diffgr:before>* section that have no counterpart in the current data instance are first inserted in the table and then deleted. Although this approach might appear a bit odd, it's probably the most sensible way to add a logically deleted row to a *DataTable* object.

Note   The *DataTable* class provides two methods to delete child rows: *Delete* and *Remove*. The *Delete* method deletes the row logically by changing the state of the row. The row no longer appears in the *Rows* collection, but it is not detached from the *DataTable* object. The *Remove* method, on the other hand, performs a physical deletion and detaches the row from the table. The detached *DataRow* object is not automatically destroyed and remains valid as long as it does not go out of scope. (Out of scope objects are automatically garbage-collected and destroyed.) Valid *DataRow* objects can be readded to the same *DataTable* object (or to another *DataTable* object) at any time.

No matter how many columns in a row have effectively been updated, in the *<diffgr:before>* section, the original row is stored in its entirety. The XML layout of the row depends on the column mappings, as shown here:

```
<diffgr:before>
  <Employees diffgr:id="Employees2" msdata:rowOrder="1">
    <employeeid>2</employeeid>
    <lastname>Fuller</lastname>
    <firstname>Andrew</firstname>
  </Employees>
</diffgr:before>
```

Although this solution is clearly not optimal, because unchanged columns are stored twice, it closely reflects the internal architecture of the *DataRow* object and, as such, speeds up the restoration of the *DataRow* object in the destination *DataTable* object.

> **Note** The *DataRow* class maintains its various versions by implementing an array of subobjects—one for the current values, one for the original version, and one for intermediate proposed values. Other internal properties indicate at any moment which is the current version and what the state of the row is.

As a final note, consider that for each column in a *DataRow* object, only the original and the current values are tracked, and no intermediate values are buffered. For example, suppose that you perform the following operation on an unchanged row:

```
// 1 is the current value of the field
row[0][field] = 2;
```

The row state changes to *Modified*, the original value (1) is persisted in the *Original* copy of the row, and the new value (2) is registered as the current value. Next the following code runs:

```
// 2 is the current value of the field
// 1 is the original value of the field
row[0][field] = 3;
// 3 is NOW the current value of the field
// 1 is the original value of the field
```

The original copy of the row remains intact, but the current version is updated. As a result, the intermediate value (2) is overwritten and is irreversibly lost.

> **Note**   Building an automatic mechanism for tracking the entire history of a row is probably unnecessary in most cases. If you need a more powerful mechanism to track changes, you can build a parallel table of changes for each row in the table. Each entry in the custom table would point to a particular *DataRow* object and contain a collection of changes organized as you prefer.

Tracking Pending Errors

The *DataRow* class provides a few methods for handling row errors. You can set a general error message on the entire row, and you can set a column-specific message. To set a general error message, you use the *RowError* property. To set a column-specific message, you use the pair of methods *SetColumnError* and *GetColumnError*. Other helper methods available are *GetColumnsInError* and *ClearErrors*.

A column or row with an error is in no way different from a column or row without pending errors. In this context, an *error* is simply a description of contents that the user, or the application, finds erroneous and inconsistent. Nothing prevents you from using error properties as general-purpose cargo variables in which to store custom information and annotations.

> **Note**   If you choose to use error properties as general-purpose cargo variables, keep in mind that some advanced Windows Forms and Web Forms controls can, in the presence of error flags, refresh their own user interfaces accordingly. For example, the Windows Forms *Data-Grid* control displays a red exclamation mark on the columns in error, as shown here:
>
>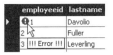

The *DataRow* Error Programming Interface

The tables in this section provide a quick overview of the properties and methods available in the *DataRow* class for setting and getting error messages. These messages arc then tracked in the *<diffgr:errors>* section of the DiffGram. Table 10-5 lists the error-related properties of the *DataRow* class.

Table 10-5   Error-Related *DataRow* Properties

Property	Description
HasErrors	Indicates whether the row contains errors
RowError	Gets or sets a custom error description for the row

The *HasErrors* property is set to *true* when either the *RowError* property contains a value or at least one column is not associated with an empty message. If you want to know about all the columns with errors, use the *GetColumnsInError* method to obtain an array containing the *DataColumn* objects with errors.

Table 10-6 shows the error-related methods of the *DataRow* class.

Table 10-6   Error-Related *DataRow* Methods

Method	Description
ClearErrors	Clears all the pending errors for the row. Does not distinguish between errors set using *RowError* and errors set using *SetColumnError*.
GetColumnError	Gets the error description for the specified column.
GetColumnsInError	Returns an array of the *DataColumn* objects with errors.
SetColumnError	Sets the error description for the specified column.

Contents of the *<diffgr:errors>* Section

A table row is assigned an element in the *<diffgr:errors>* section if its *HasErrors* property returns *true*. In this case, the element that represents the row in the data section has an extra attribute, *diffgr:hasErrors*, as shown here:

```
<Employees diffgr:id="Employees1" msdata:rowOrder="0"
  diffgr:hasErrors="true">
    <employeeid>1</employeeid>
    <lastname>Davolio</lastname>
    <firstname>Nancy</firstname>
</Employees>
```

The preceding element is coupled with another element in the *<diffgr:errors>* section in which the error messages are tracked, as follows:

```
<diffgr:errors>
  <Employees diffgr:id="Employees1" diffgr:error="Must review">
    <employeeid diffgr:error="Check the ID" />
    <lastname diffgr:error="Sounds like the wrong name" />
  </Employees>
</diffgr:errors>
```

The *diffgr:error* attribute on the row node (*<Employees>* in the preceding sample code) contains the text stored in the *RowError* property. For each column with a custom error description, a new child element is created with the name of the column and a *diffgr:error* attribute. In the sample code, the *employeeid* and *lastname* columns contain errors. Note that the *RowError* property is not automatically filled when at least one column is in error.

> **Caution**   The XML schema of the elements in the *<diffgr:errors>* section is not affected by column mappings, as is the case with the current data and the *<diffgr:before>* sections we examined earlier.

The DiffGram Viewer Application

To fully demonstrate the workings of XML DiffGrams, nothing is better than taking a *DataSet* object, entering some changes, and seeing how the corresponding DiffGram representation varies. For this purpose, I created the DiffGram Viewer Windows Forms application, shown in Figure 10-3. The application is available in this book's sample files.

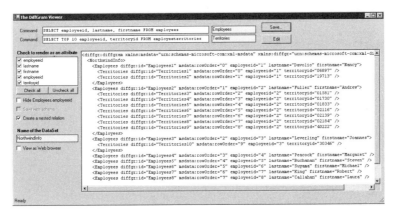

Figure 10-3   The DiffGram Viewer sample application in action.

This application executes a couple of SQL commands to obtain a *DataSet* object filled with two tables—Employees and Territories. The names of the *DataSet* object and the in-memory tables can be changed at will using text boxes. Next the application creates a relation between the tables, sets the nesting property to *true*, and creates the DiffGram.

The DiffGram is created using an in-memory string writer, and the output text is written to a multiline, read-only text box. Clicking the Edit button opens a new form with a *DataGrid* control for editing rows. The *DataGrid* control is bound to the *DataSet* object generated by the query, and is shown in Figure 10-4.

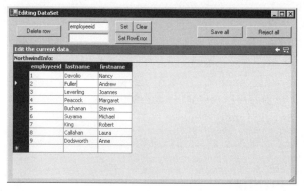

Figure 10-4 At the end of the editing phase, the updated *DataSet* object is resaved as a DiffGram and the pending changes are displayed.

The child form allows you to set errors and enter any type of changes. When the form is dismissed, the main application automatically saves the bound *DataSet* object back to a DiffGram and refreshes the user interface. As a result, you can easily test the DiffGram and view how the output varies after data changes.

A nice feature of the DiffGram Viewer application is that it lets you toggle the DiffGram view between plain text and XML. The XML view is provided by Internet Explorer, as shown in Figure 10-5.

The DiffGram Viewer application makes use of the WebBrowser ActiveX control, which is imported almost seamlessly by Microsoft Visual Studio .NET. The following code shows how to refresh such a Web view. To view the Diff-Gram using the WebBrowser control, the DiffGram must first be saved to disk as a temporary XML file.

```
void RefreshWebBrowser()
{
    // Url is a form property that points to the DiffGram file
    object o1=null, o2=null, o3=null, o4=null;
    WebBrowser.Navigate(Url, ref o1, ref o2, ref o3, ref o4);
}
```

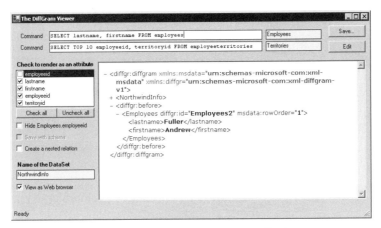

Figure 10-5   The DiffGram displayed in Internet Explorer.

A DiffGram has no trace of relationships between tables unless the *Nested* property of the *DataRelation* object is set to *true*. This system is reasonable in light of what we saw in Chapter 9. ADO.NET serializes information about tables relationships using XML Schema constructs. Because a DiffGram does not include schemas, it can't contain static information about table relationships. When the *Nested* property is set to *true*, the parent/child relationship is expressed by grouping child rows as a subtree of the parent row.

Persisting a *DataSet* Object to a DiffGram

A DiffGram is programmatically created by calling the *WriteXml* method of the *DataSet* class. To save data to a DiffGram, however, you must explicitly set the *XmlWriteMode* argument of the method to the flag *XmlWriteMode.DiffGram*, as shown in the following code. The XML data created in this way does not include schema information. We'll return to this important point in the section "Schema Information in the DiffGram," on page 461.

```
// Prepare the output stream
StreamWriter sw = new StreamWriter(fileName);
XmlTextWriter writer = new XmlTextWriter(sw);
writer.Formatting = Formatting.Indented;

// Create the diffgram
ds.WriteXml(writer, XmlWriteMode.DiffGram);
writer.Close();
```

The DiffGram contains all the rows from all the tables found in the *DataSet* object. You can create ad hoc subsets of the *DataSet* object to narrow the information being saved. In particular, you can use the *DataSet* object's *GetChanges* method to save only those rows that contain uncommitted changes, as shown here:

```
DataSet dsChanges = ds.GetChanges();
dsChanges.WriteXml(writer, XmlWriteMode.DiffGram);
```

The *GetChanges* method also has a few overloads that let you control the type of changes you are interested in. For example, the following code prepares a DiffGram containing only the rows that have been inserted:

```
DataSet dsChanges = ds.GetChanges(DataRowState.Added);
dsChanges.WriteXml(writer, XmlWriteMode.DiffGram);
```

Loading a *DataSet* Object from a DiffGram

When you try to build a *DataSet* object from an XML DiffGram, you must first ensure that the target *DataSet* object has a schema that is compatible with the data in the DiffGram.

In no case does the *ReadXml* method—the only *DataSet* method that can load a DiffGram—infer the schema or extend with new elements an existing schema. *ReadXml* works by merging the rows read from the DiffGram with existing rows in the *DataSet* object. The DiffGram row identifier (the *diffgr:id* attribute) is used to pair DiffGram and *DataSet* object rows.

Any incompatibility between the current schema of the *DataSet* object and the data in the DiffGram throws an exception and causes the merge operation to fail. As a result, you can't load a DiffGram into an empty, newly created *DataSet* object. You can create the target *DataSet* object simply by cloning an existing object that you know has the correct schema. Or, more realistically, you might want to read the schema from an external support using the *ReadXml-Schema* method. The following code snippet shows how to create a DiffGram and its schema in distinct files:.

```
// Prepare the output stream for the DiffGram
StreamWriter diffStrm = new StreamWriter(diffgramFile);
XmlTextWriter writer = new XmlTextWriter(diffStrm);
writer.Formatting = Formatting.Indented;

// Create the diffgram from the ds DataSet
ds.WriteXml(writer, XmlWriteMode.DiffGram);
writer.Close();

// Prepare the output stream for the schema
StreamWriter xsdStrm = new StreamWriter(schemaFile);
```

```
XmlTextWriter writer = new XmlTextWriter(xsdStrm);
writer.Formatting = Formatting.Indented;

// Create the schema from the ds DataSet
ds.WriteXmlSchema(writer);
writer.Close();
```

The schema written with *WriteXmlSchema* is an XML Schema and includes table, relation, and constraint definitions.

Schema Information in the DiffGram

In general, the schema and the data should be kept in separate files and handled as truly independent entities. The schema and the data are tightly coupled, and if serialization is involved, you might want to consider putting schema information in-line in the data.

In the .NET Framework, the *WriteXml* method does not provide the capability to include schema information along with the data. This is more of a design choice than an objective difficulty. An indirect confirmation comes from the XML string you get from a Web service method that returns a *DataSet* object. The output is a DiffGram extended with schema information, as shown here:

```
<DataSet>
  <xs:schema> ... </xs:schema>
  <diffgr:diffgram ... >
  ...
  </diffgr:diffgram>
</DataSet>
```

By design, the current DiffGram implementation does not include schema information. However, I can't see any reason for not providing the schema option in future versions. The *DataSet* representation you get from a Web service method offers a glimpse of what could be a possible enhancement of the DiffGram format. Technically speaking, the Web service serialization of a *DataSet* object is not a DiffGram, but rather a new XML format that incorporates a DiffGram. In addition, this new format is not produced by *WriteXml* but comes care of the XML serializer—a different breed of data formatter that we'll explore in Chapter 11.

Creating DiffGrams with Schemas

The DiffGram Viewer application includes a Save With Schema check box that enables you to persist the *DataSet* object using the XML serializer. The final output, shown in Figure 10-6, is the same as you would obtain through a Web service. (This happens because .NET Framework Web services are actually serviced by the XML serializer.)

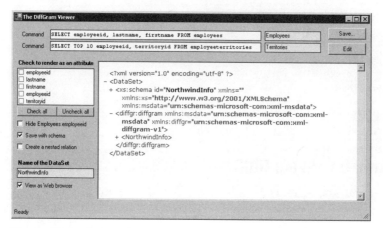

Figure 10-6 A *DataSet* object serialized through the XML serializer class.

The code that saves the *DataSet* object to a DiffGram changes as follows:

```
StreamWriter sw = new StreamWriter(fileName);
XmlTextWriter writer = new XmlTextWriter(sw);
writer.Formatting = Formatting.Indented;

// Create the diffgram
if (!bUseSchema)
    ds.WriteXml(writer, XmlWriteMode.DiffGram);
else
{
    XmlSerializer ser = new XmlSerializer(typeof(DataSet));
    ser.Serialize(writer, ds);
}
writer.Close();
```

If schema information must be included, the application makes use of the XML serializer defined in the *System.Xml.Serialization* namespace. The constructor of the XML serializer takes the type of the data to process as an argument and invokes the *Serialize* method. In Chapter 11, I'll unveil what really happens at this stage and how the XML serializer sets itself up to work on a particular data type. For now, suffice to say that once the instance of the serializer has been configured, you simply call the *Serialize* method on the object instance to be persisted. When the object is a *DataSet*, the output is a DiffGram and a schema—that is, an XML Schema and a DiffGram rooted under a common node. The name of the root matches the name of the type being serialized (for example, *DataSet*) and can't be modified programmatically.

Loading DiffGrams with Schemas

To read back a DiffGram and a schema into a *DataSet* object, you call the XML deserializer. *Deserialization* is the process of reading an XML document and building an object instance that coincides with a given XML Schema. With *DataSet* objects, the schema and the data are stored as distinct nodes under a common root. The data is expressed as a DiffGram.

To set up the serializer, follow the same steps as in the previous section. You instantiate the *XmlSerializer* class and pass the type of the object to process, as shown here:

```
XmlSerializer ser = new XmlSerializer(typeof(DataSet));
DataSet dsNew = (DataSet) ser.Deserialize(writer, ds);
```

To deserialize, call the *Deserialize* method and cast the object you get to the *DataSet* type.

DiffGrams and Remoting

When a *DataSet* object is serialized to a .NET Framework formatter, it directly controls the format of its data through the methods of the *ISerializable* interface. In particular, a serializable class implements the *GetObjectData* method, as shown here:

```
void GetObjectData(SerializationInfo info,
    StreamingContext context)
```

The class passes its data to the formatter by adding entries to the *SerializationInfo* object using the *AddValue* method. A *DataSet* object serializes itself by adding a couple of entries, as shown in the following pseudocode:

```
info.AddValue("XmlSchema", this.GetXmlSchema());
this.WriteXml(strWriter, XmlWriteMode.DiffGram);
info.AddValue("XmlDiffGram", strWriter.ToString());
```

The information stored in the *SerializationInfo* is then flushed to a binary stream or a Simple Object Access Protocol (SOAP) stream, according to the formatter in use.

The gist of this story is that a *DataSet* object is remoted using a couple of XML documents—one for the schema and one for the data—and the data is rendered using a DiffGram. To make DiffGrams really usable, the availability of schema information is vital.

A Save-and-Resume Application

As a stateful data format, a DiffGram is particularly useful for building save-and-resume applications. In this context, a *save-and-resume application* is a desktop or Web application that can work both on line and off line. For such applications, the connection to the rest of the back-end system is optional and is not guaranteed to be up all the time. From the connectivity standpoint, a save-and-resume application is intermittent and must be able to get its core data either remotely (for example, from the central system) or locally (for example, from data persisted to files).

In this section, we'll build a Windows Forms application that connects to a database, downloads some data, and disconnects. From this point on, the application works disconnected, the data it needs is stored locally, and the application can be used anywhere and shut down and resumed any number of times. All the changes made to the local data are correctly tracked and reported as insertions, deletions, and updates. At a later time, the application reconnects to the system and submits its changes.

In this description, common words such as *connection*, *back-end system*, *data*, *database*, and *updates* are treated as blanket terms that each application can implement as needed. For example, a simple query executed on a SQL Server table in the sample application can easily become a call to a middle-tier object. Similarly, a simple connection to SQL Server in the sample application could be viewed as a login in a distributed application.

> **Note**   While looking at the sample application discussed here, keep in mind that it is just a sample. Focus on the technologies involved and their interactions rather than on the implementation details. The overall context of the sample application, while representative of a common type of application, is certainly not a real-world scenario!

Setting Up the Application

The key functions of a save-and-resume application can be summarized in three categories. First, the application must be able to work disconnected, thus transparently using a local copy of the back-end database. Next, the application must allow you to review, filter, and reject changes. Finally, the application must allow you to reconnect and submit changes at any time. Figure 10-7 shows the key elements of the architecture.

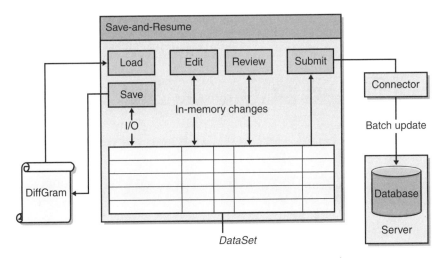

Figure 10-7   Constituent parts of a disconnected save-and-resume application.

At startup, the application loads data either from the local store or from a centralized repository. Applications can determine what route should be taken first according to their own features and requirements. Likewise, they can provide distinct user interface elements to trigger the local and remote downloads independently.

The *DataSet* object is ideal for storing a disconnected database. It can contain multiple, even indexed, tables, as well as relations and constraints. Once rebuilt, the *DataSet* object is used to populate the user interface, which also provides for editing. In this chapter and in Chapter 9 and Chapter 11, we examine the various options available for serializing a *DataSet* object: .NET Framework formatters, the ADO.NET normal form, DiffGrams, and XML serializers.

A disconnected application should allow users to accumulate and review changes to the original through several work sessions. This means that the local data store must persist the state of each change and possibly the history of each row. The *DataSet* object provides for just this situation.

The *DataSet* object is also ideal for gathering all the modified rows to be submitted to the back-end system for permanent updates. The *DataSet* object has been designed with disconnection in mind and to be used in save-and-resume applications. In save-and-resume scenarios, the serialization of the object is a critical aspect in improving overall client-side performance and efficiency.

Creating the Local Data Store

The sample application shown in Figure 10-8 is a simple Windows Forms application containing an editable *DataGrid* control. The grid is bound to a *DataSet* object that can be obtained by executing a SQL query or by reading a local Diff-Gram file.

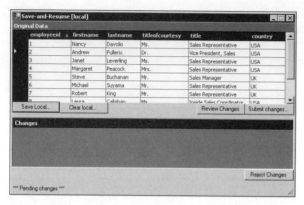

Figure 10-8   The sample save-and-resume application.

The code that populates the data grid looks like this:

```
void PopulateGrid()
{
    if (!File.Exists(m_diffgram))
        LoadFromDatabase();
    else
        LoadFromLocalStore();

    // Load methods fill the m_dataSet internal property
    grid.DataSource = m_dataSet;
    grid.DataMember = "Employees";
}
```

Once the data loads, users can start working and enter changes as appropriate. The *DataSet* object tracks any changes and signals those changes to the application through the *HasChanges* method. Here's the code to load the data from the local store:

```
private void LoadFromLocalStore()
{
    // Load the schema into the DataSet
    m_dataSet.ReadXmlSchema(m_schemaFile);

    // Load the data
    m_dataSet.ReadXml(m_diffgramFile, XmlReadMode.DiffGram);
}
```

The sample application uses a DiffGram to implement the local store. More precisely, the local store consists of two distinct files—one for the data (the DiffGram) and one for the schema. As mentioned, a DiffGram can't be used to populate a *DataSet* object without schema information. This is not your only option, however.

You can use the XML serializer to persist a *DataSet* object to a file that stores schema and data in the same place. In all these cases, the final output format is XML. If you want a more compact format, opt for the binary .NET Framework formatter and consider using a ghost class, as described in Chapter 9.

Reviewing and Rejecting Changes

Users of the sample application enter changes through the interface of the *DataGrid* control. Each change is detected, and controls in the user interface are enabled and disabled to reflect those changes. For example, the Review Changes button is enabled if there are changes to review.

Detecting Ongoing Changes

In a Windows Forms application, data sources associated with data-bound controls are managed by a special breed of component—the *binding manager*. *BindingManagerBase* is the abstract class for binding managers; the actual classes you will work with are *CurrencyManager* and *PropertyManager*.

The *PropertyManager* class keeps track of a simple binding between a data-bound control property and a data source scalar value. The *CurrencyManager* class plays a more sophisticated role. *CurrencyManager* handles complex data binding and maintains bindings between a data source and all the list controls (for example, the *DataGrid* control) that bind to it or to one of its member tables. The *CurrencyManager* class takes care of synchronizing the controls bound to the same data source and provides a uniform interface for clients to access the current item for the list. Both manager classes have a property named *Current* and fire position-related events such as *ItemChanged*. The *Current* property returns the currently selected item, whatever that is for the particular binding class. For example, for the *DataGrid* class, the current item is the *n*th bound element—that is, a *DataRow* object if a *DataTable* is bound, or a string if an array of strings is bound.

To access the binding manager for a particular data source, you use the *Form* object's *BindingContext* collection, as shown here:

```
CurrencyManager m_bmbEmployees;
m_bmbEmployees = (CurrencyManager) BindingContext[m_dataSet,
    "Employees"];
m_bmbEmployees.ItemChanged +=
    new ItemChangedEventHandler(CurrentChanged);
```

This code also registers a handler for the *ItemChanged* event. The binding manager automatically fires the event whenever an item in the bound data source—the Employees table in the grid's *DataSet* object—changes. In other words, the handler executes whenever a change occurs and refreshes the application's user interface accordingly.

Selecting Changed Rows

As mentioned, the *DataSet* object registers all the changes but retains the original values of the modified rows. Thanks to these features, setting up a form to review the current changes is not at all difficult. Let's see how to proceed.

The idea is to create a view of the table—possibly a copy of the table that includes only the changes. The *GetChanges* method can be used to obtain a copy of the *DataTable* object (or the *DataSet* object) that includes only the changed rows, as shown here:

```
DataTable dtChanges = m_dataSet.Tables["Employees"].GetChanges();
if (dtChanges == null)
    return;


DataView dv = dtChanges.DefaultView;
dv.RowStateFilter = DataViewRowState.Added |
    DataViewRowState.ModifiedOriginal |
    DataViewRowState.Deleted;
gridChanges.DataSource = dv;
```

A *DataView* object can be obtained from the table through the *DefaultView* property. Normally, the *DefaultView* property returns an unfiltered view of the table contents. The *RowStateFilter* property enables you to select the rows to be displayed in the view based on the state. With the preceding code, only the rows added and deleted are shown. In addition, the view includes the original version of the modified rows.

Because the *dtChanges* table has already been constructed to contain all the changes, a good question would be, Should we really need to set the *RowStateFilter* property to *Added*, *ModifiedOriginal*, and *Deleted*? Shouldn't such rows already be displayed in the view? This consideration applies only to added and deleted rows. By default, the modified rows are displayed with the current values, not the original values. The goal of the *Review Changes* feature is to display pending changes, so we need to display the original values to let users make comparisons with the current values. The Changes window, shown in Figure 10-9, allows you to see any changes to the data.

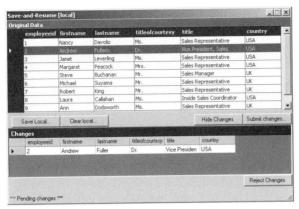

Figure 10-9   The *Review Changes* feature in action. The bottom grid shows the original version of the modified rows.

Rejecting Changes

Pending changes can be rejected by calling the *RejectChanges* method. *RejectChanges* is available on the *DataSet* class as well as on the *DataTable* and *DataRow* classes. By calling *RejectChanges* on the *DataSet* class, you cancel all the pending changes in all the tables in the *DataSet* object. Similarly, calling *RejectChanges* on a *DataTable* object rejects all the changes on the table. Finally, calling the method on the *DataRow* class simply cancels the current changes on the given row.

If *RejectChanges* performs an in-memory rollback, *AcceptChanges* does the opposite and commits all the pending changes. When changes are committed, the original values of each involved row are overwritten with the current values and the row state is reset to *Unchanged*. Uncommitted changes are key to performing a batch update to the back-end system.

Submitting Changes

Data submission is the process in which all in-memory changes are passed on to the back-end system for permanent storage and global availability. In ADO.NET, this submission does not consist of a block of data being sent to the database—SQL Server 2000 or any other database—in a single shot as an Updategram or a text stream. An ADO.NET batch update executes individual statements on the target system, one for each change that needs to be submitted. For the most part, statements will be SQL statements.

The Batch Update

The *DataSet* object can submit data to the database in batch mode by using the data adapter's *Update* method, as shown in the following code. Data can be submitted only on a per-table basis. When you call *Update* without specifying a table name, the code assumes a default name of *Table*. If no table exists with that name, an exception is raised.

```
adapter.Update(dataSet, tableName);
```

The *Update* method first examines the *RowState* property of each table row. It then prepares and calls a tailor-made *INSERT, UPDATE,* or *DELETE* statement for each inserted, updated, or deleted row in the specified *DataTable* object. The *Update* method belongs to a data adapter object, so you need a connection string, or a connection object, to proceed.

Rows are scanned and processed according to their natural order (their position in the table's *Rows* collection). If you need to process rows in a particular order, you must divide the overall update process into various subprocesses, each working on the selected rows you need. For example, if you have parent/child–related tables, you might want to start by updating rows in both tables. Next you delete rows in the child table and then in the parent table. Finally, you insert new rows in the parent table and finish with child insertions.

The following code shows how to submit only the rows that have been added to the in-memory table:

```
// Submit all the rows that have been added to a given table
DataRow[] arrayOfRows = table.Select("", "",
    DataViewRowState.Added);
adapter.Update(arrayOfRows);
```

This arrangement is made possible by the fact that one of the *Update* overloads takes an array of *DataRow* objects, which provides for the greatest flexibility.

Detecting and Resolving Update Conflicts

Data disconnection is based on a clearly optimistic vision of concurrency. What happens if, by the time you attempt to apply your changes to the back-end system, someone else has modified the same records? Technically speaking, in this case, you have a *data conflict*. How conflicts are handled is strictly application-specific, but the reasonable options can be easily summarized in three categories, as follows:

- **First-win**   The conflict is resolved by silently and automatically dropping the latest change—that is, the change that you were trying to submit. To implement a first-win approach, you simply set the *ContinueUpdateOnError* property on the data adapter to *true*. If *ContinueUpdateOnError* is set to *true*, no exception is thrown when an error occurs during the update of a row. The error information is stored in the *RowError* property of the corresponding row. The batch update process continues with subsequent rows.

- **Last-win**   Your change is applied regardless of the current status of the row. To implement this approach, you have only to ensure that the SQL command used to carry the update is not too restrictive to generate a data conflict. A data conflict occurs when the SQL command finds no row to affect. If you build the SQL command so that it updates or deletes rows that match a primary key field, no data conflict will ever be raised. Conflict-aware SQL code is code generated by ADO.NET command builders in which the *WHERE* clause ensures that the current status and the original status of the row match prior to proceeding with the statement.

- **Ask-the-user**   Take this route when neither of the two preceding options will work in all possible cases you foresee handling. By default, a data conflict raises a *DBConcurrencyException* exception. This exception is not raised if you set the *ContinueUpdateOnError* property to *true*. The *Row* property of the exception class returns a reference to the row in error. By reading the properties of such a *DataRow* object, you have access to both proposed and original values. You have no access to the underlying value, but you can obtain that value by issuing another query against the database. Resolving the conflict ultimately means opting either for a first-win or a last-win approach, but you let the user decide which. Your goal is to provide the user with enough information to make the correct choice.

The following code uses the "ask-the-user" approach for resolving update data conflicts:

```
OleDbDataAdapter da = new OleDbDataAdapter();
da.ContinueUpdateOnError = true;
da.SelectCommand = new OleDbCommand("SELECT * FROM employees",
    m_conn);
OleDbCommandBuilder cb = new OleDbCommandBuilder(da);
da.Update(m_dataSet, "Employees");
```

Figure 10 10 shows the sample application when a change fails.

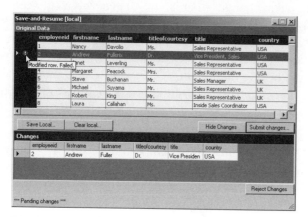

Figure 10-10 The user interface of the application when the batch update fails on a row.

Notice the custom error message on the row in error. This message is obtained using the following code:

```
// Select all the rows in error after the batch update
foreach(DataRow row in
    m_dataSet.Tables["Employees"].GetErrors())
{
    string msg = row.RowState.ToString() + " row. Failed.";
    row.RowError = msg;
}
```

Updating conflicts and reconciling tables after a batch update procedure can be expensive. Sometimes, it might be even more costly than working connected. Choosing the right application perspective is a delicate task with quite a simple guideline: go for disconnection if you have a low degree of data contention and your tables aren't updated frequently with highly volatile data.

Conclusion

If you've recently programmed data-driven applications, disconnected programming is nothing new for you. Disconnected scenarios are key in the era of the Internet, as they let you gain in scalability and mobility, bringing simplification to the software and to the user. For disconnected applications, effective local copies of the data are more than vital—they're absolutely mandatory.

For .NET Framework applications, the *DataSet* object is the ideal candidate to take the position of the client-side data container in disconnected, intermittent applications. In this chapter and in Chapter 9, we analyzed various options for serializing the contents of a *DataSet* object to output streams. In this chapter in particular, we analyzed a stateful way to persist the *DataSet* contents.

In general, there are two different angles from which you should look at the *DataSet* object's serialization. One is the physical layout of the data when stored to disk; the other is the statefulness of the format. Normally, a *DataSet* object serializes itself using a couple of XML blocks—schema and data. This data can then be saved as is to a text or SOAP output stream or saved to a more compact binary stream. In this case, however, the verbosity of XML patently wins over the compactness of binary data. As a result, the size of the final stream is often unacceptably large. You must resort to tricks such as the ghost class discussed in Chapter 9 to overcome this difficulty.

As for the data format, you can choose between the stateless ADO.NET normal form, the DiffGram format, and the DiffGram with a schema. In the first case, you take a snapshot of the current data, disregarding original values, ongoing changes, and pending row errors. The DiffGram format is stateful and maintains a history of the changes and pending errors. Unfortunately, the DiffGram format does not include schema information. Schema information is fundamental for constructing a *DataSet* object from XML data. By using the XML serializer class, you obtain a new XML format in which schema and DiffGram data are grouped under a common umbrella. Incidentally, XML serializers are the topic of Chapter 11.

Further Reading

In my book *Building Web Solutions with ASP.NET and ADO.NET* (Microsoft Press, 2002), I devoted Chapter 7 to disconnected applications and batch updates. In that chapter, I discuss save-and-resume applications from the Web perspective. A wider coverage of disconnected ADO.NET can be found in Francesco Balena's *Programming Visual Basic .NET* (Microsoft Press, 2002) and David Sceppa's *Microsoft ADO.NET Core Reference* (Microsoft Press, 2002). Both books will more than get you started, so deciding which works better for you is more of a matter of personal preference. If you want to focus on ADO.NET, go for Sceppa's book; if you want to look at ADO.NET as a part of the larger .NET Framework, pick up Balena's book.

Data binding is a key enhancement in the .NET Framework. Although based on a shared model such as ADO.NET, data binding is implemented in radically different ways in Windows Forms and Web Forms applications. Insights into Windows Forms data binding can be found in the following Microsoft Developer Network (MSDN) articles: *http://msdn.microsoft.com/library/en-us/dndive/html/data06132002.asp* and *http://msdn.microsoft.com/msdnmag/issues/02/02/cutting/cutting0202.asp*.

Part IV

Applications Interoperability

11

XML Serialization

Serialization is the run-time process that converts an object, or a graph of objects, to a linear sequence of bytes. You can then use the resultant block of memory either for storage or for transmission over the network on top of a particular protocol. In the Microsoft .NET Framework, object serialization can have three different output forms: binary, Simple Object Access Protocol (SOAP), and XML. We touched on binary serialization in Chapter 9 while examining how to work around XML DiffGram code in serialized *DataSet* and *DataTable* objects. In this chapter, we'll look briefly at SOAP serialization and then move on to the core topic—XML serialization.

Run-time object serialization (for example, binary and SOAP) and XML serialization are significantly different technologies with different implementations and, more important, different goals. Nevertheless, both forms of serialization do just one key thing: they save the contents and the state of living objects out to memory, and from there to any other storage media. Run-time serialization is governed by .NET Framework formatter objects. XML serialization takes place under the aegis of the *XmlSerializer* class.

The XML serialization process converts the public interface of an object to a particular XML schema. Such a mechanism is widely used throughout the .NET Framework as a way to save the state of an object into a stream or a memory buffer. In Chapter 10, we saw XML serialization used as a way to persist DiffGram with schema scripts that describe a *DataSet* object. Web services use the *XmlSerializer* class to encode object instances being returned by methods.

The Object Serialization Process

In the .NET Framework, object serialization is offered through the classes in the *System.Runtime.Serialization* namespace. These classes provide type fidelity and support deserialization. As you probably know, the deserialization process is the reverse of serialization. Deserialization takes in stored information and re-creates objects from that information.

Object serialization in the .NET Framework allows you to store public, protected, and private fields and automatically handles circular references. A circular reference occurs when a child object references a parent object and the parent object also references the child object. Serialization classes in the .NET Framework can detect these circular references and resolve them. Serialization can generate output data in multiple formats by using different made-to-measure formatter modules. The two system-provided formatters are represented by the *BinaryFormatter* and *SoapFormatter* classes, which write the object's state in binary format and SOAP format.

Classes make themselves serializable through formatters in two ways: they can either support the *[Serializable]* attribute or implement the *ISerializable* interface. With the *[Serializable]* attribute, the class author has nothing else to do, as the serialization takes place governed by caller applications and the class data is obtained through reflection. The *ISerializable* interface, on the other hand, enables the class author to exercise closer control over how the bits of the living object are actually persisted.

A *formatter* is the .NET Framework object that obtains the serialized data from the target object. Data is requested either by calling the *GetObjectData* method on the *ISerializable* interface or through the services of the *FormatterServices* static class. In particular, the *GetSerializableMembers* method returns all the serializable members for a particular class.

In the .NET Framework, formatters are of two types, depending on the nature of the underlying stream they use. The binary formatter (available through the *BinaryFormatter* class) saves data to a binary stream. The SOAP formatter (available through the *SoapFormatter* class) saves data to a text stream, automatically encoding information in a SOAP message before writing.

The SOAP Formatter

To use the SOAP formatter, you must reference a distinct assembly—*System.Runtime.Serialization.Formatters.Soap*. You add this separate assembly through the Add Reference dialog box or manually on the compiler's command line through the */reference* switch. In addition to linking the assembly to the project, you still have to import the namespace with the same name as the assembly, as shown here:

```
using System.Runtime.Serialization.Formatters.Soap;
```

At this point, you prepare the output stream, instantiate the SOAP formatter, and call the *Serialize* method, as follows:

```
// emp is the object instance to process
StreamWriter writer = new StreamWriter(filename);
SoapFormatter soap = new SoapFormatter();
soap.Serialize(writer.BaseStream, emp);
writer.Close();
```

Note that the *Serialize* method accepts only a stream object, which makes serializing to in-memory strings a little more difficult.

Let's consider a rather simple class, such as the following *Employee* class:

```
[Serializable]
public class Employee
{
    public int ID;
    public string FirstName;
    public string LastName;
    public string Position;
    public int[] Territories;
}
```

Upon instantiation, only the numeric *ID* field has a determined value (0). All the other members are *null*, as shown here:

```
Employee emp = new Employee();
```

After the *Employee* class has been instantiated, the SOAP formatter generates the following script:

```
<SOAP-ENV:Envelope
  xmlns:xsi="http://www.w3.org/2001/XMLSchema-instance"
  xmlns:xsd="http://www.w3.org/2001/XMLSchema"
  xmlns:SOAP-ENC="http://schemas.xmlsoap.org/soap/encoding/"
  xmlns:SOAP-ENV="http://schemas.xmlsoap.org/soap/envelope/"
  xmlns:clr="http://schemas.microsoft.com/soap/encoding/clr/1.0"
  SOAP-ENV:encodingStyle=
    "http://schemas.xmlsoap.org/soap/encoding/">
<SOAP-ENV:Body>
  <a1:Employee id="ref-1"
    xmlns:a1=
      "http://schemas.microsoft.com/clr/nsassem/XmlNet.SoapStuff/
      SoapFormatter_CS%2C%20Version%3D1.0.922.19048%2C%20
      Culture%3Dneutral%2C%20PublicKeyToken%3Dnull">
    <ID>0</ID>
    <FirstName xsi:null="1"/>
    <LastName xsi:null="1"/>
    <Position xsi:null="1"/>
    <Territories xsi:null="1"/>
  </a1:Employee>
</SOAP-ENV:Body>
</SOAP-ENV:Envelope>
```

As you can see, the class representation is perfect, and the fidelity between the SOAP description and the class is total. Information about the namespace is preserved and *null* values are listed. But what about types?

Retrieving Type Information

The formatter's *TypeFormat* property lets you indicate how type descriptions are laid out in the serialized stream. By default, *TypeFormat* is set to *TypesWhenNeeded*, which means that type information is inserted only when strictly necessary. This is true for arrays of objects, generic *Object* objects, and nonprimitive value types. If you want to force type description, use either the *TypesAlways* or the *XsdString* option. The difference between these two options is in the format used to describe the type: SOAP in the former case; XSD in the latter. All the type format options are gathered in the *FormatterTypeStyle* enumeration.

Serializing to Strings

Because the SOAP formatter and the binary formatter write only to streams, to avoid creating disk files you can use the *MemoryStream* object, as shown here:

```
// emp is the object instance to process
MemoryStream ms = new MemoryStream();
SoapFormatter soap = new SoapFormatter();
soap.Serialize(ms, emp);
```

Reading back data is a bit trickier. First you must get the size of the serialized stream. This information is stored in the *Length* property of the *MemoryStream* class. Bear in mind, however, that *Length* moves the internal pointer ahead to the end of the stream. To be able to read the specified number of bytes, you must first reset the internal pointer. The *Seek* method serves just this purpose, as shown here:

```
int size = (int) ms.Length;    // Moves the pointer forward
byte[] buf = new byte[size];
ms.Seek (0, SeekOrigin.Begin);
ms.Read(buf, 0, size);
ms.Close();
string soapText = Encoding.UTF8.GetString(buf);
```

The *MemoryStream* object reads data only as bytes. Especially in a strong-typed environment like the .NET Framework, an array of bytes and a string are as different as apples and oranges. Fortunately, the encoding classes provide for handy conversion methods. The *Encoding* static class belongs to the *System.Text* namespace.

Deserializing Objects

To rebuild a living instance of a previously serialized object, you call the *Deserialize* method on the specified formatter. The deserializer returns an object that you cast to the particular class type you need, as shown here:

```
StreamReader reader = new StreamReader(filename);
Employee emp1 = (Employee) soap.Deserialize(reader.BaseStream);
reader.Close();
```

The .NET Framework serialization mechanism also allows you to control the post-deserialization processing and explicitly handle data being serialized and deserialized. In this way, you are given a chance to restore transient state and data that, for one reason or another, you decide not to serialize. Remember that by marking a field with the *[NonSerializable]* attribute, you keep it out of the serialized stream.

By implementing the *IDeserializationCallback* interface, a class indicates that it wants to be notified when the deserialization of the entire object is complete. The class can easily complete the operation by re-creating parts of the state and adding any information not made serializable. The *OnDeserialization* method is called after the type has been deserialized.

Finally, it goes without saying that you can't serialize to, say, SOAP, and then pretend to deserialize using the binary formatter. See the section "Further Reading," on page 518, for more information about run-time binary and SOAP serialization.

From SOAP to XML Serialization

A second, very special type of .NET Framework serialization is XML serialization. Compared to ordinary .NET Framework object serialization, XML serialization is so different that it shouldn't even be considered another type of formatter. It is similar to SOAP and binary formatters because it also persists and restores the object's state, but when you examine the way each serializer works, you see many significant differences.

XML serialization is handled by using the *XmlSerializer* class, which also enables you to control how objects are encoded into elements of an XML schema. In addition to differences in goals and implementation details, the strongest difference between run-time and XML serialization is in the level of type fidelity they provide.

Run-time object serialization guarantees full type fidelity. For this reason, binary and SOAP serialization are particularly well-suited to preserving the state of an object across multiple invocations of an application. For example, .NET Framework remoting (see Chapter 12) uses run-time serialization to marshal objects by value from one AppDomain to another. Whereas run-time serialization is specifically aimed at serializing object instances, XML serialization is a system-provided (as opposed to object-provided) mechanism for serializing the data stored in an object instance into a well-formed schema.

The primary goal of XML serialization is making another application, possibly an application running on a different platform, effectively able to consume any stored data. Let's recap the key differences between run-time and XML serialization:

- **Persisted properties**   Run-time serialization takes into account any properties, regardless of the scope a property has in the context of the class. XML serialization, on the other hand, avoids private, protected, and read-only properties; does not handle circular references; and works only with public classes. In addition, if one property is set to *null* in the particular instance being serialized, the XML serializer just ignores the property. The XML serializer never includes type information.

- **Object identity**   Run-time serialization maintains information about the original class name, namespace, and assembly. All this information—the object's identity—is irreversibly lost with XML serialization.

- **Control of the output**   Run-time serialization lets you indicate the data to serialize by adding values to a cargo collection. You can't control how these values are actually written, however. The schema of the persisted data is fixed and hard-coded in the formatter. In this respect, the XML serializer is much more flexible. The XML serializer lets you specify namespaces, the name of the XML element that will contain a particular property, and even whether a given property should be rendered as an attribute, text, or an element.

> **Important**   During serialization, the .NET Framework formatters get information dynamically from the target object and write any bytes to the specified stream. The XML serializer uses any object information to create a couple of highly specialized reader and writer classes in a C# source file. The file is then silently compiled into a temporary assembly. As a result, XML serialization and deserialization for an object are actually performed using the classes in the temporary assembly. (More on this in the section "The Temporary Assembly," on page 513.)

One final note about SOAP and XML serialization: Although it's more powerful in terms of the information carried, SOAP is significantly more verbose than XML serialization and of course much less flexible. In fact, SOAP is just a particular XML dialect with vocabulary and syntax rules defined by the SOAP specification. With XML serialization, you define the schema you want, and the process is designed to return a more compact output.

The XML Serializer

The central element in the XML serialization architecture is the *XmlSerializer* class, which belongs to the *System.Xml.Serialization* namespace. The XML serialization process is articulated in the following steps:

1. The serializer generates an XSD schema for the target class that includes all the public properties and fields.

2. Using this XSD schema, the serializer generates a C# source file with a made-to-measure reader and writer class. The source file is compiled into a temporary assembly.

The *Serialize* and *Deserialize* methods are simply higher level interfaces for those writer and reader classes. This list does not cover all the features of XML serialization, but it certainly focuses on the key aspects. Let's look more closely at these key aspects before we move on to more advanced issues such as customizing the XSD schema being generated and hooking up the deserialization process.

The Programming Interface

The *XmlSerializer* class has a rather limited programming interface, with no properties, only a few methods, and a handful of events. *XmlSerializer* has several constructors with important functionalities, however. As you'll see in the following sections, the constructor is the place where most of the serializer's activity occurs.

The *XmlSerializer* Class's Constructors

Table 11-1 lists all the public constructors available in the *XmlSerializer* class. This list does not include the default class constructor because it is declared as protected and, as such, is not intended to be used directly from the user's code.

Let's review the code necessary to set up and use an XML serializer class:

```
[Serializable]
public class Employee
{
    protected int m_ID;
    public int ID
    {
        get {return m_ID;}
    }
    public string FirstName;
    public string LastName;
    public string Position;
    public int[] Territories;
    public Employee()
    {
        m_ID = -1;
    }
    public Employee(int empID)
    {
        m_ID = empID;
    }
    public override string ToString()
    {
        return LastName + ", " + FirstName;
    }
}
```

This class has one read-only member (*ID*), a couple of constructors, and a protected member. To begin, let's use the simplest constructor and see what happens:

```
Employee emp = new Employee(1);
emp.LastName = "Esposito";
emp.FirstName = "Dino";

StringWriter writer = new StringWriter();
XmlSerializer ser = new XmlSerializer(typeof(Employee));
ser.Serialize(writer, emp);
string xmlText = writer.ToString();
writer.Close();
```

The output generated is rather compact and does not include *null* and *less than* public fields, as shown here:

```
<?xml version="1.0" encoding="utf-16"?>
<Employee
  xmlns:xsd="http://www.w3.org/2001/XMLSchema"
  xmlns:xsi="http://www.w3.org/2001/XMLSchema-instance">
  <FirstName>Dino</FirstName>
  <LastName>Esposito</LastName>
</Employee>
```

The read-only *ID* property is ignored, as are all protected members. In addition, public properties set to *null* are blissfully discarded.

Table 11-1   **Constructors of *XmlSerializer***

Constructor	Description
XmlSerializer(Type)	Serializes objects of the specified type.
XmlSerializer(XmlTypeMapping)	Allows you to customize the default mapping between properties and XSD elements. Adds type information to elements. Useful if you don't have the source code for the class being serialized.
XmlSerializer(Type, string)	Serializes objects of the specified type using XML elements in the given default namespace.
XmlSerializer(Type, Type[])	Serializes objects of the specified type and all child objects listed in the specified array of extra types.
XmlSerializer(Type, XmlAttributeOverrides)	Allows you to customize the default mapping between properties and XSD elements. No type information is added to elements. Useful if you don't have the source code for the class being serialized.
XmlSerializer(Type, XmlRootAttribute)	Allows you to specify the root element of the XML output.
XmlSerializer(Type, XmlAttributeOverrides, Type[], XmlRootAttribute, string)	Sums up all the previous settings and provides a signature to set any combination of features in a single shot.

> **Caution**   If the class being serialized does not provide the default constructor, an exception is thrown and the class won't be processed further. The *XmlSerializer* class raises an *InvalidOperationException* exception stating that the class can't be successfully reflected. The true reason for the exception is slightly more subtle, however. The *XmlSerializer* class needs to create internally an instance of the target class to collect all the information necessary to create the serialization reader and writer objects. The serializer can't make assumptions about the constructors available on the class, so it always uses the default constructor. If there is no such constructor, an exception is thrown.

Configuring the Root Node

By default, the root element is defined by the serializer. However, the serializer gives you a chance to intervene and change things around a bit. For example, you can create an *XmlRootAttribute* object, set some of its properties, and pass it on to the serializer constructor, as shown here:

```
XmlRootAttribute root = new XmlRootAttribute();
root.ElementName = "NorthwindEmployee";
root.Namespace = "urn:dino-e";
root.IsNullable = true;
XmlSerializer ser = new XmlSerializer(typeof(Employee), root);
```

The subsequent output is shown here:

```
<?xml version="1.0" encoding="utf-16"?>
<NorthwindEmployee
  xmlns:xsd="http://www.w3.org/2001/XMLSchema"
  xmlns:xsi="http://www.w3.org/2001/XMLSchema-instance"
  xmlns="urn:dino-e">
  <FirstName>Dino</FirstName>
  <LastName>Esposito</LastName>
</NorthwindEmployee>
```

Alternatively, instead of creating an *XmlRootAttribute* object, you can simply set another attribute to the class being serialized, as shown here:

```
[XmlRootAttribute(ElementName="NorthwindEmployee")]
public class Employee
{ ... }
```

Although the final effect on the XML code is the same, the two approaches are not identical. To set the attribute, you must have access to the source code for the class. If you resort to the *XmlRootAttribute* object, you can change the root node of each class, including those classes available only in a compiled form.

The *XmlRootAttribute* object, both as an attribute and as an object, lets you set a default namespace for all elements in the XML document being generated. If you want to set only the namespace, however, use another constructor overload, as follows:

```
XmlSerializer ser = new XmlSerializer(typeof(Employee),
    "urn:dino-e");
```

In this case, the root node remains intact but an extra *xmlns* attribute is added.

Methods of the *XmlSerializer* Class

Table 11-2 describes the methods exposed by the *XmlSerializer* class. As you'd expect, this list does not include methods such as *ToString* and *Equals* that are inherited from *Object* and overridden.

Table 11-2 **Methods of the *XmlSerializer* Class**

Method	Description
CanDeserialize	Indicates whether the contents pointed to by the specified *XmlReader* object can be successfully deserialized using this instance of the serializer class.
Deserialize	Deserializes an XML document read from a stream, text, or an XML reader.
FromTypes	Static method that returns an array of *XmlSerializer* objects created from an array of types. Useful for speeding operations when you need to create multiple serializers for different types.
Serialize	Serializes an object into an XML document.

As with the *Deserialize* method, the output for the *Serialize* method can be a stream, text, or an XML writer.

Events of the *XmlSerializer* Class

Table 11-3 lists the events that the *XmlSerializer* class triggers during the deserialization process.

Table 11-3 **Events of the *XmlSerializer* Class**

Event	Description
UnknownAttribute	Fires when the deserializer encounters an XML attribute of unknown type.
UnknownElement	Fires when the deserializer encounters an XML element of unknown type.
UnknownNode	Fires when the deserializer encounters any XML node, including *Attribute* and *Element*.
UnreferencedObject	Fires when the deserializer encounters a recognized type that is not used. Occurs during the deserialization of a SOAP-encoded XML stream. (More on this topic in the section "Deserializing XML Data to Objects," on page 496.)

UnknownNode is a more generic event that fires for all nodes. It reaches the client application before more specific events such as *UnknownAttribute* and *UnknownElement* arrive.

Serializing Objects to XML

The *[Serializable]* attribute, which makes a class serializable through formatters, is not inheritable and must be explicitly assigned to derived classes. No such explicit conditions exclude some classes from the benefits of the XML serialization technique. This certainly does not mean that all the classes can be serialized to XML, however. The most restrictive condition in qualifying for XML serialization is not having circular references. A lot of relatively complex .NET Framework classes can't be serialized to XML for this reason. Want an illustrious example? Consider the *DataTable* class.

If you try to serialize an instance of the *DataTable* class, you get a fairly unclear error message. Try the following code:

```
DataTable dt = new DataTable();
XmlSerializer ser = new XmlSerializer(typeof(DataTable));
ser.Serialize(writer, dt);
```

The debugger stops on the constructor line and displays a message about a certain error that occurred during reflection of the *DataTable* class. Like many other Microsoft ADO.NET and XML classes, the *DataTable* class has circular references. For example, *DataTable* contains the *Rows* property, which is a collection of *DataRow* objects. In turn, each *DataRow* object has a *Table* property that points to the parent *DataTable* object. This is clearly a circular reference, and, as such, is an appropriate justification for the run-time error.

Why Is the *DataSet* Object XML-Serializable?

The *DataSet* class (and the *XmlNode* and *XmlElement* classes) contains at least one circular reference—specifically, the *Tables* collection, whose child *DataTable* objects reference the parent *DataSet* object. Nevertheless, the *DataSet* object is serializable through the *XmlSerializer* class. Why is this so?

The internal module that imports the XML schema for the type to serialize—the same module that does not handle circular references—specifically checks for the *DataSet* type. If the object turns out to be a *DataSet* object, the standard schema importation process aborts, and an alternative schema is applied. The schema importer uses the methods of the *IXmlSerializable* interface to serialize and deserialize a *DataSet* object.

The MSDN documentation only touches on the *IXmlSerializable* interface, which is defined in the *System.Xml.Serialization* namespace. This interface is not intended to be used by applications—at least not yet. *IXmlSerializable* defines three methods: *GetSchema*, *ReadXml*, and *WriteXml*. Despite their names, these *ReadXml* and *WriteXml* methods have nothing to do with the methods we saw in Chapter 9 and Chapter 10. Serialization methods are void, private, and accept only a single *XmlReader* argument.

You can serialize XML classes with no circular references, the default constructor, and at least one public property. If the class implements the *ICollection* or *IEnumerable* interface, other constraints apply. In addition to these classes, the XML serializer supports three more classes as an exception to the previous rules: *DataSet*, *XmlNode*, and *XmlElement*.

The *XmlSerializerNamespaces* Class

A few of the *Serialize* overloads can take an extra parameter that denotes the XML namespaces and prefixes that the *XmlSerializer* uses to generate qualified names. The *XmlRootAttribute* class we examined in the section "Configuring the Root Node," on page 486, is useful for defining the default namespace but provides no way for you to use more namespaces and prefixes.

The *XmlSerializerNamespaces* class can be used to cache multiple namespace URIs and prefixes that the target class will reference through attributes. You populate the namespace container as follows:

```
XmlSerializer ser = new XmlSerializer(typeof(Employee));
XmlSerializerNamespaces ns = new XmlSerializerNamespaces();
ns.Add("d", "urn:dino-e-xml");
ns.Add("x", "urn:mspress-xml");
ser.Serialize(writer, emp, ns);
```

After it is populated, the instance of the *XmlSerializerNamespaces* class is passed on to one of the overloads of the *Serialize* method. The source class can associate properties with namespaces using a couple of attributes, *XmlType* and *XmlElement*, as shown in the following code. In particular, you use *XmlType* to provide a namespace to all the members of a class. *XmlElement* applies the namespace information to only the current element. Of course, you can use *XmlType* and *XmlElement* together, but can't use *XmlType* with a property. We'll return to XML attributes in the section "The *XmlElement* Attribute," on page 501.

```
[XmlType(Namespace ="urn:dino-e-xml")]
public class Employee
{
    public string FirstName;
    [XmlElement(Namespace ="urn:mspress-xml")]
    public string LastName;
    public string Position;
    ...
}
```

The resultant XML code is shown here. All the elements have the *d* prefix except the element that maps to the *LastName* property.

```
<?xml version="1.0" encoding="utf-16"?>
<Employee xmlns:d="urn:dino-e-xml" xmlns:x="urn:mspress-xml">
  <d:FirstName>Dino</d:FirstName>
  <x:LastName>Esposito</x:LastName>
  <d:Position>CEO</d:Position>
</Employee>
```

Serializing Arrays and Collections

Class members that evaluate to an array of some type are rendered using a sub-tree of nodes in which each node renders a single array element. For example, let's initialize the *Territories* property of the *Employee* class as follows:

```
emp.Territories = (int[]) Array.CreateInstance(typeof(int), 3);
emp.Territories[0] = 1;
emp.Territories[1] = 2;
emp.Territories[2] = 3;
```

The corresponding XML serialized stream creates three child nodes below *<Territories>*, one for each element in the array, as shown in the following code. Child nodes are then serialized as instances of the particular type—in this case, *integer*.

```
<?xml version="1.0" encoding="utf-16"?>
<Employee xmlns:d="urn:dino-e-xml" xmlns:x="urn:mspress-xml">
  <d:FirstName>Dino</d:FirstName>
  <x:LastName>Esposito</x:LastName>
  <d:Position>CEO</d:Position>
  <d:Territories>
    <d:int>1</d:int>
    <d:int>2</d:int>
    <d:int>3</d:int>
  </d:Territories>
</Employee>
```

Classes that must be serialized to XML can't use most of the more common collection classes. For example, the *ArrayList* class is serializable, but *NameValueCollection*, *Hashtable*, and *ListDictionary* are not. The reason lies in the extra constraints set for the classes that implement *ICollection* and *IEnumerable*.

In particular, a class that implements *IEnumerable* must also implement a public *Add* method that takes a single parameter. This condition filters out dictionaries and hash tables but keeps *ArrayList* and *StringCollection* objects on board. In addition, the type of the argument you pass to *Add* must be polymorphic with the type returned by the *Current* property of the underlying enumerator object.

A class that implements the *ICollection* interface can't be serialized if it does not have an integer indexer—that is, a public *Item* indexed property that accepts integer indexes. The class must also have a public *Count* property of type *integer*. The type of the argument passed to *Add* (only one argument is allowed) must be compatible with the type returned by *Item*.

Serializing Enumerated Types

XML serialization supports enumerated types. The serialized stream contains the named constant that identifies the value. The *enum* value is stored as a string, and neither the actual value nor the type are serialized. During deserialization, the named value is reassociated with the underlying *enum* value through the *Enum.Parse* static method.

The Notion of Serializability

Having the *Add* method take exactly one argument is a strong, but rather inevitable, constraint that is needed to wed consistency with effectiveness of coding. Unlike run-time serialization, XML serialization never actively involves objects. XML serialization instead treats objects as passive entities. It parses their interface through reflection and irrevocably decides whether a given object can be serialized.

The basic notion of serializability is different in the two approaches. Run-time serialization is a more rigorous process based on the assumption that classes make themselves serializable by taking clear actions. XML serialization, on the other hand, is a centralized process that involves classes only for the details of the final XML schema. The XML serialization process makes assumptions about what the classes should do (or, better yet, should have done) to be serializable.

Collection classes, in particular, are seen simply as a collection of objects of a given type. By enforcing this basic concept, the XML serializer discards all collections that do not provide such an interface—that is, the *Add* method to append new objects of that type and the *Item* property (or the enumerator) to return a particular object of that type.

When designing classes destined to be serialized to XML, either avoid collection classes altogether or express their contents as an array of basic objects. One possibility is to use the *ArrayList* class as the container and a user-defined class to store element information. Alternatively, you could write your own collection class. In this case, however, consider that no public or private properties on the collection class would be serialized, only the child objects would be.

> **Tip** As mentioned, XML serialization skips over read-only data members. You can overcome this built-in behavior with a simple and inexpensive trick. Add an empty *set* accessor to a read-only property, as shown in the following code, and the serializer will treat the member as a read/write property. The empty *set* accessor will still prevent the variable from being updated, however.
>
> ```
> public int ID
> {
>     get {return m_ID;}
>     set {}
> }
> ```
>
> The only drawback is that no compile error will be raised for (innocuous) lines of code that might attempt to assign a value to the property.

Serializing Child Classes

If a class contains a public member that belongs to a nonprimitive, user-defined class, that member would be recursively serialized as an element nested within the main XML document. Let's see what happens with the following classes:

```
public class Employee
{
    ...
    public Order LastOrder;
    public ArrayList Orders;
    ...
}
public class Order
{
    public int ID;
    public DateTime Date;
    public double Total;
}
```

The *Orders* member is intended to be a collection of *Order* objects, as shown here:

```
emp.LastOrder = new Order();
emp.LastOrder.ID = 123;
emp.LastOrder.Date = new DateTime(2002,8,12);
emp.LastOrder.Total = 1245.23;
```

```
emp.Orders = new ArrayList();
Order ord1 = new Order();
ord1.ID = 98;
ord1.Date = new DateTime(2002,7,4);
ord1.Total = 145.90;
emp.Orders.Add(ord1);

Order ord2 = new Order();
ord2.ID = 101;
ord2.Date = new DateTime(2002,7,24);
ord2.Total = 2000.00;
emp.Orders.Add(ord2);
```

After initializing the members as shown in the preceding code, the final
output looks like this:

```
<?xml version="1.0" encoding="utf-16"?>
<Employee xmlns:d="urn:dino-e-xml" xmlns:x="urn:mspress-xml">
...
  <d:LastOrder>
    <d:ID>123</d:ID>
    <d:Date>2002-08-12T00:00:00.0000000+02:00</d:Date>
    <d:Total>1245.23</d:Total>
  </d:LastOrder>
  <d:Orders>
    <d:anyType d3p1:type="d:Order"
      xmlns:d3p1="http://www.w3.org/2001/XMLSchema-instance">
      <d:ID>98</d:ID>
      <d:Date>2002-07-04T00:00:00.0000000+02:00</d:Date>
      <d:Total>145.9</d:Total>
    </d:anyType>
    <d:anyType d3p1:type="d:Order"
      xmlns:d3p1="http://www.w3.org/2001/XMLSchema-instance">
      <d:ID>101</d:ID>
      <d:Date>2002-07-24T00:00:00.0000000+02:00</d:Date>
      <d:Total>2000</d:Total>
    </d:anyType>
  </d:Orders>
</Employee>
```

As you can see, the XML code being generated contains very little type information. This is not a specific feature of XML serialization, however. The run-time
object serialization process also considers type information optional—at least in
most cases. This standpoint is quite reasonable. Serialization is just a way to persist the state of an object. During deserialization, an instance of the object will be
created from the referenced assembly and its properties configured with the

stored information. The serialization process needs mapping information rather than type information.

That said, you can see in the preceding listing that the *ArrayList* object is serialized with type information in the *<anyType>* node. This happens because the *ArrayList* class manages generic object references, whereas concrete types are needed for serialization and deserialization. To force .NET Framework formatters to include type information, you simply set the *TypeFormat* property of the serializer. Let's look at how to accomplish this with the XML serializer.

Adding Type Information

One of the constructors of the *XmlSerializer* class takes a second argument of type *XmlTypeMapping*. The *XmlSerializer* class is used to encode and serialize an object to SOAP. The following code is used to add XSD type definitions to a serialized class:

```
SoapReflectionImporter imp = new SoapReflectionImporter();
XmlTypeMapping tm = imp.ImportTypeMapping(typeof(Employee));
XmlSerializer ser = new XmlSerializer(tm);
```

Let's assume the following class definition:

```
public class Employee
{
    public int ID;
    public string FirstName;
    public string LastName;
}
```

The typed XML output looks like this:

```
<?xml version="1.0" encoding="utf-8"?>
<Employee
  xmlns:xsd="http://www.w3.org/2001/XMLSchema"
  xmlns:xsi="http://www.w3.org/2001/XMLSchema-instance" id="id1">
  <ID xsi:type="xsd:int">4</ID>
  <FirstName xsi:type="xsd:string">Dino</FirstName>
  <LastName xsi:type="xsd:string">Esposito</LastName>
</Employee>
```

The final output gets a bit more complicated if custom types are involved. For example, consider the following nested classes:

```
public class Employee
{
    public int ID;
    public string FirstName;
    public string LastName;
    public Order LastOrder;
}
```

```
public class Order
{
    public int Number;
    public DateTime Date;
    public double Total;
}
```

In this case, when SOAP encoding is involved, the serializer does not generate a well-formed XML document. More precisely, the XML code is correct, but the document has no root, because the child class is written at the same level as the parent class. If you don't explicitly serialize to a writer with a user-defined root, a writing exception is thrown.

The following code demonstrates how nested classes are encoded. As you can see, without the custom *<wrapper>* element, the XML serializer would have generated only an XML fragment.

```
<wrapper>
  <Employee xmlns:xsd="http://www.w3.org/2001/XMLSchema"
    xmlns:xsi=
      "http://www.w3.org/2001/XMLSchema-instance" id="id1">
    <ID xsi:type="xsd:int">4</ID>
    <FirstName xsi:type="xsd:string">Dino</FirstName>
    <LastName xsi:type="xsd:string">Esposito</LastName>
    <LastOrder href="#id2" />
  </Employee>
  <Order id="id2" d2p1:type="Order"
    xmlns:d2p1="http://www.w3.org/2001/XMLSchema-instance">
    <Number xmlns:q1="http://www.w3.org/2001/XMLSchema"
      d2p1:type="q1:int">55</Number>
    <Date xmlns:q2="http://www.w3.org/2001/XMLSchema"
      d2p1:type="q2:dateTime">
      2002-07-04T00:00:00.0000000+02:00</Date>
    <Total xmlns:q3="http://www.w3.org/2001/XMLSchema"
      d2p1:type="q3:double">2000</Total>
  </Order>
</wrapper>
```

SOAP type mapping can also be used to map one type to another. In other words, while generating type information, you can also rename elements and slightly change the structure of the final serialized document. To exploit this feature in depth, you create attribute overrides, as shown here:

```
SoapAttributes attrib1 = new SoapAttributes();
SoapElementAttribute elem1 =
    new SoapElementAttribute("FamilyName");
attrib1.SoapElement = elem1;

SoapAttributeOverrides sao = new SoapAttributeOverrides();
sao.Add(typeof(Employee), "LastName", attrib1);
```

The preceding code creates an attribute override based on an element named *FamilyName*. This new element is added to an attribute overrides collection. In particular, the *FamilyName* attribute overrides the *LastName* element on the *Employee* type. The following code snippet shows how to hide a source element—in this case, *FirstName*:

```
SoapAttributes attrib2 = new SoapAttributes();
attrib2.SoapIgnore = true;
sao.Add(typeof(Employee), "FirstName", attrib2);
```

The attribute overrides are gathered in the *SoapAttributeOverrides* collection, which is then used to initialize the *SoapReflectionImporter* class, as shown here, and then can be used in the type mapping in the serializer:

```
SoapReflectionImporter imp = new SoapReflectionImporter(sao);
```

We'll return to this topic in the section "XML Serialization Attributes," on page 499. In particular, you'll learn how to add type information to plain XML serialization, when no SOAP-encoded types are involved.

Deserializing XML Data to Objects

The deserialization process is controlled by the *Deserialize* method for a variety of sources, including streams, XML readers, and text readers. Remember that by using the trick discussed in Chapter 2 for XML readers (packing a string into a *StringReader* object), you can also easily deserialize from strings.

Although officially you can deserialize from streams and text readers, the deserialization process is actually a matter of invoking an XML reader—more precisely, a very special breed of XML reader, optimized for serialization and for the specific class involved. Connected to the deserialization process is the *CanDeserialize* method. This method returns a Boolean value indicating whether the XML reader is correctly positioned on the start element of the XML data. In addition, *CanDeserialize* ensures that the start element of the XML data is compatible with the originally saved class.

Normally, you call *CanDeserialize* in the context of a more general strategy designed to trap as many errors and exceptions as possible. If the application always deserializes data that the XML serializer has previously created, a call to *CanDeserialize* can easily be redundant. The call becomes crucial, however, as soon as your application begins to deserialize XML data whose genuineness and quality are not guaranteed. It is worth noting that *CanDeserialize* works only on XML readers, whereas *Deserialize* can successfully handle streams and text readers too.

From a programming perspective, deserializing is not rocket science, as the following code clearly demonstrates:

```
StreamReader reader = new StreamReader(fileName);
Employee emp = (Employee) ser.Deserialize(reader);
reader.Close();
```

During the deserialization stage, a few events can be fired. In particular, the *UnknownElement*, *UnknownAttribute*, and *UnknownNode* events signal when unknown and unexpected nodes are found in the XML text being deserialized. The *UnknownNode* event is more generic than the other two and triggers regardless of the node type on which the exception is detected. In case of unknown element or attribute nodes, the *UnknownNode* event is fired first.

Hooking Up the Deserialization Process

The following code demonstrates how to register event handlers for the events described in the previous section:

```
XmlSerializer ser = new XmlSerializer(typeof(Employee));
ser.UnknownElement +=
    new XmlElementEventHandler(GotUnknownElement);
ser.UnknownAttribute +=
    new XmlAttributeEventHandler(GotUnknownAttribute);
ser.UnknownNode += new XmlNodeEventHandler(GotUnknownNode);
```

Each event requires its own event handler class and passes a distinct data structure to the client code. All the event data structures share the properties listed in Table 11-4.

Table 11-4   Common Properties of Deserialization Event Handlers

Property	Description
LineNumber	Gets the line number of the unknown XML attribute
LinePosition	Gets the column number in the line of the unknown XML attribute
ObjectBeingDeserialized	Gets the object being deserialized

In addition, the *XmlElementEventArgs*, *XmlAttributeEventArgs*, and *XmlNodeEventArgs* classes add some extra and more specific properties. Figure 11-1 shows a sample application that lets you enter some XML code.

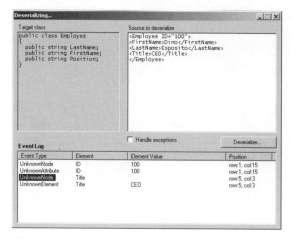

Figure 11-1 Tracing deserialization events.

The application then attempts to map the code to the following class:

```
public class Employee
{
    public string LastName;
    public string FirstName;
    public string Position;
}
```

Any exceptions are traced in the bottom pane of the window. As shown in Figure 11-1, the *ID* attribute and the *Title* node have nothing to do with the target schema. By default, the deserializer ignores unknown nodes.

The *XmlElementEventArgs* class has an extra property named *Element* whose type is *XmlElement*. Likewise, *XmlAttributeEventArgs* features an extra *Attr* property that is an instance of the *XmlAttribute* type. The *XmlNodeEventArgs* class also includes a group of additional properties that look like a subset of the *XmlNode* class properties.

Importing Unmatched Data

The most compelling reason to use deserialization events is that they enable you to attempt to fix incoming data that doesn't perfectly match your target schema. For example, our target class contains a *Position* member, so the deserializer expects to find a *<Position>* element in the source code. If a needed element is not found, no event is triggered. However, if an unexpected node is found, the user code receives a notification.

If you know that the contents of one or more unknown elements can be adapted to populate target members, an event handler is the best place in which to have your custom code plug in and do the job. For example, suppose that the node *<Title>* contains the same information as *Position*, but expressed with a different element name. The following code shows how to fix things up and have the information fill the *Position* property in the target class:

```
void GotUnknownElement(object sender, XmlElementEventArgs e)
{
    if (e.Element.Name == "Title")
    {
        Employee emp = (Employee) e.ObjectBeingDeserialized;
        emp.Position = e.Element.InnerText;
    }
}
```

You can also easily combine information coming from multiple unknown elements. In this case, however, you must figure out an application-specific way to cache crucial information across multiple invocations of the event handler. The event handler is invoked for each unknown node, although the event's *ObjectBeingDeserialized* property is cumulatively set with the results of the deserialization.

Shaping the XML Output

XML serialization enables you to shape the final form of the XML data being created. Although the code of the class is not directly involved in the generation of the output, the programmer is given a couple of tools to significantly influence the serialization process.

The first approach is fairly static and works by setting attributes on the various members of the class to be serialized. According to the attribute set, a given member can be rendered as an attribute, an element, or plain text, or it can be ignored altogether. The second approach is more dynamic and, more importantly, does not require the availability of the class source code. This approach is particularly effective for achieving a rather odd yet realistic result: shaping an XML flow you can't control to fit into a data structure you can't modify.

XML Serialization Attributes

The *XmlAttributes* class represents a collection of .NET Framework attributes that let you exercise strict control over how the *XmlSerializer* class processes an object. The *XmlAttributes* class is similar to the *SoapAttributes* class mentioned in the section "Adding Type Information," on page 494. Both classes perform the same logical operation, but the former outputs to XML, whereas the latter returns SOAP-encoded messages with type information.

Each property of the *XmlAttributes* class corresponds to an attribute class. The available *XmlAttributes* properties and their corresponding attribute classes are listed here:

- **XmlAnyAttribute** Corresponds to the *XmlAnyAttributeAttribute* attribute and applies to properties that return an array of *XmlAttribute* objects. A property marked with this attribute is populated with any unknown attribute detected during the deserialization process.

- **XmlAnyElements** Corresponds to the *XmlAnyElementAttribute* attribute and applies to properties that return an array of *XmlElement* objects. A property marked with this attribute contains all the unknown elements found.

- **XmlArray** Corresponds to the *XmlArrayAttribute* attribute and applies to all properties that return an array of user-defined objects. This attribute causes the contents of the property to be rendered as an XML array. An XML array is a subtree in which child elements are recursively serialized and appended to a common parent node.

- **XmlArrayItems** Corresponds to the *XmlArrayItemAttribute* attribute and applies to all properties that return an array of objects. Tightly coupled with the previous attribute, *XmlArrayItemAttribute* describes the type of the items in the array. *XmlArrayItemAttribute* specifies how the serializer renders items inserted into an array.

- **XmlAttribute** Corresponds to the *XmlAttributeAttribute* attribute and applies to public properties, causing the serializer to render them as attributes. By default, if no attribute is applied to a public read/write property, it will be serialized as an XML element.

- **XmlChoiceIdentifier** Corresponds to the *XmlChoiceIdentifier-Attribute* attribute and implements the *xsi:choice* XSD data structure. The *xsi:choice* data type resembles the C++ *union* structure and consists of additional properties, only one of which is valid for each instance. The *XmlChoiceIdentifierAttribute* attribute lets you express the choice of which data member to consider for serialization.

- **XmlDefaultValue** Corresponds to the *XmlDefaultValueAttribute* attribute and gets or sets the default value of an XML element or attribute.

- **XmlElement** Corresponds to the *XmlElementAttribute* attribute and forces the serializer to render a given public field as an XML element.

- ***XmlEnum*** Corresponds to the *XmlEnumAttribute* attribute and specifies the way in which an enumeration member is serialized. You use this attribute class to change the enumeration that the *XmlSerializer* generates and recognizes when deserializing.

- ***XmlIgnore*** Corresponds to the *XmlIgnoreAttribute* attribute and specifies whether a given property should be ignored and skipped or serialized to XML as the type dictates. The attribute requires no further properties to be specified.

- ***XmlRoot*** Corresponds to the *XmlRootAttribute* attribute and overrides any current settings for the root node of the XML serialization output, replacing it with the specified element.

- ***XmlText*** Corresponds to the *XmlTextAttribute* attribute and instructs the *XmlSerializer* class to serialize a public property as XML text. The property to which this attribute is applied must return primitive and enumeration types, including an array of strings or objects. If the return type is an array of objects, the *Type* property of the *XmlTextAttribute* type must be set to *string*, and the objects will then be serialized as strings. Only one instance of the attribute can be applied in a class.

- ***XmlType*** Corresponds to the *XmlTypeAttribute* attribute and can be used to control how a type is serialized. When a type is serialized, the *XmlSerializer* class uses the class name as the XML element name. The *TypeName* property of the *XmlTypeAttribute* class lets you change the XML element name. The *IncludeInSchema* property lets you specify whether the type should be included in the schema.

The *XmlElement* Attribute

The key XML attributes are *XmlElement* and *XmlAttribute*. *XmlElement*, in particular, has a few interesting properties: *IsNullable*, *DataType*, *ElementName*, and *Namespace*. *IsNullable* lets you specify whether the property should be rendered even if set to *null*. *DataType* allows you to specify the XSD type of the element the serializer will generate. *ElementName* indicates the name of the element. Finally, *Namespace* associates the element with a namespace URI. If you want to use a namespace prefix, add a reference to that namespace using the *XmlSerializerNamespaces* class, as shown here:

```
[XmlElement(Namespace ="urn:mspress-xml", IsNullable=true,
  DataType="nonNegativeInteger", ElementName="FamilyName")]
```

When the *IsNullable* property is set to *true* and the property has a *null* value, the serializer renders the element with a *nil* attribute that equals *true*, as shown here:

```
<x:FirstName xsi:nil="true"
  xmlns:xsi="http://www.w3.org/2001/XMLSchema-instance" />
```

If you specify the *DataType* attribute, the type name must match exactly the XSD type name. Specifying the *DataType* attribute does not actually change the serialization format, it affects only the schema for the member.

The *XmlAttribute* Attribute

The *XmlAttribute* attribute also supports the *DataType* and the *Namespace* properties. *IsNullable* is not supported. In addition, you can replace the default name of the attribute with the string assigned to the *AttributeName* property. As with elements, the default name of the attribute is the name of the parent class member.

The *XmlEnum* Attribute

If your class definition contains an enumeration type, the *XmlEnum* attribute lets you modify the named constants used to define each value member, as shown here:

```
public enum SeatsAvailable
{
    [XmlEnum(Name = "AisleSeat")]
    Aisle,
    [XmlEnum(Name = "CentralSeat")]
    Central,
    [XmlEnum(Name = "WindowSeat")]
    Window
}
```

You use the *Name* property to modify the name of the *enum* member.

The XML Schema Definition Tool

Installed as part of the .NET Framework SDK, the XML Schema Definition Tool (xsd.exe) has several purposes. When it comes to XML serialization, the tool is helpful in a couple of scenarios. For example, you can use xsd.exe to generate source class files that are the C# or Microsoft Visual Basic .NET counterpart of existing XSD schemas. In addition, you can make the tool scan the public interface exposed by managed executables (DLL or EXE) and extrapolate an XML schema for any of the contained classes.

In the first case, the tool automatically generates the source code of a .NET Framework class that is conformant to the specified XML schema. This feature is extremely handy when you are in the process of writing an application that must cope with a flow of XML data described by a fixed schema. In a matter of seconds, the tool provides you with either C# or Visual Basic source files containing a number of classes that, when serialized through *XmlSerializer*, conform to the schema.

Another common situation in which xsd.exe can help considerably is when you don't have the source code for the classes your code manages. In this case, the tool can generate an XML schema document from any public class implemented in a DLL or an EXE.

Overriding Attributes

A fairly common scenario for XML serialization is when you call into middle-tier class methods, get back some XML data, and then map that information onto other classes. In real-world situations, you can't control or modify the layout of the incoming XML data or the structure of the target classes.

This is certainly nothing new for experienced developers who have been involved in the design and development of distributed, multitiered systems. Normally, you resolve the issue by writing adapter components that use hard-coded logic to transform the inbound XML flow into fresh instances of the target classes. Although the map of the solution is certainly effective and reasonable, a number of submerged obstacles can make your trip through the data long and winding.

First you must parse the XML data and extrapolate significant information. Next you copy any pieces of information into a newly created instance of a target class. The XML serialization mechanism was designed to resolve this difficulty, thus making the process of initializing classes from XML data both effective and efficacious.

Adapting Data to Classes

Reading incoming XML data is itself a kind of deserialization. However, as we've seen, the XML deserializer can only re-create an instance of the type you pass when you create the *XmlSerializer* object. How can you comply with any difference in the schema of the target class and the incoming XML data? That task is handled by the attribute overrides process for the *XMLSerializer* object, shown in Figure 11-2.

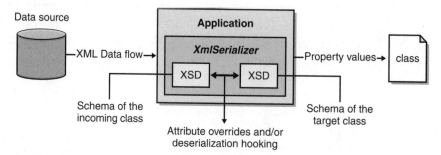

Figure 11-2   Attribute overrides are crucial architectural elements to allow effective XML-to-class mapping.

The XML serializer works on top of a particular type—the target class. While deserializing, the deserializer engine attempts to fit incoming data into the properties of the target class, taking into careful account any attributes set for the various properties. What happens if the source and the destination follow incompatible schemas? This might seem a rather odd situation—how could you deserialize data that you haven't previously serialized?—but in practice it exemplifies the real goal of XML serialization. Beyond any technological and implementation details, XML serialization is simply a way to automatically instantiate classes from XML data.

This is not simply the problem of transforming one schema into another; instead, you must transform a schema into a class. If you don't want to write an ad hoc piece of code, you have only the following few options:

■ Modify the source data to make it fit the target class through default XML serialization. This solution is impractical if you don't have access to the component that generates this flow.

■ Modify the target class with static attributes to make it support in deserialization the schema of the incoming data. This solution is impractical if you don't have access to the source code for the class—for example, if the class is deployed through an assembly.

■ Override the attributes of the target class using dynamic hooks provided by the objects you can create and store in an *XmlAttribute-Overrides* class. We'll examine this solution more closely in the section "The *XmlAttributeOverrides* Class," on page 505.

■ If the differences involve data, too, and therefore can't be addressed with schema elements, resort to deserialization events, as described in the section "Deserializing XML Data to Objects," on page 496.

Attribute overriding is a technique that lets you change the default way in which serialization and deserialization occur. In addition to the case just mentioned, attribute overrides are also useful for setting up different (and selectable) serialization/deserialization schemes for a given class.

The *XmlAttributeOverrides* Class

You pass an instance of the *XmlAttributeOverrides* class to the *XmlSerializer* constructor. As a result, the serializer will use the data contained in the *XmlAttributeOverrides* object to override the serialization attributes set on the class. The *XmlAttributeOverrides* class is a collection and contains pairs consisting of the object types that will be overridden and the changes to apply.

As shown in the following code, you first create an instance of the *XmlAttributes* class—that is, a helper class that contains all the pairs of overriding objects. Next you create an attribute object that is appropriate for the object being overridden. For example, create an *XmlElementAttribute* object to override a property. In doing so, you can optionally change the element name or the namespace. Then store the override in the *XmlAttributes* object. Finally, add the *XmlAttributes* object to the *XmlAttributeOverrides* object and indicate the element to which all those overrides will apply.

```
// Create the worker collection of changes
XmlAttributes changes = new XmlAttributes();

// Add the first override (change the element's name)
XmlElementAttribute newElem = new XmlElementAttribute();
newElem.ElementName = "New name";
changes.XmlElements.Add(newElem);

// Create the list of overrides
XmlAttributeOverrides over = new XmlAttributeOverrides();

// Fill the overrides list (Employee is the target class)
over.Add(typeof(Employee), "Element-to-Override", changes);
```

The instance of the *XmlAttributeOverrides* class is associated with the XML serializer at creation time, as shown here:

```
XmlSerializer ser = new XmlSerializer(typeof(Employee), over);
```

> **Note**   Attribute overriding also enables you to use derived classes in lieu of the defined classes. For example, suppose you have a property of a certain type. To force the serializer (both in serialization and deserialization) to use a derived class, follow the steps outlined in the preceding code but also set the *Type* property on the overriding element, as shown here:
>
> ```
> // Manager is a class that inherits from Employee
> newElem.Type = typeof(Manager);
> ```

Attribute overriding is a useful technique, and in the next section, we'll see it in action.

Mapping SQL Server Data to Classes

In Chapter 8, we saw the *ExecuteXmlReader* method exposed by the *SqlCommand* class in the SQL Server–managed provider. The *ExecuteXmlReader* method executes a command against the database and returns an XML reader if the output of the command can be expressed as a well-formed XML document or fragment. Let's see what's needed to transform that output into an instance of a class. The following code is at the heart of the example. You call into a method, the method executes an SQL XML command, the data flows into the serializer, and an instance of a particular class is returned.

```
Employee emp = LoadEmployeeData(empID);
```

The following code shows the body of the *LoadEmployeeData* method:

```
private Employee LoadEmployeeData(int empID)
{
    // Create the serializer
    XmlSerializer ser = PrepareEmployeeTypeSerializer();

    // Prepare the connection and the SQL command
    SqlConnection conn = new SqlConnection(NWindConnection);
    SqlCommand cmd = PrepareSqlCommand(empID, conn);
    conn.Open();

    // Execute the command
    Employee emp = null;
    XmlTextReader reader =
        (XmlTextReader) cmd.ExecuteXmlReader();
```

```
// Deserialize the incoming data
if(ser.CanDeserialize(reader))
    emp = (Employee) ser.Deserialize(reader);
else
    Console.WriteLine("Cannot deserialize");

// Clean-up
reader.Close();
conn.Close();

return emp;
}
```

The serializer is tailor-made for the *Employee* class shown here:

```
public class Employee
{
    public string FirstName;
    public string LastName;
    public string Position;
    public DateTime Hired;
}
```

The SQL command used in our example is shown here:

```
SELECT firstname, lastname, title, hiredate FROM employees
WHERE employeeid=@empID
FOR XML AUTO
```

The final XML output takes the following form:

```
<employees firstname="..." lastname="..." title="..."
  hiredate="..." />
```

As you can see, the class requires some attribute overrides to adapt to the actual XML stream coming from SQL Server. In general, you can modify either the SQL command or the class source to make each fit the other's structure. This is not always possible, however. When it's not possible, attribute overrides are the only safe way to make two immutable and incompatible flows of data interoperate.

Overriding the Class Name

In this scenario, the serializer is used only to deserialize data coming from SQL Server. No previous serialization has been explicitly done. The deserializer reads the inbound data and determines an ad hoc class structure. It then matches this inferred structure with the specified type to be deserialized to—in this case, *Employee*.

The first issue to consider is the name of the class. The deserializer takes the class name from the root of the stream. In our example, the inferred class name would be *employees*. This issue is easily resolved by creating an alias for the SQL Server table. Add an *AS Employee* clause to the table name, and you're done. As mentioned, however, this solution is not possible at all if you don't have enough rights to modify hard-coded SQL code. An *XmlRoot* attribute is another way to work around the problem.

The attribute can be assigned either statically or dynamically. Again, static attributes require that you have access to the class source code. Let's create attributes dynamically, as follows:

```
XmlAttributes changesRoot = new XmlAttributes();
XmlRootAttribute newRoot = new XmlRootAttribute();
newRoot.ElementName = "employees";
changesRoot.XmlRoot = newRoot;
```

You create an *XmlRootAttribute* object and set its *ElementName* property to the name of the source root tag—in this case, *employees*. Next you assign the newly created element attribute to the *XmlRoot* property of the *XmlAttributes* object that gathers all the attribute overrides for a particular element—in this case, the class as a whole. To become effective, the changes must be added to an *XmlAttributeOverrides* object, which will then be passed to the type-specific serializer's constructor, as shown here:

```
XmlAttributeOverrides over = new XmlAttributeOverrides();
over.Add(typeof(Employee), changesRoot);
```

Overriding Class Properties

Each property of the *Employee* class must be renamed and remapped to match one of the source XML attributes because we assume we're working on the data flow of a *FOR XML AUTO*, in which each field is rendered as an attribute. No remapping would be needed if you assumed the data flow of a *FOR XML AUTO ELEMENTS*, in which fields are represented with elements.

Renaming properties is necessary because the deserializer works in a strictly case-sensitive fashion and considers *firstname* completely different from *FirstName*, as you can see by running the following code:

```
XmlAttributes changesFirstName = new XmlAttributes();
XmlAttributeAttribute newFirstName =
    new XmlAttributeAttribute();
newFirstName.AttributeName = "firstname";
changesFirstName.XmlAttribute = newFirstName;
over.Add(typeof(Employee), "FirstName", changesFirstName);
```

You need a distinct *XmlAttributes* object for each element you want to override. The *XmlAttributes* object collects all the overrides you want to enter for a given element. In this case, after creating a new *XmlAttributeAttribute* object, we change the attribute name and store the resultant object in the *XmlAttribute* property of the overrides container.

When the overrides are for a specific element, you use a particular over-load of the *XmlAttributeOverrides* class's *Add* method. In this case, you specify a third argument—the name of the element being overridden. The following code replaces the current settings of the *FirstName* property:

```
over.Add(typeof(Employee), "FirstName", changesFirstName);
```

The code is slightly different if you need to override an element instead of an attribute, as shown here:

```
XmlAttributes changesFirstName = new XmlAttributes();
XmlElementAttribute newFirstName = new XmlElementAttribute();
newFirstName.ElementName = "firstname";
changesFirstName.XmlElements.Add(newFirstName);
over.Add(typeof(Employee), "FirstName", changesFirstName);
```

A different attribute class is involved—*XmlElementAttribute*—with a slightly different programming interface.

Similar code should be written for each class property you want to map to a source XML attribute or element.

> **Caution**   If the name of the XML root does not match the name of the target class, the deserializer can't proceed further, and the *CanDeserialize* method returns *false*. If the root and class names match, the deserialization can take place. Any unmatched attributes and elements are treated as unknown objects, and the proper deserialization event is fired.

Mixing Overrides and Events

Up to now, we have considered a simple scenario in which a direct mapping exists between elements in the source XML and properties in the target class. In this case, all of your overrides end up changing the structure of the XML code being deserialized. But what if you need to apply some logic in the middle of your code? Let's consider a scenario in which the XML source contains a *birth-date* field but your class contains an *Age* property instead. In this case, an attribute override is no longer useful and hooking the deserialization process is the only way.

Earlier in this chapter, we discussed deserialization events. If the *birthdate* value is expressed as an attribute, you write an *UnknownAttribute* handler; otherwise, resort to an *UnknownElement* event handler. The following code snippet shows how to determine the correct value for the *Age* property based on *birthdate*:

```
// Unknown attribute detected
if (e.Attr.Name == "birthdate")
{
    Employee emp = (Employee) e.ObjectBeingDeserialized;
    DateTime dt = DateTime.Parse(e.Attr.Value);
    emp.Age = (int) (DateTime.Now.Year - dt.Year);
}
```

Populating Collection Properties

An even more complex scenario arises when the source XML contains embedded data, the result of *INNER JOIN* operations being rendered in XML. Consider the following statement:

```
SELECT firstname, lastname, title, hiredate, birthdate,
        terr.territorydescription
FROM Employees As employees
INNER JOIN EmployeeTerritories AS empterr
    ON employees.employeeid=empterr.employeeid
INNER JOIN Territories AS terr
    ON empterr.territoryid=terr.territoryid
WHERE employees.employeeid=@empID
FOR XML AUTO
```

The XML output for the *empID* parameter that equals 1 is shown here:

```
<employees firstname="Nancy" lastname="Davolio" ...>
  <terr territorydescription="Wilton" />
  <terr territorydescription="Neward" />
</employees>
```

This output changes a little bit if you use the *ELEMENTS* clause, as follows:

```
<employees>
<firstname>Nancy</firstname>
<lastname>Davolio</lastname>
...
<terr>
  <territorydescription>Wilton</territorydescription>
```

```
<territorydescription>Neward</territorydescription>
</terr>
</employees>
```

The application is always notified of any *<terr>* elements through an *UnknownElement* event. Suppose you also want any territory description to populate a *StringCollection* property in the *Employee* class. The following code shows how to handle the event and accumulate the data for an unknown element in the string collection:

```
if (e.Element.Name == "terr")
{
    if (emp.Territories == null)
        emp.Territories = new StringCollection();

    object o =
        e.Element.Attributes["territorydescription"].Value;
    emp.Territories.Add(o.ToString());
}
```

If the territory description is not expressed as an attribute, you can use the *InnerText* property of the *terr* element to get its value.

Figure 11-3 shows the sample application in action. The application retrieves the data for a particular employee, copies the data into an instance of the *Employee* class, and then displays the data through the user interface.

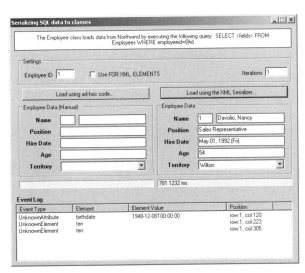

Figure 11-3   Using the XML serializer to deserialize the output of a SQL Server XML query.

> **Note** The query used in this sample application restricts the output to at most one record so that the final XML output will be an XML document instead of an XML fragment. XML fragments are not read by the XML serializer.

Performance Considerations

The first time you write test code that invokes the XML serializer, you'll notice that it takes a while to complete when compared to SOAP or binary serialization. When the serializer object is created, an unknown assembly is loaded. If you run the sample application and monitor the output window, you'll see something like this :

```
'Sql2Class_CS.exe': Loaded 'qsxgw21i', No symbols loaded.
```

The name of the first assembly varies each time you create the XML serializer, a clear sign that it is a temporary assembly created on the fly. We'll examine the internal architecture of the XML serializer in the next section.

For now, consider that each instantiation of the *XmlSerializer* class results in an ad hoc assembly being created and loaded. After that, the reading and writing performance you get from the XML serializer is not different from that of other types of reading/writing tools. The creation of the assembly takes several milliseconds—probably several hundred milliseconds—as compared to the one or two milliseconds that serializing a class might take. This means that using the XML serializer taxes you for about half a second each time you instantiate the *XmlSerializer* class.

This book's sample files include a console application named Perf-Test that demonstrates the differences in performance you get when using XML serialization and ad hoc user code. The output is the same, but custom code runs significantly faster. On the other hand, the XML serializer saves you from writing and testing complex code for complex classes. Keep these issues in mind if you are using XML serialization and want to improve the overall performance.

> **Note**   The full source code for the sample application demonstrating the deserialization of SQL Server XML queries to .NET Framework classes is available in this book's sample files. The application is named Sql2Class. The application demonstrates attribute overriding and works with *FOR XML* and *FOR XML ELEMENTS* queries. In addition, it compares the performance of the serializer and a piece of ad hoc code mapping XML data to the same class.

Inside the XML Serializer

The XML serializer is a powerful tool that can transform a fair number of .NET Framework classes into portable XML code. The key thing to note is that the serializer is a kind of compiler. It first imports type information from the class and then serializes it to the output stream. It also works the other way around. The serializer reads XML data and maps elements to the target class members.

Normally, serialization and deserialization are functions that each class implements in whatever way it determines is more convenient for its data. This is precisely what happens with run-time object serialization. XML serialization works differently, however. With the XML serializer, you have a compiler tool that takes information out of the class and conveys it to the stream. Each class is particular and, in a certain way, unique. How can a generic tool work efficiently on all possible classes? This is where the temporary assembly comes in.

The Temporary Assembly

The following listing shows the pseudocode that makes up the constructor of the *XmlSerializer* class:

```
public XmlSerializer(Type type)
{
    // Looks up for the assembly in the internal cache
    tempAssembly = Cache[type];

    // If no assembly is found, create a new one
    if (tempAssembly == null)
    {
```

(continued)

```
    // Import type mapping information
    XmlReflectionImporter importer =
        new XmlReflectionImporter();
    XmlTypeMapping map = importer.ImportTypeMapping(type);

    // Generate the assembly and add it to
    // the cache for that type
    tempAssembly = GenerateTempAssembly(map);
    Cache.Add(type, tempAssembly);
    }
}
```

The *XmlSerializer* class maintains an internal table of type/assembly pairs. If no known assembly exists to handle the type, a new assembly is promptly generated and cached; otherwise, the existing assembly is used to serialize and deserialize. (More on the assembly's contents in the next section.)

Each instance of the *XmlSerializer* class maintains a reference to the assembly to be used for reading and writing operations. In the preceding pseudocode, *tempAssembly* is the name of this data member. Both the *Serialize* method and the *Deserialize* method use this reference to obtain the tailor-made reader and writer objects to work on the particular type.

The Assembly Cache

The assembly cache is built around a hash table that contains objects of type *TempAssembly*. As the ILDASM shows in Figure 11-4, the assembly cache corresponds to a class named *TempAssemblyCache*. The *XmlSerializer* class holds a static *TempAssemblyCache* member that is shared by all instances of the *XmlSerializer* you might create.

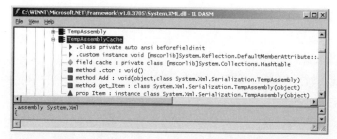

Figure 11-4   Peeking into the *System.Xml.Serialization* namespace.

The *TempAssembly* class maintains information about the assembly that provides reader and writer classes optimized to XML serialize and XML deserialize classes of a certain type. To build a type-specific assembly, the serializer needs fresh information about the type being serialized. An internal class named *Xml-*

ReflectionImporter retrieves this information through the .NET Framework reflection API. The type data is packed into an *XmlTypeMapping* structure and then passed to the internal method that provides for the assembly generation.

Caution   The main purpose of the assembly cache is to save you from repeatedly re-creating the assembly for the same type in the same application session. Unfortunately, this seems to work only if you use the simplest *XmlSerializer* constructor, as shown here:

```
XmlSerializer ser = new XmlSerializer(type);
```

All other constructors—that is, those that can accept namespaces, type mapping, and attribute overrides—never look into the cache to find matching assemblies. The net effect of this behavior is that if you use, say, attribute overrides, as we did earlier, the assembly for the type is generated each time you create the constructor, even if the type is always the same.

To work around this, use global instances of the *XmlSerializer* class, one for each type you plan to work on. This workaround is not strictly required if you use the simple constructor, but using a global serializer for each type results in slightly more efficient code because you avoid any access to the cache, and not doing so will certainly result in significantly slower code. Generating the assembly pays for itself in a single serializing or deserializing operation.

Assembly Creation

The assembly is created from dynamically generated C# source code. The code contains two classes whose names are hard-coded as *XmlSerializationReader1* and *XmlSerializationWriter1*. The former class works like a tailor-made reader for the type being deserialized. The latter class is an ad hoc writer that dumps out to XML the contents of the specified object instance. The classes are generated in the *Microsoft.Xml.Serialization.GeneratedAssembly* namespace.

The serializer's constructor uses an internal code-writer object to transform all type information stored in *XmlTypeMapping* into C# source code. The C# source file, as well as the assembly, are generated in a temporary folder—the path returned by *Path.GetTempPath*. Normally, the following temporary path is used:

```
C:\Documents And Settings\[user name]\Local Settings\Temp
```

If you monitor this folder with a tool like the one shown in Figure 11-5, you'll discover what really happens when you call the *XmlSerializer* constructor.

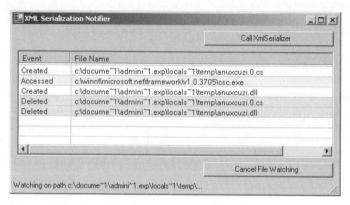

Figure 11-5 Unveiling the clandestine life of the temporary assembly.

As you can see, the first file created is a C# source file whose name has been randomly generated. Next the serializer invokes the C# compiler, and the assembly is soon created! The files are cached in memory and deleted from disk immediately after having been created. It's almost impossible to programmatically catch those files and make a copy for further perusal. The XML Serialization Notifier tool (XmlSerial_CS) shown in Figure 11-5 (and available in this book's sample files) uses the *FileSystemWatcher* class to monitor file system events that take place in a given folder. The only trick I've come up with to get my hands on the serializer's internal files is dropping the delete permission on the folder.

Figure 11-6 shows the files generated using this trick for the serializer instance shown in Figure 11-5.

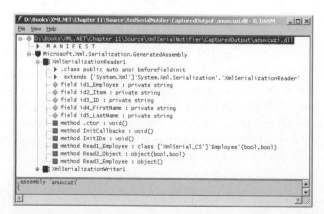

Figure 11-6 The ILDASM view of the temporary assembly's contents.

Serialization Writers and Readers

Let's take a brief look at what happens under the hood of the *XmlSerialization-Reader* and *XmlSerializationWriter* classes. The MSDN documentation touches on these two classes, which form the substrate of the classes contained in the temporary assembly. The *XmlSerializationReader* and *XmlSerializationWriter* classes are internal and are not intended to be used directly from user code. More interesting than the actual contents of the classes is how the *Serialize* and *Deserialize* methods interact with them.

Serializing to XML

The *Serialize* method first gets a reference to the class-specific type writer. An instance of the *XmlSerializationWriter1* class is returned by the *TempAssembly* class that represents the temporary assembly. Once the *Serialize* method holds a reference to the actual serialization writer, it calls the write method that outputs XML code to a text writer.

Deserializing from XML

Although a *CanDeserialize* method is provided, the *Deserialize* method never calls it. If the type is not fully serializable, or if errors occurred somewhere along the way, the *Deserialize* method fails, throwing an exception.

If no errors occur, the *Deserialize* method asks the temporary assembly to return a reference to the reader object to be used. The reader object is simply an instance of the *XmlSerializationReader1* class. The method that actually returns the object is one of the *ReadN_XXX* methods, where *N* is the method index and *XXX* is the type.

Conclusion

The XML serializer is a double-edged sword. On one hand, it lets you serialize and deserialize even complex .NET Framework classes to and from XML with very few lines of code. To accomplish this, the serializer needs to create an assembly on the fly. If you don't use a global instance of the serializer for each type, you can easily add hundreds of milliseconds of overhead to each call—definitely not a pleasant prospect.

On the other hand, appropriately used, XML serialization produces more compact code than run-time SOAP serialization. If you add type information, and SOAP type information in particular, the ratio changes, however. The moral of this story is don't ever mix XML and SOAP—use only the process you need.

Serialization is one of the new frontiers of XML. It is not clear yet whether today's SOAP, extensions to SOAP, or a brand-new dialect will become the universal platform for describing objects. Currently, XML serialization is a hybrid, incomplete, technology. Originally designed as a tool running underneath the .NET Framework implementation of Web services, XML serialization entered prime time a bit too early, or if not too early, certainly not optimized.

If you look at XML serialization as a way to save and resume objects to and from a tag-based description, the current architecture makes sense because it is fairly unobtrusive and even efficient. The apparently odd use of a temporary assembly is fully justified in a Web service context. As we'll see in Chapter 13, the return type of a Web method is serialized back to the caller using an instance of the *XmlSerializer* class. In this context, a Web service class does not need to use attribute overriding or other features that require a rich constructor. This could be just the unofficial explanation for the fact that assembly caching is enabled only for the simplest constructor. This was originally the core of what we know today as XML serialization. All the rest was untidily tacked on when someone pushed XML serialization into prime time.

If you look at object serialization from a broader perspective, you can't help wondering why run-time object serialization and XML serialization are so different. My hunch is that XML serialization was initially designed as an internal tool and was tailor-made for use with Web services. In that context, a dynamic assembly is useful and speeds up the process. The XML serializer then came to be seen, and with good reason, as a more powerful and useful tool to be made public and with a richer programming interface. This project is still incomplete. Overall, XML serialization touches a programmer's sensitive nerve, but at least in this version of the .NET Framework, it comes with a clearly inconsistent design, although with some great ideas sprinkled here and there. It's as if the technology was rushed out the door with no further thought. A glimpse of the potential future of the XML serialization is buried in the recesses of the *DataSet* object—in the *IXmlSerializable* interface. Forcing objects to make themselves XML serializable by implementing a particular interface is a clean way toward much faster, better designed, consistent, and more effective code.

Further Reading

This chapter focused on XML serialization. For a more thorough coverage of object serialization in general, look at *Programming Visual Basic .NET* by Francesco Balena (Microsoft Press, 2002). Chapter 11 of that book provides a comprehensive explanation of run-time object serialization in the .NET Framework, including XML serialization.

SOAP was also repeatedly mentioned in this chapter. A good introduction to SOAP that successfully weds philosophy and technology can be found in Don Box's article *"Young Person's Guide to the Simple Object Access Protocol: SOAP Increases Interoperability Across Platforms and Languages,"* in MSDN Magazine, March 2000.

A good source for learning about SOAP in general terms and not specifically from a .NET Web service perspective is *Understanding SOAP*, by Kennard Scribner and Mark Stiver (SAMS, 2000). For an in-depth reference discussing both SOAP and Web services from a .NET Framework angle, try *Building XML Web Services for the Microsoft .NET Platform*, by Scott Short (Microsoft Press, 2002).

12

The .NET Remoting System

The Microsoft .NET Framework infrastructure for remoting is the set of system services that enable .NET applications to communicate and exchange data and objects. In this chapter and Chapter 13, you'll find an annotated overview of the two technologies that constitute the .NET answer to the universal demand for a seamless and effective mechanism for building distributed and interoperable applications: .NET Remoting and Web services.

Before we begin our technical examination of the .NET Remoting architecture, a broader perspective is necessary to understand how .NET Remoting—that is, a non-XML technology—fits into a book about XML.

Interprocess Communications in the .NET Framework

Web services and .NET Remoting are distinct, stand-alone technologies that share a common root but have different sets of features and, more important, different goals. Both Web services and .NET Remoting let you publish functions over a network and handle incoming calls. Both share an architectural design that includes layers for request/response handling, object serialization, and data transportation. Both share underlying network protocols such as Simple Object Access Protocol (SOAP) and HTTP.

Overall, Web services and .NET Remoting are two distinct and independent sides of the same coin. Web services—a clearly XML-based technology—are a special case of the .NET Remoting infrastructure. The .NET Framework infrastructure for remoting can be seen as an abstract approach to interprocess communication. Web services and .NET Remoting are technologies that represent concrete implementations of that abstract interface. As distinct implementations, they end up using different building blocks to set up constituent features such as object serialization, type description, and reflection. The actual underlying technologies that make Web services and .NET Remoting happen are chosen according to the final goal of each technology.

Web services are targeted to cross-platform communication and heterogeneous systems. .NET Remoting doesn't allow for cross-platform communication, but it is highly optimized for .NET-to-.NET communication. In a nutshell, .NET Remoting takes in the best aspects of its Microsoft Win32 predecessor—Distributed Component Object Model (DCOM)—and elegantly fills in the gaps.

In this chapter and Chapter 13, we'll examine the major features of each technology and demonstrate that a common, platform-independent piece of code—say, a .NET Framework class—can be exposed in both models and perform in the same way in .NET Framework as well as Win32 and Linux applications.

.NET Remoting as a Better DCOM

Prior to the advent of the .NET Framework, DCOM was the underlying technology of choice for any sort of remote communication between Microsoft Windows applications. Based on a proprietary binary protocol, DCOM has suffered since its conception from a number of shortcomings. For this reason, DCOM never charmed its way into the average programmer's heart, although it did prove to be functional and effective.

DCOM is somewhat quirky to set up and configure, and under certain, but relatively frequent, circumstances, it also raises serious interoperability exceptions that basically put you in the unenviable position of having to change the connectivity engine for the sake of the application or simply give up.

> **Note** Some programmers believe that .NET Remoting is even harder to set up than DCOM. They point out that DCOM, at least, has a tool (dcomcnfg.exe) to help with the setup and configuration of remote components; .NET Remoting has no such tool (although the Control Panel applet called the .NET Framework Configuration tool [mscorcfg.msc] provides a minimal amount of configuration support). My personal opinion, however, is that the tasks required to set up a .NET Remoting application are far simpler to understand than the equivalent DCOM tasks.

Aware of the ubiquity of HTTP, which allows you to legitimately penetrate any system through the always open port 80, at a certain point users began asking more and more for distributed applications capable of interconnecting and interoperating with any sort of remote system. For a time, the most natural response to such a demand seemed to be taking the official Windows Component Object Model (COM) and attaching a logical wire to both ends. DCOM became the network extension of COM, thus building a new infrastructure on the same successful component technology. Seamless integration, a short learning curve, and a concrete possibility of retaining existing investments in COM-based applications and tools were understandably the most intriguing benefits of DCOM.

DCOM works as a wrapper for COM components. DCOM takes care of all that boring stuff about low-level network protocols and leaves you free to concentrate your efforts on the bread and butter of your business: planning and realizing great and effective solutions for customers.

DCOM is a binary protocol that has in its favor a theoretically excellent measure of performance, especially when compared to text-based interactions such as those taking place over HTTP and the Internet. DCOM applications are fundamentally location-independent, as the protocol infrastructure covers the physical distance between users in the way it finds best. For example, DCOM automatically creates a pair of proxy/stub modules for any interprocess and intermachine communication and resolves the call within the boundary of the current process, whenever this is possible and plausible. So where are the jarring notes with DCOM?

DCOM Shortcomings

In many Internet scenarios, the level of connectivity allowed between a client and a server is subject to a variety of restrictions. For example, on its way to the remote server component, a client component might run across a proxy server that filters and controls outbound network traffic. As a result, the proxy might prevent the client from properly interacting with the object of its software desire. Furthermore, a firewall might filter any incoming Internet requests to protect the server components from any unauthorized contact. A firewall normally defines the combination of network ports, packets, and protocols that is acceptable for the safety and the health of the network environment running behind it.

The ultimate effect of such restrictions is that a DCOM client and a server can set up and carry out a conversation only through a quite narrow set of protocol and port combinations. When opening a port and sending out the packets that constitute a method request, DCOM dynamically selects a network port in the range 1024 through 65,535. Unfortunately, system administrators normally prohibit inbound Internet traffic from passing through these ports and penetrating into intranet microcosms.

Using DCOM over the Internet is not particularly reliable—or, at least, not as reliable as it is in intranet scenarios. The fact that DCOM can use such a wide range of ports makes coding significantly easier. In fact, programmers don't have to worry about possible conflicts with other applications attempting to access the same port. In addition, dynamic port allocation also increases the overall level of flexibility because the particular communication port doesn't have to be hard-coded or persisted somewhere as an application-specific argument. On the down side, system administrators don't usually agree to leave such a wide range of ports open to inbound traffic because doing so could leave a major hole in security.

> **Note** The DCOM security model is based on the assumption that developers and administrators configure the security settings properly for each component. The net effect of this approach is that the same binary code works unchanged both in environments in which the security is of no concern (for example, on a local single machine) and in environments in which the code needs to be processed in a secure fashion (as in a fully distributed environment).

DCOM Extensions for the Internet

Over the years, DCOM has been extended to work around this security issue. In particular, the COM Internet Services (CIS) layer has given DCOM the capability to work over port 80 thanks to a new transportation protocol called Tunneling Transmission Control Protocol (TTCP). CIS works as an Internet Server Application Programming Interface (ISAPI) filter and requires Microsoft Internet Information Services (IIS) 4.0 or later to run on the server machine. Basically, TTCP works by fooling the firewall. At the very beginning of each DCOM operation, TTCP shakes hands with the server, declaring its intention to use HTTP over port 80. If the firewall agrees, what follows is a traffic pattern of non-HTTP packets that are blissfully delivered over port 80 of those firewalls that are lazy enough to accept binary packets over HTTP. All in all, CIS gives DCOM a good chance of entering through a window when it finds that the front door is locked. This peculiarity also affects the way DCOM components work. In fact, server components can't call back the client component to sink events or send notifications.

.NET Remoting to the Rescue

What's new and better with .NET Remoting? The advent of the .NET Framework pushed COM-related technology aside, and DCOM is no exception. The .NET Framework architecture for remoting arose completely redesigned, with two key goals to pursue: allowing for seamless and location-independent coding while providing a fully operational way of interacting with restricted servers.

> **Note**   The previous statement about the diminished status of COM-related technologies doesn't imply that existing COM components are obsolete in the new .NET world. On the contrary, the .NET Framework integrates seamlessly with COM components and the Win32 API through ad hoc interoperability mechanisms such as COM Callable Wrappers (CCWs) and P/Invoke. By adopting a "leave-no-COM-object-behind" philosophy, the .NET Framework designers ensured the continued success of existing COM-related technologies even as developers migrate to the .NET Framework.

The .NET Remoting classes allow for optimized and effective communication between .NET Framework applications. They don't offer even the possibility of being used in any other scenario. For cross-platform scenarios in which heterogeneous environments are involved, you must use Web services. But if you need to set up communication between two .NET Framework applications, nothing is better and more efficient than .NET Remoting.

What Is .NET Remoting?

The entire set of services that enable .NET Framework applications to communicate with each other falls under the umbrella of .NET Remoting. Such applications can reside on the same computer, can work on different computers in the same LAN, and can even be scattered across the world in heterogeneous networks but on homogeneous platforms—that is, platforms that can host the common language runtime (CLR) and access the .NET Framework.

The .NET Remoting architecture enables you to use different transportation protocols, serialization formats, object lifetime schemes, and modes of object creation. In addition, programmers can directly plug into the flow of messages that each communication originates and can hook up activities at various stages of the process.

At a lower level of abstraction, however, the only thing .NET Remoting can do for you is enable communication and data exchange between different application domains (AppDomains).

Application Domains

The .NET Framework CLR provides a feature-rich execution environment for code. Within the CLR, code finds available services like garbage collection, security, versioning, and threading. Executable code must be loaded into the CLR to be *managed* while running, however.

> **Note**   Currently, only the Microsoft Windows XP operating system is equipped with a CLR-aware program loader capable of running a .NET Framework executable within the context of a CLR instance. For compatibility with all non-XP Windows operating systems, all .NET Framework executables include a tailor-made stub program that operating systems automatically launch when executables don't match the current system platform. This stub passes the control to another piece of code that instantiates the CLR and loads the managed code into it. See the section "Further Reading," on page 559, for additional resources on this topic.

To run an application's code, the instance of the CLR must obtain a pointer to an AppDomain. AppDomains are separate units of processing that the CLR recognizes in a running process. All .NET Framework processes run at least one AppDomain—known as the default AppDomain—that is created during the CLR initialization. An application can have additional AppDomains. Each AppDomain is independently configured and given personal settings for security, reference paths, and configuration files.

AppDomains are separated and isolated from one another in a way that resembles process separation in Win32. The CLR enforces isolation by preventing direct calls between objects residing in different AppDomains. From the CPU perspective, AppDomains are much more lightweight than Win32 processes and provide for a more lightweight mechanism of isolation between processing units. The .NET Framework provides the remoting API as a tailor-made set of system services to access an object that resides in an external AppDomain. Figure 12-1 illustrates such an inter-AppDomain communication.

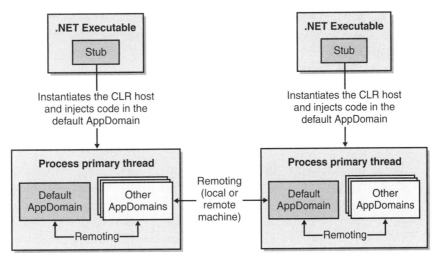

Figure 12-1   Inter-AppDomain communication in the .NET Framework.

Why AppDomains Do It Better

Managed code needs an AppDomain to run, but it must also pass through a verification process before it can be run. Code that passes such a test is said to be *type-safe*. Type-safe code never reads memory that has not been previously written, never calls a method using an incorrect number of arguments, and always assigns a return value to functions. In summary, type-safe code can't cause memory faults, which in Win32 were one of the reasons to have a physical separation between process memory contexts. The certainty of running type-safe code allows the CLR to provide a level of isolation as strong as process boundaries, but more cost-effective because an AppDomain is a logical process and as such is more lightweight than a true process.

> **Note**   Direct use of pointers is allowed in C# as long as you explicitly mark your code (classes, methods, and interfaces) as unsafe by using the *unsafe* keyword. Unsafe code loads and runs in an AppDomain, just like managed code, but isn't verified to be type-safe. Unsafe code is supported by the C# compiler only.

Unlike Win32 processes, you can have several AppDomains running within the boundaries of the same .NET Framework application. Individual domains can be stopped without stopping the entire process, but you can't unload only a single assembly within an AppDomain. Managed code running in an AppDomain is carried out by a particular thread. However, threads and App-Domains are orthogonal entities in the sense that you can have several threads active during the execution of the AppDomain's code, but a single thread is in no way limited to running only within the context of a given AppDomain.

Location Transparency

From an application's standpoint, an external AppDomain can transparently be another AppDomain in the same process, the default AppDomain in another process on the same machine, and even an AppDomain residing on a physically distant machine. All the low-level details that make each of these scenarios unique are transparently handled by .NET Remoting; the user is responsible only for higher-level aspects such as actual network paths or the URLs used to set up the communication.

Remotable Objects

The overall architecture that makes .NET Remoting happen is extremely modular and flexible enough to let you customize several aspects of the service. For example, you can decide whether remote objects should be marshaled on the local platform by value or by reference. Similarly, you can control how objects are activated and whether the activation should take place on the client or on the server. Programmers also can intervene in the object's lifetime and specify the most suitable communications channel and formatter module for transporting messages to and from remote applications.

A remotable object can be implemented in one of two ways. One possibility is that you design the class to be serializable so that its instance data can be marshaled from the server to the client. At the receiving end, the client unmarshals the data and creates another instance of the class with the same values as the instance on the server. This approach is referred to as marshal by value (MBV). The other possibility is that the class allows for its object reference to be marshaled. When unmarshaled on the client, the object reference becomes a proxy to the remote instance. This second approach is known as marshal by reference (MBR). Unlike MBV, MBR preserves the object's identity.

No matter how you design your remotable objects—MBV or MBR—a network connection must always exist between the client application and the remote object for .NET Remoting to work.

> **Note**   .NET Remoting doesn't support the automatic download of the assembly containing the type of the instance that is being marshaled (unlike other remote access technologies, such as Java's Remote Method Invocation [RMI]). Instead, the assembly for the type needs to exist on the client beforehand. How the assembly gets on the client is outside the purview of .NET Remoting.

Marshaling Objects by Value

Marshaling by value downloads the entire object's contents to the client, which uses the instance data to initialize a client-side object of that type. The client obtains a perfect local clone of the original object and can work with it completely oblivious to the fact that the object data has been downloaded from a remote location.

In general, MBV is not recommended when you have to cope with large objects with several properties. With MBV, you take the risk of consuming a significant portion of bandwidth to perform the full object's data download, thus subjecting the client to a potentially long wait to execute only one or two methods. MBV also imposes some constraints on the remotable objects. In particular, any objects that need to be consumed by value must qualify as serializable—which is not the case for all objects. In addition to objects that deliberately make themselves nonserializable, some objects are objectively hard to serialize. In this list, you certainly find classes that represent or contain database connections. More generally, the list includes all those objects that can't be reasonably represented outside their native environment. This happens when all or part of the information stored in an object does not make sense once the object is transferred to the client. If the object has any implicit dependencies on server-side resources, you can't just use it from the client. For example, if the class has a method that accesses a SQL Server table, you could call it from the client only if the same SQL Server table is accessible from the current location.

When to Marshal by Value

So how do you know when MBV is a good option? Let's say that MBV is a compelling option when the following conditions are true:

- The object is not particularly large and complex.

- You're going to make intensive use of the object.

- You have no special security concerns.

- The object has no dependencies on remote resources such as files, databases, devices, or system resources.

Some rather illustrious .NET Framework classes that support remoting through the MBV technique are the *DataSet* and *DataTable* classes.

MBV Objects

The .NET Remoting system serializes all the internal data of MBV objects and passes the stream to the calling AppDomain, as illustrated in Figure 12-2.

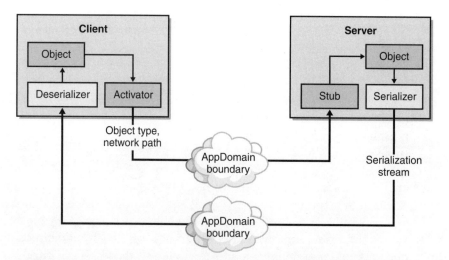

Figure 12-2   How .NET Remoting marshals objects by value.

After the data is in the client AppDomain, a new local object is instantiated and initialized and starts handling calls. To write remotable objects that are exchanged by value, you need to make them serializable, either by declaring the *SerializableAttribute* attribute or by implementing *ISerializable*. Aside from this, nothing else is required for instances of the class to be passed by value across AppDomains.

Marshaling Objects by Reference

When an object is marshaled by reference, the client process receives a reference to the server-side object, rather than a copy. This means that any call directed to the object is always resolved on the server within the native context of the object. The remoting infrastructure governs the call, collecting all information about the call and sending it to the server process. On the server, the correct object is located and asked to execute the call using the client's arguments. When the call is finished, the results are packaged and sent back to the client. Unlike MBV, MBR uses the network only for transmitting arguments and return values. Figure 12-3 shows the architecture of MBR remoting.

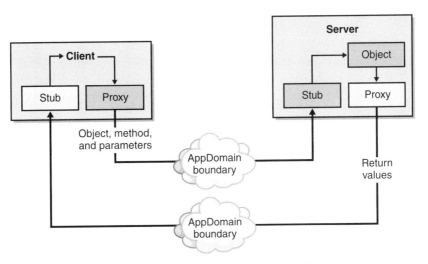

Figure 12-3   How .NET Remoting marshals objects by reference.

The .NET Remoting implementation of MBR provides for a proxy/stub pair and a physical channel for network transportation. The proxy represents the remote object to the client, as it simply mirrors the same set of methods and properties. Each client invocation of a remote method actually hits the local proxy, which, in turn, takes care of routing the call down to the server. A method invocation originates a message that travels on top of a channel and a transmission protocol.

Each message passes through a chain of hook objects (called *sinks*) on each side of the transport channel. Sinks are nearly identical to Windows hooks. By defining and registering a sink, the programmer can perform a specific operation at a specific stage of the remoting process. Because the creation of the proxy takes place automatically, the programmer has little to do other than creating an instance of the target object and issuing the call.

If the object resides in an external AppDomain, the remoting infrastructure creates a local proxy for it to perform the requested operation. But how can the code determine whether a given object is local, lives in a remote AppDomain, or just doesn't exist? In spite of the sophisticated code that constitutes the remoting infrastructure, programming remote objects is mostly a matter of setup. Once the client has been properly configured, you normally create a new instance of the remote class using the *new* operator, no matter what type of class you're calling and where it resides. Clients must declare to the CLR which classes are remote and provide connection information. Remote objects, in turn, must be publicly available and bound to a given channel.

The *MarshalByRefObject* Class

Inheriting from the *MarshalByRefObject* class is the key that enables user classes to be accessed across AppDomain boundaries in applications that support remoting. *MarshalByRefObject* is the base class for objects that communicate across AppDomains. Serializable classes that do not inherit from *MarshalByRefObject*, when instantiated from a remote assembly, are implicitly marshaled by value. Other classes are simply considered nonremotable.

So if you want to write a remote component that uses the network efficiently and always runs on the server, the only thing you have to do is create the class inheriting from *MarshalByRefObject*, as follows:

```
public class NorthwindService : MarshalByRefObject
{
    public DataSet GetSalesReport(int year);
}
```

For example, the *NorthwindService* class shown here is ideally suited to act as a remote console that clients access through transparent proxies.

> **Note**   When creating a remotable object, you normally limit the class to inheriting from *MarshalByRefObject*. In some situations, however, you might want to override some of the parent class's methods. In particular, you might want to replace the *InitializeLifetimeService* method and configure the object's lifetime. We'll return to this topic in the section "Memory Management," on page 551.

The *ObjRef* Class

When a *MarshalByRefObject* object is being remoted, the .NET Remoting system packs all the relevant information into an *ObjRef* object. An *ObjRef* object is a serializable representation of the original MBR object. This intermediary object enables the .NET Remoting system to transfer an object reference across the boundaries of AppDomains. In effect, the entire action of marshaling by reference can be summarized with the creation an *ObjRef* object.

An *ObjRef* object contains information that describes the type and the class of the object being marshaled, the exact location, and any communication-related information such as port and protocols. The *ObjRef* instance is created on the server when the MBR object is first referenced; next it is transferred into the target AppDomain, possibly in another process or on another machine. On the client, the *ObjRef* object is then deserialized, and the real proxy is created to access the remote instance of the MBR object. This operation is globally known as *unmarshaling*.

The *RealProxy* Class

RealProxy is an abstract class that represents a remoting proxy. Any remoting client transparently uses an instance of this class to issue calls to the remote object. The overall .NET Framework model for distributed programming is designed to create the illusion that remote objects are actually working locally. This is true for .NET Remoting as well as for Web services, even though the effect is obtained with radically different techniques.

Note   .NET Remoting creates the local instance of the remote object using dynamically created proxies that result from the run-time deserialization process. Basically, the deserialization of the *ObjRef* class generates a transparent proxy to handle user calls. With Web services, a proxy class is statically added to the application's project at design time when the Web service is referenced as an external library. The generation of the source code for the class and the subsequent addition to the project are automatically handled by Visual Studio .NET. However, the wsdl.exe utility (part of the .NET Framework SDK) allows you to generate the class yourself.

The *RealProxy* class hidden behind the software creates the illusion that remoting clients actually work locally. The proxy is transparently invoked whenever a method is called on the remote object. The *RealProxy* class executes the method by forwarding any calls to the real object using the remoting infrastructure.

If you want to play with the transparent proxy object yourself, you can get a reference to it by using the following code:

```
RemotingServices.GetRealProxy(localObject);
```

The variable *localObject* is the local instance of the remote object that you have created using the *new* operator. (More on this in a moment.) As mentioned, *RealProxy* is only an abstract class. The actual proxy object belongs to the *RemotingProxy* class in the *System.Runtime.Remoting.Proxies* namespace.

Building a Remote Service

Let's take the plunge into .NET Remoting and start building a service that can be exploited and consumed from remote clients. In Chapter 13, we'll extend the service to make it openly available to Internet clients too. In this way, you can really grab the essence of .NET Framework distributed programming and understand the key differences that keep .NET Remoting and Web services separate even though they're both children of a common model for remotable objects.

A .NET Remoting server and a Web service are both .NET Framework classes. As such, they can inherit from a parent class and can be left open to further inheritance. As you'll see in more detail in Chapter 13, a Web service class can optionally inherit from the *WebService* class, but there is no syntax obligation. A .NET Remoting server class must inherit from *MarshalByRefObject*.

The object-oriented nature of the .NET Framework makes sharing classes between a .NET Remoting server and a Web service straightforward. However, because of the inheritance difference just mentioned, you can't have the Web service and the .NET Remoting server descend from the same base class of functionality. The .NET Framework, in fact, does not permit inheritance from multiple classes.

We'll start by writing a helper class that constitutes the programming interface for both the .NET Remoting server in this chapter and the Web service we'll create in Chapter 13. The remote service is actually a class built around the Northwind database that lets you obtain gross sales information on a per-year basis. A nice feature of this service is that it lets you obtain information in two ways: as raw tabular data to format and analyze or as a ready-to-print, snazzy bar chart.

Writing the Data Provider Class

Because our final goal is exposing a common set of functionalities through both the .NET Remoting server and the Web service interfaces, let's group all the needed core code into a separate middle-tier class that both higher-level layers can easily call. We'll call this helper class *SalesDataProvider* and bury into its code all the details about connection strings, SQL commands, and bar chart creation. The class outline is shown here:

```
namespace XmlNet.CS
{
    public class SalesDataProvider
    {
        // Constructor(s)
        public SalesDataProvider() {...}

        // Internal properties
        private string m_conn = "DATABASE=northwind;SERVER=...;UID=sa;";
        private int m_Year = 0;

        // Returns sales details for the specified year
        public DataTable GetSalesReport(int theYear) {...}

        // Create a bar chart with the sales data for the specified year
        public string GetSalesReportBarChart(int theYear) {...}

        // INTERNAL METHODS

        // Fetch the data
        private DataTable ExecuteQuery(int theYear) {...}

        // Draw the bar chart based on the data in the specified table
        private string CreateBarChart(DataTable dt) {...}

        // Encode the specified bitmap object as BinHex XML
        private string SaveBitmapAsEncodedXml(Bitmap bmp)
    }
}
```

The class contains only a couple of public methods—*GetSalesReport* and *GetSalesReportBarChart*. These methods will also form the public interface of the .NET Remoting server we'll build in this chapter and the Web service slated for Chapter 13.

Implementation Details

GetSalesReport takes an integer that indicates the year to consider and returns a *DataTable* object with two columns—one containing employee last names and one showing total sales for the year for each employee. The method runs the following SQL query against the Northwind database:

```
SELECT e.lastname AS Employee, SUM(price) AS Sales FROM
  (SELECT o.employeeid, od.orderid, SUM(od.quantity*od.unitprice)
    AS price
    FROM Orders o, [Order Details] od
    WHERE Year(o.orderdate)=@TheYear AND od.orderid=o.orderid
    GROUP BY o.employeeid, od.orderid
  ) AS t1
  INNER JOIN Employees e ON t1.employeeid=e.employeeid
  GROUP BY t1.employeeid, e.lastname
```

The query involves three tables—*Employees*, *Orders*, and *Order Details*—and basically calculates the total amount of each order issued in the specified year by a particular employee. Finally, the amounts of all orders are summed and returned together with the employee's last name.

GetSalesReportBarChart works in two steps: first it gets the sales data by calling *GetSalesReport*, and then it uses this information to create the bar chart. The bar chart is generated as an in-memory bitmap object and is drawn using the GDI+ classes in the *System.Drawing* namespace. To make the image easily transportable over the wire for .NET Remoting clients as well as for Web service clients, the *GetSalesReportBarChart* method converts the bitmap to JPEG, encodes the bits as BinHex, and puts the results in an XML string.

Using GDI+ to Create Charts

GDI+ is the latest incarnation of the classic Windows Graphical Device Interface (GDI), a graphics subsystem that enables you to write device-independent applications. The .NET Framework encapsulates the full spectrum of GDI+ functionalities in quite a few managed classes that wrap any GDI+ low-level functions, thus making them available to Web Forms and Windows Forms applications.

GDI+ services fall into three broad categories: 2-D vector graphics, imaging, and typography. The 2-D vector graphics category includes drawing primitives such as lines, curves, and any other figures that are specified by a set of points on a coordinate system. The imaging category includes functions for displaying, manipulating, and saving pictures as bitmaps and metafiles. The typography category concerns the display of text in a variety of fonts, sizes, and styles. Only the imaging functions are key to the *GetSalesReport-BarChart* implementation.

In GDI+, the *Graphics* class represents the managed counterpart of the Win32 GDI device context. You can think of it as the central console from which you call all primitives. Everything you draw, or fill, through a *Graphics* object acts on a particular canvas. Typical drawing surfaces are the window background (including control backgrounds), the printer, and in-memory bitmaps.

The following code creates a new bitmap object and gets a *Graphics* object from it:

```
Bitmap bmp = new Bitmap(500, 400);
Graphics g = Graphics.FromImage(bmp);
g.Clear(Color.Ivory);
```

From this point on, any drawing methods called on the *Graphics* object will result in changes to the bitmap. For example, the *Clear* method clears the bitmap's background using the specified color.

Creating a bar chart is as easy as creating and filling a certain number of rectangles, as shown in the following code. We need to create a bar for each employee in the *DataTable* object and give it a height that is both proportional to the maximum value to draw and based on the scale given by the bitmap's size.

```
// Save the names of the fields to use to get data
string fieldLabel, fieldValue;
fieldLabel = dt.Columns[0].ColumnName;
fieldValue = dt.Columns[1].ColumnName;

// For each employee...
for(int i=0; i<dt.Rows.Count; i++)
{
    //
    // Set up some internal variables to determine
    // size and position of the bar and the
    // companion text
    //

    // Draw the value (top of the bar)
    g.DrawString(dt.Rows[i][fieldValue].ToString(),
        fnt, textBrush, x, yCaption);

    // Draw the bar
    Rectangle bar = new Rectangle(x, yBarTop, barWidth - 10, barHeight);
    LinearGradientBrush fill = new LinearGradientBrush(bar,
        Color.SpringGreen, Color.Yellow,
        LinearGradientMode.BackwardDiagonal);
```

(continued)

```
g.FillRectangle(fill, bar);
fill.Dispose();

// Draw the employee name (bottom of the bar)
g.DrawString(dt.Rows[i][fieldLabel].ToString(),
    fnt, textBrush, x, barBottom + textHeight);
}
```

At the end of the loop, the bar chart is completely rendered in the *Bitmap* object. The bitmap is still held in memory in an intermediate, internal format, however. Two more steps are necessary: converting the bitmap to a public format such JPEG, BMP, or GIF, and figuring out a way to persist or transfer its content.

Encoding Images as BinHex

Converting a *Bitmap* object to one of the commonly used image formats is a nonissue. You call the *Save* method on the *Bitmap* object, pick up one of the supported formats, and you're done. The real difficulty has to do with the planned use of this helper class.

Remember, we designed this class for later use within a .NET Remoting server and a Web service. When Web services in particular are involved, having the helper class save the image to persistent storage just doesn't make sense. An alternative approach would be saving the bitmap locally on the server in a location accessible for download via FTP or HTTP. Creating files on the server might pose security problems, however, and normally forces the system administrator to change default settings to allow for local files being created.

The *SalesDataProvider* helper class was designed to return the dynamically created image as an encoded text string packed in an XML document. This approach is not optimal in a .NET Remoting scenario, but it probably represents the only option if you have to also publish the function through a Web service.

As we saw in Chapter 4, the *XmlTextWriter* class provides methods for encoding and writing arrays of bytes, and an image—no matter the format—is just an array of bytes. A further step is needed to transform the *Bitmap* object into an array of bytes that make up a JPEG image. To convert a *Bitmap* object to a real-world image format, you must use the *Save* method. The *Save* method can accept only a file name or a stream, however.

To solve this problem, you first save the bitmap as a JPEG image to a memory stream. Next you read back the contents of the stream as an array of bytes and write it to an *XmlTextWriter* object as BinHex or base64 code, as shown here:

```
// Save the bitmap to a memory stream
MemoryStream ms = new MemoryStream();
bmp.Save(ms, ImageFormat.Jpeg);
```

```
int size = (int) ms.Length;

// Read back the bytes of the image
byte[] img = new byte[size];
img = ms.GetBuffer();
ms.Close();
```

The preceding code snippet converts the instance of the *Bitmap* object that contains the bar chart to an array of bytes—the *img* variable—that represents the JPEG version of the bitmap.

As the final step, you encode the bytes as BinHex (or base64, if you prefer) and write them to an XML stream, as shown here:

```
// Prepare the writer
StringWriter buf = new StringWriter();
XmlTextWriter xmlw = new XmlTextWriter(buf);
xmlw.Formatting = Formatting.Indented;

// Write the XML document
xmlw.WriteStartDocument();
xmlw.WriteComment("Sales report for " + m_Year.ToString());
xmlw.WriteStartElement("jpeg");
xmlw.WriteAttributeString("Size", size.ToString());
xmlw.WriteBinHex(img, 0, size);
xmlw.WriteEndElement();
xmlw.WriteEndDocument();

// Extract the string and close the writer
string tmp = buf.ToString();
xmlw.Close();
buf.Close();
```

The *XmlTextWriter* object is still a stream-based component that needs a destination to write to. Unlike the *Bitmap* object, however, the *XmlTextWriter* object can be forced to write the output to a string. To do that, you initialize the XML text writer with an instance of the *StringWriter* object. The final string with the XML code can be obtained with a call to the *StringWriter* object's *ToString* method.

The format of the XML text returned is shown here:

```
<?xml version="1.0" encoding="utf-16" ?>
<!-- Sales report for 1997 -->
<jpeg Size="20146">
  FFD8FF...E00010
</jpeg>
```

Notice that the comment and the size of the file are strictly call-specific parameters. The *Size* attribute refers to the size of the BinHex-encoded text. As you'd expect, this value is significantly larger than JPEG size. Having that value available is not strictly necessary, but once it's on the client, it can simplify the task of transforming the XML stream back into a JPEG image.

StringWriter and Unicode Encoding

The XML output generated by the *GetSalesReportBarChart* method uses the Unicode encoding scheme—UTF-16—instead of the default UTF-8. This would be fine if not for the fact that Microsoft Internet Explorer returns an error when you double-click the XML file. The error has nothing to do with the XML itself; it is more a bug (or perhaps even a feature) of Internet Explorer and the internal style sheet Internet Explorer uses to display XML documents.

In general, UTF-16 is used whenever you write XML text to a *StringWriter* object. When a *TextWriter* object (*StringWriter* inherits from *TextWriter*) is passed to the *XmlTextWriter* constructor, no explicit encoding argument is allowed. In this case, the *XmlTextWriter* object transparently inherits the encoding set contained in the writer object being passed. The *StringWriter* class hard-codes its *Encoding* property to UTF-16—there's no way for you to change it, because the property is marked as read-only. If you want to generate XML strings with an encoding scheme other than UTF-16, drop *StringWriter* objects in favor of memory streams.

The helper class shared by the remotable object and the Web service is now ready to use. Let's look more closely at the remote service component.

Writing the Remote Service Component

As mentioned, a remotable component has just one requirement: the class that represents the object must be inherited from *MarshalByRefObject*. Unless you need to exercise stricter control over the object lifetime, you don't need to override any of the methods defined in the base class for MBR objects.

Apart from the parent class, a remotable class is not different from any other class in the .NET Framework. All of its public methods are callable by clients, the class can implement any number and any type of interfaces, and the class can reference any other external class.

Because we already put all the core code in the *SalesDataProvider* class, writing the remote service class—*ServiceSalesProvider*—is a snap. The class is a simple wrapper for *SalesDataProvider*, as shown here:

```
public class ServiceSalesProvider : MarshalByRefObject
{
    // Properties
    protected SalesDataProvider m_dataManager;

    // Constructor
    public ServiceSalesProvider()
    {
        m_dataManager = new SalesDataProvider();
    }

    // GetSalesReport
    public DataSet GetSalesReport(int theYear)
    {
        DataSet ds = new DataSet();
        ds.Tables.Add(m_dataManager.GetSalesReport(theYear));
        return ds;
    }

    // GetSalesReportBarChart
    public string GetSalesReportBarChart(int theYear)
    {
        return m_dataManager.GetSalesReportBarChart(theYear);
    }
}
```

The *SalesDataProvider* protected member is initialized only once, when the *ServiceSalesProvider* class instance is constructed. After that, any call to the various methods is resolved using the same instance of the helper class.

The *ServiceSalesProvider* class has two public methods with the same names as the methods in *SalesDataProvider*. The implementation of these methods is straightforward and fairly self-explanatory. The only aspect worth noting is that the remotable *GetSalesReport* method adds the *DataTable* object returned by the corresponding method on the *SalesDataProvider* class to a newly created *DataSet* object. The *DataSet* object is then returned to the caller.

> **Note**   When writing remotable classes, be sure that all the methods use and return serializable classes. No extra steps are required if you decide to write your own, user-defined classes as long as they include *SerializableAttribute* or implement the *ISerializable* interface.

Publishing the Remote Service Component

To be usable in a distributed environment, a remotable class must be configured and exposed so that interested callers can reach it. A remotable object needs a running host application to handle any incoming calls. In addition, the object must specify what protocol, port, and name a potential client must use to issue its calls. All requirements that callers must fulfill are stored in the remote object's configuration file.

The Host Application

The host application can be IIS or a custom program (for example, a console application or a Microsoft Windows NT service) written by the same team that authored the class. Unlike DCOM, the .NET Remoting system does not automatically start up the host application whenever a client call is issued. To minimize network traffic, .NET Remoting assumes that the host application on the server is always up, running, and listening to the specified port. This is not an issue if you choose IIS as the host, as IIS is generally up all the time.

If you use a custom host, you must make sure it is running when a call is issued. A simple, yet effective, host program is shown here:

```
// MyHost.cs -- compiled to MyHost.exe
using System;
using System.Runtime.Remoting;

public class MyHost
{
    public static void Main()
    {
        RemotingConfiguration.Configure("MyHost.exe.config");
        Console.WriteLine("Press Enter to terminate...");
        Console.ReadLine();
    }
}
```

The key statement in the preceding code is this:

```
RemotingConfiguration.Configure("MyHost.exe.config");
```

The host program reads the given configuration file and organizes itself to listen on the specified channels and ports for calls directed to the remote object. The configuration file contains information about the remote class name, the assembly that contains the class, the required activation mode (*Client*, *Singleton*, or *SingleCall*), and, if needed, the object URI. Here is the configuration file that fully describes the *ServiceSalesProvider* class:

```
<configuration>
   <system.runtime.remoting>
      <application>
         <service>
            <wellknown mode="SingleCall"
               type="XmlNet.CS.ServiceSalesProvider, ServiceSalesProvider"
               objectUri="ServiceSalesProvider.rem" />
         </service>
         <channels>
            <channel ref="http" />
         </channels>
      </application>
   </system.runtime.remoting>
</configuration>
```

We'll look more closely at channels and activation modes in a moment. For now, keep in mind that the contents of this configuration file tell the host application (whatever it is) which channels and ports to listen to and the name and the location of the class. In this example, the host application listens to the HTTP channel, and therefore the port must be 80.

Predefined Channels

A *channel* is the element in the .NET Remoting architecture that physically moves bytes from one endpoint to the other. A channel takes a stream of bytes, creates a package according to a particular protocol, and routes the package to the final destination across remoting boundaries. A channel object listens for incoming messages and sends outbound messages. The messages it handles consist of packets written in accordance with a variety of network protocols.

The .NET Framework provides two predefined channels, *tcp* and *http*, both of which are bidirectional and work as senders and receivers. The *tcp* channel uses a binary formatter to serialize data to a binary stream and transport it to the target object using TCP through the specified port. The *http* channel transports messages to and from remote objects using SOAP and always through port 80. A channel can connect two AppDomains in the same process as well as two machines over a network.

An object can legitimately decide to listen on both channels. In this case, the *<channels>* subtree in the configuration file changes as follows:

```
<channels>
  <channel ref="http" />
  <channel ref="tcp" port="3412" />
</channels>
```

A client can select any of the channels registered on the server to communicate with the remote object. At least one channel must be registered with the remoting system on the server.

Using IIS as the Remoting Host

If you write your own host application, you can make it as flexible as you need. If you decide to use IIS as the host, some constraints apply. To use IIS instead of a handcrafted host as the activation agent, you must first create a virtual directory (say, SalesReport) and copy the object's assembly in the BIN subdirectory. The configuration file must have a fixed name—web.config—and must reside in the virtual directory's root, as shown in Figure 12-4.

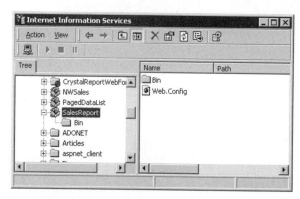

Figure 12-4 The SalesReport virtual directory created to make the remotable object accessible.

If you choose IIS as the activation agent, you must be aware of a few things. IIS can listen only to the *http* channel; any other channel you indicate is simply ignored. The way IIS applies the information read from the web.config file is hard-coded and can't be programmatically controlled or changed. However, you can create a global.asax file in the virtual folder, hook the *Application_Start* event, and then execute some custom code. In addition, the inevitable use of SOAP as the underlying protocol increases the average size of network packets.

> **Note**   As often happens, the use of IIS as the activation agent has pros and cons. You don't need to write any extra code, but you lose a bit in flexibility. Regaining the lost flexibility is still possible, but at the price of writing nontrivial code. For example, you can write an *Application_Start* event handler and apply extra binary formatters at both ends of the *http* channel. In this way, the SOAP packets will contain binary data and you'll save some bytes.

Using IIS as the activation agent is natural when you plan to expose the same remote service through .NET Remoting and Web services. So let's assume in our example application that IIS is the activation agent and SalesReport is the virtual directory.

Activation Policies

In addition to the remotable object's identity, channels, and ports, the server configuration file also contains another important piece of information—the object activation policy. An MBR remotable object can be either *server-activated* or *client-activated*. Server-activated objects are created by the server only when the client invokes the first method through the local proxy. Client-activated objects are created on the server as soon as the client instantiates the object using either the *new* operator or methods of the *System.Activator* class.

In addition, server-activated objects can be declared as *Singleton* or *SingleCall* objects. A *Singleton* object has exactly one instance to serve all possible clients. A *SingleCall* object, on the other hand, requires that each incoming call is served by a new instance of the remotable object. A remotable object declares its required activation policy in the configuration file through specific subtrees placed below the *<application>* node.

Server-Side Activation

Server-activated objects are remotable objects whose entire life cycle is directly controlled by the host application. Server-activated objects are instantiated on the server only when the client calls a method on the object. The object is not instantiated if the client simply calls the *new* operator or the methods of the *System.Activator* object. This policy is slightly more efficient than client-side activation because it saves a network round-trip for the sole purpose of creating an instance of the target object. In addition, this approach makes better use of server memory by delaying as much as possible the object instantiation.

What happens when the client code *apparently* instantiates the remote object? Consider the following client-side sample code:

```
ServiceSalesProvider ssp = new ServiceSalesProvider();
string img = ssp.GetSalesReportBarChart(theYear);
```

The remoting client treats the remote object as a local object and calls the *new* operator on it. The object has been previously registered as a *well-known* type, so the .NET Remoting system knows about it. In particular, the .NET Remoting system knows that any object of type *ServiceSalesProvider* is just a local proxy for a remote object. When the client calls *new* or *System.Activator* on the well-known type, only the remoting proxy is created in the client application domain.

The real instantiation of the object will take place on the server at a later time, when a non-*null* instance is needed to serve the first method call. Because the constructor is called implicitly and outside the control of the client, only the default constructor is supported. This means that if your class has a constructor that takes some arguments, that constructor is never taken into account by the host application and never used to create instances of the remotable class.

> **Note** As part of the .NET Framework reflection API, the *System.Activator* object provides a *CreateInstance* method that you can use to create instances of dynamically determined types. (Instantiating types this way is a kind of .NET Framework late binding.) Interestingly, this method supports a nice feature that would have fit well in the .NET Remoting system too (and hopefully will in a future version). The *CreateInstance* method has an overload that takes an array of *object* objects. It then uses the size of the array and the actual types boxed in the various objects to match one of the constructors declared on the target type. However, maybe for performance concerns or perhaps just to simplify the feature, the .NET Remoting infrastructure does not supply this facility.

If you need to publish a remotable type whose instances must be created using a specific, nondefault constructor, you should resort to client activation.

Well-Known Objects

From the perspective of a .NET Remoting client, server-activated objects are said to be well-known objects. Well-known objects have two possible working modes: *Singleton* and *SingleCall*. In the former case, one instance of the object services all calls from all clients. In the latter case, a new instance of the object is created to service each call.

A well-known object declares its working mode using the *<wellknown>* tag in the configuration file under the *<service>* tag, as shown here:

```
<service>
  <wellknown mode="SingleCall"
    type="XmlNet.CS.ServiceSalesProvider, ServiceSalesProvider"
    objectUri="ServiceSalesProvider.rem" />
</service>
```

The *mode* attribute specifies the working mode of the well-known object. Allowed values are *Singleton* and *SingleCall*, defined in the *WellKnownObject-Mode* enumeration. The *type* attribute contains two pieces of information. It is a comma-separated string in which the first token represents the fully qualified name of the remotable type and the second part of the string points to the assembly in which the remotable type is defined. You must use the display name of the assembly without the DLL extension. The assembly must be located either in the global assembly cache (GAC) or on the server in a location that the host application can reach.

If the host application is a normal console application or a Windows NT service, the directory of the application's executable is a safe place to store the remotable type's assembly. Similarly, you can store the assembly in any other path for which the host application is configured to probe when searching for assemblies. If you use IIS as the activation agent, all the assemblies needed for the remotable type must be located in the BIN directory of the host application.

Giving Well-Known Types a URI

A well-known type also needs to be identified by a unique URI. The URI must be unique for the type and not for the object. This name represents remote objects of a certain type and is the means by which the client gets a proxy pointing to the specified object. The server-side remoting infrastructure maintains a list of all published well-known objects, and the object URI is the key to access this internal table. Well-known objects must explicitly indicate the URI. For client-activated objects, a unique URI is transparently generated (and used) for a particular instance of the class.

When an object is hosted in IIS, the *objectUri* name must have a .soap or .rem extension, as shown in Figure 12-5. This naming convention enables IIS to recognize the incoming call as a remoting request that must be routed to a particular handler.

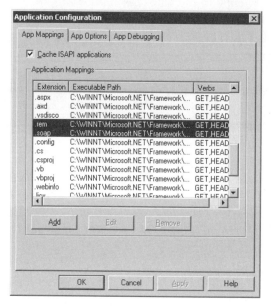

Figure 12-5   The IIS application mapping table for .rem and .soap URIs.

When IIS detects a remoting call, it passes the call to the ad hoc HTTP handler registered to handle .soap and .rem resources. Although the object URI gives the impression of being a URL—that is, a true server-side resource—it is only a name and should in no way correspond to a physical file. Whether the URI should be a string or the name of a physical resource depends on the expectations of the handler. The remoting handler uses .soap and .rem URIs as strings to retrieve the proxy for the type.

Singleton Objects

When an object declares itself as a *Singleton* type, the host application uses only a single instance of the object to service all incoming calls. So when a call arrives, the host attempts to locate the running instance of the object. If such an instance exists, the request for execution is processed. Otherwise, the host creates the unique instance of the remote class (using the default constructor) and forwards the request to it.

What happens if two requests arrive at the same time? The .NET Remoting subsystem arranges for them to be automatically serviced by distinct threads.

This requires that *Singleton* objects be thread-safe. Note that this is not a mandatory programming rule but is more of a practical guideline for real-world scenarios.

State management for *Singleton* objects is certainly possible in theory, but it must be coded in the body of the object in much the same way as you do with Active Server Pages (ASP) and Microsoft ASP.NET pages and even Web services. The idea is that you use a shared cache that all clients can access (a sort of ASP.NET *Application* object), unless you apply a filter on a per-client basis (a sort of ASP.NET *Session* object).

The lifetime of a *Singleton* well-known object is managed by the .NET Remoting system through a special module called the *lease manager* (LM). (See the section "Memory Management," on page 551, for more information.)

SingleCall Objects

A well-known type declared as a *SingleCall* object has a new instance of it created whenever a request arrives. The host application creates a new instance of the *SingleCall* object, executes the requested method, and then routes any return values back to the client. After that, the object goes out of scope and is left to the garbage collector.

Although it's not completely impossible, preserving state from one call to the next is realistically a bit impractical for *SingleCall* objects. In this case, the lifetime of the object instance is extremely short and barely covers the duration of the method call. You can try either storing information in a database (or any sort of persistent storage medium) or parking data in other objects with a different lifetime scheme.

Client-Side Activation

Client-activated objects are instantiated on the client as the result of a call to the *new* operator or to the *System.Activator* object. Each remoting client runs its own copy of the object and can control it at will. For example, the client can use any of the available constructors. In addition, persisting the state during the session is straightforward and does not require any special coding. On the down side, sharing state between clients is difficult, and to do so, you must resort to a database, a disk file, or any other global object in the current App-Domain.

The following code snippet shows how to change the contents of the *<service>* tag to reflect a client-activated object. Instead of the *<wellknown>* tag, you use the *<activated>* tag. This tag supports only the type attribute. No object URI is necessary with client-activated objects. More precisely, the URI is still necessary, but because the activation occurs on the client and at a very specific moment in time, the URI can be silently generated by the .NET Remoting infra-structure and attached to each call.

```
<service>
  <activated
    type="XmlNet.CS.ServiceSalesProvider, ServiceSalesProvider" />
</service>
```

As with *Singleton* objects, the lifetime of a client-activated object is con-trolled by the LM. The instance of the object remains active until the proxy is destroyed.

Choosing the Activation Mode That Fits

Theoretically, all the working modes examined up to now don't affect in any shape or fashion the way in which you code your remotable classes. For exam-ple, a client-activated object is in no way different from a *Singleton* object. All options can be set declaratively and, again speaking theoretically, each object can be configured to work in different ways simply by changing a few entries in the server's configuration file.

Intriguing as this possibility is, such flexibility is not realistic in practice because a real-world object might want to exploit in depth the specific features of a working mode. In other words, you should thoughtfully and carefully choose the configuration options for your remote object and then stick to that configuration as long as the user's requirements are stable. For example, if you determine that the *Singleton* mode is appropriate for your component, you will probably want to implement an internal state management engine to share some variables. When at a later time you decide to set the object to work—say, in *SingleCall* mode—the state management engine is somewhat useless.

Let's analyze our *ServiceSalesProvider* class to determine the most appro-priate options. To begin, the object needs to query a back-end database (North-wind). Even this little requirement is enough to lead us to discard the option of making the object available by value. As an MBR object, the remotable class can be client-activated or server-activated. What's better to us?

The *ServiceSalesProvider* class doesn't need a nondefault constructor, so both client-activated and server-activated modes are fine. The object is expected to work as a one-off service and has no need to maintain per-client state, so you can discard the client-activated option and go for the server-driven activation. OK, but should you opt for *Singleton* or *SingleCall*?

SingleCall—that is, a short-lived instance that serves the request and dies—is certainly an option. If you use the object as a *Singleton*, however, you can architect slightly more efficient code and avoid having to query SQL Server each and every time a request comes in. The remoting code included in this book's sample files makes use of the *ServiceSalesProvider* class configured to run as a *SingleCall* object.

Memory Management

SingleCall objects present no problems in terms of memory management. They require a new object instance that is extremely volatile and does not survive the end of the method's code. *Singleton* and client-activated objects, on the other hand, need a mechanism to determine when they can be safely destroyed. In COM, this issue was resolved by implementing reference counting. In the .NET Remoting system, the same tasks are accomplished using a new module: the LM.

Unlike reference counting, the LM works on a per-AppDomain basis and allows objects to be released even though clients still hold a reference. Let's quickly review the differences between these two approaches.

Old-Fashioned Reference Counting

Reference counting requires clients—including, of course, distributed and remote clients—to communicate with the server each time they connect or disconnect. The object maintains the number of currently active client instances, and when the count goes to 0, the object destroys itself.

In the presence of an unreliable network, however, chances are good that some objects might remain with a reference count that never goes to 0. If this weren't bad enough, the continual sequence of *AddRef/Release* calls would generate significant network traffic.

The Lease Manager (LM)

The idea behind leasing is that each object instance is leased to the client for a given amount of time fixed by the LM. The lease starts when the object is created. By default, each *Singleton* or client-activated object is given 5 minutes to process incoming calls. When the interval ends, the object is marked for deletion. During the object's lifetime, however, any processed client call resets the lease time to a fixed value (by default, 2 minutes), thus increasing or decreasing the overall lease time.

Note that leasing is managed exclusively on the server and doesn't require additional network traffic, apart from the traffic needed for normal method execution. The initial lease time and the renewal period can be set both programmatically and declaratively in the configuration file.

Getting a Sponsor

Another mechanism for controlling an object's lifetime is *sponsorship*. Both clients and server objects can register with the AppDomain's LM to act as sponsors of a particular object. Prior to marking an object for deletion when its lease expires, the .NET Remoting run time gives sponsors a chance to renew the lease. By implementing sponsors, you can control the lifetime of objects based on logical criteria rather than strict time intervals.

In summary, nothing can guarantee that clients will always find their server objects up and running. When a remoting client attempts to access an object that is no longer available, a *RemotingException* exception is thrown. One way to resolve the exception is by creating a new instance of the remote object and repeating the operation that failed.

Calling a Remote Service

Let's see what a client must do to call a method on a remote object. To begin, add a project reference to the assembly that contains the remote object by right-clicking References in Solution Explorer, choosing Add Reference from the shortcut menu, and traversing the network to locate the target assembly. The project reference lets the client application know about the types defined in the assembly.

> **Note**   Even if your remotable object is hosted by IIS, when you reference the assembly from a remoting client, choose the Add Reference option. The Add Web Reference command on the same shortcut menu is reserved for Web services and, more importantly, starts a completely different linking procedure. (More on this in Chapter 13.)

Referencing a remote assembly is only the first step to being able to call any of its methods.

Configuring the Caller

The remote object must be registered with the local application before you can successfully use it. The .NET Remoting system must be aware that objects of certain types represent instances of remote objects. In this way, ad hoc code can be generated to obtain the necessary proxy.

You configure the client application either through a configuration file or programmatically by calling the *RegisterWellKnownClientType* method on the static *RemotingConfiguration* object, as shown here:

```
RemotingConfiguration.RegisterWellKnownClientType(
    typeof(ServiceSalesProvider),
    "http://www.contoso.com/SalesReport/ServiceSalesProvider.rem");
```

To register a well-known type, you pass in the type and object URI. If the object is not server-activated, and therefore is not a well-known object, you use the *RegisterActivatedClientType* instead, as follows:

```
RemotingConfiguration.RegisterActivatedClientType(
    typeof(ServiceSalesProvider),
    "http://www.contoso.com/SalesReport");
```

In this case, you don't need to pass an explicit object URI. However, you still need to indicate the remote path for the target object. Because we are working with IIS as the host, the remote path must be the URL of the virtual directory. If a custom host is used, instead of the URL, you use a TCP address and the port, as shown here:

```
RemotingConfiguration.RegisterActivatedClientType(
    typeof(ServiceSalesProvider),
    "tcp://192.345.34.1:8082");
```

You can also direct the caller application to read setup information from a configuration file located in the same path as the executable. In this case, the convention is to give the file the same name as the executable plus a .config extension. You then pass the file name to the *Configure* method, as shown here:

```
RemotingConfiguration.Configure("MyClient.exe.config");
```

The following script shows the layout of a client configuration file:

```
<configuration>
  <system.runtime.remoting>
    <application name="MyClient" >
      <client>
        <wellknown
          type="XmlNet.CS.ServiceSalesProvider, ServiceSalesProvider"
          url="http://server/SalesReport/ServiceSalesProvider.rem" />
      </client>
      <channels>
        <channel ref="http" />
      </channels>
    </application>
  </system.runtime.remoting>
</configuration>
```

As you can see, the differences between the client and the server-side configuration files are minimal and are all related to the use of the *<client>* tag instead of *<service>*.

The server object publishes the list of supported channels, and based on that list, the client can decide which channel to use. Note that servers must register at least one channel. Clients are not required to indicate a channel. If a client doesn't indicate a channel, the .NET Remoting system uses one of the default channels. On the other hand, a client that plans to use a given channel must first register with it. The application can run the channel registration procedure personally or let it run by default under the control of the *RemotingConfiguration* object.

Channels are registered on a per-AppDomain basis and must have unique names in that context. On physical machines, however, only one channel can listen to a given port. In other words, at any time you can't have more than one channel registered to work on a given port on a given machine.

A client enabled to make remote calls on a remote object simply creates an instance of the desired class using the language-specific operator for instantiation—*new* in C# and Visual Basic. Alternatively, the client can use the *System.Activator* object—a managed counterpart of the VBScript *CreateObject* and *GetObject* functions.

Writing the Client Component

Figure 12-6 shows the initial user interface of the client application we'll use to query for sales reports and bar charts. You select the year of interest and click one of the two buttons—Get Data to display sales information as a *DataSet* object, or Get Chart to display the information as a bar chart saved as a JPEG image. The form contains a *DataGrid* control (invisible by default) and a *PictureBox* control. Needless to say, the *DataGrid* object will display the contents of the *DataSet* object, whereas the *PictureBox* object will show the image.

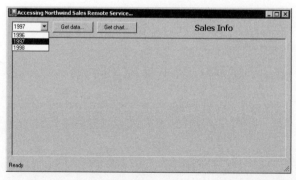

Figure 12-6   The sample application in action, waiting for user input.

Accessing the Raw Data

Once the remote assembly has been referenced by the project and the remote type configured in the form's *Load* event, you can write the client application and use the remote type as if it were a local type. The following code shows what happens when you click to get raw data:

```
private void ButtonGetData_Click(object sender, System.EventArgs e)
{
    // Get the year to process
    int theYear = Convert.ToInt32(Years.Text);

    // Instantiate the object and issue the call
    ServiceSalesProvider ssp = new ServiceSalesProvider();
    DataSet ds = ssp.GetSalesReport(theYear);

    // Turn on and fill the DataGrid control
    // Also and turn off the picture box
    PictureContainer.Visible = false;
    Data.Visible = true;
    Data.DataSource = ds.Tables[0];

    // Update the UI
    Title.Text = "Sales Report for " + theYear.ToString();
}
```

The code in boldface demonstrates that, at this point, using the remote object is in no way different from using any other local, or system, class.

Figure 12-7 shows the sales information displayed in *DataSet* format.

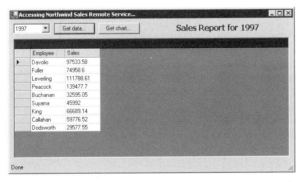

Figure 12-7   The sample application displaying downloaded sales data in *DataSet* format.

Accessing BinHex-Encoded Images

Calling the *GetSalesReportBarChart* method is not all that different from calling the *GetSalesReport* method, but more work is needed to make the downloaded data usable. As mentioned, the *GetSalesReportBarChart* method draws a bar chart, converts it to JPEG, encodes the image as a BinHex string, and packs everything into an XML document. The content of the document is then returned as a string, as shown here:

```
ServiceSalesProvider ssp = new ServiceSalesProvider();
string encImage = ssp.GetSalesReportBarChart(theYear);
```

The next step is transforming the string into a bitmap and displaying it in the *PictureBox* control. The following procedure takes the BinHex image description and creates an equivalent *Bitmap* object. Because the string is an XML document, an *XmlTextReader* object is needed to parse the contents and then decode the BinHex data.

```
private Bitmap EncodedXmlToBitmap(string encImage)
{
    Bitmap bmp = null;

    // Parse the XML data using a string reader
    StringReader buf = new StringReader(encImage);
    XmlTextReader reader = new XmlTextReader(buf);
    reader.Read();
    reader.MoveToContent();

    // The root node of the document is <jpeg>
    if (reader.LocalName == "jpeg")
    {
        // Get the size of the BinHex data
        int encodedSize = Convert.ToInt32(reader["Size"].ToString());

        // Read and decode the BinHex data
        byte[] img = new byte[encodedSize];
        reader.ReadBinHex(img, 0, encodedSize);

        // Transform the just read bytes into an Image object
        MemoryStream ms = new MemoryStream();
        ms.Write(img, 0, img.Length);
        bmp = new Bitmap(ms);
        ms.Close();

        reader.Close();
        return bmp;
    }
}
```

You decode the image data using the *ReadBinHex* method on the *XmlTextReader* class. Next you copy the resultant array of bytes into a temporary memory stream. This step is necessary because a *Bitmap* object can't be created directly from an array of bytes.

Finally, the returned *Bitmap* object is bound to the *PictureBox* control in the form, as shown in the following code:

```
PictureContainer.SizeMode = PictureBoxSizeMode.StretchImage;
PictureContainer.Image = bmp;
```

Figure 12-8 shows the results.

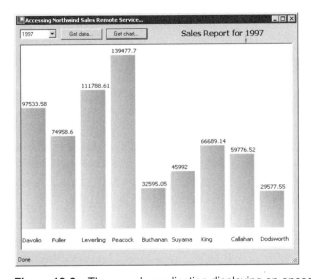

Figure 12-8   The sample application displaying an encoded bar chart.

The client can easily create a local copy of the JPEG file. The following code snippet shows how to proceed:

```
// img is the array of bytes obtained from ReadBinHex
FileStream fs = new FileStream(fileName, FileMode.Create);
BinaryWriter writer = new BinaryWriter(fs);
writer.Write(img);
writer.Close();
```

> **Tip**   When converting a *Bitmap* object to JPEG, you can control the compression ratio to obtain a better image. However, JPEG is not a compression scheme designed for text and simple figures like bar charts. In fact, JPEG was originally designed to effectively compress photographic images. To ensure a better image, you might want to use the GIF format or control the compression ratio of the final JPEG image. You can do that by using one of the overloads of the *Bitmap* object's *Save* method.

Using the *System.Activator* Class

A remoting client can obtain a proxy to make calls to a remote object in two ways: by using the *new* operator or by using methods of the *System.Activator* class. The *Activator* class provides two methods—*CreateInstance* and *GetObject*. Clients of well-known objects use *GetObject*, whereas clients of client-activated objects use *CreateInstance*.

GetObject returns a proxy for the well-known type served at the specified URL location, as shown in the following code. *GetObject* is a wrapper placed around the global *RemotingServices.Connect* method. The proxy is built on the client from the remote object metadata and exposed to the client application as the original type.

```
ServiceSalesProvider ssp;
ssp = (ServiceSalesProvider) Activator.GetObject(
    typeof(ServiceSalesProvider),
    "http://www.contoso.com/SalesReport");
```

From this relatively simple explanation, it should be clear that .NET Remoting is no less quirky than DCOM, but unlike DCOM, the .NET Framework successfully hides a great wealth of low-level details.

CreateInstance differs from *GetObject* in that it actually creates a new remote instance of the object, as shown here:

```
// Set the URL of the remote object
object[1] attribs;
attribs[0] = new Activation.UrlAttribute(url);

// Create the instance of the object
ServiceSalesProvider ssp;
ssp = (ServiceSalesProvider) Activator.CreateInstance(
    typeof(ServiceSalesProvider), null, attribs);
```

Conclusion

The .NET Remoting system enables you to access .NET Framework objects across the boundaries of AppDomains. It represents the actual implementation of a programming model designed for interprocess communication. Another facet of this model is .NET XML Web services. Although .NET XML Web services allow you to expose .NET Framework objects to any client that can use HTTP, .NET Remoting is optimized for .NET-to-.NET communication. Communication between the client and the remotable object can take place using SOAP or binary payloads transported over HTTP or TCP. .NET Remoting can transfer any serializable CLR types; it is not limited to XML Schema Definition (XSD) types or complex custom types as rendered by the .NET XML serializer.

This chapter illustrated the key features of the .NET Remoting system and showed you how to set up a remotable object that exposes nontrivial functionalities. In particular, you learned how to expose JPEG images through XML documents. Of course, if the goal of your distributed system is simply to create and return dynamic images, .NET Remoting might not be for you. But from a broader standpoint that encompasses Web services, .NET Remoting not only makes sense, it is also compelling. The example we've constructed in this chapter has two aims. First, it demonstrates that .NET Remoting and Web services are just two remoting interfaces and that the same core class can outfit both. Second, it shows that to come up with truly efficient and effective code, you must always take the most appropriate route and create specialized code instead of pursuing the promises of code universality and platform independence.

This chapter covered only the first side of remoting—.NET Remoting for CLR types. In Chapter 13, we'll look at Web services—a truly interoperable infrastructure ideal for rolling up your functionalities and making them available to a potentially infinite set of clients.

Further Reading

Although this chapter touched on all the key aspects of the .NET Remoting technology, it revealed only the tip of the iceberg. Throughout the chapter, I've noted several aspects of .NET Remoting whose coverage was simply beyond the scope of a book about XML. Principal among the resources that cover these topics in more detail is the MSDN .NET Framework documentation, but many other appropriate resources are also available.

I mentioned that Windows XP and newer systems boast a modified loader that looks directly into the source Portable Executable (PE) file to find .NET Framework–specific metadata. To understand the entire loading process of managed executables in Windows XP as well as in Windows 2000, I know just one resource: Jeffrey Richter's excellent book *Applied Microsoft .NET Framework Programming* (Microsoft Press, 2002).

In the October 2002 issue of MSDN Magazine, you can find an article of mine that, like this chapter, attempts to explain the ABCs of .NET Remoting. In that article, you'll find a deeper discussion of architectural aspects—channels, formatters, and sink chains—than we've covered here.

The internal engine that performs memory management for instances of remote objects is the lease manager (LM). Jeff Prosise, in Chapter 15 of his book *Programming Microsoft .NET* (Microsoft Press, 2002), explains a lot about it.

Finally, if you're just looking for a complete .NET Remoting book, here it is: *Microsoft .NET Remoting*, by Scott McLean, James Naftel, and Kim Williams (Microsoft Press, 2002).

13

XML Web Services

The term *Web service* is relatively new, but the idea behind Web services has been around for a while. A Web service is an interface-less Web site designed for programmatic access. This means that instead of invoking URLs representing Web pages, you invoke URLs that represent methods on remote objects. Similarly, instead of getting back colorful and animated HTML code, you get back XML Schema Definition (XSD) data types packed in XML messages. Aside from these higher-level differences, the underlying models for a Web site and a Web service are the same. In addition, any security measure you can implement on a Web site can be duplicated in a Web service. To summarize, the Web service model is just another programming model running on top of HTTP.

A Web service is a software application that can be accessed over the Web by other software. Web services are applicable in any type of Web environment, be it Internet, intranet, or extranet. All you need to locate and access a Web service is a URL. In theory, a number of Internet-friendly protocols might be working through that URL. In practice, the protocol for everyday use of Web services is always HTTP.

How is a Web service different from a remote procedure call (RPC) implementation of distributed interfaces? For the most part, a Web service is an RPC mechanism that uses the Simple Object Access Protocol (SOAP) to support data interchange. This general definition represents the gist of a Web service, but it focuses only on the core behavior. A Web service is more than just a business object available over an HTTP-accessible network. A number of evolving industry standards are supported today, including the Universal Description, Discovery, and Integration (UDDI) standard and the Web Services Description Language (WSDL); others, such as the Web Services Security (WS-Security) and the Global XML Web Services Architecture (GXA), will be supported soon. These industry standards contribute to setting up a full and powerful environment for remote object-oriented access and programming.

In this chapter, we'll look at implementing and programming Web services in the Microsoft .NET Framework. We'll also take a look at the Web infrastructure that makes these services available and at the functionalities you can obtain and publish. To demonstrate the breakthrough that Web services represent in the software industry, we'll rewrite the .NET Remoting code example from Chapter 12 to make it work as a Web service. In doing so, we'll also be able to examine the differences between the .NET Remoting and Web service architectures and determine in which scenarios each architecture is suitable.

The .NET Framework Infrastructure for Web Services

Although Web services and the .NET Framework were introduced at roughly the same time, there is no strict dependency between the two, and the presence of one does not necessarily imply the presence of the other. The .NET Framework is simply one of the platforms that support Web services and that provide effective tools and system classes to create and consume Web services. No one person invented Web services, but all the big players in the IT arena are rapidly adopting and transforming the raw idea of "software callable by other software" into something that fits their respective development platforms.

Regardless of how a Web service is created—and whether it is vendor-specific or platform-specific—the way in which a Web service is exposed to the public is the same. Any Web service can be imported and incorporated into vendor-specific and platform-specific solutions, as long as the service adheres to accepted standards, like HTTP, SOAP, and WSDL, to name a few. Web services guarantee interoperability because they are based entirely on open standards. By rolling your functionalities into a Web service, you can expose them to anyone on the Web who speaks HTTP and understands XML. Of course, for this to happen, some infrastructure that deals with Web communication and data transportation is still required. No worries, though—this is just what the major IT players are building into their development platforms.

The primary factor in industry-wide adoption of Web services is SOAP. Although it is a bit verbose, SOAP offers a standard way to define the method to call and the arguments to pass. In addition, SOAP exploits a standard, rich, and extensible type system—the XSD type system. In the .NET Framework, the XSD type system is extended with a set of .NET Framework classes—the classes that the XML serializer can handle. (Chapter 11 covers the XML serializer in detail.)

> **Note**   Web service clients are not forced to use SOAP as the protocol for issuing their calls. HTTP-GET and HTTP-POST are effective as well, and even more compact if you look at the size of the individual payload. SOAP is not a stand-alone protocol; it simply defines the XML vocabulary used to express method invocations. The SOAP payload does need a transportation protocol, however, and usually, SOAP packets travel over HTTP-POST commands.

The Simple Object Access Protocol (SOAP)

SOAP is a simple, lightweight XML-based protocol for exchanging information on the Web. SOAP defines a messaging framework that is independent from any application or transportation protocol. Although, as mentioned, SOAP packets travel mostly as HTTP-POST commands, SOAP neither mandates nor excludes any network and transportation protocol.

The most important part of the SOAP specification consists of an envelope for encapsulating data. The SOAP envelope defines a one-way message and is the atomic unit of exchange between SOAP senders and receivers. The SOAP specification also needs a request/response message exchange pattern, although it does not mandate a specific message pattern. The remaining, optional parts of the SOAP specification are data encoding rules for representing application-defined data types and a binding between SOAP and HTTP.

> **Note**   Although SOAP is often associated with HTTP alone, it has been designed according to general principles so that you can use SOAP in combination with any transportation protocol or mechanism that is able to transport the SOAP envelope, including SMTP and FTP.

The following code shows a simple SOAP envelope that invokes a *GetSalesReport* method on the specified Web server:

```
POST /salesreport/SalesReportService.asmx HTTP/1.1
Host: expo-star
Content-Type: text/xml; charset=utf-8
Content-Length: length
SOAPAction: "xmlnet/cs/0735618011/GetSalesReport"
```

(continued)

```
<?xml version="1.0" encoding="utf-8"?>
<soap:Envelope xmlns:xsi="http://www.w3.org/2001/XMLSchema-instance"
    xmlns:xsd="http://www.w3.org/2001/XMLSchema"
    xmlns:soap="http://schemas.xmlsoap.org/soap/envelope/">
  <soap:Body>
    <GetSalesReport xmlns="xmlnet/cs/0735618011">
      <theYear>int</theYear>
    </GetSalesReport>
  </soap:Body>
</soap:Envelope>
```

SOAP is not magic—it is a simple XML-based, message-based protocol whose packets normally travel over HTTP. The Web server must have a special listener ready to catch incoming calls on port 80. These listeners are integrated with the Web servers, as is the case with Internet Information Services (IIS).

IIS Support

A .NET Framework Web service is a Microsoft ASP.NET application with an .asmx extension that is accessed over HTTP. ASP.NET, as a whole, is part of the .NET Framework that works on top of IIS, taking care of files with special extensions such as .aspx and .asmx. One of the key components of the ASP.NET infrastructure is the Internet Server Application Programming Interface (ISAPI) filter that IIS involves when it gets a call for files with a certain extension. For example, Figure 13-1 shows the settings in the IIS Configuration Manager that associate .asmx files with a system module named aspnet_isapi.dll.

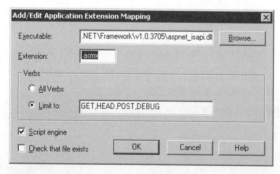

Figure 13-1   The IIS mapping between .asmx files and the appropriate ASP.NET ISAPI filter.

As mentioned, calls for Web services always come through port 80. For .NET Framework Web services, such calls are always directed to URLs with an .asmx extension. IIS intercepts these calls and passes all the related packets on to the registered ASP.NET ISAPI filter (aspnet_isapi.dll). The filter connects to a worker process named aspnet_wp.exe, which implements the HTTP pipeline that ASP.NET uses to process Web requests. Both executables are made of ordinary Win32 code. The ASP.NET layer built atop IIS is shown in Figure 13-2.

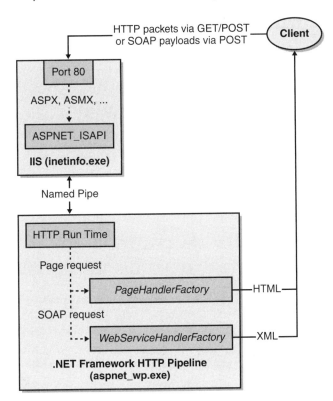

Figure 13-2   The ASP.NET architecture to process page and Web service requests.

The connection between the IIS process (the executable named inetinfo.exe) and the HTTP pipeline (the worker executable named aspnet_wp.exe) is established through a named pipe—that is, a Win32 mechanism for transferring data over a network. As you'd expect, a named pipe works just like a pipe: you enter data in one end, and the same data comes out at the other end. Pipes can be established both locally to connect processes and between remote machines.

After the ASP.NET worker process receives a request, it routes that request through the .NET Framework HTTP pipeline. The entry point of the pipeline is the *HttpRuntime* class. This class is responsible for packaging the HTTP context for the request, which is nothing more than familiar Active Server Pages (ASP) objects such as *Request, Response, Server,* and the like. These objects are packed into an instance of the *HttpContext* class, and then a .NET Framework application is started.

The *WebService* Class

In the .NET Framework, a Web service is an ordinary class with public and protected methods. The Web service class is normally placed in a source file that is saved with an .asmx extension. Web service files must contain the @ *WebService* directive that informs the ASP.NET run time about the nature of the file, the language in use throughout, and the main class that implements the service, as shown here:

```
<%@ WebService Language="C#" Class="MyWebServiceClass" %>
```

The *Language* attribute can be set to C#, VB, or JS. The main class must match the name declared in the *Class* attribute and must be public, as shown here:

```
public class MyWebService : WebService
{
    ⋮
}
```

Indicating the base class for a .NET Framework Web service is not mandatory. A Web service can also be architected starting from the ground up using a new class. Inheriting the behavior of the *WebService* class has some advantages, however. A Web service based on the *System.Web.Services.WebService* class has direct access to common ASP.NET objects, including *Application*, *Request*, *Cache*, *Session*, and *Server*. These objects are packed into an *HttpContext* object, which also includes the time when the request was made. If you don't have any need to access the ASP.NET object model, you can do without the *WebService* class and simply implement the Web service as a class with public methods. With the *WebService* base class, however, a Web service also has access to the ASP.NET server *User* object, which can be used to verify the credentials of the current user executing the method.

> **Note**   The *Class* attribute is normally set to a class residing in the same file as the @ *WebService* directive, but nothing prevents you from specifying a class within a separate assembly. In such cases, the entire Web service file consists of a single line of code:
>
> ```
> <%@ WebService Language="C#" Class="MyWebService,MyAssembly" %>
> ```
>
> The actual implementation is contained in the specified class, and the assembly that contains the class must be placed in the Bin subdirectory of the virtual folder where the Web service resides.

The @ *WebService* directive supports two additional attributes: *Debug* and *CodeBehind*. The former is a Boolean property that indicates whether the Web service should be compiled with debug symbols. The latter specifies the source file that contains the class implementing the Web service when the class is neither located in the same file nor resident in a separate assembly.

The *WebService* Attribute

The *WebService* attribute is optional and does not affect the activity of the Web service class in terms of what is published and executed. The *WebService* attribute is represented by an instance of the *WebServiceAttribute* class and enables you to change three default settings for the Web service: the namespace, the name, and the description.

The syntax for configuring the *WebService* attribute is declarative and somewhat self-explanatory. Within the body of the *WebService* attribute, you simply insert a comma-separated list of names and values, as shown in the following code. The keyword *Description* identifies the description of the Web service, whereas *Name* points to the official name of the Web service.

```
[WebService(
    Name="Northwind Sales Report Web Service",
    Description="The Northwind Sales Report Web Service")]
public class SalesReportWebService : WebService
{
    ⋮
}
```

Changing the name and description of the Web service is mostly a matter of consistency. The .NET Framework assumes that the name of the implementing class is also the name of the Web service; no default description is provided. The *Name* attribute is used to identify the service in the WSDL text that explains the behavior of the service to prospective clients. The description is not used in the companion WSDL text; it is retrieved and displayed by the IIS default page only for URLs with an .asmx extension.

Changing the Default Namespace

Each Web service should have a unique namespace that makes it clearly distinguishable from other services. By default, the .NET Framework gives each new Web service the same default namespace: *http://tempuri.org*. This namespace comes with the strong recommendation to change it as soon as possible and certainly prior to publishing the service on the Web.

> **Note**   Using a temporary name does not affect the overall functional-
> ity, but it will affect consistency and violate Web service naming con-
> ventions. Although most namespace names out there look like URLs,
> you don't need to use real URLs. A name that you're reasonably cer-
> tain is unique will suffice.

The only way to change the default namespace of a .NET Framework Web service is by setting the *Namespace* property of the *WebService* attribute, as shown in following code. This example uses a custom path that merges the namespace of the class providing the sample service with the ISBN of this book.

```
[WebService(
    Namespace="xmlnet/cs/0735618011",
    Name="Northwind Sales Report Web Service",
    Description="The Northwind Sales Report Web Service")]
```

The namespace information is used extensively in the WSDL definition of the Web service.

Building a .NET Web Service

As mentioned, a Web service is a class that optionally inherits from *WebService*. As such, the class can implement any number of interfaces and, as long as you don't need to directly access common ASP.NET objects, can also inherit from any other .NET Framework or user-defined class. The definition of the class must necessarily be coded in an .asmx file. The file is made available to poten-tial clients through a Web server virtual directory and is accessed through a URL. Any client that can issue HTTP commands can connect to the Web service unless security settings restrict the client's access to the service.

What happens after a client points to the URL is the focus of the rest of this chapter. Let's start by analyzing the internal structure of the Web service class.

Exposing Web Methods

Unlike the .NET Framework remotable classes described in Chapter 12, in a Web service class, public methods are not automatically exposed to the pub-lic. To be effectively exposed over the Web, a Web service method requires a special attribute in addition to being declared as public. Only methods marked with the *WebMethod* attribute gain the level of visibility sufficient to make them available over the Web.

The *WebMethod* Attribute

In practice, the *WebMethod* attribute represents a member modifier similar to *public, protected,* or *internal.* Only public methods are affected by *WebMethod,* and the attribute is effective only to callers invoking the class over the Web. This characteristic increases the overall flexibility of the class design. A software component allowed to instantiate the Web service class sees all the public methods and does not necessarily recognize the service as a Web service. However, when the same component is invoked as part of a Web service, the IIS and ASP.NET infrastructure ensure that external callers can see only methods marked with the *WebMethod* attribute. Any attempt to invoke untagged methods via a URL results in a failure.

The *WebMethod* attribute features several properties that you can use to adjust the behavior of the method. Table 13-1 lists the properties.

Table 13-1   Properties of the *WebMethod* Attribute

Property	Description
BufferResponse	Set to *true* by default, this property indicates that the IIS run time should buffer the method's entire response before sending it to the client. Even if set to *false,* the response is partially buffered; however, in this case, the size of the buffer is limited to 16 KB.
CacheDuration	Specifies the number of seconds that the IIS run time should cache the response of the method. This information is useful when you can foresee that the method will handle several calls in a short period of time. Set to *0* by default (meaning no caching), the caching engine is smart enough to recognize and cache page invocations that use different parameter values.
Description	Provides the description for the method. The value of the property is then embedded into the WSDL description of the service.
EnableSession	Set to *false* by default, this property makes available to the method the *Session* object of the ASP.NET environment. Depending on how *Session* is configured, using this property might require cookie support on the client or a Microsoft SQL Server 2000 installation on the server.

(continued)

Table 13-1 **Properties of the *WebMethod* Attribute** *(continued)*

Property	Description
MessageName	Allows you to provide a publicly callable name for the method. When you set this property, the resulting SOAP messages for the method target the name you set instead of the actual name. Use this property to give distinct names to overloaded methods in the event that you use the same class as part of the middle tier and a Web service.
TransactionOption	Specifies the level of COM+ transactional support you want for the method. A Web service method can have only two behaviors, regardless of the value assigned to the standard *TransactionOption* enumeration you select: either it does not require a transaction or it must be the root of a new transaction.

The following code snippet shows how to set a few method attributes:

```
[WebService(
    Namespace="xmlnet/cs/0735618011",
    Name="Northwind Sales Report Web Service",
    Description="The Northwind Sales Report Web Service")]
public class SalesReportWebService : WebService
{
    [WebMethod(CacheDuration=60,
        Description="Returns sales for the specified year")]
    public DataSet GetSalesReport(int theYear)
    {
        ⋮
    }
```

Don't be fooled by appearances: attributes must be strongly typed in the declaration. In other words, the value you assign to *CacheDuration* must be a true number and not a quoted string containing a number. This is a general rule for attributes in the .NET Framework—not a peculiarity of Web services.

Transactional Methods

The behavior of a Web service method in the COM+ environment deserves a bit of attention. The inherent reliance of Web services on HTTP inevitably prevents them from being enlisted in running transactions; in the case of a rollback, it would be difficult to track and cancel performed operations. For this reason, a Web method can do either of two things: it can work in nontransacted mode, or it can start a nondistributed transaction.

For consistency, the *TransactionOption* property of the *WebMethod* attribute takes values from the .NET Framework's *TransactionOption* enumeration. The behavior of some of the values in this enumeration, however, is different from what their names suggest. In particular, the *Disabled, NotSupported,* and *Supported* values from the *TransactionOption* enumeration always cause the method to execute without a transaction. Both *Required* and *RequiresNew,* on the other hand, create a new transaction.

> **Note**   When a transactional method throws an exception or an externally thrown exception is not handled, the transaction automatically aborts. If no exceptions occur, the transaction automatically commits at the end of the method being called.

Format of SOAP Messages for a Web Method

Although SOAP dictates that the messages being exchanged between the Web service and its clients must be in XML, it says nothing about the actual schema of the XML. The .NET Framework provides an attribute-based mechanism to let you control the format of the XML packed in the SOAP message. To customize the structure of a SOAP message, you can intervene in two places: you can modify the layout of the information being packed beneath the *<soap:body>* tag, and you can change the way in which parameter values are formatted.

The options available for formatting the body of the message are *RPC* and *Document*; the latter is the default format for the .NET Framework. The *Document* style refers to formatting the body of the method call according to an XSD schema. Typically, the body is given by a sequence of message parts whose actual syntax is specified by other properties such as *Use* and *ParameterStyle*. The *RPC* style formats the body of the SOAP message according to the formatting rules outlined in the SOAP specification, section 7.

The *SoapDocumentMethod* and the *SoapRpcMethod* attributes apply to an individual method. If you want the same attributes to apply to all methods in the Web service, use the *SoapDocumentService* and *SoapRpcService* attributes with the same syntax.

The *SoapDocumentMethod* Attribute

As mentioned, the *Document* body style is set by default. If you need to change some of its default settings, you can use the *SoapDocumentMethod* attribute implemented in the *SoapDocumentMethodAttribute* attribute class. The *Use* property of the attribute specifies whether parameters are formatted in the *Encoded* or *Literal* style. (Both values come from the *SoapBindingUse* enumeration.)

The *Literal* flag formats parameters using a predefined XSD schema for each parameter, whereas *Encoded* encodes all message parts using the encoding rules set in the SOAP specification, section 5. *Literal* is the default option.

The *ParameterStyle* specifies whether the parameters are encapsulated within a single message part following the *<soap:body>* element or whether each parameter is an individual message part. The second option is the default. To encapsulate the parameters, set the *ParameterStyle* attribute to *SoapParameterStyle.Wrapped*.

The following code snippet attempts to return a string encoded in a SOAP message instead of described by an XSD document:

```
[WebMethod(CacheDuration=60)]
[SoapDocumentMethod(Use=SoapBindingUse.Encoded)]
public string GetSalesReportBarChart(int theYear)
{
    ⋮
}
```

This script represents the SOAP request message for the method when the request is SOAP-encoded:

```
POST /salesreport/SalesReportService.asmx HTTP/1.1
Host: expo-star
Content-Type: text/xml; charset=utf-8
Content-Length: length
SOAPAction: "xmlnet/cs/0735618011/GetSalesReportBarChart"

<?xml version="1.0" encoding="utf-8"?>
<soap:Envelope
    xmlns:xsi="http://www.w3.org/2001/XMLSchema-instance"
    xmlns:xsd="http://www.w3.org/2001/XMLSchema"
    xmlns:soapenc="http://schemas.xmlsoap.org/soap/encoding/"
    xmlns:tns="xmlnet/cs/0735618011"
    xmlns:types="xmlnet/cs/0735618011/encodedTypes"
```

```
    xmlns:soap="http://schemas.xmlsoap.org/soap/envelope/">
  <soap:Body
      soap:encodingStyle="http://schemas.xmlsoap.org/soap/encoding/">
    <types:GetSalesReportBarChart
        xsi:type="types:GetSalesReportBarChart">
      <theYear xsi:type="xsd:int">int</theYear>
    </types:GetSalesReportBarChart>
  </soap:Body>
</soap:Envelope>
```

The default request for the same method is shown here:

```
POST /salesreport/SalesReportService.asmx HTTP/1.1
Host: expo-star
Content-Type: text/xml; charset=utf-8
Content-Length: length
SOAPAction: "xmlnet/cs/0735618011/GetSalesReportBarChart"

<?xml version="1.0" encoding="utf-8"?>
<soap:Envelope xmlns:xsi="http://www.w3.org/2001/XMLSchema-instance"
    xmlns:xsd="http://www.w3.org/2001/XMLSchema"
    xmlns:soap="http://schemas.xmlsoap.org/soap/envelope/">
  <soap:Body>
    <GetSalesReportBarChart xmlns="xmlnet/cs/0735618011">
      <theYear>int</theYear>
    </GetSalesReportBarChart>
  </soap:Body>
</soap:Envelope>
```

> **Caution**   The *DataSet* object can't be used with a Web service method if the parameters for the method are SOAP-encoded. This means that you can't use the *SoapRpcMethod* attribute with the method. In addition, when you use the default *SoapDocumentMethod* attribute, be sure that the *Use* property is set to *SoapBindingUse.Literal*.

The *SoapRpcMethod* Attribute

The *RPC* format is expressed by the *SoapRpcMethod* attribute and specifies that all parameters are encapsulated within a single XML element named after the Web service method, as shown in the following code. The *RPC* style does not support the *Literal* binding mode; only the SOAP-encoded binding mode (*Encoded*) is accepted.

```
POST /salesreport/SalesReportService.asmx HTTP/1.1
Host: expo-star
Content-Type: text/xml; charset=utf-8
Content-Length: length
SOAPAction: "xmlnet/cs/0735618011/GetSalesReportBarChart"

<?xml version="1.0" encoding="utf-8"?>
<soap:Envelope
    xmlns:xsi="http://www.w3.org/2001/XMLSchema-instance"
    xmlns:xsd="http://www.w3.org/2001/XMLSchema"
    xmlns:soapenc="http://schemas.xmlsoap.org/soap/encoding/"
    xmlns:tns="xmlnet/cs/0735618011"
    xmlns:types="xmlnet/cs/0735618011/encodedTypes"
    xmlns:soap="http://schemas.xmlsoap.org/soap/envelope/">
  <soap:Body
      soap:encodingStyle="http://schemas.xmlsoap.org/soap/encoding/">
    <tns:GetSalesReportBarChart>
      <theYear xsi:type="xsd:int">int</theYear>
    </tns:GetSalesReportBarChart>
  </soap:Body>
</soap:Envelope>
```

You must include the *System.Web.Services.Protocols* and *System.Web.Services.Description* namespaces in the Web service source to use SOAP formatting attributes.

> **Note**   Web service methods in which the *OneWay* property of either the *SoapRpcMethod* attribute or the *SoapDocumentMethod* attribute is set to *true* do not have access to ASP.NET objects packed in the *HttpContext* object. References to these objects are still allowed, but *null* is always returned.

The Sales Report Web Service

To see a concrete example of a Web service, let's transform the remote service created in Chapter 12 into a Web service. The Web service class makes externally available a group of functions nearly identical to that of the .NET Remoting component. In doing so, it also uses the same internal class, thus demonstrating a true reuse of code.

The SalesReportService.asmx file is located in the same virtual folder as the remote object. The following code shows the implementation of the Sales Report Web service. The main class is named *SalesReportWebService*.

```
<%@ WebService Language="C#" Class="SalesReportWebService" %>
<%@ Assembly Name="SalesDataProvider" %>

using System;
using System.Web.Services;
using System.Data;
using System.Data.SqlClient;
using XmlNet.CS;

[WebService(
    Namespace="xmlnet/cs/0735618011",
    Name="Northwind Sales Report Web Service",
    Description="The Northwind Sales Report Web Service")]
public class SalesReportWebService
{
    [WebMethod(CacheDuration=60)]
    public DataSet GetSalesReport(int theYear)
    {
        SalesDataProvider m_dataManager;
        m_dataManager = new SalesDataProvider();

        DataSet ds = new DataSet();
        ds.Tables.Add(m_dataManager.GetSalesReport(theYear));
        return ds;
    }

    [WebMethod(CacheDuration=120)]
    public string GetSalesReportBarChart(int theYear)
    {
        SalesDataProvider m_dataManager;
        m_dataManager = new SalesDataProvider();
        return m_dataManager.GetSalesReportBarChart(theYear);
    }
}
```

The class features two methods—*GetSalesReportBarChart* and *GetSales-Report*—that are simply wrappers around the same methods of the *Sales-DataProvider* class. As we saw in Chapter 12, the *SalesDataProvider* class provides the implementation of business logic, including the code necessary to draw graphics.

If you compare this code with the remotable object in Chapter 12, you can't help but notice a close resemblance. For the most part, this similarity depends on the use of an intermediate, common class. Just this fact proves the extreme flexibility of the .NET Framework. Rolling your own functionalities into an interface-less Web site is just one side of a coin that has on its other side .NET Remoting accessibility. Later in this chapter, after we finish our implementation of a Web service, we'll complete the comparison between .NET Remoting and Web services. Figure 13-3 shows the typical user interface that IIS and ASP.NET provide for Web services, mostly for testing purposes.

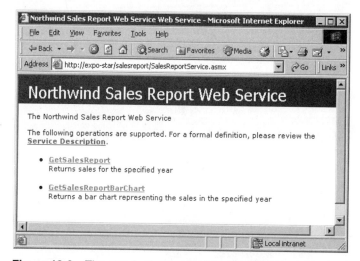

Figure 13-3 The standard user interface for .NET Framework Web services.

If you test the Web service using a Netscape browser, you might get a slightly different user interface, depending on the version of the browser and the level of support it provides for cascading style sheets (CSS). Also bear in mind that the Web service console shown in Figure 13-3 assumes that your client machine has a program registered to handle XML files. The response of the method is saved to a local XML file that is then displayed through the registered program. On many Microsoft Windows machines, the default handler of XML files is Internet Explorer.

Figure 13-4 shows what happens when you test the *GetSalesReport* method with the default (and test-only) user interface.

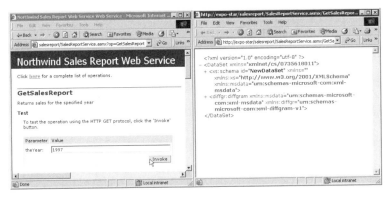

Figure 13-4   Testing the *GetSalesReport* Web method.

Under the Hood of a Web Method Call

Any call made to a Web service method is resolved by an HTTP handler module tailor-made for Web services. In the ASP.NET and IIS architectures, an HTTP handler is a Web server extension that handles all the URLs of a certain type. Once the incoming call has been recognized as a Web service call, an instance of the *WebServiceHandlerFactory* class is created. The just-created object compiles the Web service class into an assembly (only the first time). Next the Web service factory class analyzes the request bits and parses the contents of the messages (probably, but not necessarily, a SOAP payload). If successful, the request is transformed into method information. An ad hoc data structure contains information such as the name of the method, the list of formal and actual parameters, whether the method is void, and the returned type.

The method information is then passed to a call handler that will actually take care of executing the method. According to the information specified in the request, the call handler can contain context information (for example, *Session*) and work either synchronously or asynchronously. Finally, the server object is instantiated, the method is invoked, and the return value is written to the output stream. Figure 13-5 illustrates the process.

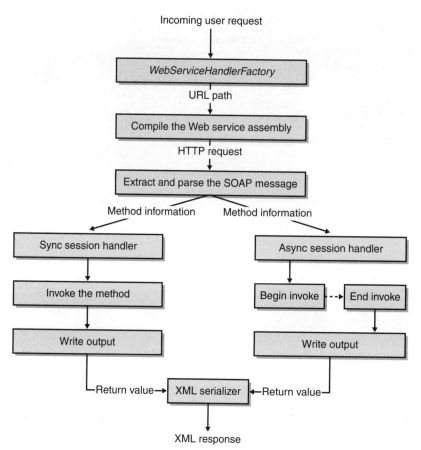

Figure 13-5 Processing a Web service call.

Setting Caching Properties

As mentioned, the *CacheDuration* property of the *WebMethodAttribute* class sets the length of time in seconds that the Web service should cache the page output. This feature demonstrates once again the tight integration between Web services and the ASP.NET run-time infrastructure. The *CacheDuration* property is implemented using the ASP.NET *Cache* object. Just before instantiating the server object, the Web service handler configures the *Cache* object. In particular, the Web service handler sets the cache to work on the server, as shown here:

```
Response.Cache.SetCacheability(HttpCacheability.Server);
```

In addition, the Web service handler sets the expiration time and configures the caching subsystem for parametric output, as follows:

```
Response.Cache.VaryByHeaders["SOAPAction"] = true;
Response.Cache.VaryByParams["*"] = true;
```

The *VaryByHeaders* property enables you to cache multiple versions of a page, depending on the value of the HTTP header (or headers) you specify—in this example, the header value is *SOAPAction*. The *VaryByParams* property, on the other hand, lets you maintain different caches for each set of distinct values of the specified parameters. In this case, using the asterisk (*) indicates that all parameters must be considered when caching a page.

> **Note**   Under certain conditions, the *CacheDuration* attribute can constitute a significant improvement for your Web services. Ideally, you might want to set this attribute when your method returns a large amount of data (for example, a *DataSet* object) but receives quite a few requests distributed throughout the day. The caching mechanism—the same mechanism available to all ASP.NET applications—lets you distinguish cached copies of the output that are also based on parameters. Under these circumstances, generating a new data set every time the method is called isn't efficient—unless, of course, user requirements mandate that you return fresh data. The advantage in performance can be relevant and significant. In my experimentation, I was able to get response times up to 8 times faster, with 2 or 3 times faster being the average.

The Role of the XML Serializer

As shown in Figure 13-5, the return value of the method call is packed as XML using the XML serializer that we saw in action in Chapter 11. The following script represents the pseudocode that creates the response for a Web service method:

```
Response.ContentType = ContentType.Compose("text/xml",
    Encoding.UTF8Encoding);
ser.Serialize(outputStream, returnValue);
```

The XML serializer can't process all .NET Framework types. Remember, the XML serializer doesn't work with types that have circular references and only packs public and read/write members. The XML serializer doesn't ensure type fidelity but simply an effective XSD (or SOAP-encoded) representation of the data.

> **Note**   A Web service can't return an ADO.NET object other than the
> *DataSet* object for the simple reason that the *XmlSerializer* class
> doesn't know how to handle them. On the other hand, *XmlSerializer*
> can normally handle arrays of primitive objects, and this can help
> when you're creating workarounds for returning complex data like that
> stored in many ADO.NET objects.

Disabling HTTP-POST and HTTP-GET

As we'll see in more detail in the section "Invoking a Web Service Through
Script," on page 586, you can invoke a Web service method using a SOAP message as well as a plain HTTP-POST or HTTP-GET command. The latter two protocols have been introduced to make accessing a Web service easier than ever.
However, leaving the Web service door open to HTTP packets can constitute a
potential security hole.

If you want to disable the HTTP-POST and HTTP-GET support on a
machine-wide basis, do as follows. First locate the machine.config file (more on
configuration files in Chapter 15) in the local system. The file is normally
located in the config subdirectory of the .NET Framework installation path. A
typical path is shown here:

```
c:\winnt\microsoft.net\framework\v1.0.3705\config\machine.config
```

The machine.config file is an XML file that contains a *<webServices>* section similar to the following:

```
<webServices>
  <protocols>
    <add name="HttpSoap"/>
    <add name="HttpPost"/>
    <add name="HttpGet"/>
    <add name="Documentation"/>
  </protocols>
  ⋮
```

To disable HTTP-POST and HTTP-GET support for all Web services on the
server, simply comment out the lines corresponding to "HttpPost" and
"HttpGet". You can also disable HTTP-POST and HTTP-GET support on a per-
service basis. In this case, do not enter any changes in the machine.config file;
instead, create a web.config file in your Web service's virtual directory and add
the following XML to the file:

```
<configuration>
  <system.web>
    <webServices>
      <protocols>
        <remove name="HttpPost" />
        <remove name="HttpGet" />
      </protocols>
    </webServices>
     ⋮
  </system.web>
   ⋮
</configuration>
```

> **Note**   If you open up the machine.config file and look in the *<webServices>* section, you can't help but notice the special *Documentation* protocol. This protocol is the key that enables the ASP.NET run time to deliver a help page, such as the one shown in Figure 13-3, when you point your browser to an .asmx resource. The default help page is generated by a file named DefaultWsdlHelpGenerator.aspx, which is located in the same folder as machine.config. The page is modifiable, but if you need to enter changes, I'd recommend that you create and register your own generator page. The generator page can be changed with the following configuration code:
>
> ```
> <webServices>
>   <wsdlHelpGenerator href="YourGeneratorPage.aspx"/>
> </webServices>
> ```
>
> Of course, the help page can be customized for all Web services by adding the preceding code to maching.config, or it can be customized for a particular Web service by adding the code to the service's web.config file.

Building a .NET Framework Web Service Client

Whether you use Microsoft Visual Studio .NET or a simple text editor to code the .asmx file, writing Web services using the .NET Framework is definitely an easy task. And as you'll see, writing client applications to use those services is even easier.

You can call a Web service through a URL using either the HTTP-GET or the HTTP-POST command. You can do that also from within an ASP.NET page using the *WebRequest* .NET Framework class. From within Visual Studio .NET, referencing a Web service is nearly identical to adding a reference to another assembly. What you get is a proxy class through which your Windows Forms or Web Forms application can reach its URL across port 80, just like a user's browser. In doing so, firewall problems disappear and HTTP on top of Secure Sockets Layer (SSL) or any other form of encryption can be used to transfer data.

Connecting to a Web service is similar to connecting to a .NET Framework remotable object in that in both cases you end up using a proxy class. The big difference is in the characteristics of the proxy. The .NET Remoting proxy is a dynamically created object that works transparently under the hood of the remote object instance. The client has the impression that it is working with a local object that silently posts all calls to the remote object.

The Web service proxy is a statically created class that must be compiled and linked to the project. The .NET Framework provides a tool to generate such a class. This tool, named wsdl.exe, takes the Web service WSDL script and generates a Microsoft Visual Basic .NET or a C# class (the default) that mirrors methods for synchronous and asynchronous calls. From the client perspective, calling into the proxy class is a local call. Each call, however, results in a round-trip to the server. The following command line generates the C# proxy for the previously written Web service:

```
wsdl.exe http://server/salesreport/salesreportservice.asmx?wsdl
```

The wsdl.exe utility is part of the .NET Framework SDK, and among its other options, it allows you to specify the protocol for the call and the language for the source code. The utility is also silently invoked by Visual Studio .NET when you reference a Web service using the Add Web Reference menu command in Solution Explorer.

The Proxy Class

The proxy class generated for a Web service is added to the project and is in effect a local class. The difference in the remoting architecture is that .NET Remoting uses a dynamically generated class whose method information is hard-coded in the object information being marshaled—the *ObjRef* object. With a Web service, there is no dynamic class creation. The following source code represents the proxy for the Sales Report Web Service:

```csharp
using System;
using System.Xml.Serialization;
using System.Web.Services.Protocols;
using System.Web.Services;

[System.Web.Services.WebServiceBindingAttribute(
    Name="Northwind Sales Report Web ServiceSoap",
    Namespace="xmlnet/cs/0735618011")]
public class NorthwindSalesReportWebService :
    SoapHttpClientProtocol
{
    public NorthwindSalesReportWebService()
    {
        // Feel free to change this URL
        this.Url =
            "http://expo-star/salesreport/salesreportservice.asmx";
    }

    [SoapDocumentMethodAttribute("xmlnet/cs/0735618011/GetSalesReport",
        RequestNamespace="xmlnet/cs/0735618011",
        ResponseNamespace="xmlnet/cs/0735618011",
        Use=SoapBindingUse.Literal,
        ParameterStyle=SoapParameterStyle.Wrapped)]
    public DataSet GetSalesReport(int theYear)
    {
        object[] results = Invoke("GetSalesReport",
            new object[] {theYear});
        return ((DataSet)(results[0]));
    }

    public IAsyncResult BeginGetSalesReport(int theYear,
        AsyncCallback callback, object asyncState)
    {
        return BeginInvoke("GetSalesReport", new object[] {
            theYear}, callback, asyncState);
    }

    public DataSet EndGetSalesReport(IAsyncResult asyncResult)
    {
        object[] results = EndInvoke(asyncResult);
        return ((DataSet)(results[0]));
    }

    [SoapDocumentMethodAttribute(
        "xmlnet/cs/073561801/GetSalesReportBarChart",
        RequestNamespace="xmlnet/cs/0735618011",
        ResponseNamespace="xmlnet/cs/0735618011",
```

(continued)

```
        Use=SoapBindingUse.Literal,
        ParameterStyle=SoapParameterStyle.Wrapped)]
public string GetSalesReportBarChart(int theYear)
{
    object[] results = Invoke("GetSalesReportBarChart",
        new object[] {theYear});
    return ((string)(results[0]));
}

public IAsyncResult BeginGetSalesReportBarChart(int theYear,
    AsyncCallback callback, object asyncState)
{
    return BeginInvoke("GetSalesReportBarChart",
        new object[] {theYear}, callback, asyncState);
}

public string EndGetSalesReportBarChart(IAsyncResult asyncResult)
{
    object[] results = EndInvoke(asyncResult);
    return ((string)(results[0]));
}
}
```

In addition to the class constructor, the proxy contains a public method for each Web method defined on the Web service. The proxy also provides a pair of *Begin* and *End* members for each Web method; these members are used to set up asynchronous calls.

> **Note**   This proxy class uses the *SoapDocumentMethod* attribute. Up to now, we've used the *SoapDocumentMethod* and *SoapRpcMethod* attributes for server files. One thing developers often miss is that the SOAP-related settings you use on the server must be repeated on the client. Normally, the wsdl.exe utility takes care of this for formatting attributes. However, if you use SOAP extensions, you have to assign the same attributes to the proxy class manually—in addition, of course, to making the necessary assemblies available on the client.

Changing the Web Service Reference

The proxy constructor sets the *Url* property of the proxy class to the original URL of the Web service. The value of the property can be changed at design time and even programmatically. The *Url* property is inherited from the base class *WebClientProtocol*—one of the proxy's ancestors.

In situations in which the URL can't be determined unequivocally or might change on a per-user basis or because of other run-time factors, you can ask the wsdl.exe utility not to hard-code the URL in the source. By using the */urlkey* command-line switch, you instruct the utility to dynamically read the Web service URL from the application's configuration file. If you use a switch such as */urlkey:ActualUrl*, the proxy class constructor changes as follows:

```
using System.Configuration;
⋮
public NorthwindInfoService()
{
    String urlSetting = ConfigurationSettings.AppSettings["ActualUrl"];
    if ((urlSetting != null))
        this.Url = urlSetting;
    else // Defaults to the URL used to build the proxy
        this.Url = "http://server/salesreport/salesreportservice.asmx";
}
```

ConfigurationSettings.AppSettings is a special property that provides access to the application settings defined in the *<appSettings>* section of the configuration file. Configuration files are XML files that allow you to change settings without recompiling the application. Configuration files also allow administrators to apply security and restriction policies that affect how applications run on various machines. (We'll cover configuration files in Chapter 15.)

The name and location of the configuration file depends on the nature of the application. For ASP.NET pages and Web services, the file is named web.config and is located in the root directory of the application. You can also have other web.config files located in child directories. Child configuration files inherit the settings defined in configuration files located in parent directories. For Windows Forms applications, the configuration file takes the name of the executable plus a .config extension. Such a file must be resident in the same folder as the main executable.

Issuing Calls to the Web Service

Once a client application is linked to the Web service, it simply creates a new instance of the proxy class and calls its methods. Consider that calling into a Web service is a potentially lengthy operation that might take a few seconds to complete. If you find that the method call is too long, go for an asynchronous call.

This book's sample files include a Windows Forms application that uses the Web service proxy to get data from the site. Surprisingly enough, the code is nearly identical to the related application we built in Chapter 12 as a remoting client. (See the following listing.) The key difference is in the name of the class to call. In addition, with a Web service you don't need to initialize the class in the form's *Load* event because the proxy class is statically linked to the project.

```
NorthwindSalesReportWebService service;
service = new NorthwindSalesReportWebService();
string img = service.GetSalesReportBarChart(theYear);
```

Figure 13-6 shows the Windows Forms client in action.

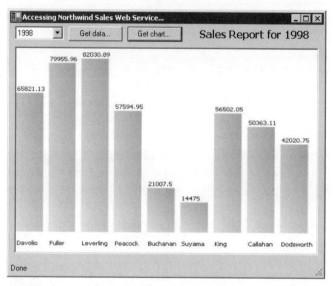

Figure 13-6 A Windows Forms Web service client in action.

Invoking a Web Service Through Script

A Web service is always invoked by using an ordinary HTTP packet that contains information about the method to call and the arguments to use. This HTTP packet reaches the Web server by traveling as a GET or POST command. You can invoke a Web service method using one of these commands:

- A POST command that embeds a SOAP request

- A POST command that specifies the method name and parameters

- A GET command whose URL contains the method name and parameters

To invoke a method in a Web service, SOAP is not strictly necessary. You can use GET or POST commands, which results in a more compact body. However, the benefits of using SOAP become clearer as the complexity of data increases. GET and POST commands support primitive types, including arrays and enumerations. SOAP, on the other hand, relies on a portable and more complex type system based on XML schemas. In addition, in the .NET Framework, Web services also support classes that the XML serializer can handle.

A Windows Script Host Example

To give you a practical demonstration of how Web services are really just HTTP-accessible software agents, let's write a Windows Script Host (WSH) script that allows plain Microsoft Visual Basic, Scripting Edition (VBScript) code to download information from a remote server. To send HTTP commands from VBScript code, we'll use the *Microsoft.XmlHttp* object—a native component of Microsoft Internet Explorer 5.0 and MSXML 3.0 and later versions. The following script calls the method *GetSalesReport* by using a GET command:

```
Const HOST = "http://expo-star/"
Const URL = "salesreport/salesreportservice.asmx/"
Const TheYear = 1997


' Create the HTTP object
Set xmlhttp = CreateObject("Microsoft.XMLHTTP")
xmlhttp.open "GET", _
    HOST & URL & "GetSalesReport?TheYear=" & TheYear, _
    False


' Send the request synchronously
xmlhttp.send ""


' Store the results in a file named RAW_OUTPUT.XML
Set fso = CreateObject("Scripting.FileSystemObject")
Set f = fso.CreateTextFile("raw_output.xml")
f.Write xmlhttp.responseText
f.Close
```

The resultant XML string—the body of the response—is stored in a local XML file.

Extracting a JPEG Image from the XML Output

We've now built a Web service that returns JPEG images, BinHex-encoded and packed in an XML string. Let's see how to get the image and save it locally as a distinct JPEG file. And because we used a GET command in our previous example, we'll use a POST command this time.

With POST commands, you have to use a URL without parameters and store the parameter information in the body of the message, as shown in the following code. In addition, you must indicate the content type of the message.

```
Const HOST = "http://expo-star/"
Const URL = "salesreport/salesreportservice.asmx/"
Const TheYear = 1997

' Create the HTTP object
Set xmlhttp = CreateObject("Microsoft.XMLHTTP")
xmlhttp.open "POST", _
    HOST & URL & "GetSalesReportBarChart", _
    False

' Set the Content-Type header to the specified value
xmlhttp.setRequestHeader "Content-Type", _
    "application/x-www-form-urlencoded"

' Send the request synchronously
xmlhttp.send "TheYear=" & TheYear

' Get the results as a XMLDOM
Set xmldoc = xmlhttp.responseXml

' Extract the XML-based image description from the response
img = xmldoc.text

' Store the results in a file named RAW_OUTPUT.XML
Set fso = CreateObject("Scripting.FileSystemObject")
Set f = fso.CreateTextFile("raw_output.xml")
f.Write img
f.Close

' Extract the JPEG image from raw output
Set shell = CreateObject("WScript.Shell")
shell.Run "jpegextractor.exe raw_output.xml image.jpg"
```

This script first invokes the method and gets the results as an XML Document Object Model (XML DOM) object. The inner text of the document is saved to a local variable and then to a temporary file (raw_output.xml). Finally, a small managed utility (jpegextractor.exe) parses the XML stream, extracts and decodes the JPEG bits, and saves them to a file. The result is a JPEG file representing the sales report for the year you specify.

> **Note** The jpegextractor.exe utility is available as source code in this book's sample files, along with the Web service, the scripts, and the client applications discussed in this chapter.

.NET Remoting vs. Web Services

Web services were designed to overcome a few Web architecture problems—particularly in the area of component interoperability. Web services are key tools for accessing otherwise inaccessible functionalities exposed over heterogeneous hardware and software platforms.

If we stopped our analysis here, the conclusion would be rather obvious: Web services are the first fundamental software development of the new millennium. Although Web services will certainly represent a milestone in the history of computer programming, the more we design them and use them, the more we realize they have serious limitations. Subsequently, and perhaps unfortunately, using a Web service isn't always the best solution.

Which Came First?

I perceive the .NET Framework Web services as a special case of .NET Remoting, but one could argue for the opposite scenario as well. Putting Web services at the center of the interoperability universe and considering .NET Remoting as a platform-specific implementation does make a lot of sense. In general, the way you look at the newest Microsoft remoting technologies depends on your individual perspective.

If you look at interoperability from a .NET Framework–specific viewpoint, you will probably agree with my perception and put Web services on a secondary plane. If your situation spans more vendors and more platforms, you'll recognize that the unquestionable similarity between the Web service API and the .NET Remoting API stems from the fact that .NET Remoting has stolen some features from the Web service specification.

So which came first, the .NET Remoting egg or the Web service chicken? If you're considering .NET Remoting, you are looking at Microsoft's remoting technologies mostly from a .NET Framework perspective. The key issue is slightly different, however. Instead of focusing on which technology came first, you should ask what each technology can do for you. And your final choice should favor the technology that most closely meets your needs.

When to Use .NET Remoting

.NET Remoting is ideal for .NET-to-.NET communication. More exactly, it's been designed for precisely that purpose. As a .NET Framework–specific technology, .NET Remoting lets you use all common language runtime (CLR) types, detects and handles local calls differently, and distinguishes the atomic unit of processing at a different level—the application domain (AppDomain) level instead of the process level. And .NET Remoting increases its performance by allowing the use of binary protocols.

The Special Case of Win32/COM

If you need to set up communication between a .NET Framework application and a Win32 or COM application, you might consider an ad hoc DLL, a COM object, or even a memory mapped file as an alternative to using Web services. In this scenario, you can't use .NET Remoting because one of the applications is either a Win32 or a COM application—that is, a non-.NET-Framework application.

When to Use Web Services

Web services are ideal in a couple of scenarios. First, they are the only safe way to go if your goal is targeting a non-Microsoft platform. If you have to access code running on Linux or want to make your .NET Framework component available to a Linux client, by all means, go for Web services. Second, you should use Web services when, irrespective of the involved platforms, the user requirements mandate that the application must be programmatically accessible through a URL.

Web Service Issues

As a software application that makes itself available only through Internet connections, a Web service is at risk of being, or becoming, a slow application. For this reason, optimization is more than ever a critical factor. Overall performance is affected mostly by the network latency but also, in small part, by the format of the protocol being used. HTTP and SOAP are both based on text, and SOAP in particular is a quite verbose protocol. This results in packets significantly larger than those typical of binary protocols such as Common Object Request Broker Architecture (CORBA) or even Distributed COM (DCOM).

When trying to improve the usability of a Web service (the area in which you should focus your optimization efforts), you should address the following tasks:

- Performing asynchronous calls

- Compressing packets using a SOAP extension

- Minimizing round-trips

- Enhancing the interface of the Web service with mobile code

Asynchronous calls let an application invoke a method and continue running as usual until the response is downloaded on the client. The mechanism exploits the features of asynchronous programming in the .NET Framework.

A SOAP extension is like a hook that you register with the Web service to access the raw SOAP XML either as it is about to be transmitted or as it is received. A SOAP extension works both on the client, by using proxy classes, and on the server. When you want to perform tricks or customize the underlying XML, SOAP extensions provide the right connection point. One valid use of SOAP extensions is for encrypting or compressing method parameters for improved performance and security.

The last two tasks, minimizing round-trips and creating mobile code, are somewhat more complex. Minimizing round-trips is a key aspect of optimization that goes deeper than simply improving performance using software tricks. Mobile code is a concept that is quite popular in the Java community and involves software agents that execute some user code on the server. Let's look at these two topics in more detail.

Minimizing Round-Trips

Each call addressing a Web service method requires a round-trip. Because all Web service activity takes place over the Internet, you can't always expect a rapid response. And because the round-trip is permanently tied to the request of an operation on the Web service, the best—and possibly the only—way to minimize round-trips is to merge more logically distinct functions. The open issue in this approach concerns using additional methods in the interface or additional parameters in the prototype of certain methods. Simple, succinct, and direct methods enhance overall design but certainly do not minimize round-trips, because to execute two functions, you need at least two round-trips.

On the other hand, incorporating more functionality in the body of a single and more complex method is effective in terms of performance but not necessarily in terms of the service usability. A client might receive more information than needed, paying the price in increased downloading time. Moreover, a client might be forced to use an overly complex signature, exposing itself to the risk of getting the requested information by trial and error.

Creating Mobile Code

Although the .NET Framework environment attempts to make you comfortable with Web service client programming, you must still call into remote methods over the Internet. Minimizing round-trips with a smart design is only the first step. What if you can't easily come up with a sequence of operations to pack into a new method? What if the next step depends on run-time conditions? In the database world, you use stored procedures to concatenate multiple SQL calls with some logic. Why can't the same concept be ported to the Web?

Mobile code technology has already been tested on other platforms, although with slightly different purposes, and sooner or later it will make its way to the .NET Framework run time. By *mobile code*, I mean the ability that certain server applications (for example, Web services) might have to execute code sent by clients. Created to allow software agents to transport code to specialized servers for longtime executions, mobile code is a concept that proves useful also in the land of Web services. Interestingly enough, mobile code can solve many problems but exacerbate others.

Mobile code allows you to send C# or Visual Basic .NET code to a Web service, where it can be compiled and executed on the fly. Once the user code has been given access to the methods of the Web service, it can execute any operations and combine the Web service calls in any suitable order—all in a single round-trip.

Mobile code is not perfect, however. But the problems it makes more acute tend to be problems that you'll have to address anyway for the sake of the Web service's stability and success. For example, using mobile code poses serious security concerns. How can you ensure that the code accepted by the Web service is safe for the Web server? You can work around this issue in several ways: You can enable the compilation feature only for authorized users. Or, better yet, you can allow the resulting dynamic assembly to run in a sort of sandbox, where potentially dangerous calls are simply forbidden.

True Interoperability

Another issue that must be consistently addressed to guarantee the widespread acceptance and success of Web service technology is data interoperability. Although several recent articles claim that interoperability is the key feature of Web services, the truth is that Web services are currently fully interoperable only within the boundaries of the .NET Framework.

At this time, you can safely transmit over the Web only primitive types that are included in the XSD type system. What happens to a .NET Framework class or a user-defined class? In the section "The Role of the XML Serializer," on page 579, you saw that the XML serializer takes care of writing the return value of a Web service method call. The XML serializer is actually responsible for the data types—custom and .NET Framework classes—that will be sent to callers. The XML serializer is not perfect, and more important, it is not standard. So how could a Java application quickly and easily understand and deserialize the XML stream it gets from the *XmlSerializer* class? Only when a recognized standard for serializing classes to XML is available will true interoperability between platforms be realized.

Conclusion

Web services are often presented as the perfect tool for today's programmers. Web services are interoperable, are based on open standards such as SOAP and WSDL, and, more importantly, are fully integrated with the .NET platform. This apparent point of strength in Web services—the perfect and seamless integration with the rest of the .NET Framework—on closer examination turns out to be, if not a weakness, a reliable indicator of where Web services are limited. Aspects such as security, interoperability, and code optimization are undermining the stability of the technology. Don't be fooled by the hype that vendors are attaching to the blanket term *Web service*. A lot of work has been done, but a lot still remains.

In this chapter, we looked at Web services from the perspective of usability instead of as a programming topic. We examined the key operations you might want to accomplish with a Web service and the core code that makes this happen. We did not touch on topics such as state management, authentication, and service discovery, which are bread and butter for serious Web service developers. Instead, we focused on comparing Web services with .NET Remoting.

In Chapter 14 and Chapter 15, we'll address some ancillary topics related to application interoperability. One of these topics regards the use of XML data from the client side of a Web application—specifically, an ASP.NET application.

Further Reading

This chapter provides an essential introductory reference to .NET Framework Web services; for a thorough guide, have a look at Scott Short's *Building XML Services for the Microsoft .NET Platform* (Microsoft Press, 2002). Concrete examples covering a possible .NET Framework implementation of the mobile code feature can be found in the article *"Using an Eval Function in Web Services,"* in the September 2002 issue of MSDN Magazine.

For more information about Web service–related standards, here are some useful URLs: You'll find the SOAP specification at *http://www.w3.org/TR/soap*. The UDDI official Web site is *http://www.uddi.org*. From that Web site, I recommend the *"UDDI Executive White Paper,"* which is available for download at *http://www.uddi.org/pubs/uddi_executive_white_paper.pdf*. Notes about the WSDL standard can be found at *http://www.w3.org/tr/wsdl*. Finally, if you need an introduction to the WS-Security initiative, get a copy of the June 2002 issue of MSDN Magazine and read the *"XML Files"* column.

14

XML on the Client

All the technologies and programming interfaces we've looked at up to now work regardless of the surrounding environment—be it the Microsoft Windows desktop, an MS-DOS console, or a Web server. As long as the Microsoft .NET Framework is available, XML-based code works just fine. When you move on to Web applications, however, things change a little bit. Using XML on the client side of a Web application poses a few extra problems and affects the browsers you can use.

In this chapter, you'll learn how to embed XML data in the body of server-side generated HTML pages and how to access that data using script code on the client. To do this, you don't need managed code or the XML classes of the .NET Framework. We'll also investigate a little-used feature of the .NET Framework and Component Object Model (COM) interaction and import a Windows Forms application into an HTML page as a special type of Microsoft ActiveX control. Finally, we'll review the possible ways to make the embedded Windows Forms application access the XML data nested in the same HTML page.

To use this chapter's Web applications included with the book's sample files, follow this procedure:

1. Copy the EmbReaders subfolder to your Web server's root (usually c:\inetpub\wwwroot).

2. Create an IIS virtual folder named EmbReaders, and point it to the preceding folder.

3. Point your browser to the dataisland.aspx and dataislandstep2.aspx files in the EmbReaders IIS virtual folder.

XML Support in Internet Explorer

Internet Explorer versions 5.0 and later provide good support for XML on the client. Among the supported features are *direct browsing* and *data islands*. Direct browsing is the browser's ability to automatically apply an Extensible Stylesheet Language Transformation (XSLT) to the XML files being viewed. In particular, Internet Explorer uses a default, built-in style sheet unless the document points to a specific style sheet. The default style sheet produces the typical tree-based view of nodes you're familiar with. If, as mentioned in Chapter 7, the XML document includes its own style sheet reference (the *xml-stylesheet* processing instruction), the direct browsing function automatically applies the style sheet and displays the resulting HTML code.

A data island is an XML document that exists within an HTML page. In general, a data island can contain any kind of text, not just XML text. Since version 5.0, Internet Explorer provides extra support for XML data islands. If you use the special *<xml>* tag to wrap the text, the browser automatically exposes the contents as an XML Document Object Model (XML DOM) object and allows you to script against the document. The XML DOM object is expressed as a COM object created by the MSXML parser. The advantage for developers is that the XML data travels with the rest of the page and doesn't have to be loaded using ad hoc script or through the *<object>* tag. On the other hand, because the XML data is an integral part of the page, the size of the page itself grows. Determining the best way to include XML data for client-side processing is application-specific, but the *<xml>* tag certainly represents an interesting and compelling option.

The Data Island (*<xml>*) Tag

The *<xml>* tag marks the beginning of a data island, and the *ID* attribute provides the name you use to reference the XML DOM object. The XML text can be inserted in the data island either in-line or through an external reference to a URL. The following code snippet shows an XML data island with in-line text:

```
<html>
<xml id="xmldoc">
<Employees>
  <Employee ID="1">
    <LastName>Davolio</LastName>
    <FirstName>Nancy</FirstName>
  </Employee>
</Employees>
</xml>
</html>
```

The *<xml>* tag simply wraps the XML data; it is not part of the data. Internet Explorer does not throw an exception if the XML text is not well-formed, but if the XML data is not well-formed, the MSXML parser fails to load it, and no XML DOM object is made available to client-side scripts.

The following code snippet demonstrates the use of the *src* attribute with the *<xml>* tag. If this attribute is specified, the XML data and the host page from the specified URL are downloaded separately.

```
<html>
<xml id="xmldoc" src="EmployeesData.xml" />
</html>
```

The contents of the XML data island are not displayed as a portion of the page. This means that if you attempt to view any of the preceding HTML pages using Internet Explorer, an empty page will be displayed. In fact, the pages have no contents other than the data island.

> **Note**   The XML data island should not include a nested *<xml>* tag. If this happens, no error is returned, but the nested end tag *</xml>* closes the data island's open *<xml>* tag. As a result, the XML text that follows the nested *<xml>* element becomes part of the HTML body and is treated as displayable contents.

The Role of the MSXML Parser

Internet Explorer uses the COM-based MSXML parser to load the contents of the XML data island into a programmable XML DOM object. The parser is included in the Internet Explorer installation, so for this feature to work, you don't have to install an additional tool. Of course, the availability of a client-side XML parser is a necessary condition for handling XML data on the client.

In the next section, we'll review alternative ways to embed nondisplayable XML data in HTML pages. Some of these tricks also work with Internet Explorer 4.0 and old Netscape browsers. Bear in mind, however, that although you can figure out several ways to embed XML data in HTML pages, you always need a client-side, script-accessible XML parser to consume that data effectively. COM objects and Java classes are probably the most popular and broadly available tools to process client-side XML. In this chapter, we'll look at a third approach that requires the availability of the .NET Framework.

Accessing Data Islands Through Script

Let's expand the previously created HTML pages with some script code to see what's needed to programmatically access the embedded XML data island. The following HTML page contains a button that, when clicked, prompts you with the XML contents of the data island:

```
<html>
<xml ID="xmldoc">
<Employees>
<Employee ID="1">
  <LastName>Davolio</LastName>
  <FirstName>Nancy</FirstName>
</Employee>
</Employees>
</xml>

<script language="javascript">
function getDataIsland() {
    alert(xmldoc.XMLDocument.xml);
}
</script>

<body>
<input type="button" value="Outer XML" onclick="getDataIsland()">
</body>
</html>
```

Figure 14-1 shows the page in action.

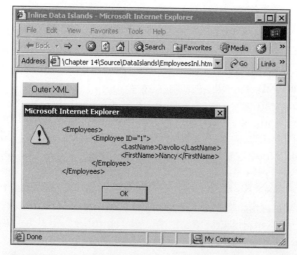

Figure 14-1 Extracting and displaying the contents of the XML data island.

As mentioned, when Internet Explorer encounters the *<xml>* tag, it extracts the XML data and initializes an *XMLDOMDocument* COM object. The object is created and returned by an internal instance of the MSXML parser. Internet Explorer calls the *loadXML* method on the parser and initializes the XML DOM object using the data island contents. The document instance is then added to the HTML object model and made available to scripts via the *document.all* collection, as shown here:

```
var doc = document.all("xmldoc");
```

The *document.all* property is a name/value collection that contains all the elements found in the HTML page. To simplify coding, Internet Explorer also provides an object instance named as the ID of the data island. The data island contents can be referenced using either the *document.all* collection or the property with the same name as the ID.

Once you hold the reference to the data island, you use the *XMLDocument* property to access the actual contents, as shown here:

```
var dataIslandText = xmldoc.XMLDocument.xml;
```

This expression demonstrates how to access the entire XML text stored in the data island. If you need to access a subset of the XML DOM object, you can narrow the set of nodes by using an XPath query or by moving to a particular root node.

Handling Parsing Errors

If errors occur during the parsing of the data island contents, Internet Explorer does not raise exceptions; any error is silently trapped and a *null* object is returned. The code shown in the previous section for accessing the data island does not produce run-time errors in the case of badly formed XML text, but an empty string is returned. To check for errors, use the *parseError* property of the *XMLDOMDocument* object.

The *parseError* property is a reference to an *XMLDOMParseError* object. The *XMLDOMParseError* object returns information about the last parser error. This information includes the error number, line number, character position, and a text description.

The following code shows a version of the script code from the previous section modified to provide error handling:

```
<script language="javascript">
function getDataIsland()
{
```

(continued)

```
    if(xmldoc.parseError.errorCode == 0)
        alert(xmldoc.XMLDocument.xml);
    else
        alert("ERROR: " + xmldoc.parseError.reason);
}
</script>
```

> **Note**   All the code we've looked at up to now as part of a static HTML page can be dynamically generated by Active Server Pages (ASP) or Microsoft ASP.NET code. Later in this chapter, in the section "Creating Data Islands in ASP.NET," on page 603, we'll examine ASP.NET pages that produce HTML code with child XML data islands.

Other Ways to Embed XML Data

The main reason for embedding XML data in a special tag is that an XML document is formed by a sequence of markup delimiters that in most cases are unrecognized by a Web browser. By using a special tag like the *<xml>* tag, you instruct the browser to treat the embedded information in an appropriate way. Note that although an XML data island is a general concept, the *<xml>* special tag is a peculiarity of Internet Explorer versions 5.0 and later. Other browsers, including older versions of Internet Explorer, don't support the *<xml>* tag and don't provide alternative specific tags.

Normally, Web browsers ignore any tag they encounter that is not part of the predefined HTML vocabulary. Most browsers don't raise errors; instead, they send all the text found between the start and end tags in the main body of the page. Consider the following HTML page:

```
<html>
<body>
<specialtext>Hello, world</specialtext>
</body>
</html>
```

This page produces the following output when viewed with Internet Explorer 5.0 and Netscape Communicator 4.5 and later versions. Neither browser recognizes the *<specialtext>* tag; they simply ignore the tag and inject the inner text in the body.

```
Hello, world
```

Data islands let you embed external blocks of data so that they have no impact on the final page being rendered but are accessible programmatically. In other words, the contents of a data island must be invisible to the user but not to the other child components of the page.

Let's look briefly at how to simulate data islands with Internet Explorer 4.0 and older HTML 3.2 browsers such as Netscape 4.x. This information will be useful if you create ASP.NET pages with embedded islands of data that can be viewed through a variety of browsers.

Data Islands in Internet Explorer 4.0

Internet Explorer 4.0 already provides great support for Dynamic HTML (DHTML). For our purposes, this means that once you've assigned an ID to a tag, you can later retrieve the tag by name and run a script against it. Internet Explorer 4.0 also provides good support for cascading style sheets (CSS), which means that you can use ad hoc attributes to control the visibility style of any tag you want.

If you plan to embed XML text in an HTML page using an ordinary tag, keeping the text invisible is only half the task. The key is forcing the browser not to process the embedded text as HTML. In Internet Explorer 4.0, the *<pre>* tag is one of few that offers this capability. When you combine display styles and implicit ID-based object references, you can write code similar to the following:

```
<pre id="xmldoc" style="display:none">
  <xmldata>XML data island</xmldata>
</pre>
```

You wrap the XML code in any HTML or custom tag you want, making sure to assign it a unique ID and set the CSS *display* attribute to *none*. As a result, the contents of the XML data island will be accessible through the expression shown here and, more important, won't affect the page rendering:

```
xmldoc.innerHTML
```

What you get using this technique is not an XML DOM object, however, but a plain string. Initializing a valid XML DOM object and actually parsing and manipulating the XML contents is completely up to you.

Using Hidden Fields

HTML 3.2–compliant browsers make things slightly more difficult. You can't count on CSS support, and you can't expect to find a rich object model attached to all tags. A good compromise can be assigning the XML source code to an *INPUT* control marked as hidden, as shown here:

```
<form>
<input name="xml" type="hidden" value="XML code">
</form>
```

Assigning a *name* attribute to the *INPUT* tag lets you retrieve the XML code later through the following code:

```
oForm = document.forms[0];
oInput = oForm["xml"];
alert(oInput.value);
```

Be sure to use the exact case for names, and be sure to wrap the *INPUT* tag in a *FORM* tag. Both things aren't necessary with Internet Explorer, but Netscape's browsers require it.

> **Note**   In general, you can name the outer form as well and use the name to select the particular form that contains the hidden field. However, bear in mind that if you use this technique from within ASP.NET pages, only one form is available.

The *<script>* Tag

Another possible trick for embedding XML data in an HTML page entails using the *<script>* tag. There are two possible ways of overloading the *<script>* element so that it accepts XML contents. The approaches differ in the trick they use to inform the *<script>* tag that it is actually handling XML data.

You can use the *language* or the *type* attribute. Set the *language* attribute to *xml*, or set the *type* attribute to *text/xml*, as shown in the following code:

```
<script type="text/xml" id="xmldoc1">
    XML content here
</script>
<script language="xml" id="xmldoc2">
    XML content here
</script>
```

You can also reference the XML data through the *src* attribute by making the attribute point to an external URL, as shown here:

```
<script language="xml" src="EmployeesData.xml"></script>
```

In all these cases, you should give the tag a unique ID and use it to access the XML data either directly or through the *document.all* collection.

> **Note**   Overall, if you can control the version of the client browser, the *<xml>* tag is by far the most preferable and flexible solution. Other- wise, I suggest that you embed any XML data in a hidden field.

Creating Data Islands in ASP.NET

To create data islands in ASP.NET, you can use the *<asp:xml>* server control to inject XML code in the body of the HTML *<xml>* tag. We saw this technique in action in Chapter 7 when we examined XSLT and used the *<asp:xml>* control to apply server-side transformations. The *<asp:xml>* control can also be used to inject plain XML code without any preliminary transformation.

The following code demonstrates an ASP.NET page that is functionally equivalent to the HTML page discussed in the previous section. The page cre- ates a couple of data islands by importing the contents of a local XML file and then using a hidden field. The page contains two buttons bound to client-side scripting to read the XML source.

```
<%@ Page Language="C#" %>
<%@ Import Namespace="System.Xml" %>
<%@ Import Namespace="System.Xml.Xsl" %>

<script runat="server">
void Page_Load(object sender, EventArgs e)
{
    button1.Attributes["onclick"] = "getDataFromXmlTag()";
    button2.Attributes["onclick"] = "getDataFromHiddenField()";
    RegisterHiddenField("xml", "<xmldata>my data</xmldata>");
}
</script>

<html>

<script language="javascript">
function getDataFromXmlTag() {
    // Get the data island content from the IE5+ <xml> tag
    if(xmldoc.parseError.errorCode == 0)
        alert(xmldoc.XMLDocument.xml);
    else
        alert("ERROR: " + xmldoc.parseError.reason);
}
```

(continued)

```
function getDataFromHiddenField() {
    // Get the data island content from a hidden field
    oForm = document.forms[0];
    oInput = oForm["xml"];
    alert(oInput.value);
}
</script>

<body>
<h1>Creating Data Islands</h1>

<!-- Client-side XML data island -->
<xml id="xmldoc">
  <asp:xml runat="server" documentsource="employees.xml" />
</xml>
<!-- End of the data island -->

<form runat="server">
  <asp:button runat="server" id="button1"
    text="From <xml> tag..." />
  <asp:button runat="server" id="button2"
    text="From hidden field..." />
</form>

</body>
</html>
```

To create a hidden field, you can use the plain *INPUT* HTML tag with the *type* attribute set to the *hidden* keyword. In ASP.NET, however, you can also use the new *RegisterHiddenField* method exposed by the *Page* object. The advantage of this technique is that you can create and add the field dynamically. The following code shows how it works:

```
RegisterHiddenField("xml", "<xmldata>my data</xmldata>");
```

The method takes two arguments: the unique name of the input field and the contents to be output. When the method executes, no actual HTML code is generated, but a reference is added to an internal collection to keep track of the hidden fields to be created. The hidden input field is actually added to the output when the HTML code for the page is rendered.

Embedding .NET Framework Components in Internet Explorer

The one key reason for creating data islands or, more generally, for embedding XML data in the folds of an HTML page is to cache data on the client to outfit some of the controls on the page. In the previous section, we saw how to embed a data island and how to retrieve its contents. Once retrieved, the XML data can be passed on to client-side components for further processing or can be manipulated via script. As you can imagine, the latter option is less effective because it is based on interpreted code and because, in general, script languages aren't particularly rich in programming features.

So far, COM objects and Java classes have been the most popular technologies used by developers to write client-side components running in the context of Web pages. COM objects and Java classes can be passed, or can directly access, XML data stored in embedded blocks and can then apply some business logic. Both COM objects and Java classes require special support from the browser.

The advent of the .NET Framework added a third option to this list. In addition to writing COM components (including ActiveX controls) or Java classes (including applets), you can now write Windows Forms controls and embed them in HTML pages and ASP.NET–generated Web forms.

In the rest of this chapter, we'll examine the foundation of Windows Forms controls and the tools and techniques you need to know to embed these controls in HTML pages. Next we'll build a sample control that imports the contents of a data island, parses the XML text using a .NET Framework reader, and finally displays the resultant data through a data-bound control.

Building Windows Forms Controls for HTML Pages

Internet Explorer versions 5.5 and later support a special syntax for the *<object>* tag that lets you embed managed objects in Web applications. The object must be an instance of a class that inherits from the *System.Windows.Forms.Control* class either directly or indirectly. The assembly that contains the class is downloaded to the client if it is not already cached. Of course, for this feature to work, the .NET Framework must be installed on the client.

The following code shows how to embed a .NET Framework user-defined class into a Web page:

```
<object id="grid"
  classid="http:DataListView.dll#XmlNet.CS.DataListView"
  height="300" width="100%">
</object>
```

The *id* attribute identifies the instance of the control, whereas the *width* and *height* properties specify the dimensions of the control's site. The key attribute to consider is *classid*. Normally, *classid* identifies the CLSID of the COM object or the ActiveX control to embed. Its typical syntax consists of the keyword *clsid* followed by a colon and the text representation of the object's CLSID, as shown here:

```
<object id="myCtl"
  classid="clsid:8AD3067A-B3FC-11CF-A560-00A0C9081C21">
```

Since version 5.5, Internet Explorer supports an extended format that looks like this:

```
classid="http:[assembly URL]#[full class name]"
```

To instruct the browser to download the *DataListView* assembly from the root of the virtual directory, use the following code snippet:

```
classid="http:DataListView.dll#XmlNet.CS.DataListView"
```

The class to instantiate is *XmlNet.CS.DataListView*. The class must be referenced with its fully qualified name. The assembly doesn't necessarily have to be a DLL; it can be an EXE file instead.

Note   The size of the object must be set explicitly; otherwise, the control will not be displayed in the HTML page. The size can be specified in one of two ways: you can set the *width* and *height* attributes of the *<object>* tag, or you can indicate a size in the control class constructor.

Locating Assemblies

The HTML document can provide information about the locations of the assemblies to download as well as a configuration file in which additional information can be stored. Applications hosted in Internet Explorer indicate the location of the configuration file through the *<link>* tag and the following syntax:

```
<link rel="Configuration" href="[location]">
```

The *href* attribute indicates the URL of the configuration file. By default, Internet Explorer creates a unique application domain (AppDomain) over the entire site that contains the HTML page, which means that all the managed components involved run in the same AppDomain. This is not necessarily a bad thing; however, it is a setting that can be overridden using configuration files. When a configuration file is specified, all pages that point to the same file are created in the same domain.

All dependent assemblies should be available in the same directory as the control—that is, the URL indicated through the *classid* attribute. If needed, however, you can download assemblies from other Web sites using the *<codebase>* setting in a configuration file. The *<codebase>* setting specifies where the common language runtime (CLR) can find a needed assembly. The syntax of the *<codebase>* setting is shown here:

```
<codeBase
  version="Assembly version"
  href="URL of assembly" />
```

To load assemblies from directories other than the application base directory, you can resort to the *<probing>* element in the configuration file. In this case, you dictate that the run time searches for assemblies in the listed subdirectories of the application base. The application base is the directory that contains the configuration file or the directory that contains the control, if no configuration file is used.

> **Note**   If your control references only assemblies stored in the global assembly cache, you don't need to take any additional measures. Those assemblies are always correctly located.

Setting Up the Virtual Directory

To successfully test HTML pages that contain managed controls, you should create an ad hoc virtual directory and access the page through Internet Information Services (IIS). In other words, you can't simply prepare an HTML document and double-click it from Windows Explorer.

In addition, the virtual directory must have the Execute Permissions setting configured to Scripts Only, as shown in Figure 14-2.

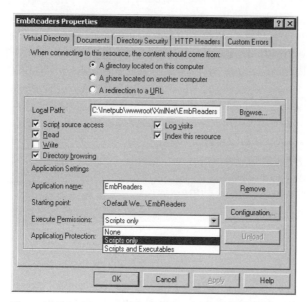

Figure 14-2 The virtual directory for the page that embeds a managed control must be configured to run only scripts.

The reason for this is that if you configure Execute Permissions to Scripts And Executables, IIS will be fooled by the assembly's .dll or .exe extension and will treat the control's assembly as an ISAPI application. As a result, the control won't be hosted by the browser.

A Data Display Custom Control

The browser control class must be derived from *Control* or from another *Control*-derived class. The control can't be a form or a Windows Forms–derived type. In addition, the control class must be publicly accessible and must contain a public default constructor that takes no parameters. Aside from these requirements, a browser-embeddable control is nothing special and does not require you to take any particular steps other than those you would take for any other kind of Windows Forms control.

Let's build a sample control named *DataListView* and make it inherit from the Windows Forms *ListView* control. We will also add a new method that receives an XML string and loads the parsed text into a *DataSet* object. If successful, the *DataSet* object will then be used to populate the view. The input XML string can be set programmatically from any source and in particular can be extracted from a data island.

The *DataListView* Control

The *DataListView* class inherits from *ListView*, but unlike the parent class, it always works in Details mode. The view mode and the font are set during the initialization phase. The following code is invoked from within the constructor:

```
protected void SetupControl()
{
    this.View = View.Details;
    this.Font = new Font("Verdana", 8f);
    this.FullRowSelect = true;
}
```

Although the control is automatically configured to work in Details mode, no columns are added to the view until the user interface is populated with data. The Details view provides clickable columns of data arranged in a grid.

Populating the Control's User Interface

Load is the key method of the *DataListView* control. It is also the only extension made to the programming interface of the parent class, as shown here:

```
public void Load(string xmldata)
```

The *Load* method expects to receive an XML string that can be successfully parsed into a *DataSet* object. The resultant object, if any, is used to populate the *ListView* class. Unlike other list controls, the *ListView* class does not fully support the .NET Framework's complex data-binding. In fact, the *ListView* class does not provide for a *DataSource* property. To populate its user interface with data read out of data-bindable object, you must loop through the rows and update the list items yourself.

The following code illustrates the behavior of the *Load* method:

```
public void Load(string xmldata)
{
    DataSet ds = new DataSet();
    StringReader reader = new StringReader(xmldata);
    ds.ReadXml(reader);
    reader.Close();

    // Store the current data source and its view object
    m_data = ds.Tables[0];
    m_viewOfData = new DataView(m_data);

    // Add columns
    this.Columns.Clear();
```

(continued)

```
for(int j=0; j<m_data.Columns.Count; j++)
{
    int size = 130;
    this.Columns.Add(m_data.Columns[j].ColumnName,
        size, HorizontalAlignment.Left);
}


// Add rows
FillTable();
}
```

The first task accomplished is transforming the input XML data into a *DataSet* object. The XML data is read and parsed by the *ReadXml* method of the *DataSet* object. *ReadXml* normally works on streams and files, but you can force it to work on a string if you specify the string through a *StringReader* object.

Once the input XML data has been transformed into a *DataSet* object, the first table in the *DataSet* object is extracted and its columns and rows processed. (In this example, the control arbitrarily processes only the first table.) For each column in the table, the *DataListView* control creates and adds a new column with default settings and size. Next the table rows are enumerated. Each row becomes a new line in the *ListView* object. The first column maps to the *ListView* primary item; the other columns are rendered as *ListView* subitems, as shown in the following code:

```
private void FillTable()
{
    // Clear existing rows
    this.Items.Clear();

    // Add new rows
    for(int i=0; i<m_viewOfData.Count; i++)
    {
        ListViewItem lvi = null;
        for(int j=0; j<m_viewOfData.Table.Columns.Count; j++)
        {
            string elem = m_viewOfData[i][j].ToString();
            if (j==0)
                lvi = this.Items.Add(elem);
            else
                lvi.SubItems.Add(elem);
        }
    }
}
```

The rows are enumerated through a *DataView* object to allow for sorting and filtering. We'll return to this topic in the upcoming section "Adding Sorting and Filtering Capabilities." For now, let's see how to connect the data island with the control.

Accessing the Data Island Contents

In the previous section, we learned how to extract the contents of an XML data island, regardless of the technique that was used to store it in an existing HTML page. The content of an XML data island is a plain string and as such can be passed on to the *Load* method for further processing. The following code demonstrates how:

```
<script language="javascript">
function getDataFromXmlTag()
{
    // Get the data island content from the IE5+ <xml> tag
    if(xmldoc.parseError.errorCode == 0)
    {
        g = document.all("grid");
        var data = xmldoc.XMLDocument.xml;
        g.Load(data);
    }
    else
        alert("ERROR: " + xmldoc.parseError.reason);
}
</script>
```

The content of the data island is extracted, parked in a temporary variable, and then passed on to *Load*. In the next section, we'll see a sample page in action.

Adding Sorting and Filtering Capabilities

To make the *DataListView* control even more useful, you can add advanced view capabilities. Adding sorting and filtering capabilities to the *DataListView* control is surprisingly simple thanks to the programming power of the .NET Framework. To add sorting and filtering features, you use the *Sort* and *RowFilter* properties of the embedded *DataView* object.

Data sorting is triggered when the user clicks on the column's header. The base *ListView* control already provides the *ColumnClick* event and an ad hoc delegate (the *ColumnClickEventHandler* class) to handle the event, as shown in the following code. The event data, gathered in the *ColumnClickEventArgs* structure, provides a *Column* member that indicates the zero-based index of the column clicked. The actual sorting of the displayed data is up to you.

```
// Execute when the user clicks on a column's header
private void SortData(object sender, ColumnClickEventArgs e)
{
    // Prepare a view with sorted data
    PrepareSortedDataView(e.Column);

    // Refresh the view to reflect sorting
    FillTable();
}


// Configure the internal DataView to support sorting
private void PrepareSortedDataView(int colPos)
{
    // Set the column to sort by
    m_viewOfData.Sort = m_data.Columns[colPos].ColumnName;

    // Arrange the auto-reverse sorting
    if (m_columnSorted == colPos)
    {
        // If the same column is clicked twice,
        // invert the direction
        m_viewOfData.Sort += " DESC";
        m_columnSorted = -1;
    }
    else
        // Store the index of the currently sorted column
        m_columnSorted = colPos;
}
```

Implementing row filtering is even easier. You simply expose a read/write property called, say, *RowFilter* and make it work as a wrapper around the *Data-View* object's *RowFilter* property, as shown here:

```
private string m_rowFilter = "";
public string RowFilter
{
    get {return m_rowFilter;}
    set
    {
        // Store the filter string
        m_rowFilter = value;

        // Pass the information on to the DataView
        m_viewOfData.RowFilter = m_rowFilter;
```

```
        // Refresh the view
        FillTable();
    }
}
```

What we have built so far is a *ListView*-based control that features data-binding functionalities along with advanced capabilities for sorting and filtering the data. This control can be initialized from an XML string that can be deserialized to a *DataSet* object. The *DataListView* control can be used with any Windows Forms application, but when embedded in an HTML or ASP.NET page, the programming interface lends itself very well to filling the control with the contents of an XML data island.

> **Tip**   To significantly improve your programming experience when developing browser-embeddable Windows Forms controls, you might want to create a simple test application that hosts the control. Only when the control works as expected should you write the test HTML or ASP.NET page. Testing a control embedded in Internet Explorer can be quite frustrating because the CLR does not redownload assemblies that already figure in the cache. This means that you have to physically empty the assembly cache or replace the local copy of the assembly before you can see changes in action.

Putting It All Together

The *DataListView* control is an effective tool for displaying a snapshot of data cached on the client. An ASP.NET page that makes use of the *DataListView* control differs in some respects from any other ordinary data-bound ASP.NET page. First and foremost, using the *DataListView* control or similar controls in a Web application requires a rich client such as Internet Explorer and requires that the .NET Framework is installed on the client. As you might expect, these requirements make such a Web application more suitable for controlled environments like an intranet than for the Internet.

On the other hand, caching data on the client allows you page through data, as well as sort and filter rows, without repeated access to the database and without tying up Web server memory with server-side cached objects. Writing a browser-managed control also lets you exploit the power of the .NET Framework on the client, although with some limitations. The *DataListView* control will run as partially trusted code, and although the control can administratively receive more privileges and permissions, the core code you write should not presume itself to be more than a partially trusted application. In particular, this means that file I/O should be avoided to the extent that it is possible and replaced with isolated storage whenever data persistence becomes a strong necessity.

> **Note** The *GetSalesReportBarChart* method of the Web service built in Chapter 13 creates the JPEG image that represents the chart as an in-memory image just to avoid security restrictions for file I/O. For the most part, the location of the assembly determines the restrictions it will be subject to. Locations are articulated in zones, including MyComputer, Intranet, and Internet.

Registry, clipboard, and network access are restricted also. Network access is restricted to the URL from which the control's assembly was downloaded. Printing is allowed only through the Windows Forms common dialog box, and no direct access to the resource is permitted. Finally, both run-time and XML serialization are considered restricted functionalities whose full access is reserved for fully trusted applications.

With these considerations in mind, let's finalize the *DataListView* control and build an ASP.NET page that makes use of it. A sneak preview of the final page is shown in Figure 14-3.

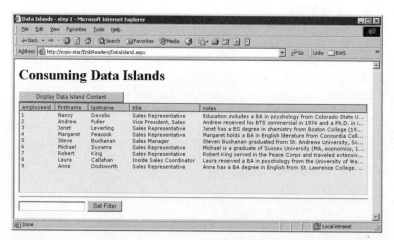

Figure 14-3 An ASP.NET page that creates and consumes an XML data island.

Serializing *DataSet* Objects to Data Islands

The sample page shown in Figure 14-3 is named dataisland.aspx and is available in this book's sample files, along with the source code for the *DataListView* control. The following code shows the body of the page. Key parts of the code are shown in boldface—in particular, the data island definition and the managed control declaration.

```
<html>
<body>
<h1>Consuming Data Islands</h1>

<!-- Client-side XML data island -->
<xml id="xmldoc">
  <asp:xml runat="server" documentsource="employees.xml" />
</xml>
<!-- End of the data island -->

<form runat="server">
  <input type="button" value="Display Data Island Content"
    onclick="getDataFromXmlTag()">

  <object id="grid"
    classid="http:DataListView_CS.dll#XmlNet.CS.DataListView"
      height="300" width="100%">
  </object>
</form>

</body>
</html>
```

The data island is created using the *<asp:xml>* server control, which reads a previously created XML file. The employees.xml file is simply the XML normal form of a *DataSet* object. The *DataSet* object is serialized to the data island, and the page is sent to the browser. On the client, some Javascript code takes care of extracting the data island contents as XML text and passing it on to a method—*Load*—on the managed control. Internally, the *Load* method rebuilds the *DataSet* object and uses it to populate its own user interface. Figure 14-4 shows the ASP.NET page in action, with a filter applied and with the data sorted in ascending order by last name.

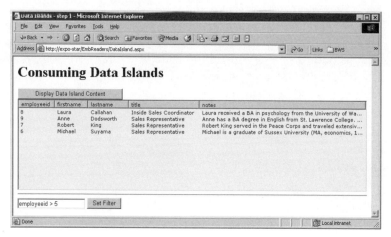

Figure 14-4   Sorting and filtering data on the client.

> **Note**   When embedding script code in Web pages to be consumed over the Internet, you should use the Javascript language to reach the widest possible range of browsers. VBScript is limited to Internet Explorer. In this example, however, we're making serious assumptions about the capabilities of the client—.NET Framework installed, support for the extended syntax of the *<object>* tag, and ability to host managed code. This means that your browser must be Internet Explorer 5.5 or, more likely, Internet Explorer 6.0 or later. So in this case you can reasonably drop Javascript in favor of VBScript.

From MSXML Documents to .NET XML Documents

When Internet Explorer detects the *<xml>* tag in a client page, it automatically extracts the page's contents, creates an internal instance of the MSXML parser, and makes the data available through an *XMLDOMDocument* object. Note that *XMLDOMDocument* is not a managed object created from any of the .NET Framework classes but rather an instance of a COM object that constitutes the XML DOM representation of the data island contents. The following pseudocode, written in JScript, illustrates this point; the variable *xmldoc* is an *XMLDOMDocument* object.

```
// Extract the data island contents
// xmldoc is the ID of the <xml> tag
var xmldata = document.all("xmldoc").innerHTML;
```

```
// Instantiate MSXML
var parser = new ActiveXObject("Microsoft.XMLDOM");

// Parse the contents of the data island and makes
// it available as a XML DOM object. The object is given
// the same name as the <xml> tag's ID
var xmldoc = parser.loadXML(xmldata);
```

If your final goal is consuming the data island within the body of a managed control, there is no need to pass through a COM-based intermediate representation of the XML data. In this case, in fact, the parser that will actually process the data is the .NET Framework XML reader. The reader needs only a string of XML data, not a COM object. On the other hand, whenever you use the *<xml>* tag, Internet Explorer automatically creates the *XMLDOMDocument* object. So if the final destination of the data island is a Windows Forms control, you might want to speed things a little bit by not using the *<xml>* tag, which will produce a useless COM XML DOM object. Using a hidden field offers the same functionality at a lower price. But keep in mind that this option is valid only if you plan to consume the data island contents through embedded managed code.

The Role of Script Code

To establish a connection between the host environment and the managed control, you must use script code—Javascript in particular. For this reason, while you're designing the interface of the managed control, don't forget what the actual callers of those methods will be. A Javascript client has different capabilities than a .NET Framework client, so you should keep the signature of public methods as simple as possible and avoid using arrays and other complex and user-defined types.

In the dataisland.aspx sample code, the connection between the data island and the managed control is made through the *Load* method. The *Load* method accepts a simple string, which results in a signature that the Javascript code can easily match, as shown here:

```
// At this point, Internet Explorer has already created
// the XMLDOMDocument. You can retrieve the content of the
// data island either through the XMLDocument object or
// the innerHTML property.
var data = xmldoc.XMLDocument.xml;

// Pass the data island content to the managed control
var listView = document.all("grid");
listView.Load(data);
```

Avoiding Problems with Submit Buttons

While developing the sample ASP.NET page to test the *DataListView* object, I ran into an interesting snag. I originally used the *<asp:button>* tag to insert a button to load the data island into the control. As a result, the data island was correctly read and the control filled, but a moment later the page refreshed, and the control lost its state and was displayed as empty. What happened? The reason for this strange behavior is that the *<asp:button>* tag always generates a submit button, as shown here:

```
<input type="submit" name="button1" value="Click me" />
```

As a result, the page first executes the client-side script associated with the HTML button and fills the control with the XML data. Next the browser posts the page back to the server as the submit button type mandates. This behavior is undesired for a couple of reasons. First, it produces an unneeded round-trip to the Web server. Second, the round-trip cancels the changes to the user interface that have been made on the client and that constitute the core of our efforts and our main reason for building and using a managed control. On the other hand, the Windows Forms control is not a server-side control and does not have access to the *ViewState* property to control its state when the page posts back.

This problem has a simple workaround: don't use the *<asp:button>* tag to insert a button that is expected to interact with the managed control through client-side script code. Instead, use the *<input>* tag and explicitly set the *type* attribute to *button*, as shown in the following code:

```
<input type="button" value="Display Data Island Content"
  onclick="getDataFromXmlTag()">
```

Also, don't set the *runat* attribute; if you do, the *onclick* attribute will be mistaken for server-side code to be executed. In this way, the browser executes the associated client-side script code and refreshes the page accordingly, but no postback occurs.

Using Hidden Fields and SQL Queries

Despite the fact that the *<xml>* tag is the official way of defining XML data islands with Internet Explorer, a hidden field is probably a better solution. With a hidden field, Internet Explorer doesn't preprocess the XML data into a COM-based XML DOM object. This feature is welcome if you are going to process the XML data using script code. No parsing is needed if you only plan to pass the XML data island to a managed control, however. Using a hidden field or a hidden tag is a valid approach to inserting XML data in the body of an HTML page.

The following code illustrates how to create a hidden field that contains dynamically generated XML data. The data is the output you get from the XML normal form of a *DataSet* object. In this sample code, the *DataSet* object is obtained by running a query against the Customers table in the Northwind database.

```
<script runat="server">
private void Page_Load(object sender, EventArgs e)
{
    if (!IsPostBack)
    {
        string xmldata = GetDataAsXml();
        RegisterHiddenField("xml", xmldata);
    }
}

private string GetDataAsXml()
{
    SqlDataAdapter adapter = new SqlDataAdapter(
        "SELECT customerid, companyname, contactname,
         contacttitle, city, country FROM customers",
        "SERVER=localhost;DATABASE=northwind;UID=sa;");
    DataSet ds = new DataSet();
    adapter.Fill(ds);
    return ds.GetXml();
}
</script>
```

Figure 14-5 shows the sample page in action.

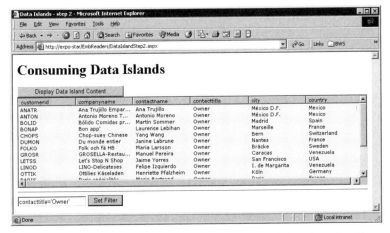

Figure 14-5   The sample page now shows filtered data from the Customers table. The XML data has been carried using a hidden field.

> **Note**   Another key technique you can use to refresh the page using client-side data leverages DHTML. Although this approach can be effective and powerful, it doesn't combine well with managed code. DHTML refers to the page object model and is designed for scripting. The page object model is exposed as a suite of COM objects, and driving it from within managed code is certainly possible but not particularly easy.

Conclusion

Using XML data islands to import sensitive data into HTML pages is a technique that deserves further investigation. Creating XML data islands is easier with ASP.NET but was not rocket science even prior to the advent of the .NET Framework. Accessing the contents of a data island on the client is still based on Javascript code, and therefore is not a feature that has been affected by the .NET Framework. So what's the problem with using XML and the .NET Framework on the client?

The .NET Framework classes provide a far richer object model that has a lot to offer in terms of XML data manipulation, as we saw in Chapter 8, Chapter 9, and Chapter 10. Exploiting this bounty of functions on the client is possible thanks to the browser-deployable Windows Forms controls that we examined in this chapter. Code that uses XML and the .NET Framework on the client, although based on ASP.NET code, is not Internet-oriented because it imposes two key restrictions on the client environment: the browser must be Internet Explorer 5.5 (or later), and the .NET Framework must be installed on the client machine. (Because you often end up installing Internet Explorer 6.0 with the .NET Framework, this is really a single requirement.)

Passing data to managed controls is relatively easy; each component can define its own interface. However, any interaction between the user and the control can take place only through script code. Keep this in mind when you're designing the programming interface of the managed controls.

The key concept that this chapter has pursued is that you can split your Web functions and balance them between the client and the server without renouncing managed code and the power of the .NET Framework. To do so, you create a Windows Forms rich client and embed it in an HTML or ASP.NET page using the *<object>* tag. Next you pass server-side data (for example, the results of a SQL query) to the client using XML data islands and script code to invoke properties and methods on the managed controls.

Admittedly, the concepts illustrated in this chapter are probably not the most common way to use XML in a .NET Framework environment. In my ADO.NET and XML seminars, however, I often get questions that touch on, directly or indirectly, the use of XML in a client-side scenario. This chapter should answer some of the most frequently asked questions.

In Chapter 15, we'll finish our examination of XML in the .NET Framework, including application configuration, the format of .config files, and ways to extend and customize them.

Further Reading

In an article published in *MSDN Magazine* in June 2000 ("Creating and Optimizing Performance for XML Document/View Web Applications"), I discussed ways to use XML on the client using COM technologies. In particular, I explored XML implementations of the document/view architecture. The book *XML Programming Core Reference* (Microsoft Press, 2002) also contains chapters that illustrate the use of XML on the client.

Internet Explorer has played a key role in this chapter as the richest browser available today. You can get an inside look at the expanded capabilities of Internet Explorer 6.0 through the *Microsoft Internet Explorer 6 Resource Kit*, (Microsoft Press, 2001).

Finally, Jason Clark's excellent piece "Code Access Security and Distribution Features in .NET Enhanced Client-Side Apps" (*MSDN Magazine*, June 2002) celebrates the return of the rich client in the Windows Forms platform. Among other things, this article covers .NET Framework browser controls and provides a handful of useful caveats and tips.

15

.NET Framework Application Configuration

To the extent that it is possible, all applications, regardless of platform, should be designed in a parametric way and should read some of their settings from an external file. Simply by updating the configuration file, developers and system administrators can change the way in which the application works as well as elements of the user interface. In Microsoft Windows 3.x, user preferences and application settings were usually stored in INI files located in the Windows folder or in the application's main directory. This practice was retained in Microsoft Win32, although since Windows 95, the system registry has become the recommended store for Win32 and Component Object Model (COM) application settings. With both INI files and the registry, however, the developer had a certain degree of freedom in designing the layout of the data. Various guidelines have been suggested over time, but in fact the structure of INI files and registry subtrees was different from one application to the next.

The Microsoft .NET Framework defines a tailor-made, XML-based API to access configuration files and, in doing so, forces developers to adopt a common, rich, and predefined schema for storing application settings. Using configuration files, administrators can control which resources a user can access, which versions of assemblies an application will use and from where, and which connection strings should be used. Configuration files can also include application-specific settings such as the buttons to be displayed on the toolbar, the size and position of controls, and other, more specific, state information. Using configuration files, you give your application a bunch of dynamic properties and eliminate the need to recompile every time different settings should be applied.

.NET Framework configuration files are XML files saved with the .config extension and named and located according to the type of the application. Managed code can use the classes in the *System.Configuration* namespace to read settings from the configuration files but not to write settings to those files. Configuration files are considered plain XML files, and appropriate XML writers should be used to edit their contents.

In this chapter, we'll delve into the .NET Framework configuration engine, reviewing the characteristics of the main classes involved and how key tasks are accomplished. We'll analyze the various types of configuration files and their overall schemas, and you'll learn how to customize a .config file with custom tags and custom contents.

Configuration Files

The .NET Framework provides three basic types of configuration files: machine, application, and security. Despite their different contents and goals, all configuration files are XML files and share the same schema. For example, all configuration files begin with a *<configuration>* node and then differentiate their contents and child nodes according to the final goal and the information contained. In this chapter, we'll focus primarily on application configuration files, but this section also provides a quick introduction to the other types of configuration files.

The XML Schema for Configuration Settings

As mentioned, configuration files are standard XML files that follow a particular schema. This schema defines all possible configuration settings for machine, security, and application configuration files. The .NET Framework provides you with ad hoc classes to read configuration settings, but no writing can be performed. You need to be familiar with XML readers and writers if you want to directly edit the configuration files. (In light of this, bear in mind that XML elements and attribute names are case-sensitive.)

All the configuration files are rooted in the *<configuration>* element. Table 15-1 lists the first-level children of the *<configuration>* element. Each node has a specified number of child elements that provide a full description of the setting. For example, the *<system.web>* element optionally contains the *<authorization>* tag, in which you can store information about the users who can safely access the URL resources.

Table 15-1   Children of the <configuration> Element

Element	Description
<appSettings>	Contains custom application settings in the specified XML format.
<configSections>	Describes the configuration sections for custom settings. If this element is in a configuration file, it must be the first child of the *<configuration>* root.
<mscorlib> \<cryptographySettings>	Cryptography schema; describes the elements that map friendly algorithm names to classes that implement cryptography algorithms.
<runtime>	Run-time settings schema; describes the elements that configure assembly binding and run-time behavior.
<startup>	Startup settings schema; contains the elements that specify which version of the common language runtime (CLR) must be used.
<system.diagnostics>	Describes the elements that specify trace switches and listeners that collect, store, and route messages.
<system.net>	Network schema; specifies elements to indicate how the .NET Framework connects to the Internet, including the default proxy, authentication modules, and connection parameters.
<system.runtime.remoting>	Settings schema; configures the client and server applications that implement remoting.
<system.web>	Microsoft ASP.NET configuration section schema; contains the elements that control how ASP.NET Web applications behave.

Because we're focusing on application configuration files in this chapter, for our purposes, two of these elements have particular importance: *<appSettings>* and *<configSections>*. The *<configSections>* element defines the sections that will be used in the rest of the document to group information. The *<appSettings>* element contains user-defined nodes whose structure has been previously defined in the *<configSections>* node.

Armed with this working knowledge of the internal layout of configuration files, let's learn a bit more about the two configuration file types that won't receive an in-depth exposure in this chapter—machine and security configuration files.

Machine Configuration Files

Machine configuration files are named machine.config and are located in the CONFIG subdirectory of the .NET Framework installation path. A typical path is shown here:

```
C:\WINNT\Microsoft.NET\Framework\v1.0.3705\CONFIG
```

The machine.config file contains machine-wide settings that apply to assembly binding, built-in remoting channels, and the ASP.NET runtime. In particular, the machine.config file contains information about the browser capabilities, registered HTTP handlers, and page compilation. The following listing provides an excerpt from a machine.config file:

```xml
<?xml version="1.0" encoding="UTF-8"?>
<configuration>
    <configSections>
        <section name="runtime"
            type="System.Configuration.IgnoreSectionHandler, System,
                Version=1.0.3300.0, Culture=neutral,
                PublicKeyToken=b77a5c561934e089" allowLocation="false" />
        <section name="mscorlib"
            type="System.Configuration.IgnoreSectionHandler, System,
                Version=1.0.3300.0, Culture=neutral,
                PublicKeyToken=b77a5c561934e089" allowLocation="false" />
        <section name="appSettings"
            type="System.Configuration.NameValueFileSectionHandler, System,
                Version=1.0.3300.0, Culture=neutral,
                PublicKeyToken=b77a5c561934e089" />
        ⋮
    </configSections>
    ⋮
</configuration>
```

The machine.config file typically contains remoting, ASP.NET, and diagnostics sections, plus the *<configSections>* element. Declaring a section in the machine.config file enables you to use that section in any configuration file on that computer, unless the setting is explicitly overwritten in the application configuration file.

Security Configuration Files

Security configuration files contain information about the code groups and the permission sets associated with a policy level. A policy level describes all the security measures for a given context. There are three policy levels for security: enterprise, machine, and user. The CLR grants permissions to an assembly based on the minimum set of permissions granted by any of the policy levels.

> **Note**   A *code group* is a logical grouping of code that specifies certain conditions for membership. Any code that meets the given criteria can be included in the group. Code groups have associated permission sets. A permission set, in turn, defines the resources that can be accessed at execution time.

The name and the location of the security configuration file depend on the policy level. The configuration file for the enterprise policy level is named enterprisesec.config and resides in the same directory as the machine.config file. Contained in the same folder but with a different name, the security.config file characterizes the machine policy level. The enterprise level groups security settings for the entire enterprise; the machine policy level, on the other hand, defines the security for the local machine. Both levels can be configured only by an administrator.

The user policy configuration file is configurable by the current logged-on user. It is named security.config and resides in a folder under the user profile subtree. A typical path is shown here:

```
C:\Documents and Settings\[UserName]\Application Data\Microsoft\CLR Security Co
nfig\v1.0.3705
```

> **Note**   The paths for security configuration files are specific to each operating system. The paths mentioned here refer to Microsoft Windows 2000. For other systems' paths, refer to the MSDN documentation.

Editing the contents of the file, and thereby modifying the security poli-cies, is a potentially critical task that should be accomplished using the .NET Framework Configuration tool (a Control Panel applet named mscorcfg.msc) or the Code Access Security Policy tool (caspol.exe).

Application Configuration Files

As the name suggests, application configuration files are designed to contain settings specific to an application. The settings stored in the file are consumed by the CLR as well as by the application itself. The CLR reads information such as assembly binding policy, the location of remoted objects, and ASP.NET set-tings, if applicable. The application reads settings that correspond to the param-eters it needs to work.

The name and the location of the application configuration file depend on the application's model, which can be one of the following: Windows Forms or console executable, ASP.NET application or Web service, or Internet Explorer–hosted application.

The Configuration File for Executables

For Windows Forms and console-based applications, the configuration file resides in the same directory as the application. The name of the file is the name of the application (including the .exe extension) followed by a .config extension. For example, if the application is named MyProgram.exe, the config-uration file must be named MyProgram.exe.config.

> **Note**   Windows Forms applications, as well as any other type of .NET Framework applications, can in some situations use a configura-tion file with a custom name and format. This is possible when the only information stored in the file is application-specific settings.

The ASP.NET web.config File

ASP.NET and Web service configuration files are named web.config and are located in the root of the virtual directory. When you request a particular page, however, the ASP.NET runtime determines the correct settings by looking at all web.config files found, proceeding from the virtual folder root down to the actual path of the requested resource—typically a child directory.

Innermost configuration files can overwrite settings defined at an outer level. Likewise, pages located in internal folders inherit the settings of configuration files found at upper levels. For example, you have two web.config files, one in the root of the Web application and one in the OtherPages subfolder. The innermost configuration file is in no way involved when the URL points to a page in the root folder. However, when a page in the OtherPages subfolder is requested, the contents of the two web.config files are merged. In the case of conflicting settings, the innermost values win.

Internet Explorer–Hosted Applications

As we saw in Chapter 14, managed controls hosted in Internet Explorer can also have a configuration file. The name of this file doesn't have to follow specific rules, but the location of the file must be in the same virtual directory as the application. You simply indicate the file and its location using the *<link>* tag, as shown here:

```
<link rel="configuration" href="location">
```

In this declaration, *location* is a placeholder that denotes the URL to the actual configuration file. Whatever the name of the file, the format must be compliant with the standard XML schema described in the section "The XML Schema for Configuration Settings," on page 624.

Managing Configuration Settings

Application settings, including general user preferences and state information, are saved in the *<appSettings>* section of a configuration file. The following code snippet shows some typical output:

```
<configuration>
   <appSettings>
      <add key="LastLeftTopPosition" value="100,200" />
      <add key="LastSize" value="300,400" />
   </appSettings>
</configuration>
```

The settings in the preceding sample file refer to the position and size of a window when the application is closed. The syntax of the *<appSettings>* section is defined as follows:

```
<appSettings>
   <add key="..." value="..." />
   <remove key="..." />
   <clear />
</appSettings>
```

The *<add>* element adds a new setting to the internal collection. This new setting has a value and is identified by a unique key. The *<remove>* element removes a specified setting from the collection. The setting is identified using the key. Finally, the *<clear>* element clears all the settings that have previously been defined in the section.

> **Note** The *<remove>* and the *<clear>* elements are particularly useful in ASP.NET configuration files in which a hierarchy of files can be created. For example, you can use the *<clear>* element to remove all settings from your application that were defined at a higher level in the configuration file hierarchy.

In general, the requirement that an application setting must be composed of a name/value pair is arbitrary. By default, the *<appSettings>* section is configured to use the name/value form. All sections used in a configuration file, including the *<appSettings>* section, must be declared in the initial *<configSections>* block. The following code snippet demonstrates the standard declaration of the *<appSettings>* section:

```
<configSections>
   <section
      name="appSettings"
      type="System.Configuration.NameValueFileSectionHandler, ..." />
</configSections>
```

The *<section>* element takes two attributes—*name* and *type*. The *name* attribute denotes the name of the section being declared. The *type* attribute indicates the name of the managed class that reads and parses the contents of the section from the configuration file. The value of the *type* attribute is a comma-separated string that includes the class name and the assembly that contains it.

The *<section>* element also has two optional attributes: *allowDefinition* and *allowLocation*. These attributes apply only to ASP.NET applications and are ignored when other types of applications are running. *AllowDefinition* specifies in which configuration files the section can be used—everywhere, the machine configuration file only, or the machine and the application configuration file. This attribute provides a way to control ASP.NET settings inheritance. The *<allowLocation>* attribute specifies whether the section can be used within the *<location>* section.

> **Note**   User applications don't need to declare the *<appSettings>* section because the section is already declared in the system's machine.config file, as we saw in the section "Machine Configuration Files," on page 626. You don't need to repeat the *<appSettings>* declaration unless you want to modify some of the attributes, including the name/value format of the settings.

The *ConfigurationSettings* Class

To programmatically read application settings, you use the *ConfigurationSettings* class. *ConfigurationSettings* is a small, sealed class that simply provides one static method (*GetConfig*) and one static property (*AppSettings*).

The *AppSettings* property is a read-only *NameValueCollection* object designed to get the information stored in the *<appSettings>* section. If no setting is specified, or if no *<appSettings>* section exists, an empty collection is returned.

> **Note**   To have a read-only *NameValueCollection* object, you need to use a class that derives from *NameValueCollection* and sets the protected member *IsReadonly* to *true*. This is exactly what happens under the hood of the *AppSettings* property. The helper collection class that the *AppSettings* property returns is an undocumented class named *ReadOnlyNameValueCollection*.

The *GetConfig* method returns the configuration settings for the specified section, as shown here:

```
public static object GetConfig(string sectionName);
```

Although the method signature indicates an *object* return type, the actual return value you get from a call to *GetConfig* is a class derived from *NameValueCollection*. In particular, the class is *ReadOnlyNameValueCollection* if the section is *<appSettings>*.

> **Note** In general, the object returned by *GetConfig* is determined by the handler class specified for the section. If the handler is *NameValueSectionHandler* or a related class, you get settings stored in a name/value collection. As we'll see chapter in the section "Types of Section Handlers," on page 640, other options exist that could result in a different way of packing settings for applications.

The *AppSettings* property acts as a wrapper for the *GetConfig* method. The actual implementation of the property consists of a call to *GetConfig* in which the section name defaults to *<appSettings>*. The following pseudocode demonstrates:

```
public static NameValueCollection AppSettings
{
   get {return GetConfig("appSettings");}
}
```

The real code is a bit more sophisticated than this, however. After *GetConfig* returns, the *get* accessor verifies that the returned value is not *null*. *GetConfig* returns *null* if the specified section is empty or does not exist. If the returned object is *null*, the *get* accessor of the *AppSettings* property creates an empty collection and returns that to the caller. The pseudocode is shown here:

```
public static NameValueCollection AppSettings
{
   get
   {
      ReadOnlyNameValueCollection o = GetConfig("appSettings");
      if (o == null)
      {
         o = new ReadOnlyNameValueCollection();
         o.IsReadOnly = true;
      }

   return o;
   }
}
```

Internally, the *GetConfig* method first determines the name and location of the configuration file to access and then proceeds by creating a specialized XML text reader to operate on the XML document. Each XML node read is parsed and the contents stored as name/value pairs in a *ReadOnlyNameValueCollection* object. To parse the contents of each XML node found, the method uses an instance of the section handler class specified in the section declaration within the *<configSections>* block. To read the *<appSettings>* section, *GetConfig* resorts to the *NameValueSectionHandler* handler. This handler parses all the *<add>* nodes below *<appSettings>* and adds entries to the collection. We'll look at section handler objects in more detail in the section "Customizing the XML Schema for Your Data," on page 646.

The *<appSettings>* Section Handler

In our sample machine.config file, the *<appSettings>* section is read through an instance of the *NameValueFileSectionHandler* class. What's the difference between this class and the *NameValueSectionHandler* class?

The MSDN documentation doesn't provide further information about the *NameValueFileSectionHandler* class; it notes only that the class is intended to be used only by the .NET Framework. But the *NameValueFileSectionHandler* class is actually a wrapper for *NameValueSectionHandler* class, which provides an extra, although undocumented, feature. In particular, the *NameValueFile-SectionHandler* section handler allows the application settings to be stored in a separated file in accordance with the following syntax:

```
<appSettings file="myfile.config" />
```

The file pointed to by the *file* attribute is read as if it is an *<appSettings>* section in the configuration file. Note that the root element of the myfile.config file must match the section that refers to it. So if the *file* attribute belongs to the *<appSettings>* section, the root element of the file being pointed to must be named *<appSettings>*.

The *NameValueFileSectionHandler* object processes the contents of the embedded file using the *NameValueSectionHandler* class. If no file is embedded in the *<appSettings>* section but the default documented schema is used, the two section handlers are functionally equivalent.

Although undocumented, the following code represents a perfectly valid schema for the application's configuration file. The sample application AppSettings, available in this book's sample files, demonstrates how to take advantage of this syntax.

```
<configuration>
   <appSettings file="myfile.config" />
</configuration>
```

The myfile.config file contains the actual settings, as shown here:

```
<appSettings>
   <add key="LastLeftTopPosition" value="100,200" />
   <add key="LastSize" value="300,400" />
</appSettings>
```

Using Settings Through Code

Now that you know how to read settings, let's create a sample application that uses persistent settings to refresh its own user interface. This application, shown in the following code, is a simple Windows Forms program that always appears at the same size and in the same position as when it was last closed. The settings are stored in a myfile.config file and are read using the *AppSettings* property of the *ConfigurationSettings* class.

```
private void Form1_Load(object sender, System.EventArgs e)
{
    // Read settings
    string wndPos =
        ConfigurationSettings.AppSettings["LastLeftTopPosition"];
    string wndSize = ConfigurationSettings.AppSettings["LastSize"];

    // Update internal members
    string[] tmp;
    if (wndPos != null)
    {
        int m_top, m_left;
        tmp = wndPos.Split(',');
        m_left = Convert.ToInt32(tmp[0]);
        m_top = Convert.ToInt32(tmp[1]);
        this.Location = new Point(m_left, m_top);
    }

    if (wndSize != null)
    {
        int m_width, m_height;
        tmp = wndSize.Split(',');
        m_width = Convert.ToInt32(tmp[0]);
        m_height = Convert.ToInt32(tmp[1]);
        this.Size = new Size(m_width, m_height);
    }
}
```

At loading, the form reads the settings from the configuration file, extracts position and size information, and updates the *Location* and *Size* properties. Next the form is displayed in the same location and at the same size as when it was closed.

Enumerating All Settings

The *AppSettings* property is a static member shared by all instances of *ConfigurationSettings* running in the application domain (AppDomain). If you need to access all the application settings, or simply to count them, you don't need to read one property after the next. The property already contains all the settings in an easily manageable *NameValueCollection* object. The following code shows how to enumerate all the settings in a drop-down list:

```
foreach(string s in ConfigurationSettings.AppSettings)
   SettingList.Items.Add(s);
SettingList.SelectedIndex = 0;
```

Figure 15-1 shows the sample application in action. The drop-down list contains all the settings.

Figure 15-1   Reading and using configuration settings programmatically.

Updating Settings

The .NET Framework does not provide any facilities for updating a configuration file. How you create and maintain the application's file is up to you and might require different approaches for different cases. As long as the size of the file is limited to just a few KB, loading the entire document into an *Xml-Document* object is plausible and results in an effective and familiar programming interface. To add new nodes, you use the methods of the XML Document Object Model (XML DOM); to locate a particular node to update, you use XPath queries. (XML DOM is covered in Chapter 5, and XPath expressions are covered in Chapter 6.)

Let's proceed to persisting the location and size of the form. When the form is about to close, a *Closing* event is fired to let users perform some clean-up operations and other finalizing tasks—for example, persisting state information. The following code illustrates the event handler used in the sample application:

```
private void Form1_Closing(object sender, CancelEventArgs e)
{
    // Load the config file as an XML document
    // (Assume that the config file exists)
    string configFile;
    configFile = Assembly.GetExecutingAssembly().Location + ".config";
    XmlDocument doc = new XmlDocument();
    doc.Load(configFile);
```

(continued)

```
// Some internal variables
XmlNodeList settings;
XmlElement node, appSettingsNode;
string query;

// Get the <appSettings> node
query = "configuration/appSettings";
appSettingsNode = (XmlElement) doc.SelectSingleNode(query);
if (appSettingsNode == null)
    return;
    ⋮
}
```

This code first loads the configuration file into an instance of the *Xml-Document* class. The name of the file is obtained by combining the name of the currently executing assembly with the .config extension. Next the code gets a reference to the *<appSettings>* node. The reference to the *<appSettings>* node is obtained through an XPath query executed by *SelectSingleNode*. By design, the *<appSettings>* subtree is always a direct child of the *<configuration>* root node. The following code demonstrates how to update—or, if needed, to create—a setting.

```
// Get the LastLeftTopPosition setting
query = "configuration/appSettings/add[@key='LastLeftTopPosition']";
settings = doc.SelectNodes(query);

// If the node does not exist, create it
if (settings.Count >0)
    node = (XmlElement) settings[0];
else
{
    // Create the node <add key="..." value="..." />
    node = doc.CreateElement("add");
    XmlAttribute attKey = doc.CreateAttribute("key");
    attKey.Value = "LastLeftTopPosition";
    node.Attributes.SetNamedItem(attKey);
    XmlAttribute attVal = doc.CreateAttribute("value");
    node.Attributes.SetNamedItem(attVal);

    // Append the node
    appSettingsNode.AppendChild(node);
}

// Update the value attribute
node.Attributes["value"].Value = String.Format("{0},{1}",
    this.Left, this.Top);
```

Finally, you save the file and persist the changes, as shown here:

```
doc.Save(configFile);
```

The *XmlDocument* class is particularly useful for performing this kind of task because it allows you to selectively access a particular node. If you have dozens of settings to persist, you might want to take a different route and rewrite the configuration file from scratch each time. In this case, using an XML writer can result in more effective code.

If the configuration file contains information other than application settings and this information takes up a lot of room, referencing an external configuration file from the *<appSettings>* node can become an attractive option. Although the *<appSettings>* node's *file* attribute is not documented, it works just fine and enables you to separate application and user settings from the rest of the settings.

The *AppSettingsReader* Class

A more specialized tool for reading application settings is the *AppSettings-Reader* class. This class provides a single method, named *GetValue*, for reading values of a particular type from the configuration file. The *GetValue* method takes two arguments—the name of the setting to retrieve and the type to return—as shown here:

```
public object GetValue(string key, Type type);
```

The *GetValue* method retrieves the value of the given setting using the *AppSettings* property and then performs an automatic cast to the specified type. Unlike the *AppSettings* property of the *ConfigurationSettings* object, which always returns a string, the *GetValue* method works in a strongly typed way. Suppose that you have the following setting:

```
<add key="ReleaseDate" value="10-9-02" />
```

You can load the value directly into a *DateTime* object. Here's how:

```
AppSettingsReader reader = new AppSettingsReader();
DateTime relDate = (DateTime) reader.GetValue("ReleaseDate",
   typeof(DateTime));
MessageBox.Show(relDate.ToShortDateString());
```

Note that the *GetValue* method is not marked as static, which means that you need a fresh instance of the *AppSettingsReader* class to call the method. As mentioned, the *GetValue* method is a simple wrapper for the *AppSettings* property, which is a static member. If you plan to use *AppSettingsReader* in your application, you're better off instantiating the object only once during the startup phase.

Creating New Configuration Sections

The *<appSettings>* section is one of many predefined configuration sections provided by the .NET Framework. Programmers can also create their own sections. To create a new section, you need to accomplish two basic tasks: declare the section in the *<configSections>* block, and fill the section with custom data.

One of the key bits of information you need to specify while declaring a new section is the name of the section handler class. The section handler class can be one of the predefined classes provided by the .NET Framework or a class that you write from scratch or inherit from an existing class. The section handler object is responsible for reading and parsing the actual contents of the setting.

Declaring a New Section

The *<configSections>* node contains the declarations of all the sections in the various configuration files. The predefined sections are declared in the machine.config file that the .NET Framework installs. Custom sections must be registered by the application that plans to use them. The application's configuration file is a good place for inserting this information.

The *<configSections>* node can accept up to four child nodes: *<section>*, *<sectionGroup>*, *<remove>*, and *<clear>*. The *<remove>* element removes a previously defined section, or a section group, from the *<configSections>* block. The *<clear>* element clears all previously defined sections and section groups.

> **Note**   The *<remove>* and *<clear>* elements don't affect the actual data stored in the configuration file. Removing a section doesn't erase the related data from the file, but the data becomes unreachable because of the missing section declaration.

A new section is registered using the *<section>* element. As mentioned, the *name* attribute of this element specifies the name of the section and the *type* attribute specifies the name of the section handler class. The name of the configuration section class should contain full assembly information, including version, culture, and public key token, if any. All the predefined handlers are defined in the same assembly and therefore share the same information, as in the following example:

```
System, Version=1.0.3300.0, Culture=neutral,
    PublicKeyToken=b77a5c561934e089
```

> **Note**   When you create a custom assembly with no strong name (a strong name is necessary if you want to put the assembly in the global assembly cache), the version number is defined in the assemblyinfo file that Microsoft Visual Studio .NET automatically adds to the project. The culture is *neutral*, and the public key token is *null*. Here's an example:
>
> ```
> AppSettings_CS, Version=1.0.9.0, Culture=neutral,
>     PublicKeyToken=null
> ```

The custom section follows the *<configSections>* block and contains the actual configuration settings. The following code creates a new section named *userPreferences* that accepts name/value pairs:

```
<configuration>
    <configSections>
        <section name="userPreferences"
            type="System.Configuration.NameValueFileSectionHandler, ⇥
                System, Version=1.0.3300.0, Culture=neutral, ⇥
                PublicKeyToken=b77a5c561934e089" />
    </configSections>
    <userPreferences>
        <add key="ReleaseDate" value="10-9-02" />
    </userPreferences>
</configuration>
```

Sections can be grouped under a *<sectionGroup>* element. Declaring a section group creates a namespace and ensures that no naming conflicts arise with other configuration sections defined by someone else. Section groups can also be nested within each other. The following code snippet declares the *userPreferences* section nested in the *AppName* group:

```
<sectionGroup name="AppName">
   <section name="userPreferences"
      type="System.Configuration.NameValueSectionHandler, →
         system, Version=1.0.3300.0, Culture=neutral, →
         PublicKeyToken=b77a5c561934e089" />
</sectionGroup>
```

A node with the group name must also wrap the settings subtree, as shown here:

```
<AppName>
   <userPreferences>
      <add key="ReleaseDate" value="10-9-02" />
   </userPreferences>
</AppName>
```

To read the settings of a custom section, you use the *GetConfig* method, passing the fully qualified name of the section to retrieve. For example, the following code returns the settings in the *<userPreferences>* section:

```
NameValueCollection settings;
settings = ConfigurationSettings.GetConfig("AppName/userPreferences");
MessageBox.Show(setting["ReleaseDate"]);
```

> **Note** A new section, or section group, that is defined in the machine.config file is visible to all applications. This setting can be changed using the *allowDefinition* attribute for ASP.NET applications only. In contrast, sections defined in the application configuration file are visible only to the local application.

Types of Section Handlers

A *section handler* is a .NET Framework class that implements the *IConfigurationSectionHandler* interface. It interprets and processes the configuration settings stored in a configuration section and returns a configuration object based on the configuration settings. The returned object is accessed by the *GetConfig* method. The data type returned by the *GetConfig* method depends on the section handler defined for the particular section.

The .NET Framework provides a few predefined section handlers, listed in Table 15-2. All of these section handlers belong to the *System.Configuration* namespace and are implemented in the *System* assembly.

Table 15-2   Predefined Section Handlers

Class	Description
DictionarySectionHandler	Reads name/value pairs and groups them in a hash table object.
IgnoreSectionHandler	The *System.Configuration* classes ignore the sections marked with this handler because their contents will be processed by other components. This handler is an alternative to using and declaring custom handlers.
NameValueFileSectionHandler	Reads name/value pairs from a file referenced in the *<appSettings>* section and groups them in a *NameValueCollection* object.
NameValueSectionHandler	Reads name/value pairs and groups them in a *NameValueCollection* object.
SingleTagSectionHandler	Reads settings from attributes stored in a single XML node. The data is returned as a hash table.

In the .NET Framework, the classes in the *System.Configuration* namespace are responsible for parsing the contents of the configuration files. These classes are designed to process the entire contents of the configuration files. The classes also throw an exception when a configuration section lacks a corresponding entry in the *<configSections>* block and when the layout of the data does not match the declaration.

Of the five section handlers, we have examined *NameValueSectionHandler* and *NameValueFileSectionHandler*. The *DictionarySectionHandler* class is very similar; it differs only in that it stores settings in a hash table instead of in a *NameValueCollection* object. Collection objects are more efficient if they are used to store a small number of items (ideally fewer than 10), whereas a hash table provides better performance with large collections of items. The *IgnoreSectionHandler* and *SingleTagSectionHandler* classes deserve a bit more attention, and we'll look at them next.

The *IgnoreSectionHandler* Section Handler

A few subsystems in the .NET Framework store configuration data in the machine.config file but process the data themselves, without relying on the services provided by the *System.Configuration* classes. For example, the machine.config file contains remoting and startup information that is processed outside the configuration engine. To prevent the configuration file from parsing exceptions, you can use a dummy section handler—*IgnoreSectionHandler*. This handler handles sections of configuration data rather than relying on the classes in *System.Configuration*. It could be argued that such data should be stored in a system configuration file, like the machine.config file, or in a custom file. Looking at the following excerpt from the machine.config file, you can see that remoting configuration settings are processed by the remoting classes, whereas HTTP run-time configuration settings are processed by a custom handler:

```
<!-- Tell the .NET Framework to ignore these sections -->
<section name="system.runtime.remoting"
    type="System.Configuration.IgnoreSectionHandler, System,
    Version=1.0.3300.0, Culture=neutral,
    PublicKeyToken=b77a5c561934e089" />


<!-- Employ a custom section handler -->
<section name="httpRuntime"
    type="System.Web.Configuration.HttpRuntimeConfigurationHandler,
    System.Web, Version=1.0.3300.0, Culture=neutral,
    PublicKeyToken=b03f5f7f11d50a3a" />
```

In both cases, configuration settings need a customized and more sophisticated layout than name/value pairs. In the first scenario, the handler is embedded in the remoting subsystem; in the second scenario, the handler conforms to the configuration guidelines but is simply not one of the predefined handlers. As mentioned, because by design the configuration classes read through all the contents of a configuration file and throw exceptions whenever they encounter something wrong, custom settings handled outside the configuration namespace must have a section handler, although one that does nothing—the *IgnoreSectionHandler* handler.

The *SingleTagSectionHandler* Section Handler

The *SingleTagSectionHandler* class supports a simpler schema for storing configuration settings. Unlike *NameValueSectionHandler*, which supports name/value pairs defined within *<add>* nodes, the *SingleTagSectionHandler* class uses a single XML node with as many attributes as needed. Each attribute maps to a setting, and the name of the attribute is also the key to access the value.

In other words, the *SingleTagSectionHandler* class provides an attribute-based view of the configuration settings, whereas the *NameValueSectionHandler* class (and *DictionarySectionHandler* as well) provides an element-based representation. The following code shows the way in which settings are stored by a single tag section handler:

```
<configuration>
    <configSections>
        <section name="MyCountries"
            type="System.Configuration.SingTagSectionHandler" />
    </configSections>
    <MyCountries country1="USA"
                 country2="Italy"
                 country3="Iceland" />
</configuration>
```

Under the Hood of Section Handlers

As mentioned, a configuration section handler is simply a managed class that implements the *IConfigurationSectionHandler* interface. The classes that implement the *IConfigurationSectionHandler* interface define the rules for transforming pieces of XML configuration files into usable objects. The created objects can be of an arbitrary type. The following code shows the interface signature:

```
public interface IConfigurationSectionHandler
{
    object Create(object parent, object configContext,
        XmlNode section);
}
```

The interface includes a single method, *Create*, that configuration readers call to obtain an object that represents the contents of a particular setting. This method takes three arguments: a parent object, a context object, and a section XML node. In general, the configuration object can be obtained by combining the information read and composed in a parent directory with the current settings. This information is stored in the *parent* argument. A configuration setting can't always have a parent path, however; this is possible only with web.config files, which are specifically designed to support configuration inheritance. For all other configuration files, the *parent* argument of the *Create* method is always *null*. The *parent* argument being passed should not be altered, and if a modification is necessary, you first clone the object and then modify it.

> **Note**   If it isn't *null*, the *parent* argument is guaranteed to be an object returned by a previous call made to the *Create* method on the same section handler object. Therefore, by design, the type of the *parent* argument is identical to the return type of the current implementation of *Create*. For example, if the *Create* method returns a *NameValueCollection* object, the *parent* argument can only be an object of type *NameValueCollection* or *null*.

A section handler object might be used in any configuration file, including a web.config file. For this reason, when implementing the *IConfigurationSectionHandler* interface, you should check the value in the *parent* argument and act accordingly. We'll look at an example of this in the section "Implementing the *DataSet* Section Handler," on page 653.

The *configContext* argument is non-*null* only if you use the section handler within a web.config file in an ASP.NET application. In this case, the argument evaluates to an object of type *HttpConfigurationContext*, whose only significant member is a property named *VirtualPath*. The *VirtualPath* property contains the virtual path to web.config with respect to the ongoing Web request. In this way, you can determine the level of configuration nesting at which your handler is called to operate.

Finally, the *section* argument is the XML DOM node object rooted at the section to be handled. The argument is an XML DOM subtree that represents the data to be processed.

> **Note**   To better understand the rather symbolic role played by the *IgnoreSectionHandler* section handler class, consider what the implementation of its *Create* method looks like:
>
> ```
> object Create(object parent, object context, XmlNode section)
> {
>     return null;
> }
> ```
>
> No information is returned, but neither is an exception thrown.

Customizing Attribute Names

Configuration settings are stored using predefined attribute names: *key* for the setting's name, and *value* for the actual contents. Such names are hard-coded as protected members in the *NameValueSectionHandler* and *DictionarySectionHandler* classes. Their associated properties are named *KeyAttributeName* and *ValueAttributeName*, respectively. To customize those names, you must derive a new class, override the properties, and use the new class as your section handler.

The following code demonstrates a class that inherits from *NameValueSectionHandler* and simply renames the attributes to be used for the settings. Instead of the default names *key* and *value*, *SettingKey* and *SettingValue* are used.

```
public class CustomNameValueSectionHandler : NameValueSectionHandler
{
   public CustomNameValueSectionHandler() : base()
   {
   }

   protected override string KeyAttributeName
   {
      get{return "SettingKey";}
   }
   protected override string ValueAttributeName
   {
      get{return "SettingValue";}
   }
}
```

Note that the *KeyAttributeName* and *ValueAttributeName* properties are read-only, protected, and virtual. You must retain the same modifier and override the properties in a new class. There is no need to make the properties read/write. The preceding class is defined in the sample application AppSettings_CS available in this book's sample files and enables you to access the configuration file shown here:

```
<configuration>
  <configSections>
    <sectionGroup name="AppName">
      <section name="CustomSection"
          type="AppSettings_CS.CustomNameValueSectionHandler,
             AppSettings_CS" />
    </sectionGroup>
```

(continued)

```
    </configSections>
    <AppName>
       <CustomSection>
           <add SettingKey="Property" SettingValue="My value" />
       </CustomSection>
    </AppName>
</configuration>
```

The beauty of these section handlers is that they encapsulate all the logic necessary to access settings in the configuration file. The application is not affected by the actual layout of the setting. As a result, reading the preceding value requires the same high-level code, regardless of the attribute names you use, as shown here:

```
NameValueCollection coll;
coll = ConfigurationSettings.GetConfig("AppName/CustomSection");
MessageBox.Show(coll["Property"]);
```

Customizing the XML Schema for Your Data

The predefined XML schema for configuration files fits the bill in most cases, but when you have complex and structured information to preserve across application sessions, none of the existing schemas appear to be powerful enough. At this point, you have two possible workarounds. You can simply avoid using a standard configuration file and instead use a plain XML file written according to the schema that you feel is appropriate for the data. Alternatively, you can embed your XML configuration data in the standard application configuration file but provide a tailor-made configuration section handler to read it. A third option exists. You could insert the data in the configuration file, register the section with a null handler (*IgnoreSectionHandler*), and then use another piece of code (for example, a custom utility) to read and write the settings.

Before we look more closely at designing and writing a custom configuration handler according to the XML schema you prefer, let's briefly compare the various approaches. In terms of performance and programming power, all approaches are roughly equivalent, but some key differences still exist. In theory, using an ad hoc file results in the most efficient approach because you can create made-to-measure, and subsequently faster, code. However, this is only a possibility—if your code happens to be badly written, the performance of your whole application might still be bad. The *System.Configuration* classes are designed to serve as a general-purpose mechanism for manipulating settings. They work great on average but are not necessarily the best option when an effective manipulation of the settings is key to your code. On the other hand, the *System.Configuration* classes, and the standard configuration files, require you to write a minimal amount of code. The more customization you want, the more code you have to write, with all the risks (mostly errors and bugs) that this introduces.

As a rule of thumb, using the standard configuration files should be the first option to evaluate. Resort to custom files only if you want to control all aspects of data reading (for example, if you want to provide feedback while loading), if performance is critical, or if you just don't feel comfortable with the predefined section handlers. Finally, although it's reasonable to use the *Ignore-SectionHandler* handler in the context in which the .NET Framework uses it, I don't recommend using *IgnoreSectionHandler* in user applications. A custom section handler or a custom file is preferable.

If you're considering creating a custom file based on a customized XML schema, *DataSet* objects present an interesting option. Assuming that the data to be stored lends itself to being represented in a tabular format, you could write an XML configuration file using the Microsoft ADO.NET normal form and load that data into a *DataSet* object. Loading data requires a single call to the *ReadXml* method, and managing data is easy due to the powerful interface of the *DataSet* class. We'll look at an example of the *DataSet* section handler next.

> **Note**   In the section "Customizing Attribute Names," on page 645, we analyzed a custom section handler inherited from the *NameValueSec-tionHandler* class. That trivial handler was simply aimed at overriding some of the standard features of one of the predefined handlers. A truly custom section handler is a more sophisticated object that uses an XML reader to access a portion of the configuration file and parse the contents.

Creating a *DataSet* Section Handler

Let's look at a practical example of a new section handler named *DatasetSec-tionHandler*. This section handler reads XML data from a configuration file and stores it in a new *DataSet* object. The data must be laid out in a format that the *ReadXml* method can successfully process. The typical format is the ADO.NET normal form that we examined in Chapter 9.

Along with the custom section handler, let's write an application that can handle configuration data through a *DataSet* object. Suppose you have a Windows Forms application that can be extended with plug-in modules. We won't look at the details of how this could be done here; instead, we'll focus on how to effectively store configuration data as XML. (In the section "Further Reading," on page 655, you'll find a reference to a recent article that addresses this topic fully.) We'll analyze the plug-in engine for Windows Forms applications only, but the same pattern can be easily applied to Web Forms applications as well.

Extending Windows Forms Application Menus

The sample application shown in Figure 15-2 allows users to add custom menu items below the first item on the Tools menu. Such menu items are linked to external plug-in modules. In this context, a plug-in module is simply a class dynamically loaded from an assembly. More generally, the plug-in class will need to implement a particular interface, or inherit from a given base class, because the application needs to have a consistent way to call into any plug-in class. (For more information and a complete example of extensible .NET Framework applications, check out the article referenced in the section "Further Reading," on page 655. In our sample application, we'll limit ourselves to creating a context-sensitive *MessageBox* call for each new registered plug-in.

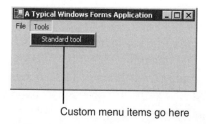

Custom menu items go here

Figure 15-2   A Windows Forms application that can be extended with plug-in modules that integrate with the menu.

At loading, the sample application calls the following routine to set up the menu:

```
private void SetupMenu()
{
    // Access the menu config file
    string path = "TypicalWinFormsApp/PlugIns";
    DataSet configMenu = (DataSet) ConfigurationSettings.GetConfig(path);

    // Add dynamic items to existing popup menus
    if (configMenu != null)
        AddMenuToolsPlugIns(configMenu);
}
```

The configuration settings—that is, the menu items to be added to the Tools menu—are read from the configuration file using the *ConfigurationSettings* class, as usual. Nothing in the preceding code reveals the presence of a custom section handler and a completely custom XML schema for the settings. The only faint clue is the use of a *DataSet* object.

After it has been successfully loaded from the configuration file, the *DataSet* object is passed to a helper routine, *AddMenuToolsPlugIns*, which will modify the menu. We'll return to this point in the section "Invoking Plug-In Modules," on page 650; in the meantime, let's review the layout of the configuration file.

The XML Layout of the Configuration Settings

The data corresponding to plug-in modules is stored in a section group named *TypicalWinFormsApp*. The actual section is named *PlugIns*. Each plug-in module is identified by an assembly name, a class name, and display text. The display text constitutes the caption of the menu item, whereas the assembly name and the class name provide for a dynamic method call. As mentioned, in a real-world scenario, you might force the class to implement a particular interface so that it's clear to the calling application which methods are available for the object it is instantiating.

Here is a sample configuration file for the application shown in Figure 15-2:

```
<configuration>
   <configSections>
      <sectionGroup name="TypicalWinFormsApp">
         <section name="PlugIns"
            type="XmlNet.CS.DatasetSectionHandler,
               DatasetSectionHandler" />
      </sectionGroup>
   </configSections>
   <appSettings>
      <add key="LastLeftTopPosition" value="358,237" />
      <add key="LastSize" value="472,203" />
   </appSettings>
   <TypicalWinFormsApp>
      <PlugIns>
         <MenuTools>
            <Text>Add new tool...</Text>
            <Assembly>MyToolsPlugIns</Assembly>
            <Class>MyPlugIn.AddNewTool</Class>
         </MenuTools>
         <MenuTools>
```

(continued)

```
        <Text>Special tool...</Text>
        <Assembly>MyToolsPlugIns</Assembly>
        <Class>MyPlugIn.SpecialTool</Class>
      </MenuTools>
    </PlugIns>
  </TypicalWinFormsApp>
</configuration>
```

I deliberately left a few standard application settings (the *<appSettings>* section) in this listing just to demonstrate that custom sections can happily work side by side with standard system and application settings. In particular, the sample application depicted in Figure 15-2 also supports the same save and restore features described in the section "Using Settings Through Code," on page 634.

The *<section>* element points to the class *XmlNet.CS.DatasetSectionHandler*, which is declared and implemented in the *DatasetSectionHandler* assembly. The net effect of this section declaration is that whenever an application asks for a *PlugIns* section, the preceding section handler is involved, its *Create* method is called, and a *DataSet* object is returned. We'll look at the implementation of the section handler in the section "Implementing the *DataSet* Section Handler," on page 653.

Invoking Plug-In Modules

The *AddMenuToolsPlugIns* procedure modifies the application's Tools menu, adding all the items registered in the configuration file. The following code shows how it works:

```
private void AddMenuToolsPlugIns(DataSet ds)
{
    DynamicMenuItem mnuItem;
    DataTable config;

    // Get the table that represents the settings for the menu
    config = ds.Tables["MenuTools"];
    if (config == null)
        return;

    // Add a separator
    if (config.Rows.Count >0)
        menuTools.MenuItems.Add("-");

    // Start position for insertions
    int index = menuTools.MenuItems.Count;
```

```
// Populate the Tools menu
foreach(DataRow configMenuItem in config.Rows)
{
    mnuItem = new DynamicMenuItem(configMenuItem["Text"].ToString(),
        new EventHandler(StdOnClickHandler));
    mnuItem.AssemblyName = configMenuItem["Assembly"].ToString();
    mnuItem.ClassName = configMenuItem["Class"].ToString();
    menuTools.MenuItems.Add(index, mnuItem);
    index += 1;
}
}
```

The *DataSet* object that the section handler returns is built from the XML code rooted in *<PlugIns>*. This code originates a *DataSet* object with one table, named *MenuTools*. The *MenuTools* table has three columns: *Text*, *Assembly*, and *Class*. Each row in the table corresponds to a plug-in module.

The preceding code first adds a separator and then iterates on the rows of the table and adds menu items to the Tools menu, as shown in Figure 15-3. *MenuTools* is just the name of the Tools pop-up menu in the sample application.

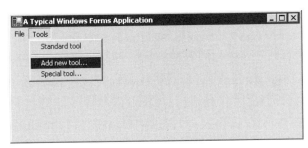

Figure 15-3   Registered plug-in modules appear on the Tools menu of the application.

To handle a click on a menu item in a Windows Forms application, you need to associate an event handler object with the menu item. Visual Studio .NET does this for you at design time for static menu items. For dynamic items, this association must be established at run time, as shown here:

```
DynamicMenuItem mnuItem;
mnuItem = new DynamicMenuItem(
    configMenuItem["Text"].ToString(),
    new EventHandler(StdOnClickHandler));
```

A menu item is normally represented by an instance of the *MenuItem* class. What is that *DynamicMenuItem* class all about then? *DynamicMenuItem* is a user-defined class that extends *MenuItem* with a couple of properties particularly suited for menu items that represent calls to plug-in modules. Here's the class definition:

```
public class DynamicMenuItem : MenuItem
{
    public string AssemblyName;
    public string ClassName;

public DynamicMenuItem(string text, EventHandler onClick) :
    base(text, onClick)
    {}
}
```

The new menu item class stores the name of the assembly and the class to use when clicked. An instance of this class is passed to the event handler procedure through the *sender* argument, as shown here:

```
private void StdOnClickHandler(object sender, EventArgs e)
{
    // Get the current instance of the dynamic menu item
    DynamicMenuItem mnuItem = (DynamicMenuItem) sender;

    // Display a message box that proves we know the corresponding
    // assembly and class name
    string msg = "Execute a method on class [{0}] from assembly [{1}]";
    msg = String.Format(msg, mnuItem.ClassName, mnuItem.AssemblyName);
    MessageBox.Show(msg, mnuItem.Text);
}
```

In a real-world context, you can use the assembly and class information to dynamically create an instance of the class using the *Activator* object that we encountered in Chapter 12, as follows:

```
// Assuming that the class implements the IAppPlugIn interface
// asm is the assembly name, cls is the class name
IAppPlugIn o = (IAppPlugIn) Activator.CreateInstance(asm, cls).Unwrap()

// Assume that the IAppPlugIn interface has a method Execute()
o.Execute();
```

Figure 15-4 shows the message box that appears when you click a custom menu item in the sample application. All the information displayed is read from the configuration file.

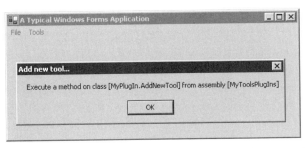

Figure 15-4   The message box that appears when a custom menu item is clicked.

Implementing the *DataSet* Section Handler

To top off our examination of section handlers, let's review the source code for the custom section handler that we've been using, shown here:

```
using System;
using System.Data;
using System.Xml;
using System.Configuration;

namespace XmlNet.CS
{
    public class DatasetSectionHandler : IConfigurationSectionHandler
    {
        // Constructor(s)
        public DatasetSectionHandler()
        {
        }

        // IConfigurationSectionHandler.Create
        public object Create(object parent,
            object context, XmlNode section)
        {
            DataSet ds;

            // Clone the parent DataSet if not null
            if (parent == null)
                ds = new DataSet();
            else
                ds = ((DataSet) parent).Clone();
```

(continued)

```
    // Read the data using a node reader
    DataSet tmp = new DataSet();
    XmlNodeReader nodereader = new XmlNodeReader(section);
    tmp.ReadXml(nodereader);

    // Merge with the parent and return
    ds.Merge(tmp);
    return ds;
  }
 }
}
```

The *DatasetSectionHandler* class implements the *IConfigurationSectionHandler* and provides the default constructor. The most interesting part of this code is the *Create* method, which reads the current section specified through the section argument and then merges the resultant *DataSet* object with the parent, if a non-*null* parent object has been passed. Because configuration inheritance proceeds from top to bottom, the base *DataSet* object for merging is the parent.

The XML data to be parsed is passed via an *XmlNode* object—that is, an object that represents the root of an XML DOM subtree. To make an XML DOM subtree parsable by the *DataSet* object's *ReadXml* method, you must wrap it in an *XmlNodeReader* object—that is, one of the XML reader objects that we encountered in Chapter 2 and Chapter 5. When called to action on the configuration file from the section "The XML Layout of the Configuration Settings," on page 649, the *XmlNode* object passed to the handler points to the *<PlugIns>* node.

Conclusion

The .NET Framework API for reading configuration settings is designed to greatly simplify the code needed on the client. This API represents the perfect example of smooth XML integration. No matter how the configuration data is organized and where the data is located, the code you use to access the data is nearly identical. The only significant drawback I've noticed in the current implementation of the configuration API is that you can't rely on a common and official API to update settings. However, as this chapter showed, using XML writers or, better yet, XML DOM documents provides a quick and effective workaround.

In this chapter, we reviewed the fundamentals of the .NET Framework configuration subsystem, the files in which it is articulated, and their related locations. Next we reviewed the properties and methods commonly used to access configuration settings. The final part of the chapter addressed the topics and the tasks involved in an in-depth customization of configuration files. In particular, you learned how to create new sections and new section handlers, and we examined a comprehensive example.

Further Reading

The configuration API is described in detail in the MSDN documentation. I've noticed only a few omissions and a few points about which that text is unclear, and I've tried to include that information in this chapter. The final example presented in this chapter represents a hot topic for many developers: building desktop applications that can be extended with external plug-in modules. I discussed this topic at length and with extensive code examples in an article that appeared in the "Cutting Edge" column of the July 2002 issue of *MSDN Magazine*.

Afterword

While writing this book, I accumulated a few thoughts that I'd like to share with you as my final considerations about XML and the Microsoft .NET Framework. If you consider these ideas individually, they might appear completely unrelated to one another, but considered all together, they form a sort of filter through which you can reconsider and review this book's contents from a higher level perspective. These are the four main concepts:

- XML is a native data type in the .NET Framework.

- We need a parsing model that falls in the middle between the XML Document Object Model (XML DOM) and Simple API for XML (SAX).

- The capability to query data effectively is key.

- We need more than the Simple Object Access Protocol (SOAP) and the XML Schema Definition (XSD) for true interoperability.

Some of these ideas address cross-platform issues whose solution is beyond the capabilities and interests of individual vendors. The W3C is working on XQuery, an evolution of the XPath query language, which will provide a data model for XML documents as well as a set of operators for that data model and a query language based on these operators. (For more information, refer to *http://www.w3.org/XML/Query.*)

To date, the recent WS-I initiative (see *http://www.ws-i.org*) appears to be the Web services counterpart to the W3C. The goal of the consortium behind the WS-I initiative is to promote true interoperability across Web services implementations. To the extent that I can envision things, the most effective way to make this happen is by defining new XML-based standards at least for security and object representation.

Native XML in the .NET Framework

Prior to the advent of the .NET Framework, we were used to writing XML-driven Microsoft Windows applications based on the MSXML COM-based library. Unlike classes in the .NET Framework, however, MSXML is a bolted-on API that communicates with the rest of the application but does not really integrate with it. *Communication* entails the activity or the process of passing information to others. It is based on some set of signals that both parties understand and that encode the information being exchanged. *Integration*, on the other hand, means that items are combined so that they are closely linked and form one unit. This distinction is significant.

The MSXML library can be imported into your code but remains an external, self-contained black box that acts as a server component. .NET Framework applications, on the other hand, use XML classes along with other classes in the .NET Framework, resulting in a homogeneous combination of "equal-sized" pieces. As a self-contained component, the MSXML must provide itself with advanced features such as asynchronous parsing. This feature is *apparently* lacking in the XML classes of the .NET Framework. By integrating XML classes with other classes in the .NET Framework, however, you can easily obtain the same functionality and even gain more control over the overall process.

Neither XML DOM nor SAX

The .NET Framework supports the XML DOM but not SAX. The XML DOM is the classic way to process XML documents, but it also turns out to be ineffective for certain classes of documents—mostly very large and volatile documents. The SAX model was developed to provide an alternative approach. The idea behind SAX is great; the actual programming model is much less ideal. SAX uses the push model, whereas a pull model is certainly more effective and flexible.

The .NET Framework provides a third parsing model based on the concept of the reader. The reader is a kind of read-only, forward-only cursor that doesn't cache anything—it just reads as quickly as possible.

Programmers need classes that implement the XML DOM because the XML DOM is a recognized standard and because it is useful in a number of realistic scenarios. However, XML DOM can't be the only API available to work with XML documents. A lower level set of tools is needed. The .NET reader is just this. In fact, the XML DOM implementation in the .NET Framework is built using readers.

Query Is Key

An XML document is primarily a repository of information and as such must be searchable. But how? XPath was the first answer to the demand for a query tool to extract node-sets out of XML documents. But more powerful tools are needed. Today, XPath 2.0 is on the way, with XQuery 1.0 running close behind.

XPath as we know it today, and as supported by the .NET Framework, is a language for addressing parts of an XML document. XPath 2.0 presents itself as an expression language for processing sequences of text. It also comes with built-in support for querying XML documents. But what's the difference between addressing and querying? And between XPath and XQuery?

I think that the difference between addressing and querying can be summarized by resorting to a SQL metaphor. A simple SELECT statement with a WHERE clause addresses a subset of rows; a more complex SELECT statement that includes UNION, GROUP BY, INNER JOIN, and temporary tables does much more and actually performs a query.

XPath 1.0 addresses parts of the documents; XQuery performs complex queries and supports more data types. From a syntax point of view, XPath 2.0 is a subset of XQuery but with a number of key features already included. Stepping from XPath 1.0 to XPath 2.0 positions you nicely for a further jump to XQuery when it becomes a W3C recommendation.

A good reference for clearing up any confusion you might have about XPath and XQuery is the following: *http://www.xml.com/pub/a/2002/03/20/xpath2.html.*

The Dream of True Interoperability

That XML can be exchanged between heterogeneous platforms and understood anywhere is a fact. Web services are a relatively new type of software that exploits this aspect of XML. The rub lies in the fact that in the real world, data must be used once it has been transferred. XML data must be converted to usable objects. But which tool can take care of this mapping process? An easy answer would be the parser, but the parser is a generic tool that processes XML data and returns an XML-specific object, not an application-specific object. For example, while parsing employee data, the parser can create an XML DOM object that contains a tree of nodes set to employee data. There is no way for the parser to return an application-specific object such as an *Employee* class with properties and methods.

Just as SOAP provides a universal technique for defining a method call, another protocol should provide the ability to describe a class. I'd like to have a simple class definition protocol that would let servers and clients exchange documents that contain structure and data of a given class instance. A specialized type of parser would be needed with the extra ability to deserialize the class description into a valid instance of a type. Sound confusing? Think of the .NET Framework XML serializer (or the SOAP formatter). The XML serializer provides the ability to save and restore instances of classes. The saved data contains information about the structure of the class and its instance data. I believe that the .NET Framework already contains a prototype of the parser of the future.

It will be interesting to see how many of the features predicted or called for in this book will find their place in the next version of the .NET Framework (code-named Whidbey).

Index

Symbols and Numbers

@ (at sign), abbreviation for the attribute axis type, 252

@ (at sign) WebService directive, 566–67

"." expression in XPath, 301

. (period), indicating the context node, 252

.. (double-dot) symbol in XPath, 301

.. (two periods), referring to the parent, 252

/ (forward slash), beginning an absolute location path, 250

< (less than sign), not allowed in an XSLT expression, 324

(number sign) in a fragment identifier, 253

[ ] (square brackets), enclosing a predicate, 251

* (wildcard character), indicating all nodes in a given axis, 251

2-D vector graphics category of GDI+, 536

A

abbreviated form of a location path, 250

absolute location path, 250

absolute URI, 46

abstract classes, 26

abstract methods, overriding, 60

AcceptChanges method, 452

Action field in XmlNodeChangedEventArgs, 213

<activated> tag, 549–50

activation agent, choosing IIS as, 544–45

activation mode, choosing, 550–51

activation policies of remotable objects, 545

Activator class, 390, 558

Activator object, 652

ad hoc assembly, created and loaded by XmlSerializer, 512

ad hoc virtual directory, setting up to test HTML pages, 607–8

<add> element of a configuration file, 630

Add method

of the NameTable class, 49

of the XmlSchemaCollection object, 92

Add Reference option in Solution Explorer, 552

AddAttributeChange method of XmlTextReadWriter, 183

Added state of a DataRow object, 452

AddExtensionObject method of XsltArgumentList, 325

AddMenuToolsPlugIns procedure, 650–51

AddParam method of XsltArgumentList, 325

addresses, creating a schema for, 112–13

address.xml file, inferring the schema for, 118

address.xsd schema, 114–15, 116

AddSort method of XPathExpression, 273, 277–79

AddValue method of SerializationInfo, 463

adLongVarWCharADO data type, 178

ADO recordset, XML format for, 105–6

ADO Recordset objects

importing contents of, 170–71

node layout of, 173

persisting to XML, 101–2

processing contents of, 175–76

XML version of, 329–31

ADO Recordset XML writer, 170–71

ADO style sheet, 328–32

ADO types, compared to predefined XDR data types, 178

ADO XML Recordset object, 176–77

ADO-driven applications, recognizing XML files created with XmlRecordsetWriter, 177–78

ADO.NET

batch update, 469

classes, 8

data reader classes, 16

as a key XML area in the .NET Framework, 5

normal form, 8, 404, 433–34

object model, 360, 399

serializing objects, 422

two-way binding with ADO, 171

types of constraints, 413

ADO.NET DataSet objects. *See* DataSet objects

AdoNetXmlSerializer class library, 418, 420–21

ADO-specific XML file, 171

aliases, defining for columns, 356

all element for a complex type, 114

allowDefinition attribute for ASP.NET applications, 640

AllowDefinition attribute of the <section> element, 630

allowLocation attribute of the <section> element, 630

ancestor axis, 247

ancestor element nodes, 271

annotated schemas, 359

Annotation element for an XML schema file, 113

annotations, 448

Any type in XPath, 274, 275

anySimple Type class, 108, 109

anyType generic type, 108, 109

AppDomains, 526–28

AppendChild method of XmlNode, 213, 218

Dino Esposito

Dino Esposito is Wintellect's ADO.NET and XML expert and a trainer and consultant who specializes in .NET and Web applications. A frequent speaker at popular industry events such as Microsoft TechEd, VSLive!, DevConnections, and WinSummit, Dino is also a prolific author writing the monthly "Cutting Edge" column for *MSDN Magazine* and the "Diving into Data Access" column for *MSDN Voices*. He also regularly contributes to a number of other magazines, including *Visual Studio Magazine*, *CoDe Magazine*, and *asp.netPRO Magazine* (*http://www.aspnetpro.com*). During a few rare moments of spare time, Dino cofounded *http://www.vb2themax.com*, a Web site for Visual Basic and Visual Basic .NET developers.

Fond of sea and beaches, Dino lives in Italy, precisely in the Rome area, with his wife, Silvia, and two children—Francesco and Michela.

Tubing Sizer

Scientists and engineers use tubing of various sizes to transport a vast variety of liquids and gases. The tubing they use can be made of materials as basic as cellulose wood fiber, natural latex rubber, and glass or as exotic as polyvinyl chloride (PVC), nalgene, or platinum-cured silicone plastic. No matter what material their tubing is made of, if they need to measure its outsize diameter, they will use a *tubing sizer* to measure tubing, connecting pieces, rods, test tubes, and more. In the same way, no matter what kind of Web-based application a modern software developer is trying to build, they will probably use XML as the "tubing" to transport its data.

At Microsoft Press, we use tools to illustrate our books for software developers and IT professionals. Tools very simply and powerfully symbolize human inventiveness. They're a metaphor for people extending their capabilities, precision, and reach. From simple calipers and pliers to digital micrometers and lasers, these stylized illustrations give each book a visual identity, and a personality to the series. With tools and knowledge, there's no limit to creativity and innovation. Our tagline says it all: the tools you need to put technology to work.

The manuscript for this book was prepared and galleyed using Microsoft Word. Pages were composed by Microsoft Press using Adobe FrameMaker + SGML for Windows, with text in Garamond and display type in Helvetica Condensed. Composed pages were delivered to the printer as electronic prepress files.

Cover Designer:	Methodologie, Inc.
Interior Graphic Designer:	James D. Kramer
Principal Compositor:	Gina Cassill
Interior Artist:	Rob Nance
Prinicpal Copy Editor:	Jennifer Harris
Proof reader:	nSight, Inc.
Indexer:	Richard Shrout